Algorithms for Data and Computation Privacy

Alex X. Liu • Rui Li

Algorithms for Data
and Computation Privacy

 Springer

Alex X. Liu
Chief Scientist
Ant Group
Hangzhou, Zhejiang, China

Rui Li
School of Cyberspace Security
Dongguan University of Technology
Dongguan, Guangdong, China

ISBN 978-3-030-58898-4   ISBN 978-3-030-58896-0   (eBook)
https://doi.org/10.1007/978-3-030-58896-0

This Springer imprint is published by the registered company Springer Nature Switzerland AG
The registered company address is: Gewerbestrasse 11, 6330 Cham, Switzerland

*Dedicated with love and respect
to my parents
Yuhai Liu (God rest his soul) and Shuxiang
Wang,
to my wife
Chenyang Li,
to my twin sons
Max Boyang and Louis Boyang,
to whom I owe
all that I am and all that I have
accomplished.*

– Alex X. Liu

*To my dearest wife Jian Zhou, my son Zixuan
Li, and my parents Jixiang Li and Yuqiong Li.
Thanks for your support and understanding.*

–Rui Li

Contents

Part IV   Breaking Privacy

Acronyms

ACL	Access control list
AM	Anonymization module
ASPE	Asymmetric scalar-product-preserving encryption
BDD	Binary decision diagram
BMAB	Budget-limited multi-armed bandit
CDCF	Cross-domain cooperative firewall
COLD	COmmunication Link De-anonymization
CTL	Computation tree logic
DP	Differential privacy
EVC	Eigenvector centrality
FDD	Firewall decision diagram
GSR	Galvanic skin response
IBF	Indistinguishable Bloom filter
IBtree	Indistinguishable binary tree
ICA	Independent component analysis
IDD	Interval decision diagram
IM	Instant messaging
IND-CKA	Indistinguishability against chosen keyword attack
IND-CPA	Indistinguishability against chosen plain-text attack
IND-OCPA	Indistinguishable under ordered chosen plain-text attack
IPSes	Intrusion prevention systems
ISP	Internet service provider
kNN	k-nearest neighbor
LSH	Locality sensitive hashing
MAB	Multi-armed bandit
MCS	Mobile crowd sensing
MSE	Average mean squared error
MSU	Michigan State University
NAT	Network address translation
OAR	Overall approximation ratio
OSN	Online social network

PASStree	Pattern aware secure search tree
PBtree	Privacy Bloom filter tree
PCA	Principal component analysis
PCC	Principal component centrality
PPT	Probabilistic polynomial time
QoS	Quality of service
SANE	Secure architecture for the networked enterprise
SecEQP	Secure and efficient query processing
SNN	Secure nearest neighbor
SP	Sub-string prefix
SRA	Secure RPC authentication
SSE	Searchable symmetric encryption
TF-IDF	Term-frequency inverse-document-frequency
VPN	Virtual private network

Part I
Privacy Preserving Queries

Chapter 1
Range Queries over Encrypted Data

1.1 Introduction

1.1.1 Background and Motivation

Driven by lower cost, higher reliability, better performance, and faster deployment, data and computing services have been increasingly outsourced to clouds such as Amazon EC2 and S3 [1], Microsoft Azure [2], and Google App Engine [3]. However, privacy has been the key road block to cloud computing. On one hand, to leverage the computing and storage capability offered by clouds, we need to store data on clouds. On the other hand, due to many reasons, we may not fully trust the clouds for data privacy. First, clouds may have corrupted employees who do not follow data privacy policies. For example, in 2010, a Google engineer broke into the Gmail and Google Voice accounts of several children [4]. Second, cloud computing systems may be vulnerable to external malicious attacks, and when intrusions happen, cloud customers may not be fully informed about the potential implications on the privacy of their data. Third, clouds may base services on facilities in some foreign countries where privacy regulations are difficult to enforce.

In this chapter, we consider the following popular cloud computing paradigm: a data owner stores data on a cloud, and multiple data users query the data. For a simple example, a user stores his own data and queries his own data on the cloud. For another example, multiple doctors in a clinic store and query patient medical records in a cloud. Figure 1.1 shows the three parties in our model: a data owner, a cloud, and multiple data users. Among the three parties, the data owner and data users are trusted, but the cloud is not fully trusted. The problem addressed in this chapter is range query processing on clouds in a privacy preserving and yet scalable manner. For a set of records where all records have the same attribute $\mathbb{A}$, which has numerical values or can be represented as numerical values, given a range query specified by an interval $[a, b]$, the query result is the set of records whose $\mathbb{A}$ attribute

A. X. Liu, R. Li, *Algorithms for Data and Computation Privacy*,
https://doi.org/10.1007/978-3-030-58896-0_1

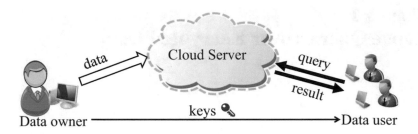

Fig. 1.1 Cloud computing model

falls into the interval. Range queries are fundamental operations for database SQL queries and big data analytics. In database SQL queries, the `where` clauses often contain predicates specified as ranges. For example, SQL query `select * from patients where 20 <= age and age <= 30` means to find all records of the patients whose age is in the range of [20, 30]. In big data analytics, many analyses involve range queries along dimensions such as time and human age.

Given data items $d_1, \ldots, d_n$, the data owner encrypts these data using a symmetric key K, which is shared between the data owner and data users, generates an *index*, and then sends both the encrypted data denoted $(d_1)_k, \ldots, (d_n)_k$ and the index to the cloud. Given a query, the data user generates a *trapdoor* and then sends it to the cloud. The index and the trapdoor should allow the cloud to determine which data items satisfy the query. Yet, in this process, the cloud should not be able to infer *useful information* about the data and queries. The useful information in this context includes the values of the data items, the content of the queries, and the statistical properties of the data items. Other than encrypted data and queries, together with query results, the cloud may have information obtained from other channels, such as domain knowledge about the data (e.g., age distribution). However, even with such information, a privacy preserving range query scheme should not allow the cloud to infer additional information about the data based on past query results.

Besides privacy guarantees, a privacy preserving range query scheme should be efficient in terms of query processing time, storage overhead, and communication overhead. The query processing time needs to be small because many applications require real-time queries. The storage overhead refers to the data that cloud needs to store other than encrypted data items. It needs to be small because the volume of data stored on the cloud is typically large. The communication overhead refers to the data transferred between the data owner and the cloud, other than encrypted data items, and the data transferred between data users and the cloud, other than the precise query results. It needs to be small due to bandwidth limitations and the extra time involved in uploading and downloading.

1.1.2   Threat Model

For the cloud, we assume that the cloud is *semi-honest* (also called *honest-but-curious*), which was proposed by Canetti et al. in [5] and has been widely adopted including prior privacy preserving range and keyword query work [6–18]. A cloud is semi-honest means that it does follow required communication protocols and execute required algorithms correctly, but it may attempt to obtain information about data items and the content of user queries with the help of domain knowledge about the data items and the queries (such as the distribution of data items and queries). For the data owner and the data users, we assume that they are trusted.

1.1.3   Security Model

We adopt the IND-CKA security model proposed in [13], which has been widely accepted in prior privacy preserving keyword query work. This model has two key requirements: *index indistinguishability (IND)* and *security under chosen keyword attacks (CKA)*. Informally, a range query scheme is secure under the IND-CKA model if an adversary $\mathcal{A}$ chooses two different sets S_1 and S_2 of data items, where the two sets have the same number of data items and they may or may not overlap, lets an oracle simulating the data owner to build indexes for S_1 and S_2, but $\mathcal{A}$ cannot distinguish which index is for which data set. The rationale is that if the problem is distinguishing the indexes for S_1 and S_2 is hard, then deducing at least one data item that S_1 and S_2 do not have in common must also be hard. In other words, if $\mathcal{A}$ cannot determine which data item is encoded in an index with probability non-negligibly different from 1/2, then the index reveals nothing about the data items. Such indexes are called *secure indexes*. The IND-CKA model aims to prevent an adversary $\mathcal{A}$ from deducing the plaintext values of data items from the index, other than what it already knows from previous query results or from other channels. Note that secure indexes do not hide information such as the number of data items. For applications that demand the privacy of data item numbers, they can inject dummy data items into small data sets to make all data sets to have equal sizes. Also, note that we are not interested in hiding search patterns, where a search pattern is defined as the set of trapdoors corresponding to different user queries. So far there are no searchable symmetric encryption schemes that can hide the statistical patterns of user searches because trapdoors are generated deterministically (i.e., the same trapdoor will always be generated for the same keyword) [18].

1.1.4   Summary and Limitation of Prior Art

Prior privacy preserving query schemes fall into two categories according to their query types: range queries, which query all data items that fall into a given range, and keyword queries, which query all text documents that contain a given keyword. Privacy preserving range query schemes can also be called *range searchable symmetric encryption schemes*, and privacy preserving keyword query schemes can also be called *keyword searchable symmetric encryption schemes*. Prior privacy preserving range query schemes for the single-data-owner-multiple-data-user cloud paradigm fall into two categories: bucketing schemes [6–8] and order preserving schemes [9–11]. In bucketing schemes, the data owner partitions the whole data domain (e.g., [0, 150] of human ages) into multiple buckets of varying sizes (e.g., four buckets of [0, 12], [13, 22], [23, 60], [61, 150]). The index consists of pairs of a bucket ID and the encrypted data items in the bucket. The trapdoor of a range query (e.g., [10, 20]) consists of the IDs of the buckets that overlaps with the range (e.g., bucket IDs 1 and 2). All data items in a bucket are included in the query result as long as the bucket overlaps with the query. Bucketing schemes have two key limitations: weak privacy protection and high communication cost. Their privacy protection is weak because the cloud can statistically estimate the actual value of both data items and queries using domain knowledge and historical query results, as pointed out in [7]. Their communication cost is high because many data items in the query result do not satisfy the query. Reducing bucket sizes helps to reduce communication costs, but will worsen privacy protection because the number of buckets becomes closer to that of data items.

Order preserving schemes use encryption functions that preserve the relative ordering of data items even after encryption. For any two data items a and b, and an order preserving encryption function f, $a \leq b$ if and only if $f(a) \leq f(b)$. In order preserving schemes, the index for data items $d_1, \ldots, d_n$ are $f(d_1), \ldots, f(d_n)$, and the trapdoor for query $[a, b]$ is $[f(a), f(b)]$. Order preserving schemes have weak privacy protection because they allow the cloud to statistically estimate the actual values of both data items and queries [19].

The fundamental reason that the privacy protection provided by the above prior schemes is weak is because their indexes are distinguishable for the same number of data items but with different distributions. In bucketing schemes, for the same number of data items, different distributions in data values will cause buckets to have different distributions in sizes because they need to balance the number of items among buckets. In order preserving schemes, for the same number of data items, different distributions in data values will cause cipher-texts to have different distribution in the projected space. Leveraging domain knowledge about data distribution, both bucketing schemes and order preserving schemes allow the cloud to statistically estimate the values of data and queries.

1.1.5   Proposed Approach

In this chapter, we propose the first privacy preserving range query scheme that achieves index indistinguishability. Our key idea for achieving index indistinguishability is to organize all indexing elements in a complete binary tree where each node is represented using a Bloom filter, which we call a *PBtree* (where "P"stands for privacy and "B" stands for Bloom filter). PBtrees allow us to achieve index indistinguishability because it has two important properties. First, a PBtree has the property of *structure indistinguishability*, that is, two sets of data items have the same PBtree structure if and only if the two sets have the same number of data items. The structure of the PBtree of a set of data items is determined solely by the set cardinality, not the value of data items. Second, a PBtree has the property of *node indistinguishability*, that is, for any two PBtrees constructed from data sets of the same cardinality, which have the same structure, and for any two corresponding nodes of the two PBtrees, the values of the two nodes are not distinguishable. Thus, our scheme prevents cloud from performing statistical analysis on the index even with domain knowledge.

1.1.6   Technical Challenges and Solutions

There are two key technical challenges. The first challenge is the *construction* of PBtrees by data owners. We address this challenge by first transforming less-than and bigger-than comparisons into set membership testing (i.e., testing whether a number is in a set), which involves only equal-to comparisons, and then organize all the sets hierarchically in a PBtree. This transformation helps us to achieve node indistinguishability because the less-than or bigger-than relationship among PBtree nodes is no longer statistically meaningful. The second challenge is the *optimization* of PBtrees for fast query processing on the cloud. We address this challenge by two ideas: *PBtree traversal width minimization* and *PBtree traversal depth minimization*. The idea of *PBtree traversal width minimization* is to minimize the number of paths that the cloud needs to traverse for processing a query. We prove that the PBtree traversal width minimization problem is NP-hard, and propose an efficient approximation algorithm. The idea of *PBtree traversal depth minimization* is to minimize the traversal depth of the paths that the cloud needs to traverse for processing a query; in other words, we want the traversal of many paths to terminate as early as possible.

1.1.7   Key Contributions

We make three key contributions. First, we propose the first privacy preserving range query scheme and prove that it is secure under the widely adopted IND-CKA model. Second, we propose PBtrees, basic PBtree construction and query processing algorithms, and two PBtree optimization algorithms. Third, we implemented and evaluated our scheme on a large real world data set with 5 million data items. Experimental results show that our scheme is both fast and scalable. For example, for a query whose results contain ten data items, it takes only 0.17 ms.

1.2   Related Work

There are some privacy preserving range query work that does not fit into our cloud computing paradigm and cannot be used to solve the problem addressed in this chapter. In the public-key domain, the approach in [20] supports range querying using identity based encryption primitives [21, 22]. Their encryption scheme allows a network gateway to encrypt summaries of network flows before submitting them to an untrusted repository; when a network operator suspects that an intrusion happens, a trusted third party can release a key to the operator to allow the operator to decrypt flows whose attributes fall within specified ranges, but not other flows. However, the user query privacy is not preserved.

A significant amount of work has been done in privacy preserving keywordand ranked keyword queries [12–18, 23–30]. However, these solutions are not optimized for range queries.

Prior work on outsourced databases has addressed problems such as secure kNN processing [31–33], privacy preserving data mining [34, 35], and query result integrity verification [36]. In [31–33], order preserving encryption techniques were used to compute the k-nearest neighbors of a given encrypted query point in an encrypted database. For the privacy preserving clustering mechanisms in [34, 35], certain confidential numerical attributes are perturbed in a uniform manner so that preserve the distances between any two points. Significant work has been done on query result integrity verification [36]. The basic idea is to include verifiable digital signatures for each returned tuple, which allow the client to verify the integrity of query results.

1.3   PBtree Construction

In this section, we first present our PBtree construction algorithm, which is executed by the data owner. This algorithm consists of three steps: prefix encoding, tree construction, and node randomization using Bloom filters. Second, we present our algorithm for computing the trapdoor for a given query, which is executed by the data users. With the PBtree of n data items and the trapdoor for a given query, the cloud is able to process the query on the PBtree without knowing the value of the data items and the query.

1.3.1 Prefix Encoding

The key idea of this step is to convert the testing of whether a data item falls into a range to the testing of whether two sets have common elements, where the basic step is testing whether two numbers are equal. To achieve this, we adopt the prefix membership verification scheme in [37]. Given a number x of w bits whose binary representation is $b_1 b_2 \cdots b_w$, its prefix family denoted as $F(x)$ is defined as the set of $w + 1$ prefixes $\{b_1 b_2 \cdots b_w, b_1 b_2 \cdots b_{w-1}*, \ldots, b_1 * \cdots *, ** \ldots *\}$, where the i-th prefix is $b_1 b_2 \cdots b_{w-i+1} * \cdots *$. For example, the prefix family of number 6 of 5 bits is $F(6) = F(00110) = \{00110, 0011*, 001**, 00***, 0****, *****\}$. Given a range $[a, b]$, we first convert the range $[a, b]$ to a minimum set of prefixes, denoted $S([a, b])$, such that the union of the prefixes is equal to $[a, b]$. For example, $S([0, 8]) = \{00***, 1000\}$. Given a range $[a, b]$, where a and b are two numbers of w bits, the number of prefixes in $S([a, b])$ is at most $2w - 2$ [38]. For any number x and range $[a, b]$, $x \in [a, b]$ if and only if there exists prefix $p \in S([a, b])$ so that $x \in p$ holds. Furthermore, for any number x and prefix p, $x \in p$ if and only if $p \in F(x)$. Thus, for any number x and range $[a, b]$, $x \in [a, b]$ if and only if $F(x) \cap S([a, b]) \neq \emptyset$. From the above examples, we can see that $6 \in [0, 8]$ and $F(6) \cap S([0, 8]) = \{00***\}$. In this step, given n data items $d_1, \ldots, d_n$, the data owner computes the prefix families $F(d_1), \ldots, F(d_n)$; given a range $[a, b]$, the data user computes $S([a, b])$.

1.3.2 Tree Construction

To achieve sub-linear search efficiency, we organize $F(d_1)$, ..., $F(d_n)$ in a tree structure that we call *PBtree*. We cannot use existing database indexing structures like $B+$ trees because of two reasons. First, searching on such trees (such as $B+$ trees) requires the operation of testing which of two numbers is bigger; however, PBtrees cannot support such operations for the cloud because otherwise PBtrees will share the same weaknesses with prior order preserving schemes [6–8]. Second, their structures for different sets of data items are often different even if the two sets have equal sizes; however, for any two sets of the same size, their PBtrees are required to have the same structure, i.e., the two PBtrees are indistinguishable. In this chapter, we organize $F(d_1), \ldots, F(d_n)$ using our PBtree structure.

Definition 1.1 (PBtree) A PBTree for n data items is a full binary tree with n terminal nodes and $n - 1$ nonterminal nodes, where all n terminal nodes form a linked list from left to right and each node is represented using a Bloom filter. Each terminal node contains one data item, and each nonterminal node contains the union of its left and right children. For any nonterminal node, the size of its left child either equals to that of its right child or exceeds by one.   □

According to this definition, a PBtree is a highly balanced binary search tree. The height of the PBtree for n data items is $\lfloor \log n \rfloor + 1$. We construct the PBtree from $F(d_1), \ldots, F(d_n)$ in a top-down fashion. First, we construct the root node, which is labeled with the n prefix families $\{F(d_1), \ldots, F(d_n)\}$. Second, we partition the set of n prefix families $\{F(d_1), \ldots, F(d_n)\}$ into two subsets of prefix families S_{left} and S_{right} such that $|S_{\text{left}}| = |S_{\text{right}}|$ if n is even and $|S_{\text{left}}| = |S_{\text{right}}| + 1$ if n is odd, and then construct two child nodes for the root, where the left child is labeled with S_{left} and the right child is labeled with S_{right}. We recursively apply the above step to the left child and the right child, respectively, until every terminal node contains only one prefix family. At the end, we link all terminal nodes by a linked list. Figure 1.2 shows the PBtree for the set of prefix families $S = \{F(1), F(6), F(7), F(9), F(11), F(12), F(13), F(16), F(20), F(25)\}$.

Algorithm 1: PBtreeConstruction(S)

Input: S
Output: PBtree constructed for value set S

1 $root :=$ PBtreeNodeConstruction(S);
2 PBtreeLeafLinking($root$);
3 return $root$;

The key property of PBtrees is stated in Theorem 2.1, which is straightforward to prove according to its construction algorithm. Note that the constraint $0 \leq |S_{\text{left}}| - |S_{\text{right}}| \leq 1$ makes the structure of the PBtree for a set of data items to solely depend on the number of data items.

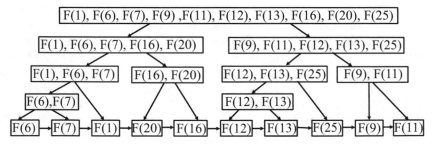

Fig. 1.2 PBtree example

Algorithm 2: PBtreeNodeConst(S)

Input: $S = \{d_1, d_2, \ldots, d_n\}$
Output: A PBtree T without linked list in leaf nodes

1   v:=new PBtreeNode;
2   $\forall d_i \in S, v.B := F(d_i)$;
3   **if** $|S| = 1$ **then**
4       $\lfloor$ $v.left := null; v.right := null$

5   **else**
6   partition S into S_1, S_2 so that $0 \leq |S_1| - |S_2| \leq 1$;
7       $v.left :=$ PBtreeNodeConst(S_1);
8       $v.right :=$ PBtreeNodeConst(S_2);

9   return v;

Algorithm 3: PBtreeLeafLinking(T, pre)

Input: A PBtree T without linked list in leaf nodes, leaf node pre which is the predecessor
      of the first leaf node in T
Output: A PBtree T with linked list in leaf nodes

1   **if** T *is a leaf node* **then**
2       $T.SetLeftChild(pre)$;
3   **if** $pre! = NULL$ **then**
4           $\lfloor$ $pre.SetRightChild(T)$;

5       $pre = T$;

6   PBtreeLeafLinking($T.LeftChild$, pre);
7   PBtreeLeafLinking($T.RightChild$, pre);

Theorem 1.1 (Structure Indistinguishability) *For any two sets of data items S_1 and S_2, their PBtrees have exactly the same structure if and only if $|S_1| = |S_2|$.* □

We now describe the query processing algorithm on the above tree. For a PBtree T, we use $T.root$ to denote the root node of T, $T.left$ to denote the left subtree of T, and $T.right$ to denote the right subtree of T. For a node v, we use $L(v)$ to denote the label of v, which is a set of prefix families, and $U(v)$ to denote the union of all prefix families in $L(v)$. For example, if $L(v) = \{F(6), F(7)\}$, then $U(v) = F(6) \cup F(7)$. Given a range $[a, b]$, starting from the root $T.root$ of a PBtree T, where $L(T.root) = \{F(d_1), \ldots, F(d_n)\}$ and $U(T.root) = F(d_1) \cup \cdots \cup F(d_n)$, we check whether $U(T.root) \cap S([a, b]) = \emptyset$. If $U(T.root) \cap S([a, b]) = \emptyset$, then none of the n data items $d_1, \ldots, d_n$ falls into the range of $[a, b]$ and therefore we do not need to continue searching tree T. If $U(T.root) \cap S([a, b]) \neq \emptyset$, then there exists at least one of the n data items $d_1, \ldots, d_n$ falls into the range of $[a, b]$; thus, we need to continue to recursively conduct the same search on $T.left$ and $T.right$, if they exist. The pseudocode of the algorithm is in Algorithm 4.

We now analyze the time complexity of our query processing algorithm and show that it is sub-linear in the number of data items. Let n be the number of data items indexed by the PBtree, $[a, b]$ be the query, and R be the query result. The average

---

Algorithm 4: PBtreeSearch(T, a, b)

Input: S

Output: PBtree nodes whose data item is in $[a, b]$

1 if $U(T.root) \cap S([a, b]) = \emptyset$ **then**

2 $\quad \lfloor$ **return** null ;

3 else

4 $\quad$ **if** T *is leaf* **then**

5 $\qquad \lfloor$ **return** L(T.root);

6 $\quad$ **else**

7 $\qquad \lfloor$ PBtreeSearch($T.left, [a, b]$); PBtreeSearch($T.right, [a, b]$);

---

run-time of the search algorithm depends on $|R|$, query result size. Theoretically, if $|R| = 0$, then only the root of the PBtree needs to be checked and the time complexity is $O(1)$; if $|R| = n$, then all data items indexed by the PBtree need to be traversed via the linked list and the time complexity is $O(n)$. In reality, we have $|R| \ll n$ as n is typically large. For each data item in R, we need to traverse at most $2 \log n - 1$ nodes. Thus, the time complexity is $O(|R| \log n)$.

1.3.3   Node Randomization Using Bloom Filters

Next, we present a solution based on secure keyed hash functions (HMAC) and Bloom filters to make our PBtree privacy preserving. For each node v, we use a Bloom filter denoted by $v.B$ to store the prefixes of a node's prefix families. We assume that the data owner and the users share r secret keys, denoted $k_1, \ldots, k_r$, other than the symmetric key for encrypting and decrypting data items. Consider a PBtree node v, where set $L(v)$ consists of n prefix families and set $U(v)$ consists of m prefixes $p_1, \ldots, p_m$. Let w be the number of bits that each data item contains. Our node randomization algorithm consists of three steps.

One-wayness   For each prefix p_i, we use the r secret keys to compte r hashes: HMAC(k_1, p_i), $\ldots$, HMAC(k_r, p_i). The purpose of this step is to achieve one-wayness, that is, given prefix p_i and the r secret keys, it is computationally efficient to compute the r hashes; but given the r hashes, it is computationally infeasible to compute the r secret keys and p_i; furthermore, even given the r hashes and p_i, which is the case in chosen plaintext attacks (CPA), it is still computationally infeasible to compute the r secret keys.

Decorrelation   For node v, we generate a random number $v.R$, which has the same number of bits as a secret key. We use $v.R$ to compute r hashes: HMAC($v.R$, HMAC(k_1, p_i)), $\ldots$, HMAC($v.R$, HMAC(k_r, p_i)). For each prefix p_i and for each $1 \leq j \leq r$, we let $v.B[$HMAC($v.R$, HMAC(k_j, p_i)) $mod\ M] := 1$. The purpose of the random number that is unique for each node is to eliminate the

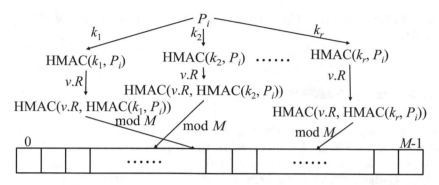

Fig. 1.3 Secure Hashing in Bloom filters

correlation among different Bloom filters for different nodes. For the same prefix p, this random number allows us to hash p independently for different Bloom filters. Without the use of this random number, if prefix p_i is shared by $U(v_1)$ and $U(v_2)$ of two different nodes v_1 and v_2, then for all the r locations HMAC(k_1, p_i) mod M, ..., HMAC(k_r, p_i) mod M, both Bloom filters have the value 1. Although two Bloom filters both having one for all these r locations does not necessarily mean that $U(v_1)$ and $U(v_2)$ share a common prefix, without the use of this random number, if two Bloom filters have more 1s at the same locations than other pairs, then the probability that they share common prefixes is higher. Figure 1.3 shows the above hashing process for Bloom filters.

Padding If $m < (w + 1) * n$, which means that some prefix families share common prefixes, we generate $((w + 1) * n - m) * r$ random numbers and for each number x, $v.B[x \; mod \; M] := 1$. At last, we use this Bloom filter together with the random number $v.R$ to replace the label of v. The purpose of this step is to avoid a Bloom filter to expose the information how much its prefix families share common prefixes. Without the padding, some Bloom filters are inserted with less number of elements than others, which will cause it to have less 1s than others in the statistical sense.

By now the PBtree is fully constructed from data items $d_1, \ldots, d_n$ by the data owner. The data owner sends the encrypted data items and the PBtree to the cloud.

1.3.4   Trapdoor Computation

Given a query $[a, b]$, suppose $S([a, b])$ consists of z prefixes $p_1, \ldots, p_z$, for each prefix p_i, $1 \leq i \leq z$, the data user computes r hashes: HMAC(k_1, p_i), ..., HMAC(k_r, p_i). The trapdoor for query $[a, b]$, denoted as $M_{[a,b]}$, is a matrix of $z * r$ hashes: HMAC$(k_1, p_1), \ldots,$ HMAC$(k_r, p_1), \ldots,$ HMAC$(k_1, p_z), \ldots,$ HMAC(k_r, p_z). We organize these $z * r$ hashes in a matrix because the cloud needs to know which r hashes are all correspond to the same prefix. The trapdoor of p_i corresponds to the

ith row of the trapdoor matrix. After the computation, the data user sends $M_{[a,b]}$ to the cloud.

1.3.5   Query Processing

After receiving a query represented as a trapdoor, the cloud uses the trapdoor to search over the PBtree. The query processing algorithm on PBtrees still applies except that the checking of whether $U(v) \cap S([a,b]) \neq \emptyset$ is implemented as checking whether there exists a row $i(1 \leq i \leq z)$ in matrix $M_{[a,b]}$ so that for every j ($1 \leq j \leq r$) we have $v.B[\text{HMAC}(v.R, \text{HMAC}(k_j, p_i))\ mod\ M] = 1$. The straightforward implementation of the above query processing algorithms requires to check each row of $M_{[a,b]}$ at each visited PBTree node. For a row i in $M_{[a,b]}$, if there exists j ($1 \leq j \leq r$) so that $v.B[\text{HMAC}(v.R, \text{HMAC}(k_j, p_i))\ mod\ M] = 0$, then $U(v) \cap p_i = \emptyset$. If $U(v) \cap p_i = \emptyset$, then for any descendent node v' of node v, we have $U(v') \cap p_i = \emptyset$ because $U(v') \subset U(v)$. Thus, when we take $M_{[a,b]}$ to search over the PBtree, for any such row in $M_{[a,b]}$, we remove it from $M_{[a,b]}$ when we continue to search the descendent nodes of v. The searching process terminates when $M_{[a,b]}$ becomes empty or we finishes searching terminal nodes.

1.3.6   False Positive Analysis

As each node in a PBtree is represented by a Bloom filter, which inherently has false positives, the query result on a PBtree may contain false positives. For simplicity, consider a PBtree with $n = 2^h$ leaf nodes, where the height of the PBtree is $h + 1$. Let R be the query result, which is a set of data items. We color all the terminal and nonterminal nodes on the path from a data item in R to the root of the PBtree to be grey and others to be white. Figure 1.4 shows such a marked PBtree where $d_j \in R$. Let f be the false positive rate of a Bloom filter in the PBtree. Note that although nodes of different levels in a PBtree may have a Bloom filter of different length, we

Fig. 1.4 PBtree example

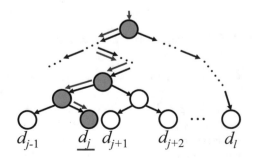

always choose the number of hash functions r to be $\frac{m}{n} \times \ln 2$ to minimize the false positive rate to be $(1 - (1 - \frac{1}{m}^{rn})^r \approx (1 - e^{-rn/m})^r = 2^{-r} \approx 0.6185^{m/n}$; thus, by choosing the same m/n value for each node, the false positive of the Bloom filter at each node is the same. For any node $d_i \notin R$, let $\texttt{len}(d_i, R)$ be the number of white nodes on the path from d_i to the root, the probability that d_i is a false positive is $f^{\texttt{len}(d_i, R)}$. Thus, the expected number of false positives is $\Sigma_{d_i \notin R} f^{\texttt{len}(d_i, R)}$. Among all possible query result sets R of the same size a, we use M_a be denote the maximum expected number of false positives. Thus,

$$M_a = \max_{\forall R}(\sum_{d_i \notin R} f^{\texttt{len}(d_i, R)}) \tag{1.1}$$

For $a = 0$, we have

$$M_0 = 2^h \times p^{h+1} \tag{1.2}$$

For $a = 1$, say $d_j \in R$ as illustrated by Fig. 1.4, the values of $\texttt{len}(d_i, R)$ for $d_i \notin R$ are $1, 2, 2, 3, 3, 3, 3, \cdots$. Thus, we have:

$$M_1 = f + 2f^2 + \cdots + 2^{h-1} f^h = f\frac{1 - (2f)^h}{1 - 2f} \tag{1.3}$$

For $1 < a < n$, according to Eq. (1.1), M_a corresponds to the case where in the $(\lceil \log a \rceil + 1)$-th layer there are a nodes colored grey and for each subtree rooted at these a nodes, there is one and only one terminal node is colored grey. Considering the $2^{\lceil \log a \rceil}$ subtrees rooted at the $(\lceil \log a \rceil + 1)$-th layer, the a subtrees have only one grey terminal node each and the rest $2^{\lceil \log a \rceil} - a$ subtrees have no grey terminal nodes. For each of the a subtrees, we can calculate the maximum expected number of false positives based on Eq. (1.3); similarly, for each of the rest $2^{\lceil \log a \rceil} - a$ subtrees, we can calculate that based on Eq. (1.2). Thus, M_a can be calculated as follows:

$$M_a = af \times \frac{1 - (2f)^{h - \lceil \log a \rceil}}{1 - 2f} + (2^{\lceil \log a \rceil} - a)f(2f)^{h - \lceil \log a \rceil}$$

Figure 1.5 shows the relation between M_a and a, where we choose $f = 0.05$ and $h = 13$.

1.4   PBtree Search Optimization

In this section, we optimize PBtree searching efficiency by minimizing the number of nodes that a query needs to traverse both horizontally and vertically.

Fig. 1.5 Relation between M_a and a

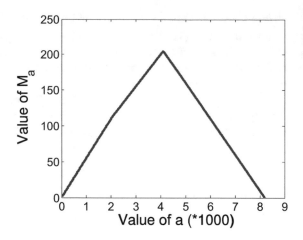

1.4.1 Traversal Width Optimization

Recall that in the PBtree construction algorithm in Sect. 1.3.2, for a nonterminal node with prefix family set S, we partition this node into two child nodes S_1, S_2 so that $0 \leq |S_1| - |S_2| \leq 1$. This partition is critical for the performance of query processing on the PBtree because querying the common prefixes that both S_1 and S_2 share will lead to the traversal of both subtrees. Thus, in partitioning S into S_1, S_2, besides satisfying the condition $0 \leq |S_1| - |S_2| \leq 1$, we want to minimize $Max\{F_i \cap F_j | F_i \in S_1, F_j \in S_2\}$, which is the maximum number of prefixes in the intersection of two prefix families that one from S_1 and the other from S_2. This condition is to let those prefix families that share more prefixes to be partitioned in the same set. We call this problem *Equal Size Prefix Family Partition*. We next formally define this problem and prove that it is NP-hard.

Definition 1.2 (Equal Size Prefix Family Partition) Given a set S of prefix families, we want to partition S into S_1, S_2, such that the following two conditions are satisfied:

1. $0 \leq ||S_1| - |S_2|| \leq 1$;
2. $Max\{F_i \cap F_j | F_i \in S_1, F_j \in S_2\}$ is minimized. □

Theorem 1.2 *The Equal Size Prefix Family Partition problem is NP-hard.* □

Proof The decision version of the Equal Size Prefix Family Partition Problem is the following: "Is it possible to partition a set S of prefix families into S_1 and S_2 such that $0 \leq ||S_1| - |S_2|| \leq 1$ and $Max\{F_i \cap F_j | F_i \in S_1, F_j \in S_2\} < k$?" We reduce the *Set Partition Problem*, a known NP-Complete problem, to the decision version of Equal Size Prefix Family Partition Problem. The Set Partition Problem is as follows: "For a multiset of positive numbers $A = \{a_1, a_2, \ldots, a_n\}$, is it possible to partition A into A_1 and A_2 such that $\sum_{a_i \in A_1} a_i = \sum_{a_j \in A_2} a_j$".

Given an instance of the set partition problem with positive number multiset $A = \{a_1, a_2, \ldots, a_n\}$, we convert it to an instance of our Equal Size Prefix Family Partition Problem with prefix family set S as follows. Let a_{max} be the largest number in A. For each number a_i in A, we first generate a_i data items $d_1, d_2, \ldots, d_{a_i}$ where each data item has $\lceil \log n \rceil + \lceil \log a_{max} \rceil$ bits, and for each data item d_j ($1 \leq j \leq a_i$), the value of the first $\lceil \log n \rceil$ bits is i and the value of the last $\lceil \log a_{max} \rceil$ bits is $j - 1$. For example, suppose $A = \{2, 3, 4\}$, for number 2 in A, we generate 2 data items 0000 and 0001 in their binary representation. Second, for each data item d_j ($1 \leq j \leq a_i$), we generate its prefix family $F(d_j)$. Finally, we map each number a_i in A to a_i prefix families $F(d_1), F(d_2), \ldots, F(d_{a_i})$ in S, and let $k = \lceil \log n \rceil$.

Suppose the prefix family set S constructed above has an equal size prefix family partition solution S_1 and S_2 with $Max\{F_i \cap F_j | F_i \in S_1, F_j \in S_2\} \leq k = \lceil \log n \rceil$. We next prove that A has a set partition solution. Note that if $\sum_{a_i \in A} a_i$ is odd, then the set partition problem has no solution. Thus, we only need to consider cases where $\sum_{a_i \in A} a_i$ is even, which means that $|S_1| = |S_2|$. A notable property of the a_i prefix families $F(d_1), F(d_2), \ldots, F(d_{a_i})$ constructed above is that any two of these prefix families share at least $\lceil \log n \rceil$ prefixes. For example, $F(0001)$ and $F(0001)$ share 3 prefixes. Thus, $Max\{F_i \cap F_j | F_i \in S_1, F_j \in S_2\} \leq k = \lceil \log n \rceil$ implies that for any a_i in A, the constructed a_i prefix families $F(d_1), F(d_2), \ldots, F(d_{a_i})$ are either all in S_1 or all in S_2. Otherwise, suppose $F(d_1) \in S_1$ and $F(d_2) \in S_2$, then $|F(d_1) \cap F(d_2)| \geq \lceil \log n \rceil = k$. Thus, $|S_1|$ is equal to the sum of some numbers in A and $|S_1|$ is equal to the sum of the remaining numbers in A. Finally, $|S_1| = |S_2|$ implies that A has a set partition solution. Thus, the Set Partition Problem $\leq_p$ the decision version of Equal Size Prefix Family Partition Problem, which means that the Equal Size Prefix Family Partition Problem is NP-hard. $\square$

Next, we present our approximation algorithm to the equal size prefix family partition problem. Our algorithm consists of two phases: *partition phase* and *re-organization phase*. In the partition phase, we partition the input prefix family set into two or three subsets so that the size of each subset is no larger than $\lceil \frac{n}{2} \rceil$, where n is the size of the prefix family set. In the re-organization phase, if the first phase outputs two subsets, then we do nothing because the two subsets must satisfy the condition of $0 \leq ||S_1| - |S_2|| \leq 1$; if the first phase outputs three subsets, then we first choose one subset to split into multiple smaller subsets, and then merge these new subsets with the two other subsets to obtain two subsets that satisfy the condition of $0 \leq ||S_1| - |S_2|| \leq 1$.

To help to present the details of these two phases, we first define two concepts: *longest common prefix* and *child prefixes*. The longest common prefix of a set of prefix families $S = \{F_1, F_2, \ldots, F_n\}$, denoted by $LCP(S)$, is the longest prefix in $F_1 \cap F_2 \cap \cdots \cap F_n$. For example, the longest common prefix of $\{F(1101), F(1100)\}$ is 110*. Note that for any set of prefix families, it has only one longest common prefix because no prefix family consists of two prefixes of the same length. For any prefix $b_1 b_2 \cdots b_{w-i+1} * \cdots *$, it has two child prefixes $b_1 b_2 \cdots b_{w-i+1} 0 * \cdots *$ and $b_1 b_2 \cdots b_{w-i+1} 1 * \cdots *$, which are obtained by replacing the first * by 0 and 1 and called child-0 and child-1 prefixes, respectively. For example, prefix $11 * *$ has two child prefixes 110∗ and 111∗. For any prefix p, we use p^0 and p^1 to denote p's child-0 and child-1 prefixes, respectively.

Given a set of prefix families $S = \{F_1, F_2, \ldots, F_n\}$, the partition phase of our approximation algorithm works as follows. First, we compute $LCP(S)$, the longest common prefix of S. Second, we partition S into two subsets, one subset whose each prefix family contains $LCP(S)^0$ and one subset whose each prefix family contains $LCP(S)^1$. If any of the two subsets has a larger size than $\lceil \frac{n}{2} \rceil$, then we recursively apply the above two partition process to that subset. This process terminates when all subsets have a smaller size than $\lceil \frac{n}{2} \rceil$. Third, for any two subsets whose union has a size smaller than $\lceil \frac{n}{2} \rceil$, we call them *mergeable* and we merge them (i.e., union them into one set). This process terminates when no two subsets are mergeable. Thus, we result in either two subsets or three subsets. It is impossible to result in four subsets or more because otherwise there are at least two subsets can be merged.

If the partition phase results in two subsets, then the re-organization phase does nothing. Let S_1 and S_2 be the two subsets. Because $|S_1| + |S_2| = n$, $|S_1| \leq \lceil \frac{n}{2} \rceil$, and $|S_2| \leq \lceil \frac{n}{2} \rceil$, we have $0 \leq ||S_1| - |S_2|| \leq 1$. Thus, S_1 and S_2 represent the final partition result.

If the partition phase results in three subsets, then the re-organization phase chooses one subset to split into multiple smaller subsets, and then union these new subsets with the two other subsets to obtain two subsets S_1 and S_2 that satisfy the condition of $0 \leq ||S_1| - |S_2|| \leq 1$. Let S_1, S_2, and S_3 be the three subsets. We choose the subset whose longest common prefix is the smallest, that is, the subset whose prefix families share the least number of prefixes. Let S_3 be the subset that we choose. We first compute its longest common prefix $LCP(S_3)$. Note that for any prefix family in S_3, it contains either $LCP(S_3)^0$ or $LCP(S_3)^1$. Second, we split S_3 into two subsets S_{31}, whose each prefix family contains $LCP(S_3)^0$, and S_{32}, whose each prefix family contains $LCP(S_3)^1$. Without loss of generality, we suppose $|S_{31}| \leq |S_{32}|$. Thus, either S_1 or S_2 can be merged with S_{31}. Otherwise, if both $|S_1| + |S_{31}| > \lceil \frac{n}{2} \rceil$ and $|S_2| + |S_{31}| > \lceil \frac{n}{2} \rceil$, then $|S_1| + |S_2| + |S_3| = |S_1| + |S_2| + |S_{31}| + |S_{32}| \geq |S_1| + |S_2| + |S_{31}| + |S_{31}| = (|S_1| + |S_{31}|) + (|S_2| + |S_{31}|) > \lceil \frac{n}{2} \rceil + \lceil \frac{n}{2} \rceil \geq n$. Again, suppose $|S_1| \geq |S_2|$ and S_1 can be merged with S_{31}, we merge S_1 with S_{31}. After merging S_1 with S_{31}, we check whether S_2 can be merged with S_{32}. If they can, we merge them and output the partition result $S_1 \cup S_{31}$ and $S_2 \cup S_{32}$. If S_2 and S_{32} can not be merged, we further split S_{32}, and repeat the above process. If S_1 can not be merged with S_{31}, we merge S_{31} with S_2 and split S_{32}, and then repeat the above process.

We now analyze the worst case computational complexity of our prefix family partition algorithm. Let n be the size of the input set of prefix families and $T(n)$ be the corresponding time complexity. Each set partition operation takes $O(n)$ time and each subset merging takes $O(1)$ time. The worse case computational complexity is when each set partition operation produces two subsets where the size of one subset is one. Thus, we have: $T(n) = T(n - 1) + O(n)$. The computational complexity of this algorithm is therefore $O(n^2)$ in the worst case.

Set splitting and merging operations are performed in both phases of our prefix family partition algorithm. To analyze the partition results, we combine these two phases together, and view the whole algorithm as two parts: set splitting and subsets reorganization. The subsets are produced in a top-down fashion. For any prefix family $F_i \in S_i$, $F_j \in S_i$, and $F_k \notin S_i$, we have $|F_i \cap F_j| > |F_i \cap F_k|$. We state the properties of the subsets generated by our algorithm in Theorem 1.3. Before we present Theorem 1.3, we first introduce and prove Lemma 1.4.1.

Lemma 1.4.1 *For any three prefix families $F(d_1)$, $F(d_2)$, and $F(d_3)$, if $|F(d_1) \cap F(d_2)| \geq |F(d_1) \cap F(d_3)|$ and $|F(d_1) \cap F(d_2)| \geq |F(d_2) \cap F(d_3)|$, then $F(d_1) \cap F(d_3) = F(d_2) \cap F(d_3) \subseteq F(d_1) \cap F(d_2)$.*   □

Proof Let $|F(d_1) \cap F(d_3)| = k \geq 0$ and $F(d_1) \cap F(d_2)| = m \geq k$, which means the first k bits of d_1 and d_3 are the same and the first m bits of d_1 and d_2 are the same. Because $m \geq k$, the first k bits of d_1 and d_3 share is also the first k bits of d_1 and d_2 share, which means $F(d_1) \cap F(d_3) \subseteq F(d_1) \cap F(d_2)$. Similarly, $F(d_2) \cap F(d_3) \subseteq F(d_1) \cap F(d_2)$. Because d_1 and d_3 share exactly the first k bits of d_1, d_1 and d_2 share exactly the first m bits of d_1, and $m \geq k$, d_2 and d_3 also share exactly the first k bits of d_1. Thus, $F(d_1) \cap F(d_3) = F(d_2) \cap F(d_3)$.   □

Theorem 1.3 *For any three prefix family sets S_1, S_2, and S_3 produced in our prefix family partition algorithm, we have:*

1. $|F_p \cap F_l| = |F_q \cap F_l| = |\cup_{F_i \in S_i} \cap \cup_{F_j \in S_j}|$, where $F_p \in S_i$, $F_q \in S_i$, and $F_l \in S_j$.
2. *if* $|\cup_{F \in S_1} F \cap \cup_{F \in S_2} F| \geq |\cup_{F \in S_1} F \cap \cup_{F \in S_3} F|$ *and* $|\cup_{F \in S_1} F \cap \cup_{F \in S_2} F| \geq |\cup_{F \in S_2} F \cap \cup_{F \in S_3} F|$, *then* $\cup_{F \in S_1} F \cap \cup_{F \in S_3} F = \cup_{F \in S_2} F \cap \cup_{F \in S_3} F \subseteq \cup_{F \in S_1} F \cap \cup_{F \in S_2} F$.   □

Based on Lemma 1.4.1 and its proof, it is straightforward to prove Theorem 1.3. According to Theorem 1.3, subset production is optimized in our partition algorithm, but subset reorganization is not because the number of common prefixes shared between subsets is not considered.

1.4.2   Traversal Depth Optimization

Our idea for optimizing searching depth is based on the following observation: for any internal node v with label $\{F(d_1), F(d_2), \ldots, F(d_m)\}$ that a query prefix p traverses, if $p \in F(d_1) \cap F(d_2) \cap \cdots \cap F(d_m)$, then all terminal nodes of the subtree rooted at v satisfy the query; thus, we can directly jump to the left most terminal node of this subtree and collect all terminal nodes using the linked list, skipping the traversal of all nonterminal node under v in this subtree. This optimization opportunity is the motivation that we chain the terminal nodes in PBtrees. Note that here $F(d_1) \cap F(d_2) \cap \cdots \cap F(d_m) \neq \emptyset$ because it must contain the prefix of w *s. Furthermore, our searching width optimization technique significantly increases the probability that the prefix families in a nonterminal node share more than one common prefix.

For a node v labeled with $\{F(d_1), F(d_2), \ldots, F(d_m)\}$, we split $\bigcup_{i=1}^{m} F(d_i)$ into two sets: the *common set* $\mathbb{C} = \bigcap_{i=1}^{m} F(d_i)$ and the *uncommon set* $\mathbb{N} = \bigcup_{i=1}^{m} F(d_i) - \bigcap_{i=1}^{m} F(d_i)$. With this splitting, query processing at node v is modified to be the following. First, we check whether $p \in \mathbb{N}$. If $p \in \mathbb{N}$, then we continue to use the query processing algorithm in Sect. 2.3.5 to search p on v's left and right child nodes. If $p \notin \mathbb{N}$, then we further check $p \in \mathbb{C}$; if $p \notin \mathbb{N}$ but $p \in \mathbb{C}$, then we directly jump to the bottom to collect all terminal nodes in the subtree rooted at v; if p is in neither set, then we skip the subtree rooted at v.

The key technical challenge in searching depth optimization is how to store the common set $\mathbb{C}$ and the uncommon set $\mathbb{N}$ for each nonterminal node using Bloom filters. The straightforward solution is to use two Bloom filters, storing $\mathbb{C}$ and $\mathbb{N}$, respectively. However, this will not be space efficient as we need two bit vectors. In this chapter, we propose an space efficient way to represent two Bloom filters using two sets of k hash functions $\{hc_1, hc_2, \ldots, hc_r\}$ and $\{hn_1, hn_2, \ldots, hn_r\}$ but only one bit vector B of m bits. In the PBtree construction phase, for a prefix $p \in \mathbb{C} \cup \mathbb{N}$, if $p \in \mathbb{C}$, we set $B[hc_1(p)], B[hc_2(p)], \ldots, B[hc_r(p)]$ to be 1; if $p \in \mathbb{N}$, we set $B[hn_1(p)], B[hn_2(p)], \ldots, B[hn_r(p)]$ to be 1. Thus, we check whether a $p \in \mathbb{C}$ by checking whether $\wedge_{i=1}^{r}(B[hc_i(p)] == 1)$ holds and check whether $p \in \mathbb{N}$ by checking whether $\wedge_{i=1}^{r}(B[hn_i(p)] == 1)$ holds.

Next, we analyze the false positives of this Bloom filter with two sets of r hash functions and a bit vector B of m bits. Suppose we have inserted n elements (i.e., $|\mathbb{C}| + |\mathbb{N}| = n$) into this bloom filter. Recall that our query processing algorithm conducts two times of set membership testing of a query prefix p at node v: first, we test whether $p \in \mathbb{N}$; second, on the condition that $p \notin \mathbb{N}$, we test whether $p \in \mathbb{C}$. Let $f_\mathbb{N}$ be the probability of a false positive occurs at the first membership testing, and $f_\mathbb{C}$ be the probability of a false positive occurs at the second membership testing. As the n elements are randomly and independently inserted into the bit vector B, the false positive probability at the first membership testing is the same as the false positive probability of the standard Bloom filter. Thus, we have

$$f_\mathbb{N} = (1 - (1 - \frac{1}{m})^{rn})^r = (1 - e^{-\frac{rn}{m}})^r \tag{1.4}$$

As the second testing is only performed on the condition that $p \notin \mathbb{N}$, and similarly, when the condition $p \notin \mathbb{N}$ holds, the false positive probability at testing whether $p \in \mathbb{C}$ is the same as that at testing whether $p \in \mathbb{N}$, we have

$$f_\mathbb{C} = (1 - f_\mathbb{N}) \times (1 - (1 - \frac{1}{m})^{rn})^r = (1 - (1 - e^{-\frac{rn}{m}})^r) \times (1 - e^{-\frac{rn}{m}})^r \tag{1.5}$$

To further reduce the false positive probability in testing $p \in \mathbb{C}$ at node v, when we collect the leaves of the subtree rooted at v, we can randomly choose x leaf nodes to test whether they indeed match p; if any of the leaf nodes does not match p, which means that $p \notin \mathbb{C}$, then we exclude all leaves of the subtree rooted at v from the query result. Thus, with the testing of the x leaf nodes, the false positive probability in testing whether $p \in \mathbb{C}$ becomes the following:

$$f_{\mathbb{C}} \times (1 - e^{-\frac{rn}{m}})^{rx} = (1 - (1 - e^{-\frac{rn}{m}})^r) \times (1 - e^{-\frac{rn}{m}})^{rx+r} \qquad (1.6)$$

Note that we test $p \in \mathbb{N}$ first and only when $p \notin \mathbb{N}$ we test $p \in \mathbb{C}$. Otherwise, if we use the above mentioned leaf testing method to further reduce the false positive probability in testing $p \in \mathbb{C}$, we may introduce false negatives, which is not allowed in our scheme. Suppose we first test $p \in \mathbb{C}$ first and only when $p \notin \mathbb{C}$ we test $p \in \mathbb{N}$. For a query prefix p, if $p \in \mathbb{N}$ and $p \notin \mathbb{C}$, but false positive occurs in testing $p \notin \mathbb{C}$, when we collect the leaves of the subtree rooted at v, if we test a leaf node and find it is not in $\mathbb{C}$, according to the above leaf testing method, we exclude all leaves of the subtree rooted at v from the query result; however, as $p \in \mathbb{N}$, some of these excluded leaves should be included in the query result, which are false negatives.

1.5 PBtree Update

Databases are typically subject to changes including record insertion, modification, and deletion. In this section, we present algorithms for inserting a new data item into a PBtree, modifying an existing data item, and deleting an existing data item from a PBtree. Note that all these operations are taken place on the data owner side, not in the cloud. After finishing the update operations, the data owner sends the modified part of the PBtree to the cloud. And the cloud updates PBtree index correspondingly. Although we support PBtree update, after a number of changes to a PBtree, we suggest to reconstruct the PBtree offline to improve query processing efficiency.

1.5.1 PBtree Insertion Algorithm

According to the definition of PBtrees, given a new data item and a PBtree, the location of the new data item on each level of the new PBtree is predetermined. In the process of inserting this new data item, the prefixes of the new data item need to be inserted into the bloom filers along the path from the root to the corresponding leaf node. Figure 1.6 shows an example PBtree and that after inserting item 24.

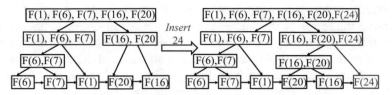

Fig. 1.6 PBtree insertion example

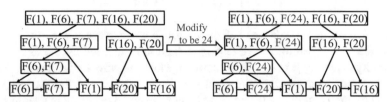

Fig. 1.7 PBtree modification example

Algorithm 5: PBtreeInsert(T, F_i)

Input: A PBtree T, prefix family F_i
Output: A PBtree T with F_i in it

1 Collect all leaf nodes of T into set S;
2 Allocate a new bloom filter B_T for T;
3 Insert all prefix families in S into B_T;
4 Insert F_i into B_T;
5 **if** $|S| == 1$ **then**
6   New two terminal nodes p_1 and p_2;
7   Insert the prefix family in S into p_1's bloom filter;
8   Insert F_i into p_2's bloom filter;
9   Return;
10 **if** $|S|$ *is even* **then**
11   PBtreeInsert($T.LeftChild, F_i$);
12 **else**
13   PBtreeInsert($T.RightChild, F_i$);

1.5.2   PBtree Modification Algorithm

In the process of modifying an existing old data item to be a new data item, we first compute the different prefixes between the old data and the new data item. In the bloom filters along the path from the root to the corresponding leaf node, the prefixes which only belongs to the old data item are deleted and the prefixes which only belongs to the new data item are inserted. Figure 1.7 shows an example PBtree and that after modifying data item $F(7)$–$F(24)$.

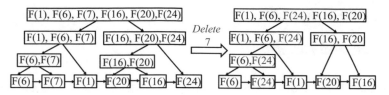

Fig. 1.8 PBtree deletion example

1.5.3   PBtree Deletion Algorithm

As deletion can happen to any data item in a PBtree, the key technical challenge is to preserve the structural indistinguishability of the PBtree after deletion; that is, for a PBtree constructed from n data items, after deleting one data item, the structure of the resulting PBtree should be the same as any PBtree constructed from $n - 1$ data items. To address this challenge, instead of directly deleting the data item d that we want to delete, we first delete a data item d' in the original PBtree so that after deleting d', the structural indistinguishability of the PBtree after deletion is preserved; second, we modify d to be d' in the resulting PBtree after deleting d'. Semantically, this two-step process is equivalent to directly delete d; structurally, we preserve the indistinguishability of the PBtree after deletion. Figure 1.8 shows an example PBtree and that after deleting one data item 7, during which process we first delete 24 from the PBtree and then use 24 to replace 7 in the PBtree and modify the corresponding bloom filters

Bloom filters only support data insertion directly. When processing modification and deletion on the PBtree, the corresponding Bloom filters need to be rebuild. Let n be the number of prefix families in the root. For insertion algorithm, we only need to insert the prefixe family of the inserted data item in the corresponding bloom filters. And the number of bloom filters is equal to the height of the PBtree, which is $\log n$. Thus, the complexity of insertion is $O(\log n)$. The computation complexities of modification and deletion algorithms are similar. For each of these two algorithms, we need to rebuild the Bloom filters along the root to one or two terminals. The total number of prefix families that we need to deal with is $n+n/2+n/4+\cdots+1 = O(n)$. As the number of prefixes in a prefix family and the number of hash function in a Bloom filter are two constants, the complexity of each of these two algorithms is $O(n)$. Note that the updating operations reveal the hash locations of updated data items in the related Bloom filters, which can be partially hidden by choosing new padding bits for the updated Bloom filters.

1.6   Security Analysis

1.6.1   Security Model

To achieve IND-CKA security, our PBtree uses HMAC as the pseudo-random function, which is a *keyed* hash function whose output cannot be distinguished from the output of a truly random function with non-negligible probability [39]. Let $g : \{0, 1\}^n \times \{0, 1\}^s \rightarrow \{0, 1\}^m$ be a keyed function, which takes as input n-bit strings and s-bit keys and maps to m-bit strings. Let $G : \{0, 1\}^n \rightarrow \{0, 1\}^m$ be a random function, which maps n-bit strings to m-bit strings. Function g is pseudo-random if satisfies the following two conditions. First, $g(x, k)$ can be computed efficiently from input $x \in \{0, 1\}^n$ and $k \in \{0, 1\}^s$. Second, for any probabilistic polynomial-time (PPT) adversary $\mathcal{A}$, $|Pr[\mathcal{A}^{g(\cdot, k)} = 1 | k \leftarrow \{0, 1\}^s] - Pr[\mathcal{A}^r | r \leftarrow G : \{0, 1\}^n \rightarrow \{0, 1\}^m]| \leq negl(m)$, where $negl(m)$ is a negligible function. The IND-CKA secure model captures the notion that an adversary cannot deduce the contents of a data set from its index, other than what it already knows from previous query results or from other channels. Let (keygen, BuildIndex, Trapdoor, SearchIndex) be an index scheme. The set difference of A and B is defined as $A \bowtie B = (A - B) \cup (B - A)$. We use the following game between a challenger C and a PPT adversary $\mathcal{A}$ to define IND-CKA security for a dynamic range query scheme.

Setup C creates a set S of data items and gives it to $\mathcal{A}$. $\mathcal{A}$ generates a collection S^* of subsets by choosing a number of subsets from S. $\mathcal{A}$ sends S^* to C. C runs keygen to generate the private key set K_{priv} and builds indexes for each subset in S^* using BuildIndex. Finally, C sends all indexes with their associated subsets to $\mathcal{A}$.

Queries $\mathcal{A}$ issues a range query $[a, b]$ to C. C computes a trapdoor $t_{[a,b]}$ for $[a, b]$ via Trapdoor and returns it to $\mathcal{A}$. With $t_{[a,b]}$, $\mathcal{A}$ searches an index $\mathcal{I}$ via SearchIndex and acquires the corresponding query result.

Updates $\mathcal{A}$ issues an update request to C on index $\mathcal{I}$ for inserting, modifying, or deleting a specified data item. C updates $\mathcal{I}$ to $\mathcal{I}'$ and returns $\mathcal{I}'$ to $\mathcal{A}$.

Challenge After making some queries and updates, $\mathcal{A}$ decides on a challenge by picking a non-empty subset $S_0 \in S^*$ and generating another subset S_1 from S such that $|S_0 - S_1| \neq 0$, $|S_1 - S_0| \neq 0$, and $|S_0| = |S_1|$. Note that $\mathcal{A}$ must not have queried C for the trapdoor of any range query $[a, b]$ such that $\exists d_i \in S_0 \bowtie S_1$ and $a \leq d_i \leq b$, and $\mathcal{A}$ also must have not updated data item d_j such that $d_j \in S_0 \bowtie S_1$. $\mathcal{A}$ sends S_0 and S_1 to C. C choose $b \leftarrow \{0, 1\}$ and builds an index $\mathcal{I}_b$ for S_b via BuildIndex and sends $\mathcal{I}_b$ to $\mathcal{A}$. After the challenge is issued, $\mathcal{A}$ is not allowed to query C for the trapdoor of any query $[a, b]$ such that $\exists d_i \in S_0 \bowtie S_1, a \leq d_i \leq b$ and to update d_j such that $d_j \in S_0 \bowtie S_1$.

Response $\mathcal{A}$ guesses which subset that I_b is built for and outputs a bit b' as its guess for b. The advantage of $\mathcal{A}$ in winning this game is defined as $\text{Adv}_{\mathcal{A}} = |Pr[b = b'] - 1/2|$.

We say that $\mathcal{A}$ breaks an index if $\text{Adv}_{\mathcal{A}}$ is not negligible. We show next that no PPT adversary $\mathcal{A}$ can break the PBtree scheme and thereby, prove its security under the IND-CKA model.

1.6.2 Security Proof

Theorem 1.4 *The PBtree scheme is IND-CKA secure.* □

Proof We prove this theorem by contradiction. Suppose PBtree is not IND-CKA secure, then there exists a PPT algorithm $\mathcal{A}$ that can break it. We construct a PPT algorithm $\mathcal{B}$ using $\mathcal{A}$ as a sub-routine to distinguish a pseudo-random function from a truly random function with non-negligible probability. The algorithm $\mathcal{B}$ works as follows. Given an unknown function g, g is either truly random or pseudo-random, a challenger C replaces HMAC with g in the PBtree scheme. Note that the challenger C has access to an Oracle O_g for the unknown function g that takes as input $\{0, 1\}^n$ and returns $g(x) = \{0, 1\}^m$. The algorithm $\mathcal{B}$ calls the algorithm $\mathcal{A}$ as a subroutine in the following game.

PBtree Construction The challenger C creates a data set S by randomly picking up a number of data items from $\{0, 1\}^n$ and sends to $\mathcal{B}$. $\mathcal{B}$ calls $\mathcal{A}$ to generates a collection S^* of subsets by choosing polynomial number of subsets of S and returns to C. After choosing r secret keys, C builds a PBtree for each subset $S_i \in S^*$ using the PBtree Construction algorithm. C sends all PBtrees with their associated subsets to $\mathcal{B}$.

Queries $\mathcal{B}$ calls $\mathcal{A}$ to generate a range query $[a, b]$ to C. C computes a trapdoor $M_{[a,b]}$ for $[a, b]$ and returns it to $\mathcal{B}$. With $M_{[a,b]}$, $\mathcal{B}$ calls $\mathcal{A}$ to search an index I using PBtree searching algorithm and gets the corresponding query results.

Updates $\mathcal{B}$ calls $\mathcal{A}$ to generate update operations to C on a PBtree I of inserting new data item d_i, deleting existing data item d_i, or modifying existing data item d_i to new data item d_j. C executes the corresponding updating algorithms and returns the updated index I' to $\mathcal{B}$.

Challenge After making some queries and updates, $\mathcal{B}$ calls $\mathcal{A}$ to pick a non-empty subset $S_0 \in S^*$ and generates another subset S_1 from S such that $|S_0 - S_1| \neq 0$, $|S_1 - S_0| \neq 0$, $|S_1| = |S_0|$, no such queries $[a, b]$ have been queried such that $\exists d_i \in S_0 \bowtie S_1$ and $a \leq d_i \leq b$, and no such data item d_j is involved in the updating processes such that $d_j \in S_0 \bowtie S_1$. $\mathcal{B}$ sends S_0 and S_1 to C. C randomly chooses a subset $S_b(b = 0, 1)$ and builds a PBtree I_b for S_b. C sends I_b to $\mathcal{B}$ and $\mathcal{B}$ is not allowed to query C for the trapdoor of any query $[a, b]$ such that $\exists d_i \in S_0 \bowtie S_1$

and $a \leq d_i \leq b$, and $\mathcal{B}$ is not allowed to update $\mathcal{I}_b$ involving data item d_j such that $d_j \in S_0 \bowtie S_1$.

Response $\mathcal{B}$ calls $\mathcal{A}$ to guess which subset that $\mathcal{I}_b$ is built for. $\mathcal{A}$ outputs a bit b' as its guess for b. If $b' = b$, $\mathcal{B}$ outputs 1, indicating that it guesses that g is pseudo-random. Otherwise, $\mathcal{B}$ outputs 0.

Next, we show that $\mathcal{B}$ can determine whether g is a pseudo-random function or a random function with advantage greater than $negl(m)$ by proving the following claims.

Claim 1 When g is a pseudo-random function, then $|Pr[\mathcal{B}^{g(\cdot,k)} = 1|k \leftarrow \{0,1\}^s] - \frac{1}{2}| > negl(m)$.

Claim 2 When g is a random function, then $Pr[\mathcal{B}^g(n) = 1|g \leftarrow \{G : \{0,1\}^n \rightarrow \{0,1\}^m\}] = \frac{1}{2}$.

The proof of Claim 1 is directly. When g is pseudo-random, $\mathcal{B}$ calls $\mathcal{A}$ as a subroutine on IND-CKA game. Therefore, Claim 1 follows by the definition of $\mathcal{A}$.

We prove Claim 2 from following aspects.

First, the PBtrees of other subsets in S^* reveal no information about S_0 and S_1. Recall that each node v in a PBtree is assigned a different random number $v.R$ and g uses $v.R$ to map a hash string s into the bloom filter B_v of node v. We view B_v which s has been mapped into by g as a string output by g. If g is pseudo-random function, then for any PPT algorithm $\mathcal{A}'$, $|Pr[\mathcal{A}'^{(g(s))} = 1|s \leftarrow \{0,1\}^n] - Pr[\mathcal{A}'^r = 1|r \leftarrow \{0,1\}^m]| < negl(m)$, which means a string output by a pseudo-random function is computationally indistinguishable from a random string. Thus, given two different bloom filters B_i and B_j, each of which a string has been mapped into by g, it is infeasible for any PPT algorithm to distinguish whether a same string or two different strings are mapped into them. Note that, it does not matter that whether B_i and B_j belong to a same PBtree or two different PBtrees. Since g is a random function, it is impossible for $\mathcal{A}'$ to correlate codewords across different Bloom filters. That is, $\mathcal{A}'$ learns nothing about $S_0 \bowtie S_1$ from other subsets in S^* and their corresponding PBtrees.

Second, the issued trapdoors reveal no information about the difference between the challenge subsets. With the restriction on the choice of queries during the game, no data item $d_i \in S_0 \bowtie S_1$ falls in any query result. Thus, no issued trapdoors reveal the difference between S_0 and S_1.

Third, the updating operations reveal no useful information for distinguishing the challenge subsets. Given a PBtree, the updating algorithms do not change its structure and also, no data item $d_j \in S_0 \bowtie S_1$ is involved in the updating operations. Thus, no useful information for distinguishing challenge subsets is revealed from the tree structure and the updated data items. When performing an updating operation, some changes are made to the related Bloom filters and the adversary $\mathcal{A}'$ can learn these changes by comparing corresponding Bloom filters. Without losing generality, we assume that $\mathcal{A}'$ learns the hash locations of a data item d_i in Bloom filter B_x. When g is pseudo-random, $\mathcal{A}'$ can not predict the hash locations of d_i in a new

Bloom filter B_y, also, $\mathcal{A}'$ cannot predict the hash locations of $d_j (d_j \neq d_i)$ in B_x, which follows by the definition of a pseudo-random function. Thus, $\mathcal{A}'$ cannot predict hash locations for any data item $d_k \in S_0 \bowtie S_1$ in any Bloom filter of $\mathcal{I}_b$. Since g is truly random, it is impossible for $\mathcal{A}'$ to predict hash locations for any data item $d_i \in S_0 \bowtie S_1$ in any Bloom filter of $\mathcal{I}_b$. That is, $\mathcal{A}'$ learns nothing to distinguish S_0 and S_1 from updating operations.

Now, we only need to consider the challenge subsets to prove Claim 2. As $|S_0| = |S_1|$, according to Theorem 2.1, no information is revealed from the structure of $\mathcal{I}_b$. Without loss of generality, we assume that $S_0 \bowtie S_1$ only contains two data items d_i and d_j, where $d_i \in S_0$ and $d_j \in S_1$. Suppose $\mathcal{A}$ can guess b correctly with advantage θ, then at least there exists one Bloom filter B_i in $\mathcal{I}_b$ that $\mathcal{A}$ can determine d_i or d_j in B_i with advantage θ, which is impossible. Therefore, $\mathcal{A}$ guesses b correctly with probability $1/2$. It follows that $Pr[\mathcal{B}^g = 1 | g \leftarrow \{G : \{0,1\}^n \rightarrow \{0,1\}^m\}] = \frac{1}{2}$, thus proving Claim 2.

It follows from Claims 1 and 2 that $|Pr[\mathcal{B}^{g(\cdot,k)} = 1 | k \leftarrow \{0,1\}^s] - Pr[\mathcal{B}^g = 1 | g \leftarrow \{G : \{0,1\}^n \rightarrow \{0,1\}^m\}]| > negl(m)$, i.e. $\mathcal{B}$ can distinguish a pseudo-random function from a truly random function with non-negligible probability, which is impossible. Thus, we proved that our PBtree scheme is IND-CKA secure.

$\square$

1.7 Experimental Evaluation

1.7.1 Experimental Methodology

To evaluate the performance of PBtree, we considered four factors and generated various experimental configurations. The metrics considered are: the data sets, the type of PBtree construction, the type of queries, and the operations of updating. Based on these metrics, we have comprehensively evaluated the construction cost of the PBtree, the query evaluation time, the observed false positive rates, and the time and the communication cost for updating.

1.7.1.1 Data Sets

We chose the Gowalla [40] data set, which consists of 6,442,890 check-in records of users, over the period of Feb. 2009–Oct. 2010, and extracted the time stamps. Now, given that each time stamp is represented as a tuple: $\langle year, month, date, hour, minute, second \rangle$, we performed a binary encoding for each of these attributes and treated the concatenation of the respective binary strings as a 32-bit integer value, while ignoring the unused bit positions. The details of encoding are as follows: $year$ is represented with a single bit as the value for $year$ is either 2009 or 2010; $month$, $date$ and $hour$ are represented using 5 bits each; and *minute, second* are represented using 6 bits each. We perform the construction and querying experiments on 10 fixed size data sets varying from 0.5 to 5 million records with a scaling factor of 0.5 million records, respectively, chosen uniformly at random from the 6 million-plus total records in the Gowalla data set. For the update experiments, we choose data items randomly from the data set records, which have not been used during the PBtree construction phase.

1.7.1.2 PBtree Types

We performed experiments with three variants of the PBtree: the basic PBtree without any optimizations, denoted as PB_B, the PBtree with width optimization, denoted as PB_W, and the PBtree with both depth and width optimizations, denoted as PB_WD. We have not performed experiments for the case of the PBtree with only depth optimization due to the following reasoning: when searching on a Bloom filter we may need to perform two checks, which is twice the effort. If a query prefix is not found in the Bloom filter, then we need to perform a second check, using a different set of hash functions, to check if the prefix is a common prefix in the Bloom filter. As a result, depth optimization is more effective when combined with width optimization because width optimization aggregates the common prefixes in a systematic manner. Therefore, we focus only on the performance evaluation of PB_B, PB_W and PB_WD.

1.7.1.3 Query Types

The performance evaluation of PBtree is dependent on two factors: query types and query results size. We consider two query types: prefix and range queries. A prefix query is a query specified as a single binary prefix, whereas, a range query is specified as a numerical range and is likely to generate more than one binary prefixes. The prefix queries are effective in evaluating the performance of PBtree under the two types of optimizations we have described, and the range queries are effective to evaluate the performance of PBtree against other known approaches in literature. For each data set, we generate a distinct collection of 10 prefix query sets, where each prefix set contains 1000 prefixes, and similarly, we generate 10 distinct range query sets, where each set contains 1000 range queries. The average number of prefixes for denoting a range in our range query sets vary from 5.93 to 9.6 prefixes, respectively.

The query result size is another important factor since the worst-case run-time search complexity of PBtree is given by $O(r. \log N)$ where r is the query result size. But the challenge is that, since the data values are not in any particular sequence, it is difficult to know which range queries can generate the desired query result sizes after the PBtree is built. To handle this issue, prior to the PBtree construction, we sort the data items and determine the appropriate range queries, which will result in the desired query result sizes and use these queries in our experiments. For our experiments, we chose query ranges which result in query result sizes varying from 10 to 90 data items.

1.7.1.4 Implementation Details

We conducted our experiments on desktop PC running Windows 7 Professional with 32 GB memory and 3.5 GHz *Intel(R) Core(TM) i7-4770k* processor. We used $HMAC - SHA1$ as the pseudo-random function for the Bloom filter encoding and implemented the PBtree using C++. We set the Bloom filter parameter, $m/n = 10$, where m is the Bloom filter size and n is the number of elements, and the number of Bloom filter hash functions as seven. Although we have also experimented with other values of m/n, because of the limited space, we only show the results for $m/n = 10$.

1.7.2 Evaluation of PBtree Construction

Our experimental results show that, the cost of PBtree construction is reasonable, both in terms of time and space. For the chosen datasets, Fig. 1.9a shows that, the average time for generating, the PB_B is 276–3443 s, the PB_W is 338–7500 s, and the PB_WD is 357–14027 s, respectively. The average time required for the PB_WD construction is higher due to the equal-size partition algorithm and common prefix computation overhead involved. However, as we show later, the query processing time for PB_WD is smaller compared to the other two variants of the PBtree, and the false positive rate is lower as well. Figure 1.9b shows that, the PBtree sizes range from 1.598 GB to 18.494 GB for the data sets, and also, for a specific data set size, the PB_B, PB_W, and PB_WD index structures are of the

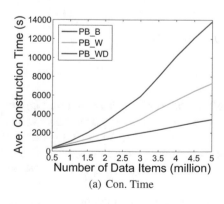

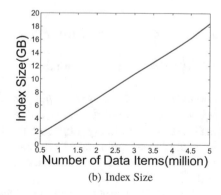

(a) Con. Time

(b) Index Size

Fig. 1.9 Time and Size. (**a**) Con. Time. (**b**) Index Size

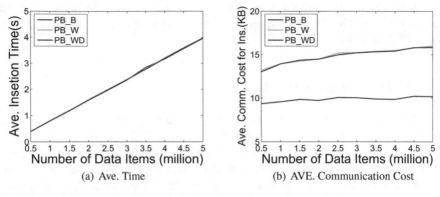

(a) Ave. Time   (b) AVE. Communication Cost

Fig. 1.10 Insertion. (**a**) Ave. Time. (**b**) AVE. communication cost

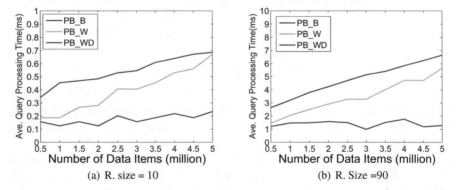

(a) R. size = 10   (b) R. Size =90

Fig. 1.11 Ave. query time of prefix queries. (**a**) R. size = 10. (**b**) R. Size =90

same size, respectively. Finally, the PBtree construction incurs a one-time off-line construction overhead.

1.7.3   Query Evaluation Performance

1.7.3.1   Prefix Query Evaluation

Our experimental results show that, the width and the depth optimizations are highly effective in reducing the query processing time and the false positive rates. We denote the average query result size as "R.Size" in the figures. Figures 1.11 and 1.12 show the average prefix query processing times and false positive rates, respectively, on different data sets, for prefix queries issued on the corresponding PB_B, PB_W and PB_WD structures.

The PB_WD structure exhibits higher query processing efficiency and records lower false positive among all PBtree structures. From the figures, we note that, for

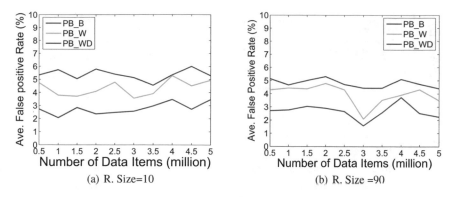

Fig. 1.12 Ave. false positive rate of prefix queries. (**a**) R. Size=10. (**b**) R. Size =90

the same the query result sizes, PB_WD executes, 2.153 and 2.533 times faster than PB_B, respectively; and the corresponding false positive rates in PB_WD are 0.88 and 0.83 times smaller than in PB_B. In comparison, for the same query result sizes, PB_W executes 0.516 and 0.444 times faster than PB_B, respectively; and the corresponding false positive rates in PB_W are 0.25 and 0.21 times smaller than PB_B.

1.7.3.2   Range Query Evaluation

Compared with existing schemes, our experimental results show that PB_WD has smaller range query processing times and lower false positive rates. We compared the speed of PB_WD with two plain text schemes: *linear search*, in which we examine each item from the unsorted data set to match the range query, and *binary search*, in which we execute the range query over the sorted data using the binary search algorithm. To evaluate the accuracy of PB_WD, we compared the recorded false positive rates with those observed in the *bucket* scheme of [7]. In our experiments, both the data items and the queries follow uniform distribution and hence, each bucket contains same number of data items with bucket sizes ranging from 10 to 90. Figures 1.13 and 1.14 show the average range query processing time and the false positive rates, respectively for different query result sizes on the experimental data sets. We observed that, for the three query result sizes, the plan-text binary search is, respectively, 116 and 110 times, faster than the corresponding search results on the PB_WD structure. On the other hand, PB_WD performs, 14.8 and 1.748 times, faster query processing than the linear search scheme. Note that we use logarithmic coordinates in Fig. 1.13.

In terms of accuracy PB_WD outperforms the bucket scheme [7] by orders of magnitude. For instance, for the maximum query result size of 90 in our experiments, the false positive rates recorded by PB_WD are, 2.12 and 39.96 times lesser than the bucket scheme with respective bucket sizes being 10 and 90.

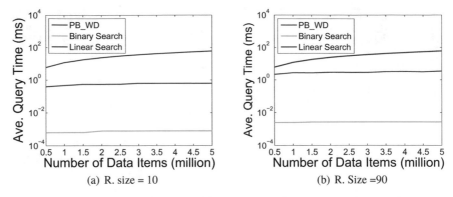

Fig. 1.13 Ave. query time of range queries. (**a**) R. size = 10. (**b**) R. Size =90

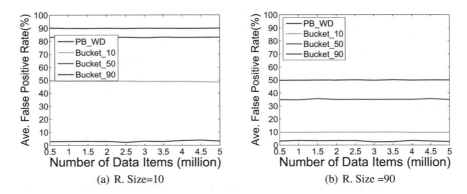

Fig. 1.14 Ave. false positive rate of range queries. (**a**) R. Size=10. (**b**) R. Size =90

1.7.4   Experimental Results on Updating

We measured the average update time and the communication cost, for inserting, modifying, and deleting one data item on the PBtree structures built on the data sets. Note that, in our experiments, we only measure the update cost for the data owner and not for the cloud server. This is because, the cloud server only needs to change the Bloom filter values specified by the data owner, and this is a negligible overhead for the cloud server.

1.7.4.1   Average Time of Updating

Our experiments confirm that the update time increases in proportion to the size of the data set. Figures 1.10a, 1.15a, and 1.16a show the average time of inserting, modifying, and deleting one data item on the corresponding PBtree, respectively. Among the three operations, due to the design of the Bloom filter, inserting an

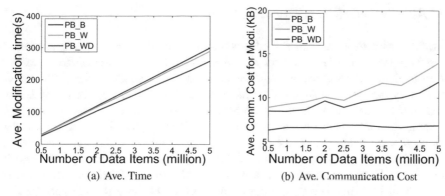

(a) Ave. Time

(b) Ave. Communication Cost

Fig. 1.15 Modification. (**a**) Ave. Time. (**b**) Ave. communication cost

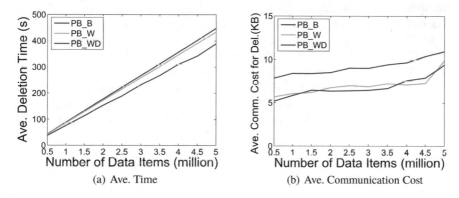

(a) Ave. Time

(b) Ave. Communication Cost

Fig. 1.16 Deletion. (**a**) Ave. time. (**b**) Ave. communication cost

element is the most efficient, while modifying and deleting elements are the most expensive operations.

Regardless of the type of PBtree, PB_WD, PB_W, or PB_B, the insertion time is observed to be identical, i.e., as the data set sizes progressively increase from 0.5 to 5 million data items, the insertion time increases from 0.396 to 3.96 s, respectively. We note that a similar trend is observed for modifying an element, i.e., the modification time is nearly similar across all three PBtree variants with minor differences. For the experimental data sets, with increasing data set sizes, the modification time of PB_WD increases from 25.011 to 258.687 s, and the modification time of PB_W and PB_B increases from 28.388 to 289.666 s. However, deleting an element from PB_WD is slightly faster than deleting an element from PB_W and PB_B. As the data set sizes increase, the average time for deleting an element from PB_WD increases from 37.656 to 389.484 s, and the deletion time for PB_W and PB_B increases from 42.597 to 434.183 s.

1.7.4.2   Communication Cost of Updating

Our experiments show that the communication cost for the update operation is practical and grows slowly with the data set size. The communication cost is measured by the information size that the data owner sends to the cloud server to modify the specified Bloom filter locations in the PBtree. Figures 1.10b, 1.15b, and 1.16b show the average communication cost of inserting, modifying, and deleting one data item on the corresponding PBtree, respectively. To inform the cloud server of the update, the data owner uses a 9-byte meta-data structure, in which the first 4 bytes specify the Bloom filter ID, the next four bytes specify the cell location in the Bloom filter, and the last byte contains the new bit-value to be updated to the cell location. The update communication costs for PB_WD and PB_W are almost similar, and are slightly smaller when compared to communication cost for updating PB_B. For inserting a data item, as the data set sizes increase, the observed communication cost for PB_WD and PB_W increases from 12.98 KB to 15.82 KB, and the communication cost for PB_B increases from 9.34 KB to 10.16 KB. Similarly, the communication cost for modifying an item in PB_WD and PB_W increases from 8.47 KB to 11.82 KB, and the communication cost for PB_B increases from 6.32 KB to 6.9 KB. Finally, as the data set sizes increase, the communication cost of deleting an item from PB_WD and PB_W increases from 5.186 KB to 9.39 KB, and the cost for PB_B increases from 7.84 KB to 10.93 KB.

1.8   Conclusions

In this chapter, we propose the first range query processing scheme that achieves index indistinguishability, under the IND-CKA [13], which provides strong privacy guarantees. The key novelty of this chapter is in proposing the PBtree data structure and associate algorithms for PBtree construction, searching, optimization, and updating. We implemented and evaluated our scheme on a real world data set. The experimental results show that our scheme can efficiently support real time range queries with strong privacy protection.

References

1. Amazon Web Services. https://aws.amazon.com
2. Microsoft azure. www.microsoft.com/azure
3. Google App Engine. https://code.google.com/appengine
4. Google Fires Engineer for Privacy Breach. Fired engineer for privacy breach (2010). http://www.cnet.com/news/google
5. R. Canetti, U. Feige, O. Goldreich, M. Naor, Adaptively secure multi-party computation, in *Proceedings of the 28th ACM Symposium on Theory of Computing (STOC)* (ACM, New York, 1996), pp. 639–648

6. H. Hacigumus, B. Iyer, C. Li, S. Mehrotra, Executing SQL over encrypted data in the database-service-provider model, in *Proceedings of the 2002 ACM SIGMOD International Conference on Management of Data* (2002)
7. B. Hore, S. Mehrotra, G. Tsudik, A privacy-preserving index for range queries, in *Proceedings of the Thirtieth International Conference on Very large Data Bases* (2004), pp. 720–731
8. B. Hore, S. Mehrotra, M. Canim, M. Kantarcioglu, Secure multidimensional range queries over outsourced data. VLDB J. **21**(3), 333–358 (2012)
9. J. Li, E.R. Omiecinski, Efficiency and security trade-off in supporting range queries on encrypted databases, in *IFIP Annual Conference on Data and Applications Security and Privacy* (Springer, Berlin, 2005), pp. 69-83
10. A. Boldyreva, N. Chenette, Y. Lee, A. O'Neill, Order-preserving symmetric encryption, in *Annual International Conference on the Theory and Applications of Cryptographic Techniques* (Springer, Berlin, 2009), pp. 224–241
11. A. Boldyreva, N. Chenette, A. O'Neill, Order-preserving encryption revisited: Improved security analysis and alternative solutions, in *Annual Cryptology Conference (CRYPTO)* (Springer, Berlin, 2011), pp. 578-595
12. D. Song, D. Wagner, A. Perrig, Practical techniques for searches on encrypted data, in *Proceedings of the IEEE S&P Symposium* (2000)
13. E. Goh, Secure indexes, in *Stanford University Technical Report* (2004)
14. D. Boneh, G. Di Crescenzo, R. Ostrovsky, G. Persiano, Public key encryption with keyword search, in *International Conference on the Theory and Applications of Cryptographic Techniques* (2004), pp. 506–522
15. Y.-C. Chang, M. Mitzenmacher, Privacy preserving keyword searches on remote encrypted data, in *Proceedindg of the 3rd International Conference on Applied Cryptography and Network Security (ACNS)* (2005)
16. M. Bellare, A. Boldyreva, A. Oeill, Deterministic and efficiently searchable encryption, in *Proceedings of the CRYPTO* (2007)
17. R. Curtmola, J.A. Garay, S. Kamara, R. Ostrovsky, Searchable symmetric encryption: improved definitions and efficient constructions. J. Comput. Secur. **19**, 895–934 (2011)
18. S. Kamara, C. Papamanthou, T. Roeder, Dynamic searchable symmetric encryption, in *Proceedings of the ACM CCS* (2012)
19. R. Agrawal, J. Kiernan, R. Srikant, Y. Xu, Order preserving encryption for numeric data, in *Proceedings of the ACM SIGMOD* (ACM, New York, 2004), pp. 563–574
20. E. Shi, J. Bethencourt, T.-H.H. Chan, D. Song, A. Perrig, Multi-dimensional range query over encrypted data, in *Proceedings of the IEEE S&P Symposium* (2007)
21. A. Shamir, Identity-based cryptosystems and signature schemes, in *Proceedings of the CRYPTO*, vol. 84 (1985), pp. 47–53
22. X. Boyen, B. Waters, Anonymous hierarchical identity-based encryption (without random oracles), in *Proceedings of the CRYPTO* (2006)
23. O. Goldreich, R. Ostrovsky, Software protection and simulation on oblivious rams. J. ACM **43**(3), 431–473 (1996)
24. E. Damiani, S.C. Vimercati, S. Jajodia, S. Paraboschi, P. Samarati, Balancing confidentiality and efficiency in untrusted relational DBMSS, in *Proceedings of the CCS* (2003), pp. 93–102
25. M. Kantarcioglu, C. Clifton, Security issues in querying encrypted data, in *Proceedings of the DBSec* (2005)
26. P. Golle, J. Staddon, B. Waters, Secure conjunctive keyword search over encrypted data, in *Applied Cryptography and Network Security* (2004)
27. D.J. Park, K. Kim, P. Lee, Public key encryption with conjunctive field keyword search, in *Proceedings of the Information Security Applications* (2005), pp. 73–86
28. L. Ballard, S. Kamara, F. Monrose, Achieving efficient conjunctive keyword searches over encrypted data, in *Proceedings of the Information and Communications Security* (2005), pp. 414–426
29. N. Cao, C. Wang, M. Li, K. Ren, W. Lou, Privacy-preserving multi-keyword ranked search over encrypted cloud data, in *Proceedings of the IEEE INFOCOM* (2011)

30. C. Wang, N. Cao, K. Ren, W. Lou, Enabling secure and efficient ranked keyword search over outsourced cloud data. IEEE TPDS **23**(8), 1467–1479 (2012)
31. W.K. Wong, D.W.-L. Cheung, B. Kao, N. Mamoulis, Secure kNN computation on encrypted databases, in *Proceedings of the 2009 ACM SIGMOD International Conference on Management of data* (2009), pp. 139–152
32. L. Sweeney, K-anonymity: a model for protecting privacy. Int. J. Uncertain. Fuzziness Knowl. Based Syst. **10**(5), 557–570 (2002)
33. N. Li, T. Li, S. Venkatasubramanian, t-closeness: privacy beyond k-anonymity and l-diversity, in *Proceedings of the IEEE 23rd International Conference on Data Engineering (ICDE 2007)* (2007), pp. 106–115
34. R. Agrawal, R. Srikant, Privacy-preserving data mining, in *Proceedings of the ACM SIGMOD* (ACM, New York, 2000), pp. 439–450
35. S. Oliveira, O. Zaïane, Privacy preserving clustering by data transformation. JIDM **1**(1), 37–52 (2010)
36. F. Li, M. Hadjieleftheriou, G. Kollios, L. Reyzin, Authenticated index structures for outsourced databases, in *Handbook of Database Security* (2008), pp. 115–136
37. A.X. Liu, F. Chen, Collaborative enforcement of firewall policies in virtual private networks, in *Proceedings of the ACM PODC* (2008)
38. P. Gupta, N. McKeown, Algorithms for packet classification. IEEE Netw. **15**(2), 24–32 (2001)
39. J. Katz, Y. Lindell, *Introduction to Modern Cryptography* (Chapman and Hall/CRC, New York, 2007)
40. E. Cho, S.A.Myers, J. Leskovec, Friendship and mobility: User movement in location-based social networks, in *Proceedings of the 17th ACM SIGKDD International Conference on Knowledge Discovery and Data Mining(KDD)* (ACM, New York, 2011), pp. 1082–1090

Chapter 2
Fast and Scalable Range and Keyword Query Processing Over Encrypted Data with Provable Adaptive Security

2.1 Introduction

2.1.1 Motivation and Problem Statement

Both enterprises and end users have been increasingly outsourcing their data and computing services to public clouds such as Amazon EC2 and S3, Microsoft Azure, and Google App Engine for lower cost, higher reliability, better performance, and faster deployment. However, privacy has become the key concern as data owners may not fully trust public clouds. First, clouds may have corrupt employees. For example, in 2010, a Google engineer broke into the Gmail and Google Voice accounts of several children. Second, clouds may be hacked and customers may not be informed. Third, some cloud facilities may be operated in some foreign countries where privacy regulations are difficult to enforce.

In this chapter, we adopt the cloud computing paradigm in Chap. 1 where a data owner stores data on a cloud and multiple data users query the data. Among the three parties, the data owner and data users are trusted, but the cloud is not fully trusted.

In this chapter, we consider the fundamental problem of processing conjunctive queries that contain both keyword conditions and range conditions on public clouds in a privacy preserving manner. The query conditions in the *where* clauses of SQLs are often conjunctive conditions of keywords and ranges. A disjunctive query can be easily converted into multiple conjunctive queries. For example, in the SQL query `select * from patient where NAME="John" and age` ≤ 30, the `where` clause contains a *keyword* condition NAME=`"John"` and a *less-than* condition age `< 30`, which can be converted into range condition age $\in$ [0, 30]. In particular, we consider Searchable Symmetric Encryption (SSE) schemes as symmetric encryption based privacy preserving schemes are significantly more efficient than asymmetric ones. In SSE, the data owner builds a *secure index* I for a

A. X. Liu, R. Li, *Algorithms for Data and Computation Privacy*,
https://doi.org/10.1007/978-3-030-58896-0_2

data set D, and encrypts each data item $d_i \in D$ into $(d_i)_K$ using a secret key K that is shared between the data owner and data users. Then, the data owner outsources the secure index I along with the set of encrypted data $\{(d_1)_K, (d_2)_K, \cdots, (d_n)_K\}$ to the cloud. Given a conjunctive query q, the data user generates a *trapdoor* t_q for q, and sends t_q to the cloud. Base on t_q and the secure index I, the cloud can determine which encrypted data items satisfy q without knowing the content of the data and query. Yet, in this process, the cloud should not be able to infer privacy information about the data items and queries such as data content, query content, and the statistical properties of attribute values. The index I should leak no information about the data items in D. Note that a data item d_i could be a record in a rational database table or a text document in a document set.

2.1.2   Threat Model

We assume that the cloud is *semi-honest* (also called *honest-but-curious*), which was proposed by Canetti et al. in [1] and has been widely adopted by prior privacy preserving keyword and range query work [2–13]. A cloud is semi-honest means that it follows required communication protocols and execute required algorithms correctly, but it may attempt to obtain information about data items and the content of user queries. The data owner and data users are trusted.

2.1.3   Security Model

In this chapter, we adopt the *adaptive IND-CKA* security model proposed in [8], which is by far the strongest security model for SSE based keyword query schemes. Here IND-CKA means that the index is *indistinguishable (IND)* under *chosen keyword attack (CKA)*. Non-adaptive and adaptive IND-CKA models differ in how keywords are chosen. The IND-CKA model is based on two facts. First, the outputs of a truly random function contains no meaningful information. Second, the outputs of a pseudo-random function are not distinguishable from the outcomes of a truly random function by any polynomial-time adversary. An index I constructed by a pseudo-random function is $\mathcal{L}$-secure under the IND-CKA model if and only if there exists a simulator S that is constructed from the information leaked by leakage function $\mathcal{L}$ using a truly random function and can simulate I with the queries chosen by a polynomial-time adversary $\mathcal{A}$ so that to $\mathcal{A}$, the query results from $\mathbb{I}$ are not distinguishable from the outputs of S (i.e., $\mathcal{A}$ can correctly guess whether the query result is obtained from I or S with a negligible probability over $\frac{1}{2}$). The leakage function $\mathcal{L}$ usually includes the information such as input queries, output query results, the index size, and the data size.

In the non-adaptive IND-CKA model, the adversary chooses the queries without considering the previously chosen queries along with their trapdoors and query results. An adversary $\mathcal{A}$ sends a data set D with a set of chosen queries Q to a challenger C. The challenger C builds a secure index I for D, generates trapdoor t_q for each query $q \in Q$, processes queries using t_q and I, and sends back the query results to the adversary $\mathcal{A}$. The index I is secure in this non-adaptive IND-CKA model if and only if (1) there exists a simulator S that can simulate I by returning query results for the queries in Q and (2) $\mathcal{A}$ cannot distinguish the results returned by I from the outputs returned by S.

In the adaptive IND-CKA model, the adversary $\mathcal{A}$ chooses each query based on the previously chosen queries along with their trapdoors and query results. An adversary $\mathcal{A}$ sends a data set D to a challenger C. The challenger C builds a secure index I for D. Then the adversary begins the query process as follows. First, $\mathcal{A}$ chooses a query q_1 and sends to the challenger C. Second, C computes t_{q_1} for q_1, processes the query with t_{q_1} and I, and returns the query results R_1 back to $\mathcal{A}$. Third, based on I, t_{q_1}, and R_1, $\mathcal{A}$ chooses query q_2 and repeats the above query process. These query processes repeat a polynomial number of times. The index I is secure in this adaptive IND-CKA model if and only if (1) there exists a simulator S that can simulate I by returning query results for the queries chosen by $\mathcal{A}$ and (2) $\mathcal{A}$ cannot distinguish the results returned by I from the outputs returned by S.

The key differences between non-adaptive IND-CKA model and adaptive IND-CKA model are threefolds. First, the requirements for simulators are different. The simulator in the non-adaptive IND-CKA model only needs to simulate an index for a set of *known* queries. The simulator in the adaptive IND-CKA model needs to simulate an index for both *known* and *unknown* queries. Second, on what queries the results returned by I are undistinguishable from the outputs returned by S are different. For the non-adaptive IND-CKA model, only for the set of known queries, the results returned by I are guaranteed to be undistinguishable from the outputs returned by S. For the adaptive IND-CKA model, for a polynomial number of both previously known and previously unknown queries, the results returned by I are guaranteed to be undistinguishable from the outputs returned by S. Third, the level of securities are different. A non-adaptive secure scheme only provides security if the search queries are independent of the secure index I and previous search results. An adaptive secure scheme guarantees security even the search queries are not independent of the secure index I and of previous search results[10]. A query scheme is secure under the adaptive IND-CKA model, then it is also secure under the non-adaptive IND-CKA model, but not vice versa.

2.1.4 Limitation of Prior Art

A practical privacy preserving conjunctive query scheme that supports keyword conditions, range conditions, and their conjunctions should satisfy the three requirements of *adaptive security under the IND-CKA model, efficient query processing time,* and *scalable index size with respect to the number of data items.* However, no prior scheme satisfies all these requirements. The schemes in [14, 15] achieve adaptive security and scalable index sizes, but are extremely inefficient because they use Yao's Garbled Circuits [16] to evaluate query conditions and require multiple rounds of communication to process a query. The schemes in [11, 13] achieve efficient query processing time and scalable index sizes, but are not adaptively secure; the Constant schemes proposed in [17] cannot achieve adaptive security under IND-CKA model; the scheme proposed in [18] supports incremental, query-triggered adaptive indexing over encrypted numeric data. None of the schemes in [13, 17, 18] supports conjunctive queries. The scheme in [11] cannot process range queries. The schemes in [12, 19–22] and the SSE-2 scheme in [8] are adaptively secure, but they all only support keyword queries; furthermore, the schemes in [19–22] have an unscalable index size of $O(mn)$, where m is the total number of all possible keywords that can be queried, which can be extremely large, and n is the total number of all documents. The CryptDB system in [23] makes use of property-preserving encryption schemes such as deterministic (DTE) and order preserving encryption (OPE) to support keyword and range queries. However, property-preserving encryption schemes have been proved to be fundamentally insecure by Naveed et al. in CCS 2015 [24].

2.1.5 Proposed Approach

In this chapter, we propose the first SSE based conjunctive query scheme that supports both keyword conditions and range conditions and satisfies the three requirements of adaptive security, efficient query processing time, and scalable index sizes. To achieve adaptive security, we propose a data structure called *Indistinguishable Bloom Filter (IBF)* for storing index elements. Each element in an IBF has two cells: one is used for storing index information and the other is for masking, which help us to achieve node indistinguishability and enable the simulator of an IBF to simulate future unknown queries in a random oracle model. The key difference between IBFs and Bloom filters is that IBFs have the ability to simulate future unknown queries while Bloom filters cannot. To achieve *efficient query processing time* and *structure indistinguishability*, we propose a highly balanced binary tree structure called *Indistinguishable Binary Tree (IBtree)* whose structure solely depends on the number of index elements regardless of their values. To optimize searching efficiency, we propose a traversal width minimization algorithm and a traversal depth minimization algorithm to minimize the number of nodes need to be traversed in an IBtree for processing queries. To achieve scalable index sizes, we propose an IBtree space compression algorithm to remove redundant information in the IBFs. To support range queries, we transform range query processing into keyword query processing by transforming range membership testing (i.e. testing whether a number belongs to a range), which involves less-than and bigger-than comparison, into set membership testing (i.e. testing whether a keyword is in a set), which only involves equality comparison. Furthermore, we formally prove that our scheme achieves adaptive security.

2.1.6 Novelty and Advantages Over Prior Art

Our scheme is the first SSE based conjunctive query scheme that achieves adaptive security, efficient query processing time, and scalable index sizes. The key technical novelty of this chapter is five-fold. First, our IBF data structure is novel. It helps us to achieve node indistinguishability and adaptive security for the whole scheme. Second, our IBtree data structure is novel. It helps us to achieve structure indistinguishability and make sublinear query processing time possible. Third, our trapdoor generation method is novel. It overcomes the range expansion problem. Fourth, our multidimensional partition algorithm is novel. It improves searching efficiency significantly, especially in the case of large number of dimensions. Fifth, our IBtree space compression algorithm is novel. It reduces index size by orders of magnitude.

2.2 Related Work

Non-SSE Based Privacy Preserving Query Schemes Dan Boneh et al. proposed a predicate encryption named Hidden Vector Encryption (HVE) to support conjunctive, subset, and range query processing [25]. Elaine Shi et al. proposed a scheme named MRQED using identity based encryption to handle multidimensional range queries [26]. Bharath K. Samanthula et al. proposed a privacy-preserving query processing scheme based on homomorphic encryption and garbled circuit techniques that supports complex queries over encrypted data [27]. However, these three schemes have linear query processing time with respect to the total number of data records. Boyang Wang et al. proposed a multidimensional range query processing scheme achieving sublinear query processing time, based on HVE and R-trees [28]; however, it reveals query conditions to the cloud. Furthermore, the schemes proposed in [25–28] are asymmetric cryptography based approaches, which have a high computing complexity. For example, the scheme in [27] requires several seconds to test whether a data item satisfies a query condition. The scheme in [29] adopts the ASPE approach [30] to encrypt query ranges; however, the security of ASPE is not secure against chosen plain text attack [31]. Oblivious RAMs proposed by Goldreich and Ostrovsky can be used to support complex query processing with adaptive security; however, this scheme requires multiple rounds of interaction for each read and write, which makes it extremely inefficient [32]. Arasu et al. described the design of Cipherbase system and presented the design of Cipherbase secure hardware and its implementation using FPGAs [33], which is different from our secure model as we do not consider to equip special hardwares in cloud servers.

SSE Based Privacy Preserving Keyword Query Schemes Besides the keyword query schemes mentioned in Sect. 2.1.4, there are other SSE based privacy preserving keyword query schemes such as the ones in [4, 5, 7] and the one in [8]. In [34], the authors proposed a scheme for privacy preserving string matching. But all of them only achieve non-adaptive security. Seny Kamara et al. proposed a scheme to process SQL queries over encrypted data for a relational database [35]. But the scheme in [35] does not supports privacy preserving conjunctive queries that contain range conditions.

SSE Based Privacy Preserving Range Query Schemes All prior SSE based privacy preserving range query schemes, no matter one-dimensional or multidimensional, cannot achieve adaptive security. Bucketing based range query schemes [36, 37] and order preserving encryption/hash function based range query schemes [2, 3, 38–40] cannot achieve provably security, no matter under the non-adaptive or the adaptive security model.

2.3   Basic IBtree Algorithms

In this section, we first introduce the key generation algorithm and data encryption algorithm. Second, we introduce our index element encoding algorithm both for numeric and non-numeric index elements, which is executed by the data owner. Third, we introduce our IBF data structure and its construction algorithm, which is executed by the data owner. Fourth, we introduce our IBtree and its construction algorithm, which is executed by the data owner. Fifth, we present our trapdoor computation algorithm, which is executed by data users. At last, we present our query processing algorithm, which is executed by the cloud.

2.3.1   Index Element Encoding

There are two types of index elements for indexing data: non-numeric and numeric. Given a non-numeric index element, we encode it into a keyword by concatenating its corresponding attribute name. For example, we encode people's name "John" into keyword "NAME:John", where "NAME" is the attribute of "John". Given a numeric index element, we first adopt the prefix membership verification scheme to compute its prefix family. The prefix membership verification scheme helps us to convert the testing of whether a numeric data item falls into a range to the testing of whether two sets have common elements. Given a w-bit number x whose binary representation is $b_1 b_2 \cdots b_w$, its prefix family denoted as $F(x)$ is defined as the set of $w+1$ prefixes $\{b_1 b_2 \cdots b_w, b_1 b_2 \cdots b_{w-1}*, \cdots, b_1 * \cdots *, ** \ldots *\}$, where the i-th prefix is $b_1 b_2 \cdots b_{w-i+1} * \cdots *$. For example, the prefix family of 4-bit number 4 is $F(4) = F(0100) = \{0100, 010*, 01**, 0***, ****\}$. Each prefix denotes a range. For example, the prefix $01**$ denotes the range $[0100, 0111]$. Given a range $[a, b]$, we convert it into the minimum set of prefixes, denoted by $S([a, b])$, such that the union of the ranges denoted by all prefixes in $S([a, b])$ is equal to $[a, b]$. For example,

$S([1, 7])=\{0001, 001*, 01 * *\}$. For any number x and range $[a, b]$, $x \in [a, b]$ if and only if there exists prefix $p \in S([a, b])$ so that $x \in R(p)$ holds, where $R(p)$ is the range denoted by p. Furthermore, for any number x and prefix p, $x \in R(p)$ if and only if $p \in F(x)$. Thus, for any number x and range $[a, b]$, $x \in [a, b]$ if and only if $F(x) \cap S([a, b]) \neq \emptyset$. From the above examples, we see that $4 \in [1, 7]$ and $F(4) \cap S([0, 8])=\{01**\}$. After the prefix family computation, we encode each prefix into a keyword by concatenating its corresponding attribute name. For the above example, assuming the attribute of "4" is "AGE", we encode each prefix in $F(4)$ into keywords "AGE:0100", "AGE:010*", "AGE:01**", "AGE:0***", and "AGE:****".

2.3.2 IBF Construction

Bloom filters (BFs) are space-efficient probabilistic data structures for fast set membership verification. The one-wayness property of Bloom filters has been exploited for preserving data privacy in prior work [5, 13]. However, neither of these two schemes achieves adaptive security. The reason stems from the difficulty of creating Bloom filters that can simulate in advance, an index for the adversary that will be consistent with future unknown queries. In this chapter, we propose a new data structure called *Indistinguishable Bloom filters (IBF)*, which enables the simulator of an IBF to simulate future unknown queries, to achieve adaptive security.

Definition (Indistinguishable Bloom Filter) An indistinguishable bloom filter (IBF) is an array B of m twins, k pseudo-random hash functions $h_1, h_2, \cdots, h_k$, and a hash function H. Each twin consists of two cells where each cell stores one bit and the two bits remain the opposite. For each twin, the hash function H determines which cell is chosen in a random fashion. For every twin, the chosen cell is initialized to 0 and the unchosen cell is set to 1. Given one keyword w, we hash it to k twins $B[h_1(w)], B[h_2(w)], \cdots, B[h_k(w)]$, and for each of these k twins, we set its chosen cell to 1 and set its unchosen cell to 0. □

An IBF with m twins always has m 1s and the chosen cell in a twin is determined randomly. Thus, a polynomial-time adversary $\mathcal{A}$ can correctly guess which cell is chosen from a twin with a negligible probability over $\frac{1}{2}$. Figure 2.1 shows an example IBF, where grey cells are chosen cells.

Fig. 2.1 An example IBF

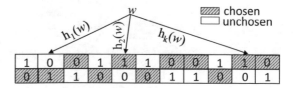

Given a set of keywords, our IBF construction algorithm outputs the IBF B that probabilistically represents the keyword set. Let $W=\{w_1, w_2, \cdots, w_g\}$ be the given set of keywords. We assume that the data owner and the data users share $k + 1$ secret keys, $K_1, K_2, \cdots, K_k, K_{k+1}$. We construct k pseudo-random hash functions $h_1, h_2, \cdots, h_k$ using the keyed-hash message authentication code HMAC, where $h_i(.)=\text{HMAC}_{K_i}(.)\%m$ for $1 \leq i \leq k$). We construct a hash function H using the pseudo-random hash function SHA1 as $H(.)=\text{SHA1}(.)\%2$. We consturct another pseudo-random hash function h_{k+1} using the keyed-hash message authentication code HMAC where $h_{k+1}(.)=\text{HMAC}_{K_{k+1}}(.)$. For each keyword w_i, we hash it to k twins $B[h_1(w_i)], B[h_2(w_i)], \cdots, B[h_k(w_i)]$. For each of these k twins $B[h_j(w_i)]$ $(1 \leq j \leq k)$, we first use the pseudo-random hash function H to determine the chosen cell location $H(h_{k+1}(h_j(w_i)) \oplus r_B)$ where r_B is a random number associated with IBF B; then, we assign its value to be 1 and the other cell's value to 0 (i.e., $B[h_j(w_i)][H(h_{k+1}(h_j(w_i)) \oplus r_B)]:=1$ and $B[h_j(w_i)][1 - H(h_{k+1}(h_j(w_i)) \oplus r_B)]:=0$). For an IBF B, *the value of its i-th twin* is the value of the chosen cell.

The IBF constructed from a keyword set W preserves W's privacy for two reasons. First, through the use of secure one-way hash functions, our construction algorithm achieves one-wayness. That is, given a keyword set W, we can easily compute the IBF, but given an IBF, it is computationally infeasible to compute W. Second, through the use of the hash function $H(.)$, our construction algorithm achieves equivocation for each element in an IBF. For each twin in an IBF, the cell that we choose for storing the BF bit is totally random. Note that we associate a random number with an IBF to eliminate the correlation among different IBFs.

2.3.3   IBtree Construction

Given n data items $d_1, d_2, \cdots, d_n$, where each d_i has a keyword set $W(d_i)$, we organize the keyword sets into our *IBtree* data structure. Figure 2.2 shows an IBTree for the data set $D=\{d_1, d_2, d_3, d_4, d_5, d_6, d_7\}$.

Definition 2.1 (IBtree) An IBTree constructed from n data items is a highly balanced full binary tree with n terminal nodes and $n - 1$ nonterminal nodes. All n

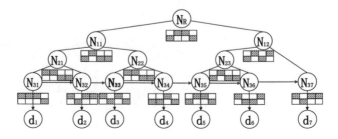

Fig. 2.2   IBtree example

terminal nodes form a linked list from left to right. Each terminal and nonterminal node is an IBF. Each terminal node is an IBF constructed from the keyword set of one data item, and each nonterminal node is an IBF constructed from the union of all keyword sets represented by its left and right children. For any nonterminal node, its left child has the same number of terminal nodes as its right child or its left child has one more terminal node than its right child. All IBFs in this tree have the same size.   □

The IBtree data structure gives us structure indistinguishability because the structure of an IBtree solely depends on the number of data items. The key property of IBtrees is stated in Theorem 2.1, which is straightforward to prove according to the IBtree definition.

Theorem 2.1 (IBtree Structure Indistinguishability) *For any two sets of data items D_1 and D_2, their IBtrees have exactly the same structure if and only if $|D_1| = |D_2|$.*

Given a set of data items $D = \{d_1, d_2, \cdots, d_n\}$, we first encrypt each data item $d_i \in D$ by calling $\mathcal{E}.Enc(d_i, K_d)$, where $\mathcal{E}$ is an CPA-security encryption scheme such as AES and k_d is a secret key shared by the data owner and data users. Then we construct an IBtree in two stages. In the first stage, we build the tree structure in a top-down fashion. First, we compute the root node, which is labeled with the complete set D. Second, we partition D into two subsets D_l and D_r so that $0 \leq |D_l| - |D_r| \leq 1$. Third, we construct two child nodes for the root, where the left child is labeled with D_l and the right child is labeled with D_r. We recursively apply the above three steps to the left and right children, respectively, until each node contains only one data item. And all these nodes that contain only one data item form the leaf nodes in the IBtree. At last, we link all leaf nodes into a list.

In the second stage, we construct an IBF for each node in the IBtree in a bottom-up fashion. First, for each terminal node v labeled with a data item d, we construct an IBF from $W(d)$ using our IBF construction algorithm. Second, for each nonterminal node v whose left child and right child have constructed their IBFs, we construct v's IBF from the two IBFs of two children using the logical OR operation. Let B_l and B_r denote the two constructed IBFs of v's left and right child, respectively. We now construct the IBF of v, denoted B_v, as follows: for each $1 \leq i \leq m$, the value of B_v's i-th twin is the logical OR of B_l's i-th twin and B_r's i-th twin. That is, $B_v[i][H(h_{k+1}(i) \oplus r_{B_v})]:=B_l[i][H(h_{k+1}(i) \oplus r_{B_l})] \vee B_r[i][H(h_{k+1}(i) \oplus r_{B_r})]$. This process repeats until we construct the IBFs for all nonterminal nodes. Note that same $k + 1$ secret keys are used for constructing all IBFs in an IBtree.

2.3.4   Trapdoor Computation

We first present our trapdoor computation algorithm for multidimensional keyword queries. Single keyword queries are special cases of multidimensional keyword queries. Given a u-dimensional keyword query $q = e_1 \wedge e_2 \cdots \wedge e_u$, the data user first encodes each index element $e_i (1 \le i \le u)$ into a keyword w_{e_i} by concatenating its attribute. Second, the data user computes k locations $h_1(w_{e_i}), h_2(w_{e_i}), \cdots, h_k(w_{e_i})$ for w_{e_i}. Third, for each location $h_j(w_{e_i})$ $(1 \le j \le k)$, the data user computes hash $h_{k+1}(h_j(w_{e_i}))$. The sub-trapdoor for e_i is a k-pair of the locations and hashes: $\{(h_1(w_{e_i}), h_{k+1}(h_1(w_{e_i}))), \cdots, (h_k(w_{e_i}), h_{k+1}(h_k(w_{e_i})))\}$. Then, the $(u \times k)$-pair of locations and hashes are formed the trapdoor t_q for q.

Now we present our trapdoor computation algorithm for multidimensional range queries. One-dimensional range queries are special cases of multidimensional range queries too. Given a query $q=[a_1, b_1][a_2, b_2] \cdots [a_u, b_u]$, we first consider the case where each range $[a_i, b_i]$ $(1 \le i \le u)$ is a prefix range (i.e., can be represented by one prefix). For such a multidimensional prefix range q, we compute its trapdoor t_q as follows. First, for each $1 \le i \le u$, we encode range $[a_i, b_i]$ to a keyword $A_i |[a_i, b_i]$, where A_i is the attribute of dimension i. Second, for each keyword $A_i |[a_i, b_i]$, we use the $k + 1$ hash functions in IBtree construction algorithm to compute k-pair of locations and hashes. Then, for a u dimensional prefix range, we compute $u \times k$ ordered pairs as the trapdoor t_q for q.

We now consider the case where there exist $1 \le i \le u$ so that $[a_i, b_i]$ is not a prefix range. A straight-forward solution is to convert query q to a set of multidimensional prefix ranges whose union is q. For each multidimensional prefix range, we can compute its trapdoor as above. However, this solution suffers from the range expansion problem explained below. Let w be the number of bits for representing each a_i and b_i. In the worst case, the minimum number of prefixes to represent an arbitrary $[a_i, b_i]$ is $2w - 2$ [41]. Thus, for a u-dimensional range $[a_1, b_1][a_2, b_2] \cdots [a_u, b_u]$, in the worst case, it requires a minimum of $(2w - 2)^u = O(w^u)$ prefixes. To address the prefix expansion problem, we observe that there is always a minimum multidimensional prefix range, denoted by q_s, that contains the multidimensional non-prefix range $[a_1, b_1][a_2, b_2] \cdots [a_u, b_u]$. Let $q_c = q_s - [a_1, b_1][a_2, b_2] \cdots [a_u, b_u]$. We observe that q_c can be represent by $O(wu)$ multidimensional prefix ranges. Now we compute q_s and q_c. For each arbitrary range $[a_i, b_i]$, let $[\hat{a}_i, \hat{b}_i]$ be the minimum prefix range that contains $[a_i, b_i]$. The minimum multidimensional prefix range that contains $[a_1, b_1][a_2, b_2] \cdots [a_u, b_u]$ is therefore $[\hat{a}_1, \hat{b}_1][\hat{a}_2, \hat{b}_2] \cdots [\hat{a}_u, \hat{b}_u]$. For each $1 \le i \le u$, we use $\overline{[a_i, b_i]}$ denote $[\hat{a}_i, \hat{b}_i] - [a_i, b_i]$. Thus, $q_c = \overline{[a_1, b_1]}[\hat{a}_2, \hat{b}_2] \cdots [\hat{a}_u, \hat{b}_u] \cup [\hat{a}_1, \hat{b}_1]\overline{[a_2, b_2]}[\hat{a}_3, \hat{b}_3] \cdots [\hat{a}_u, \hat{b}_u] \cup \cdots \cup [\hat{a}_1, \hat{b}_1][\hat{a}_2, \hat{b}_2] \cdots [\hat{a}_{u-1}, \hat{b}_{u-1}]\overline{[a_u, b_u]}$. This is because for any data item $d = (d^1, d^2, \cdots, d^u)$, if there exist i so that $d^i \notin [a_i, b_i]$, then $(d^1, d^2, \cdots, d^u) \notin [a_1, b_1][a_2, b_2] \cdots [a_u, b_u]$, regardless of the values of $d^1, d^2, \cdots, d^{i-1}, d^{i+1}, \cdots, d^u$. As $\overline{[a_i, b_i]}$ can be represented by at most 2 ranges, in the worst case, the minimum number of prefixes that can represent $\overline{[a_i, b_i]}$ is $4w - 4$. Thus, in the worst case, the minimum number of prefix ranges that can represent q_c is $(4w - 4)u = O(wu)$. By representing query q as $q_s - q_c$, we address the range expansion problem by converting the multiplicative effect to additive effect. Our idea of processing query $q = q_s - q_c$ is to first find all data items that satisfy q_s and then prune the data items that satisfy query q_c. Thus, we call q_s the *searching component* of q and q_c the *checking component* of q.

The trapdoor t_q consists of both t_{q_s} and t_{q_c}. For q_s, which is a multidimensional prefix range, we use the above trapdoor computation method to compute $u \times k$ ordered pairs as t_{q_s}. For q_c, we only need to compute $u \times k$ ordered pairs for each $\overline{[a_i, b_i]}$ because if a data item d satisfies q_s, then we only need to check whether there exists $1 \le i \le u$ such that $d^i \in \overline{[a_i, b_i]}$. For each $1 \le i \le u$, we first convert $\overline{[a_i, b_i]}$ to a minimum set of prefix ranges, and then for each of these prefix ranges, we convert it to a keyword, and use the $k + 1$ hash functions to compute k ordered pairs as t_{q_c}.

To compute a trapdoor for a conjunctive query that contains both keywords and ranges, the data user first adopts the above two trapdoor computation algorithms to compute sub-trapdoors for keywords and ranges, respectively, and then combines them together to form the trapdoor for the conjunctive query.

Discussion A limitation of known SSE construction is that the same trapdoors are always generated for the same queries. This means that searches leak statistical information about data user search patterns. In comparison, our trapdoor computation algorithm can be amended to partially overcome this limitation. When computing t_{q_s} for query q, the data user randomly chooses $k'(k' < k)$ hash functions from $\{h_1, h_2, \cdots, h_k\}$ to compute k' location-hash pairs and pads the trapdoor to k location-hash pairs by adding $k\text{-}k'$ location-hash pairs that do not result false negatives. We observe that for each prefix p in q_s, any prefix p' that contains p (i.e., $R(p) \subset R(p')$) can be used for computing paddings, where $R(p)$ is the range denoted by p. For each $\overline{[a_i, b_i]}$ in q_c, the data user randomly inserts some location-hash pairs generated from the prefixes that contains $[\hat{a}_j, \hat{b}_j]$, where $1 \le j \le u$. Thus, different trapdoors can be generated for the same query. This trapdoor computation algorithm may increase false positives in query results. However, false positive is helpful for thwarting inference attacks via *access pattern*, which is described in [42]. We leave the study as our future work that combines the mitigation scheme in [42] and our amended trapdoor computation algorithm to partially hide *search patterns* and *access patterns*. Our IBtree can be combined with the mitigation scheme in [42] to prevent the inference attack in [42].

2.3.5 Query Processing

The query processing algorithm is as follows. After receiving the trapdoor t_q from a data user for query $q = q_s - q_c$, the cloud first processes query q_s using t_{q_s}. This querying process starts from the root of the IBtree. Let B_p denote the IBF of the IBtree root, $t_{qs}[i]$ denote the i-th ordered pair in t_{q_s}, $t_{q_s}[i].f$ and $t_{q_s}[i].s$ denote the first and second hash of the ordered pair $t_{q_s}[i]$, respectively. For each IBF that the cloud checks against using t_{q_s}, for each ordered pair of hashes in t_{q_s}, the first hash locates the twin that the corresponding keyword is hashed to and the second hash locates the cell in the twin. If there exists $1 \le i \le u \times k$ so that $B_p[t_{q_s}[i].f][H(t_{q_s}[i].s \oplus r_p)] = 0$, then t_{q_s} does not match any of the data items. If the cloud determines that t_{q_s} matches no data items, the query processing terminates. Otherwise, the cloud processes t_{q_s} against the left and right children of the root. The above process recursively applies to subtrees in the IBtree. The search process terminates when the cloud determine that t_{q_s} matches no data items or we finish searching at terminal nodes. When the search process reaches a terminal node N_j, which is associated with IBF B_j and random number r_j, and the cloud determines that t_{q_s} matches the data item associated with N_i, then the cloud processes each checking sub-trapdoor in the checking component t_{q_c} to determine whether the data item associated with N_j, denoted by d_j, should be included in the query result of t_q. If there exists one checking sub-trapdoor $t_{q_c}^x \in t_{q_c}$ such that for each $1 \leq i \leq k$, $B_j[t_{q_c}^x[i].f][H(t_{q_c}^x[i].s \oplus r_j)]=1$, then d_j is excluded from the result of t_q. Otherwise the result includes d_j.

We now analyze the time complexity of our query processing algorithm in the worst case and show that it is sub-linear in the number of data items. Let n be the number of data items indexed by the IBtree, u be the number of dimensions, q_s be the searching component of q and $q_s = q_1 \wedge q_2 \wedge \cdots q_u$, R_i be the query result of $q_i (1 \leq i \leq u)$, and R be the query result of q_s. Thus, $R = \cap_{i=1}^{u} R_i$. Let $|R_x|$ be the minimum among $|R_1|, \cdots, |R_u|$. In the worst case, there are at most $|R_x|$ internal nodes in a same layer of the IBtree whose IBFs satisfy the query q_s. The search time for each data item in R_x is $O(\log n)$. Thus, the time complexity of our query processing algorithm is $O(|R_x| \log n)$. In reality, $|R_x| \ll n$ as n is typically large and $|R_x|$ is the minimum among $R_1, \cdots, R_u$. Thus, our query processing time is sublinear.

2.4   Optimized IBtree Algorithms

2.4.1   IBtree Traversal Width Minimization

Recall that in the IBtree construction algorithm in Sect. 2.3.3, for a nonterminal node with data set D, we partition D into two subsets D_l and D_r so that $0 \leq |D_l| - |D_r| \leq 1$. This partition is critical for the performance of query processing on the IBtree because a sub query $q_i \subseteq W(D_l) \cap W(D_r)$ will lead to the traversal of both subtrees. Thus, in partitioning D into D_l and D_r in addition to satisfying the condition $0 \leq |D_l| - |D_r| \leq 1$, we want to minimize $|W(D_l) \cap W(D_r)|$. We call this problem *Equal Size Data Set Partition*, which is a general version of *Equal Size Prefix Family Partition* defined in [13]. According to the theory of NP-Completeness, the *Equal Size Data Set Partition* is NP-hard as its special case *Equal Size Prefix Family Partition* is NP-hard.

We next formally define this problem and prove that it is NP-hard.

Definition (**Equal Size Data Set Partition**) Given a data set $D = \{d_1, d_2, \cdots, d_n\}$, we want to partition D into D_l and D_r so that $0 \leq |D_l| - |D_r| \leq 1$ and $|W(D_l) \cap W(D_r)|$ is minimized.   □

Theorem 2.2 *The equal size data set partition problem is NP-hard.*

Proof The decision version of the equal size data set partition problem is the following: can data set D be partitioned into D_l and D_r so that $0 \le |D_l| - |D_r| \le 1$ and $|W(D_l) \cap W(D_r)| \le k$? To prove its NP-hardness, we reduce the well known NP-hard set partition problem into our equal size data set partition problem. The set partition problem is the following: given a positive integer set $S = \{a_1, a_2, \cdots, a_n\}$, can we partition S into two subsets S_1 and S_2 so that $\sum_{a_i \in S_1} a_i = \sum_{a_j \in S_2} a_j$?" Given an instance of the set partition problem, we transform it into an instance of the decision version of our equal size data set partition problem with $k = 0$ as follows: for each integer $a_i \in S$, we generate a data set D_i with a_i data items so that (1) for any two data items d_p and d_q in D_i, we have $W(d_p) \cap W(d_q) \ne \phi$, and (2) for any two data items $d_x \in D_i$ and $d_y \in D_j$ ($D_i \ne D_j$), $W(D_x) \cap W(D_y) = \phi$. Suppose the data set $D = \bigcup_{i=1}^{n} D_i$ can be partitioned into two subsets D_1 and D_2 in polynomial time so that $||D_1| - |D_2|| \le 1$ and $|W(D_l) \cap W(D_r)| \le k = 0$. This means that no two data items that share keywords will be grouped into two different subsets; otherwise we have $|W(D_l) \cap W(D_r)| > 0$. This implies that S can be partitioned into two subsets S_1 and S_2 so that $\sum_{a_i \in S_1} a_i = \sum_{a_j \in S_2} a_j$. Thus, the set partition problem $\le_p$ the equal size data set partition problem, which means the equal size data set partition problem is NP-hard. □

Next, we present our approximation algorithm to the equal size data set partition problem. For a multidimensional data set D, as $|W(D)|$ is many times larger than $|D|$, partitioning a multidimensional data set is more complicated than partitioning a 1-dimensional data set of equal size. We have the following two observations. First, a search processing for a query q_s is terminated on an internal node v of an IBtree if there exists at least one component q_s^j of q_s such that no data item in D_v satisfies q_s^j, where D_v is the data set labeled with node v in an IBtree. Second, because in order to construct an IBtree for a multidimensional data set D, we need to partition D into multiple subsets in an recursive manner till each subset only contains one data item, given a multidimensional data set D, we only need to choose one dimension in a turn to partition D, which remarkably reduces the size of the keyword set that needs to be dealt with in the partition process, and we alternatively choose different dimensions in turn to partition.

The pseudo-code of the whole data set partition, which is treated as data preprocessing for IBTree construction, is shown in Algorithm 6, where l and r denote the beginning and end partition position in D, respectively, *cur_dim* denotes the dimension that is chosen in the current turn to partition data set, and u denotes the dimension number of data items. *Equal Data Set Partition*(D, l, r, cur_dim) is an algorithm that partitions $D_{l,r}$ into $D_{l,(l+r)/2}$ and $D_{(l+r)/2+1,r}$ according to *cur_dim*-th dimension, where $D_{i,j}$ denotes the data set that contains the data items from i-th position to j-th position in D. At the very beginning, we let $l := 1$ and $r := n$.

Algorithm 6: preProcessData(D, l, r, cur_dim, u)

Input: $D = \{d_1, d_2, \cdots, d_n\}, l, r, cur\_dim, u$
Output: A preprocessed data set D

1 **if** $(r - l) \leq 2$ **then**
2 $\quad \lfloor$ return;

3 EqualDataSetPartition(D, l, r, cur_dim);
4 $cur\_dim := ((cur\_dim + 1) modu) + 1$;
5 preProcessData($D, l, (l + r)/2, cur\_dim, u$);
6 preProcessData($D, (l + r)/2 + 1, r, cur\_dim, u$);

There are two types of attributes: numeric and non-numeric. For numeric attributes, we use the partition algorithm proposed in [13]. Next, we propose a graph based keyword partition algorithm to deal with non-numeric attributes.

Given a data set $D = \{d_1, d_2, \cdots, d_n\}$, suppose the x-th attribute is non-numeric, we construct a weighted undirected graph $G = (V, E)$ as follows. For each data item d_i, we create a node v_i with label $L(v_i) = \{d_i\}$. Let the *size* of a node v_i be the number of data items in v_i, i.e., $|L(v_i)|$. Thus, at this initial stage, the size of each node is 1. For any two different data items d_i and d_j, we create an edge $e_{i,j}$ between v_i and v_j where the weight of $e_{i,j}$ is $|W(d_i^x) \cap W(d_j^x)|$, i.e., the number of common keywords shared by d_i and d_j on x-th attribute.

After graph $G = (V, E)$ is constructed, we perform node merging as follows. Our goal is to merge the n nodes into two nodes, which represents our partition of the n data items. For any two nodes v_i and v_j, if $|L(v_i)| + |L(v_j)| \leq \lceil n/2 \rceil$, then we say v_i and v_j are *mergeable*. Among all mergeable pairs of nodes, we select the pair whose edge has the largest weight. For any two nodes v_i and v_j that we choose to merge, we merge them into a new node $v_{i,j}$ with label $L(v_{i,j}) = L(v_i) \cup L(v_j)$ and then update the weight of all edges connected with this new node. For any node v connected by an edge with node $v_{i,j}$, we update the weight of the edge to be $W(L(v)^x) \cap W(L(v_{i,j})^x)$. This merging process repeats until no two nodes can be merged.

When there are no two nodes that can be merged, the resulting graph has either exactly two nodes or exactly three nodes because of the mergeable condition $|L(v_i)| + |L(v_j)| \leq \lceil n/2 \rceil$. It cannot be merged into only one node as otherwise the node size n is larger than $\lceil n/2 \rceil$. The resulting graph will not have four or more nodes because it must be able to further merge. For example, if the resulting graph has four nodes v_1, v_2, v_3, v_4 and no two nodes can be merged, then $|L(v_1)| + |L(v_2)| > \lceil n/2 \rceil$ and $|L(v_3)| + |L(v_4)| > \lceil n/2 \rceil$; thus, we have $|L(v_1)| + |L(v_2)| + |L(v_3)| + |L(v_4)| > n$, which contracts with the fact that $\Sigma_{i=1}^{4}|L(v_i)| = n$.

Next, we discuss these two cases. If the resulting graph has exactly two nodes v_1, v_2, without loss of generality, assuming $|L(v_1)| \geq |L(v_2)|$, then the equal size partition solution is $D_l = L(v_1)$ and $D_r = L(v_2)$. Note that $0 \leq |D_l| - |D_r| \leq 1$ because $|D_l| \leq \lceil n/2 \rceil$, $|D_r| \leq \lceil n/2 \rceil$, and $|D_l| \geq |D_r|$. If the resulting graph

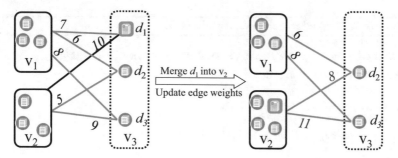

Fig. 2.3 Node redistribution example

has exactly three nodes v_1, v_2, v_3, without loss of generality, assuming $|L(v_1)| \geq |L(v_2)| \geq |L(v_3)|$, we redistribute the data items in $L(v_3)$ into nodes v_1 and v_2 as follows so that the resulting two nodes represent the equal size partition solution. For each data item d_g in $L(v_3)$, we calculate its *distance values* to v_1 and v_2, namely $|W(d_g^x) \cap |W(L(v_1)^x)|$ and $|W(d_g^x) \cap |W(L(v_2)^x)|$, respectively. Among all these distance values, we choose the highest distance value. Suppose it is the distance between data item d_g and node v_1. If $|L(v_1)| + 1 \leq \lceil n/2 \rceil$, we first redistribute d_g into node v_1 and then for each remaining data item in $L(v_3)$, we recalculate its new distance values to v_1 and v_2 and repeat this redistribution process. If $|L(v_1)| + 1 > \lceil n/2 \rceil$, then we redistribute all nodes in $L(v_3)$ to node v_2 and the redistribution process terminates.

Figure 2.3 shows an example illustrating this redistribution process. Note that we use the union-find data structure to implement the set union operation.

We now analyze the worst case computational complexity of our equal size data set partition algorithm. Let n be the size of the given data set. We first need $O(n^2)$ time to build the graph G. The node merging process takes $O(|E|)$ time, where E is the set of edges in G and we have $|E| \leq n^2$. The data item redistribution process takes a maximum of $O(n)$ time. Thus, the time complexity of our algorithm is $O(n^2)$.

2.4.2 IBtree Traversal Depth Minimization

Our basic idea for minimizing IBtree traversal depth is based on the following observation: for any nonterminal node v with label $L(v) = \{d_1, d_2, \cdots, d_g\}$ that a sub query q_i of a conjunctive query q traverse, if $q_i \subseteq W(d_1) \cap W(d_2) \cap \cdots \cap W(d_g)$, then all terminal nodes of the subtree rooted at v satisfy the query; thus, instead of traversing this subtree level by level downward, we can directly jump to the left most terminal node of this subtree and use the link list pointers to collect all data items of this subtree. This is why we link all leaf nodes of an IBtree together.

Algorithm 7: Equal size data set partition (D)

Input: $D = \{d_1, d_2, \cdots, d_n\}$
Output: D_1 and D_2, where $D_1 \cup D_2 = D$, $D_1 \cap D_2 = \phi$, and $||D_1| - |D_2|| \leq 1$

1 **for** *each $d_i (1 \leq i \leq n)$ in D* **do**
2 　⌊ create a node v_i in V, $L(v_i) = \{d_i\}$

3 .**for** *each pair of $v_i \in V$ and $v_j \in V$* **do**
4 　**if** $(W(d_i^x) \cap W(d_j^x) \neq \phi)$ **then**
5 　　⌊ Create $e_{i,j} \in E$, $w(e_{i,j}) := |W(d_i^x) \cap W(d_j^x)|$.

6 **for** *Each $e \in E$* **do**
7 　⌊ Insert e into MaxHeap H.

8 **while** $(|H| \neq \phi)$ **do**
9 　Removing $e_{i,j}$ with maximum weight from H.
10 　**if** $|L(v_i)| + |L(v_j)| \leq \lceil((|D|+1)/2)\rceil$ **then**
11 　　Merge v_i and v_j into $v_{i,j}$, let $L(v_{i,j}) = L(v_i) \cup L(v_j)$.
12 　　**if** $\exists e_{z,i} \in E || \exists e_{z,j} \in E$ **then**
13 　　　Removing $e_{z,i}$ or $e_{z,j}$ from H; Insert $e_{ij,z}$ into H, where
　　　　$W(e_{ij,z}) = |L(v_{i,j}) \cap L(v_z)|$.

14 $v_{c1} := v_i$, where $v_i \in V$.
15 **for** $\forall v_z \in V$ **do**
16 　**if** $(|v_{c1}| < |v_z|)$ **then**
17 　　⌊ $v_{c1} := v_z$.

18 $k := |W(L(v_y)) \cap W(L(v_{c1}))|$, where $v_y \in V - \{v_{c1}\}$. **for** $\forall v_z \in V - \{v_{c1}\}$ **do**
19 　**if** $(k > |W(L(v_z)) \cap W(L(v_{c1}))|)$ **then**
20 　　⌊ $k := |W(L(v_z)) \cap W(L(v_{c1}))|$.

21 $v_{c2} := v_j$, where $v_j \in \{v_y || W(L(v_y)) \cap W(L(v_{c1}))| = k\}$.
22 **for** $\forall v_z \in \{v_y || W(L(v_y)) \cap W(L(v_{c1}))| = k\}$ **do**
23 　**if** $(|v_{c2}| < |v_z|)$ **then**
24 　　⌊ $v_{c2} := v_z$.

25 **while** $(|V| > 3)$ **do**
26 　**for** *each $v_i \in V - \{v_{c1}, v_{c2}\}$* **do**
27 　　**if** $|L(v_i)| + |L(v_{cb})| \leq \lceil((|D|+1)/2)\rceil$ **then**
28 　　　⌊ Merge v_i into v_{cb}, here $b = 1, 2$.

29 **if** $(|V| = 2)$ **then**
30 　⌊ **return** $D_1 = L(v_{c1})$ *and* $D_2 = L(v_{c2})$.

31 **else**
32 　Let $v_z := V - \{v_{c1}, v_{c2}\}$
33 　**while** $(|L(v_{cb})| < \lceil((|D|+1)/2)\rceil)$ **do**
34 　　**for** *Each $D_i \in L(v_z)$* **do**
35 　　　**if** $(|W(D_i) \cap W(L(v_{cb}))|$ *is largest*$)$ **then**
36 　　　　⌊ Remove D_i from $L(v_z)$ and merge $L(v_{cb}) := L(v_{cb} \cup \{D_i\}$, here $b = 1, 2$.

37 　Return $D_1 = L(v_{c1})$ and $D_2 = L(v_{c2})$.

The key challenge is that when we traverse to node v in processing q_i, we need to quickly determine whether $q_i \subseteq W(d_1) \cap W(d_2) \cap \cdots \cap W(d_g)$. Note that the IBF of node v allows us to determine whether $q_i \subseteq W(d_1) \cup W(d_2) \cup \cdots \cup W(d_g)$. Our solution is to precompute such information when we construct the IBtree and extend the IBF data structure to store this extra information in IBF twins. Specifically, for each nonterminal node v whose IBF is denoted as B_v and for each twin $B_v[i]$, we extend the twin to store one indicator bit denoted as $B_v[i].\texttt{ind}$ whose value is 1 if and only if for every node in the subtree rooted at v, we have $B_u[i].\texttt{ind} = 1$. For any terminal node u, $B_u[i].\texttt{ind} = 1$ if and only if the value of the i-th twin $B_u[i]$ is 1. With all indicator bits in place, when we process q_i at node v, if for all the twins representing q_i, their indicator bits are all 1s, then we know that $q_i \subseteq W(d_1) \cap W(d_2) \cap \cdots \cap W(d_g)$.

In addition to helping IBtree traversal depth minimization, the indicator bits also help to improve query processing efficiency. When we process q_i at nonterminal node v and j is the location in t_{q_i}, if $B_v[i].\texttt{ind} = 1$, then when we process q_i at any node in the subtree rooted at v, we do not need to examine the value of the i-th twin of the IBF for that node because its value must be 1. This saves the operations of computing HMAC and SHA1 values.

2.4.3   IBtree Compression

When the number of dimensions and the number of bits for each dimension are constants, both the space and time complexity for constructing an IBtree over a data set D are $O(n^2)$ because the IBtree contains $2n - 1$ nodes and each node contains an IBF of size $O(n)$, where n is the number of data items in D. We now present our IBtree space compression algorithm to make our IBtree data structure scalable in terms of both space and time. Our basic idea is to remove the twins whose stored information is redundant from IBFs. There are two types of information redundancy in the IBFs of an IBtree: 0-redundancy and 1-redundancy.

0-redundancy: Let B_v be the IBF of a nonterminal node v, B_l and B_r be the IBFs of v's left and right child, respectively. According to our IBtree construction algorithm, for each twin $B_v[i]$, its value is the logical OR of the corresponding twins of B_l and B_r. Thus, if the value of $B_v[i]$ is 0, then the values of both $B_l[i]$ and $B_r[i]$ are 0. Applying this analysis recursively, if the value of $B_v[i]$ is 0, then for any node u in the subtree rooted at node v, the value of $B_u[i]$ is 0. For any sub query q_i that involves checking $B_v[i]$, because the value of $B_v[i]$ is 0, which means that $q_i \nsubseteq W(L(v))$, we will not further process the query against the subtree rooted at v. Thus, for any node u in the subtree rooted at node v, the information stored in $B_u[i]$ is redundant.

1-redundancy: According to our IBtree traversal depth minimization algorithm, when we process sub query q_i at nonterminal node v, if $B_v[i].\texttt{ind} = 1$, then when we process q_i at any node in the subtree rooted at v, we do not need to examine the value of the i-th twin of the IBF for that node because its value must be 1. Thus, if $B_v[i].\text{ind} = 1$, then for any node u in the subtree rooted at v, the information stored in $B_u[i]$ is redundant.

Eliminating 0-redundancy and 1-redundancy from an IBtree can save a large amount of space because the number of elements inserted to the IBFs in an IBtree reduces exponentially on average from top down based on the definition of IBtrees (assuming that the number of keywords in each data item is similar). Space saving will result time saving as the main part time for construction an IBtree is spending on initializing IBFs.

After removing both 0-redundancy and 1-redundancy from an IBF/IBtree, we call the resulting IBF a *compressed IBF/IBtree*. It is challenging to process a query against a compressed IBF because eliminating even one twin from an IBF changes the location of each twin after that eliminated twin. Thus, processing a sub query against a compressed IBF can no longer be based on the output of the c hash functions of the IBF. Recall that it is the data user who computes the c location-selector pairs using the k hash functions and then sends the c pairs to the cloud. Note that by definition the root IBF contains neither 0-redundancy nor 1-redundancy. This means that the root IBF remains the same after IBtree compression. Thus, processing a query on the root IBF is still based on the c twin locations received from the data user.

Next, we present our fast algorithm for processing a sub query q_i on a compressed IBF B_c whose uncompressed version is denoted by B_u. Basically we need to build a one to one mapping from the k locations $l_1, l_2, \cdots, l_k$, for each $1 \le i \le k$) that corresponds to the uncompressed IBF B_u to k new values $l'_1, l'_2, \cdots, l'_k$ that corresponds to the compressed IBF B_c so that for each $1 \le i \le k$, we have $B_u[l_i] = B_c[l'_i]$. We build this one to one mapping using perfect hashing functions constructed as follows. For each l_i, we first calculate $h_{k+1}(l_i)$. To maintain structure indistinguishability, we compress all IBFs in an IBtree, except the root IBF, into IBFs of the same size. Let m' be the size of the compressed IBFs. Second, for each $1 \le j \le g$ where g is a constant, we calculate $\text{SHA1}(h_{k+1}(l_i), j)\%m'$. Here we hash g times to allow each l_i to have g mapping options. Third, we use the Hungary algorithm to construct a bipartite matching from the k locations $l_1, l_2, \cdots, l_k$ to the k new locations $l'_1, l'_2, \cdots, l'_k$ in the compressed IBF of size m'. After this bipartite matching, each l_i chooses one of the g options. Suppose l_i is mapped to $\text{SHA1}(h_{k+1}(l_i), j)\%m'$, then we store j as the mapping option information in the corresponding twin of the parent IBF. We allocate an auxiliary IBF B_a for an IBtree to deal with mapping fails. If a location l_i cannot find a position in corresponding child IBFs, we map l_i into B_a by hashing. Given a data set, we can construct a compressed IBtree directly, instead of constructing an uncompressed IBtree and then compress it.

To support IBtree space compression, the chosen cell of a twin needs to store more information. The information includes the value of the twin, the indicator information, and the mapping option information. In practice, we combine two bits for denoting twin value and indicator information and two bits for the mapping option information. Thus, we can allocate one byte for a twin. We randomly generate 4-bit value for the unchosen cell in a twin.

Now we analyze the space complexity and time complexity of a compressed IBtree for n data items. The worst case space complexity is calculated in a bottom-up fashion as follows. Let c be the maximum number of keywords contained in one data item and k be the number of hash functions for IBFs. In a leaf IBF, the maximum number of twins whose value is 1 is ck. Now consider a nonterminal node whose two children are terminal nodes. The case that achieves the least compression is the following: for each twin with value 1 in one child, the corresponding twin in the other child has a value of 0. Suppose that we only perform compression to remove 0-redundancy. In this case, for the parent IBF, the number of twins of value 1 is $2ck$. Recursively applying this analysis, the number of twins of value 1 is $2ckn$ at each level. As the IBtree has $O(\log n)$ levels, the total number of twins of value 1 is $O(2ckn \log n) = O(n \log n)$ as both c and k are constants. Thus, the worst case space complexity of our compressed IBtree construction algorithm is $O(n \log n)$.

In basic IBtree construction algorithm, the main part time is consumed by initializing IBFs. We only allocate a few IBFs with $O(n)$ size, and reuse these IBFs in the whole construction of a compressed IBtree to reduce the time complexity. The time consumed in the construction of a compressed IBtree can be divided into two parts: initializing new IBFs and mapping elements by Hungary algorithm. We have analyzed that the number of cells of all IBFs in an IBtree is $O(n \log n)$. Also, there are $O(n \log n)$ keywords need to be mapped in the whole construction procedure. The time complexity of Hungary algorithm depends on the ratio n_p/n_e, where n_p and n_e denote the number of available positions for mapping and the number of elements to be mapped, respectively. When a proper value is given to the ratio such as $n_p/n_e \geq 1.2$, the most of elements can find a place in g testing without affecting the already mapped elements, here g is the number mapping options. Thus the time complexity of Hungary algorithm is almost linear. Combining the IBF initializing part and element mapping part, the complexity of our compressed IBtree construction is $O(n \log n)$.

Note that our IBtree is significantly different from PBtree in [13]. First, their data structures for storing indexing elements are different. IBtree uses IBFs proposed in this chapter, whereas PBtree uses Bloom filters. Note that IBF is critical in making IBtree scheme adaptively secure. Second, their tree construction methods are different. An IBtree needs two stages to be built, whereas a PBtree only needs one stage to be built. The space compression issue is unique for IBtree. Third, their query processing algorithms are different. For IBtree, the trapdoor for a query is a set of location-hash pairs, whereas for PBtree, the trapdoor for a query is a set of hashes. The range expansion issue in trapdoor computation is unique for IBtree. Fourth, their optimization techniques are different. In traversal width optimization, IBtree needs to deal with multidimensional data partition for both numeric and non-numeric indexing elements, whereas PBtree only needs to deal with single dimensional data partition for numerical indexing elements.

2.5   Security Analysis

We now prove that our IBtree based privacy preserving keyword query scheme is secure under the adaptive IND-CKA model. We use HMAC and SHA1 to implement the hash functions $h_1, h_2, \cdots, h_{k+1}$ and the hash function H, respectively. Both HMAC and SHA1 are pseudo-random hash functions. A function is a pseudo-random hash function if and only if the output of this function and the output of a truly random function are not distinguishable to a probabilistic polynomial time adversary [19, 43]. Let $G : \{0, 1\}^e \times \{w_1, w_2, \cdots, w_m\} \rightarrow \{0, 1\}^e$ be a function that takes as input a keyword and an e-bit key and maps to an e-bit string. Let $g : \{w_1, w_2, \cdots, w_m\} \rightarrow \{0, 1\}^s$ be a truly random function that takes as input a keyword and maps it to an e-bit string. Here G is a pseudo-random hash function if and only if, for a fixed value $k \in \{0, 1\}^e$, $G(x, k)$, where $x \in \{w_1, w_2, \cdots, w_m\}$, can be computed efficiently and a probabilistic polynomial time adversary $\mathcal{A}$ with access to r chosen evaluations of G, i.e., $(x_i, G(x_i, k))$ where $i \in [1, r]$, cannot distinguish the value $G(x_{r+1}, k)$ from the output of g. A privacy preserving query scheme is secure if a probabilistic polynomial time adversary cannot distinguish the output of a real index, which uses pseudo-random functions, from the output of a simulated index, which uses truly random functions. We next construct such a simulator for IBtree scheme and prove that our IBtree scheme is adaptive IND-CKA secure under the random oracle model. Note that an IBF can also be viewed as an IBtree that has only the root node. Thus, if our IBtree scheme is adaptive IND-CKA secure, our IBF is adaptive IND-CKA secure too.

We view an IBtree as a set of IBFs that are organized in a tree structure where each IBF stores a set of keywords. We consider an *adaptive adversary*, who can choose queries as a function of previously obtained trapdoors and query results. In essence, to prove a scheme is secure under the adaptive IND-CKA model, we need to prove that there exists a simulator for this secure index that has the ability to simulate future unknown queries and the adversary can not distinguish between the results of the real secure index and those of the simulator. We define two leakage functions as follows:

$\mathcal{L}_1(\text{I}, \text{D})$: Given the index I and data set D, this function outputs the size of each IBF, the number of data items n in D, the data item identifiers $ID = \{id_1, id_2, \cdots, id_n\}$, and the size of each encrypted data item encrypted by a CPA-secure encryption scheme.

$\mathcal{L}_2(\text{I}, \text{D}, q_i, t)$: This function takes as input the index I, the set of data items D, and a sub query q_i as a query at time t. It outputs two types of information: the *search pattern*, which is the information about whether the same search was performed before time t or not, and the *access pattern*, which is the information about which data items contain q_i at time t.

Theorem 2.3 (Security) *The optimized IBtree is adaptive IND-CKA ($\mathcal{L}_1, \mathcal{L}_2$)-secure in the random oracle model.*

Proof We first construct a simulator S that can build a simulated index based on the information revealed by the leakage function $\mathcal{L}_1(\mathtt{I}, D)$ as follows. It simulates the encrypted data items $D = \{d_1, d_2, \cdots, d_n\}$ using the simulator S_E, which is guaranteed to exist by the CPA-security of Enc, together with the value n and the size of each encrypted date item, which are both included in the output of $\mathcal{L}_1(\mathtt{I}, D)$. To simulate IBtree index $\mathtt{I}$, it constructs an IBtree T according to IBtree Definition 2.1 using the identifiers $ID = \{id_1, id_2, \cdots, id_n\}$ included in the leakage function. It then picks m random e-bit strings $(s_1, s_2, \cdots, s_m)$ as m keys for the m twin numbers to be used for choosing cells. Note that m is included in the leakage function $\mathcal{L}_1$.

Now for each node v in T, the simulator sets up an IBF B_v with the same size of the corresponding IBF in $\mathtt{I}$. In the i-th twin of B_v, the simulator stores either 0 at $B_v[i][0]$ and 1 at $B_v[i][1]$, or vice verse. This is decided for each twin by flipping a coin. The simulator also store the information of coin values locally. Finally, the simulator outputs this simulated index T to the adversary.

Next, we show how the simulator simulates queries on T. Let B_p denote the IBF in the root of T. If $B_p[l_i]=1$ and for any IBF B that is in the path from the root to the leaf node for data item d, B has a location l_i^B corresponding to l_i by a random hash function and $B[l_i^B]=1$, then we say d can be reached by l_i. The data set of location l_i, denoted as $D(l_i)$, is the set of all data items that can be reached by l_i. Suppose the simulator receives a query q_i. According to the leakage function $\mathcal{L}_2(\mathtt{I}, D, q_i, t)$, the simulator knows whether this query has been performed before or not due to the revealed search pattern in $\mathcal{L}_2$. If it has been performed before, the simulator outputs the same trapdoor t_{q_i} to the adversary. Otherwise, the simulator generates a new trapdoor t_{q_i} as follows. Recall that each sub-trapdoor in a trapdoor for a query is the set of c locations determined by k' secure hashes. The simulator associates an e-bit string for each twin to simulate the secure hashes. The simulator knows the value of c from the leakage function $\mathcal{L}_2$. Suppose the trapdoors issued by the simulator have a total of p locations. Note that the simulator has stored locally the data sets of these p locations. From the access pattern revealed in $\mathcal{L}_2$, the simulator knows the query result set R_{q_i} for each sub query q_i. If the simulator can find a new combination of c locations $\{l_1, l_2, \cdots, l_c\}$ from the p locations so that these c locations satisfy the condition $D(l_1) \cap D(l_2) \cap \cdots \cap D(l_c) = R_{q_i}$, then the simulator issues these c locations with their corresponding c random e-bit strings as the trapdoor for q_i. Otherwise, the simulator randomly chooses $h(h < c)$ locations $l_y, l_{y+1}, \cdots, l_{y+h-1}$ so that these h locations satisfy the condition $R_{q_i} \subseteq D(l_j)(1 \leq j \leq h)$. Then, the simulator chooses c-h locations $l_x, l_{x+1}, \cdots, l_{x+c-h-1}$ from the rest m-p unused locations, and associates a unique data set with each of these c-h locations so that the following condition is satisfied: $D(l_x) \cap \cdots \cap D(l_{x+c-h-1}) \cap D(l_y) \cap \cdots \cap D(l_{y+h-1}) = R(q_i)$.

The goal of associating a data set $D(l_i)$ with an unused location l_i in B_p for satisfying the above equation can be achieved by using the random oracle. The bit b that the random oracle outputs for a twin in the IBF of a tree node v is programmed by the simulator as follows: if a data item d_x needs to be included in $D(l_i)$ and v

is on the path from the root to the leaf node for d_x, then the simulator let b be the bit so that $B_v[l_i^{Bv}][b]=1$ and randomly select an unused location in both its left and child IBFs to correspond to l_i^{Bv}, respectively, where B_v is the IBF of node v and l_i^{Bv} is the location in B_v that corresponds to l_i in B_p. Otherwise, if for any leaf node of data item d in $D(l_i)$ where $d \neq d_x$, v is not in the path from the root to this leaf node and the parent node of v is in that path, then the simulator let b to be the bit so that $B_v[l_i^{Bv}][b]=0$ and choose no locations in the IBFs of its left and right child nodes to correspond to l_i^{Bv}.

Now if a probabilistic polynomial time adversary issues a query, the simulator can generate a trapdoor for this query as above. The trapdoor given by the simulator and the query result produced by the simulated index T are indistinguishable to the adversary because of the pseudo-random function and CPA-secure encryption algorithm. Thus, our scheme is adaptive IND-CKA secure under the random oracle model.   □

2.6 Experimental Evaluation

2.6.1 Experimental Methodology

The key factors that affect the performance of an IBtree are data set sizes, IBtree types, dimension numbers, and query types. Base on these factors, we generated various experimental configurations and comprehensively evaluated construction time, index sizes, and query processing time.

Data Sets: We chose two data sets to evaluate our schemes. One data set that we choose is the Gowlla data set [44], which is used in [13]. Gowlla data set consists of 6,442,890 check-in records of users over the period of Feb. 2009 to Oct. 2010. We extracted time stamps to form 1-dimensional data sets, time stamps and User IDs to form 2-dimensional data sets, and time stamps, User IDs, and locations to form 3-dimensional data sets. We performed a binary encoding for each attribute and then computed a keyword set for each dimension value in a data set. We generated two categories of data sets, where each category has 10 data sets. The data set sizes in Category I range from 1 to10K. We generated these 10 data sets of small sizes because our basic IBtree scheme cannot support data sets containing large number of data items. The data set sizes in Category II range from 0.5 million to 5million. Each data set was chosen randomly from the 6 million-plus total records in the Gowalla data set. We generated these 10 data sets of large sizes for testing the scalability and efficiency of our optimized IBtree scheme and for comparing our optimized IBtree scheme with $PBtree\_WD$, which is the optimized range query processing scheme in [13].

The other data set is the America NSF Research Award Abstract set [45], which consists of 129K abstracts describing NSF awards from 1990–2003. We extract keywords from each abstract. The number of keywords in a document ranges from 15 to 454 and the average number of keywords in a document is 99.27. We generate one category named Category III of data sets that contains 10 document sets with sizes ranging from 1 to 10K. We compare our optimized IBtree scheme with KRB scheme proposed in [19] on the data sets in this category for keyword query processing. We generate these 10 documents sets of small sizes because the KRB scheme cannot support document sets of large sizes due to the unscalable space requirement.

IBtree Types: To evaluate the effectiveness of our IBtree optimization algorithms, we compared the performance of the following three schemes: (1) `IBtree_Basic`, which is the basic IBtree scheme without any optimization, (2) `IBtree_C`, which is the IBtree with space compression, (3) `IBtree_CQ`, which is the `IBtree_C` plus traversal width and depth minimization. As `IBtree_Basic` is unscalable, we first evaluated all these three schemes on data sets in Category I, then we evaluated `IBtree_C` and `IBtree_CQ` on data sets in Category II. Note that space compression is critical for scaling our IBtree scheme to data sets of large sizes.

Query Types: We generated three kinds of queries: conjunctive queries, range queries, and keyword queries. We experimented two-dimensional and three dimensional conjunctive queries that contain both keyword conditions and range conditions on different IBtree schemes. For 2-dimensional queries, we generated keyword query conditions for user IDs and range query conditions for time-stamps. For 3-dimensional queries, we generated keyword query conditions for user IDs and range query conditions for both time stamps and locations. We experimented range queries on $IBtree\_CQ$ and $PBtree\_WD$ and keyword queries on $IBtree\_CQ$ and KRB tree. For each data set in Category I, Category II, and Category III, we generated a distinct collection of 11 query sets, where each query set contains 1000 queries, and the average query result sizes in these query sets range from 0 to 100.

Implementation Details: We conducted our experiments on a PC server running Windows server 2008 R2 Enterprise with 160 GB memory and two *Intel(R) Xeon(R) E5-2609 2.4* GHz processors. We used $HMAC - SHA1$ as the pseudo-random function for IBFs and our space reduction algorithm. We implemented IBtree schemes using C++. We let each dimension of each data item has 32 bits. Thus, the number of unique keyword-record pairs is up to 495 million for the 3-dimensional data set containing 5 million records. There are two parameters that need to be assigned with proper values when we conduct our experiments on data sets of large sizes. One is the IBFs' parameter m/n, where n is the total number of keywords that we need to store in the root IBF and m is the size of the root IBF, and the other is ratio n_p/n_e in Hungary algorithm mentioned in Sect. 2.4.3. We chose proper values for m/n and n_p/n_e via experiments. We let m/n vary from 2 to 11 with a scaling factor 3. Experimental results show that the index size and query processing time increase as m/n increases. No false negative is observed when $m/n \geq 2$. However, when $m/n = 2$, the average false positive rate is 1.39%, while $m/n \geq 5$, no false positive is observed. We let n_p/n_e vary from 1.1 to 1.6 with a scaling factor 0.1. Experimental results show that matching fail happens to some elements when $n_p/n_e \leq 1.3$. We observed that when $n_p/n_e = 1.1$, the average number of matching fail elements in a data set containing 10K elements is 429, while no mismatching elements is observed when $n_p/n_e \geq 1.4$. Thus, we set m/n=5 and n_p/n_e=1.4. Note that to achieve structure indistinguishable, given a data set D, we estimate the value of n_e for IBFs in each layer of the IBtree built for D in advance and let each IBF in same layers have same size.

2.6.2 Index Size

Experimental Results Show that the Index Size of IBtree_CQ *Is Scalable* With 2 and 3 dimensional data set sizes growing from 1 to 10K, the index sizes of IBtree_CQ grows from 2.4 to 26.8 MB, and from 3.5 to 41 MB, respectively. With 2 and 3 dimensional data set sizes growing from 0.5 million to 5 million, the index sizes of IBtree_CQ grows from 1.21 to 10.28 GB, and from 2.02 to 17.95 GB, respectively.

Experimental Results Show that Our Space Reduction Algorithm Significantly Reduces Index Space IBtree_CQ and IBtree_C consume orders of magnitude less space than IBtree_Basic. For example, for 2-dimensional data sets of 10K, the index sizes of IBtree_CQ, IBtree_C, and IBtree_Basic, are 26.8, 34.4 MB, and 14.9 GB, respectively. Figure 2.4, which uses logarithmic coordinates, shows the index sizes for these three schemes.

Experimental Results Show That Our Traversal width and Depth Minimization Algorithms Also Reduce Index Size For example, for 2-dimensional data sets of 5 million, the index sizes of IBtree_CQ and IBtree_C are 10.28 and 20.40 GB, respectively. Figure 2.5 shows the index sizes of these two schemes.

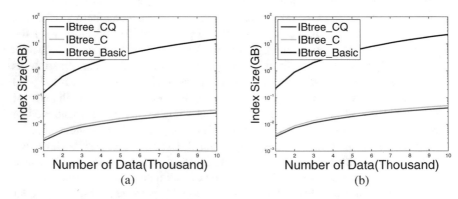

Fig. 2.4 Index size on category I. (**a**) Two-dimensional data. (**b**) Three-dimensional data

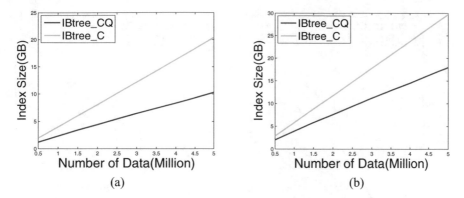

Fig. 2.5 Index size on category II. (**a**) Two-dimensional data. (**b**) Three-dimensional data

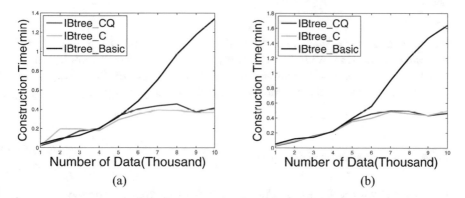

Fig. 2.6 Index construction time on category I. (**a**) Two-dimensional data. (**b**) Three-dimensional data

2.6.3 Index Construction Time

Experimental Results Show That the Index Construction Time of IBtree_CQ *Is Practically Acceptable* With 2 and 3 dimensional data set sizes growing from 1 to 10K, the index construction time of IBtree_CQ grows from 0.02 to 0.41 min, and from 0.05 to 1.21 min, respectively. With 2 and 3 dimensional data set sizes growing from 0.5 million to 5 million, the index construction time of IBtree_CQ grows from 9.6 to 284.3 min, and from 17.2 to 661.4 min, respectively.

Experimental Results Show That Our Space Reduction Algorithm Significantly Reduce Index Construction Time The index construction time of IBtree_CQ and IBtree_C are also orders of magnitude less than that of IBtree_Basic. For example, for 2-dimensional data sets of $10K$, the index construction time of IBtree_CQ, IBtree_C, and IBtree_Basic are 0.41, 0.37, and 1.34 min, respectively. Figure 2.6 shows the construction time for these three schemes.

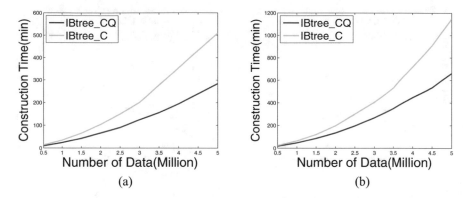

Fig. 2.7 Index construction time on category II. (**a**) Two-dimensional data. (**b**) Three-dimensional data

Experimental Results Show That Our Traversal Width and Depth Optimization Algorithms Also Can Reduce Index Construction Time For example, for 2-dimensional data sets of 5 million, the construction time of IBtree_CQ and IBtree_C are 284.3 and 509.2 min, respectively, as shown in Fig. 2.7.

2.6.4   Query Processing Time

Experimental Results Show That the Query Processing Time of IBtree_CQ *Is in the Millisecond Scale* When we fixed the query result size to be 50, with 2 and 3 dimensional data set sizes growing from 0.5 million to 5 million, the average query processing time of IBtree_CQ grows from 2.2 to 7.4 ms, and from 4.7 to 38.1 ms, respectively. When we fix the data set size to be 5 million, with 2 and 3 dimensional data set sizes growing from 0 to 100, for that of 2-dimensional data, the average query processing time of IBtree_CQ grows from 4.1 to 11.1 ms, and from 9.1 to 83.2 ms, respectively.

Experimental Results Show That Our Traversal Width and Depth Minimization Algorithms Significantly Improve Searching Efficiency The time consumed in processing queries by IBtree_CQ is orders of magnitude less than IBtree_C. When we fixed the query result size to be 50, with data set sizes growing from 0.5 million to 5 million, for the average query processing time of 2-dimensional data, IBtree_CQ grows from 2.2 to 7.4 ms, whereas IBtree_C grows from 123.7 to 3996.4 ms; for that of 3-dimensional data, IBtree_CQ grows from 4.7 to 38.1 ms, whereas IBtree_C grows from 166 to 17911 ms. When we fix the data set size to be 5 million, with result set sizes growing from 0 to 100, for that of 2-dimensional data, IBtree_CQ grows from 4.1 to 11.1 ms, whereas IBtree_C grows from 1049.4 to 5621.5 ms; for that of 3-dimensional data, IBtree_CQ grows from 9.1

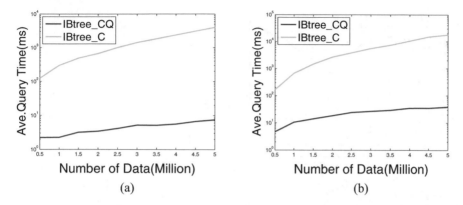

Fig. 2.8 Ave. query time when $|R| = 50$. (**a**) Two-dimensional data. (**b**) Three-dimensional data

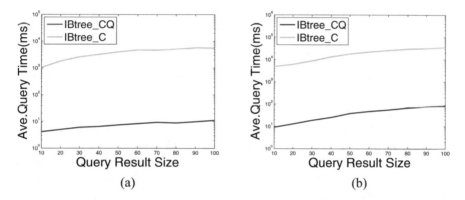

Fig. 2.9 Ave. query time when $|D| = 5$ million. (**a**) Two-dimensional data. (**b**) Three-dimensional data

to 83.2 ms, whereas `IBtree_C` grows from 4791 to 34350 ms. Figures 2.8 and 2.9, both of which use logarithmic coordinates, show the average query processing time for these two schemes.

2.6.5 Compared with PBtree and KRB

We compared `IBtree_CQ` with *PBtree*_WD on data sets in Category II with range queries and `IBtree_CQ` with KRB on data sets in Category III with keyword queries. As the space limitation, we only show the experimental results of index sizes and query processing time with query result size $|R| = 50$.

Experimental Results Show That `IBtree_CQ` *Consumes Less Space Than PBtree*_WD With $|D|$ growing from 0.5 million to 5 million, the `IBtree_CQ`

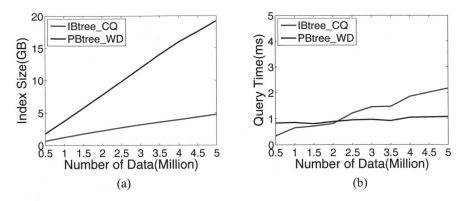

Fig. 2.10 Compared with PBtree. (**a**) Index size. (**b**) Query time ($|R| = 50$)

size grows from 0.659 to 4.744 GB. Whereas, the PBtree sizes grows from 1.785 to 19.243 GB. When data sets of size 0.5million, IBtree_CQ consumes 1.708 times less space than $PBtree$_WD. When data sets of size 5 million, IBtree_CQ consumes 3.056 times less space than $PBtree$_WD. Figure 2.10a shows the index size for these two schemes.

Experimental Results Show That IBtree_CQ *Is as Fast as* $PBtree$_WD *on Query Processing* When $|D| = 0.5$million and $|R| = 50$, the average query processing time of IBtree_WD and $PBtree$_WD tree are 0.342 and 0.843 ms, respectively. When $|D| = 2.5$million and $|R| = 50$, the average query processing time of IBtree_WD and $PBtree$_WD are 1.217 and 0.952 ms, respectively. When $|D| = 5$million and $|R| = 50$, the average query processing time of IBtree_WD and $PBtree$_WD are 2.168 and 1.075 ms, respectively. Figure 2.10b shows the query time for these two schemes. Note that the Bloom ration in $PBtree$_WD is 10.

Experimental Results Show That the Space Consumed by $IBtree$_CQ *Is Orders of Magnitude Less Than KRB* With $|D|$ growing from 1 to 10K, the IBtree_WD size grows from 3.84 to 43.26 MB, whereas KRB grows from 704.96 MB to 24.24 GB. For document sets of size 1 and 10 K, IBtree_WD consumes 181.96 and 572.73 times less space than KRB, respectively. Figure 2.11a shows the average index size for these three schemes. Note that we use logarithmic coordinates in Fig. 2.11a.

Experimental Results Show That IBtree_WD *Is as Fast as KRB on Query Processing* When $|D| = 1$K and $|R| = 50$, the average query processing time of IBtree_WD and KRB are 0.307 and 0.158 ms, respectively. When $|D| = 5$K and $|R| = 50$, the average query processing time of IBtree_WD and KRB are 0.456 and 0.465 ms, respectively. When $|D| = 10$K and $|R| = 50$, the average query processing time of IBtree_WD and KRB are 0.614 and 0.624 ms, respectively. Figure 2.11b shows the query time of these two schemes.

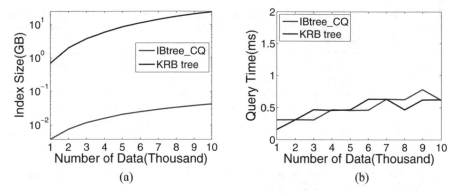

Fig. 2.11 Compared with KRB tree. (**a**) Index size. (**b**) Query time ($|R| = 50$)

2.7 Conclusions

We make three key contributions in this chapter. First, we propose the first privacy preserving conjunctive query processing scheme that achieves all three requirements of adaptive security, efficient query processing, and scalable index size. Our scheme embraces several novel ideas such as IBFs and IBtrees, which can be used in other applications. We formally prove that our scheme is adaptively secure under a random oracle model. Second, we propose several optimization algorithms such as IBtree traversal width and depth minimization algorithms and the IBtree space compression algorithm. Third, we implemented our scheme in C++ and evaluated its performance on two real-world data sets. Experimental results show that our scheme is fast in terms of query processing time and scalable in terms of index size.

References

1. R. Canetti, U. Feige, O. Goldreich, M. Naor, Adaptively secure multi-party computation, in *STOC'96: Proceedings of the Twenty-Eighth Annual ACM Symposium on Theory of Computing* (ACM, New York, 1996), pp. 639–648
2. J. Li, E.R. Omiecinski, Efficiency and security trade-off in supporting range queries on encrypted databases, in *Proceedings of 19th IFIP Annual Conference on Data and Applications Security and Privacy* (2005), pp. 69–83
3. A. Boldyreva, N. Chenette, A. O'Neill, Order preserving encryption revisited: improved security analysis and alternative solutions, in *Proceedings of CRYPTO* (2011), pp. 578–595
4. D.X. Song, D. Wagner, A. Perrig, Practical techniques for searches on encrypted data, in *Proceedings of IEEE Symposium on Security and Privacy (S&P)* (IEEE, Piscataway, 2000), pp. 44–55
5. E. Goh, Secure indexes. Stanford University Tech. Report (2004)
6. D. Boneh, G.D. Crescenzo, R. Ostrovsky, G. Persiano, Public key encryption with keyword search, in *Proceedings of EUROCRYPT* (2004), pp. 506–522

7. Y.-C. Chang, M. Mitzenmacher, Privacy preserving keyword searches on remote encrypted data, in *Third International Conference on Applied Cryptography and Network Security (ACNS)* (2005), pp. 442–455

8. R. Curtmola, J. Garay, S. Kamara, R. Ostrovsky, Searchable symmetric encryption: improved definitions and efficient constructions, in *CCS'06: Proceedings of the 13th ACM Conference on Computer and Communications Security* (2006), pp. 79–88

9. M. Bellare, A. Boldyreva, A. OfNeill, Deterministic and efficiently searchable encryption, in *Proceedings of Advances in Cryptology - CRYPTO'07* (2007), pp. 535–552

10. S. Kamara, C. Papamanthou, T. Roeder, Dynamic searchable symmetric encryption, in *CCS'12: Proceedings of the 2012 ACM Conference on Computer and Communications Security* (2012), pp. 965–976

11. D. Cash, S. Jarecki, C. Jutla, H. Krawczyk, M.-C. Rosu, M. Steiner, Highly-scalable searchable symmetric encryption with support for boolean queries, in *Proceedings of Advances in Cryptology - CRYPTO* (2013), pp. 353–373

12. D. Cash, J. Jaeger, S. Jarecki, C. Jutla, H. Krawczyk, M.-C. Rosu, M. Stiner, Dynamic searchable encryption in very-large databases: data structures and implementation, in *Proceedings of Network and Distributed System Security Symposium (NDSS)*. (ISOC, Reston, 2014)

13. R. Li, A. X.Liu, L. Wang, B. Bezawada, Fast range query processing with strong privacy protection for cloud computing, in *Proceedings of 40th International Conference on Very Large Data Bases* (IEEE, Piscataway, 2014), pp. 1953–1964

14. V. Pappas, F. Krell, B. Vo, V. Kolesnikov, T. Malkin, S.G. Choi, W. George, A. Keromytis, S. Bellovi, Blind seer: a scalable private DBMS, in *Proceedings of IEEE Symposium on Security and Privacy (S&P)* (IEEE, Piscataway, 2014), pp. 359–374

15. B.V. Ben Fisch, F. Krell, A. Kumarasubramanian, V. Kolesnikov, T. Malkin, S.M.Bellovin, Malicious client security in blind seer: a scalable private DBMS, in *Proceedings of IEEE Symposium on Security and Privacy (S&P)* (IEEE, Piscataway, 2015), pp. 395–410

16. A. Yao, How to generate and exchange secrets, in *Proceedings of 27th Annual Symposium on Foundations of Computer Science (FOCS)* (IEEE, Piscataway, 1986), pp. 162–167

17. I. Demertzis, S. Papadopoulos, O. Papapetrou, Practical private range search revisited, in *SIGMOD'16: Proceedings of the 2016 International Conference on Management of Data* (ACM, New York, 2016), pp. 185–198

18. P. Karras, A. Nikitin, M. Saad, R. Bhatt, D. Antyukhov, S. Idreos, Adaptive indexing over encrypted numeric data, in *Proceedings of the 2016 International Conference on Management of Data* (ACM, 2016), pp. 171–183

19. S. Kamara, C. Papamanthou, Parallel and dynamic searchable symmetric encryption, in *Proceedings of Financial Cryptography and Data Security (FC)* (2013), pp. 258–274

20. M. Chase, S. Kamara, Structured encryption and controlled disclosure, in *Proceedings of Theroy and Application of Cryptology and Information Security(ASIACRYPT)* (2010), pp. 577–594

21. K. Kurosawa, Y. Ohtaki, UC-secure searchable symmetric encryption, in *Proceedings of the Financial Cryptography (FC)* (2012), pp. 285–298

22. P.V. Liesdonk, S. Sedghi, J. Doumen, P. Hartel, W. Jonker, Computationally efficient searchable symmetric encryption, in *Proceedings of Secure Data Management (SDM)* (2010), pp. 87–100

23. R.A. Popa, C.M.S. Redfied, N. Zeldovich, H. Balakrish, Cryptdb: protecting confidentiality with encrypred query processing, in *Proceedings of ACM Symposium on Operating Systems Principles (SOSP)* (ACM, New York, 2011), pp. 85–100

24. M. Naveed, S. Kamara, C.V.Wright, Inference attack on property-preserving encrypted databases, in *CCS'15: Proceedings of the 22nd ACM SIGSAC Conference on Computer and Communications* (ACM, New York, 2015), pp. 644–655

25. D. Boneh, B. Waters, Conjunctive, subset, and range queries on encrypted data, in *Proceedings of 4th Theory of Cryptography Conference (TCC)* (2007), pp. 535–554

26. E. Shi, J. Bethencourt, T.-H.H. Chan, D. Song, A. Perrig, Multi-dimensional range queries over encrypted data, in *Proceedings of IEEE Symposium on Security and Privacy (S&P)* (2007), pp. 350–364

27. B.K. Samanthula, W. Jiang, E. Bertino, Privacy-preserving complex query evaluation over semantically secure encrypted data, in *Proceedings of European Symposium on Research in Computer Security (ESORICS)* (Springer, Berlin, 2014), pp. 400–418

28. B. Wang, Y. Hou, M. Li, H. Wang, H. Li, Maple: scalable multi-dimensional range search over encrypted cloud data with tree-based index, in *Proceedings of ACM Symposium on Information, Computer and Communication Security (ASIACCS)* (2014), pp. 111–122

29. P. Wang, C. Ravishankar, Secure and efficient range queries on outsourced databases using R-trees, in *IEEE 29th International Conference on Data Engineering (ICDE)* (IEEE, Piscataway, 2013), pp. 314–325

30. W.K. Wong, D.W.-L. Cheung, B. Kao, N. Mamoulis, Secure kNN computation on encrypted databases, in *SIGMOD'09: Proceedings of the 2009 ACM SIGMOD International Conference on Management of Data* (2009), pp. 139–152

31. B. Yao, F. Li, X. Xiao, Secure nearest neighbor revisited, in *IEEE 29th International Conference on Data Engineering (ICDE)* (IEEE, Piscataway, 2013), pp. 733–744

32. O. Goldreich, R. Ostrovsky, Software protection and simulation on oblivious RAMs. J. ACM **43**(3), 431–473 (1996)

33. A. Arasu, S. Blanas, K. Eguro, R. Kaushik, Orthogonal security with cipherbase, in *6th Biennial Conference on Innovative Data Systems Research (CIDR'13)* (2013)

34. B. Bezawada, A.X. Liu, B. Jayaraman, A. Wang, R. Li, Privacy Preserving string matching for cloud computing, in *IEEE 35th International Conference on Distributed Computing Systems ICDCS* (2015), pp. 609–618

35. S. Kamara, T. Moataz, SQL on structurally-encrypted databases. IACR ePrint 2016/453

36. H. Hacigumus, B. Iyer, C. Li, S. Mehrotra, Executing sql over encrypted data in the database-service-provider model, in *SIGMOD'02: Proceedings of the 2002 ACM SIGMOD International Conference on Management of Data* (2002), pp. 216–227

37. B. Hore, S. Mehrotra, M. Canim, M. Kantarcioglu, Secure multidimensional range queries over outsourced data. VLDB J. **21**(3), 333–358 (2012)

38. R. Agrawal, J. Kiernan, R. Srikant, Y. Xu, Order preserving encryption for numeric data, in *SIGMOD'04: Proceedings of the 2004 ACM SIGMOD International Conference on Management of Data* (ACM, New York, 2004), pp. 563–574

39. F. Kerschbaum, A. Schropfer, Optimal average-complexity ideal-security order-preserving encryption, in *CCS'14: Proceedings of the 2014 ACM SIGSAC Conference on Computer and Communications* (2014), pp. 275–286

40. R.A. Popa, F.H. Li, N. Zeldovich, An ideal-security protocol for order-preserving encoding, in *Proceedings of IEEE Symposium on Security and Privacy (S&P)* (2013), pp. 463–477

41. P. Gupta, N. McKeown, Algorithms for packet classification. IEEE Netw. **15**(2), 24–32 (2001)

42. M.S. Islam, M. Kuzu, M. Kantarcioglu, Access pattern disclosure on searchable encryption: ramification, attack and mitigation, in *Proceedings of Network and Distributed System Security Symposium (NDSS)* (ISOC, Reston, 2012)

43. J. Katz, Y. Lindell, *Introduction to Modern Cryptography* (Chapman & Hall/CRC Press, Boca Raton, 2007)

44. E. Cho, S.A. Myers, J. Leskovec, Friendship and mobility: user movement in location-based social networks, in *KDD'11: Proceedings of the 17th ACM SIGKDD International Conference on Knowledge Discovery and Data* (ACM, New York, 2011), pp. 1082–1090

45. K. Bache, M. Lichman, UCI machine learning repository (2013). http://archive.ics.uci.edu/ml

Chapter 3
Nearest Neighbor Queries over Encrypted Data

3.1 Introduction

Public clouds, such as Amazon EC2 and S3, Microsoft Azure, and Google App Engine, attract enterprises and users with lower cost, higher reliability, better performance, and faster deployment. However, privacy is the key roadblock as data owners may not fully trust public clouds. First, clouds may have corrupt employees. For example, in 2010, a Google engineer broke into the Gmail and Google Voice accounts of several children. Second, clouds may be hacked. For example, in 2014, Apple iCloud got hacked and hundreds of private pictures of various celebrities were posted on the Internet. Third, some cloud facilities may be operated in some foreign countries where privacy regulations may be difficult to enforce.

The cloud computing paradigm considered in this chapter contains three parties: a data owner, a cloud, and multiple data users, where the data owner stores data on the cloud and multiple data users query the data. Among the three parties, the data owner and data users are trusted, but the cloud is not fully trusted. We assume that the cloud is *semi-honest* (also called *honest-but-curious*), which means that the cloud follows required communication protocols and executes required algorithms correctly, but it may attempt to obtain information about data points and the content of user queries with the help of some domain knowledge about the data points and the queries (such as data point distribution). This threat model was proposed by Canetti et al. in [1] and has been widely adopted by prior privacy preserving work [2–7].

The computational problem considered in this chapter is nearest neighbor searching: given a set of multi-dimensional Euclidean points $D = \{d_1, d_2, \ldots, d_n\}$ and a query q specified as a multi-dimensional point, the *nearest neighbor* searching problem is to find the point in D that has the minimum distance to q. This fundamental problem arises in many fields such as spatial databases, machine learning, and computer vision.

A. X. Liu, R. Li, *Algorithms for Data and Computation Privacy*, https://doi.org/10.1007/978-3-030-58896-0_3

The *Secure Nearest Neighbor (SNN)* problem is as follows. Given a data point set $D = \{d_1, d_2, \ldots, d_n\}$, the data owner first encrypts each data point $d_i \in D$ into $(d_i)_K$ using a key K that is shared between the data owner and data users, builds a *secure index* Γ for the data points in D, and sends both the encrypted data points $\{(d_1)_K, (d_2)_K, \ldots, (d_n)_K\}$ and the secure index Γ to the cloud. Given a query q, the data user generates a *trapdoor* t_q and sends it to the cloud. The cloud uses the trapdoor to search over the secure index Γ and finds the data points that satisfy the query. In this process, with encrypted data, trapdoors, query results, the cloud should not be able to infer useful information about the data and queries, such as the values of the data points, the content of the queries, and the statistical properties of the data points.

In SIGMOD 2009 [8], Wong et al. proposed the first SNN scheme called Asymmetric Scalar-Product-Preserving Encryption (ASPE) and informally argued that it is secure against known-plaintext attacks. ASPE is one of the most influential SNN schemes as it has been used as the building block for a variety of privacy preserving query schemes such as keyword queries [9, 10], range queries [11], graph queries [12], biometric identification [13], and XML queries [14].

In this chapter, we formally prove that ASPE is actually insecure against even ciphertext only attacks. The fundamental reason that ASPE is insecure is that in ASPE, which represents data as matrices, the encryption process of data is a linear combination of the multiple dimensions of the data. Our key insight is that if we treat each dimension of the data as a source signal, each dimension of the encrypted data encrypted by ASPE can be viewed as a set of observed signals that are generated by combining the source signals linearly, thus we can use signal processing theory to break ASPE.

Yao et al. proved that "it is impossible to construct an SNN scheme even in much relaxed standard security models such as IND-OCPA (*indistinguishable under ordered chosen plaintext attack*)" [15]. In this chapter, we advance the state-of-the-art understanding of the hardness of SNN by pointing out the flaws of the hardness proof by Yao et al. in [15].

3.2   Insecurity of ASPE

Although in [15], Yao et al. showed that the ASPE schemes proposed in [8] are insecure against *chosen plaintext attacks*, but the authors in [8] only claimed that their ASPE schemes are secure against *known plaintext attacks* and *ciphertext-only attacks*. In this section, we first briefly introduce ASPE schemes; then we give a *ciphertext only attack* method; finally we show our experimental results on attacking ASPE schemes.

3.2.1 ASPE I and II

Wong et al. proposed two versions of ASPE: ASPE I and ASPE II [8]. ASPE is based on the fact that $p^T \cdot q = p^T \cdot I \cdot q$, where p, q are two n-dimensional column vectors and I is an $n \times n$ identified matrix. The identity matrix I can be decomposed into $M \cdot M^{-1}$, where M is an $n \times n$ matrix and M^{-1} is the inverse matrix of M. Thus, $p^T \cdot q = p^T \cdot I \cdot q = (p^T \cdot M) \cdot (M^{-1} \cdot q)$. To preserve privacy for p, q and compute the scalar product of $p \cdot q$ in a privacy preserving manner, they use M and M^{-1} as two keys to encrypt p and q into $p^T \cdot M$ and $M^{-1} \cdot q$, respectively. ASPE is an encryption scheme that uses different matrices as keys to encrypt data points and query points for preserving the privacy of the scalar product. ASPE I works as follows. For each data point p, the data owner computes $\|p\|^2$, creates a new data point $\hat{p}^T = (p^T, -\frac{1}{2}\|p\|^2)$, and encrypts the new data point using M. For each query point q, the data user uses a random factor $r > 0$ to create a new query point $\hat{q} = r \times (q^T, 1)^T$, and then uses M^{-1} to encrypt $\hat{q}$. Wong et al. informally argued that ASPE I is secure against known sample plaintext attack.

ASPE II improves upon ASPE I by introducing randomness to both data points and query points. Given an n-dimensional point p, two random points p_a and p_b, which are called shared points of p, are generated as follows. The data owner first randomly chooses some dimensions from all these n dimensions to split. Suppose the i-th ($1 \leq i \leq n$) dimension of data points is chosen to split, for each data point p, $p[i]$ is randomly split into two parts $p_a[i]$ and $p_b[i]$ satisfying $p[i] = p_a[i] + p_b[i]$, where $p[i]$ denotes the i-th dimensional value of p and $1 \leq i \leq n$. Otherwise, the data owner lets $p_a[i] = p_b[i] = p[i]$. Accordingly, for each query point q, the data user also generate two shared query points q_a and q_b, in a way that is exactly the opposite for shared data points. If the i-th dimension of data points is chosen to split, for each query point q, $q[i]$ is not split, i.e. they let $q[i] = q_a[i] = q_b[i]$. Otherwise, $q[i]$ is randomly split into two parts $q_a[i]$ and $q_b[i]$ satisfying $q[i] = q_a[i] + q_b[i]$. It is easy to prove that $p^T \cdot q = p_a{}^T \cdot q_a + p_b{}^T \cdot q_b$. Note that it is predefined and kept as a secret that which dimensions are split or not. Second, they increase the number of dimensions of data points and query points by adding artificial dimensions. To ensure the correctness of KNN query results, the artificial dimensional values added in data points and query points satisfy the condition that the results of scalar product over these artificial dimensions are always zeros. Artificial dimensions are treated the same as non-artificial dimensions in the split process. Wong et al. informally argued that ASPE II is secure against known plaintext attack. Readers can refer to [8] for more details about these two schemes.

3.2.2 Attack Method

Our ciphertext only attacks on ASPE uses Independent Component Analysis (ICA), which is used for blind source separation in signal processing. As an observed signal often consists of several source signals, when the contributed source signals are statistically independent from each other, we can use ICA to separate them from the observed signal. Our basic idea is to treat each dimension as a signal, which can be modeled by a random variable, and use ICA to recover each dimension value of data items from the cipher texts. Let $(E(p_j))^T = p_j^T \cdot M$. Each dimension value in $E(p_j)$ is a lineal combination result of all the dimension values in p_j. The i-th dimension value $p_j[i]$ can be viewed as the value generated by the i-th source signal in a given time t_j, where $1 \le i \le n$. We view each dimension as a source signal. Thus, each dimension value in $E(p_j)$ can be viewed as an observed signal value that is generated by linearly combining n source signal values at time t_j. If source signals are independent from each other, we can use ICA to separate them from the n observed signals.

Let $S = (s_1, s_2, \ldots, s_n)^T$ being n mutually independent signals whose distributions are unknown. Each $s_i (i = 1, 2, \ldots, n)$ represent an unknown source signal. Let $X = x_1, x_2, \ldots, x_m$ with each $x_j (j = 1, 2, \ldots, m)$ being an observed signal measuring a linear combination of the n source signals. Then, X can be expressed in a vector form as:

$$X = AS, \tag{3.1}$$

where A is am $m \times n$ matrix.

The blind source separation is to find a linear filter B for computing an l−dimensional random vector $Y = (y_1, y_2, \ldots, y_l)$ that satisfy:

$$Y = BX, \tag{3.2}$$

where B is an $l \times m$ matrix. Combining both Eqs. (3.1) and (3.2), we get:

$$Y = CS, \tag{3.3}$$

where $C = B \times A$ is an $l \times n$ matrix. Equation (3.3) shows that Y has a linear structure. Ideally, if C is an $n \times n$ identity matrix, then $y_i = s_i$.

By treating each dimension of the data points as a source signal, each dimension of the encrypted data points by ASPE can be viewed as a set of observed signals that are generated by combining the source signals linearly. Thus, we reduce the problem of attacking the two ASPE schemes to the problem of blind source separation. Note that although ASPE II has two cipher text sets, we can choose either of them to attack. Thus, our ICA based method for attacking ASPE I and II is the same. Further note that we treat non-artificial attributes and artificial attributes equally. Recall that in ASPE schemes, the data points is of the form $\hat{p}_i = (p_i^T, -\frac{1}{2}||p_i||^2)^T$, which can be written as $\hat{p}_i = (p_i^1, p_i^2, \ldots, p_i^n, p_i^{n+1})^T$. When we view each dimension as a source signal, a data point $\hat{p}_i$ can be viewed as a tuple recording the values of the $n + 1$ source signals at a given time t_i. Let $P = (P^1, P^2, \ldots, P^{n+1})$, where P^i $(1 \le i \le n + 1)$ is the i-th attribute of the generated data points. Each generated data point $\hat{p}$ is an instance of P. We rephrase the encrypting operation as:

$$Enc(P) = P^T \cdot M, \qquad (3.4)$$

where M is a secret matrix used as a key. Accordingly, the cipher text of a generated data point is an instance of $Enc(P)$. Equation (3.4) can be rephrased to

$$\{Enc(P)\}^T = M^T \cdot P, \qquad (3.5)$$

which is of the same form as Eq. (3.1).

Let $\dot{P} = (\dot{P}_1, \dot{P}_2, \dots, \dot{P}_{n+1})$ denote the separated results. Suppose that $\dot{P}_i$ matches P_j, then the waveform of $\dot{P}_i$ will be highly similar to that of P_j. The precision of separated results is highly related to the independence of the attributes. The more independent the data point dimensions are, the more insecure ASPE schemes are. Although ASPE II is proposed as an optimization of ASPE I, ASPE II is less secure than ASPE I because the randomness splitting introduced in ASPE II actually increases the independence of data point dimensions, which improves the accuracy of the separated results significantly.

3.2.3 Experimental Results

Data Sets To evaluate the effectiveness of our attack method, we chose four different data sets from UCI machine learning repository [16]: Pseudo Periodic Synthetic Time Series Data Set (PPSTS), PAMAP2 Physical Activity Monitoring Data Set (PAMAP2), Dataset for Sensor-less Drive Diagnosis Data Set (SDD), Corel Image Features Data Set (CIF). We added some artificial attributes in these data sets for ASPE II. Table 3.1 shows the detailed information about the data sets and record numbers that were used in our experiments. Note that we removed some dimensions of the data points in SDD and PAMAP2 as they are either constant or non-numerical.

Metrics We use Pearson product-moment correlation coefficient to evaluate the linear correlation between a dimension of a set of data point and a dimension of the results separated by FastICA algorithm. The Pearson product-moment correlation coefficient $\rho_{X,Y}$ for two variables X and Y is defined as:

Table 3.1 Data sets

Data sets	Data set attribute number	Chosen attribute number	Artificial attribute number	Chosen record number
SDD	49	42	10	10,000
CIF	89	89	10	10,000
PAMAP2	52	37	10	10,000
PPSTS	10	10	5	10,000

$$\rho_{X,Y} = |\frac{cov(X, Y)}{\sigma_X \sigma_Y}|. \tag{3.6}$$

In Eq. (3.6), $cov(X, Y)$ denotes the covariance between X and Y, σ_X and σ_Y denote the standard deviations of X and Y, respectively. The value of $\rho_{X,Y}$ is between 1 and 0, where 1 is total correlation and 0 is no correlation.

Setup We implemented ASPE I and ASPE II using C++. We use ASPE I and ASPE II to encrypted the four data sets, respectively. We use the FastICA algorithm [17] on the cipher texts encrypted by ASPE I and ASPE II, respectively, and obtain their corresponding separated data points. Given a data set D and its corresponding D', for each dimension A of D, we computed a Pearson product-moment correlation coefficient for each pair attributes (A, A'), where A' is an attribute of D', and identified the corresponding attribute A' in D' for A.

Results *The experimental results show that both ASPE I and ASPE II are vulnerable to ciphertext only attacks because for each dimension, the original data points before being encrypted by ASPE and the data points obtained by our ICA based attack method from the ASPE encrypted data points are highly correlated.* For ASPE I, the maximum coefficients in these four data sets are larger than 0.995 and the average coefficients are larger than 0.49. Figure 3.1 shows the two waveforms of a dimension and its corresponding separated attribute in CIF and SDD, respectively. For ASPE II, the maximum coefficients in these four data sets are larger than 0.997 and the average coefficients are larger than 0.845. Figure 3.2 shows two waveforms of a dimension and its corresponding separated attribute in

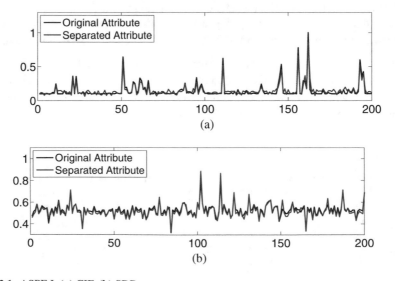

Fig. 3.1 ASPE I. (**a**) CIF. (**b**) SDD

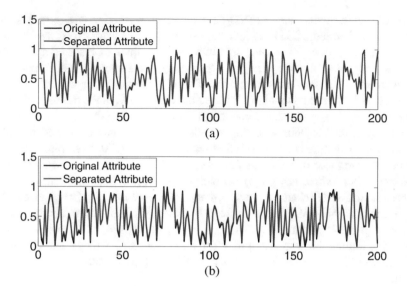

Fig. 3.2 ASPE II. (**a**) PPSTS. (**b**) PAMAP2

Table 3.2 Experimental results

Data Set	ASPE I		ASPE II	
	Ave.$\rho_{X,Y}$	MAX.$\rho_{X,Y}$	Ave.$\rho_{X,Y}$	MAX.$\rho_{X,Y}$
SDD	0.8157	0.9955	0.9618	0.9983
CIF	0.5930	0.9271	0.8851	0.9974
PAMAP2	0.4931	0.9023	0.8752	0.9987
PPSTS	0.6130	0.8243	0.8455	0.9997

PPSTS and PAMAP2, respectively. Our experimental results show that ASPE II is more insecure than ASPE I as the independence of each attribute increases after introducing randomness. Table 3.2 shows the results. Note that the x-axis in Figs. 3.1 and 3.2 are the number of records. Because of space limitation, for each data set, we only show the correlation of 200 original values and separated values in one attribute.

3.3 Hardness Analysis

While it is believed that "it is impossible to construct an SNN scheme even in much relaxed standard security models such as IND-OCPA" as proved by Yao et al. in [15], in this section, we show that their hardness proof is flawed.

Yao et al. proved the hardness of the SNN problem by reducing the order-preserving encryption (OPE) problem to the SNN problem because the OPE hardness has been proved in [18, 19], i.e., no truly secure OPE scheme exists in standard secure models such as IND-CPA and even relaxed secure models such as IND-OCPA. The reduction is as follows. Giving a set of values $\{m_1, m_2, \ldots, m_n\}$, where $m_1 < m_2 < \cdots < m_n$, they map these values to a set of special one-dimensional points $D = \{p_1, p_2, \ldots, p_n, p_{n+1}\}$ by a special hash function $h(.)$ that guarantees that the nearest neighbor of $h(m_i)$ is $h(m_{i+1})$ for any $i \in [1, n-1]$, where m_{i+1} is the successor of m_i. By the hash function $h(.)$, the problem of finding the successor of m_i is converted into the problem of finding the nearest neighbor of $h(m_i)$. Thus, the problem of testing whether $m_j > m_i$ can be solved by calling the method of finding the nearest neighbor in iteratively. For example, if $h(m_j)$ is the nearest neighbor of the nearest neighbor of $h(m_i)$ i.e. $h_{m_j} = nn(nn(h(m_i)))$, then $m_j > m_i$, where $nn(h(m_i))$ denotes the nearest neighbor of $h(m_i)$. If there exists a secure SNN scheme E under a standard secure model $\mathcal{M}$, then given $E(q)$, the nearest neighbor of q in D, denoted by $nn(q, D)$, can be efficiently found in a privacy preserving manner i.e. $\mathcal{B}(E(q), E(D) \rightarrow E(nn(q, D)))$, where $\mathcal{B}$ is the method of finding the nearest neighbor for $E(q)$ from $E(D)$, they construct an OPE $\mathcal{E}$ by letting $\mathcal{E}(.) = E(h(.))$. Readers can refer to [15] for more details about the proof.

The proof in [15] is based on the assumption that the encrypted data point $E(p_i)$ should be directly used as the trapdoor for p_i, which is actually incorrect for SSE schemes. In an SSE scheme, only the data owner or the authorized data users, who have the keys for generating trapdoors, can generate a trapdoor t_q for a given query q. The trapdoors and the corresponding query results known by the cloud are included in the *search pattern* and the *access pattern*, respectively. In an SSE scheme, encrypted data point $E(p_i)$ cannot be directly used as the trapdoor for p_i. Otherwise, the cloud knows a large number of trapdoors and corresponding query results without processing any queries for data users. If $E(p_i)$ can not be directly used as the trapdoor for p_i, we cannot use $\mathcal{B}(E(p_i), E(D))$ to find the nearest neighbor of $E(p_i)$ and the *traverse(E(p_i))* algorithm in [15], which is used for finding the index value i for $E(p_i)$ in $E(D)$, does not work in their proof. Thus, the hardness analysis for the SNN problem in [15] is flawed.

3.4   Conclusions

We make following two contributions in this chapter. First, we formally prove and experimentally demonstrate that the widely adopted SNN scheme ASPE is insecure against even ciphertext only attack. Second, we point out the flaws of hardness analysis of SecNN in [15]. Our future work is to design an efficient SNN scheme for multi-dimensional data that can achieve security under a standard security model.

References

1. R. Canetti, U. Feige, O. Goldreich, M. Naor, Adaptively secure multi-party computation, in *Proceedings of the 28th ACM Symposium on Theory of Computing (STOC)* (ACM, New York, 1996), pp. 639–648

2. S. Kamara, C. Papamanthou, Parallel and dynamic searchable symmetric encryption, in *Proceedings of the Financial Cryptography and Data Security (FC)* (Springer, Okinawa, 2013), pp. 258–274

3. R. Li, A.X. Liu, L. Wang, B. Bezawada, Fast range query processing with strong privacy protection for cloud computing, in *Proceedins of the 40th International Conference on Very Large Data Bases (VLDB)* (IEEE, Hawaii, 2014), pp. 1953–1964

4. I. Demertzis, S. Papadopoulos, O. Papapetrou, Practical private range search revisited, in *Proceedings of the International Conference on Management of Data (SIGMOD)* (ACM, San Francisco, 2016), pp. 185–198

5. P.V. Liesdonk, S. Sedghi, J. Doumen, P. Hartel, W. Jonker, Computationally efficient searchable symmetric encryption, in *Proceedings of the 7th VLDB Conference on Secure Data Management (SDM)* (Springer, Singapore, 2010), pp. 87–100

6. D. Cash, J. Jaeger, S. Jarecki, C. Jutla, H. Krawczyk, M.-C. Rosu, M. Stiner, Dynamic searchable encryption in very-large databases: data structures and implementation, in *Proceedings of the Network and Distributed System Security Symposium (NDSS)* (The Internet Society, California, 2014)

7. B. Vo, B. Fisch, F. Krell, A. Kumarasubramanian, V. Kolesnikov, T. Malkin, S.M. Bellovin, Malicious client security in blind seer: a scalable private DBMS, in *Proceedings of the IEEE Symposium on Security and Privacy (S&P)* (IEEE Computer Society, California, 2015), pp. 395–410

8. W. Wong, D.W.L. Cheung, B. Kao, N. Mamoulis, Secure kNN computation on encrypted databases, in *Proceedings of the International Conference on Management of Data (SIGMOD)* (ACM, Providence, 2009), pp. 139–152

9. N. Cao, C. Wang, M. Li, K. Ren, W. Lou, Privacy-preserving multi-keyword ranked search over encrypted cloud data, in *Proceedings of the IEEE International Conference on Computer Communications (INFOCOM)* (IEEE, New York, 2011), pp. 829–837

10. Y. Ren, Y. Chen, J. Yang, B. Xie, Privacy-preserving ranked multi-keyword search leveraging polynomial function in cloud computing, in *Proceedings of the Global Communications Conference (GLOBECOM)* (IEEE, New York, 2014), pp. 594–600

11. P. Wang, C. Ravishankar, Secure and efficient range queries on outsourced databases using r-trees, in *Proceedings of the IEEE International Conference on Data Engineering (ICDE)* (IEEE, New York, 2013), pp. 314–325

12. N. Cao, Z. Yang, C. Wang, K. Ren, W. Lou, Privacy-preserving query over encrypted graph-structured data in cloud computing, in *Proceedings of the International Conference on Distributed Computing Systems (ICDCS)* (IEEE, New York, 2011), pp. 393–402

13. J. Yuan, S. Yu, Efficient privacy-preserving biometric identification in cloud computing, in *Proceedings of the IEEE International Conference on Computer Communications (INFOCOM)* (IEEE, New York, 2013), pp. 2652–2660

14. J. Cao, F.Y. Rao, M. Kuzu, Efficient tree pattern queries on encrypted xml documents, in *Proceedings of the International Conference on Extending Database Technology (EDBT)* (ACM, New York, 2013), pp. 111–120

15. B. Yao, F. Li, X. Xiao, Secure nearest neighbor revisited, in *Proceedings of the IEEE International Conference on Data Engineering (ICDE)* (IEEE Computer Society, Brisbane, 2013), pp. 733–744

16. K. Bache, M. Lichman, UCI Machine Learning Repository (2013). http://archive.ics.uci.edu/ml

17. A. Hyvarinen, Fast and robust fixed-point algorithms for independent component analysis. IEEE Trans. Neural Netw. **10**(3), 626–634 (1999)

18. A. Boldyreva, N. Chenette, Y. Lee, A. O'Neill, Order-preserving symmetric encryption, in *Proceedings of the International Conference on the Theory and Applications of Cryptographic Techniques (EUROCRYPT)* (Springer, Cologne, 2009), pp. 224–241
19. A. Boldyreva, N. Chenette, A. O'Neill, Order-preserving encryption revisited: improved security analysis and alternative solutions, in *Proceedings of the International Cryptology Conference (CRYPTO)* (Springer, California, 2011), pp. 578–595

Chapter 4
K-Nearest Neighbor Queries Over Encrypted Data

4.1 Introduction

4.1.1 Motivations

In location-based services, a user sends his/her current location to a location service provider, and the service provider then responds the user with the query results (such as the top five nearest restaurants). For lower cost, higher performance, and better flexibility, location service providers often host their geospatial data on public clouds. However, in this service model, security and privacy are major concerns as public clouds are typically not fully trusted. The confidential geospatial data and querier location information may be leaked or inferred by the cloud service providers. These storage clouds may have financial incentives (e.g., delivering advertisements to users) to collect or infer their customer sensitive information by analyzing the stored data and user queries. Moreover, these public storage clouds may be compromised and all of the stored information is further leaked by hackers. For example, it is reported that Dropbox is hacked and more than 68 million Dropbox account information is now for sale on the DarkNet marketplace [1].

In this chapter, we focus on secure k nearest neighbor (SkNN) query. The location-based kNN search is one of the most widely used location-based services. The state-of-the-art solutions are either not sufficiently efficient or non-strong-provable-secure to perform the location-based kNN searches over the encrypted geospatial data on cloud. Therefore, it is crucial to develop a scheme that provides strong provable security against the untrusted clouds, while still preserving the cloud's ability to efficiently perform location-based kNN queries over the encrypted geospatial data.

A. X. Liu, R. Li, *Algorithms for Data and Computation Privacy*, https://doi.org/10.1007/978-3-030-58896-0_4

4.1.2   Problem Formulation

- **Threat Model.** We consider a service model which consists of a data owner, a cloud, and multiple users. The data owner will store the geospatial data on the cloud. The cloud will serve the users' location-based queries. The adversary we consider is the cloud, which is assumed to be honest-but-curious. More specifically, the cloud provides reliable data and query services as the protocol specification, but it is curious about data it stores and queries it receives. Therefore, to protect data privacy and users' location privacy, the data owner needs to encrypt data before outsourcing and the data users need to encrypt the queries before submitting to the cloud.
- **Geospatial Data.** We consider that the data owner stores geospatial data items. Each data item consists of spatial information (e.g., the location of a restaurant) and non-spatial information (e.g., the rating of a restaurant). Data items can be represented and indexed by their spatial information. Formally, they are represented by points $p_1, \cdots, p_n$ in the two-dimensional geographical space.
- **Approximate kNN.** The secure kNN problem is modeled as how the cloud finds the top-k nearest points of $q \in U$ given by a user, as well as provides both the data owner and the user with the security guarantee. It should be ensured that the honest-but-curious cloud cannot deduce any useful information from the data it stores. Meanwhile, when the data user submits its current location to the cloud to launch a kNN query, the honest-but-curious cloud cannot learn the data user's location. In SecEQP, we use the Euclidean distance as the distance metric. To reduce query latency, SecEQP does not aim to discover strict accurate results but acceptable approximate results (e.g., the error is limited to 10%). Note that an approximate answer of kNN with a small error is still very useful in some use scenarios. For example, a user wants to find the top five nearest restaurants within 1 km for lunch. SecEQP may return five nearest restaurants within 1.1 km. The approximate results can still help the user to find a nearby restaurant (s)he likes.

4.1.3   Service Model and Design Goals

We propose SecEQP scheme to address the aforementioned secure kNN problem. The service model and design goals of SecEQP scheme are elaborated below.

- **Service Model.** The proposed SecEQP service model is depicted in Fig. 4.1. In SecEQP scheme, data owner delegates the query service to authenticated data users by sharing the secret keys with them. Each Geospatial data item hosted by the data owner consists of location information (spatial attributes) and other information (non-spatial attributes). In order to preserve the ability to query and retrieve the data efficiently, the data owner extracts the spatial attributes

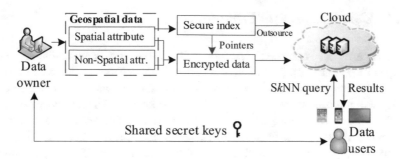

Fig. 4.1 SecEQP service model

of each data item and builds a secure index and then encrypts the entire data items by using the shared keys. Because queries are processed on the secure index, the data items can be encrypted by any encryption algorithms including the standard encryption algorithms with strongest security assurance (e.g., AES). Each secure index item should contain the identifier information (i.e., a pointer) to record the association between the secure index item and the encrypted data item. Afterward, the data owner outsources both the secure index items and the encrypted data items to the powerful cloud, which provides both storage and search services. After the cloud receives the secure index and encrypted data items, the authorized data users can use the shared keys to generate valid search tokens and search for the corresponding SkNN results.

- **Design Goals.** There are three design goals: security, efficiency, and accuracy, which are described in detail as follows.

  1. *Security.* SecEQP should preserve the following three types of privacy. (1) Data privacy: from the encrypted data items, the adversary cannot reveal any useful information about the data. (2) Index privacy: from the secure index, the adversary cannot learn any useful information about the spatial information of the data items. (3) Token privacy: from the encrypted search token, the adversary cannot infer any information about the query point's location.
  2. *Efficiency.* SecEQP should satisfy two types of efficiency requirements. (1) Low query latency: the data user can get the result within a reasonable amount of time. (2) Low interaction: the protocol should be non-interactive, or it just requires a small constant number of interactions between the data user and the cloud server.
  3. *Accuracy.* Let o_i be the ith nearest point returned by SecEQP scheme, and let o_i^* be the ground truth, i.e., the actual ith nearest point. We can compute their distances between the query point q, denoted as $\|q, o_i\|$ and $\|q, o_i^*\|$, respectively. SecEQP should keep that $\|o_i, q\|$ is as close as possible to $\|o_i^*, q\|$ (for all $i = 1, \cdots, k$). A formal definition of accuracy metric can be found in Sect. 4.5.

4.1.4   Comparison with Prior Arts

We compare our proposed SecEQP with other six state-of-the-art SkNN schemes [2–7] based on features that a secure kNN scheme is expected to satisfy, such as the support of strong security (i.e., the data privacy and users' location privacy will not be disclosed or inferred), the support of sublinear query processing time (i.e., the query running time is in $O(k \log n)$), etc. The results are summarized in Table 4.1. Among these features, the two important ones are the support of strong security and the support of sublinear query processing time. The major limitation for most of the previous secure kNN schemes is that it is hard to achieve both of them simultaneously. Wang et al. [6] proposed a secure kNN scheme based on order-preserving encryption (OPE) [8], which is a deterministic encryption scheme whose encryption function preserves numerical ordering of the plaintexts. A similar method called distance-recoverable encryption (DRE) is leveraged in [2] and [3] to support secure kNN search. The DRE enables anyone to recover the distance between two points by running a function over their encrypted data. The OPE and DRE are two cases of property-preserving encryptions, which only provide weak privacy protection. They are vulnerable to various serious attacks, as analyzed in [9]. Elmehdwi et al. [5] proposed a novel protocol over encrypted data based on a twin-cloud model [10] and Paillier cryptosystem [11]. This protocol employs too many heavy cryptographic operations, so its query latency is too long, rendering it impractical for large datasets. The private information retrieval (PIR)-based

Table 4.1 The comparison among previous schemes and SecEQP

Features	Wong et al. [2]	Hu et al. [3]	Yi et al. [4]	Elmehdwi et al. [5]	Wang et al. [6]	Yao et al. [7]	Our SecEQP
Strong security	×	×	×	✓	×	✓	✓
Sublinear query latency	×	✓	×	×	✓	✓	✓
Result accuracy	Accurate	Accurate	Accurate	Accurate	Accurate	Accurate	Approximate[a]
kNN or 1NN	k	k	k	k	k	1	k
High-dimensional data	✓	✓	×	✓	✓	×	×[b]
No local index	✓	×	✓	✓	✓	×	✓
Single server	✓	✓	✓	×	✓	✓	✓
Rounds of interaction	1	$O(\log n)$	1	1	1	2	1

[a]SecEQP can achieve high result accuracy by well-developed strategies
[b]Handling data with dimensionality more than two is not required for location-based services

schemes [4] mainly consider how to protect query privacy but not data privacy. Besides, the inefficiency of PIR significantly increases the total search time. Yao et al. [7] designs a solution that can support secure nearest neighbor search by exploiting Voronoi diagram [12] for space partition. Voronoi-based schemes require each data user to download and maintain a copy of the large-size index locally for query processing, which seriously impedes its real-world applications. Besides, the generation of order-k Voronoi diagram for kNN is very computational intensive, as analyzed in [13].

Different from the previous works, SecEQP scheme can support the two most important features (i.e., strong security and sublinear query processing time). However, we would like to point out that SecEQP still has two downsides: (1) returning approximate results to a query instead of accurate ones and (2) only supporting 2-dimensional data, which may not fit all use scenarios (e.g., requiring strict accurate results or 3-dimensional data).

4.1.5 Technical Challenges and Proposed Solutions

There are three technical challenges SecEQP shall deal with.

- **C1:** *How to achieve strong data privacy while still supporting efficient kNN query processing?* To measure the proximity of two encrypted points, the straightforward approach is to compute their distance over the encrypted data. A dilemma arises: on one hand, to ensure low query latency requires the data is weakly encrypted (e.g., using order-preserving encryption); on the other hand, if strong encryption (e.g., fully homomorphic encryption (FHE) [14]) is used, the query latency will be prohibitively long. To address the dilemma, we propose the projection-based space encoding method to build a secure index. In SecEQP, the geospatial data can be formally encrypted by standard encryption methods to achieve strong data privacy (e.g., CPA-secure [15]). The secure index enables SecEQP to circumvent heavy computation over encrypted data while still supports secure kNN query processing (Sect. 4.2).
- **C2:** *How to design a secure index for sublinear query latency while preserving the index privacy?* Building a secure index is not enough for secure kNN query processing. Without any index optimization, the cloud may linearly scan each encrypted data item in the database to evaluate its distance with the queried location. The linear query latency is prohibitively slow for a large dataset (e.g., a million locations are stored in the cloud). To tackle this challenge, we first propose the prefix-free encoding technique to turn the kNN query processing problem to be the keywords query problem. Then, we exploit the indistinguishable Bloom filter (IBF) tree data structure for the secure index building, which can ensure the protocol to be secure and sublinear (Sect. 4.4).
- **C3:** *How to develop effective strategies to improve the result accuracy of SecEQP?* SecEQP can only return approximate query results. How to satisfy the high query result accuracy demands is not an easy task. In order to solve this

problem, we leverage the observed successive inclusion property to develop an effective strategy to improve the result accuracy (Sect. 4.5.4).

4.1.6   SecEQP Scheme Overview

Figure 4.2 sketches the SecEQP scheme. We first turn the kNN problem into the equality checking problem via the projection-based space encoding technique (Sect. 4.2). We further translate the equality checking problem into the keywords query problem by the prefix-free encoding technique (Sect. 4.4.1). Finally, we employ the indistinguishable Bloom filter (IBF) tree data structure for index building (Sect. 4.4.3) which can ensure our SecEQP to be secure and efficient (i.e., the results to kNN queries are given in sublinear time). The details of provable security are provided in (Sect. 4.4.5); we prove that SecEQP is secure in the random oracle model. Moreover, the accuracy of SecEQP results is adaptive and configurable. By leveraging the observed successive inclusion property (Sect. 4.3), the accuracy of query results can be further improved (Sect. 4.5.4).

4.1.7   Main Contributions

In this chapter, we make the following main contributions.

- We leverage a projection-based approach to realize space encoding over two-dimensional space. Space encoding enables the cloud to perform the proximity test between the queried location and the locations in the database by just equality checking operations.

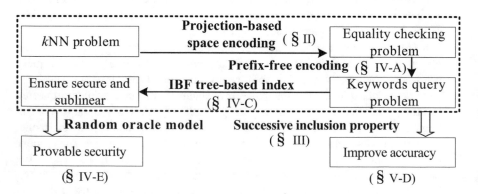

Fig. 4.2 SecEQP scheme overview

- We design a prefix-free encoding method to embed the codes into an indistinguishable Bloom filter tree to build a secure index. By using the binary search over the indistinguishable Bloom filter tree, our protocol can ensure a sublinear search time.
- We formalize the information leakage functions and formally prove that the SecEQP scheme achieves strong provable security in the random oracle model.

4.2 Space Encoding

In this section, we propose the space encoding technique, which can be used to build a secure index for secure kNN query processing. In the following, we first introduce our customized primitive projection function. Then, we introduce how to encode/stipulate a searching region with infinite space by a single primitive projection function and how to encode/stipulate a searching region with finite space by projection function composition (i.e., multiple primitive projection functions). Moreover, we will introduce how to perform proximity testing between two locations by using the generated codes.

4.2.1 Projection Function Introduction

The projection function is defined as follows.

Definition 4.1 (Primitive Projection Function) The primitive projection function $h : \mathbb{R}^2 \rightarrow \mathbb{Z}$ maps a two-dimensional vector $\mathbf{q}$ to an integer,

$$h(\mathbf{q}) = \lfloor \frac{\mathbf{a} \cdot \mathbf{q} + b}{d} \rfloor, \tag{4.1}$$

where $\mathbf{a} = (\theta, r)$ denotes a two-dimensional vector in polar coordinate form, where the angle θ is chosen uniformly from the range $[0, 2\pi)$ and the radius $r = 1$. The parameter b is chosen uniformly from the range $[0, d)$.

- **Geometric Interpretation.** The primitive projection function has a simple geometric interpretation. As shown in Fig. 4.3, suppose that $\mathbf{a}$ crosses the origin and its slope is identical with the straight line in the figure. So the projection of a point q is a point A onto the line $\mathbf{a}$. By viewing the vector along $\mathbf{a}$ as a new coordinate axis, A can be represented by its distance from the origin, i.e., $A = \mathbf{a} \cdot \mathbf{q}$. The point B is also on the line by shifting A a distance of b. Then, the straight line is divided by discrete intervals of length d. The projected value is the ID of the interval containing B. The farthest bound that B can reach is C, where $C = \mathbf{a} \cdot \mathbf{q} + d$, i.e., $B \in [A, C)$ along the line.

Fig. 4.3 Geometric illustration of the primitive projection function

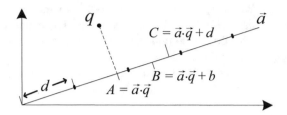

- **Comparison with LSH.** The primitive projection function in Eq. (4.1) has a similar form with locality sensitive hashing (LSH) defined in [16], where the LSH is defined to map a high-dimensional data to an integer. The parameter **a** is a high-dimensional vector with entries chosen independently from a p-stable distribution. The traditional usage of LSH is to reduce the dimensionality of high-dimensional data for accelerating similarity search without security considerations. Different from traditional usage, SecEQP exploits multiple primitive projection functions to project two-dimensional data to high-dimensional data (i.e., the data has a high-dimensional vector representation) for secure kNN search.

4.2.2   Space Encoding via a Single Primitive Projection Function

We now illustrate how to use a single primitive projection function to encode an infinite geometric region.

Definition 4.2 (Feasible Region) Given a point q in the two-dimensional space and a projection function h, we define the feasible region of **q** with respect to the projection function h as consisting of all the possible points **p**, such that $h(\mathbf{q}) = h(\mathbf{p})$, denoted as **FR**$(h(\mathbf{q}))$.

Figure 4.4a shows an example to illustrate the feasible region with respect to a single primitive projection function. Consider a projection function $h(\mathbf{q}) = \lfloor \frac{\mathbf{a_1}\cdot\mathbf{q}+b}{d} \rfloor$ with $b = 0$. Given a point $q \in \mathbb{R}^2$, suppose that $d \leq \mathbf{a_1} \cdot \mathbf{q} < 2d$, so we have $h(\mathbf{q}) = 1$. As shown in Fig. 4.4a, for any point in the shadowed area will be projected to be 1. Therefore, the feasible region of q is an infinite region between two parallel lines l_1 and l_2. The distance of l_1 and l_2 is exactly d. In more general cases, the properties of the feasible region are identified by the following Theorem.

Theorem 4.1 *Given a point $q \in \mathbb{R}^2$, the feasible region of q is between two parallel lines l_1 and l_2 that are perpendicular to* **a**, *as shown in Fig. 4.4a. Define the width of the feasible region* wid *as the distance of l_1 and l_2, we have $wid = d$, which is independent of the location of q and the choice of b.*

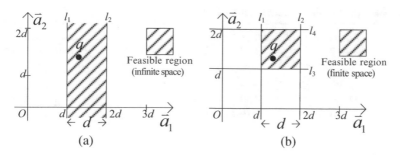

Fig. 4.4 Two examples to illustrate the feasible region. (**a**) The feasible region with respect to a single primitive projection function. (**b**) The feasible region with respect to two orthogonal projection functions

The projected code value enables us to test whether two points p, q are in the same infinite d-width space by checking $h(\mathbf{q}) \stackrel{?}{=} h(\mathbf{p})$. For example, as shown in Fig. 4.4a, if $h(\mathbf{q}) = h(\mathbf{p})$, then point q must locate in the feasible region (shadowed area). Note that the proximity testing by using a single projected code is not accurate because the encoded space is infinite. Two far away points may have the same projected code.

4.2.3 Projection Function Composition Introduction

We use two kinds of compositions: AND-composition and OR-composition, which are defined as follows.

Definition 4.3 (AND-Composition and OR-Composition)

- AND-composition: Consider there are v projection functions $h_1, \cdots, h_v$. A new composite projection function g can be constructed as the AND-composition of them, denoted as $g = AND(h_1, \cdots, h_v)$. *Equal criterion*: given any two points q and p, $g(\mathbf{q}) = g(\mathbf{p})$ if and only if $h_i(\mathbf{q}) = h_i(\mathbf{p})$ for all $i \in [v]$, where $[v]$ denotes the set $\{1, \cdots, v\}$.
- OR-composition: Consider there are t projection functions $h_1, \cdots, h_t$. A new composite projection function g can be constructed as the OR-composition of them, denoted as $g = OR(h_1, \cdots, h_t)$. *Equal criterion*: given any two points q and p, $g(\mathbf{q}) = g(\mathbf{p})$ if and only if $h_i(\mathbf{q}) = h_i(\mathbf{p})$ for at least one $i \in [t]$, where $[t]$ denotes the set $\{1, \cdots, t\}$.

The outputs of a composite projection function can be represented in many ways (e.g., it can be represented by a hierarchical table, as shown in Table 4.2). We give the following example to illustrate how to determine if two composite projection functions equal or not.

Table 4.2 An example to illustrate equal criterion

Point q	$f_1(\mathbf{q}) = OR(g_{1,1}(\mathbf{q}), g_{1,2}(\mathbf{q}))$			
	$g_{1,1}(\mathbf{q}) = AND(h_{1,1,1}(\mathbf{q}), h_{1,1,2}(\mathbf{q}))$		$g_{1,2}(\mathbf{q}) = AND(h_{1,2,1}(\mathbf{q}), h_{1,2,2}(\mathbf{q}))$	
	$h_{1,1,1}(\mathbf{q}) = 1$	$h_{1,1,2}(\mathbf{q}) = 2$	$h_{1,2,1}(\mathbf{q}) = 1$	$h_{1,2,2}(\mathbf{q}) = 2$
Point p	$f_1(\mathbf{p}) = OR(g_{1,1}(\mathbf{p}), g_{1,2}(\mathbf{p}))$			
	$g_{1,1}(\mathbf{p}) = AND(h_{1,1,1}(\mathbf{p}), h_{1,1,2}(\mathbf{p}))$		$g_{1,2}(\mathbf{p}) = AND(h_{1,2,1}(\mathbf{p}), h_{1,2,1}(\mathbf{p}))$	
	$h_{1,1,1}(\mathbf{p}) = 1$	$h_{1,1,2}(\mathbf{p}) = 2$	$h_{1,2,1}(\mathbf{p}) = 3$	$h_{1,2,2}(\mathbf{p}) = 4$

- **An Example to Illustrate Equal Criterion.** Table 4.2 shows an example
  to illustrate equal criterion for the composite projection function. Consider
  there are 4 primitive projection functions $h_{1,1,1}, h_{1,1,2}, h_{1,2,1}, h_{1,2,2}$. Suppose
  that $g_{1,1}$ is constructed by AND-composition of $h_{1,1,1}, h_{1,1,2}$ denoted as
  $g_{1,1} = AND(h_{1,1,1}, h_{1,1,2})$. Likewise, suppose that $g_{1,2}$ is AND-composition of
  $h_{1,2,1}, h_{1,2,2}$ denoted as $g_{1,2} = AND(h_{1,2,1}, h_{1,2,2})$. Let f_1 be constructed by
  OR-composition of $g_{1,1}, g_{1,2}$, i.e., $f_1 = OR(g_{1,1}, g_{1,2})$. In the example, given
  two points q and p, since $h_{1,1,1}(\mathbf{q}) = h_{1,1,1}(\mathbf{p}), h_{1,1,2}(\mathbf{q}) = h_{1,1,2}(\mathbf{p})$, we have
  $g_{1,1}(\mathbf{q}) = g_{1,1}(\mathbf{p})$. Because $h_{1,2,1}(\mathbf{q}) \neq h_{1,2,1}(\mathbf{p})$, we have $g_{1,2}(\mathbf{q}) \neq g_{1,2}(\mathbf{p})$.
  Moreover, it holds that $f_1(\mathbf{q}) = f_1(\mathbf{p})$, because either $g_{1,1}(\mathbf{q}) = g_{1,1}(\mathbf{p})$ or
  $g_{1,2}(\mathbf{q}) = g_{1,2}(\mathbf{p})$ will lead to $f_1(\mathbf{q}) = f_1(\mathbf{p})$.

4.2.4   Space Encoding via Projection Function Composition

In this section, we illustrate how to use projection function composition to encode a
finite space.

- **Space Encoding by only AND-composition.** Given a point $q \in \mathbb{R}^2$, we now
  study the feasible region of q with respect to a projection function g, where g is
  AND-composition of v primitive projection functions. Taking the simplest case
  $v = 2$ as an example, let

$$g(\mathbf{q}) = AND(h_1(\mathbf{q}), h_2(\mathbf{q})), \tag{4.2}$$

  where $h_1(\mathbf{q}) = \lfloor \frac{\mathbf{a}_1 \cdot \mathbf{q} + b_1}{d} \rfloor$ and $h_2(\mathbf{q}) = \lfloor \frac{\mathbf{a}_2 \cdot \mathbf{q} + b_2}{d} \rfloor$, $b_1 = b_2 = 0$, $\mathbf{a}_1$ and $\mathbf{a}_2$ are
  orthogonal vectors (i.e., $\mathbf{a}_1 \perp \mathbf{a}_2$), $d \leq \mathbf{a}_1 \cdot \mathbf{q} < 2d$, and $d \leq \mathbf{a}_1 \cdot \mathbf{q} < 2d$.
  As shown in Fig. 4.4b, the feasible region of q with respect to h_1 is an infinite
  region between l_1 and l_2. Likewise, the feasible region of q with respect to h_2
  is an infinite region between l_3 and l_4. Therefore, the feasible region of q with
  respect to $g = AND(h_1, h_2)$ is the intersection region (i.e., a d-width square),
  as shown in Fig. 4.4b (shadowed area).

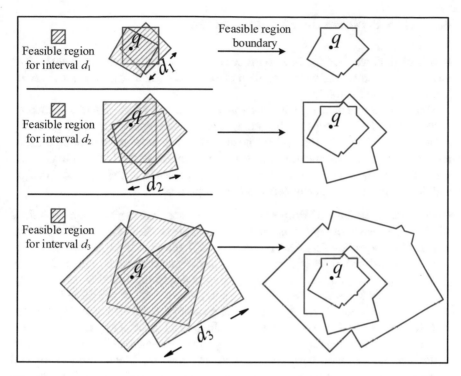

Fig. 4.5 An example to illustrate successive inclusion property ($\mathbf{FR}(f_1(q)) \subset \mathbf{FR}(f_2(q)) \subset \mathbf{FR}(f_3(q))$)

- **Space Encoding by first AND-composition and then OR-composition.** Given a point $q \in \mathbb{R}^2$, where is the feasible region of q with respect to a projection function which is constructed by first AND-composition and then OR-composition? We consider there are two projection functions $g_1(\mathbf{q})$ and $g_2(\mathbf{q})$, which are constructed by AND-composition in the same way as Eq. (4.2). Let $f = OR(g_1, g_2)$. Because each of $g_1(\mathbf{q})$ and $g_2(\mathbf{q})$ specifies a square feasible region of q as shown in Fig. 4.4b. Therefore, the feasible region of q with respect to f is the union of two d-width square feasible regions. For instance, Fig. 4.5 shows feasible regions generated by the union of three square feasible regions with different choices of parameter d.

    In analogy to the single primitive projection function-based space encoding, the composite projection function code values enable us to perform proximity testing over a finite two-dimensional space. More concretely, we can test whether a point p is in the feasible region $\mathbf{FR}(f(\mathbf{q}))$ of q by checking $f(\mathbf{q}) \overset{?}{=} f(\mathbf{p})$. The proximity testing over a finite space can get a much more accurate result than proximity testing over an infinite space.

4.3 kNN Protocol for Plaintext Domain

In this section, we describe how to process kNN queries in plaintext domain (i.e., no data encryption is enforced) and then elaborate on how to transform it to secure kNN protocol in Sect. 4.4.

Our kNN protocol design is developed on the top of an essential property: successive inclusion property. It can be used to generate a series of gradually enlarged feasible regions for a point. The cloud can search from the smallest feasible region to the largest one and gradually find the k nearest points. In the following, we will introduce the successive inclusion property, present our kNN protocol design, and discuss two critical parameters used in our protocol.

- **Successive Inclusion Property.** We construct three projection functions f_1, f_2, f_3, each of which is constructed by first AND-composition of two primitive projection functions (as in Eq. (4.2)) and then three OR-composition. In the construction of f_1, f_2, and f_3, three parameters d_1, d_2, and d_3 are used to generate the corresponding primitive projection function, respectively. Suppose that $d_1 < d_2 < d_3$, Fig. 4.5 shows an example of the feasible regions of q with respect to f_1, f_2, and f_3, respectively. It is shown in Fig. 4.5 that $\mathbf{FR}(f_1(\mathbf{q})) \subset \mathbf{FR}(f_2(\mathbf{q})) \subset \mathbf{FR}(f_3(\mathbf{q}))$. In general, consider there is a series of composite projection function $f_1, \cdots, f_L$ (with the same first AND-composition and then OR-composite patterns), which are constructed by a series of interval lengths $(d_1, \cdots, d_L)$ (with $d_1 < \cdots < d_L$), respectively. If the gap between two successive values in $d_1, \cdots, d_L$ is sufficiently large, it holds that

$$\mathbf{FR}(f_1(\mathbf{q})) \subset \mathbf{FR}(f_2(\mathbf{q})) \subset \cdots \subset \mathbf{FR}(f_L(\mathbf{q})). \tag{4.3}$$

We call the property exhibited in Formula (4.3) as successive inclusion property.

4.3.1 kNN Protocol Design

We next elaborate on our kNN protocol high-level design rationale and present its main algorithms in detail.

- **High-level Design Rationale.** Consider the service model as depicted in Fig. 4.1. The data owner hosts a dataset of n data items in plaintext, then (s)he extracts the spatial attributes, denoted as $p_1, \cdots, p_n$, to build an index for kNN search. The data owner chooses a series of composite projection functions with successive increasing interval lengths $(d_1, \cdots, d_L)$. Given composite projection functions and a data point p_i, the data owner computes a series of feasible regions with successive increasing interval lengths $(d_1, \cdots, d_L)$. Each feasible region is represented by its composite projection function codes, which is outsourced to the cloud to serve as the index. For a query point q, the data user computes a series of the above chosen composite projection functions outputs, and send the codes to cloud for results. Upon reception of the query from the data user, the cloud evaluates the proximity of q and p_i by comparing whether their corresponding composite projection function output codes equal. The cloud searches from the smallest feasible region of q to the largest one until k points are found. Figure 4.7 shows an example of three feasible regions of q that satisfy the successive inclusion property (i.e., $\mathbf{FR}(f_1(\mathbf{q})) \subset \mathbf{FR}(f_2(\mathbf{q})) \subset \mathbf{FR}(f_3(\mathbf{q})))$). Each feasible region is generated by first two AND-composition and then three OR-composition, as shown in Fig. 4.5. For the query point q, the cloud searches from the smallest feasible region $\mathbf{FR}(f_1(\mathbf{q}))$ to the largest feasible region $\mathbf{FR}(f_3(\mathbf{q}))$ to gradually find the closest points.

- *k*NN **Protocol in Detail.** The *k*NN protocol design involves in choosing a group of composite projection functions. We first define the following mathematical notations to facilitate our description. Then, we describe *k*NN protocol in detail.

Definition 4.4 (Projection Function Family)

- $\mathcal{H}_{1,1}^{d_i}$: We define $\mathcal{H}_{1,1}^{d_i}$ to be the primitive projection function family which contains all of primitive projection functions generated by Eq. (4.1) (with $d = d_i$). Let $h \leftarrow \mathcal{H}_{1,1}^{d_i}$ be the process of randomly sampling a projection function h from $\mathcal{H}_{1,1}^{d_i}$, where the randomness comes from the random choices of the vector **a** and b in Eq. (4.1).

- $\mathcal{H}_{v,1}^{d_i}$: We define $\mathcal{H}_{v,1}^{d_i}$ to be AND-composite projection function family which contains all of composite projection functions generated by the AND-composition of v randomly chosen primitive projection functions $h_1, \cdots, h_v$, where $h_i \leftarrow \mathcal{H}_{1,1}^{d_i}$ for all $i \in [v]$. Let $g \leftarrow \mathcal{H}_{v,1}^{d_i}$ be the process of randomly sampling a composite projection function g from $\mathcal{H}_{v,1}^{d_i}$.

- $\mathcal{H}_{v,t}^{d_i}$: We define $\mathcal{H}_{v,t}^{d_i}$ to be the Or-composite projection function family which contains all of composite projection functions generated by the OR-composition of t randomly chosen AND-composite projection functions $g_1, \cdots, g_t$, where $g_i \leftarrow \mathcal{H}_{v,1}^{d_i}$ for all $i \in [t]$. Let $f \leftarrow \mathcal{H}_{v,t}^{d_i}$ be the process of randomly sampling a composite projection function f from $\mathcal{H}_{v,t}^{d_i}$.

With the above notations, the proposed *k*NN protocol is described as follows. First, the data owner setups several global parameters including v, t, and L successive increasing interval lengths $(d_1, \cdots d_L)$. Second, the data owner invokes Algorithm 1 (Index-Building) to compute and store the projection function output values of each point in the index matrix $\mathbb{I}'$. Afterward, the index $\mathbb{I}'$ is sent to the cloud for storage. Then, the data user calls the Algorithm 2 (Token-Generation) to compute and store the projection function output values of the query point in the token array $\mathbb{T}'$. Recall that whether two points are in the same feasible region or not can be deduced by comparing their projection function output values, the cloud calls Algorithm 3 (Query-Processing) to check whether $p_i (i \in [n])$ is in the smallest feasible region $\mathbf{FR}(f_1(\mathbf{q}))$ of query point q via checking $f_1(\mathbf{q}) \stackrel{?}{=} f_1(\mathbf{p}_i)$ (i.e., $\mathbb{T}'(1) \stackrel{?}{=} \mathbb{I}'(i, 1)$) (step 3 in Algorithm 3). According to the successive inclusion property, the cloud searches from the smallest feasible region of q (i.e., $\mathbf{FR}(f_1(\mathbf{q}))$) to the largest one (i.e., $\mathbf{FR}(f_L(\mathbf{q}))$) and stops until at least k distinct points are found. Suppose that the search stops when $k'(k \geq k)$ points are found, the data user computes their accurate distance to the query point q and sorts them to figure out the top-k closest points as the query results.

Algorithm 1: Index-building

Input: $v, t, L, (d_1, \cdots, d_L), p_1, \cdots, p_n$
Output: $\mathbb{I}'$
1 **for** $(i = 1; i \leq L; i + +)$ **do**
2     $f_i \leftarrow \mathcal{H}_{v,t}^{d_i}$;
3 **for** $(i = 1; i \leq n; i + +)$ **do**
4   **for** $(j = 1; j \leq L; j + +)$ **do**
5   compute $\mathbb{I}'(i, j) = f_j(p_i)$;
        /* $\mathbb{I}'(i, j)$ represents the composite projection function
           output values for data point p_i with $d = d_j$ */

Algorithm 2: Token-generation

Input: q and $f_1, \cdots, f_L$
Output: $\mathbb{T}'$
1 **for** $(j = 1; j \leq L; j + +)$ **do**
2   compute $\mathbb{T}'(j) = f_j(q)$;
    /* $\mathbb{T}'(j)$ represents the composite projection function
        output values for query point q with $d = d_j$ */

4.3.2 Analysis of kNN Protocol Parameters

In our kNN protocol, there are two critical parameters: v (the number of AND-composition) and t (the number of OR-composition). We discuss how they influence the performance of kNN protocol as follows.

- **Geometric Analysis of v.** Setting up a larger v implies an improvement of the proximity measurement precision. In order to precisely measure the proximity between two points in two-dimensional space, it is desirable that points p and q

---

Algorithm 3: `Query-processing`

Input: k, L, $\mathbb{I}'$, $\mathbb{T}'$ and $p_1, \cdots, p_n$
Output: $\mathbb{R}'$
    /* $\mathbb{R}'$ represents the set of returned points   */
1 Initialization: $\mathbb{R}' = Null$; $i = j = 1$; $result\_num = 0$;
2 **while** $(result\_num < k$ && $j \leq L)$ **do**
3   **if** $(\texttt{Is\_equal}(\mathbb{T}'(j), \mathbb{I}'(i, j)) ==$ True$)$ && $(p_i \notin \mathbb{R}')$ /* search for the
          data point p_i in $\mathbf{FR}(f_j(\mathbf{q}))$ */
4   **then**
5 $\mathbb{R}' = \mathbb{R}' \cup p_j$, $result\_num + +$;
6   **if** $(i == n)$ /* if $\mathbf{FR}(f_j(\mathbf{q}))$ have been searched, then search in
          $\mathbf{FR}(f_{j+1}(\mathbf{q}))$ */
7   **then**
8 $j + +, i = 1$;
9   **else**
10 $i + +$;
          /* search for the next data point p_{i+1} in $\mathbf{FR}(f_j(\mathbf{q}))$ */

Fig. 4.6 Circle-based
accurate *k*NN search process

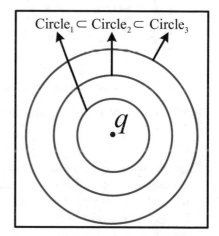

are projected to more random directions on the two-dimensional plane and then compare their projection function output values. As a result, a larger v implies an improvement of the proximity measurement precision.

- **Geometric Analysis of** t. Setting up a larger t implies an improvement of the result accuracy. For the query point q, if the cloud searches from a series of concentric circle regions (centered at the point q), then the cloud always gets the accurate results. Figure 4.6 shows an example of the ideal accurate *k*NN search process. For the query point q, the cloud first searches from the smallest circle Circle₁ to the largest circle Circle₃ to gradually find the closest points. In comparison, Fig. 4.7 shows the projection-based approximate *k*NN search process. In order to increase the result accuracy, it is desirable that the feasible

Fig. 4.7 Projection-based
approximate kNN search
process

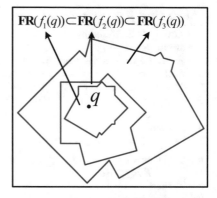

$$\mathbf{FR}(f_1(q)) \subset \mathbf{FR}(f_2(q)) \subset \mathbf{FR}(f_3(q))$$

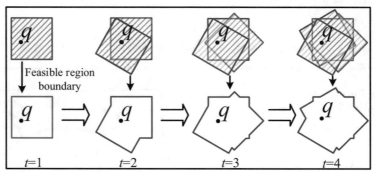

Fig. 4.8 The feasible region is getting closer to a circle by increasing the number of OR-composition t

regions are close to circles with point q at the center. Figure 4.8 shows that
increasing the number of OR-composition t can make the feasible region closer
to a circle. Therefore, a larger t implies an improvement of the result accuracy.

- **An Optimization in Projection Function Generation.** In the AND-composite
function g generation, SecEQP chooses t random primitive projection functions
with t random directions for a point to project. In order to better measure the
proximity of two points p, q in the space, it is expected that p, q are projected in
many different directions over the space. The difference between two directions
$\mathbf{a}_1$ and $\mathbf{a}_2$ can be represented by their angle, denoted as $\widehat{\mathbf{a}_1, \mathbf{a}_2}$. Random projection
direction choices may lead to many pairs of similar directions (e.g., $\widehat{\mathbf{a}_1, \mathbf{a}_2}$ is very
small). To increase the difference between projected directions, we refine our
direction choice process by first choosing a random direction $\mathbf{a}_1 = (\theta, 1)$, and
then choose the remaining $v - 1$ vectors to equally divide the space. For example,
if there are three chosen directions $\mathbf{a}_1$, $\mathbf{a}_2$, and $\mathbf{a}_3$, an optimized solution is to keep
$\widehat{(\mathbf{a}_1, \mathbf{a}_2)} = \widehat{(\mathbf{a}_2, \mathbf{a}_3)} = \pi/3$.

4.4   Transforming kNN to Secure kNN

In this section, we describe how to transform the above kNN protocol to be a secure and sublinear protocol. Our approach is to leverage searchable symmetric encryption (SSE) for keyword query [17]. It allows data users to have secure keyword query processing on the cloud. In order to harness SSE, there are three technical issues need to be addressed.

- *How to generate keywords?* Our solution is to design a prefix-free encoding method (Sect. 4.4.1) to encode the projection function output values to generate keywords.
- *How to perform search operations over the index?* Our solution is to do the operation transformation (Sect. 4.4.2) which transforms the Is_equal evaluation in Algorithm 3 to be Is_exist evaluation.
- *How to build a secure index?* Our solution is to use the indistinguishable Bloom filter (IBF) tree based secure index (Sect. 4.4.3) which provides the sublinear search time as well as a strong security guarantee.

In the following, we will elaborate on our remedies to the above technical issues in detail and finally present how to apply them to the SkNN protocol (i.e., SecEQP) design (Sect. 4.4.4).

4.4.1   Prefix-Free Encoding

In Algorithm 3 (Query-Processing), for two points p and q, in order to know whether p locates in the feasible region $\mathbf{FR}(f_i(\mathbf{q}))$ of q, we need to evaluate the logic expression

$$\text{Is\_equal}(f_i(\mathbf{q}), f_i(\mathbf{p})), \tag{4.4}$$

where $f_i = OR(g_{i,1}, \cdots, g_{i,t})$. Then, the logic expression (4.4) can be translated to

$$\text{Is\_equal}(g_{i,1}(\mathbf{q}), g_{i,1}(\mathbf{p})) \vee \cdots \vee \text{Is\_equal}(g_{i,t}(\mathbf{q}), g_{i,t}(\mathbf{p})). \tag{4.5}$$

Consider $g_{i,j} = AND(h_{i,j,1}, \cdots, h_{i,j,v})$, we let $str(g_{i,j}(\mathbf{q})) = h_{i,j,1}(\mathbf{q})||\cdots||$ $h_{i,j,v}(\mathbf{q}))$, where "$||$" denotes the string concatenation. In order to circumvent Is_equal evaluation, we construct two sets by prefix encoding as

$$\begin{aligned} Q_i &= \{i||1||str(g_{i,1}(\mathbf{q})), \cdots, i||t||str(g_{i,t}(\mathbf{q}))\}, \\ P_i &= \{i||1||str(g_{i,1}(\mathbf{p})), \cdots, i||t||str(g_{i,t}(\mathbf{p}))\}. \end{aligned} \tag{4.6}$$

For each component in the coding, we reserve a fix number of bit to ensure that the code is prefix-free. The prefix-free encoding ensures if one element in the set Q_i equals to another element in set P_i, then their each coding component must equal to each other. For example, suppose that $h_{1,1,1}(\mathbf{q}) = 1, h_{1,1,2}(\mathbf{q}) = 11, h_{1,1,1}(\mathbf{p}) = 11$, and $h_{1,1,2}(\mathbf{p}) = 1$, a direct encoding will lead to $1||1||str(g_{i,j}(\mathbf{q})) = $ "1"+"1"+ "11"+"1" = "11111" and $1||1||str(g_{i,j}(\mathbf{p})) = $ "1"+"1"+"1"+"11" = "11111". This leads to $str(g_{i,j}(\mathbf{q})) = str(g_{i,j}(\mathbf{p}))$ despite $g_{i,j}(\mathbf{q}) \neq g_{i,j}(\mathbf{p})$. However, if we fix 2 digits to encode each component, then we have $01||01||str(g_{i,j}(\mathbf{q})) = $ "01"+"01"+"11"+"01" = "01011101" and $01||01||str(g_{i,j}(\mathbf{p})) = $ "01"+"01"+ "01" + "11" = "01010111", so $str(g_{i,j}(\mathbf{q})) \neq str(g_{i,j}(\mathbf{p}))$. Therefore, prefix-free encoding preserves the equal relationship after coding. In the above example, we choose 2 digits for each coding component. However, in real applications, the data owner should choose a number which is not less than the maximum number of digits for each coding component.

4.4.2 Operation Transformation

With the prefix-free encoding, the following Theorem holds immediately.

Theorem 4.2 *Logic expression (4.4) and (4.5) are* True $\Longleftrightarrow Q_i \cap P_i \neq \emptyset$, *where* "$\Longleftrightarrow$" *denotes logical equivalence.*

Let us reuse the settings in Table 4.2 as an example. According to prefix-free encoding described in Eq. (4.6), we have $Q_1 = \{01010102, 01020102\}$ and $P_1 = \{01010102, 01020304\}$, where we fix 2 bits for each component in coding. Because $Q_1 \cap P_1 = \{01010102\} \neq \emptyset$, we have $f_1(\mathbf{q}) = f_1(\mathbf{p})$. Based on Theorem 4.2, we can employ Is_exist evaluation to replace Is_equal evaluation. That is, we can know whether query point p is located in the feasible region $\mathbf{FR}(f_i(\mathbf{q}))$ of q by checking $Q_i \cap P_i \overset{?}{=} \emptyset$. In order to check $Q_i \cap P_i \overset{?}{=} \emptyset$, we can traverse every element in Q_i and then test whether it exists in P_i.

4.4.3 Indistinguishable Bloom Filter Tree Based Secure Index

The secure index used in SecEQP is built based on a data structure called indistinguishable Bloom filter (IBF) tree. In the following, we will provide the primer of indistinguishable bloom filter and then introduce how to construct an IBF tree for the secure index. Finally, we will discuss why IBF-based index is secure and efficient.

- **Indistinguishable Bloom Filter.** The indistinguishable Bloom filter (IBF) is a data structure that is extended from Bloom filter [18]. It can be used to test whether an element is a member of a set or not. IBF is defined as follows.

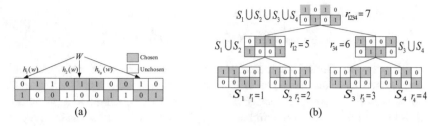

Fig. 4.9 Indistinguishable Bloom filter and indistinguishable Bloom filter tree examples. (**a**) An simplified example of indistinguishable Bloom filter. (**b**) An simplified example of indistinguishable Bloom filter tree

Definition 4.5 (IBF [19]) An IBF is an array B of m twins, k_B different hash functions $h_1, h_2, \cdots, h_{k_B}$, and a random oracle H. Each twin consists of two cells where each cell stores either 0 or 1 and the two cells should be different. The two cells in a twin are named as 0-cell and 1-cell, respectively. For each twin, the oracle H determines which cell is chosen in a random fashion. For every twin, the chosen cell is initialized to 0 and the unchosen cell is set to 1. Given one keyword w, we hash it to k_B twins $B[h_1(w)], B[h_2(w)], \cdots, B[h_{k_B}(w)]$, and for each of these k_B twins, we set its chosen cell to 1 and the unchosen cell to 0.

Figure 4.9a shows an example of IBF. Let us describe how to embed a keyword w_i into an IBF. We assume that the data owner and data users share $k_B + 1$ secret keys $K_1, \cdots, K_{k_B+1}$. We construct k_B hash functions using the keyed hash message authentication code (HMAC), where $h_i(\cdot) = \mathrm{HMAC}_{K_i}(\cdot) \mod m$, for $i \in [k_B]$. We construct another hash function as $h_{i+1}(\cdot) = \mathrm{HMAC}_{K_{B+1}}(\cdot)$. The random oracle is instantiated as $H(\cdot) = \mathrm{SHA1}(\cdot) \mod 2$. An IBF can be viewed as a two-dimensional array B with two rows and m columns. Let $B[i][j]$ be the value in the ith row and jth column of the IBF B. To embed a keyword w_i into the IBF B, we set

$$B[H(h_{k_B+1}(h_j(w_i)) \oplus r_B)][h_j(w_i)] = 1,$$
$$B[1 - H(h_{k_B+1}(h_j(w_i)) \oplus r_B)][h_j(w_i)] = 0, \tag{4.7}$$

for all $j \in [k_B]$, where r_B is a random number associated with IBF B. To test whether a keyword w_i is in the IBF B, we just need to compute the corresponding hashes and test whether the positions indicated by these hashes are all 1. If all positions are 1, then w_i is in the IBF, otherwise not.

- **Indistinguishable Bloom Filter Tree.** IBFs can be organized into a binary tree structure to achieve sublinear search time. Figure 4.9b shows an example of IBF tree. An IBF tree is constructed as follows. Suppose that B_v is the father IBF of two children IBFs: B_l (left child) and B_r (right child), then B_v is constructed as follows: for each $i \in [m]$, the value of B_v's ith twin is the logical OR of B_l's ith twin and B_r's ith twin. That is

$$B_v[H(h_{k_B+1}(i) \oplus r_{B_v})][i] =$$
$$B_l[H(h_{k_B+1}(i) \oplus r_{B_l})][i] \vee B_r[H(h_{k_B+1}(i) \oplus r_{B_r})][i]. \tag{4.8}$$

By this way, the IBF tree can be constructed from a number of leaf nodes until there is one root node. As shown in Fig. 4.9b, if B_l is an IBF representing set S_1 and B_r is an IBF representing set S_2, then we have that B_v is an IBF representing set $S_1 \cup S_2$ while the random numbers, r_1, r_2, and r_{12}, for S_1, S_2, and $S_1 \cup S_2$ are 1, 2, and 5, respectively. More examples and the illustration about how to build a Bloom filter tree can be found in [20, 21]. This property enables us to perform a binary search from the root IBF in the tree to the leaf IBF to test whether a keyword is embedded in a leaf IBF in $O(\log(n))$ time.

The security intuition behind IBF tree-based index is that the positions of 0-cell and 1-cell are determined by the random oracle H, so an IBF tree is a completely random data structure consists of an equal number of 1s and 0s. Moreover, a node-specific random number r_B (see Eq. (4.7)) is adopted while each IBF node is generated. With this design, even if there are two points at the same location, their IBF nodes are likely to be different unless their random numbers are equivalent. This approach thus prevents the cloud from inferring the projected values or the closeness of locations in geospatial database by analyzing their IBF nodes in the IBF tree-based index. Therefore, intuitively, the IBF tree-based index can achieve index privacy (the formal index indistinguishability proof is elaborated in Step 2 of Theorem 4.3).

4.4.4   SkNN Protocol (SecEQP) Design

We next introduce the SecEQP design which employs the aforementioned prefix-free encoding, operation transformation, and IBF-tree based security index techniques.

- *Index-Building.* For each data point in the database, the data owner computes its projection function output values (exactly the same process as described in Algorithm 1). Then, the data owner employs the prefix-encoding (according to the method described in Eq. (4.6)) to generate a set of codes for each point. The set of codes are grouped by a series of sets P_i, for $i \in [L]$. Each point's codes are embedded into a distinct IBF (in the way as described by Eq. (4.7)). All IBFs generated by data points now serve as the leaf nodes to construct a balanced IBF tree (in the way as described by Eq. (4.8)). Each IBF node in the IBF tree is associated with a random number as shown in Eqs. (4.7) and (4.8). The IBF tree along with the random number for each IBF node in the tree serve as the secure index, which is outsourced and stored in the cloud.
- *Token-Generation.* Given the query point q, the data user computes projection function values and employs the prefix-encoding to generate a set of codes for each point (according to the method described in Eq. (4.6)). The set of codes

are grouped by a series of sets Q_i, for $i \in [L]$. The set of codes serve as a series of keywords. Note that the keywords in Q_{i_1} are put before keywords in Q_{i_2} if $i_1 < i_2$. For a keyword w_i, the data user computes k_B locations $h_j(w_i)$, for $j \in [k_B]$. For each location $h_j(w_i)$, the data user computes hash $h_{K_B+1}(h_j(w_i))$. The search token t_{w_i} of keyword w_i is a k_B-pair of hashes and locations: $\{h_{K_B+1}(h_j(w_i)), h_j(w_i)\}$, for $j \in [k_B]$. The data user generates search tokens in the above way for all keywords in Q_i ($i \in [L]$) and sends these search tokens to the cloud for results. Because these hash functions are one-way, it is hard for the cloud to deduce the useful information of the query point by viewing these search tokens.

- *Query-processing.* On receipt of a search token t_{w_i} for keyword w_i from the data user, the cloud performs the query processing, which is described as follows. Let $t_{w_i}[j]$ denote the jth ordered pair in t_{w_i}, i.e., $t_{w_i}[j] = \{h_{K_B+1}(h_j(w_i)), h_j(w_i)\}$. Let $t_{w_i}[j].f$ and $t_{w_i}[j].s$ be the first and second hash in $t_{w_i}[j]$, respectively. For an IBF B that the cloud checks against t_{w_i}, if there exist $j \in [k_B]$ such that $B[H(t_{w_i}[j].f \oplus r_B)][t_{w_i}[j].s] = 0$, then t_{w_i} does not match any of the items embedded in the IBF. If the cloud determines that t_{w_i} does not match the IBF B, the query processing terminates. Otherwise, the cloud processes t_{w_i} against the left and right children of the IBF B. The search begins from the root IBF until the cloud reaches the leaf IBF and get the corresponding encrypted data item. The cloud searches from the first keyword-generated tokens to the last keyword-generated tokens and stops until at least k distinct IBF leaf nodes are found. Last, the cloud returns the corresponding encrypted data item to the data user for further processing.

4.4.5 Security Analysis

In this section, we first describe the adopted security model and related notations. Then, we define leakage functions and perform security proof for SecEQP.

- *Secure Model and Notations.* We adopt the widely used adaptive indistinguishability under chosen-keyword attack (IND-CKA) secure model [17]. Let $\mathbf{D} = \{d_1, \cdots, d_n\}$ denote the set of data items. Let $\mathbb{I}$ and $\mathbf{T}$ denote the index and search token, respectively. Suppose that SecEQP employs a CPA-secure encryption scheme [15] to encrypt each data items.
- *Leakage Functions.* Before we carry out the formal security proof, we introduce two leakage functions. (1) $\mathcal{L}_1(\mathbb{I}, \mathbf{D})$: Given the index $\mathbb{I}$ and dataset $\mathbf{D}$, this function outputs the size of each IBF m, the number of data items n in $\mathbf{D}$, the data item identifiers $ID = (id_1, \cdots, id_n)$, and the size of each encrypted data item. (2) $\mathcal{L}_2(\mathbb{I}, \mathbf{D}, q_i)$: This function takes as input the index $\mathbb{I}$, the set of data items $\mathbf{D}$, and a query q_i. It outputs two types of information: the *search pattern*, which is the information about whether the same search was performed before

or not, and the *access pattern*, which is the information about which data item identifiers that match query q_i.

Theorem 4.3 *SecEQP scheme is adaptive IND-CKA $(\mathcal{L}_1, \mathcal{L}_2)$-secure in the random oracle model.*

Proof In the proof, we first describe a simulator S that can simulate a view $A_v^* = (\mathbb{I}^*, \mathbf{T}^*, \mathbf{c}^*)$ with the help of information accessible in the leakage functions $\mathcal{L}_1$ and $\mathcal{L}_2$. Next, we show that a probabilistic polynomial-time (PPT) adversary cannot distinguish between the simulated view $A_v^* = (\mathbb{I}^*, \mathbf{T}^*, \mathbf{c}^*)$ and the real adversary view $A_v = (\mathbb{I}, \mathbf{T}, \mathbf{c})$.

- Step (1): Simulate $\mathbf{c}^*$ (which captures the requirement for data privacy). To simulate the encrypted data items $D = \{d_1, \cdots, d_n\}$, the simulator first learns the value n and the size of each encrypted data item from the leakage function $\mathcal{L}_1$. Then, the simulator generates the simulated ciphertext with randomly selected plaintext and the known CPA-secure encryption algorithm. The simulator needs to ensure that the simulated ciphertext has the same size as the real ciphertext. Because the CPA-secure encryption algorithm achieves ciphertext indistinguishability, a PPT adversary cannot distinguish the simulated ciphertext with the real ciphertext.
- Step (2): Simulate $\mathbb{I}^*$ (which captures the requirement for index privacy). To simulate the IBF tree T, the simulator S constructs an identically structured IBF tree first. Then, for each node v in T, the simulator S sets up an IBF B_v with the same size as in the IBF in the index $\mathbb{I}$. Note that the simulator S can learn the IBF size from the leakage function $\mathcal{L}_1$. In the ith twin of B_v, the simulator S stores either 0 at $B_v[0][i]$ and 1 at $B_v[1][i]$, or vice versa. For each twin, how to assign 0-cell and 1-cell is decided by fairly tossing a coin. Next, for each IBF node, the simulator S generates a random number to associate with it. Finally, the simulator S outputs the IBF tree T and its associated random number as the simulated index $\mathbb{I}^*$ to the adversary. The simulated index $\mathbb{I}^*$ has exactly the same structure with the real index $\mathbb{I}$. The IBF nodes in either $\mathbb{I}^*$ or $\mathbb{I}$ have the same size and equally distributed 0-cell and 1-cell. Hence, a PPT adversary cannot distinguish between the simulated index $\mathbb{I}^*$ and the real index $\mathbb{I}$.
- Step (3): Simulate $\mathbf{T}^*$ (which captures the requirement for token privacy). Suppose that the simulator S receives a query q_i. From the leakage function $\mathcal{L}_2$, the simulator S knows whether this query has been searched before or not. If it has been searched before, the simulator S outputs the previous searched token t_{q_i} to the adversary. Otherwise, the simulator S generates a new search token t_{q_i} as follows. The search token for a query is the set of k_B-pair of hashes and locations. Because the simulator S can learn access pattern from the leakage function $\mathcal{L}_2$, the simulator S knows which leaf IBF node in the index matches the search token t_{q_i}. For the leaf IBF node that matches the search token t_{q_i}, the simulator S can program the bit output by the random oracle $H(\cdot)$ to select k_B-pair of hashes and locations and ensure that the selected k_B-pair of hashes and locations match the leaf IBF node v. For the leaf IBF node that does not match the search token

t_{q_i}, the simulator $\mathcal{S}$ is able to ensure that the simulated search token does not match the IBF node by programming the bit output by the random oracle. By this way, the simulator $\mathcal{S}$ can output the generated k_B-pair of hashes and locations as the simulated search token $\mathbf{T}^*$. Since the search token is k_B-pair of hashes and locations which are produced by the random hash functions, the simulated search token $\mathbf{T}^*$ is indistinguishable from the real search token $\mathbf{T}$ by a PPT adversary.

In summary, the simulated view $A_v^* = (\mathbb{I}^*, \mathbf{T}^*, \mathbf{c}^*)$ and the real view $A_v = (\mathbb{I}, \mathbf{T}, \mathbf{c})$ are indistinguishable by a PPT adversary. Therefore, SecEQP scheme is adaptive IND-CKA $(\mathcal{L}_1, \mathcal{L}_2)$-secure in the random oracle model. □

4.5 Performance Evaluation

In this section, we first introduce parameter settings, datasets, performance metrics, and implementation. Then, we evaluate the performance of SecEQP and compare it with other two schemes (Elmehdwi et al. [5] and Yao et al. [7]) with the strong security assurance. Last, we describe a strategy to improve the result accuracy to meet a variety of location service demands.

4.5.1 Parameters Settings

Table 4.4 summarizes the default parameter settings in the experiment. Among these parameters, the choices of $(d_1, \cdots, d_L)$ are not straightforward, because they affect the size of the feasible region. If they are set to be too small, too few or even no points are inside the feasible region. if they are set to be too large, then too many points are inside the feasible region, this would make the post-processing inefficient. Accordingly, we design a parameter training algorithm (run by the data owner) for choosing appropriate $(d_1, \cdots, d_L)$. The design rationale of the parameters training algorithm is that it uses the knowledge of the dataset to adjust $(d_1, \cdots, d_L)$ to be appropriate values to ensure that an appropriate number of points can be returned in the search. We skip the details of the parameters training algorithm due to space limitations.

4.5.2 Datasets, Metrics, and Implementation

- **Datasets.** (1) **NY** is a real-world dataset contains 1 million spatial data in the state of New York (NY) from OpenStreetMap Project [22], which collects geographical data from volunteered mobile device carriers. (2) **CA** is a real-world dataset contains 1 million spatial data in California (CA) from OpenStreetMap

Project. (3) **UF** is a synthetic dataset contains 1 million spatial data generated
from uniform (UF) distribution. More specifically, each data is denoted as
(X_{UF}, Y_{UF}), where $X_{UF} \sim U[0, 10^9]$ and $Y_{UF} \sim U[0, 10^9]$.

- **Metrics.** Three metrics are used: (1) query latency, (2) query result accuracy, and
  (3) query cost. The query latency is defined as the time for the cloud to respond
  to an SkNN query. The result accuracy of an SkNN query can be reflected by
  Overall Approximation Ratio (OAR) [23], which is defined as $\frac{1}{k}\sum_{i=1}^{k} \frac{\|o_i, q\|}{\|o_i^*, q\|}$,
  where q is the query point, o_i is the ith nearest point in the search results and o_i^* is
  the ground truth (i.e., the actual ith nearest point in the dataset). Theoretically, the
  high result accuracy means OAR should be close to 1. The query cost consists of
  the communication cost and the size of the secure index maintained in the cloud.
- **Implementation.** The SecEQP implementations are achieved by C++. We carry
  out the experiments on a cluster node (serves as the cloud) equipped with 128 GB
  RAM and two 2.5Ghz 10-core Intel Xeon E5-2670v2 CPU. In our experiments,
  unless otherwise stated, when we vary the value of one parameter in concern, we
  keep all other parameters at their default values, which are displayed in Table 4.4.

4.5.3 Experiment Results

We first evaluate the performance of SecEQP in terms of query latency, result
accuracy, and query cost. Then we compare SecEQP with other two schemes
(Elmehdwi et al. [5] and Yao et al. [7]) with the strong security assurance.

- **Query Latency.** The query latency as a function of n (i.e., the number of points
  in a dataset) and k (i.e., the number of nearest points required in a query) is shown
  in Figs. 4.10 and 4.11. It can be observed that the query latency grows sublinear
  with n and a slightly faster than linear with k. While $k = 50$, the query latency
  for a dataset contains 1 million points with is less than 50 ms.

Fig. 4.10 SecEQP query
latency by varying the
parameter n

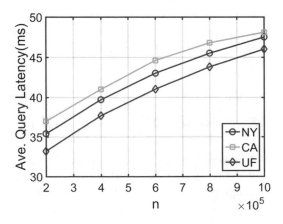

Fig. 4.11 SecEQP query latency by varying the parameter k

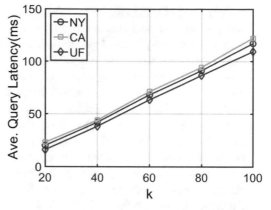

Fig. 4.12 SecEQP OAR by varying the parameter v

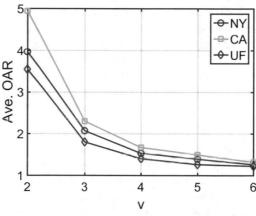

Fig. 4.13 SecEQP OAR by varying the parameter t

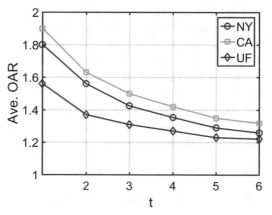

- **Result Accuracy.** Let n' be the total number of inserted items in the root node of the IBF. Figures 4.12 and 4.13 exhibit OAR as a function of v and t, respectively. The OAR is monotonically decreasing with increasing v and t. Hence, increasing v and t can improve the result accuracy. As shown in Fig. 4.12, if $v = 6$ and $t =$

6, the average OAR is about 1.3. This means that the average distance between the queried point and returned results is 1.3 times longer than the ground truth. Note that a strategy is developed to further improve the result accuracy (i.e., OAR can be improved to be 1.1) in Sect. 4.5.4.

- **Query Cost.** For the query cost, we consider the communication volume and the size of the secure index which helps to accelerate the query processing in the cloud. The communication volume consists of the transmission of the search token and the encrypted data items. Since the size of encrypted data items is independent of the adopted SecEQP scheme, we only consider the communication volume of the search token. Table 4.3 shows the token size in an SkNN query for different schemes. The token size of SecEQP is computed based on the parameter settings in Table 4.4. It is shown that all of the schemes have a constant token size for an SkNN query. The search token only takes 6.93 KB, indicating a very small communication volume. For index size, SecEQP employs the existing IBF tree compression algorithms [19] to compress the index size. The index size varies with dataset sizes. While the dataset contains 10^4, 10^5, and 10^6 points, the index will take 0.44, 3.13, and 15.8 GB, respectively.

- **Comparison with other schemes.** We compare SecEQP with two schemes with strong security assurance. The experiment results for query latency are average over the three datasets. The results are summarized in Table 4.3. We have five observations.

First, while $k = 1$ (i.e., 1NN), Yao et al. [7] has the shortest query latency over three database sizes (10^4, 10^5, 10^6), ranges from 5 to 12 ms, whereas SecEQP has a comparable query latency (i.e., from 9 to 31 ms). Second, while $k = 50$, SecEQP has the shortest query latency, ranges from 12 to 47 ms, which is not significantly increased with k, whereas Elmehdwi et al. [5] do (e.g., 14.3 sec→11.78 min). Note that Yao et al. [7] does not support the use scenarios while $k > 1$. Third, the average OAR for both Yao et al. [7] and Elmehdwi et al. [5] is 1, whereas SecEQP is about 1.3. Forth, all of three schemes do not create large tokens. The token size ranges from 8 bytes (Yao et al. [7]) to 6.9 KB (SecEQP). Fifth, SecEQP's index is the largest one compared with other schemes. In a dataset contains 10^6 points, SecEQP's index takes 15.8 GB, whereas Yao et al. [7] and Elmehdwi et al. [5] use 20.3 and 0 MB, respectively. There are two causes. First, Elmehdwi et al. [5] does not employ the index mechanism for the query acceleration. Second, SecEQP supports the use scenarios while $k > 1$; however, Yao et al. [7] does not.

4.5.4   Improve Result Accuracy

In this section, we first illustrate the top nearest accuracy property and then describe how to use it to develop an effective strategy to improve the result accuracy.

- **Top Nearest Accuracy Property.** It is observed in the experiments that the closer the point, the less probability it is missed in the searching. We call

Table 4.3 Compare SecEQP with other schemes (Na: Not applicable)

Scheme	Query latency						Query cost				Accuracy (OAR)
	k = 1			k = 50			Communication volume	Index size			
	$n = 10^4$	$n = 10^5$	$n = 10^6$	$n = 10^4$	$n = 10^5$	$n = 10^6$	(token size + data items size)	$n = 10^4$	$n = 10^5$	$n = 10^6$	
SecEQP	9 ms	21 ms	31 ms	12 ms	32 ms	47 ms	6.93 **KB** + data item size	0.44 GB	3.13 GB	15.8 GB	≈1.3
Yao et al. [7]	5 ms	9 ms	12 ms	Na	Na	Na	8 byte + data items size	14.8 MB	17.4 MB	20.3 MB	1
Elmehdwi et al. [5]	0.15 sec	1.44 sec	14.3 sec	0.12 min	1.18 min	11.78 min	16 byte + data items size	Na	Na	Na	1

Table 4.4 Parameter settings

Notations	Meanings	Default values
n	The number of points	100,000
k	The number of nearest points required in a query	50
m	The number of twins in the root node of IBF tree	$10Ltn$
k_B	The number of hash functions in an IBF	7
v	The number of AND-composition	6
t	The number of OR-composition	6
L	The number of interval lengths	5

Fig. 4.14 SecEQP OAR by varying the parameter k

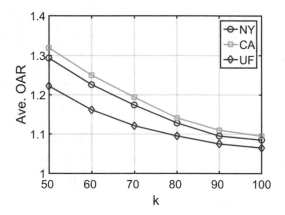

this top nearest accuracy property. Theoretically, this property is caused by the successive inclusion property as exhibited in Formula (4.3). The following example is helpful for understanding. Suppose that the query processing stops after searching $\mathbf{FR}(f_5(q))$. For the points in $\mathbf{FR}(f_1(q))$, they are searched for 5 times; ...; for the points in $\mathbf{FR}(f_5(q))$, they are searched for only 1 time. This repeated filtering process leads to top nearest accuracy property.

- **Improve Accuracy Strategy.** The top nearest accuracy property indicates a strategy to improve the result accuracy of SecEQP scheme. The strategy is that if we want to get kNN, we can query k'NN, where $k' > k$, and figure out the top-k nearest points as the query results. To evaluate this strategy, we conduct an experiment as follows. We query kNN, where $k = 50, \cdots, 100$, and select the top 50 nearest points as the final query results for 50NN. The experiment results are plotted in Fig. 4.14. We observe that the result accuracy is improved by increasing k. If we let $k = 100$, the average OAR is less than 1.1, which demonstrates that this strategy is effective in improving the result accuracy.

4.6 Related Work

- Location Obfuscation Approach. Schemes based on location obfuscation [24], and data transformation [2, 25] do not use strong standard encryption algorithm. Therefore, they suffer from weak privacy.
- Private Information Retrieval Approach. The Private Information Retrieval (PIR)-based solutions [4] mainly consider protecting query privacy but not data privacy. Besides, PIR-based solutions suffer from long query latency for large-scale dataset.
- Fully Homomorphic Encryption Approach. Fully homomorphic encryption (FHE) [14] enables cloud to perform kNN computation directly over the encrypted data. However, current FHE solutions still lack efficiency.
- Property-preserving Encryption Approach. Distance-recoverable encryption (DRE)-based schemes [2, 3] and Order-preserving encryption (OPE)-based SkNN schemes [2, 6] achieve weak security, as analyzed in [9].
- Voronoi Diagram Approach. Voronoi-based scheme [7] requires each data user to download and maintain a copy of the large-size index locally for query processing, which seriously impedes its real-world applications.

4.7 Conclusions

In this chapter, we proposed a novel SecEQP scheme which supports practical SkNN query processing over encrypted geospatial data in cloud computing. The key novelty of our scheme is in applying projection function composition to encode two-dimensional data to test the proximity of two points by only equality checking operations. We formulated the related theory and explained it via various illustrative graphic examples. We implemented and evaluated SecEQP scheme on both real-world and synthetic datasets. It is shown that SecEQP scheme can achieve strong security, high-efficiency, and high result accuracy. We hope that our study will invite more research in the current era of big data meeting security.

References

1. Dropbox hack, http://www.troyhunt.com/the-dropbox-hack-is-real/
2. W.K. Wong, D.W. Cheung, B. Kao, N. Mamoulis, Secure kNN computation on encrypted databases, in *SIGMOD'09: Proceedings of the 2009 ACM SIGMOD International Conference on Management of Data* (2009), pp. 139–152
3. H. Hu, J. Xu, C. Ren, B. Choi, Processing private queries over untrusted data cloud through privacy homomorphism, in *IEEE 27th International Conference on Data Engineering (ICDE)* (2011), pp. 601–612
4. X. Yi, R. Paulet, E. Bertino, V. Varadharajan, Practical k nearest neighbor queries with location privacy, in *IEEE 30th International Conference on Data Engineering (ICDE)* (2014), pp. 640–651

5. Y. Elmehdwi, B.K. Samanthula, W. Jiang, Secure k-nearest neighbor query over encrypted data in outsourced environments, in *IEEE 30th International Conference on Data Engineering (ICDE)* (2014), pp. 664–675
6. B. Wang, Y. Hou, M. Li, Practical and secure nearest neighbor search on encrypted large-scale data, in *The 35th Annual IEEE International Conference on Computer Communications (INFOCOM)* (2016), pp. 1–9
7. B. Yao, F. Li, X. Xiao, Secure nearest neighbor revisited, in *IEEE 29th International Conference on Data Engineering (ICDE)* (2013), pp. 733–744
8. R. Agrawal, J. Kiernan, R. Srikant, Y. Xu, Order preserving encryption for numeric data, in *SIGMOD'04: Proceedings of the 2004 ACM SIGMOD International Conference on Management of Data* (2004), pp. 563–574
9. M. Naveed, S. Kamara, C.V. Wright, Inference attacks on property-preserving encrypted databases, in *CCS'15: Proceedings of the 22nd ACM SIGSAC Conference on Computer and Communications* (2015), pp. 644–655
10. S. Bugiel, S. Nurnberger, A. Sadeghi, T. Schneider, Twin clouds: an architecture for secure cloud computing, in *Workshop on Cryptography and Security in Clouds (WCSC)* (2011)
11. P. Paillier, Public-key cryptosystems based on composite degree residuosity classes, in *International Conference on the Theory and Applications of Cryptographic Techniques (ICTACT)* (1999)
12. A. Okabe, B. Boots, K. Sugihara, S.N. Chiu, *Spatial Tessellations: Concepts and Applications of Voronoi Diagrams* (Wiley, Hoboken, 2009)
13. S. Choi, G. Ghinita, H.-S. Lim, E. Bertino, Secure knn query processing in untrusted cloud environments, in *IEEE Transactions on Knowledge and Data Engineering (IKDE)* (2014), pp. 2818–2831
14. C. Gentry, Fully homomorphic encryption using ideal lattices, in *STOC'09: Proceedings of the Forty-First Annual ACM Symposium on Theory of Computing* (2009), pp. 169–178
15. J. Katz, Y. Lindell, *Introduction to Modern Cryptography: Principles and Protocols*. Cryptography and Network Security (Chapman & Hall/CRC, Boca Raton, 2008)
16. M. Datar, N. Immorlica, P. Indyk, V.S. Mirrokni, Locality-sensitive hashing scheme based on p-stable distributions, in *SCG'04: Proceedings of the Twentieth Annual Symposium on Computational Geometry* (2004), pp. 253–262
17. R. Curtmola, J. Garay, S. Kamara, R. Ostrovsky, Searchable symmetric encryption: improved definitions and efficient constructions, in *CCS'06: Proceedings of the 13th ACM Conference on Computer and Communications Security* (2006), pp. 79–88
18. B.H. Bloom, Space/time trade-offs in hash coding with allowable errors. Commun. ACM **13**, (1970), pp. 422–426
19. R. Li, A.X. Liu, Adaptively secure conjunctive query processing over encrypted data for cloud computing, in *IEEE 33rd International Conference on Data Engineering (ICDE)* (2017), pp. 697–708
20. E.-J. Goh et al., Secure indexes. IACR Cryptology ePrint Archive (2003), p. 216
21. R. Li, A.X. Liu, A.L. Wang, B. Bruhadeshwar, Fast range query processing with strong privacy protection for cloud computing. *Proceedings of 40th International Conference on Very Large Data Bases (PVLDB)* (2014), pp. 1953–1964
22. Openstreetmap. http://www.openstreetmap.org/
23. Y. Tao, K. Yi, C. Sheng, P. Kalnis, Quality and efficiency in high dimensional nearest neighbor search, in *SIGMOD'09: Proceedings of the 2009 ACM SIGMOD International Conference on Management of Data* (2009), pp. 563–576
24. M.F. Mokbel, C.-Y. Chow, W.G. Aref, The new casper: query processing for location services without compromising privacy, in *VLDB'06: Proceedings of the 32nd International Conference on Very Large Data Bases* (2006), pp. 763–774
25. A. Khoshgozaran, C. Shahabi, Blind evaluation of nearest neighbor queries using space transformation to preserve location privacy, in *International Symposium on Spatial and Temporal Databases (SSTD)* (2007), pp. 239–257

Chapter 5
Top-k Queries for Two-Tiered Sensor Networks

5.1 Introduction

5.1.1 Motivation

Two-tiered sensor networks have been widely adopted for their scalability and energy efficiency. A large number of sensors [1–5], equipped with limited storage and computating capacity, are deployed in fields. Some storage nodes, equipped with large storage and powerful computating capacity, are deployed among sensors for storing measurement data from the neighboring sensors, as shown in Fig. 5.1. A sink serves as a terminal device that sends queries to the storage nodes and retrieves the sensor data of interest. Due to the importance of two-tiered sensor network architecture, several commercial storage nodes, such as StarGate [6] and RISE [7], have also been developed.

The storage nodes offer two major benefits compared to an unstructured sensor network model. First, the storage nodes are responsible for the collection, storage and transmission of the sensory data from the sensors to the sink. The sensors save a significant amount of energy by eliminating sensor to sensor relay transmissions towards the sink and prolong the life of the network. Second, the storage nodes have more computing power and storage capacity than the sensors. Therefore, the sink can issue complex queries, such as the range or top-k queries, to retrieve several data items in a single query. This saves the sensor nodes' energy and network bandwidth required for answering the sink queries. However, due to their importance in network operations, the storage nodes are more vulnerable to attack and compromise. Attackers can not only steal the sensitive information on the storage node, but also leverage the query processing functionality of the storage node to feed false information to the sink.

© The Editor(s) (if applicable) and The Author(s), under exclusive license to
Springer Nature Switzerland AG 2021
A. X. Liu, R. Li, *Algorithms for Data and Computation Privacy*,
https://doi.org/10.1007/978-3-030-58896-0_5

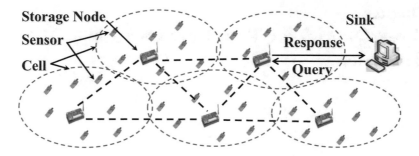

Fig. 5.1 Architecture of two-tired sensor networks

5.1.2 Problem Statement

We address the problem of privacy and integrity preserving top-k queries in two-tiered sensor networks to protect against storage node compromise. Our goal is to design scheme to enable storage nodes to process top-k queries correctly without knowing the actual value of data stored in them and allow the sink to detect misbehavior of storage nodes. Top-k query processing, i.e., finding the k smallest or largest data items collected from a specified sensed area, is a fundamental operation in sensor networks [8–10]. Such top-k queries enable users to get their most desired environmental information such as pollution index, temperature, humidity and so on. Our choice of the top-k query problem is motivated from the fact that it can be viewed as a generalized version of range query, which allows the sink to learn several values with a single query. We consider a storage node N_i and a set of sensors in its neighborhood $\{S_1, S_2, \cdots, S_g\}$ where each S_j collects a set of data items $D(S_j) = \{d_1^j, d_2^j, \cdots, d_c^j\}$. When the sink issues a top-k query to N_i, the storage node responds with the top-k largest or smallest data items from the stored data: $\cup_{j=1}^g D(S_j)$. Now, to preserve privacy of data in the event of storage node compromise, a sensor S_j encrypts the each sensed data item d_x^j into $(d_x^j)_{k_j}$ using a secret key k_j shared with the sink and builds an index I_j for $D(S_j)$. Then, S_j submits the index I_j along with the set of encrypted data items $\{(d_1^j)_{k_j}, (d_2^j)_{k_j}, \cdots, (d_c^j)_{k_j}\}$ to the storage node N_i. With this background, we state the problem of privacy and integrity preserving top-k queries as follows.

For a top-k query, the sink generates a trapdoor t_k for k, which is the query condition in an encrypted form, and sends t_k to N_i. Based on t_k and the indexes $I_1, I_2, \cdots, I_a$, N_i should be able to determine a set of encrypted data items satisfying the query condition without having to decrypt either t_k or $\{(d_1^j)_{k_j}, (d_2^j)_{k_j}, \cdots, (d_c^j)_{k_j}\}$. To preserve integrity, given the top-k results from a storage node N_i, the sink should be able to verify the validity of the results using some information embedded in the top-k query results.

5.1.3   Adversary and Security Model

In this work, we adopt the *semantic security against chosen-keyword attack*, i.e., *IND-CKA* security model proposed in [11], which has been widely accepted in privacy preserving techniques like [12–15]. Specifically, our model uses the refined simulation based definition by Curtmola et al. in [14]. Using the standard definitions from [16], we consider a probabilistic polynomial-time (PPT) adversary who attempts to leak the privacy of the secure index I of a given set of data items. The adversary is allowed to generate a sample *history*, $\mathcal{H} = \{D, d\}$ where D is a set of data items of the adversary's choice and d is a polynomial sized set of chosen queries. Now, if there exists a polynomial-time simulator that can simulate the actions of a secure index given only $\mathcal{H}$, then the secure index is *semantically secure against adaptive chosen keyword attacks*. We consider the case where the adversary is not allowed to see the secure index or any secure trapdoors or any data items, prior to generating $\mathcal{H}$ and this adversary is called *non-adaptive* adversary [14]. Briefly, the simulation proceeds thus: the adversary submits $\mathcal{H}$ to a challenger, who has access to a secure index algorithm and a simulator, and either generates a secure index using D or simulates the secure index using the simulator. In the challenge phase, the adversary obtains trapdoors for d from either the real index or the simulator and is asked to distinguish between them with non-negligible probability [16]. The existence of such a simulator proves the security of the index scheme and we show such a simulator for our index in this work.

5.1.4   Limitations of Prior Art

Previous works that are in two-tiered sensor networks and closely related to ours are privacy preserving top-k queries [17, 18] and privacy preserving range queries [3, 19–22]. Broadly, these works fall into two categories: bucketing schemes [3, 20, 22] and order preserving encryption based schemes [17–19, 21]. Note that we classify SafeQ [19] into order preserving scheme because in SafeQ scheme, sensors sort their measurement data before encryption and the encrypted data items are kept in an ordered manner in the storage nodes to facilitate the secure queries.

In bucketing schemes, sensors partition the whole data domain into multiple buckets of various sizes. The data submitted to storage nodes consist of pairs of a bucket ID and the encrypted data items belong to the bucket. The trapdoor of a query consists of the IDs of the buckets that overlap with the query condition. The query result includes all data items that their corresponding bucket IDs are in the trapdoor. However, the privacy protection of bucketing schemes is weak because attackers can statistically estimate the actual value of both the data items and the queries using domain knowledge and historical query results, as pointed out in [23]. Also, the communication cost is high in these schemes because a query result includes many false positive data items. Reducing bucket sizes helps to reduce communication cost between storage nodes and the sink, but will increase communication between sensors and storage nodes. As sensors need to submit more empty buckets to storage nodes and as a result, this approach weakens privacy protection due to the number of buckets becoming closer to the data items.

Order preserving encryption schemes describe techniques to preserve the relative ordering of data even after data encryption. Given any two data items d_1 and d_2, and an order preserving encryption function f, $f(d_1) \leq f(d_2)$ if and only if $d_1 \leq d_2$. For each $d_i^j \in D(S_j)$, sensor S_j computes $f(d_i^j)$ and submits it with $(d_i^j)_{k_j}$ to a storage node. Note that different sensors may have different order preserving encryption functions [18, 21]. In [24], the authors pointed out that the privacy preserving schemes based on order preserving encryptions are not secure.

5.1.5 Technical Challenges and Proposed Approach

Our approach for privacy and integrity preserving top-k query processing consists of a novel approach to sensor data processing that we combine with symmetric key-based techniques to achieve the desired data privacy and integrity verification. Our data processing approach helps to solve the two important challenges of privacy preserving *top-k querying* over arbitrary distributions of sensor data and *integrity verification* of the query results.

The first challenge of top-k querying on the stored data is that the sensor data is in an encrypted format on the storage node and hence, the storage node cannot execute a top-k query without the ability to compare the data items with each other. To address this challenge, we note that a top-k query can be approximated by an appropriate range query and the uniformly distribution of sensor data facilitates this approximation. First, we describe a data distribution transformation method to transform the arbitrary sensor data distribution into an approximate uniform distribution. Second, to preserve privacy of sensor data, we describe an algorithm to build an IND-CKA secure privacy preserving index on the transformed data using pseudo-random one-way hash functions and Bloom filters. Third, using prefix based techniques, we transform *lesser than* and *greater than* comparisons into *equality* checking, which only involves set membership verification operation on the Bloom filter indexes. Finally, we describe a range estimation algorithm to transform a top-k query into a special range query, called *top-range* query, and enable the storage node to process the query on the secure Bloom filter indexes.

The second challenge is to verify the integrity of the query results. Towards this, we propose a novel data partition algorithm to partition the data items into intervals. We describe an embedding technique to embed the interval information into the corresponding data items before encrypting them. We present an index selection method to guarantee that the encrypted data items are embedded with the appropriate interval information needed for integrity verification by the sink node.

The interval information allows the sink to detect whether storage nodes have made any modification to the query results.

Our proposed scheme addresses the limitation of prior arts by providing IND-CKA security through a combination of range approximation and data index generation techniques. The index indistinguishability prevents attackers to statistically infer data values from the query processing information.

5.1.6 Key Contributions

The key contributions of our work are fourfold. First, we propose the first privacy and integrity preserving top-k query processing scheme in two-tiered sensor networks that is secure under IND-CKA security model. Second, we describe a novel approach to sensor data transformation and partitioning to index the data appropriately. Third, we propose a query transformation algorithm to transform top-k queries into top-range queries. Fourth, we implemented and evaluated our scheme thoroughly on a real data set. Experimental results show that our scheme is efficient and scalable.

The rest of the chapter proceeds as follows. We discuss related work in Sect. 11.2. In Sect. 5.3, we describe our system model and assumptions. In Sect. 12.3, we describe our data processing approach. In Sect. 5.5, we describe our approach for privacy preserving index construction. In Sect. 5.6, we describe the trapdoor generation by the sink node, query processing by storage nodes, and the integrity verification by the sink. In Sect. 9.6, we formally prove the security of our scheme. In Sect. 9.7, we present our experimental results. We conclude this chapter in Sect. 8.8.

5.2 Related Work

Related schemes to our approach can be found similar in cloud computing and database domains. These works can be divided into three classes: bucketing schemes, order preserving schemes, and public-key schemes. Hacigumus et al. proposed the first bucket partition scheme [25] to query encrypted data items without allowing the server to know the exact data values. Bijit Hore et al. investigated the problem of optimal bucket partitioning and proposed two secure query schemes, one for one-dimensional data [23] and the other for multi-dimensional data [26]. Agrawal et al. adopted the bucketing scheme's idea and proposed an order preserving scheme to further protect data privacy [27]. Boldyreva et al. proposed two order preserving schemes [28, 29]. However, these schemes have the security weaknesses as discussed in Sect. 5.1.4. In [30], Rui Li et al., propose a privacy preserving range query processing scheme for outsourced data items in cloud computing, which is proved to be secure under IND-CKA security model.

However, this scheme cannot perform top-k querying with intergrity verification for sensor networks.

In the public key cryptography based schemes, Boneh and Waters proposed a database privacy-preserving scheme to support conjunctive, subset and range queries [31]. Shi et al. proposed a range query scheme using identity based encryption primitives [32]. However, public-key cryptography is generally unaffordable in two-tiered sensor networks for its computational complexity (software implementation) and system setup/maintenance cost (hardware implementation).

A significant amount of work has been proposed to preserve integrity for query results in two-tiered sensor networks [3, 10, 19–22]. All of these works require redundant information and an extra verification mechanism in addition to the query results. We show that our integrity verification mechanism is less expensive than these approaches.

5.3   System Model and Assumptions

We adopt the system model used in existing privacy preserving querying approaches [3, 20–22] for two-tiered sensor networks.

First, we assume that, all the sensors and the storage nodes are loosely synchronized. Under this assumption, we divide the time into a series of fixed length time slots. In each time slot, a sensor collects multiple integer data items, whose minimal and maximal possible values are known. At the end of a time slot, the sensor submits these data items to its closest storage node. Second, each sensor shares two symmetric keys with the sink: a common key and a secret key. The common key is shared among all the sensors and the sink. The secret key is shared between a given sensor and the sink. These two keys are stored in tamper-proof hardware and therefore, would not be compromised even if the sensors are captured by attackers. Third, the sensors may collect multi-dimensional data. In this case, the sensors compute a score for each multi-dimensional data, and then allow the sink to query on these scores, an approach adopted in previous approaches [10, 17, 18]. Without loss of generality, we assume that the top-k queries are performed on one-dimensional data and the sink is interested in the k smallest data items in the sensed data.

Let $d_1^j, d_2^j, \cdots, d_{n_j}^j$ denote the data items collected by sensor S_j in a time slot. For all sensors $S_1, S_2, \cdots, S_g$ that are close to a storage node N_i, we have:

$$\sum_{j=1}^{g} n_j = n, \tag{5.1}$$

which means totally n data items are submitted to N_i after the time slot. We define a lower bound variable d_0 and an upper bound variable d_{n+1}, such that for all j,

$d_0 \leq \min\{d_1^j, d_2^j, \cdots, d_{n_j}^j\}$ and $\max\{d_1^j, d_2^j, \cdots, d_{n_j}^j\} \leq d_{n+1}$. The possible range for all data items is $[d_0, d_{n+1}]$.

We represent a data item d as a w-bit binary string $b_1 b_2 \cdots b_w$ where $b_i \; \forall i \leq w$ denotes the bit-value at position i in the string. A k-prefix of d is the first k bits of d and the remaining $w - k$ bits are not cared, i.e., $*$s, which can be 0 or 1. For example, for the numeric value 4 represented in 4-bits as 0100, the 2-prefix is denoted by $01**$. A prefix $[\{0, 1\}^k \{*\}^{w-k}$ denotes the interval $[\{0, 1\}^k \{0\}^{w-k}, \{0, 1\}^k \{1\}^{w-k}]$. For example, $01**$ denotes $[0100, 0111]$, i.e., the interval between the minimum and the maximum values that this prefix denote. The prefix family of d, denoted by $F(d)$, is defined as the prefix set generated by replacing each right-most bit value by $*$, i.e., $F(d) = \{b_1 b_2 \cdots b_w, b_1 b_2 \cdots b_{w-1}*, \cdots, b_1 * \cdots *, ** \ldots *\}$. For example, for the value 4 represented in 4-bits, the prefix family is: $F(4) = \{0100, 010*, 01**, 0***, ****\}$. For any k-prefix, $b_1 b_2 \cdots b_k * \cdots *$, we define two prefixes, *child-0* prefix, obtained by replacing first $*$ by 0, i.e., $b_1 b_2 \cdots b_k 0* \cdots *$ and *child-1* prefix, obtained by replacing first $*$ by 1, i.e., $b_1 b_2 \cdots b_k 1 * \cdots *$. For example, for $01**$, the child-0 prefix is $010*$ and the child-1 prefix is $011*$. We use p^0 and p^1 to denote child-0 and child-1 prefixes of p, respectively. Finally, we define a *head prefix* as a prefix with a 0 before the first $*$, e.g., $010*$ and a *tail prefix* as a prefix with a 1 before the first $*$, e.g., $011*$.

5.4   Sensor Data Pre-Processing: Mapping and Partitioning

Our data processing involves four important steps: approximating uniform data distribution, data partitioning, interval embedding and index selection. In Sect. 5.4.1, we describe a method to transform the arbitrary sensor data into an approximate uniform data distribution. In Sect. 5.4.2, we describe a data partitioning algorithm, which enables us to generate the necessary information for integrity verification. In Sect. 5.4.3, we show the method to embed the interval information required for integrity verification of the query results. In Sect. 5.4.4, we show the index value selection for building the secure index for top-k querying.

5.4.1   Approximating Uniform Distribution

Our approach to executing top-k queries is to view the sensor data into a uniformly distributed data and execute specially crafted range queries, which we call *top-range* queries. As sensor data follows an arbitrary distribution, it is difficult to execute top-k queries without the use of expensive homomorphic operations or order preserving encryption that enable comparison on the encrypted data. Therefore, in this step, we transform the arbitrary distribution of the sensor data into an approximately uniform distribution. The major advantage of this transformation is that the sink node can transform a top-k query by an appropriately chosen range query, a top-*range* query, which will retrieve the expected top-k data items.

For achieving the desired transformation, we adopt the well-known approach from [27] while ensuring that it suits the sensor network domain. To approximate the arbitrary sensor data distribution, say over $[d_0, d_{n+1}]$, to a uniform distribution, say over $[d'_0, d'_{n+1}]$, the approach in [27] is to define a uniform distribution over $[d'_0, d'_{n+1}]$ with the same number of data items in $[d_0, d_{n+1}]$ and map the new data items to the arbitrarily distributed sensor data items in $[d_0, d_{n+1}]$. First, we partition $[d_0, d_{n+1}]$ into multiple intervals such that every interval contains the same number of data items. Different intervals could vary in length. Second, for a given $[d'_0, d'_{n+1}]$, we partition this range into the same number of intervals as we partition $[d_0, d_{n+1}]$. In this partition, every interval has the same length. Third, we project the data values in $[d_0, d_{n+1}]$ to new data values in $[d'_0, d'_{n+1}]$, according to a projection relationship [27] between the corresponding intervals. Figure 5.2 illustrates the idea of data distribution transformation. After the transformation, the n new data values in $[d'_0, d'_{n+1}]$ form an approximate uniform distribution. We note down the transforming relationship as a table and store it in each sensor. Thus, a top-k query can be approximated by a range query that fetches roughly k data items.

Note that, using this transformation as part of our privacy preserving scheme does not make our final scheme vulnerable to the privacy concerns inherent in [27], due to the following reasons. First, each sensor constructs a privacy preserving index (cf. Sect. 5.5) using these new data values. As our indexes are IND-CKA secure, an adversary cannot reveal the contents of the index with non-negligible probability. Also, as the mapping of the sensor data to the uniform distribution is kept secret by the sensors, an adversary cannot infer the measurement data from the indexes, even if the adversary is able to learn some of the data items in the index. This holds true even in the case where adversary is allowed to generate an arbitrary number of indexes from his guesses of measurement data values. Also, the sink and sensors can agree upon the transformation at network initialization or can exchange this information securely using the common network secret key.

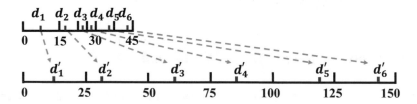

Fig. 5.2 Approximation to uniform distribution

5.4.2 Data Partitioning for Integrity Verification

In this section, we describe our approach to verify the integrity of the results returned due to the top-k query by the sink node. Intuitively, our integrity verification approach is to partition the data into distinct intervals and securely embed the interval information along with the data item. Note that, due to the transformation of the sensor data into uniform distribution, the indexing is performed on the new index values derived from the uniform distribution. However, even though the top-k query will be executed on the new data items, the storage node will send back the corresponding original data items to the sink node. This implies that the sink node needs to be able to verify that received data items correspond to the mapped data items, on which the top-k query was executed. Towards this, we describe an efficient data partition algorithm that partitions the new data items, in the uniform distribution, into different intervals depending on the data item values. At the time of index generation, we embed this interval information inside the original sensor data items returned to the sink node and use this information to verify their integrity. Since the sink node is aware of the uniform distribution mapping approach, it will be able to derive the corresponding uniform data values and subsequently, the corresponding interval information, which enables the verification of the embedded interval information in the received data items. We describe the details of the partitioning next.

Our data partition algorithm consists of two phases: *partition phase* and *merging phase*. In the *partition phase*, starting with the n distinct data items distributed in the range $[d'_0, d'_{n+1}]$, we partition the range $[d'_0, d'_{n+1}]$ into n intervals that satisfy the following conditions. (1) Each interval contains exactly one data item. (2) The union of the intervals is the range. (3) There is no overlap between intervals. In the *merging phase*, we merge the empty intervals with their neighboring intervals.

Partition Phase The first phase of our partition algorithm is as follows. Suppose the data set to be partitioned is $S = \{d_1, d_2, \cdots, d_n\}$. If $|S| > 1$, we first generate a prefix $p = \{*\}^w$. Then, we partition S into S_0 and S_1, where $S_0 = \{\forall d_i | (p^0 \in F(d_i)) \cap (d_i \in S)\}$ and $S_1 = \{\forall d_i | (p^1 \in F(d_i)) \cap (d_i \in S)\}$. If $|S_i| > 1$, we generate child-0 and child-1 prefixes for p^i and the partition process iteratively goes on, here $i = 0, 1$. Figure 5.3 demonstrates an example of the partitioning process. In this example, there are 6 4-bit data items $S = \{2, 5, 6, 7, 10, 11\}$. First, we generate prefix $p = ****$. Second, we compute $p^0 = 0***$ and $p^1 = 1***$ for p. Finally, we divide these 6 data items into $S_0 = \{2, 5, 6, 7\}$ and $S_1 = \{10, 11\}$ according to p^0 and p^1. Because both S_0 and S_1 contain more than one data item, the partition process continues. At the end of this phase, we have 8 intervals as shown in Fig. 5.3. And each interval is represented by a prefix.

Merging Phase In the merging phase, we eliminate empty intervals by merging. If the prefix representing the empty interval is a head prefix, we merge this interval with its right-closest interval; if the prefix representing the empty interval is a tail prefix, we merge this interval with its left-closest interval. For example, in

**** [0,15]							
2	5	6	7		10	11	
0***[0,7]				1***[8,15]			
2	5	6	7		10	11	
00**[0,3]	01**[4,7]			10**[8,11]			11**[12,15]
2	5	6	7		10	11	E1
00**	010*	011*		100*	101*		11**
2	5	6	7	E2	10	11	E1
00**	010*	0110	0111	100*	1010	1011	11**
2	5	6	7	E2	10	11	E1

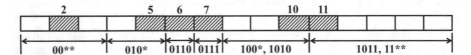

Fig. 5.3 Prefix partition

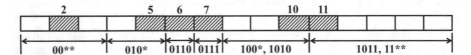

Fig. 5.4 The merging result

Fig. 5.3, there are two empty intervals $E1$ and $E2$ represented by $11**$ and $100*$, respectively. The interval represented by $11**$ will be merged with the interval represented by 1011; and the interval represented by $100*$ will be merged with the interval represented by 1010. Figure 5.4 shows the partition result of the data set $S = \{2, 5, 6, 7, 10, 11\}$.

5.4.3 Embedding Intervals with Data

In this step, we embed the interval information, to which a transformed data item belongs, into the original data item sent to the sink. Suppose a data item d_j is transformed into d'_j and partitioned into the interval R_j. The properties of prefix ensure that there are only two cases: (1) R_j is represented by one prefix; (2) R_j is represented by two prefixes. Considering these two cases, we use the form $d'_j | (b_j, e_j)$ to represent the interval information, where b_j means the last b_j bits of d'_j should be replaced by 0 to get the beginning value of R_j and e_j means the last e_j bits of d'_j should be replaced by 1 to get the ending value of R_j. If d'_j is a w-bit number, b_j and e_j only need $\log w + 1$ bits to represent. We use $N(p)$ to denote the number of $*$ in p. If R_j is represented by one prefix p, we let $b_j = e_j = N(p)$. If R_j is represented by two prefixes p_h and p_t and d'_j is in the interval denoted by p_h, we let $b_j = N(p_h)$ and $e_j = N(p_t)+1$; otherwise, we let $b_j = N(p_h)+1$ and $e_j = N(p_t)$. For example, in Fig. 5.4, data item 2, whose binary form is 0010, is in the interval represented by $00**$, we use $0010|(010, 010)$ to denote the interval; data item 11, whose binary form is 1011, is in the interval represented by $1011, 11**$ and 11 is in the interval denoted by prefix 1011, we use $1011|(000, 011)$ to represent the interval. The sensor S_i encrypts d_j with $d'_j|(b_j, e_j)$ into the form $(d_j|d'_j|(b_j, e_j))_{k_i}$. We use $E_i(d_j)$ to denoted $(d_j|d'_j|(b_j, e_j))_{k_i}$ in the following description. The sink decrypts $E_i(d_j)$ to recover the data value d_i and get the interval information via $d'_j|(b_j, e_j)$. Next, we describe our data indexing strategy, which will allow the sink node to generate the necessary interval information for integrity verification.

5.4.4 Index Selection

In the following discussion, the data items under consideration are from the approximate uniform distribution, which resulted from the original sensor data items. To guarantee that the interval information needed for verifying the integrity of a query result is included in the result, we need to include the interval information of all data items covered by the top-k query. Our approach is to select the lower bound value of the interval containing the index data item. The rationale is that, a suitably chosen prefix corresponding to the lower bound value of the interval can be used to represent the entire range of the interval. Consider Fig. 5.4 where six data items 2, 5, 6, 7, 10, 11 are partitioned into six intervals [0, 3], [4, 5], [6, 6], [7, 7], [8, 10], [11, 15], respectively, using our partitioning algorithm. For instance, to index 2, we consider the interval [0, 3] and choose 0 as the indexing point. This is because the prefix $00 * *$, generated from the 4-bit binary representation of 0, can represent the entire interval [0, 3]. We use d_i^m to denote the index of data d'_i.

5.5 Privacy Preserving Index Generation

In this section, we describe our solution for generating the privacy preserving index upon which the sink can issue top-k queries without revealing the query contents. We present our solution using Bloom filters for indexing the data and keyed pseudo-random hash functions for preserving privacy.

5.5.1 Prefix Encoding and Bloom Filter Indexing

Note that, to execute the top-k query, our approach is to convert the top-k query in a specially crafted range query, i.e. top-range query. But, if each data item is represented by a numeric value, to execute a top-range query, we need three comparison operations, *less-than*, *bigger-than*, and *equal-to*, to test if this data item falls in the query range. To solve this problem, we adopt the prefix membership testing scheme in [33] in combination with the Bloom filter [34], which is a popular data structure for solving the prefix membership problem. The key advantage of the prefix membership testing approach is that we only need to check if a given query prefix is present inside a set of stored prefixes and therefore, we only need to implement the *equal-to* operation. We choose the Bloom filter structure for the prefix membership problem as it provides an elegant solution, which is efficient in time as well as space.

For a given range $[a, b]$, we can find a prefix set S such that the union of the intervals represented by the prefixes in S is equal to $[a, b]$. The *minimum prefix set* for $[a, b]$, $S([a, b])$, is defined as the prefix set of minimum cardinality such that the union of the prefixes is equal to $[a, b]$. For example, $S([0, 4]) = \{00**, 1000\}$.

Following the definitions of *prefix family* and *minimum prefix set*, the following two properties hold. First, given a prefix p, an integer d falls into the interval represented by p if and only if $p \in F(d)$. Second, for a data item d and a range $[a, b]$, $d \in [a, b]$ if and only if there exists a prefix p, $p \in F(d)$ such that $p \in S[a, b]$. Therefore, for any integer data d and a range $[a, b]$, we can test whether $d \in [a, b]$ by testing whether

$$F(x) \cap S([a, b]) \neq \phi. \tag{5.2}$$

For example, $3 \in [0, 4]$ and $F(3) \cap S([0, 4]) = \{00**\}$. Based on this discussion, we now describe how the prefix membership testing is implemented using the Bloom filter structure [34]. A Bloom filter structure consists of an M-bit array, where the bits are initially set to 0 and a set of r independent hash functions h_i $1 \le i \le r$ such that, $h_i : N \times N \to \{0, M - 1\}$.

For each data item d'_j $(0 \le j \le n)$, we use a Bloom filter B_j to store the prefix family of its corresponding indexing value d_j^m, i.e., we store $F(d_j^m)$ in B_j. Each $p \in F(d_j^m)$ is hashed with each of the r hash functions and the corresponding locations in the Bloom filter B_j are set to 1. To verify if a Bloom filter contains a queried data item, a verifier hashes the item using each of the r hash functions and tests if all the hashed locations in the Bloom filter are set to 1 or not.

But, directly storing the data items into Bloom filters can enable the storage node to breach the privacy of the stored data in two different ways. First, since the sensor data are bounded within a finite domain and given that the Bloom filter hash functions are public, the storage node can brute force the stored data items. Second, the storage node can compare the common bit locations of Bloom filters of different sensors and find out the common readings across the two Bloom filters. Therefore, to prevent the privacy leakage due to these attacks, we describe a secure randomization approach that generates our privacy preserving index structure.

5.5.2   Randomizing Bloom Filter Indexes

In this phase, we describe an approach to store the index data item in such a way that it is not possible for a storage node to gain any information regarding the stored values using the brute-force or inference attacks described in the previous section.

Note that, in time slot t, we assume that all sensors share an l-bit symmetric secret key k_t with the sink.

First, to protect against brute-force attack, we encode a secure value of a given prefix into the Bloom filter. For each prefix $p_i \in F(d_j)$, we compute a secure one-way hash, using the HMAC keyed-hash function and the secret key k_t, as follows $h_t(p_i) = \text{HMAC}_{k_t}(p_i)$, here h_t denotes the use of HMAC with k_t. The purpose of this step is to achieve one-way-ness, i.e., given prefix p_i and the secret key k_t, it is computationally efficient to compute the hash result; but giving the hash result, it is computationally infeasible to reverse compute the secret key k_t and p_i. Now, instead of encoding the original prefix into the Bloom filter, we encode the securely hashed version. This prevents the brute-force attack as it is easy to compute $h_t(p_i)$ from p_i and h_t, but the vice-versa is not possible.

Second, to prevent inference attacks across two given Bloom filters, we devise an approach to encode a common prefix into different random locations across any two given Bloom filters. We generate r distinct numbers from the encryption of the corresponding data item. For a data item d_j, sensor S_i first computes the r hash values $\text{SHA}(1||E_i(d_j)), \cdots, \text{SHA}(r||E_i(d_j))$, where $||$ denotes catenation operation. Then, sensor S_i chooses the first l bits of each hash $\text{SHA}(k||E_i(d_j)$ to generate a unique number R_x, where $1 \leq x \leq r$. Assume that there are no two collected data items in a time slot are equal (the encryptions of two equal data items can be different by concatenating a measurement datum with its sequence number before encryption). Using these r numbers and HMAC, we construct r pseudo-random hash functions $h_1, h_2, \cdots, h_r$ where $h_x(.) = \text{HMAC}_{R_x}(.) mod\ M$ and M is the number of cells in a bloom filter. We compute r hashes: $h_1(h_t(p_i)), h_2(h_t(p_i)), \cdots, h_r(h_t(p_i))$. Let B_j be an M bits bloom filter. For each prefix p_i and for each $1 \leq x \leq r$, we let $B_j[h_x(h_t(p_i))] := 1$. The purpose of choosing r unique numbers is to eliminate the correlation among different Bloom filters. For the same prefix p, these unique random numbers allow us to hash p independently for different Bloom filters. Without the use of these numbers, if prefix p_i is shared by $F(d_1)$ and $F(d_2)$ of two different data items d_1 and d_2, then for all the r locations $h_1(h_t(p_i))$, $h_2(h_t(p_i)), \cdots, h_r(h_t(p_i))$, both Bloom filters have the value 1. Although two Bloom filters both having 1 for all these r locations does not necessarily mean that $F(d_1)$ and $F(d_2)$ share a common prefix, without the use of these unique numbers, if two Bloom filters have more 1s at the same locations than other pairs, then the probability that they share common prefixes is higher. Figure 5.5 shows the above hashing process for Bloom filters.

Finally, our privacy preserving index approach can be summarized as follows. Suppose that sensor S_i collects n_i data items in time slot t, in the end of this time slot, S_i executes the following six steps to encrypt the data items and build privacy preserving index. First, for each collected data item $d_j(1 \leq j \leq n_i)$, S_i computes d'_j for it according to the transformation table. Second, S_i runs the partition algorithm to partition each distinct data item d'_j into a unique interval and embeds the interval information as the form $d'_j|(b_j, e_j)$. Third, S_i encrypts d_j with $d'_j|(b_j, e_j)$ into $E_i(d_j)$ using key k_i. Fourth, S_i computes d''_j for d_j by choosing the lower bound of

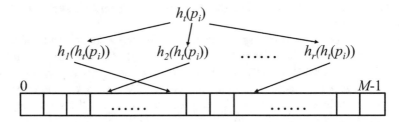

Fig. 5.5 Secure hashing in bloom filters

the interval containing d'_j. Fifth, S_i creates a Bloom filter B_j for storing d^m_j. Finally, S_i sends $(B_1, B_2, \cdots, B_{n_i})$ along with $(E_i(d_1), E_i(d_2), \cdots, E_i(d_{n_i}))$ to the nearby storage node.

5.6 Trapdoor Computation and Query Processing

In this section, we describe the process of trapdoor generation for top-k queries at the sink node, which has two important steps, and the corresponding query execution by the storage node. In Sect. 5.6.1, we show how the sink transforms a top-k query to a special query called the *top-range* query, which is a variant of range query. In Sect. 5.6.2, we show how the sink prepares the encrypted query for transmission to the storage nodes. In Sect. 5.6.3, we describe the process of query execution and results generation at the storage node. Finally, in Sect. 5.6.4, we show how the sink verifies the integrity of a query result.

5.6.1 Top-k to Top-Range Query

Our approach to executing top-k queries on the sensor data is to convert the top-k query into a *top-range* query. The intuition behind this is that, directly performing top-k queries on a set of sensor data items requires comparisons among them. But, given the prefix membership scheme from the previous section, we can check if a particular range of query prefixes are matched by any of the stored prefixes in the Bloom filter. This forms the basis of our approach wherein we transform the top-k query into a suitably crafted range query, which will obtain the same results as the top-k query. We describe the details of this transformation in the following.

Now, for the approximated uniform distribution of the sensor values on $[d'_0, d'_{n+1}]$, the sink node needs to accurately estimate a range $[d'_0, d']$, which is equivalent to the top-k query over $[d_0, d_{n+1}]$. We call such ranges top-ranges as they always start from the lower bound d'_0. The value of d' is important as it denotes the reference value for the top-k items to be retrieved. We note that, the probability that a data item falls in the range $[d'_0, d']$ is

$$p = \frac{d' - d'_0}{d'_{n+1} - d'_0}. \tag{5.3}$$

The probability that there are less than k data items in range $[d'_0, d']$ is denoted as $f(d')$, which follows from:

$$f(d') = \sum_{j=0}^{k-1} \binom{n}{j} p^j (1-p)^{n-j}. \tag{5.4}$$

$f(d')$ is the probability that the sink fails to get all k smallest data items in one top-range query with the range $[d'_0, d']$. If we require $f(d') \leq c$, where c is suitably chosen constant, the lower bound of d' can be obtained by solving Eq. (5.4) for $f(d') = c$. However, since solving this equation analytically is difficult we describe a binary search approach to compute the value of d'.

Based on the observation that $f(d')$ decreases with the increasing values of d', we use a binary search algorithm, shown in Algorithm 1, to compute d'. The binary search narrows down the searching range for the value of d' to one point. The starting value of d' will be chosen from range $[d'_0, d'_{n+1}]$. In the initial stage, we let $d' = (d'_0 + d'_{n+1})/2$ and calculate $f(d')$ according to Eq. (5.4). If $f(d') \leq c$, we let the new range to be $[d'_0, (d'_0 + d'_{n+1})/2 - 1]$ and d' to be the middle value of this new range; Otherwise, we let the new range to be $[(d'_0 + d'_{n+1})/2 + 1, d'_{n+1}]$ and d' to be the middle value of this new range. This process continues until the value of the low bound and the upper bound of a searching range become equal, and then the equal bound value is returned as the value for d'.

When the sink wants to query k smallest data items, it executes the binary search algorithm to compute d' and then sends the range $[d'_0, d']$ instead of the numeric value of k to the storage node. In the end, the storage node returns a query result containing k' data items to the sink. There are three possible cases. (1) $k' = k$. In this case, the result is exactly the top-k query result that the sink needs. (2) $k' > k$. In this case, the result contains some false positives, and the sink gets the top-k results by neglecting the false positives. (3) $k' < k$. In this case, the sink needs to query for more data. The problem is reduced as to find out top-$(k - k')$ data items from $n - k'$ data items, which uniformly spread in $[d' + 1, d'_{n+1}]$. Therefore, the sink again executes binary search on input $([d', d'_{n+1}], n - k', k - k', c)$ to compute a new range $[d' + 1, d'']$, and performs another range query.

Algorithm 1: Top-range computation

Input: $[d'_0, d'_{n+1}], n, k, c$
Output: $[d'_0, d']$

1 $low := d'_0; high := d'_{n+1}$;
2 while $low \leq high$ **do**
3 $m = (low + high)/2$;
4 $p = \frac{m - d'_0}{d'_{n+1} - d'_0}$;
5 $f(d') = \sum_{j=0}^{k-1} \binom{n}{j} p^j (1-p)^{n-j}$;
6   **if** $f(d') \leq c$ **then**
7 $high := m - 1$;
8   **else**
9 $low := m + 1$;

10 $d' := low$;
11 return $[d'_0, d']$;

5.6.2 Trapdoor Computation

In this phase, we describe our trapdoor generation approach at the sink node to optimize the query results and reduce the false positives. We notice that if prefix p_i is in a Bloom filter B_j and p_i has child-0 prefix p_i^0 and child-1 prefix p_i^1, then at least one of p_i^0 and p_i^1 is in B_j. Otherwise, none of p_i^0 and p_i^1 should be in B_j. When p_i has no child-0 or child-1 prefixes, and p_i is in Bloom filter B_j, then p_i^*, which is obtained by replacing the last 0 or 1 with $*$, must be in B_j. To reduce false positives in query results, for a top-range query with range $[d'_0, d']$, the sink executes the following three steps to compute the trapdoor denoted as $Q_{[d'_0, d']}$. Firstly, the sink computes $S([d'_0, d']) = \{p_1, \cdots, p_z\}$ for the top-range $[d'_0, d']$. Secondly, for each prefix p_i, $p_i \in S([d'_0, d'])$, if p_i has child-0 and child-1, the sink computes p_i^0 and p_i^1; otherwise the sink first computes p_i^* and $\bar{p}_i$, which is obtained by replacing the first bit value of p_i with $*$ and is impossible to be in any Bloom filters. The results are organized as a 3-tuple of the form (p_i, p_i^0, p_i^1) or $(p_i, p_i^*, \bar{p}_i)$. Finally, for each 3-tuple (p_i, p_i^0, p_i^1) or $(p_i, p_i^*, \bar{p}_i)$, the sink computes $h_t(p_i)$, $h_t(p_i^0)$, $h_t(p_i^1)$ or $h_t(p_i), h_t(p_i^*), h_t(\bar{p}_i)$. And then, the sink organizes these hashes as a matrix $Q_{[d'_0, d']}$. The trapdoor of p_i corresponds to the ith row of $Q_{[d'_0, d']}$. After the trapdoor computation, the sink sends $Q_{[d'_0, d']}$ to the storage nodes.

5.6.3 Query Execution

To describe the query execution at a storage node, we consider the scenario where a sensor S_i has submitted the Bloom filter indexes, $(B_1, B_2, \cdots, B_{n_i})$ and the encrypted data items, $(E_i(d_1), E_i(d_2), \cdots, E_i(d_{n_i}))$, to the storage node. Now, if the storage node receives the trapdoor matrix $Q_{[d'_0, d']}$ from the sink, the storage node executes following steps to test whether an encrypted data item $E_i(d_j)(1 \leq j \leq n_i)$ is in the query result. First, the storage node generates r numbers $R_1, R_2, \cdots, R_r$ from $E_i(d_j)$ using the method from Sect. 5.5.2. Second, the storage node checks whether there exists two hashes H_{xy} in a same row $x(1 \leq x \leq z, 1 \leq y \leq 3)$ in $Q_{[a,b]}$ such that for every $q(1 \leq q \leq r)$, $B_i[h_q(H_{xy})] := 1$. If this condition holds, the storage node puts $E(d_j)$ into the query result. After performing the querying over all the indexes of all the sensors, the storage node transmits the query results to the sink.

5.6.4   Integrity Verification for Query Results

Finally, upon receiving a query result of the query trapdoor $Q_{[d'_0, d']}$ from a storage node, the sink verifies the integrity for the query result as the follows. The sink divides the received data items into groups according to their source sensors. Next, the sink recovers the interval information for these data items and calculates the union of intervals for each group, denoted as R_i^U for the group of data items originates from the i-th sensor. Third, the sink tests all R_i^U for two things: (1) whether $R_i^U \cap [d'_0, d']$ is a continuous range; (2) whether $[d'_0, d'] \subseteq R_i^U$. If either test fails for any R_i^U, based on the assumption that sensors are trusted, the sink can conclude that the storage node does not faithfully return all data items according to the query. The rationale behind this verification is: a complete query result must include every data item that its interval overlaps with $[d'_0, d']$. We note that, the query result may include data items that their intervals do not overlap with $[d'_0, d']$, due to the false positives of Bloom filters.

5.6.5   False Positive Rate Analysis

As each index is represented by a Bloom filter, the query results inevitably have false positives. In our scheme, we choose the number of hash functions r to control the false positive rate. When $r = \frac{m}{n} \times \ln 2$, we have the false positive rate of a single bloom filter as

$$f = (1 - (1 - \frac{1}{m})^{rn})^r \approx (1 - e^{-rn/m})^r \approx 0.6185^{m/n}. \tag{5.5}$$

Let n be the number of index, z be the number of rows in the trapdoor $Q_{[d'_0, d']}$, and a be the size of the query result excluding false positives. We use F_a to denote the expected false positives. If p_i has child-0 and child-1 prefixes, and p_i is in Bloom filter B_j, then at least one of child-0 and child-1 prefixes is in B_j. Otherwise, none of child-0 and child-1 prefixes should be in B_j. $\bar{p}_i$ is impossible to be in any Bloom filters for storing index. When p_i has no child-0 or child-1 prefixes, and p_i is in Bloom filter B_j, then p_i^* must be in B_j; otherwise, the probability that p_i^* in B_j is very small. As we use $(p_i, p_i{}^0, p_i{}^1)$ or $(p_i, p_i^*, \bar{p}_i)$ to search, we have:

$$F_a \approx 2 * z * f^2 * (n - a), \tag{5.6}$$

where $p_i \in S[d_0', d']$). If we only use $p_i(p_i \in S[d_0', d'])$ to search, The expected false positive rate F'_a is:

$$F'_a = z * (n - a) * f. \tag{5.7}$$

When f is small and $n \neq a$, F_a is much smaller than F'_a. For example, when $f = 1\%$, $F_a/F'_a = \frac{1}{50}$.

5.7 Security Analysis

In this section, we prove that our proposed scheme is secure under the IND-CKA secure model. We use SHA − 1 as the hash function in our scheme. SHA − 1 is a keyed *pseudo-random* hash function whose output cannot be distinguished from a truly random function with non-negligible probability by a probabilistic polynomial time adversary [11]. According to [14], a searchable symmetric encryption scheme is secure if a probabilistic polynomial time adversary cannot distinguish between the output of a real index, which uses pseudo-random functions, and a simulated index, which uses truly random functions, with non-negligible probability. We first introduce some definitions from [14], and then construct a simulated index for our scheme and thereby, prove its security under the IND-CKA model.

History H_l Let $D = \{d_1, d_2, \cdots, d_n\}$ be a data set, $Q_l = \{q_1, q_2, \cdots, q_l\}$ be l top-range queries. A l-query history over D is a tuple $H_l = \{D, Q_l\}$.

View A_v A_v is the view of the adversary of the history H_l. It includes the secure Index I for D, the encrypted data set $ENC_K(D) = \{ENC_K(D_1), ENC_K(D_2), \cdots, ENC_K(D_n)\}$, and the trapdoors $T = \{t_{q_1}, t_{q_2}, \cdots, t_{q_l}\}$ for Q_l. The trapdoor for each top-range $q_i = [d_0', d_i']$ is a matrix t_{q_i}. Formally, $A_v = \{I, T, ENC_K(D)\}$.

Trace The trace is the *access* and *search* patterns observed by the adversary after T is matched against the encrypted index I. The access pattern is the set of matching data item set, $M(T) = \{m(t_{q_1}), m(t_{q_2}), \cdots, m(t_{q_l})\}$, where $m(t_{q_i})$ denotes the set of matching data item identifiers for trapdoor t_{q_i}. The search pattern is a symmetric binary matrix Π_T defined over T, such that, $\Pi_T[q_i, q_j] = 1$ if $t_{q_i} = t_{q_j}$. We denote the matching result trace over H_l as: $M_{(H_l)} = \{M(q_{1:l}), \Pi_T\}$. The adversary can only see a set of matching data items for each trapdoor, which is captured using these two patterns. In other words, each Bloom filter can be viewed as a match for a distinct set of trapdoors. According to the definition of prefix family, we know that each Bloom filter stores exactly the same number of prefixes. And, we consider a *non-adaptive adversary* in this chapter. A non-adaptive adversary is not allowed to see the index or the trapdoors prior to submitting the history.

Theorem *The scheme proposed in this chapter is IND-CKA secure under the pseudo-random function f and the encryption algorithm Enc.* □

Proof Consider a sample adversary view $A_v(H_l)$ and a real matching result trace $M_{(H_l)}$. It is possible to construct a polynomial time simulator $S = \{S_0, S_l\}$ that can simulate this view with non-negligible probability. We denote the simulated adversary view as $A_v^*(H_l)$, the simulated index as $\mathcal{I}^*$, the simulated encrypted documents as $Enc_K(D^*)$, and the trapdoors as $\mathbf{T}^*$. Each Bloom filter matches a distinct set of trapdoors, which are visible in the result trace of the query. The final result of the simulator is to output trapdoors based on the chosen top-range query history submitted by the adversary.

Step 1. Index Simulation To simulate the index, $\mathcal{I}^*$, as the size and the number of Bloom filters are known from $\mathcal{I}$, we generate bit-arrays, B^*, where random bits are set to 1 while ensuring that each Bloom filter has equal number of bits. Next, we generate, $Enc_K(D^*)$, such that each simulated data item has same size as an original encrypted data item in $Enc_K(D)$ and $|Enc_K(D^*)| = |Enc_K(D)|$. For each Bloom filter, we randomly associate a data item in $Enc_K(D^*)$ with it. Different Bloom filters will associate with different data items.

Step 2. Simulator State S_0 For H_l, where $l = 0$, we denote the simulator state by S_0. We construct the adversary view as follows: $A_v^*(H_0) = \{Enc_K(D^*), \mathcal{I}^*, T^*\}$, where T^* denotes the set of trapdoors. To generate T^*, each data item in $Enc_K(D^*)$ corresponds to a set of matched trapdoors. The length of each trapdoor is given by the pseudo-random function f, and the maximum possible size of trapdoors matching the data item is given by the size of the prefix family of the data item: $s + 1$ where, s is the bit number in a data item. Therefore, we generate $(s + 1) * |Enc_K(D^*)|$ random trapdoors of length $|f(.)|$ each. Now, with a uniform probability defined over these trapdoors, we associate at most $s + 1$ trapdoors for each data item in $Enc_K(D^*)$. Note that, some trapdoors might repeat, because two data items might match the same trapdoor.

For each Bloom filter in $\mathcal{I}^*$, we consider the data items and the union of the trapdoors. This distribution is consistent with the trapdoor distribution in the original index $\mathcal{I}$. Now, given that f is pseudo-random, and the probability of trapdoor distribution is consistent, this distribution is indistinguishable by any probabilistic polynomial time adversary.

Step 3. Simulator State S_l For H_l where $l \geq 1$, we denote the simulator state as S_l. The simulator constructs the adversary view as follows: $A_v^*(H_l) = \{Enc_K(D^*), \mathcal{I}^*, T^*, T_{q_l}\}$ where T_{q_l} are trapdoors corresponding to the query trace. To construct $\mathcal{I}^*$, given $M(q_{1:l})$, consider the set of matching data items for each trapdoor, $M(T_{q_i})=\{m(t_{q_i},1), m(t_{q_i},2), \cdots, m(t_{q_i},r_i)\}$ where $1 \leq i \leq l$. Let

$M(q_{1:l})$ contain p unique data items. For each data item in the trace, $Enc_K(D_p)$, the simulator associates the corresponding trapdoor from $M(T_{q_i})$. If more than one trapdoor matches the data item, then the simulator generates a union of the trapdoors. Since $p < |D|$, the simulator generates $1 \leq i \leq |D| - l + 1$ random strings, $Enc_K^*(D_i)$ of size $|Enc_K(D)|$ each and associates up to $s + 1$ trapdoors uniformly, as done in Step 2, ensuring that these strings do not match any strings from $M(T_{q_i})$. The simulator maintains an auxiliary state ST_l to remember the association between the trapdoors and the matching data items. The simulator outputs: $\{Enc_K(D^*), I^*, T^*, T_l\}$. Note that, all the steps performed by the simulator are polynomial and hence, the time complexity of the whole simulation processes run by the simulator is polynomial.

Now, if a probabilistic polynomial time adversary issues a top-range query over any data item matching the set $M(q_{1:l})$, the simulator can give the correct trapdoors. For any other data item, the trapdoors given by a simulator are indistinguishable due to pseudo-random function f. Finally, since each Bloom filter contains exactly same number of prefixes, our scheme is proven secure under the IND-CKA model.   □

There are three important security properties of our scheme. First, our scheme can be simulated by any polynomial time simulator since each Bloom filter encapsulates collections of encrypted data items and does not depend on exact matching of trapdoors to encrypted data items. Hence, regardless of the type of adversary queries, the Bloom filter will return any matching element as a positive result as long as the result falls within the issued top-range query. Second, we can prove the existence of *non-singular* histories[14], which are histories $H \neq H'$ but $M(T, H) = M(T, H')$. To prove this, we observe that, any given top-range query can be expressed as multiple sub-queries. This implies that we can generate different sets of trapdoors, which correspond to prefixes in our approach, for the same top-range query, while being consistent with the secure index. Therefore, by definition, the matching result traces M of these range queries will be identical. Finally, since a top-range query represents a *collection of data items*, the query for any given data item can be transformed into a different trapdoor depending on the size of the top-range query and the position where the data item might occur. Regardless of the trapdoor generated, the correctness of our approach is guaranteed by the basic privacy preserving range intersection technique. This is a key difference when compared to existing keyword-based solutions [11, 12, 14, 15, 35].

Our approach is resilient to *estimation exposure* attack wherein the attacker doesn't need to learn the actual data items but is able to infer the approximate values with a certain level of confidence. Typically, bucketing based schemes are vulnerable to such attacks as the buckets tend to reveal the distribution of various data items. For instance, if a scheme contains four buckets, [0–100], [101–200], [201–300], and [301–400], with buckets storing, 10, 20, 100, and 30, respectively, the attacker gains valuable information regarding the distribution of values. Our approach is resilient to such attacks due to the use of the following three techniques. First, the data items are encrypted using a secret key and a pseudo-random one-way hash function. This implies that we are transforming the original data distribution into a nearly random distribution thereby, eliminating the statistical estimation attacks. Second, we do not reveal the encrypted values to the storage node at the time of storage and only reveal the Bloom filters. The encrypted values might be revealed at run-time by the sink node but, due to encryption, there is no any additional advantage to the attacker. Third, the Bloom filters are randomized sufficiently so that it is difficult for storage node to check if any two sensors are storing the same values.

5.8 Performance Evaluation

To evaluate the performance of our scheme, we considered two main parameters: one is the number of data items to be queried, denoted as n and another is the number of desired data items in the top-k query, i.e., k. For various n and k, we comprehensively evaluated the top-k transformation method, the privacy preserving scheme, and the combination of these two. As we transform top-k queries to top-range queries, we compare our top-range query processing with the state-of-the-art range query processing schemes QuerySec [21] and SafeQ [19]. We use the average bandwidth cost, both for data submission from sensors to storage nodes and for query processing between storage nodes and the sink, as the performance metric.

5.8.1 Experimental Setup

We implemented our proposed scheme, QuerySec, and SafeQ using TOSSIM [36]. The implementations of QuerySec and SafeQ are according to [21] and [19], respectively. Our experimental configuration is as follows.

Data set: We chose the same data set as used in [3, 19, 21]. The data set was collected by Intel Lab [37], between 01/03/2004 to 03/10/2004, and consists of temperature, humidity and voltage data collected from 44 sensor nodes. We conducted our experiments on a single dimensional data (temperature). Similar to the methodology in QuerySec and SafeQ , we divided the 44 sensors into four groups and deployed a storage node in each group. We varied time slot period from 10 to 80 min to create different distributions on the number of data items that can be queried.

Top-k Query Transformation: We first mapped the data items to a range [0, 10000] using the method introduced in Sect. 5.4.1. Then, we used our query transformation approach, from Sect. 5.6.1, to convert top-k queries to top-range queries. For each trial, considering that each group consists 11 sensors, we chose the values for k from 20 to 200. Our approach is simple but conservative, which results in high false positive rate in the query results. To reduce false positives, we adopted a *press on towards* method to estimate the range in experiments. We first used $k * 70\%$ to compute a range $[d_0', d_1']$ from $[d_0', d_{n+1}']$ and get k_1 data items. If $k_1 < k$, then we used $(k - k_1) * 90\%$ to compute a range $[d_1' + 1, d_2']$ from $[d_1', d_{n+1}']$ and got k_2 data items. If $k_1 + k_2 < k$, we used $(k - k_1 - k_2)$ to compute a range $[d_2' + 1, d_3']$ from $[d_3', d_{n+1}']$. Finally, we evaluated the results based on the average query times and average false positive rates.

Privacy Preserving Index Generation: We used AES cipher to encrypt data on every sensor, which is affordable with modern sensor hardware. We used SHA-1 as the pseudo-random one-way hash function for the Bloom filter. We set the Bloom filter parameter $m/n = 8$, where m is the Bloom filter size and n is the number of elements, and the number of hash functions as 6. We used 14 bits to represent the data values in the [0, 10000]. Therefore, the number of possible prefixes in a prefix family of a data value is 15. The size of a Bloom filter is $15 * m/n$, i.e., 15 bytes.

5.8.2 Summary for Experimental Results

We tested the efficiency of our optimization technique on the reduction of the false positive rates in top-k query to top-range query transformation. False positives in the query transformation cause data items below top-k to be transferred from storage nodes to the sink, and therefore, waste bandwidth. Note that, the false positive rate here is not the false positive rate introduced by Bloom filters. The experimental results show that our proposed scheme can control the false positive rates to a practically acceptable range. Figure 5.6 shows comparison of the false positive rate that we use our query transform approach to estimate top-range for a top-k query with *Press on Towards* strategy and the false positive rate that we use our query transformation without *Press on Towards* strategy. We set the time slot size to 40 min for the experiments. The *Press on Towards* strategy averagely reduces 2.54 times false positive rate against the highly conservative query transform approach and limit the false positive rate well below 25%.

Fig. 5.6 False positive rates for range estimation strategy

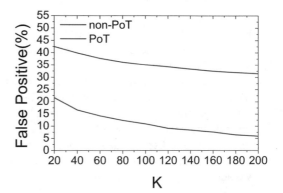

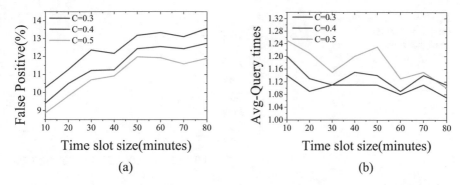

Fig. 5.7 False positive rates and query times for values of c. (**a**) Parameter c. (**b**) Query times

The experimental Results Show That Parameter c in Algorithm of Converting Top-k to Top-Range Affects the False Positive Rates Figure 5.7 shows the false positive rates and average number of top-range queries (query times) needed for a top-k query, when *Press on Towards* strategy is used. The average false positive rate of a top-k query for $c = 0.5$, $c = 0.4$, and $c = 0.3$ are 10.96%, 11.57%, and 12.4%, respectively. And, the average query times of a top-k query for $c = 0.5$, $c = 0.4$, and $c = 0.3$ are 1.22, 1.17, and 1.12, respectively.

The Experimental Results Show That the Bloom Filter Operations Also Introduce False Positives That Lead to non Top-k Data Items to be Transmitted to Sink Using different number of hash functions results in different false positive rates. Figure 5.8 shows the false positive rates, against the case where we used three hashes and the case where we used one hash, on Bloom filter testing. Using three hash functions, on an average, can reduce 91.7% false positive rate when using one hash function. When $m/n = 8$, the false positive rate caused by Bloom filters can be controlled below 10%.

The Experimental Results Show That the Total False Positive Rate Is the Combined Effect of the False Positives Caused by Imprecise Top-Range Estimation and the False Positives Caused by Bloom Filter Mismatches Figure 5.9 shows the false positive rate comparison among the top-range estimation, Bloom filter searching, and the combination of these two effects. According to Fig. 5.9, it is clear that the top-range estimation is the main contributor for the total false positive rate.

5.8.3 Comparison with Prior Art

We also compared our proposed scheme with two previously proposed secure query processing schemes, QuerySec and SafeQ. The experimental results show that *our proposed scheme has practical accepted bandwidth cost.* Figure 5.10 shows the

Fig. 5.8 False positive rates
from Bloom filter
configurations

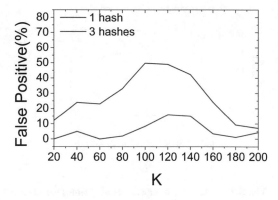

Fig. 5.9 Comparing factors
that result in false positive
rates

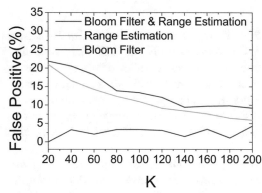

Fig. 5.10 Comparing
bandwidth cost for
sensor-storage nodes

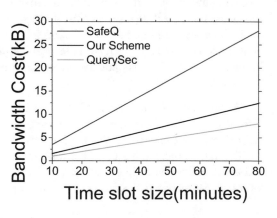

average bandwidth cost between a sensor and its nearby storage node in a time slot.
The size of time slot varies from 10 to 80 min. The experiment results indicate that
our scheme consumes 0.55 times more bandwidth than QuerySec and spends 1.22
times less bandwidth of SafeQ. Figure 5.11 shows the average bandwidth cost of
a top-k query between the sink and 4 storage nodes, using three different schemes.
Figure 5.11a shows the experiment result that we fix $k = 100$ and time slot size

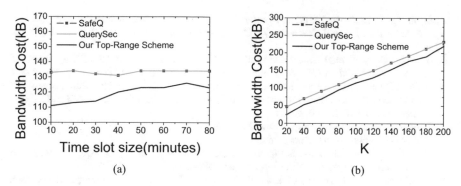

Fig. 5.11 Comparison for total bandwidth cost in three schemes. (a) $k = 100$. (b) $t = 40\,\text{min}$

ranging from 10 to 80 min, and Fig. 5.11b shows the experiment result that we fix time slot $t = 40\,\text{min}$ and k ranging from 20 to 200. In both experiments, our proposed scheme consumes less bandwidth than the other two schemes in all the tested cases.

5.9 Conclusions

In this chapter, we propose the first secure top-k query processing scheme that is secure under the IND-CKA security model. The data privacy is guaranteed by encryption as well as a careful generation of data indexes. We make two key contributions in this chapter. The first contribution is to transform a top-k query to a top-range query and adopt membership testing to test whether a data item should be included in the query result or not. This transformation allows the storage node to find k smallest or biggest data values without using numerical comparison operations, which is a key technique for the scheme to be secure under the IND-CKA security model. The second contribution is the data partition, index selection, and interval information embedding technique. This technique guarantees that at least one data item of each sensor collected data will be included in a query result and allows the sink to verify the integrity of query result without extra verification objects. Experiments show that the proposed scheme is bandwidth efficient and highly practical.

References

1. P. Desnoyers, D. Ganesan, H. Li, P. Shenoy, Presto: a predictive storage architecture for sensor networks, in *10th Workshop on Hot Topics in Operating Systems(HotOS)* (2005)
2. S. Ratnasamy, B. Karp, S. Shenker, D. Estrin, R. Govindan, L. Yin, F. Yu, Data-centric storage in sensornets with ght, a geographic hash table. Mobile Netw. Appl. **8**(4), 427–442 (2003)

3. B. Sheng, Q. Li, Verifiable privacy-preserving range query in two-tiered sensor networks, in *27th IEEE International Conference on Computer Communications (INFOCOM)* (2008), pp. 46–50

4. B. Sheng, Q. Li, W. Mao, Data storage placement in sensor networks, in *7th ACM International Symposium on Mobile Ad Hoc Networking and Computing (MobiHoc)* (2006), pp. 344–355

5. D. Zeinalipour-yazti, S. Lin, V. Kalogeraki, D. Gunopulos, W.A. Najjar, Microhash: an efficient index structure for flash-based sensor devices, in *4th USENIX Conference on File and Storage Technologies (FAST)* (2005), pp. 31–44

6. Stargate gateway (spb400). http://www.xbow.com

7. Rise project. http://www.cs.ucr.edu/rise

8. I.F. Ilyas, G. Beskales, M.A. Soliman, A survey of top-k queries processing techniques in relational database system. ACM Comput. Surv. **40**(4), 11:1–11:58 (2008)

9. A. Silberstein, R. Braynard, C. Ellis, K. Munagala, J. Yang, A sampling-based approach to optimizing top-k queries in sensor networks, in *22nd International Conference on Data Engineering(ICDE)* (2006), pp. 68–68

10. R. Zhang, JingShi, Y. Zhang, X. Huang, Secure top-k query processing in unattended tiered sensor networks. IEEE Trans. Veh. Technol. **63**(9), 4681–4693 (2014)

11. E. Goh, Secure indexes. Stanford University Technical Report (2004)

12. N. Cao, C. Wang, M. Li, K. Ren, W. Lou, Privacy-preserving multi-keyword ranked search over encrypted cloud data. IEEE Trans. Parallel Distrib. Syst. **25**, 222–233 (2014)

13. B. Bezawada, A. Liu, B. Jayaraman, A. Wang, R. Li, Privacy Preserving string matching for cloud computing, in *35th IEEE International Conference on Distributed Computing System (ICDCS)* (2015), pp. 609–618

14. R. Curtmola, J. Garay, S. Kamara, R. Ostrovsky, Searchable symmetric encryption: improved definitions and efficient constructions. J. Comput. Secur. **19**(5), 895–934 (2011)

15. P. Golle, J. Staddon, B. Waters, Secure conjunctive keyword search over encrypted data, in *2nd International Conference on Applied Cryptography and Network Security(ACNS)* (2004), pp. 31–45

16. O. Goldreich, *Foundations of Cryptography: Basic Tools* (Cambridge University Press, Cambridge, 2001)

17. X. Liao, J. Li, Privacy-preserving and secure top-*k* query in two-tiered wireless sensor, in *55th IEEE Global Communications Conference (GLOBECOM)* (2012), pp. 335–341

18. C.-M. Yu, G.-K. Ni, I.-Y. Chen, E. Gelenbe, S.-Y. Kuo, Top-k query result completeness verification in tiered sensor networks. IEEE Trans. Inf. Forensics Secur. **9**(1), 109–124 (2014)

19. F. Chen, A.X. Liu, SafeQ: secure and efficient query processing in sensor networks, in *29th IEEE International Conference on Computer Communications(INFOCOM)* (2010), pp. 2642–2650

20. J. Shi, R. Zhang, Y. Zhang, Secure range queries in tiered sensor networks, in *28th IEEE International Conference on Computer Communications (INFOCOM)* (2009), pp. 945–953

21. Y. Yi, R. Li, F. Chen, A.X. Liu, Y. Lin, A digital watermarking approach to secure and precise range query processing in sensor networks, in *32th IEEE International Conference on Computer Communications (INFOCOM)* (2013), pp. 1998–2006

22. R. Zhang, J. Shi, Y. Zhang, Secure multidimensional range queries in sensor networks, in *10th ACM International Symposium on Mobile Ad Hoc Networking and Computing (MobiHoc)* (2009), pp. 197–206

23. B. Hore, S. Mehrotra, G. Tsudik, A privacy-preserving index for range queries, in *30th International Conference on Very Large Data (VLDB)* (2004), pp. 720–731

24. M. Naveed, S. Kamara, C.V. Wright, Inference attacks on property-preserving encrypted databases, in *22nd ACM Conference on Computer and Communication Security (CCS)* (2015), pp. 644–655

25. H. Hacigumus, B. Iyer, C. Li, S. Mehrotra, Executing SQL over encrypted data in the database-service-provider model, in *21st ACM International Conference on Management of Data (SIGMOD)* (2002), pp. 216–227

26. B. Hore, S. Mehrotra, M. Canim, M. Kantarcioglu, Secure multidimensional range queries over outsourced data, in *21st International Conference on Very Large Data (VLDB)* (2012), pp. 333–358

27. R. Agrawal, J. Kiernan, R. Srikant, Y. Xu, Order preserving encryption for numeric data, in *23rd ACM International Conference on Management of Data (SIGMOD)* (2004), pp. 563–574

28. A. Boldyreva, N. Chenette, Y. Lee, A. O'Neill, Order-preserving symmetric encryption, in *23rd International Conference on the Theory and Applications of Cryptographic Techniques (EUROCRYPT)* (2009), pp. 224–241

29. A. Boldyreva, N. Chenette, A. O'Neill, Order-preserving encryption revisited: improved security analysis and alternative solutions, in *31st International Cryptology Conference (CRYPTO)* (2011), pp. 578–595

30. R. Li, A.X. Liu, L. Wang, B. Bezawada, Fast range query processing with strong privacy protection for cloud computing, in *40th International Conference on Very Large Data Bases (VLDB)* (IEEE, Piscataway, 2014), pp. 1953–1964

31. D. Boneh, B. Waters, Conjunctive, subset, and range queries on encrypted data, in *4th Theory of Cryptography Conference(TCC)* (2007), pp. 535–554

32. E. Shi, J. Bethencourt, T.-H.H. Chan, D. Song, A. Perrig, Multi-dimensional range query over encrypted data, in *28th IEEE Symposium on Security and Privacy* (2007), pp. 350–364

33. A. X. Liu, F. Chen, Collaborative enforcement of firewall policies in virtual private networks, in *27th ACM SIGACT-SIGOPS Symposium on Principles of Distributed Computing (PODC)* (2008), pp. 887–895

34. B.H. Bloom, Spacetime tradeoffs in hash coding with allowable errors. Commun. ACM **13**, 422–426 (1970)

35. Y.-C. Chang, M. Mitzenmacher, Privacy preserving keyword searches on remote encrypted data, in *3rd International Conference on Applied Cryptography and Network Security(ACNS)* (2005), pp. 442–455

36. Tossim. http://www.cs.berkeley.edu/pal/research/tossim.html

37. Intel lab data. http://berkeley.intel-rescarch.net/labdata

Part II
Privacy Preserving Computation

Chapter 6
Collaborative Enforcement of Firewall Policies in Virtual Private Networks

6.1 Introduction

6.1.1 Background and Motivation

Virtual Private Network (VPN) is a widely deployed technology that allows roaming users to securely use a remote computer on the public Internet as if that computer were residing on their organization's network, which henceforth allows roaming users to access some resources that are only accessible from their organization's network. VPN works in the following manner. Suppose IBM sends a field representative to one of its customers, say Michigan State University (MSU). Assume that MSU's IP addresses are in the range 1.1.0.0–1.1.255.255 and IBM's IP addresses are in the range 2.2.0.0–2.2.255.255. To access resources (say a confidential customer database server with IP address 2.2.0.2) that are only accessible within IBM's network, the IBM representative uses an MSU computer (or his laptop) with an MSU IP address (say 1.1.0.10) to establish a secure VPN tunnel to the VPN server (with IP address 2.2.0.1) in IBM's network. Upon establishing the VPN tunnel, the IBM representative's computer is temporarily assigned a virtual IBM IP address (say 2.2.0.25). Using the VPN tunnel, the IBM representative can access any computer on the Internet as if his computer were residing on IBM's network with IP address 2.2.0.25. The payload of each packet inside the VPN tunnel is another packet (to or from the newly assigned IBM IP address 2.2.0.25), which is typically encrypted. Figure 6.1 illustrates an example packet that traverses from the IBM representative's computer on MSU's network to the customer database server in IBM's network.

While the VPN tunnel is very useful for the IBM representative, it imposes security threats on MSU's network because MSU's firewall does not know what traffic is flowing inside the VPN tunnel. For example, if MSU's firewall blocks access to a remote site (say *www.malicious.com*) or disallows machines to run peer-

A. X. Liu, R. Li, *Algorithms for Data and Computation Privacy*, https://doi.org/10.1007/978-3-030-58896-0_6

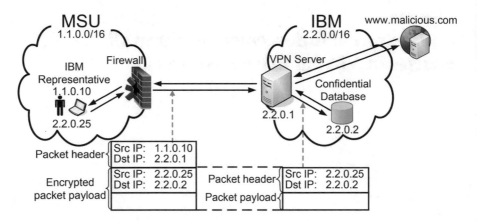

Fig. 6.1 A typical VPN example

to-peer applications due to copyright concerns, MSU's firewall cannot enforce its
policies on the IBM representative's computer although that computer is physically
on MSU's network. Thus, the VPN tunnel opens a hole to MSU's firewall that may
allow unwanted traffic to flow in and out. Having such a hole is very dangerous
because viruses or worms could flood in through it to the IBM representative's
computer first and then further spread to other computers on MSU's network.

6.1.2   Technical Challenges

This problem is technically challenging. First, MSU cannot simply block VPN
connections because otherwise the IBM representative may fail to perform his
duties. Second, MSU cannot share its firewall policy with IBM. Firewall policies
are typically kept confidential due to security and privacy concerns. Knowing the
firewall policy of a network could allow attackers to easily spot the security holes
in the policy and launch corresponding attacks. A firewall policy also reveals the
IP addresses of important servers, which are usually kept confidential to reduce
the chance of being attacked. Furthermore, from a firewall policy, one may derive
the business relationship of the organization with their partners. Third, IBM cannot
share the traffic in its VPN tunnel with MSU due to security and privacy concerns.
For example, IBM may want to keep the IP address of its customer database server
confidential to reduce the likelihood of being attacked. One main purpose of VPN
is to achieve such confidentiality.

   The fundamental problem in the above application is: *how can we collaboratively
enforce firewall policies in a privacy preserving manner for VPN tunnels in an
open distributed environment*? A satisfactory solution to this problem should meet

the following three requirements: (1) The request owner cannot gain any more knowledge on the policy after any number of runs of the protocol than they would by brute force probing of the policy. We refer to this requirement as *policy privacy*. (2) It should be computationally infeasible for the policy owner to reveal a request. We refer to this requirement as *request privacy*. (3) The overhead of the solution should be marginal. Timely processing of every request (or packet) is critical for distributed applications. We refer to this requirement as *protocol efficiency*. Throughout this chapter, we use "MSU" to represent the policy owner and "IBM" to represent the request owner.

6.1.3 Limitations of Prior Art

Although this is a fundamentally important problem, it is largely underinvestigated. The state-of-the-art on this problem is the seminal work in [7], where Cheng et al. proposed a scheme called CDCF. However, CDCF is vulnerable to selective policy updating attacks, by which the policy owner can quickly reveal the request of the other party. Furthermore, CDCF is inefficient because it uses commutative encryption functions (such as the Pohlig-Hellman Exponentiation Cipher [25] and Secure RPC Authentication (SRA) [17]), which are extremely expensive in nature, as the core cryptography primitive.

6.1.4 Our Solution

In this chapter, we present VGuard, a secure and efficient framework for collaborative enforcement of firewall policies. In VGuard, different from CDCF, the policy owner does not know which rule matches which request; thus, it makes the selective policy updating attacks infeasible. Furthermore, unlike CDCF, VGuard obfuscates rule decisions, which prevents MSU from knowing the decision for the given packet. To make VGaurd efficient, we propose a new oblivious comparison scheme, called Xhash, which uses XOR and secure hash functions. Xhash is three orders of magnitude faster than the commutative encryption scheme used in CDCF. Moreover, VGuard uses decision diagrams to process packets, which is much faster than the linear search used in CDCF. By side by side comparison, our experimental results show that VGuard is 552 times faster than CDCF on MSU side and 5035 times faster than CDCF on IBM side.

6.1.5   Key Contributions

We make the following three key contributions in this chapter. First, we propose Xhash, a very efficient oblivious comparison scheme that simply uses XOR and secure hash functions. Second, we propose VGuard, a privacy preserving framework for collaborative enforcement of firewall policies. Third, we implement both VGuard and CDCF and perform extensive experiments to evaluate their performance.

6.2   Threat Model

First, we assume that the two parties of policy owner MSU and request owner IBM are semi-honest; that is, they follow the preestablished VGuard protocol, but the policy owner may attempt to reveal the request and the request owner may attempt to reveal the policy. In particular, the enforcement party IBM does enforce the decision made by MSU. The assumption that the two parties follow the VGuard protocol can be realized by the service level agreement between MSU and IBM. Furthermore, we assume that neither MSU nor IBM has the computational power to break secure hash functions such as HMAC-MD5 or HMAC-SHA1 [11, 19, 26]. Second, we assume that there exists a third party that facilitates the execution of our protocol. This third party shares a secret key with MSU. We assume that this third party follows our protocol and will collude with neither MSU nor IBM. Third, we assume that between any two of the three parties, MSU, IBM, and the third party, there exists a reliable and secure channel. These channels can be established using protocols such as SSL. Our VGuard protocol runs inside these channels. Thus, we do not consider the network level attacks on the communication channels that VGuard is built upon.

6.3   Background

We first formally define the concepts of fields, packets, and firewalls. A *field* F_i is a variable of finite length (i.e., of a finite number of bits). The domain of field F_i of w bits, denoted $D(F_i)$, is $[0, 2^w - 1]$. A *packet* over the d fields $F_1, \cdots, F_d$ is a d-tuple $(p_1, \cdots, p_d)$ where each p_i $(1 \leq i \leq d)$ is an element of $D(F_i)$. Firewalls usually check the following five fields: source IP address, destination IP address, source port number, destination port number, and protocol type. The lengths of these packet fields are 32, 32, 16, 16, and 8 respectively. We use Σ to denote the set of all packets over fields $F_1, \cdots, F_d$. It follows that Σ is a finite set and $|\Sigma| = |D(F_1)| \times \cdots \times |D(F_d)|$, where $|\Sigma|$ denotes the number of elements in set Σ and $|D(F_i)|$ denotes the number of elements in set $D(F_i)$.

Table 6.1 An example firewall

Rule	Src. IP	Dest. IP	Src. Port	Dest. Port	Prot.	Action
r_1	1.2.*.*	192.168.0.1	*	25	TCP	Accept
r_2	*	*	*	*	*	Discard

A *rule* has the form $\langle predicate \rangle \rightarrow \langle decision \rangle$. A $\langle predicate \rangle$ defines a set of packets over the fields F_1 through F_d, and is specified as $F_1 \in S_1 \wedge \cdots \wedge F_d \in S_d$ where each S_i is a subset of $D(F_i)$ and is specified as either a prefix or a range. A *prefix* $\{0, 1\}^k\{*\}^{w-k}$ with k leading 0s or 1s for a packet field of length w denotes the range $[\{0, 1\}^k\{0\}^{w-k}, \{0, 1\}^k\{1\}^{w-k}]$. For example, prefix 01** denotes the range $[0100, 0111]$. A rule $F_1 \in S_1 \wedge \cdots \wedge F_d \in S_d \rightarrow \langle decision \rangle$ is a *prefix rule* if and only if each S_i is represented as a prefix. In firewall rules, source IP addresses, destination IP addresses, and protocol types are typically specified as prefixes, and source ports and destination ports are typically specified as ranges. A packet $(p_1, \cdots, p_d)$ *matches* a predicate $F_1 \in S_1 \wedge \cdots \wedge F_d \in S_d$ and the corresponding rule if and only if the condition $p_1 \in S_1 \wedge \cdots \wedge p_d \in S_d$ holds. For firewalls, the typical decisions include permit, deny, permit with logging, and deny with logging. A rule $F_1 \in S_1 \wedge \cdots \wedge F_d \in S_d \rightarrow \langle decision \rangle$ is called a singleton rule if and only if $|S_i| = 1$ for every i.

A sequence of rules $\langle r_1, \cdots, r_n \rangle$ is *complete* if and only if for any packet p, there is at least one rule in the sequence that p matches. To ensure that a sequence of rules is complete and thus is a firewall, the predicate of the last rule is usually specified as $F_1 \in D(F_1) \wedge \cdots \wedge F_d \in D(F_d)$. A *firewall* is a sequence of rules that is complete. Two rules in a firewall may overlap; that is, there exists at least one packet that matches both rules. Furthermore, two rules in a firewall may conflict; that is, the two rules not only overlap but also have different decisions. Firewalls typically resolve conflicts by employing a first-match resolution strategy where the decision for a packet p is the decision of the first (i.e., highest priority) rule that p matches in the firewall. Table 6.1 shows an example firewall. The format of these rules is based upon the format used in Cisco Access Control Lists.

6.4 Oblivious Comparison

In this section, we consider the following *oblivious comparison* problem. Suppose we have two parties, denoted MSU and IBM, where MSU has a private number N_1 and IBM has a private number N_2. MSU wants to compare whether $N_1 = N_2$; however, neither MSU nor IBM wants to disclose its number to others. If $N_1 \neq N_2$, no party should learn the value of the other party. This is a technically challenging problem because MSU needs to have some information about N_2 to enable the comparison; yet, such information about N_2 should not allow MSU to reveal the value of N_2. Next, we introduce the concept of oblivious comparison functions and an oblivious comparison protocol based on such functions.

Oblivious Comparison Functions Two functions f_1 and f_2 are called a pair of oblivious comparison functions if and only if they satisfy the following four properties:

1. Secrecy: Neither $f_1(x, K)$ nor $f_2(x, K)$ reveals the values of x and K.
2. Nondeducibility: Given x and $f_2(x, K)$, it is computationally infeasible to compute K.
3. Commutativity: For any x, K_1, K_2, we have $f_2(f_1(x, K_1), K_2) = f_2(f_1(x, K_2), K_1)$.
4. Distinguishability: For any x, y, and K, if $x \neq y$, then we have $f_1(x, K) \neq f_1(y, K)$ and $f_2(x, K) \neq f_2(y, K)$.

Here f_1 is called the *inner oblivious comparison function* and f_2 is called the *outer oblivious comparison function*. We discuss the construction of f_1 and f_2 later.

Oblivious Comparison Protocol Assuming that we have a pair of oblivious comparison functions f_1 and f_2, MSU and IBM can achieve oblivious comparison in the following three steps. Assume that MSU has a secret key K_1 and IBM has a secret key K_2. First, MSU computes $f_1(N_1, K_1)$ and sends the result to IBM. Because of the secrecy property of f_1, IBM cannot reveal the values of N_1 and K_1. Second, after receiving $f_1(N_1, K_1)$ from MSU, IBM computes $f_2(f_1(N_1, K_1), K_2)$ and sends the result to MSU. Because of the nondeducibility property of f_2, MSU cannot compute the value of IBM's secret key K_2. Third, IBM computes $f_1(N_2, K_2)$ and sends the result to MSU. Because of the secrecy property of f_1, from $f_1(N_2, K_2)$, MSU cannot reveal the values of N_2 and K_2. After receiving $f_1(N_2, K_2)$ from IBM, MSU computes $f_2(f_1(N_2, K_2), K_1)$ and compares the result with $f_2(f_1(N_1, K_1), K_2)$, which was received from IBM in the second step. Because of the commutativity and distinguishability properties of f_1 and f_2, $N_1 = N_2$ if and only if $f_2(f_1(N_1, K_1), K_2) = f_2(f_1(N_2, K_2), K_1)$. Figure 6.2 shows the oblivious comparison protocol.

The Xhash Protocol We propose a simple and efficient protocol, called Xhash, to achieve oblivious comparison. Xhash works as follows. First, MSU sends $N_1 \oplus K_1$ to IBM. Then, IBM computes $HMAC_k(N_1 \oplus K_1 \oplus K_2)$ and sends the result to MSU. Second, IBM sends $N_2 \oplus K_2$ to MSU. Third, MSU computes $HMAC_k(N_2 \oplus K_2 \oplus K_1)$ and compares it with $HMAC_k(N_1 \oplus K_1 \oplus K_2)$, which was received from IBM.

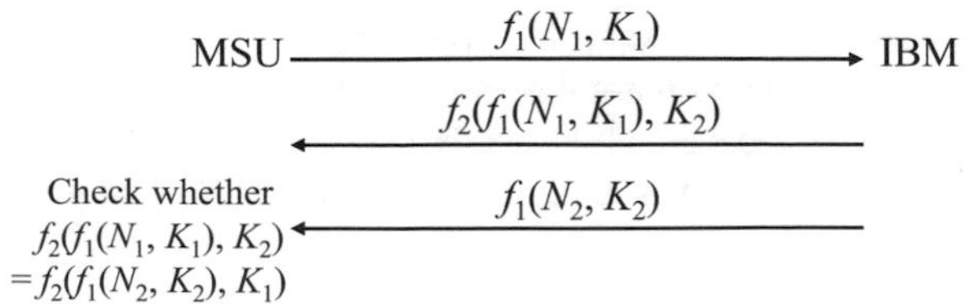

Fig. 6.2 The oblivious comparison protocol

Fig. 6.3 The Xhash protocol

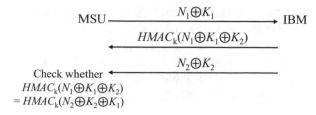

Finally, the condition $N_1 = N_2$ holds if and only if $HMAC_k(N_2 \oplus K_2 \oplus K_1) = HMAC_k(N_1 \oplus K_1 \oplus K_2)$. Figure 6.3 illustrates the Xhash protocol.

The above function HMAC is a keyed-Hash Message Authentication Code, such as HMAC-MD5 or HMAC-SHA1, which satisfies the one-wayness property (i.e., given $HMAC_k(x)$, it is computationally infeasible to compute x and k) and the collision resistance property (i.e., it is computationally infeasible to find two distinct numbers x and y such that $HMAC_k(x) = HMAC_k(y)$. Note that the key k is shared between MSU and IBM. Although hash collisions for HMAC do exist in theory, the probability of collision is negligibly small in practice. Furthermore, by properly choosing the shared key k, we can safely assume that HMAC has no collision.

To prevent brute force attacks, we need to choose key K to be sufficiently long. In our implementation, we choose K to be 128 bits. Note that in our framework x is at most 38 bits. To meet the length of K such that x can be XORed with K, we first use a pseudo random generation function R to generate $x_1 = R(x)$. Second, we apply R to x_1 to generate $x_2 = R(x_1)$. Repeat this process until we can concatenate $x, x_1, x_2, \cdots$ to form a bit string that meets the length of K. Extra bits in the concatenation beyond the length of K are discarded.

The correctness of Xhash follows from the commutative property of XOR operation (i.e., $x \oplus K_1 \oplus K_2 = x \oplus K_2 \oplus K_1$) and the one-wayness and collision resistance properties of HMAC functions.

Nondeducibility Property of f_1   Note that if f_1 does not satisfy the nondeducibility property, when $N_1 = N_2$, MSU is able to compute K_2 because MSU knows both $f_1(N_2, K_2)$ and N_2. This is fine if MSU and IBM only want to compare two numbers where K_2 will be used only once. However, in VGuard, MSU and IBM need to compare MSU's firewall with all the packets in the VPN tunnel rather than comparing two numbers. IBM will apply f_1 to all the packets with its key K_2. In this case, as long as MSU reveals K_2, it can compute the plaintext of all these packets. To address this issue, we have two options. The first option is that we can introduce a third party to prevent MSU from knowing $f_1(N_2, K_2)$ such that MSU cannot reveal K_2. The second option is that instead of introducing the third party, we find a function f_1 that satisfies the nondeducibility property. To our best knowledge, the only function that satisfies the nondeducibility property and the four properties of oblivious comparison functions is the commutative encryption function such as the Pohlig-Hellman Exponentiation Cipher [25]. A commutative encryption function satisfies the following four properties, where $(x)_K$ denotes the encryption of x using key K: (1) Given x and $(x)_K$, it is computationally infeasible to compute the value of K. (2) Given x, K_1, and K_2, we have $((x)_{K_1})_{K_2} = ((x)_{K_2})_{K_1}$. (3) Given x, y, and K, if $x \neq y$, we have $(x)_K \neq (y)_K$. (4) Given K, $(x)_K$ can be decrypted in polynomial time. However, such commutative encryption functions are computationally too expensive. Thus, we choose the first option in our VGuard framework. We defer the discussion of preventing MSU from knowing K_2 in Sect. 6.6.

6.5   Bootstrapping Protocol

In the bootstrapping protocol, MSU first converts its firewall policy to a set of non-overlapping prefix rules. Second, MSU converts each prefix to a number. Third, MSU applies an XOR operation to every number using its secret key K_1. Finally, MSU sends the anonymized policy to IBM. IBM then applies XOR and HMAC operations to every number in the received policy using its secret key K_2, obfuscates the decision of each rule, and shuffle the resulting rules. To complete the process, IBM sends the resulting policy back to MSU. Figure 6.4 illustrates the bootstrapping protocol.

Converting a firewall policy to a set of non-overlapping prefix rules consists of four steps: FDD construction, range conversion, prefix numericalization, and rule generation.

6.5.1   FDD Construction

In this step, MSU converts its firewall policy to an equivalent *Firewall Decision Diagram* [14]. A *Firewall Decision Diagram* (FDD) with a decision set *DS* and over fields $F_1, \cdots, F_d$ is an acyclic and directed graph that has the following five properties: (1) There is exactly one node that has no incoming edges. This node is called the *root*. The nodes that have no outgoing edges are called *terminal* nodes.

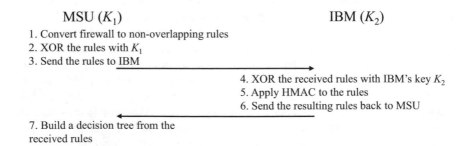

Fig. 6.4   The bootstrapping protocol

Fig. 6.5 Example of
bootstrapping at MSU

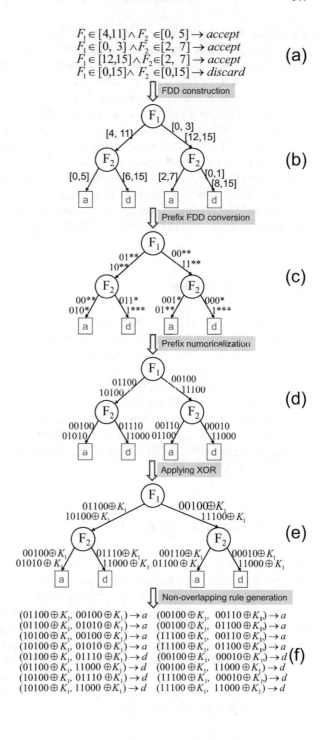

(2) Each node v has a label, denoted $F(v)$. If v is a nonterminal node, then $F(v) \in \{F_1, \cdots, F_d\}$. If v is a terminal node, then $F(v) \in DS$. (3) Each edge $e{:}u \rightarrow v$ is labeled with a nonempty set of integers, denoted $I(e)$, where $I(e)$ is a subset of the domain of u's label (i.e., $I(e) \subseteq D(F(u))$). (4) A directed path from the root to a terminal node is called a *decision path*. No two nodes on a decision path have the same label. (5) The set of all outgoing edges of a node v, denoted $E(v)$, satisfies the following two conditions: (a) *Consistency*: $I(e) \cap I(e') = \emptyset$ for any two distinct edges e and e' in $E(v)$. (b) *Completeness*: $\bigcup_{e \in E(v)} I(e) = D(F(v))$. Figure 6.5a shows an example firewall policy over two fields F_1 and F_2, where the domain of each field is [0, 15]. The FDD that is semantically equivalent to this firewall policy is shown in Fig. 6.5b. Note that in labeling terminal nodes, we use "a" as a shorthand for "*accept*" (i.e., "*permit*") and "d" as a shorthand for "*discard*" (i.e., "*deny*"). The algorithm for converting a firewall to an FDD is in [21].

6.5.2 Range Conversion

For every edge e in the FDD, MSU converts its label $I(e)$ to the minimum set of prefixes whose union is equal to $I(e)$. As one prefix can be converted to one range, a range may be converted to multiple prefixes. In converting a range to prefixes, we want to find the minimum set of prefixes such that the union of the prefixes is equal to the range. For example, given range [0001, 1110], the corresponding minimum set of prefixes would be $0001, 001*, 01**, 10**, 110*, 1110$. The minimum number of prefixes for representing an integer interval $[a, b]$, where a and b are two numbers of w bits, is at most $2w - 2$ [15]. We call such FDDs, where each edge is labeled by a set of prefixes, *prefix FDDs*. Figure 6.5c shows the prefix FDD converted from the FDD in Fig. 6.5b.

6.5.3 Prefix Numericalization

In this step, MSU converts each prefix in the FDD to a concrete number. This process is called *prefix numericalization*. A prefix numericalization function f needs to satisfy the following two properties: (1) for any prefix $\mathcal{P}$, $f(\mathcal{P})$ is a binary string; (2) for any two prefixes $\mathcal{P}_1$ and $\mathcal{P}_2$, $f(\mathcal{P}_1) = f(\mathcal{P}_2)$ if and only if $\mathcal{P}_1 = \mathcal{P}_2$. There are many ways to do prefix numericalization. We use the prefix numericalization scheme used in [4]. Given a prefix $b_1 b_2 \cdots b_k * \cdots *$ of w bits, we first insert 1 after b_k. The bit 1 represents a separator between $b_1 b_2 \cdots b_k$ and $* \cdots *$. Second, we replace every * by 0. Note that if there is no * in a prefix, we add 1 at the end of this prefix. For example, $101*$ is converted to 10110. After prefix numericalization, the FDD in Fig. 6.5c becomes the one in Fig. 6.5d.

6.5.4 Applying XOR by MSU

After prefix numericalization, MSU applies XOR to every number in the numericalized FDD using its secret key K_1. Figure 6.5e shows the numericalized and XORed FDD. Then, MSU generates non-overlapping rules from the numericalized and XORed FDD. From each decision path in the FDD, MSU generates a set of non-overlapping rules. For example, from the left-most decision path in Fig. 6.5e, MSU generates the following four non-overlapping rules:

$$F_1 \in 01100 \oplus K_1 \wedge F_2 \in 00100 \oplus K_1 \rightarrow a,$$

$$F_1 \in 01100 \oplus K_1 \wedge F_2 \in 01010 \oplus K_1 \rightarrow a,$$

$$F_1 \in 10100 \oplus K_1 \wedge F_2 \in 00100 \oplus K_1 \rightarrow a,$$

$$F_1 \in 10100 \oplus K_1 \wedge F_2 \in 01010 \oplus K_1 \rightarrow a,$$

Figure 6.5f shows the disjoint rules generated from the FDD in Fig. 6.5e.

After non-overlapping rules are generated, MSU sends the resulting policy to IBM. If MSU needs to prevent IBM from knowing the number of non-overlapping prefix rules that MSU's firewall is converted to, MSU can randomly insert some dummy rules formulated by out-of-range dummy numbers and random decisions into the set of non-overlapping numerical rules before applying XOR. An out-of-range dummy number is a number that corresponds to no prefix. Thus, no packet will match a dummy rule that consists of at least one out-of-range dummy number. According to our prefix numericalization scheme, there is only one dummy number in which every bit is 0. To create more dummy numbers, we can simply add extra bits. Note that IBM knowing the number of converted rules is not much a concern. As we will show in the experimental results, the number of non-overlapping prefix rules that a firewall is converted to far exceeds the number of original rules.

6.5.5 Applying XOR and HMAC by IBM

Upon receiving a sequence of non-overlapping numerical rules from MSU, IBM further applies XOR and HMAC to every number in the received policy using its secret key K_2. To destroy the correspondence between the rules after applying XOR and HMAC and the rules received from MSU, IBM randomly shuffles the resulting rules after applying XOR and HMAC. To prevent MSU from knowing the decision of IBM's packet, IBM obfuscates the decision of each rule by mapping each decision to another distinct decision. More formally, the decision obfuscation is a one-to-one mapping function f from the set of all decisions to the same set of all decisions. IBM stores the mapping function f in its decision obfuscation table and replaces the decision of each rule in r_i, say d_i, by $f(d_i)$. To prevent MSU from statistically discovering the obfuscation mapping function f, for any decision d_i, IBM needs

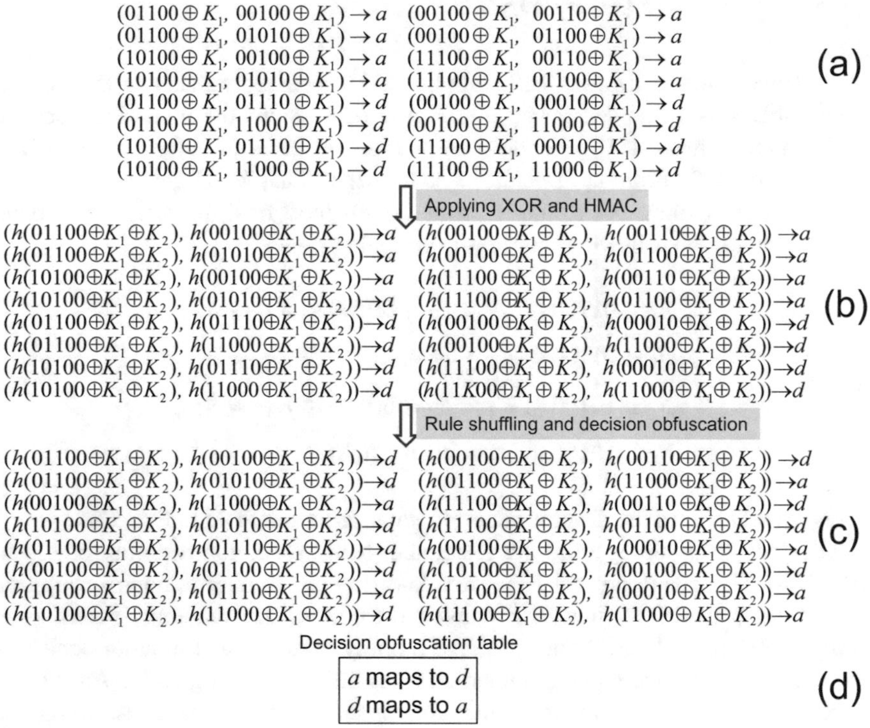

$(01100 \oplus K_1, 00100 \oplus K_1) \to a \quad (00100 \oplus K_1, 00110 \oplus K_1) \to a$
$(01100 \oplus K_1, 01010 \oplus K_1) \to a \quad (00100 \oplus K_1, 01100 \oplus K_1) \to a$
$(10100 \oplus K_1, 00100 \oplus K_1) \to a \quad (11100 \oplus K_1, 00110 \oplus K_1) \to a$
$(10100 \oplus K_1, 01010 \oplus K_1) \to a \quad (11100 \oplus K_1, 01100 \oplus K_1) \to a$
$(01100 \oplus K_1, 01110 \oplus K_1) \to d \quad (00100 \oplus K_1, 00010 \oplus K_1) \to d$
$(01100 \oplus K_1, 11000 \oplus K_1) \to d \quad (00100 \oplus K_1, 11000 \oplus K_1) \to d$
$(10100 \oplus K_1, 01110 \oplus K_1) \to d \quad (11100 \oplus K_1, 00010 \oplus K_1) \to d$
$(10100 \oplus K_1, 11000 \oplus K_1) \to d \quad (11100 \oplus K_1, 11000 \oplus K_1) \to d$

(a)

⇩ Applying XOR and HMAC

$(h(01100 \oplus K_1 \oplus K_2), h(00100 \oplus K_1 \oplus K_2)) \to a \quad (h(00100 \oplus K_1 \oplus K_2), h(00110 \oplus K_1 \oplus K_2)) \to a$
$(h(01100 \oplus K_1 \oplus K_2), h(01010 \oplus K_1 \oplus K_2)) \to a \quad (h(00100 \oplus K_1 \oplus K_2), h(01100 \oplus K_1 \oplus K_2)) \to a$
$(h(10100 \oplus K_1 \oplus K_2), h(00100 \oplus K_1 \oplus K_2)) \to a \quad (h(11100 \oplus K_1 \oplus K_2), h(00110 \oplus K_1 \oplus K_2)) \to a$
$(h(10100 \oplus K_1 \oplus K_2), h(01010 \oplus K_1 \oplus K_2)) \to a \quad (h(11100 \oplus K_1 \oplus K_2), h(01100 \oplus K_1 \oplus K_2)) \to a$
$(h(01100 \oplus K_1 \oplus K_2), h(01110 \oplus K_1 \oplus K_2)) \to d \quad (h(00100 \oplus K_1 \oplus K_2), h(00010 \oplus K_1 \oplus K_2)) \to d$
$(h(01100 \oplus K_1 \oplus K_2), h(11000 \oplus K_1 \oplus K_2)) \to d \quad (h(00100 \oplus K_1 \oplus K_2), h(11000 \oplus K_1 \oplus K_2)) \to d$
$(h(10100 \oplus K_1 \oplus K_2), h(01110 \oplus K_1 \oplus K_2)) \to d \quad (h(11100 \oplus K_1 \oplus K_2), h(00010 \oplus K_1 \oplus K_2)) \to d$
$(h(10100 \oplus K_1 \oplus K_2), h(11000 \oplus K_1 \oplus K_2)) \to d \quad (h(11K00 \oplus K_1 \oplus K_2), h(11000 \oplus K_1 \oplus K_2)) \to d$

(b)

⇩ Rule shuffling and decision obfuscation

$(h(01100 \oplus K_1 \oplus K_2), h(00100 \oplus K_1 \oplus K_2)) \to d \quad (h(00100 \oplus K_1 \oplus K_2), h(00110 \oplus K_1 \oplus K_2)) \to d$
$(h(01100 \oplus K_1 \oplus K_2), h(01010 \oplus K_1 \oplus K_2)) \to d \quad (h(01100 \oplus K_1 \oplus K_2), h(11000 \oplus K_1 \oplus K_2)) \to a$
$(h(00100 \oplus K_1 \oplus K_2), h(11000 \oplus K_1 \oplus K_2)) \to a \quad (h(11100 \oplus K_1 \oplus K_2), h(00110 \oplus K_1 \oplus K_2)) \to d$
$(h(10100 \oplus K_1 \oplus K_2), h(01010 \oplus K_1 \oplus K_2)) \to d \quad (h(11100 \oplus K_1 \oplus K_2), h(01100 \oplus K_1 \oplus K_2)) \to d$
$(h(01100 \oplus K_1 \oplus K_2), h(01110 \oplus K_1 \oplus K_2)) \to a \quad (h(00100 \oplus K_1 \oplus K_2), h(00010 \oplus K_1 \oplus K_2)) \to a$
$(h(00100 \oplus K_1 \oplus K_2), h(01100 \oplus K_1 \oplus K_2)) \to d \quad (h(10100 \oplus K_1 \oplus K_2), h(00100 \oplus K_1 \oplus K_2)) \to d$
$(h(10100 \oplus K_1 \oplus K_2), h(01110 \oplus K_1 \oplus K_2)) \to a \quad (h(11100 \oplus K_1 \oplus K_2), h(00010 \oplus K_1 \oplus K_2)) \to a$
$(h(10100 \oplus K_1 \oplus K_2), h(11000 \oplus K_1 \oplus K_2)) \to d \quad (h(111 00 \oplus K_1 \oplus K_2), h(11000 \oplus K_1 \oplus K_2)) \to a$

(c)

Decision obfuscation table

a maps to d
d maps to a

(d)

Fig. 6.6 Example of bootstrapping at IBM

to ensure that the number of rules that have decision d_i is the same. This can be easily achieved by adding dummy rules. Due to the rule shuffling and decision obfuscation, MSU cannot correlate the received rules with the original rules, and also cannot identify the decision of each rule. Figure 6.6b shows the rules after IBM applies XOR and HMAC, and Fig. 6.6c shows the rules after IBM shuffles rules and obfuscates decisions. The obfuscation mapping function is shown in Fig. 6.6d. Note that in these figures h denotes the HMAC function. Finally, IBM sends the resulting rules to MSU.

6.6 Filtering Protocol

In the filtering protocol, each time IBM receives a packet that originated from or was sent to its representative, IBM first converts the packet to prefixes and then further converts each prefix to a number using the same prefix numericalization scheme. Then, IBM XORs every number in the packet with its secret key K_2, then sends the resulting packet to the third party. The third party further applies XOR and HMAC to

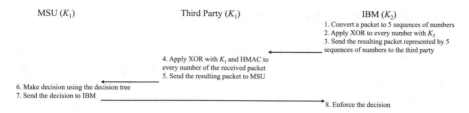

Fig. 6.7 The filtering protocol

the received packet with the secret key K_1. Note that the third party and MSU share key K_1. Then, the third party sends the resulting packet to MSU. MSU then searches the obfuscated decision for the packet using the received firewall policy from IBM in the bootstrapping protocol. Finally, MSU sends the obfuscated decision to IBM and IBM finds the original decision using its decision obfuscation table. Figure 6.7 shows the filtering protocol.

6.6.1 Address Translation

When the IBM VPN server sends (or receives) a packet on behalf of its representative in MSU, the source (or destination) IP address of the packet is an IBM IP address that the IBM VPN server assigned to the IBM representative's computer in MSU. To inquiry the decision for this packet from MSU, IBM needs to replace the source (or destination) IP address in the packet by IBM representative's MSU IP address. Otherwise, it is likely that MSU firewall policy blocks all incoming packets that are not sent to MSU and all outgoing packets that are not originated from MSU. Take the example in Fig. 6.1, the packet that IBM should ask MSU for a decision has a source IP 1.1.0.10 and a destination IP 2.2.0.2.

6.6.2 Prefix Membership Verification

We first define two concepts: k-prefix and prefix family. We call the prefix $\{0, 1\}^k \{*\}^{w-k}$ with k leading 0s and 1s followed by $w - k$ *s a k-prefix. If a value x matches a k-prefix, the first k bits of x and the k-prefix are the same. For example, if $x \in 01 * *$ (i.e., $x \in [0100, 0111]$), then the first two bits of x must be 01. Given a binary number $b_1 b_2 \cdots b_w$ of w bits, the prefix family of this number is the set of $w + 1$ prefixes $\{b_1 b_2 \cdots b_w, b_1 b_2 \cdots b_{w-1}*, \cdots, b_1 * \cdots *, * * \ldots *\}$, where the i-th prefix is $b_1 b_2 \cdots b_{w-i+1} * \cdots *$. We use $PF(x)$ to represent the prefix family of x. For example, $PF(0101) = \{0101, 010*, 01 * *, 0 * **, * * **\}$. Based on the above definitions, it is easy to draw the following conclusion: given a number x and a prefix $\mathcal{P}$, $x \in \mathcal{P}$ if and only if $\mathcal{P} \in PF(x)$.

6.6.3   Packet Preprocessing by IBM

For each of the d fields of a packet, IBM first generates its prefix family. Second, IBM converts each prefix to a number using the same prefix numericalization scheme in the bootstrapping protocol. Third, IBM applies XOR to each number using its secret key K_2. Last, IBM sends a sequence of d sets of numbers, which corresponds to the d fields of the packet, to the third party. For example, given a packet (0101, 0011) as shown in Fig. 6.8a, the prefix family of each field is shown in Fig. 6.8b. The result of prefix numericalization is shown in Fig. 6.8c. The final two sequences of numbers are shown in Fig. 6.8d.

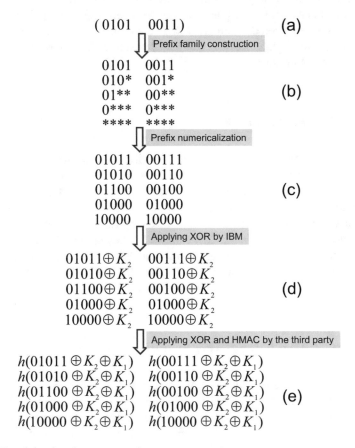

Fig. 6.8 Example of packet preprocessing

6.6.4   Packet Preprocessing by The Third Party

Upon receiving the packet as d sequences of numbers from IBM, the third party further applies XOR using key K_1 and HMAC to each number and then sends the resulting packet to MSU. Here we choose the third party, instead of MSU, to apply XOR and HMAC for the purpose of preventing MSU from knowing the IBM's XOR results (e.g., Fig. 6.8d) before applying HMAC. Otherwise, MSU may break IBM's secret key K_2 and further reveal packet headers. If MSU knows IBM's XOR results, to break K_2, MSU first stores its rules before anonymization in the bootstrapping protocol (e.g., the rules generated from Fig. 6.5d). Let $\langle r_1, \cdots, r_n \rangle$ denote these rules, where each rule r_j ($1 \leq j \leq n$) is in the form $(m_1^j, \cdots, m_d^j) \rightarrow \langle dec^j \rangle$. In the filtering protocol, when MSU finds that a packet $(p_1, p_2, \cdots, p_d)$ matches a rule, according to the property of prefix membership verification, for each $1 \leq i \leq d$, there must be a number n_i in $PF(p_i)$ that is equal to one number in the set $\{m_i^1, \cdots, m_i^n\}$. Third, for each $1 \leq i \leq d$, MSU XORs $n_i \oplus K_2$ received from IBM with every number in the set $\{m_i^1, \cdots, m_i^n\}$. Because one of the numbers in $\{m_i^1, \cdots, m_i^n\}$ is equal to n_i, then the resulting set, denoted S_i, must contains K_2. For example, if $m_i^1 = n_i$, then $m_i^1 \oplus n_i \oplus K_2 = K_2$. Thus, for each packet P, we can compute a set $S(P) = S_1 \cap \cdots \cap S_d$, which contains K_2. When MSU receives a large set of packets $P_1, \cdots, P_g$, the set $S(P_1) \cap \cdots \cap S(P_g)$ may only contains K_2. After finding K_2, MSU can reveal packet headers by applying XOR to every number of packets received from IBM using K_2. However, in VGuard, using the third party to apply XOR and HMAC to packets eliminates this possibility.

6.6.5   Packet Processing by MSU

Upon receiving the packet from the third party, MSU searches the obfuscated decision for the packet using the resulting firewall rules from the bootstrapping protocol. Recall that each rule is represented as d numbers and an obfuscated decision. A packet $(p_1, \cdots, p_d)$ matches a rule $(m_1, \cdots, m_d) \rightarrow \langle obfuscated\ decision \rangle$ if and only if the condition $m_1 \in PF(p_1) \wedge \cdots \wedge m_d \in PF(p_d)$ holds. Therefore, MSU can use linear search to find the first rule that the packet matches. Then, MSU sends the obfuscated decision to IBM and IBM finds the original decision using its decision obfuscation table. Because all the firewall rules resulted from the bootstrapping protocol are non-overlapping, there exists one and only one rule that the packet matches. For example, given the resulting firewall rules in Fig. 6.6c and the preprocessed packet in Fig. 6.8e, the only rule that matches the packet is $(h(01100 \oplus K_2 \oplus K_1), h(00100 \oplus K_2 \oplus K_1)) \rightarrow d$.

To improve search efficiency, MSU can use the following two techniques: decision tree and hash table. First, MSU converts the non-overlapping rules resulted from the bootstrapping protocol to an equivalent decision tree. For example, Fig. 6.9 shows the decision tree constructed from the firewall in Fig. 6.6c. Thus, MSU can

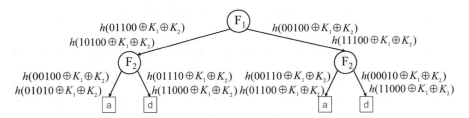

Fig. 6.9 Decision tree constructed from Fig. 6.6c

search the decision for a packet using the decision tree. Second, for the basic operation of testing $m_i \in PF(p_i)$, MSU builds one hash table for each $PF(p_i)$ and then tests whether m_i is in the hash table that constructed from $PF(p_i)$.

6.7   VGuard for Deep Packet Inspection

With the growing need to filter malicious packets, advanced firewalls, as well as intrusion detection/prevention systems such as Snort [27], Bro [24], 3Com's TippingPoint X505 [31], and a variety of Cisco Systems [8], examine not only packet headers but also packet payload by checking whether its payload contains some predefined strings in a signature database. More formally, given a string $a_1 a_2 \cdots a_n$ and a packet payload $s_1 s_2 \cdots s_m$ where each a_i ($1 \le i \le n$) and s_j ($1 \le j \le m$) are characters, we want to check whether the string $s_1 s_2 \cdots s_m$ contains the sub-string $s_{k+1} s_{k+2} \cdots s_{k+n}$ that is the same as the string $a_1 a_2 \cdots a_n$. If so, the packet payload $s_1 s_2 \cdots s_m$ matches the string $a_1 a_2 \cdots a_n$.

We can adapt our VGuard framework to deal with the cases where MSU's firewall performs deep packet inspection. The basic idea is that MSU and IBM apply Xhash protocol to each character of every string in the signature database and each character of the packet payload, and check whether the resulting packet payload contains the resulting string.

6.7.1   The Bootstrapping Protocol

In the bootstrapping protocol, MSU first applies XOR to every character of the strings in its signature database using its secret key K_1, and then sends the resulting strings to IBM. To prevent IBM from knowing the number of strings in its signature database, MSU adds some random strings and XORs them with K_1. Upon receiving the anonymized strings from MSU, IBM further applies XOR and HMAC operations to each character using its secret key K_2. To prevent MSU from identifying the original string that a packet matches by comparing the number of characters in each resulting string with that in each original string, IBM adds some dummy strings and XORs them with its secret key K_2. Then, IBM obfuscates the decision associated with each string and shuffles the strings. At last, IBM sends the resulting strings back to MSU. Note that all the random strings added by MSU and the dummy strings added by IBM should have the default action, which is *"permit"*. Figure 6.10 shows the bootstrapping protocol for deep packet inspection. Suppose a intrusion detection system has n rules and the i-th $(1 \le i \le n)$ rule has c_i characters. In the bootstrapping protocol, the computation overhead of MSU and IBM is $O(\sum_{i=1}^{n} c_i)$, and the communication overhead between MSU and IBM is also $O(\sum_{i=1}^{n} c_i)$.

Considering three strings *"eb, ebf, ecg"* in Fig. 6.11a, b shows the anonymized string s after MSU applies XOR to these strings. Figure 6.11c shows the resulting strings after MSU adds the random string $r_1 r_2$, where r_1 and r_2 denote two random characters. Figure 6.11d shows the resulting strings after IBM adds the dummy string $d_1 d_2$, where d_1 and d_2 denote two random characters. Figure 6.11e shows the strings after IBM applies XOR and HMAC, and Fig. 6.11f shows the strings after IBM shuffles rules and obfuscates decisions.

As the dummy strings that IBM generated are unlikely to match any packet, MSU may identify them and then delete them. To prevent MSU from identifying such strings, IBM can generate fake packets that match the dummy strings and periodically send them to MSU.

6.7.2   The Filtering Protocol

In the filtering protocol, each time IBM receives a packet originated from or sent to its representative, IBM first applies XOR to every character in the packet payload using K_2 and sends the resulting packet to the third party, which further applies XOR and HMAC to the packet payload using key K_1 and then sends the resulting packet to MSU. String matching algorithms have been investigated for many years and several famous algorithms have been proposed, such as Aho-Corasick algorithm [2] and Commentz-Walter algorithm [9]. MSU can use these algorithms to search the obfuscated decision for the packet based on the received strings from IBM in the bootstrapping protocol. Finally, MSU sends the obfuscated decision to IBM and IBM finds the original decision using its decision obfuscation table.

For example, given a packet that contains strings *"ebkf"* as shown in Fig. 6.12a, the packet payload after IBM applies XOR is in Fig. 6.12b. Figure 6.12c shows the result payload after the third party applies XOR and HMAC. For the resulting strings in Fig. 6.11f, the only string in the signature database that matches the packet payload is $h(e \oplus K_1 \oplus K_2), h(b \oplus K_1 \oplus K_2) \to d$.

Fig. 6.10 Bootstrapping for deep packet inspection

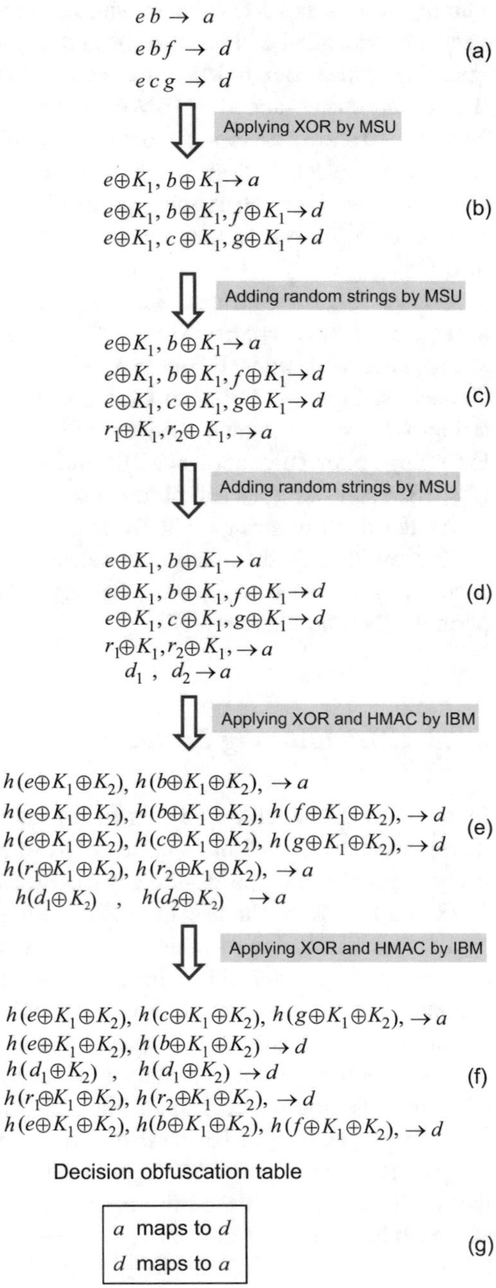

Fig. 6.11 Example of string processing

$$e\,b \rightarrow a$$
$$e\,b\,f \rightarrow d \quad\quad (a)$$
$$e\,c\,g \rightarrow d$$

⇩ Applying XOR by MSU

$$e \oplus K_1,\, b \oplus K_1 \rightarrow a$$
$$e \oplus K_1,\, b \oplus K_1,\, f \oplus K_1 \rightarrow d \quad\quad (b)$$
$$e \oplus K_1,\, c \oplus K_1,\, g \oplus K_1 \rightarrow d$$

⇩ Adding random strings by MSU

$$e \oplus K_1,\, b \oplus K_1 \rightarrow a$$
$$e \oplus K_1,\, b \oplus K_1,\, f \oplus K_1 \rightarrow d$$
$$e \oplus K_1,\, c \oplus K_1,\, g \oplus K_1 \rightarrow d \quad\quad (c)$$
$$r_1 \oplus K_1,\, r_2 \oplus K_1,\, \rightarrow a$$

⇩ Adding random strings by MSU

$$e \oplus K_1,\, b \oplus K_1 \rightarrow a$$
$$e \oplus K_1,\, b \oplus K_1,\, f \oplus K_1 \rightarrow d \quad\quad (d)$$
$$e \oplus K_1,\, c \oplus K_1,\, g \oplus K_1 \rightarrow d$$
$$r_1 \oplus K_1,\, r_2 \oplus K_1,\, \rightarrow a$$
$$d_1,\; d_2 \rightarrow a$$

⇩ Applying XOR and HMAC by IBM

$$h(e \oplus K_1 \oplus K_2),\, h(b \oplus K_1 \oplus K_2),\, \rightarrow a$$
$$h(e \oplus K_1 \oplus K_2),\, h(b \oplus K_1 \oplus K_2),\, h(f \oplus K_1 \oplus K_2),\, \rightarrow d$$
$$h(e \oplus K_1 \oplus K_2),\, h(c \oplus K_1 \oplus K_2),\, h(g \oplus K_1 \oplus K_2),\, \rightarrow d \quad\quad (e)$$
$$h(r_1 \oplus K_1 \oplus K_2),\, h(r_2 \oplus K_1 \oplus K_2),\, \rightarrow a$$
$$h(d_1 \oplus K_2) \;,\; h(d_2 \oplus K_2) \; \rightarrow a$$

⇩ Applying XOR and HMAC by IBM

$$h(e \oplus K_1 \oplus K_2),\, h(c \oplus K_1 \oplus K_2),\, h(g \oplus K_1 \oplus K_2),\, \rightarrow a$$
$$h(e \oplus K_1 \oplus K_2),\, h(b \oplus K_1 \oplus K_2) \rightarrow d$$
$$h(d_1 \oplus K_2) \;,\; h(d_1 \oplus K_2) \rightarrow d$$
$$h(r_1 \oplus K_1 \oplus K_2),\, h(r_2 \oplus K_1 \oplus K_2),\, \rightarrow d \quad\quad (f)$$
$$h(e \oplus K_1 \oplus K_2),\, h(b \oplus K_1 \oplus K_2),\, h(f \oplus K_1 \oplus K_2),\, \rightarrow d$$

Decision obfuscation table

a maps to d
d maps to a

(g)

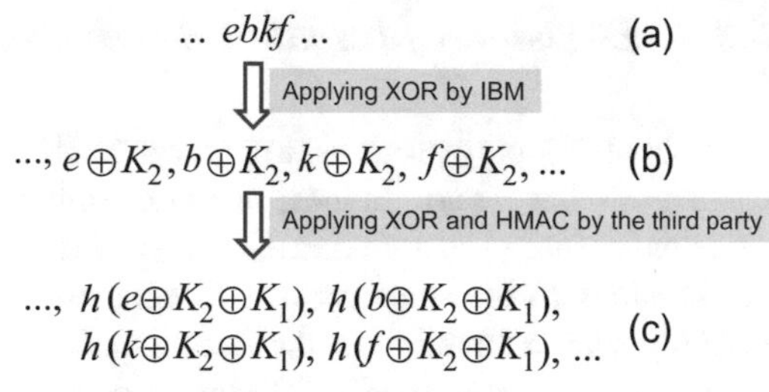

Fig. 6.12 Example of packet
payload processing

$$... \; ebkf \; ... \qquad \text{(a)}$$

⇓ Applying XOR by IBM

$$..., e \oplus K_2, b \oplus K_2, k \oplus K_2, f \oplus K_2, ... \qquad \text{(b)}$$

⇓ Applying XOR and HMAC by the third party

$$..., \; h(e \oplus K_2 \oplus K_1), \; h(b \oplus K_2 \oplus K_1),$$
$$h(k \oplus K_2 \oplus K_1), \; h(f \oplus K_2 \oplus K_1), ... \qquad \text{(c)}$$

6.8   Discussion

6.8.1   Firewall Updates

When MSU updates its firewall policy, MSU and IBM need to run the bootstrapping protocol again. To prevent IBM from identifying the unchanged rules, in each run of the bootstrapping protocol, MSU and IBM should change their secret keys K_1 and K_2. Thus, the rules that IBM receives in each run of the bootstrapping protocol are totally different. Note that MSU and IBM do not need to run the bootstrapping protocol as long as MSU's firewall remains the same.

6.8.2   Decision Caching

A packet contains a header (with fields of source and destination IP addresses, source and destination port numbers, and protocol type) and a payload. For different packets with the same header, IBM only needs to ask MSU once and then cache the packet header along with its decision. Whenever the IBM representative builds a connection through the VPN tunnel, IBM first checks whether its cache has an entry that corresponds to the connection. If yes, then IBM executes that decision; if no, IBM asks MSU for the decision using the filtering protocol and then adds an entry into its cache. Because IBM may have multiple collaborators, IBM should record the name of its collaborator (which is "MSU" in this case) to every entry in the cache. Thus, IBM only needs to maintain one cache. When MSU updates its firewall policy and reruns the bootstrapping protocol, IBM needs to delete all the entries that corresponds to MSU. IBM can implement caches efficiently using hash tables or by counting Bloom filters [12].

6.8.3 Decision Obfuscation vs. Decision Encryption

In the bootstrapping protocol, to prevent MSU from knowing the decision of IBM's packet, we have two choices, decision obfuscation and decision encryption. A decision obfuscation function is a one-to-one mapping function from the set of all decisions to the same set of all decisions. The idea of decision obfuscation is to apply such a function to the decisions of the rules sent from IBM to MSU in the bootstrapping protocol. The idea of decision encryption is to concatenate each decision dec with a number i and then encrypt the decision $dec|i$ using another secret key K, i.e., $(dec|i)_K$.

Although decision encryption obfuscates the decisions well, it can be exploited. Using decision encryption, IBM can add more information to the decision and then encrypt it. In particular, if IBM attaches the identification number of a rule to each decision, IBM can identify the exact rule that matches the packet. This would help IBM compute MSU's secret key K_1 and further reveal the exact context of the rule. More formally, IBM can store the anonymized rules received from MSU in the bootstrapping protocol. These anonymized rules are in the form $(m_1 \oplus K_1, m_2 \oplus K_1, \cdots, m_5 \oplus K_1) \rightarrow \langle dec \rangle$ (where each m_i is a number). If IBM can identify the one rule that matches the packet $(p_1, p_2, \cdots, p_5)$, IBM can generate prefix family for each attribute of the packet $PF(p_i)$ $(1 \leq i \leq 5)$. Due to the property of prefix membership verification, there should be one number n_i in each $PF(p_i)$ that is equal to m_i. Therefore, IBM can compute MSU's secret key K_1 by applying XOR to the number $m_i \oplus K_1$ using n_i. If $m_i = n_i$, then $m_i \oplus K_1 \oplus n_i = K_1$. After finding K_1, IBM can reveal the exact context of non-overlapping rules in MSU firewall policy by applying XOR to every number of anonymized rules using K_1. Because of the above security problem, we use the decision obfuscation technique.

6.8.4 Special Treatment of IP Addresses

As we discussed previously, for every packet from (or to) the IBM representative, IBM needs to translate the source (or destination) IP from an address in IBM's domain to the address in MSU's domain. Thus, for each packet that IBM asks MSU for a decision, either the source or the destination IP of the packet is the IP that MSU assigns to the IBM representative. This IP address is known to MSU, MSU can use it to compute the secret key K_2 of IBM, which henceforth violates the packet privacy. Note that $x \oplus K_2 \oplus x = K_2$.

To prevent this type of attacks, we modify VGuard as follows. First, MSU chooses five secret keys $K_1, K_2, \cdots, K_5$ that correspond to the five packet fields (source IP, destination IP, source port, destination port, and protocol type), and similarly IBM chooses five secret keys $K_1', K_2', \cdots, K_5'$ as well. Second, in the bootstrapping protocol, for each non-overlapping rule $(m_1, m_2, \cdots, m_5) \rightarrow \langle dec \rangle$ (where each m_i is a number), MSU applies XOR to each m_i using key K_i. Thus, the rule becomes $(m_1 \oplus K_1, m_2 \oplus K_2, \cdots, m_5 \oplus K_5) \to \langle dec \rangle$. Then, MSU sends these rules to IBM. For each rule $(m_1 \oplus K_1, m_2 \oplus K_2, m_3 \oplus K_3, m_4 \oplus K_4, m_5 \oplus K_5) \to \langle dec \rangle$ that IBM receives from MSU, assuming that m_1 corresponds to the field of source IP and m_2 corresponds to the field of destination IP, IBM creates the two rules:

$$(m_1 \oplus K_1, HMAC_k(m_2 \oplus K_2 \oplus K_2'), HMAC_k(m_3 \oplus K_3 \oplus K_3'),$$

$$HMAC_k(m_4 \oplus K_4 \oplus K_4'), HMAC_k(m_5 \oplus K_5 \oplus K_5')) \to \langle dec \rangle$$

$$(HMAC_k(m_1 \oplus K_1 \oplus K_1'), m_2 \oplus K_2, HMAC_k(m_3 \oplus K_3 \oplus K_3'),$$

$$HMAC_k(m_4 \oplus K_4 \oplus K_4'), HMAC_k(m_5 \oplus K_5 \oplus K_5')) \to \langle dec \rangle$$

Basically, IBM keeps the source IP field unchanged in the first rule and keeps the destination IP field unchanged in the second rule. At last, IBM sends two sets of rules back to MSU, where in one set the source IP is unchanged and in the other set the destination IP is unchanged. Third, in the filtering protocol, when IBM receives a packet, without loss of generality assuming that the packet is originated from its representative, IBM applies XOR to four fields of the packet (destination IP, source port, destination port, and protocol type) using its four corresponding keys K_2', K_3', K_4', and K_5'. In other words, when the source IP of the packet is the MSU IP address, IBM does not apply XOR to that field. When the resulting packet (p_1, $p_2 \oplus K_2'$, $p_3 \oplus K_3'$, $p_4 \oplus K_4'$, $p_5 \oplus K_5'$) is sent to the third party, IBM asks the third party to apply only XOR to p_1 using key K_1 and process $p_2 \oplus K_2'$, $p_3 \oplus K_3'$, $p_4 \oplus K_4'$, $p_5 \oplus K_5'$ as usual using keys K_2, K_3, K_4 and K_5 respectively. Then, the third party sends the resulting packet to MSU. Finally, MSU searches the decision for the packet in the rule set where the source IP field was not processed by IBM. Thus, leaving the source (or destination) IP field unprocessed by IBM, MSU cannot break any secret key of IBM.

6.8.5 Securing Keys of MSU

In our VGuard, IBM only knows $m_i \oplus K_i$ ($1 \le i \le 5$) but doesn't know m_i. However, if MSU's firewall policy has popular values in a field, say the j-th field ($1 \le j \le 5$), IBM may reveal K_j by XORing these popular values with $m_j \oplus K_j$ of all non-overlapping rules received from MSU. To prevent such attack, when MSU's firewall has some popular values, MSU can XOR each popular value using a different key in the bootstrapping protocol. The reason is that for the j-th field, although IBM can obtain a set of values through the above attack, it cannot distinguish the keys of each popular value from that set.

Similarly, for deep packet inspection, if MSU has some popular strings in its signature database, IBM may reveal MSU's secret key. The strings that MSU needs to keep confidential are the ones that are specific to MSU needs. However, if some strings are popular among signature databases, it is unlikely that MSU needs to keep them confidential. Thus, to prevent such attack, MSU can simply tell IBM these popular strings and ask IBM to check whether a packet payload matches these strings.

6.8.6 Stateful Firewalls

So far we have assumed that firewalls are stateless. A stateful firewall is a firewall that keeps track of the state of network connections across the firewall. When a stateful firewall receives a packet, it first checks its connection table to see whether the packet belongs to an ongoing connection. If yes, the packet is permitted right away. If no, the packet needs to be checked with its stateless rules to determine whether the packet should be permitted; if the stateless rules allows the packet to be permitted, then a new connection is built and inserted into the connection table of the firewall. Such stateful firewalls typically allow inside non-server computers (i.e., the computers that are not servers) to initiate connection with outside computers but disallow outside computers to initiate connection with non-server computers. When an inside non-server computer sends a packet to an outside computer, the stateful firewall uses its stateless rules to decide whether the packet should be permitted; if yes, the firewall adds an entry in its connection table that will allow subsequent packets sent from that outside computer to the inside computer. When an outside computer sends a packet to an insider non-server computer, if there is no corresponding entry in the connection table, the firewall will use its stateless rules to make a decision, which is typically *deny*.

Our framework can be extended to handle stateful firewalls. The basic idea is to let IBM maintain a connection table for its representative. If MSU's firewall is stateful, in the extended framework, when IBM receives a packet from or to its representative, IBM first consults its connection table to see whether the packet belongs to an ongoing connection. If yes, the packet is accepted right away. If no, IBM asks MSU for the decision for this packet; if the packet is permitted, IBM adds an entry into the connection table. Note that the connection table is different from IBM's decision cache. If MSU's firewall is stateless, for every connection, with the help of cache, IBM needs to ask MSU the decision for two packets that go in exactly the opposite direction. If MSU's firewall is stateful, with the help of the cache and the connection table, IBM only needs to ask MSU the decision for one packet, which is the one that initiates the connection.

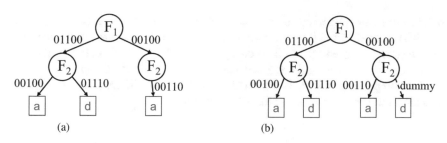

Fig. 6.13 An example of statistical analysis attack

6.8.7 Statistical Analysis Attack and Countermeasures

MSU could launch a statistical analysis attack to reduce the number of possible
rules that a packet matches. This attack works as follows. After non-overlapping
rule generation, MSU calculates the frequency for each number in the rules. The
frequency of each number is preserved in processing the policy by MSU and IBM
in the bootstrapping protocol. MSU could exploit such frequency information to
reduce the number of possible rules that an IBM packet can match. For example,
considering the numericalized FDD in Fig. 6.13a, the frequency of the number
01100 in the generated non-overlapping rules is 2, and none of the other numbers
have the same frequency. Thus, MSU can identify which rules received from IBM
correspond to the left branch of the FDD. Interestingly, MSU cannot correlate any
rule received from IBM with the right most decision path of this FDD because of
the use of dummy rules.

The statistical analysis attack is based on the assumption that the frequency of
each number remains the same before and after IBM's processing. Actually, to
prevent statistical analysis attacks, IBM can also make a statistical analysis of the
hashed rules and add some dummy rules to disturb the statistical properties of the
rules. Taking the example numericalized FDD in Fig. 6.13a, IBM can easily destroy
the frequency information of the number in the FDD by adding a dummy number to
the right F_2 node as shown in Fig. 6.13b. Basically, IBM generates dummy rules to
make all the numbers for each field have the same frequency. This will prevent MSU
from launching statistical analysis attacks. Recall that dummy rules use out-of-range
numbers and they cannot be matched by any packet.

6.8.8 Hash Collision

The chance of having hash collisions for HMAC is extremely small. However, to
be on the safe side, we propose the following solution to the problem. Our solution
is based on the observation that the bootstrapping protocol in our framework can
detect hash collisions easily. Recall that the bootstrapping protocol converts firewall

policies to non-overlapping rules. If hash collision happens, then among the rules that MSU receives from IBM, there exist at least two rules that are exactly the same. This fact can be used by MSU to easily detect whether hash collision happens. In the case that hash collision does happen, MSU and IBM can simply rerun the bootstrapping protocol, in which they will choose different secret keys and henceforth the hash collision is most likely removed.

6.9 Related Work

6.9.1 Secure Function Evaluation

Secure Function Evaluation (SFE) was first introduced by Yao with the famous "Two-Millionaire Problem" [32]. A secure function evaluation protocol enables two parties, one with input x and the other with y, to collaboratively compute a function $f(x, y)$ without disclosing one party's input to the other. The classical solutions for SFE are Yao's "garbled circuits" protocol [33] and Goldreich's protocol [23]. The method provided by Yao has a computational cost of $O(2^b)$, where b is the number of bits needed to encode x and y. Later, the Secure Function Evaluation problem was generalized to the Secure Multiparty Computation (SMC) problem. Chaum et al. proved that any multiparty protocol problem can be solved if there is an authenticated secrecy channel between every pair of participants [5]. Zero-knowledge protocols [3, 10, 22] also aims to provide the privacy between two parties. A zero knowledge protocol is an interactive method for one party (suppose IBM) to prove to another (suppose MSU) that a statement is true without revealing anything other than the veracity of the statement. Although we could use SFE or SMC solutions to solve this problem as well as the problem of checking whether a value is in a range, the $O(2^b)$ complexity makes such solutions infeasible.

Li et al. proposed Oblivious Attribute Certificates (OACerts) [20]. In OACerts, a credential holder uses his attributes in an oblivious manner to access resources if and only if the attributes in his credential satisfy the server's policy, and the server does not learn anything about the attribute values of the credential holder, no matter whether the values satisfy the policy or not. Our framework VGuard differs from Li's scheme in many ways. First, the computational cost of VGuard is much lower than that of Li's scheme because VGuard is based on efficient XOR and HMAC functions and Li's scheme is based on expensive PKI operations. Second, the communication cost of VGuard is much lower than that of Li's scheme because VGuard uses one round of message exchange for processing one packet and Li's scheme only compares one bit in each round of communication for evaluating *greater or equal* and *less or equal* functions.

6.9.2 CDCF Framework

Prior work that is closest to ours is the Cross-Domain Cooperative Firewall (CDCF) framework [7]. The CDCF framework also consists of a bootstrapping protocol and a filtering protocol. In CDCF bootstrapping protocol, for each firewall rule specified as $F_1 \in S_1 \wedge \cdots \wedge F_d \in S_d$ where each S_i is a range, MSU first converts each range S_i to a set of prefixes and then converts each prefix to a concrete number using their numericalization scheme. Second, MSU and IBM use a commutative encryption function (such as the Pohlig-Hellman Exponentiation Cipher [25] and Secure RPC Authentication (SRA) [17]) to encrypt each number generated from the prefixes with MSU's secret key K_1 and IBM's secret key K_2, respectively. A commutative encryption function satisfies the following four properties, where K_1 and K_2 are two secret keys: (a) For any x and K, given x and $(x)_K$, it is computationally infeasible to compute the value of K. (b) For any x, K_1, K_2, we have $((x)_{K_1})_{K_2} = ((x)_{K_2})_{K_1}$. (c) For any x, y, and K, if $x \neq y$, then we have $(x)_K \neq (y)_K$. (d) For any x and K, given K, $(x)_K$ can be decrypted in polynomial time. Finally, MSU stores the resulting firewall rules after commutative encryption. In the filtering protocol of CDCF, for each packet $p_1, p_2, \cdots, p_d$, IBM first computes the prefix family $PF(p_i)$ $(1 \leq i \leq d)$ and then converts each prefix in $PF(p_i)$ to a number. Second, for each number y, IBM computes $(y)_{K_2}$ using commutative encryption. Third, IBM sends d sequences of numericalized and encrypted prefixes to MSU. Upon receiving the d sequences, for each number $(y)_{K_2}$, MSU computes $((y)_{K_2})_{K_1}$. Finally, based on the properties of prefix membership verification and commutative encryption, MSU checks which rule that matches the received packet and hence finds the decision for the packet.

There are five major differences between VGuard framework and CDCF framework.

(1) The computation and communication costs of CDCF is much more expensive than those of VGuard because of the following two reasons. First, to achieve oblivious comparison, VGuard uses the Xhash protocol and CDCF uses commutative encryption functions, which are computationally expensive. Second, VGuard uses firewall decision diagrams to speed up the processing of packets, while CDCF uses the straightforward sequential search.
(2) CDCF allows MSU to discover the original firewall rule that a packet matches, which jeopardizes packet privacy. This is particularly dangerous if the matching rule is a singleton rule, which will allow MSU to immediately know the corresponding value in the matching packet. In comparison, VGuard does not allow MSU to discover the original firewall rule that a packet matches. The key operation in VGuard is that it converts the original firewall rules to non-overlapping rules, which enables IBM to shuffle the rules. Thus, MSU cannot reveal the correspondence between the original rules and the received rules from IBM. Because a firewall policy follows first-match semantics, without such a conversion, IBM cannot disturb the order among rules in CDCF.

(3) CDCF allows MSU to know the decision for each IBM's packet, while VGuard does not. Knowing both the original rules and the decision of a packet p, MSU could guess what packets that p could be.

(4) CDCF does not perform the address translation that we discussed in Sect. 6.6.1, which could render MSU's firewall policy ineffective for IBM's packets. However, the address translation procedure could be easily added to CDCF.

(5) CDCF is vulnerable to a type of attacks that we call *selective policy updating attacks*. Such attacks allow MSU to quickly discover the field values in a packet in the following manner. When MSU receives a double encrypted packet p, assuming p matches the prefix rule $F_1 \in S_1 \wedge \cdots \wedge F_d \in S_d \to \langle decision \rangle$, MSU splits each prefix S_i into two prefixes by instantiating the first $*$ by 0 and 1 respectively, and therefore converts the rule to a maximum of 2^d rules. For example, suppose a packet p from IBM matches the prefix rule $F_1 \in 10 *$ $* \wedge F_2 \in 001* \to a$. Then, MSU splits the rule into the following four rules: $F_1 \in 100*\wedge F_2 \in 0010 \to a$, $F_1 \in 101*\wedge F_2 \in 0010 \to a$, $F_1 \in 100*\wedge F_2 \in$ $0011 \to a$, $F_1 \in 101 * \wedge F_2 \in 0011 \to a$. Then, MSU requests to rerun the CDCF protocol due to firewall update. In the new run of CDCF, MSU replaces the above rule by the rules after splitting. (Note that d is typically 4 or 5.) After MSU receives the double encrypted rules from IBM in the new run, MSU compares p with the split rules again. One of the split rules must match p. The above process repeats with a maximum of 32 times before p matches a singleton rule at the end. To counter the selective policy updating attacks, CDCF can be fixed by updating the secret keys on both MSU and IBM sides in each run of the CDCF protocol.

(6) CDCF does not support deep packet inspection while VGuard supports it.

6.9.3   Secure Queries

Secure queries in outsourced database systems have been studied in prior work (e.g., [1, 16, 18]). These work aims to design a scheme for querying encrypted data in the outsourced database system where sensitive data are outsourced to an untrusted server. Later, researchers extended these work to securely process range queries in two-tiered sensor networks [6, 28, 29, 34], where storage nodes gather data from nearby sensors and answer queries from the sink. They proposed different schemes for preventing compromised storage nodes from gaining information from the sensitive data and forging query results to the sink. These schemes cannot be directly applied to the problem in this chapter for two reasons. First, both outsourced database systems and two-tiered sensor networks only deal with one untrusted party, i.e., untrusted servers or untrusted storage nodes, while in this chapter two parties MSU and IBM don't trust each other. Second, firewall policies are different from the data stored in database or collected by sensors in terms of both structure and semantics.

Some prior work (e.g., [13, 30]) has investigated keyword searching on encrypted data, where a keyword is a word of a natural language and data are text.

6.10 Experimental Results

In this section, we evaluate the performance of our schemes on both real-life and synthetic firewall policies. In particular, we implemented our schemes without and with adding dummy rules. For ease presentation, we use *VGuard* and *VGuard+* to denote our schemes without and with adding dummy rules, respectively. Then, we compared VGuard, VGuard+, and CDCF, side by side. We implemented VGuard, VGuard+, and CDCF using Java 1.6.3. Our experiments were carried out on a desktop PC running Windows XP SP2 with 3G memory and dual 3.4 GHz Intel Pentium processors. On real-life firewall policies, for processing packets, our experimental results show that VGuard is 552 times faster than CDCF on MSU side and 5035 times faster than CDCF on IBM side; VGuard+ is 544 times faster than CDCF on MSU side and 5021 times faster than CDCF on IBM side. On synthetic firewall policies, for processing packets, our experimental results show that VGuard is 252 times faster than CDCF on MSU side and 5529 times faster than CDCF on IBM side; VGuard+ is 248 times faster than CDCF on MSU side and 5513 times faster than CDCF on IBM side.

6.10.1 Efficiency on Real-Life Firewall Policies

We conducted experiments on 16 real-life firewall policies that we collected from a variety of sources. Each firewall examines five packet fields of source IP, destination IP, source port, destination port, and protocol type. The number of rules ranges from dozens to hundreds. We measured the computational cost of the two parties MSU and IBM for both bootstrapping and filtering protocols. We also measured the communication overhead for both bootstrapping and filtering protocols. For fair comparison, in implementing CDCF, we used the same parameters as in [7], i.e., we used the Pohlig-Hellman algorithm [25] with a 1024-bit prime modulus and 160-bit encryption keys. In implementing VGuard and VGuard+, we chose the HMAC-MD5 hash function with 128-bit keys.

Figure 6.14 shows the communication overhead in the bootstrapping protocol for VGuard, VGuard+, and CDCF. We observe that the communication overhead in the bootstrapping protocol of VGuard is similar as that of CDCF for all firewalls. We have two explanations. First, CDCF needs to convert the range to prefix numbers for every field in the firewall rules. Recall that the minimum number of prefixes for representing an integer $[a, b]$, where a and b are two numbers of w bits, is at most $2w - 2$. For example, the minimum number of prefixes for representing the range of IP address that has 32 bits is at most 62. Thus, the number of prefix rules converted

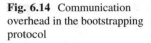

Fig. 6.14 Communication overhead in the bootstrapping protocol

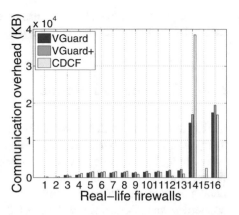

from a firewall rule can be at most $62 \times 62 \times 30 \times 30 \times 14 = 48,434,400$. Second, every prefix number will be encrypted to be 1024 bits in CDCF instead of 128 bits in VGuard. Therefore, even though the ratio between the number of non-overlapping firewall rules and the number of original firewall rules is large (i.e., in the 16 real-life firewall policies, the average ratio between the number of non-overlapping firewall rules and the number of original firewall rules is 887), the communication overhead in the bootstrapping protocol of VGuard is still similar as that of CDCF. We also observe that on average, the communication overhead in the bootstrapping protocol of VGuard+ is 15% higher than that of VGuard because of adding dummy rules. In the filtering protocol, the only difference between CDCF and VGuard is that the encryption method is different. CDCF applies double encryption to every prefix number, and VGuard applies Xhash to every prefix number. Therefore, in the filtering protocol, the overhead of CDCF is 1024/128=8 times higher than that of VGuard. Similarly, in the filtering protocol, the overhead of CDCF is 8 times higher than that of VGuard+.

Figure 6.15a and b show the computational cost of MSU and IBM respectively in the bootstrapping protocol for VGuard, VGuard+, and CDCF. We observe that the bootstrapping costs of VGuard and VGuard+ are lower than that of CDCF for most firewalls. Although the Xhash scheme is three orders of magnitude faster than the commutative encryption scheme, the bootstrapping costs of VGuard and VGuard+ are not three orders of magnitude lower than CDCF because VGuard and VGuard+ convert the given firewall policy to non-overlapping prefix rules, which result in a significant expansion. Note that the bootstrapping protocol only needs to run once between MSU and IBM unless MSU updates its firewall policy. The performance of the bootstrapping protocol is less critical than that of the filtering protocol.

Figure 6.16a and b show the computational cost of MSU and IBM respectively in the filtering protocol for VGuard, VGuard+, and CDCF. Note that the vertical axis of these two figures are in a logarithmic scale. We observe that the filtering costs of VGuard and VGuard+ are significantly lower than that of CDCF. On average, VGuard is 552 times faster than CDCF on MSU side and 5035 times faster than CDCF on IBM side; VGuard+ is 544 times faster than CDCF on MSU side and

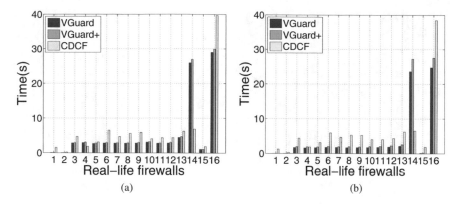

Fig. 6.15 The bootstrapping time on real-life firewalls. (**a**) MSU. (**b**) IBM

5021 times faster than CDCF on IBM side. Note that the packet processing time for CDCF on both MSU and IBM side in these two figures seems constant, instead of increasing as the number of rules increases. This is because in processing each packet on both MSU and IBM side, for CDCF, the encryption time, which is roughly constant for each packet, is about 20 times more than the time for performing a linear search in the firewall.

6.10.2 Efficiency on Synthetic Firewall Policies

Firewall policies are considered confidential due to security concerns. It is difficult to get a large number of real-life firewall policies to experiment with. To further evaluate the performance of VGuard and VGuard+ in comparison with CDCF, we generated a large number of synthetic firewall policies and conducted experiments on them. Every predicate of a rule in our synthetic firewall has five fields: source IP address, destination IP address, source port number, destination port number, and protocol type. We first randomly generated a list of values for each field. For IP addresses, we generated a random class C address then generated single IP addresses within the class C addresses; for ports we generated a random range; for protocols, we choose either TCP, UDP, or ICMP. Every field also has the "*" value included in the list. We then generated a list of predicates by taking the cross product of these five lists and randomly selected from the cross product until we reached our desired classifier size by including a final default predicate. Finally, we randomly assigned one of two decisions, accept or discard, to each predicate to make a complete rule. We generated firewall policies with the number of rules ranging from 100 to 1000, where for each number we generated ten synthetic firewall policies.

Figure 6.17a and b show the computational cost of MSU and IBM in the bootstrapping protocol for VGuard, VGuard+, and CDCF. Figure 6.18a and b show the computational cost of MSU and IBM respectively in the filtering protocol for

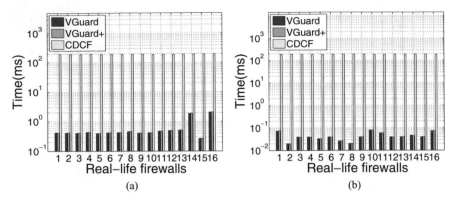

Fig. 6.16 The filtering time on real-life firewalls. (**a**) MSU. (**b**) IBM

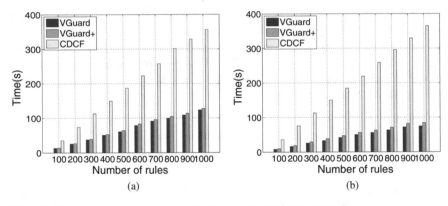

Fig. 6.17 The bootstrapping time on synthetic firewalls. (**a**) MSU. (**b**) IBM

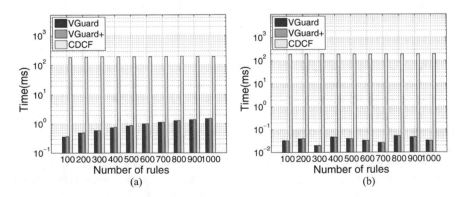

Fig. 6.18 The filtering time on synthetic firewalls. (**a**) MSU. (**b**) IBM

VGuard, VGuard+, and CDCF. On average, for these synthetic firewall policies, VGuard is 252 times faster than CDCF on the MSU side and 5529 times faster than CDCF on the IBM side; VGuard+ is 248 times faster than CDCF on MSU side and 5513 times faster than CDCF on IBM side.

6.11 Concluding Remarks

In this chapter, we propose VGuard, a privacy preserving framework for collaborative enforcement of firewall policies. In terms of security, compared with the state-of-the-art CDCF scheme, VGuard is more secure because of two major reasons. First, VGuard converts a firewall policy of an ordered list of overlapping rules to an equivalent non-ordered set of non-overlapping rules, which enables rule shuffling and consequently MSU cannot identify which original rule matches the given packet. Second, VGuard obfuscates rule decisions, which prevents MSU from knowing the decision for the given packet. In terms of efficiency, compared with the state-of-the-art CDCF scheme, VGuard is hundreds of times faster than CDCF in processing packets because of two reasons. First, VGuard uses a new oblivious comparison scheme proposed in this chapter, which is three orders of magnitude faster than the commutative encryption scheme used in CDCF. Second, VGuard uses firewall decision diagrams for processing packets, which is much faster than the linear search used in CDCF. We want to emphasize that the VGuard framework can be applied to other types of security policies as well. It is also worth noting that the Xhash scheme can be used for other applications that require oblivious comparison.

References

1. R. Agrawal, J. Kiernan, R. Srikant, Y. Xu, Order preserving encryption for numeric data, in *Proc. ACM Int. Conf. on Management of Data (SIGMOD)* (2004), pp. 563–574
2. A.V. Aho, M.J. Corasick, Efficient string matching: an aid to bibliographic search. Commun. ACM **18**(6), 333–340 (1975)
3. F. Boudot, Efficient proofs that a committed number lies in an interval, in *Proc. Advances in Cryptology (EUROCRYPT)*. Lecture Notes in Computer Science, vol. 1807, May 2000
4. Y.-K. Chang, Fast binary and multiway prefix searches for packet forwarding. Comput. Netw. **51**(3), 588–605 (2007)
5. D. Chaum, C. Crepeau, I. Damgard, Multiparty unconditionally secure protocols, in *Proc. ACM Symposium on Theory of Computing* (1988), pp. 11–19
6. F. Chen, A.X. Liu, SafeQ: secure and efficient query processing in sensor networks, in *Proc. IEEE Int. Conf. on Computer Communications (INFOCOM)* (2010)
7. J. Cheng, H. Yang, S.H.Y. Wong, S. Lu, Design and implementation of cross-domain cooperative firewall, in *Proc. IEEE Int. Conf. on Network Protocols (ICNP)* (2007)
8. Cisco ios ips deployment guide, www.cisco.com
9. B. Commentz-Walter, A string matching algorithm fast on the average, in *Proc. Colloquium, on Automata, Languages and Programming* (1979), pp. 118–132

10. R. Cramer, M.K. Franklin, B. Schoenmarks, M. Yung, Multi-authority secret-ballot elections with linear work, in *Proc. Advances in Cryptology (EUROCRYPT)*. Lecture Notes in computer Science, vol. 1070 (1996)
11. D. Eastlake, P. Jones, Us secure hash algorithm 1 (SHA1). RFC 3174, 2001
12. L. Fan, P. Cao, J. Almeida, A. Broder, Summary cache: a scalable wide-area web cache sharing protocol, in *Proc. ACM SIGCOMM*, Sept 1998
13. P. Golle, J. Staddon, B. Waters, Secure conjunctive keyword search over encrypted data, in *Proc. Int. Conf. on Applied Cryptography and Network Security (ACNS)* (2004), pp. 31–45
14. M.G. Gouda, A.X. Liu, Structured firewall design. Comput. Netw. J. **51**(4), 1106–1120 (2007)
15. P. Gupta, N. McKeown, Algorithms for packet classification. IEEE Netw. **15**(2), 24–32 (2001)
16. H. Hacigümüş, B. Iyer, C. Li, S. Mehrotra, Executing SQL over encrypted data in the database-service-provider model, in *Proc. ACM Int. Conf. on Management of Data (SIGMOD)* (2002), pp. 216–227
17. D.K. Hess, D.R. Safford, D.L. Schales, Secure RPC authentication (SRA) for TELNET and FTP. Technical report, 1993
18. B. Hore, S. Mehrotra, G. Tsudik, A privacy-preserving index for range queries, in *Proc. Int. Conf. on Very Large Data (VLDB)* (2004), pp. 720–731
19. H. Krawczyk, M. Bellare, R. Canetti, HMAC: Keyed-hashing for message authentication. RFC 2104, 1997
20. J. Li, N. Li, OACerts: oblivious attribute certificates, in *Proc. Conf. on Applied Cryptography and Network Security (ACNS)*, June 2005, pp. 301–317
21. A.X. Liu, M.G. Gouda, Diverse firewall design, in *Proc. Int. Conf. on Dependable Systems and Networks (DSN)*, June 2004, pp. 595–604
22. W. Mao, Guaranteed correct sharing of integer factorization with off-line shareholders, in *Proc. Public Key Cryptography (PKC)*. Lecture Notes in Computer Science, vol. 1431, Feb 1998
23. S. Micali, O. Goldreich, A. Wigderson, How to play any mental game, in *Proc. ACM Conf. on Theory of Computing* (1987)
24. V. Paxson, Bro: a system for detecting network intruders in real-time. Comput. Netw. **31**(23–24), 2435–2463 (1999)
25. S.C. Pohlig, M.E. Hellman, An improved algorithm for computing logarithms over GF(p) and its cryptographic significance. IEEE Trans. Inf. Syst. Secur. **24**, 106–110 (1978)
26. R. Rivest, The MD5 message-digest algorithm. RFC 1321 (1992)
27. M. Roesch, Snort: lightweight intrusion detection for networks, in *Proc. Systems Administration Conference (LISA), USENIX Association* (1999), pp. 229–238
28. B. Sheng, Q. Li, Verifiable privacy-preserving range query in two-tiered sensor networks, in *Proc. IEEE Int. Conf. on Computer Communications (INFOCOM)* (2008), pp. 46–50
29. J. Shi, R. Zhang, Y. Zhang, Secure range queries in tiered sensor networks, in *Proc. IEEE Int. Conf. on Computer Communications (INFOCOM)* (2009)
30. D.X. Song, D. Wagner, A. Perrig, Practical techniques for searches on encrypted data, in *Proc. IEEE Symposium on Security and Privacy* (2000)
31. Tippingpoint x505, www.tippingpoint.comproducts_ips.html
32. A.C. Yao, Protocols for secure computations, in *Proc. IEEE Symposium on the Foundations of Computer Science (FOCS)* (1982), pp. 160–164
33. A.C. Yao, How to generate and exchange secrets, in *Proc. IEEE Symposium on Foundations of Computer Science (FOCS)* (1986), pp. 162–167
34. R. Zhang, J. Shi, Y. Zhang, Secure multidimensional range queries in sensor networks, in *Proc. ACM Int. Symposium on Mobile Ad Hoc Networking and Computing (MobiHoc)* (2009)

Chapter 7
Privacy Preserving Quantification of Cross-Domain Network Reachability

7.1 Introduction

7.1.1 Background and Motivation

Network reachability for a given network path from the source subnet to the destination subnet is defined as the set of packets that are allowed by all network devices on the path. Network reachability quantification is important for understanding end-to-end network behavior and detecting the violation of security policies. Several critical concerns like router misconfiguration, policy violations and service availability can be verified through an accurate quantification. Quantifying network reachability is a difficult and challenging problem for two reasons. First, various complex mechanisms, such as Access Control Lists (ACLs), dynamic routing, and network address translation (NAT), have been deployed on network devices for restricting network reachability. To perform an accurate analysis, administrators need to collect all the reachability restriction information from these network devices. However, collecting such information is very difficult due to the privacy and security concerns. Second, the explosion of the Internet has caused an increase in the complexity and sophistication of these devices, thus, making reachability analysis computationally expensive and error-prone.

The current practice of reachability management is still "trial and error" due to the lack of network reachability analysis and quantification tools. This approach leads to significant number of configuration errors and has been shown to be the major cause of failure for Internet services [28]. Industry research also shows that a significant percentage of human effort and monetary resources are employed in maintaining the operational status of the network. Reports place the revenue losses per hour for media, banking and brokerage industry to 1.2, 2.6 and 4.5 million dollars, respectively [19]. Several critical business applications and sensitive communications are severely affected due to network outages caused by

© The Editor(s) (if applicable) and The Author(s), under exclusive license to
Springer Nature Switzerland AG 2021
A. X. Liu, R. Li, *Algorithms for Data and Computation Privacy*,
https://doi.org/10.1007/978-3-030-58896-0_7

misconfiguration errors. These events place a tremendous amount of pressure on network operators to debug the problems quickly. Thus, systematic analysis, and, tools for quantification of network reachability are needed for understanding end-to-end network behavior and detecting configuration errors.

7.1.2 Limitation of Prior Art

The current practice of determining network reachability through probing has two major drawbacks. First, probing is expensive because it needs to generate and send a significant amount of probe packets. Second, probing is inaccurate, e.g., it cannot probe the open ports with no server listening on them. Due to these drawbacks, many approaches were proposed to address the reachability problem [2, 18, 26, 27, 33, 35, 36]. The main assumption in all these approaches is that the reachability restriction information of each network device and configuration state are known to a central network analyst, who is quantifying the network reachability. However, in practice, it is common that the network devices along a given path belong to different domains where the reachability restriction information cannot be shared with others including the network analyst. Figure 7.1 shows a typical scenario of network reachability, where User$_1$ wants to know what packets he can send to User$_2$ through the given path. The network devices deployed along this path belong to three different parties, i.e., S_1 and FW_1 belong to Subnet$_1$, FW_2, FW_3, and R_1 belong to ISP, FW_4 and S_2 belong to Subnet$_2$.

Keeping the reachability restriction information private is important for two reasons. First, such information is often mis-configured and has security holes that can be exploited by attackers if it is disclosed. In reality, most firewall policies have security holes [34]. Disclosing ACLs allows attackers to analyze and utilize the vulnerabilities of subnets along a given path. For example, if ACLs along a path from Subnet$_1$ to Subnet$_2$ do not block some worm traffic, attackers can break into Subnet$_2$ from Subnet$_1$. In practice, neither ISPs nor private networks disclose their ACLs. Second, the reachability restriction information of a network device contains private information, e.g., the ACLs of a network device contain the IP

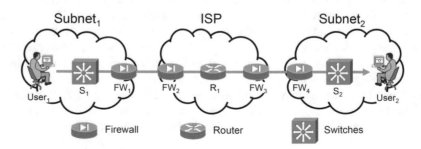

Fig. 7.1 An example of end-to-end network reachability

addresses of servers, which can be used by attacker to launch more targeted attacks. In practice, even within an organization, often no employees other than the firewall administrators are allowed to access their firewall policies. Hence, safe-guarding the privacy of network devices is a critical requirement in network reachability quantification.

7.1.3 Cross-Domain Quantification of Reachability

To our best knowledge, no prior work has addressed the problem of privacy-preserving network reachability quantification. We propose the first privacy-preserving protocol for quantifying network reachability for a given network path across multiple domains. First, for the network devices belonging to each party, we convert the reachability restriction information of these devices to an access control list (ACL) by leveraging an existing network reachability quantification tool [26]. This tool takes as input the reachability restriction information, including ACLs, all possible network transforms (e.g., NAT and PAT), and protocol states (e.g., connection-oriented and state-less), and outputs an ACL. Note that ACLs are actually the most important security components for network devices, such as network routers, firewalls, and layer 3 switches, to filter the network traffic. The network devices in each party may include multiple ACLs and also other reachability restriction information. Considering the example in Fig. 7.1, Fig. 7.2 shows the three resulting ACLs, A_1, A_2, and A_3, for Subnet$_1$, ISP, and Subnet$_2$, respectively. For ease of presentation, in the rest of this chapter, we use "ACL" to denote the resulting ACL converted from multiple ACLs as well as other reachability restriction information in one party. Second, we calculate the set of packets that are accepted by all the resulting ACLs on a given network path in a privacy-preserving manner. Typically, an ACL consists of multiple rules and each rule has several fields, such as source and destination IP addresses e.g., with an accept or discard decision. Given this, the network reachability quantification requires the comparison of the rules of adjacent ACLs. However, a direct comparison of the ACL rules is complex and error-prone as there may be several overlapping rules which require further analysis. For example, a single rule in one ACL may overlap with multiple rules in another ACL. Determining the exact nature of the overlap is important for accurate quantification of network reachability.

Our proposed cross-domain quantification approach of network reachability can be very useful for many applications. We illustrate this using two example scenarios. First, a global view of the network reachability can help Internet service providers (ISPs) to define better QoS policies to improve traffic management. For example, the knowledge of the different paths through which a particular type of traffic is allowed by the ACLs can help the ISPs to maintain a rated list of the best-quality paths in case of path failures. Second, since network reachability is crucial for many companies that provide their services over the Internet, performing a privacy-

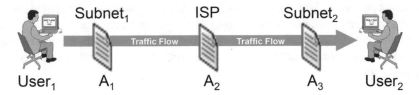

Fig. 7.2 Three resulting ACLs converted from Fig. 7.1

preserving computation of the network reachability could become a new business for the ISPs and other parties that involve in this computation. The ISPs can answer the reachability queries of these companies using this global knowledge and even provide some information regarding the quality of various paths.

Note that ACLs (also called stateless firewalls), stateful firewalls, and Intrusion Prevention Systems (IPSes) are three different mechanisms for packet filtering. ACLs are stateless by definition as they make the decision for accepting or discarding a packet based on the packet itself and do not consider the packets that they see in the past. They mainly check the well known five tuple of the packet header: source IP address, destination IP address, source port number, destination port number, and protocol type and make a decision regarding the packet. Stateful firewalls make the decision for accepting or discarding a packet based on both the current packet and the packets that they have seen in the past. They consider previous packets by checking whether the connection has been established and allow only those packets which have a matching connection in the past. Intrusion Prevention Systems (IPSes) make decision on accepting or discarding packets based on packet payload. They check packet payload mainly by performing regular expression matching where the regular expressions correspond to malicious packet signatures. The scope of this chapter is on network reachability based on packet headers. Thus, the technical discussion of this chapter is primarily based on ACLs. We will also discuss how to adapt our solutions to deal with stateful firewalls in Sect. 7.6.

7.1.4 Technical Challenges

There are four key challenges in the privacy preserving quantification of network reachability. (1) It is computationally expensive. An ACL may consist of many rules, and each rule consists of multiple fields. Therefore, comparing multiple ACLs with a large number of rules can be quite expensive, even if only a few ACLs are involved in the process. Furthermore, the complexity of comparison can be expensive due to overlapping rules resulting in many comparisons. (2) Protecting the privacy of the ACL rules is crucial. Since a rule has to be sent to other parties to enable comparison, it is necessary to propose a protocol that will not reveal the rule but still allows the different ACLs to calculate the intersection. (3) Communication cost is high as even calculating the intersection of a small number of ACLs is a tedious process and requires a number of messages to be exchanged among different parties. (4) Computing the reachability information when ACLs are updated is an important performance related issue. It is necessary to explore optimization approaches in such scenarios without sacrificing the privacy of individual ACLs.

7.1.5 Our Approach

We propose the first cross-domain privacy-preserving protocol for quantifying network reachability. We note that, the domains could be connected through multiple ISPs or they could be independently administered domains within the same ISP. We consider n ACLs, $A_1, \cdots, A_n$, $n \geq 2$, in a given network path where each ACL belongs to a distinct party. Our protocol consists of three phases: ACL preprocessing, ACL encoding and encryption, and ACL comparison.

In the first phase, we transform all the ACLs into an equivalent representation, Firewall Decision Diagram (FDD) [15, 16], and then extract the non-overlapping rules with accept decisions. In the second phase, to perform privacy preserving comparison, we reduce the problem to that of computing privacy-preserving intersection of two numerical ranges. Accordingly, we first transform the rules, which are represented as ranges, into a sequence of prefix numbers and then encrypt these numbers with secret keys of different parties. This phase enables different parties to compute the intersection of non-overlapping rules in their ACLs without revealing these rules.

In the third phase, the destination ACL computes the intersection of its non-overlapping rules with the rules from its adjacent ACL, and then the adjacent ACL further repeats this computation with its adjacent ACL until the source ACL is reached. Finally, all the ACLs collaboratively decrypt the encrypted intersection of the non-overlapping rules, but only the first party (with the source ACL) obtains the result.

To reduce the computation and communication cost, we use the divide-and-conquer strategy to divide the problem of computing reachability of n ACLs to the problem of computing reachability of three ACLs. The initial intersection is performed among the rules of three adjacent ACLs that are located in a sequence along the network path. Subsequent comparisons are grouped in a similar manner, i.e., the intersection of three ACLs can be treated as a new ACL and the process is repeated among three new ACLs. This optimization technique reduces the number of ACL encryptions and the number of messages in our protocol from $O(n^2)$ to $O(n)$.

To handle the issue of changes to ACL rules, we analyze various plausible scenarios and use the approach from [8] to localize the reachability computation. We show that our approach is effective in reducing reachability computation across the entire network in the event of such ACL updates.

7.1.6   Summary of Experimental Results

We performed extensive experiments over real and synthetic ACLs. Our experimental results show that the core operation of our protocol is efficient and suitable for real applications. The on-line processing time of an ACL with thousands of rules is less than 25 s and the comparison time of two ACLs is less than 5 s. The communication cost between two ACLs with thousands of rules is less than 2100 KB.

7.1.7   Key Contributions

The following are our key contributions. (1) We propose the first cross-domain privacy-preserving protocol to quantify network reachability across multiple domains. Our protocol can accurately compute the intersection of the rules among the ACLs along a given network path without the need to share these rules across those domains. This is the first step towards privacy-preserving quantification of network reachability and it can be extended to other network metric measurements that are sensitive in nature. Furthermore, we propose an optimization technique to reduce computation and communication cost of our protocol. It reduces the number of ACL encryptions and the number of messages from $O(n^2)$ to $O(n)$. (2) We describe an approach to handle ACL updates in an effective manner. (3) We conducted extensive experiments on both real and synthetic ACLs and the results show that our protocol is efficient and suitable for real applications.

7.2   Related Work

7.2.1   Network Reachability

Several existing approaches [2, 18, 26, 27, 33, 35, 36] have studied the problem of quantifying network reachability. The key challenges in network reachability include, misconfiguration of ACLs, changes of routing policies, and link failures, which could prevent accessibility to essential network services. To estimate reachability, existing approaches analyze ACLs while considering other critical parameters like dynamic routing policies, packet transforms, and variations in protocol operations. To estimate the bounds on reachability, Xie et al. [35] defined union and intersection operations over ACLs while taking into account the routing decisions, packet transforms, and link failures. This approach, however, over approximates and does not yield exact bounds. Ingols et al. [18] used Binary Decision Diagrams (BDDs) to reduce the complexity of handling ACLs and to estimate reachability more accurately. Matousek et al. [27] described a formal model using Interval Decision Diagrams (IDDs) to analyze network reachability under all possible network failure conditions. However, the approach is not scalable as it performs an exhaustive evaluation of failure scenarios that may or may not occur. Al-Shaer et al. [2] proposed a more accurate model using BDDs. They applied symbolic model checking techniques on properties specified in computation tree logic (CTL) [11], to verify reachability across the network for any given packet. Sung et al. [33] studied the effect of reachability constraints on class-of-service flows, where the packets are subjected to an additional constraint based on their class-of-service. Liu et al. [26] used Firewall Decision Diagrams (FDDs) to quantify reachability while considering all possible network transforms like NAT, PAT as well as protocol states like connection-oriented, state-less and so on.

While most solutions operate on static configurations, some work has been proposed for estimating reachability in an on-line manner. Bandhakavi et al. [3] analyzed the network reachability using a simulated routing environment, i.e., they constructed a routing graph which represents the possible paths that could be taken by routing advertisements under the current router configurations. Analysis of this graph helps to identify violations in security policies and in verifying reachability. Zhang et al. [36] described a real-time monitoring and verification system for network reachability. A monitoring software runs on all the routers and collects up-to-date ACL and forwarding state information, which enables the network administrator to determine instantaneous reachability between any source destination pair.

Several other works have been proposed to reduce the complexity of managing networks and to verify network configurations. Casado et al. [5] described a novel architecture for enterprise, Secure Architecture for the Networked Enterprise (SANE), which comprises of a centralized authentication server that allows authorized users to access services. In SANE, the ACLs can be specified in a natural way so as to capture the semantics clearly. Le et al. [21] used data mining techniques to analyze security policies and to detect possible mis-configurations in the policies. They considered the notion of association rule mining to extract usable safe configurations of routers and detect anomalies in other routers using the extracted patterns. Benson et al. [4] described complexity metrics to evaluate relative complexity among alternate network designs. The metrics allow network operators to compare configurations with standard configurations and identify errors.

All these approaches are based on the same assumption, that, there is a central network analyst who has the complete knowledge of the network configuration and other critical information. However, in reality, this assumption is not true for a network where network devices belong to different independent domains and whose network configuration cannot be shared with other domains due to privacy concerns. Therefore, these approaches cannot quantify network reachability across a network spanning different domains.

7.2.2   Privacy Preserving Set Operation

The other work partly related to our work is on privacy preserving set operations. These solutions enable n parties, where each party has a private set S_i, to collaboratively compute the intersection of all sets, $S_1 \cap \cdots \cap S_n$, without disclosing more information of one party's private set beyond the intersection to other parties [12, 20, 31]. Although it is possible to explore the application of these solutions to solve the problem of privacy preserving network reachability, the communication cost of these solutions is prohibitive due to the messages exchanged during the privacy preserving set operations. In privacy preserving set operations, after the computation, every party needs to know the final result, i.e., $s_1 \cap \cdots \cap s_n$, while in privacy preserving network reachability, only the first party needs to know the result. This requirement significantly alters the communication cost of the resulting protocol. Under the semi-honest model [14], the state-of-the-art solution for privacy preserving set operations [20] can achieve $O(ndw^2m^d)$ for n parties, each party with an ACL of m rules over d w-bit domains, while our solution can achieve $\min(O(ndwm^d), O(n2^w))$, which is far more efficient when w is large. Such complexity analysis will be discussed in Sect. 7.7.2.

7.2.3   Privacy Preserving Collaborative Firewall Enforcement in VPN

Previous work on collaborative firewall enforcement in virtual private networks (VPN) [9, 22, 23] differs from our work from three perspectives. First and most importantly, the problems being addressed are different. Such work focuses on enforcing firewall policies over encrypted VPN tunnels without leaking the privacy of the remote network's firewall policy, whereas our work focuses on privacy-preserving calculation of the intersection of multiple ACLs, which is a new problem. Second, the privacy requirements are different. Such work preserves only the privacy of the remote network's policy, whereas our work preserves the privacy of all parties that are involved in the quantification of network reachability. Last but not least, previous approaches do not require decryption or decoding because their comparison result is whether a packet matches a rule, whereas our work requires decryption of network reachability that is represented by a set of ACLs.

7.3 Problem Statement and Threat Model

7.3.1 Access Control Lists (ACLs)

We consider quantifying network reachability using the ACLs of different domains which are converted to enable this computation. Each ACL A is an ordered list of *rules* and each rule is composed of a *predicate* over d *fields*, $F_1, \cdots, F_d$ and a *decision* for the packets that match the predicate. Typically, an ACL checks five fields, source IP (32 bits), destination IP (32 bits), source port (16 bits), destination port (16 bits), and protocol type (8 bits). A packet over the d fields $F_1, \cdots, F_d$ is a d-tuple $(p_1, \cdots, p_d)$ where each p_i is an element of the domain of field F_i, denoted as $D(F_i)$. A $\langle predicate \rangle$ specifies a set of packets over the d fields, $F_1 \in S_1 \wedge \cdots \wedge F_d \in S_d$, where each $S_i \subseteq D(F_i)$ and is specified as either a prefix or a range. A packet $(p_1, \cdots, p_d)$ *matches* a rule $F_1 \in S_1 \wedge \cdots \wedge F_d \in S_d \rightarrow \langle decision \rangle$ if and only if the condition $p_1 \in S_1 \wedge \cdots \wedge p_d \in S_d$ holds. Typical decisions include: accept, discard, accept with logging, and discard with logging. Without loss of generality, we only consider *accepting rules*, i.e., rules with accept decisions, and *discarding rules*, i.e., rules with discard decisions. Two rules in an ACL may conflict, i.e., they have different decisions and there is at least one packet that matches both rules. To resolve these conflicts, ACLs usually employ a first-match semantics, i.e., the decision of the first-matching rule is enforced on the packet. The matching set of r_i, $M(r_i)$, is the set of all possible packets that match the rule r_i [24]. Table 7.1 shows an example ACL, the format of which is based upon the format of Cisco Access Control Lists.

7.3.2 Problem Statement

We focus on quantifying the end-to-end network reachability for a given network path with multiple network devices belonging to different parties. The network devices are connected with physical interfaces for filtering outgoing packets and incoming packets. A network path is a unidirectional path for transferring packets from the source to the destination. Along the given network path, there are multiple ACLs for filtering these packets. There may be multiple ACLs that are enforced by the same domain. To convert them to a single ACL for one party, we first employ the existing network reachability approach, Quarnet [26], and generate reachability

Table 7.1 An example ACL

Rule	Src. IP	Dest. IP	Src. Port	Dest. Port	Prot.	Action
r_1	123.24.*.*	242.168.0.1	*	80	TCP	Accept
r_2	219.27.*.*	242.168.0.2	*	25	TCP	Discard
r_3	*	*	*	*	*	Discard

matrices. Second, we use the query language of Quarnet to obtain a set of packets that can pass through the given path within the party. Finally, we convert the set of packets to a single ACL. Without loss of generality, in the rest of this chapter, we use the term "ACL" to denote the resulting ACL converted from multiple ACLs in one party. Given an ACL A, let $M(A)$ denote the set packets that are accepted by A. Given a network path with n ACLs $A_1, A_2, \ldots, A_n$ for transferring packets from A_1 to A_n, where A_i belongs to the party P_i $(1 \leq i \leq n)$, quantifying the network reachability is computing the intersection among $M(A_1), \cdots, M(A_n)$, i.e., $M(A_1) \cap M(A_2) \cdots \cap M(A_n)$.

In our context, we aim to design a privacy preserving protocol which enables the first party P_1 to compute the intersection of n ACLs , $n \geq 2$, $M(A_1) \cap M(A_2) \cdots \cap M(A_n)$ without revealing rules in an ACL A_i $(1 \leq i \leq n)$ to any other party P_j $(j \neq i)$. We make the following assumptions. (1) The destination of the network path cannot be an intermediate network device. In other words, the destination ACL A_n should filter the packets to end users but not to another network device. (2) All parties follow the privacy-preserving protocol for quantifying the network reachability.

Note that if one party does not want to involve or only wants to provide part of its ACL rules, the party P_1 can still run the protocol to compute network reachability among the remaining ACLs. This requirement is very important especially for the party who really cares about the security of its private network, e.g., a bank who will not share with other parties the information about which packets are allowed to enter into its private network.

7.3.3   Threat Model

We consider the semi-honest model, where each party follows our protocol correctly but it may try to learn the ACL rules of other parties [7, 14]. For example, the party P_1 may use the intermediate results to reveal the ACL rules of other parties. The semi-honest model is realistic in our context because a malicious party cannot gain benefits by providing a forged ACL or not following our protocol. For instance, in [7], the benefit of launching active collusion attacks is almost negligible, and even damaging to the individual parties. A similar scenario is present in our protocol, where launching such attacks neutralizes the benefits of computing network reachability, especially if the other ACL might undergo changes in a short period of time.

7.4 Privacy-Preserving Quantification of Network Reachability

To compute the network reachability from A_1 to A_n, our privacy-preserving protocol consists of three phases, *ACL preprocessing*, *ACL encoding and encryption*, and *ACL comparison*. In the first phase, ACL preprocessing, each party converts its ACL to a sequence of accepting rules. The union of the matching sets of these accepting rules is equal to the set of packets that are accepted by the ACL. In the second phase, ACL encoding and encryption, each party encodes and encrypts each field of its accepting rules for preserving the privacy of its ACL. In the third phase, ACL comparison, all parties compare their ACLs and finally the party P_1 finds out the set of packets that are accepted by all ACLs. Particularly, P_{n-1} compares the encoded and encrypted accepting rules from A_{n-1} with those from A_n, and finds out the multiple accepting rules whose union is equal to the intersection of $M(A_n)$ and $M(A_{n-1})$. Then, P_{n-2} compares the accepting rules from ACL A_{n-2} with the resulting accepting rules in the first step, and finds out the multiple accepting rules whose union is equal to $M(A_n) \cap M(A_{n-1}) \cap M(A_{n-2})$. This step is repeated until P_1 finds out the multiple accepting rules whose union is equal to $M(A_1) \cap \cdots \cap M(A_n)$. Note that, the resulting accepting rules of each step are in an encrypted format which prevents any party from revealing these rules by itself. To reveal the final accepting rules, P_1 requires all other parties to decrypt these rules with their private keys and then, P_1 decrypts these rules.

We assume that each S_i in an ACL rule $S_1 \wedge \cdots S_i \wedge \cdots \wedge S_n$, is represented in the range format. Therefore, the basic problem of privacy-preserving network reachability is to compute the intersection among the multiple ranges of the ACL rules belonging to different parties in a privacy preserving manner. This problem boils down to the problem of computing intersection of two ranges $[a, b]$ and $[a', b']$, denoted as $[a, b] \cap [a', b']$. Thus, we first describe the privacy-preserving protocol for computing $[a, b] \cap [a', b']$, and then describe the three phases in our network reachability protocol.

7.4.1 Privacy-Preserving Range Intersection

To compute the intersection of a range $[a, b]$ from A_i and a range $[a', b']$ from A_j, our basic idea is to check which range among $[min, a-1]$, $[a, b]$, and $[b+1, max]$ includes a' or b', where min and max are the minimum and maximum numbers, respectively. Thus, the problem of computing $[a, b] \cap [a', b']$ reduces to the problem of checking whether a number is in a range, e.g., $a' \in [min, a-1]$, which can be solved by leveraging the prefix membership verification scheme in [22]. Our scheme consists of five steps. We label each step with the party that is performing that step.

7.4.1.1   [P_i]: Range Transformation

The party P_i transforms each range $[a, b]$ to three ranges $[min, a - 1]$, $[a, b]$, and $[b + 1, max]$, where min and max are the minimum and maximum numbers of the corresponding field's domain, respectively. For example, [5,7] is converted to [0,4], [5,7], and [8,15], where 0 and 15 are the minimum and maximum numbers. Note that $[min, a - 1]$ and $[b + 1, max]$ may not exist. If $a = min$, then $[min, a - 1]$ does not exist; if $b = max$, then $[b + 1, max]$ does not exist.

7.4.1.2   [P_i]: Range to Prefix Set Conversion

The party P_i converts each range to a minimum set of prefixes, whose union corresponds to the range. Let $\mathcal{S}([min, a - 1])$, $\mathcal{S}([a, b])$, and $\mathcal{S}([b + 1, max)$ denote the resulting sets of prefixes for the three ranges, respectively. For example, $\mathcal{S}([5, 7])$={0101, 011*}, where "*" denotes that this bit can be 0 or 1.

7.4.1.3   [P_j]: Prefix Family Generation

The party P_j generates the *prefix families* of a and b, denoted as $\mathcal{F}(a)$ and $\mathcal{F}(b)$. The *prefix family* $\mathcal{F}(a)$ consists of a and all the prefixes that contains a. Assuming w is the bit length of a, $\mathcal{F}(a)$ consists of $w + 1$ prefixes where the l-th prefix is obtained by replacing the last $l - 1$ bits of a by *. For example, as the binary representation of 6 is 0110, we have $\mathcal{F}(6)$={0110, 011*, 01**, 0***, ****}. It is easy to prove that $a' \in [a, b]$ if and only if $\mathcal{F}(a') \cap \mathcal{S}([a, b]) \neq \emptyset$.

7.4.1.4   [P_i, P_j]: Prefix Numericalization

P_i and P_j convert the resulting prefixes to numbers so that they can encrypt them in the next step. We use the prefix numericalization scheme in [6]. This scheme basically inserts 1 before *s in a prefix and then replaces every * by 0. For example, 01** is converted to 01100. If the prefix does not contain *s, we place 1 at the end of the prefix. For example, 1100 is converted to 11001. Given a set of prefixes S, we use $\mathcal{N}(S)$ to denote the resulting set of numericalized prefixes. Thus, $a' \in [a, b]$ if and only if $\mathcal{N}(\mathcal{F}(a')) \cap \mathcal{N}(\mathcal{S}([a, b])) \neq \emptyset$.

7.4.1.5   [P_i, P_j]: Private Set Intersection

Checking whether $\mathcal{N}(\mathcal{F}(a')) \cap \mathcal{N}(\mathcal{S}([a, b])) \neq \emptyset$ is basically checking whether an element from $\mathcal{N}(\mathcal{F}(a'))$ is equal to an element from $\mathcal{N}(\mathcal{S}([a, b]))$. We use commutative encryption (e.g., [29, 30]) to do this check. Given a number x and two encryption keys K_i and K_j, a commutative encryption satisfies the property

$((x)_{K_i})_{K_j} = ((x)_{K_j})_{K_i}$, i.e., encryption with K_i and then K_j is equivalent to encryption with K_j and then K_i. For ease of presentation, we use $(x)_{K_{ij}}$ to denote $((x)_{K_i})_{K_j}$.

[P_i]: *Commutative Encryption of* $N(S([a, b]))$ In our scheme, to check whether $N(\mathcal{F}(a')) \cap N(S([a, b])) \neq \emptyset$, P_i encrypts numbers in $N(S([a, b]))$ with its private key K_i, and sends it to P_j. Then, P_j further encrypts them by its private key K_j and sends them back to P_i. Let $N(S([a, b]))_{K_{ij}}$ denote the result.

[P_j]: *Commutative Encryption of* $N(\mathcal{F}(a'))$ P_j encrypts numbers in $N(\mathcal{F}(a'))$ with K_j, sends it to P_i. Then, P_i encrypts them by K_i. Let $\mathcal{F}(a')_{K_{ji}}$ denote the result. Finally, P_i can check whether there is a common element in two sets $N(S([a, b]))_{K_{ij}}$ and $\mathcal{F}(a')_{K_{ji}}$. Through the previous steps, P_i knows which range among $[min, a - 1]$, $[a, b]$, and $[b + 1, max]$ includes a' or b'. Then, P_i can compute $[a, b] \cap [a', b']$. For example, if $a' \in [min, a - 1]$ and $b' \in [a, b]$, $[a, b] \cap [a', b'] = [a, b]$. Note that a' and b' are in the form of $\mathcal{F}(a')_{K_{ji}}$ and $\mathcal{F}(b')_{K_{ji}}$. P_i cannot reveal a' and b' without knowing P_j's private key K_j. Figure 7.3 illustrates the intersection computation of $[5, 7]$ (in A_1) and $[6, 15]$ (in A_2).

7.4.2   ACL Preprocessing

In the ACL preprocessing phase, each party P_i $(1 \leq i \leq n)$ computes the set of packets $M(A_i)$ that are accepted by its ACL A_i. To achieve this purpose, P_i first converts its ACL to an equivalent sequence of non-overlapping rules. Non-

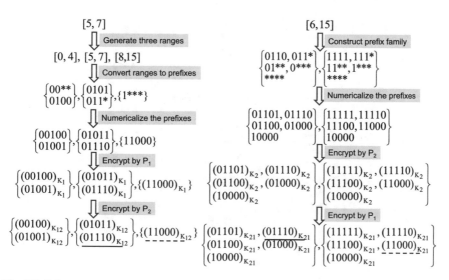

Fig. 7.3 Privacy-preserving range intersection

overlapping rules have an important property, that is, for any two non-overlapping rules nr and nr', the intersection of the two corresponding matching sets is empty, i.e., $M(nr) \cap M(nr') = \emptyset$. Thus, any packet p matches one and only one non-overlapping rule converted from A_i and the decision of this non-overlapping rule is the decision of A_i for the packet p. Therefore, instead of computing the set $M(A_i)$, P_i only needs to retrieve all non-overlapping accepting rules because the union of matching sets of these rules is equal to $M(A_i)$. The preprocessing of each A_i includes three steps:

(1) P_i converts its ACL A_i to an equivalent acyclic directed graph, called firewall decision diagram (FDD) [15]. An FDD construction algorithm, which converts an ACL to an equivalent FDD, is presented in [25]. Figure 7.4b shows the FDD constructed from Fig. 7.4a.

(2) P_i extracts non-overlapping accepting rules from the FDD. We do not consider non-overlapping discarding rules because the packets discarded by any ACL A_i cannot pass through the path. Figure 7.4c shows the non-overlapping accepting rules extracted from the FDD in Fig. 7.4b.

(3) Next, P_1 needs to compare its accepting rules from A_1 with those from the other $n - 1$ ACLs. Without loss of generality, in the next two subsections, we use a simplified example in Fig. 7.5 to show that how to compute the network reachability among three ACLs. Each ACL has only one field and the domain for the field is [0,15]. Note that in Fig. 7.5, $nr_1^{(i)}$ and $nr_2^{(i)}$ denote two non-overlapping accepting rules for ACL A_i ($1 \leq i \leq 3$). Clearly, the network reachability among these three ACLs can be denoted as two accepting rules $F_1 \in [0, 2] \rightarrow a$ and $F_1 \in [6, 7] \rightarrow a$. Next, we will show how to compute these two rules in a privacy preserving manner.

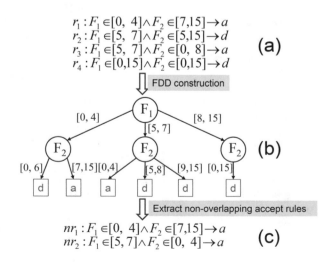

Fig. 7.4 The conversion of A_1

Fig. 7.5 The example three adjacent ACLs

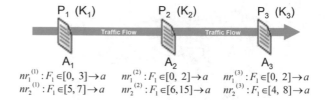

$$P_1\ (K_1) \qquad P_2\ (K_2) \qquad P_3\ (K_3)$$

$$A_1 \qquad A_2 \qquad A_3$$

$$nr_1^{(1)}: F_1 \in [0,\,3] \to a \qquad nr_1^{(2)}: F_1 \in [0,\,2] \to a \qquad nr_1^{(3)}: F_1 \in [0,\,2] \to a$$
$$nr_2^{(1)}: F_1 \in [5,\,7] \to a \qquad nr_2^{(2)}: F_1 \in [6,\,15] \to a \qquad nr_2^{(3)}: F_1 \in [4,\,8] \to a$$

7.4.3   ACL Encoding and Encryption

In the ACL encoding and encryption phase, all parties need to convert their non-overlapping accepting rules to another format such that they can collaboratively compute the network reachability while one party cannot reveal the ACL of any other party. Recall the privacy-preserving range intersection scheme in Sect. 8.4.1, two parties employ different encoding methods, one converts a range $[a, b]$ to a set of prefixes $S([a, b])$, and another converts a number a' to its prefix family $\mathcal{F}(a')$. Assume that each party P_i ($1 \le i \le n$) has a private key K_i. Let $\mathcal{H}$ denote the encoding function used by the party P_j ($1 \le j \le n - 1$). Let $F_1 \in [a_1, b_1] \wedge \cdots \wedge F_d \in [a_d, b_d]$ denote the predicate of an accepting rule over d fields. The encoding and encryption result of this accepting rule for A_j is $\mathcal{H}_{K_{j\cdots n}}([a_1, b_1]) \wedge \cdots \wedge \mathcal{H}_{K_{j\cdots n}}([a_d, b_d])$. Let $\mathcal{L}$ denote the encoding function used by the party P_n. Considering the above accepting rule, the result is $\mathcal{L}_{K_n}([a_1, b_1]) \wedge \cdots \wedge \mathcal{L}_{K_n}([a_d, b_d])$. We discuss the procedure of these two encoding and encryption methods in detail as follows.

7.4.3.1   Encoding and Encryption of ACL A_j ($1 \le j \le n - 1$)

(a) For each non-overlapping accepting rule $F_1 \in [a_1, b_1] \wedge \cdots \wedge F_d \in [a_d, b_d]$, P_j performs *Range Transformation* as described in Sect. 8.4.1(1). Figure 7.6b shows the ranges generated from Fig. 7.6a.

(b) P_j uses the approach in Sect. 8.4.1(2) to convert each range into sets of prefixes. Figure 7.6c shows the prefixes generated from Fig. 7.6b. That is, for the three ranges converted from $[a_l, b_l]$, compute $S([min_l, a_l - 1])$, $S([a_l, b_l])$, $S([b_l + 1, max_l])$.

(c) P_j unions all these prefix sets and permutes these prefixes. Figure 7.6d shows the resulting prefix set. This step has two benefits. First, it avoids encrypting and sending duplicate prefixes, and hence, significantly reduces the computation and communication costs for the next two steps. Second, it enhances the security, any other parties except P_j cannot reconstruct the non-overlapping accepting rules, because it is difficult to correlate the prefixes to their corresponding rules without the knowledge of the original ACL.

(d) P_j uses the *Prefix Numericalization* approach of Sect. 8.4.1(4) to numericalize and encrypt each number using K_j. Figure 7.6e and f show the numericalized and encrypted prefixes.

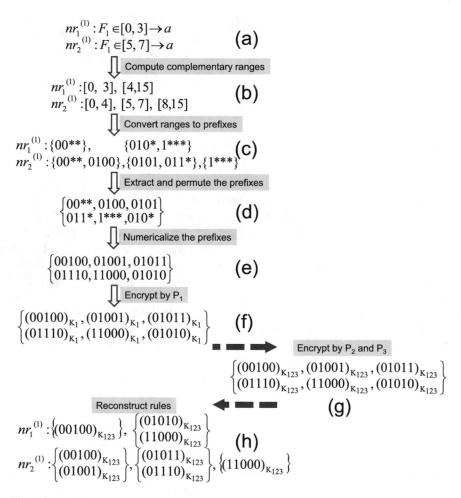

Fig. 7.6 Encoding and encryption of ACL A_1

(e) P_j sends the resulting encrypted prefixes to P_{j+1} which further encrypts them with its private key K_{j+1}. Then, P_{j+1} sends the resulting values to P_{j+2} which further encrypts them with K_{j+2}. This process is repeated until P_n encrypts them. Finally, P_n sends to P_j the resulting prefixes that are encrypted $n - j + 1$ times. Figure 7.6f shows the result after encrypting by P_1 and Fig. 7.6g shows the result after encrypting by P_2 and P_3.

(f) P_j reconstructs the non-overlapping accepting rules from the multiple encrypted prefixes because P_j knows which prefix belongs to which field of which rule.

Based on the above steps, the encoding and encryption function used by P_j ($1 \leq j \leq n - 1$) is defined as $\mathcal{H}_{K_{j\cdots n}}([a_l, b_l]) = (\mathcal{N}(\mathcal{S}(min_l, a_l - 1))_{K_{j\cdots n}}, \mathcal{N}(\mathcal{S}(a_l, b_l))_{K_{j\cdots n}}, \mathcal{N}(\mathcal{S}(b_l + 1, max_l))_{K_{j\cdots n}})$, where $[a_l, b_l]$ is the range in the l-

th field of a rule in A_j. Figure 7.8a illustrates the encoding and encryption result of ACL A_2 in Fig. 7.5. The only difference between operations for A_1 and A_2 is that A_1's numericalized prefixes are encrypted by all the three parties while A_2's numericalized prefixes are only encrypted by two parties P_2 and P_3.

7.4.3.2 Encoding and Encryption of ACL A_n

(a) For each range $[a_l, b_l]$ of a non-overlapping rule, P_n generates two prefix families $\mathcal{F}(a_l)$ and $\mathcal{F}(b_l)$ using the *Prefix Family Generation* approach from Sect. 8.4.1(3). Figure 7.7b shows the result from Fig. 7.7a.

(b) P_n uses the *Prefix Numericalization* approach from Sect. 8.4.1(4) to numericalize and then, encrypts the prefixes using its private key K_n. Figure 7.7c shows the resulting prefixes.

Based on the above steps, the encoding and encryption function used by A_n is defined as $\mathcal{L}_{K_n}([a_l, b_l]) = (\mathcal{N}(\mathcal{F}(a_l))_{K_n}, \mathcal{N}(\mathcal{F}(b_l))_{K_n})$ where $[a_l, b_l]$ is the range in the l-th field of a rule.

7.4.4 ACL Comparison

In the ACL comparison phase, we need to compare the n sequences of encrypted non-overlapping accepting rules or encrypted numbers from every two adjacent ACLs. Without loss of generality, we only present the comparison between A_{n-1} and A_n. Figure 7.8a shows the encrypted non-overlapping rules converted from A_2 in Figs. 7.5 and 7.8b shows the encrypted numbers converted from A_3 in Fig. 7.5. The comparison includes four steps:

(1) P_n sends the resulting sequence to P_{n-1} which further encrypts them with its private key K_{n-1}. Let $\mathcal{L}_{K_n}([a_1', b_1']) \wedge \cdots \wedge \mathcal{L}_{K_n}([a_d', b_d'])$ denote the encoded and encrypted result of the accepting rule nr' from A_n. P_{n-1} encrypts it with

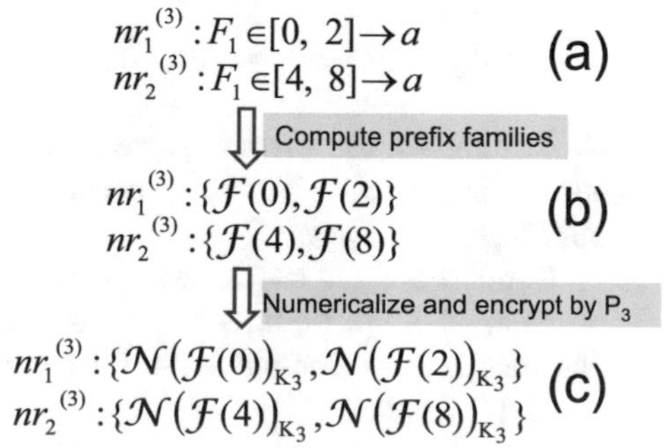

Fig. 7.7 Encoding and encryption of ACL A_3

$$nr_1^{(3)} : F_1 \in [0, 2] \to a$$
$$nr_2^{(3)} : F_1 \in [4, 8] \to a \qquad \textbf{(a)}$$

⇓ Compute prefix families

$$nr_1^{(3)} : \{\mathcal{F}(0), \mathcal{F}(2)\}$$
$$nr_2^{(3)} : \{\mathcal{F}(4), \mathcal{F}(8)\} \qquad \textbf{(b)}$$

⇓ Numericalize and encrypt by P_3

$$nr_1^{(3)} : \{\mathcal{N}(\mathcal{F}(0))_{K_3}, \mathcal{N}(\mathcal{F}(2))_{K_3}\}$$
$$nr_2^{(3)} : \{\mathcal{N}(\mathcal{F}(4))_{K_3}, \mathcal{N}(\mathcal{F}(8))_{K_3}\} \qquad \textbf{(c)}$$

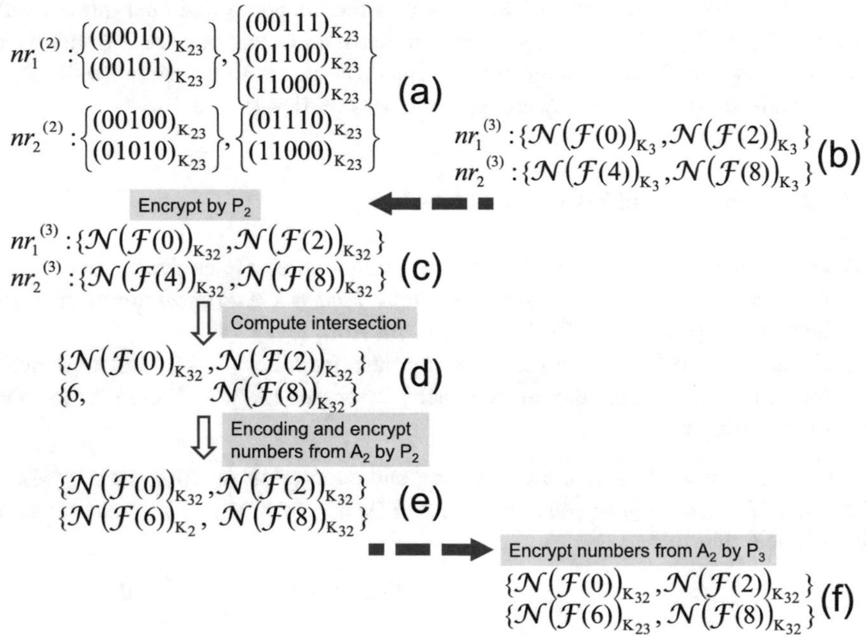

$$nr_1^{(2)} : \left\{ \begin{array}{c} (00010)_{K_{23}} \\ (00101)_{K_{23}} \end{array} \right\}, \left\{ \begin{array}{c} (00111)_{K_{23}} \\ (01100)_{K_{23}} \\ (11000)_{K_{23}} \end{array} \right\} \quad \textbf{(a)}$$

$$nr_2^{(2)} : \left\{ \begin{array}{c} (00100)_{K_{23}} \\ (01010)_{K_{23}} \end{array} \right\}, \left\{ \begin{array}{c} (01110)_{K_{23}} \\ (11000)_{K_{23}} \end{array} \right\}$$

$$nr_1^{(3)} : \{ \mathcal{N}(\mathcal{F}(0))_{K_3}, \mathcal{N}(\mathcal{F}(2))_{K_3} \}$$
$$nr_2^{(3)} : \{ \mathcal{N}(\mathcal{F}(4))_{K_3}, \mathcal{N}(\mathcal{F}(8))_{K_3} \} \quad \textbf{(b)}$$

Encrypt by P_2 ◀ ▬ ▬ ▪

$$nr_1^{(3)} : \{ \mathcal{N}(\mathcal{F}(0))_{K_{32}}, \mathcal{N}(\mathcal{F}(2))_{K_{32}} \}$$
$$nr_2^{(3)} : \{ \mathcal{N}(\mathcal{F}(4))_{K_{32}}, \mathcal{N}(\mathcal{F}(8))_{K_{32}} \} \quad \textbf{(c)}$$

⇩ Compute intersection

$$\{ \mathcal{N}(\mathcal{F}(0))_{K_{32}}, \mathcal{N}(\mathcal{F}(2))_{K_{32}} \}$$
$$\{6, \qquad \mathcal{N}(\mathcal{F}(8))_{K_{32}} \} \quad \textbf{(d)}$$

⇩ Encoding and encrypt numbers from A_2 by P_2

$$\{ \mathcal{N}(\mathcal{F}(0))_{K_{32}}, \mathcal{N}(\mathcal{F}(2))_{K_{32}} \}$$
$$\{ \mathcal{N}(\mathcal{F}(6))_{K_2}, \mathcal{N}(\mathcal{F}(8))_{K_{32}} \} \quad \textbf{(e)}$$

▪ ▬ ▶ Encrypt numbers from A_2 by P_3

$$\{ \mathcal{N}(\mathcal{F}(0))_{K_{32}}, \mathcal{N}(\mathcal{F}(2))_{K_{32}} \}$$
$$\{ \mathcal{N}(\mathcal{F}(6))_{K_{23}}, \mathcal{N}(\mathcal{F}(8))_{K_{32}} \} \quad \textbf{(f)}$$

Fig. 7.8 Comparison of ACLs A_2 and A_3

K_{n-1}, i.e., computes $\mathcal{L}_{K_{n(n-1)}}([a_1', b_1']) \wedge \cdots \wedge \mathcal{L}_{K_{n(n-1)}}([a_d', b_d'])$. Figure 7.8c shows the encrypted result from Fig. 7.8b.

(2) For each non-overlapping accepting rule nr from A_{n-1}, P_{n-1} computes $nr \cap nr'$. Let $\mathcal{H}_{K_{(n-1)n}}([a_1, b_1]) \wedge \cdots \wedge \mathcal{H}_{K_{(n-1)n}}([a_d, b_d])$ denote the encoded and encrypted result of nr.

To compute $nr \cap nr'$, for each field l ($1 \leq l \leq d$), P_{n-1} compares $\mathcal{H}_{K_{(n-1)n}}([a_l, b_l])$ with $\mathcal{L}_{K_n(n-1)}([a_l', b_l'])$ where

$$\mathcal{H}_{K_{(n-1)n}}([a_l, b_l]) = (\mathcal{N}(\mathcal{S}(min_l, a_l - 1))_{K_{(n-1)n}}$$
$$\mathcal{N}(\mathcal{S}(a_l, b_l))_{K_{(n-1)n}}, \mathcal{N}(\mathcal{S}(b_l + 1, max_l))_{K_{(n-1)n}})$$

$$\mathcal{L}_{K_{n(n-1)}}([a_l', b_l']) = (\mathcal{N}(\mathcal{F}(a_l'))_{K_{n(n-1)}}, \mathcal{N}(\mathcal{F}(b_l'))_{K_{n(n-1)}}).$$

According to the privacy-preserving range intersection, to check whether $a_l' \in [min_l, a_l - 1]$, P_{n-1} checks whether $\mathcal{N}(\mathcal{S}(min_l, a_l - 1))_{K_{(n-1)n}} \cap \mathcal{N}(\mathcal{F}(a_l'))_{K_{n(n-1)}} = \emptyset$.

Similarly, P_{n-1} checks whether $a_l' \in [a_l, b_l]$, $a_l' \in [b_l + 1, max_l]$, and whether $b_l' \in [min_l, a_l - 1]$, $b_l' \in [a_l, b_l]$, $b_l' \in [b_l + 1, max_l]$. Based on the result, P_{n-1} computes the intersection between $[a_l, b_l]$ and $[a_l', b_l']$, i.e., $[a_l, b_l] \cap [a_l', b_l']$.

Let T_l denote $[a_l, b_l] \cap [a'_l, b'_l]$. For example, if $a'_l \in [a_l, b_l]$ and $b'_l \in [b_l + 1, max_l]$, the condition $a_l \leq a'_l \leq b_l < b'_l$ holds and hence $T_l = [a'_l, b_l]$. If for any T_l $(1 \leq l \leq d)$ the condition $T_l \neq \emptyset$ holds, then $nr \cap nr' = T_1 \wedge \cdots \wedge T_d$.

Note that the party P_{n-1} cannot reveal a'_l and b'_l through this comparison because P_{n-1} doesn't know P_n's private key K_n. Thus, if $T_l = [a'_l, b_l]$, P_{n-1} only knows $N(\mathcal{F}(a'_l))_{K_{n(n-1)}}$ and b_l. We denote the information that P_{n-1} knows about T_l as $\{N(\mathcal{F}(a'_l))_{K_{n(n-1)}}, b_l\}$. Figure 7.8d shows the result after comparing A_2 and A_3.

Note that the result may contain the field values from A_{n-1}'s non-overlapping accepting rules, which are not encrypted, e.g., the field value 6 in Fig. 7.8d. This is caused due to only part of the rule in A_{n-1} intersecting with the rule from the A_n. In such cases, the privacy of these values is important and P_{n-1} needs to protect these values as well. To preserve the privacy of A_{n-1}, the party P_{n-1} encodes and encrypts such values from A_{n-1}'s non-overlapping accepting rules, and before sending the final intersection results to P_n. To ensure correctness of the protocol, for a number a_l, P_{n-1} computes its corresponding prefix family and encrypts it as follows: $N(\mathcal{F}(a_l))_{K_{(n-1)}}$. Figure 7.8e shows the result after encoding and encrypting the value 6.

(3) To facilitate the next comparison with A_{n-2}, P_{n-1} sends the comparison result to P_n and then P_n encrypts the numbers from A_{n-1}'s non-overlapping accepting rules. Figure 7.8f shows the encryption result.

These three steps are repeated to further compare A_{n-2} with the result stored in P_n. The comparison phase of the protocol terminates after all parties finish the comparisons, where P_n has the comparison end result. Let $\{N(\mathcal{F}(a_l))_{K_{1\cdots n}}, N(\mathcal{F}(b_l))_{K_{1\cdots n}}\}$ denote the l-th field of an encrypted rule in the result. To decrypt this rule, P_n first decrypts it with K_n and sends the values to P_{n-1}. Then, P_{n-1} decrypts it with K_{n-1} and sends the values to P_{n-2} and so on. This step is executed until P_1 decrypts the rule. Finally, P_1 has the result $F_1 \in [a_1, b_1] \wedge \cdots \wedge F_d \in [a_d, b_d]$. The comparison result of three ACLs in Fig. 7.5 is $\{N(\mathcal{F}(0))_{K_{123}}, N(\mathcal{F}(2))_{K_{123}}\}$, and $\{N(\mathcal{F}(6))_{K_{123}}, N(\mathcal{F}(7))_{K_{123}}\}$. Figure 7.9 shows the decryption process of the comparison result.

7.5 Incremental Updates of ACLs

An update to an ACL implies that either a rule is added, removed, or modified. Due to this it may be necessary to update the network reachability accordingly. Note that, in practice, these updates are usually performed within a network defined interval i.e., they need to be done manually and it is not possible to automate this process. Regardless of the type of ACL updates, without loss of generality, there are two outcomes of ACL updates. The affected rule either causes additional packets to be accepted or to be discarded at the router. Note that, this discussion can be extended to multiple rule updates in a straightforward manner. To optimize the process, we

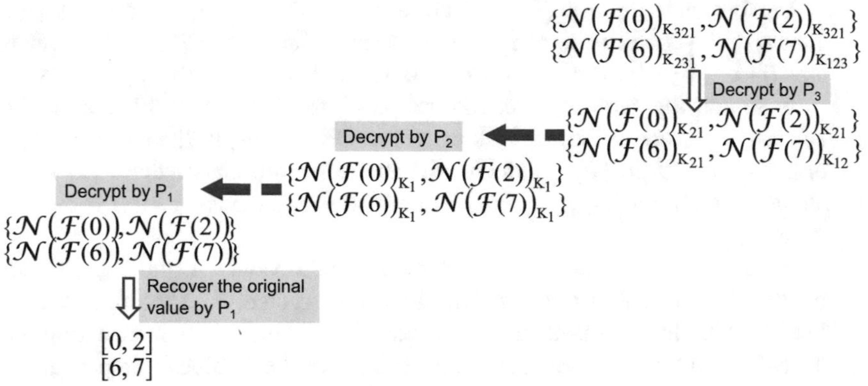

$$\{\mathcal{N}(\mathcal{F}(0))_{K_{321}}, \mathcal{N}(\mathcal{F}(2))_{K_{321}}\}$$
$$\{\mathcal{N}(\mathcal{F}(6))_{K_{231}}, \mathcal{N}(\mathcal{F}(7))_{K_{123}}\}$$

⇓ Decrypt by P_3

Decrypt by P_2 ◄ ■
$$\{\mathcal{N}(\mathcal{F}(0))_{K_{21}}, \mathcal{N}(\mathcal{F}(2))_{K_{21}}\}$$
$$\{\mathcal{N}(\mathcal{F}(6))_{K_{21}}, \mathcal{N}(\mathcal{F}(7))_{K_{12}}\}$$

Decrypt by P_1 ◄ ■
$$\{\mathcal{N}(\mathcal{F}(0))_{K_1}, \mathcal{N}(\mathcal{F}(2))_{K_1}\}$$
$$\{\mathcal{N}(\mathcal{F}(6))_{K_1}, \mathcal{N}(\mathcal{F}(7))_{K_1}\}$$

$$\{\mathcal{N}(\mathcal{F}(0)), \mathcal{N}(\mathcal{F}(2))\}$$
$$\{\mathcal{N}(\mathcal{F}(6)), \mathcal{N}(\mathcal{F}(7))\}$$

⇓ Recover the original value by P_1

$$[0, 2]$$
$$[6, 7]$$

Fig. 7.9 Decryption process of the comparison result

consider the effect of all the rule updates, i.e. batch updates, prior to processing the ACL.

7.5.1 Addition of Rules with Accept Decision

If the new rule is an accepting rule, then there is no need to update the reachability information for a given source, since this rule does not affect the existing set of accepted packets. Note that, this rule may increase the set of accepted packets along this path. However, calculating the updated set of accepted packets requires the execution of the privacy-preserving protocol along the path since it is possible that there are discarding rules, either upstream or downstream, that might neutralize the effect of the newly added rule(s). Hence, for all practical purposes, we assume that the nodes will not repeat the reachability protocol execution in this case and that this information will be reflected during the next reachability computation.

7.5.2 Addition of Rules with Discard Decision

If the new rule is a discarding rule, it will result in the following situations. First, the discard rule can overlap with any of the ACLs of its upstream nodes. In this case, adding this rule will not affect the current reachability information as the set of discarding packets remains constant.

Second, the new rule starts discarding packets that were allowed earlier. In this case, the source node needs to update the network reachability information. Note that, the new discarding rule affects the set of accepting rules of the intermediate firewall. Since the packets allowed by the intermediate firewall are dependent on its accepting rules, it is necessary to see if any change in these accepting rules affects the reachability information of the source node. To check this, the source node initiates a privacy-preserving firewall comparison [8] with the affected intermediate node using the accepting rules calculated during the reachability analysis. Using this computation, the source node computes the updated reachability information as follows. All rules that are not in the intersection of the two ACLs but are present in the previous reachability accepting rule set are discarded. The removed rules are the rules that are affected due to the addition of the discarding rule of the intermediate rule. We note that, this approach however cannot scale well if more than one node updates its firewall. This localized approach ensures that all the nodes along the path need not participate in the privacy-preserving reachability computation, and hence, saves bandwidth and computational overhead.

7.5.3 Addition of New Routers

If new routers with ACLs are introduced in the network, our protocol checks if the existing reachability is affected due to the introduction of the new ACL. This case is equivalent to the case where new rules are added to an existing ACL. Therefore, the rules of the new router are treated in a similar fashion as described earlier and the update protocol is run on this new network configuration.

7.6 Stateful Firewalls

We have discussed privacy preserving quantification of intersection of multiple ACLs across different domains. However, a party on the path may have a stateful firewall to check not only its ACL, but also its state table. The state table includes the information of whether the connection from source to destination or from destination to source has been established. When a packet that does not match any entry in the state table, the packet is discarded and the connection will fail.

We assume that the network is path-coupled on stateful firewalls. Path-coupled network means that the path from source to destination and the path from destination to source contain the same set of network devices. Most networks are path-coupled. If a party P_i ($1 \leq i \leq n$) has a stateful firewall with its ACL A_i and its state table A_{S_i}, at any moment, P_i can calculate $M(A_i \cap A_{S_i})$, which denotes the set of TCP packets that can pass through the network device of P_i. Thus, if any party P_i ($1 \leq i \leq n$) on the path has a stateful firewall, for any given moment, we can use $A_i \cap A_{S_i}$ to denote its ACL rules instead of A_i. Then, use our proposed approach to quantifying the network reachability from source to destination.

7.7 Security and Complexity Analysis

7.7.1 Security Analysis

The security of our protocol is based on the two important properties of the commutative encryption. (1) *Secrecy*: for any x and key K, given $(x)_K$, it is computationally infeasible to compute K. (2) *Indistinguishability*: the distribution of $(x)_K$ is indistinguishable from the distribution of x.

Based on the first property, without knowing P_j's secret key K_j, the party P_i $(i \neq j)$ cannot decrypt the encrypted numbers from P_i. Furthermore, one party P_i cannot statistically analyze encrypted numbers from A_j $(i \neq j)$ because each party P_j $(1 \leq j \leq n-1)$ unions the encrypted prefix numbers into one set before sending them to P_i for further encryption. Therefore, after the first and second phases of our protocol, i.e., *ACL preprocessing* and *ACL encoding and encryption*, the party P_i cannot reveal the ACL of any other party. Based on the second property, we can prove that after the third phase, i.e., *ACL comparison*, the party P_i only learns the limited information of the ACLs of other parties, but such information cannot help it reveal them.

Without loss of generality, we consider the comparison between ACLs A_{n-1} and A_n. For each non-overlapping rule nr from A_{n-1}, let $V_{F_l,h}(nr)$ denote the h-th ($1 \leq h \leq 3$) prefix set for the field F_l ($1 \leq l \leq d$), e.g., , in Fig. 7.8a, $V_{F_l,1}(nr_1^{(2)})$ denotes $\{00010, 00101\}$. Let $N(\mathcal{F}(a_l))$ denote one set of prefixes for the field F_l, e.g., , $N(\mathcal{F}(0))$ in Fig. 7.8c. The basic operation of the third phase is to compare whether two sets from different ACLs, e.g., , $V_{F_l,h}(nr)$ and $N(\mathcal{F}(a_l))$, have a common element. According to the theorems in multi-party secure computation [1, 13] and the theorem in [8], we can prove that after the three phases, the party P_{n-1} only learns $V_{F_l,h}(nr) \cap N(\mathcal{F}(a_l))$ and the size of $N(\mathcal{F}(a_l))$.

To prove this claim, based on the theorems of multi-party secure computation [1, 13], we only need to prove that the distribution of the P_{n-1}'s view of our protocol cannot be distinguished from a simulation that uses only $V_{F_l,h}(nr)$, $V_{F_l,h}(nr) \cap N(\mathcal{F}(a_l))$, and the size of $N(\mathcal{F}(a_l))$. The theorem in [8] proves that P_{n-1}'s view of our protocol

$$Y_R = \{\underbrace{(x_1)_{K_{n-1}}, \cdots, (x_m)_{K_{n-1}}}_{x_i \in V_{F_l,h}(nr) \cap N(\mathcal{F}(a_l))}, \underbrace{(x_{m+1})_{K_{n-1}}, \cdots, (x_t)_{K_{n-1}}}_{x_i \in V_{F_l,h}(nr) - N(\mathcal{F}(a_l))}\}$$

cannot be distinguished from the simulation

$$Y_S = \{\underbrace{(x_1)_{K_{n-1}}, \cdots, (x_m)_{K_{n-1}}}_{x_i \in V_{F_l,h}(nr) \cap N(\mathcal{F}(a_l))}, \underbrace{z_{m+1}, \cdots, z_t}_{t-m=|V_{F_l,h}(nr) - N(\mathcal{F}(a_l))|}\}$$

where $z_{m+1}, \cdots, z_t$ are random values and uniformly distributed in the domain of encrypted numbers.

Knowing $V_{F_l,h}(nr) \cap N(\mathcal{F}(a_l))$ and the size of $N(\mathcal{F}(a_l))$, P_{n-1} cannot reveal the rules in A_n for two reasons. First, a numericalized prefix in $V_{F_l,h}(nr) \cap N(\mathcal{F}(a_l))$ can be generated from many numbers. Considering a numericalized prefix of 32-bit IP addresses $b_1 b_2 \cdots b_k 10 \cdots 0$, the number of possible IP addresses that can generate such prefix is 2^{32-k}. Furthermore, after the comparison, P_{n-1} sends to P_n the comparison result which is encrypted with P_{n-1}'s secret key K_{n-1}. Without knowing K_{n-1}, P_n cannot reveal the comparison result, and hence, cannot reveal the values from A_{n-1}. Second, the size of $N(\mathcal{F}(a_l))$ cannot be used to reveal the rules in A_n because for any a_l or b_l in the field F_l of A_n, the size of $N(\mathcal{F}(a_l))$ or $N(\mathcal{F}(b_l))$ is constant.

At the end of our protocol, only P_1 knows the intersection of n ACLs, which includes some information (i.e., numbers) from other ACLs. However, our goal is to preserve the privacy of ACLs, not the privacy of the intersection result. Knowing such numbers cannot help P_1 to reveal an ACL rule of other parties for two reasons. First, a real ACL typically consists of hundreds of rules and no one consists of only one rule. Second, P_1 does not know which numbers belong to A_j ($2 \leq j \leq n$), which two numbers form an interval, and which d intervals form a rule in A_j. The number of possible combinations can be extremely large. Considering the intersection in Fig. 7.9, P_1 cannot know which ACL, A_2 or A_3, contains the number 2 or the number 6.

7.7.2 Complexity Analysis

In this section, we analyze the computation, space, and communication costs in our protocol. Let m_i be the number of rules in ACL A_i ($1 \leq i \leq n$) and d be the number of fields. For ease of presentation, assume that different fields have the same length, i.e., w bits. We first analyze the complexity of processing ACLs $A_1, \cdots, A_{n-1}$ and then analyze the complexity of processing ACL A_n. The maximum number of non-overlapping rules generated from the FDD is $(2m_i - 1)^d$ [25]. Each non-overlapping rule consists of d w-bit intervals, each interval can be converted to at most three ranges, and each range can be converted to at most $2w - 2$ prefixes [17]. Thus, the maximum number of prefixes generated from these non-overlapping rules is $3d(2w - 2)(2m_i - 1)^d$. Recall that P_i ($1 \leq i \leq n - 1$) unions all prefixes into one set. Then, the number of prefixes cannot exceed 2^{w+1}. Therefore, for processing A_i ($1 \leq i \leq n - 1$), the computation cost of encryption by $P_i, \cdots, P_n$ is $\min(3d(2w - 2)(2m_i - 1)^d, 2^{w+1}) = \min(O(dwm_i^d), O(2^w))$, the space cost of P_i is $O(dw(m_i)^d)$, and the communication cost is $\min(O(dw(m_i)^d), O(2^w))$. For processing P_n, each interval of the non-overlapping rules is converted to two prefix families and each prefix family includes $w + 1$ prefixes. Thus, the maximum number of prefixes converted from A_n is $2d(w + 1)(2m_n - 1)^d$. Therefore, for processing A_n, the computation, space, and communication costs of P_n is $O(dw(m_n)^d)$.

7.8   Protocol Optimization

To reduce the computation and communication costs, we use the divide-and-conquer strategy to reduce the problem of computing reachability of n ACLs to the problem of computing reachability of two ACLs. Then the intermediate results are aggregated hierarchically to obtain the final reachability result. Let Q_i ($1 \leq i \leq n$) denote the set of non-overlapping accepting rules from ACL A_i. In the ACL encoding and encryption phase, Q_i is encrypted $n - i + 1$ times, i.e., encrypted by $P_i, P_{i+1}, \cdots, P_n$. Thus, the number of encryptions for $Q_1, \cdots, Q_n$ is $n + (n - 1) + \cdots + 1 = O(n^2)$. Similarly, the number of messages in this phase is $O(n^2)$. To reduce the number of encryptions and messages, we first divide n ACLs into $\lfloor n/2 \rfloor$ groups. The j-th ($1 \leq j \leq \lfloor n/2 \rfloor$) group includes two adjacent ACLs A_{2j-1} and A_{2j}. The last group includes adjacent ACLs $A_{2\lfloor n/2 \rfloor -1}, \cdots, A_n$. For example, 5 ACLs can be divided into two groups $\{A_1, A_2\}$ and $\{A_3, A_4, A_5\}$. Second, for the ACLs in each group, we run the proposed protocol to compute the network reachability. The result for each group is actually a new set of non-overlapping accepting rules. Therefore, we obtain $\lfloor n/2 \rfloor$ sets of non-overlapping accepting rules. Repeat these two steps until we obtain the reachability for all n ACLs. Overall, there are $\lfloor n/2 \rfloor + \lfloor n/2^2 \rfloor + \ldots + 1 = O(n)$ groups, and for each group with two ACLs, the number of ACL encryptions and messages is $2 + 1 = 3$. Thus, the number of ACL encryptions and messages is reduced from $O(n^2)$ to $O(n)$.

To further reduce the computation and communication costs, we compress the sequence of prefix families from A_n and then encrypt and send them to other parties in the ACL comparison phase. The sequence of prefix families from A_n could have many duplicate numbers. For example, in Fig. 7.7c, the sequence of prefix families, $\mathcal{F}(0), \mathcal{F}(2), \mathcal{F}(4)$, and $\mathcal{F}(8)$ has duplicated prefixes $00**, 0***$, and $****$. To reduce the costs, P_n first unions all the prefix families from A_n to one set, i.e., remove all duplicated prefixes. Second, P_n replaces each prefix in a prefix family converted from A_n with the index of this number in the set. Let m denote the total number of prefixes in the set. Then k ($1 \leq k \leq m$) is the index of the k-th encrypted number in the set. The sequence of prefix families from A_n is represented as a set of prefixes with the sequence of indexes. Next, P_n only needs to encrypt the set of prefixes and then sends to other parties the encrypted result with the sequence of indexes.

7.9   Experimental Results

We evaluated the efficiency and effectiveness of our protocol on 10 real ACLs and 100 synthetic ACLs. Both real and synthetic ACLs examine five fields, source IP, destination IP, source port, destination port, and protocol type. For real ACLs, the number of rules ranges from hundreds to thousands, and the average number of rules is 806. Due to security concerns, it is difficult to obtain many real ACLs. Thus, we generated a large number of synthetic ACLs based on Singh et al.'s technique [32].

To create a rule in a synthetic ACL, we randomly pick two prefixes from a set of values which follow the same distribution as in real ACLs, one for the source IP and one for the destination IP. Then, we randomly pick source port, destination port, and protocol type from a set of all the values in real ACLs. Finally, we randomly add the decision, accept or discard, to the rule. For synthetic ACLs, the number of rules ranges from 200 to 2000, and for each number, we generated 10 synthetic ACLs. In implementing the commutative encryption, we used the Pohlig-Hellman algorithm [29] with a 1024-bit prime modulus and 160-bit encryption keys. Our experiments were implemented using Java 1.6.0 and carried out on a PC running Linux with 2 Intel Xeon cores and 16GB of memory.

To evaluate the effectiveness, we verified the correctness of our protocol because we knew all the ACLs in the experiments. The results show that our protocol is deterministic and accurate with the given ACLs. Thus, in this section, we focus on the efficiency of our protocol. Recall that processing ACL A_i ($1 \leq i \leq n-1$) is different from processing the last destination ACL A_n. Therefore, we evaluate the computation and communication costs of the core operations of our protocol, processing ACL A_i ($1 \leq i \leq n-1$), processing the destination ACL A_n, and comparing A_i and A_n. The computation cost is the execution time for each step in our approach and the communication cost is the size of messages exchanged between two parties. We note that, the computation cost includes the cost of converting the ACLs to FDDs, which is relatively smaller compared to the cost incurred due to the commutative encryption. Knowing the performance of our protocol, we can easily estimate time and space consumption for a given network path with n ACLs belonging to n parties.

7.9.1 Efficiency on Real ACLs

Our protocol is efficient for processing real ACL A_i ($1 \leq i \leq n-1$). Figure 7.10a shows for processing A_i the computation cost of P_i and the average computation cost of other parties $P_{i+1}, \cdots, P_n$. The computation cost of P_i is less than 2 s and the computation cost of P_j ($i+1 \leq j \leq n$) is less than 1.5 s. Note that, for processing A_i, the computation cost of P_i is one-time offline cost because P_i knows A_i, while the computation cost of P_j ($i+1 \leq j \leq n$) is online cost. Figure 7.10b shows the average communication cost between any two adjacent parties P_j and P_{j+1} ($i \leq j \leq n$) for processing ACL A_i, which is less than 60 KB. Note that, the computation costs of different parties P_j ($i+1 \leq j \leq n$) are similar because they encrypt the same number of prefixes from A_i. Hence, we only show the average computation cost of parties $P_{i+1}, \cdots, P_n$. Similarly, the communication costs between every two adjacent parties P_j and P_{j+1} are the same.

Our protocol is efficient for processing real ACL A_n. Figure 7.11a shows that for processing A_n, the computation cost of P_n and the average computation cost of other parties. The computation cost of P_n is less than 10 s. The average computation cost of other parties is less than 6 s. Similarly, for processing A_n, the computation

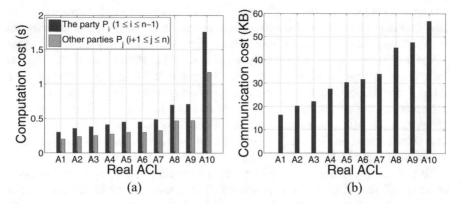

Fig. 7.10 (**a**, **b**) Computation and communication costs for processing real ACL A_i ($1 \leq i \leq n - 1$)

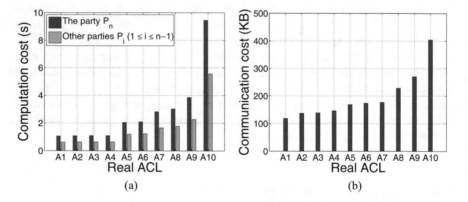

Fig. 7.11 (**a**, **b**) Computation and communication costs for processing real ACL A_n

cost of P_n is one-time offline cost, while the computation costs of other party is online cost. Figure 7.11b shows the average communication cost between P_n and P_i ($1 \leq i \leq n - 1$), which is less than 410 KB.

Our protocol is efficient for real ACL comparison. The comparison time between two ACLs is less than 1 s, which is much less than the computation cost of processing ACLs. Because the commutative encryption is more expensive than checking whether two sets have a common element.

7.9.2 Efficiency on Synthetic ACLs

To further evaluate the efficiency, we executed our protocol over every 10 synthetic ACLs with the same number of rules, and then measured the computation and

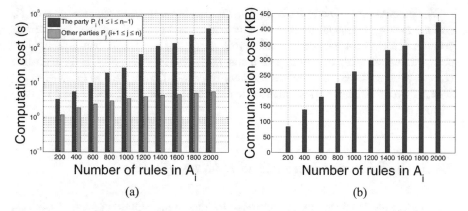

Fig. 7.12 Computation and communication costs for processing synthetic ACL A_i $(1 \le i \le n-1)$. (**a**) Ave. computation cost. (**b**) Ave. communication cost

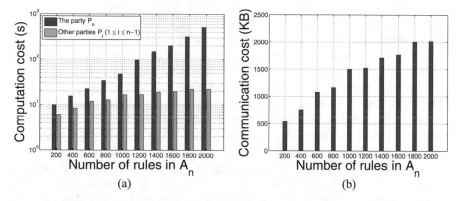

Fig. 7.13 Computation and communication costs for processing synthetic ACL A_n. (**a**) Ave. computation cost. (**b**) Ave. communication cost

communication costs of operations on synthetic ACLs A_1 to A_n for different parties. Particularly, we measured computation and communication costs for processing each synthetic ACL A_i $(1 \le i \le n-1)$, processing synthetic ACL A_n, and the comparison time for every two ACLs. Note that the vertical axis of two Figs. 7.12a and 7.13a are in a logarithmic scale.

For processing synthetic ACL A_i $(1 \le i \le n-1)$, Fig. 7.12a shows the computation cost of P_i and the average computation cost of parties $P_{i+1}, \cdots, P_n$ and Fig. 7.12b shows the average communication cost between P_j and P_{j+1} $(i \le j \le n)$. The one-time off-line computation cost, i.e., the computation cost of P_i, is less than 400 s, and the on-line computation cost, i.e., the average computation cost of other parties P_j, is less than 5 s. The average communication cost between any two adjacent parties P_j and P_{j+1} is less than 450 KB.

For processing synthetic ACL A_n, Fig. 7.13a shows the computation cost of P_n and the average computation cost of other parties and Fig. 7.13b shows the average communication cost between P_n and P_i ($1 \leq i \leq n - 1$). The one-time off-line computation cost, i.e., the computation cost of P_n, is less than 550 s, and the on-line computation cost, i.e., the average computation cost of other parties $P_1, \cdots, P_{n-1}$, is less than 25 s. The average communication cost between P_n and P_i is less than 2100 KB.

7.9.3   Efficiency of Incremental Updates of ACLs

To evaluate the efficiency of our approach to handle incremental updates of ACLs, we employed the technique of mutation testing [10] to introduce incremental updates of real and synthetic ACLs. This is a well-accepted technique for carrying out testing experiments in real practice. Given a real and a synthetic ACL, we used mutation testing to randomly create an incremental update of the ACL. Particularly, we randomly changed the some ranges of a rule in this ACL. Note that using this technique, the incremental update of the ACL may result in the equivalent to the original ACL, that is, the FDD of the new ACL is the same as that of the original ACL. In such a case, we created another incremental update of this ACL until the FDD of the new ACL was different from the original ACL. Overall, for each real and synthetic ACL, we generated an incremental update of this ACL in our experiments. Then, we applied our approach proposed in Sect. 7.5 to process each incremental update of an ACL.

Our protocol is efficient for processing incremental update of real ACL A_i ($1 \leq i \leq n - 1$). Figure 7.14a shows for processing incremental update of A_i the computation cost of P_i and the computation cost of P_n. Note that only two parties, P_i and P_n, are involved in this process. The computation cost of P_i is less than 0.4 s and the computation cost of P_n is less than 0.2 s. Both costs are at least 5 times less than those of running the entire protocol in Sect. 7.4. Figure 7.14b shows the average communication cost between two parties P_i and P_n for processing incremental update of ACL A_i, which is less than 20 KB. These communication costs also show an equivalent reduction to that of the computational cost in terms of magnitude.

Similarly, our protocol is efficient for processing incremental update of synthetic ACL A_i ($1 \leq i \leq n - 1$). Figure 7.15a shows the computation cost for processing incremental update of A_i for P_i and the computation cost for P_n. The computation cost of P_i is less than 100 s and the computation cost of P_n is less than 2 s. Figure 7.15b shows the average communication cost between two parties P_i and P_n for processing incremental update of ACL A_i. The communication cost is less than 120 KB. These computation and communication costs are far less than those of running the entire protocol.

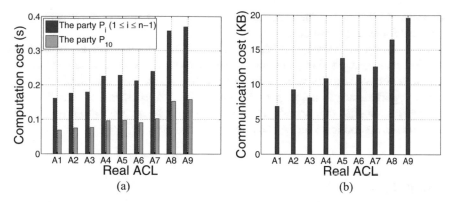

Fig. 7.14 Computation and communication costs for processing updates of real ACL A_i. (**a**) Ave. computation cost. (**b**) Ave. communication cost

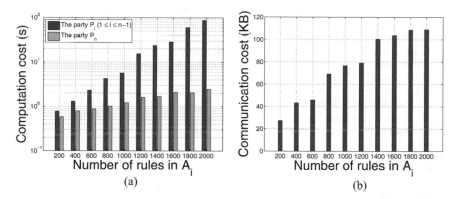

Fig. 7.15 Computation and communication costs for processing updates of synthetic ACL A_i. (**a**) Ave. computation cost. (**b**) Ave. communication cost

7.10   Conclusions

In this chapter, we addressed the problem of privacy preserving quantification of network reachability across different domains. Protecting the privacy of access control configuration is important as the information can be easily abused. We propose an efficient and secure protocol to quantify the network reachability accurately while protecting the privacy of ACLs. We use the divide-and-conquer strategy to decompose the reachability computation which results in a magnitude reduction of the computation and communication costs. To validate our protocol, we conducted the experiments on both real and synthetic ACLs, which demonstrate that our protocol has the benefits of fast computation and low communication overhead, and is suitable for deployed networks. We showed that ACL modifications can be handled effectively. The experimental results demonstrate that our approach is practical for real applications.

Network reachability quantification is an important requirement for effective network management. It has a number of applications like configuration verification and discovery of security vulnerabilities in network. The process might have to be repeated periodically in a time period to ensure that all services are accessible. This requirement implies that quantification process must be secure as well as efficient, i.e., no information leaks due to the possibility of abuse.

References

1. R. Agrawal, A. Evfimievski, R. Srikant, Information sharing across private databases, in *Proc. SIGMOD* (2003), pp. 86–97
2. E. Al-Shaer, W. Marrero, A. El-Atawy, K. ElBadawi, Network configuration in a box: towards end-to-end verification of network reachability and security, in *Proc. ICNP* (2009), pp. 123–132
3. S. Bandhakavi, S. Bhatt, C. Okita, P. Rao, Analyzing end-to-end network reachability, in *Proceedings of IFIP/IEEE International Conference on Symposium on Integrated Network Management* (2009), pp. 585–590
4. T. Benson, A. Akella, D. Maltz, Unraveling the complexity of network management, in *Proc. NSDI* (2009), pp. 335–348
5. M. Casado, T. Garfinkel, A. Akella, M.J. Freedman, D. Boneh, N. McKeown, S. Shenker, Sane: a protection architecture for enterprise networks, in *Proc. Usenix Security Symposium* (2006), pp. 137–151
6. Y.-K. Chang, Fast binary and multiway prefix searches for packet forwarding. Comput. Netw. **51**(3), 588–605 (2007)
7. R. Chen, I.E. Akkus, P. Francis, SplitX: high-performance private analytics, in *Proc. SIG-COMM* (2013), pp. 315–326
8. F. Chen, B. Bruhadeshwar, A.X. Liu, Cross-domain privacy-preserving cooperative firewall optimization. IEEE/ACM Trans. Netw. **21**, 857–868 (2013)
9. J. Cheng, H. Yang, S.H. Wong, S. Lu, Design and implementation of cross-domain cooperative firewall, in *Proc. ICNP* (2007), pp. 284–293
10. R.A. DeMillo, R.J. Lipton, F.G. Sayward, Hints on test data selection: help for the practicing programmer. IEEE Comput. **11**(4), 34–41 (1978)
11. E.A. Emerson, Temporal and modal logic, in *Handbook of Theoretical Computer Science* (Elsevier, Amsterdam, 1990), pp. 995–1072
12. M. Freedman, K. Nissim, B. Pinkas, Efficient private matching and set intersection, in *Proc. EUROCRYPT* (2004), pp. 1–19
13. O. Goldreich, Secure multi-party computations, version 1.4, Working draft, 2002
14. O. Goldreich, *Foundations of Cryptography: Volume II (Basic Applications)* (Cambridge University Press, Cambridge, 2004)
15. M.G. Gouda, A.X. Liu, Firewall design: consistency, completeness and compactness, in *Proc. ICDCS* (2004), pp. 320–327
16. M.G. Gouda, A.X. Liu, Structured firewall design. Comput. Netw. J. **51**(4), 1106–1120 (2007)
17. P. Gupta, N. McKeown, Algorithms for packet classification. IEEE Netw. **15**(2), 24–32 (2001)
18. K. Ingols, R. Lippmann, K. Piwowarski, Practical attack graph generation for network defense, in *Proc. ACSAC* (2006), pp. 121–130
19. Z. Kerravala, As the value of enterprise networks escalates, so does the need for configuration management. Enterprise Computing & Networking, The Yankee Group Report, 2004

20. L. Kissner, D. Song, Privacy-preserving set operations, in *Proc. CRYPTO* (2005), pp. 241–257
21. F. Le, S. Lee, T. Wong, H.S. Kim, D. Newcomb, Detecting network-wide and router-specific misconfigurations through data mining. IEEE/ACM Trans. Netw. **17**(1), 66–79 (2009)
22. A.X. Liu, F. Chen, Collaborative enforcement of firewall policies in virtual private networks, in *Proc. PODC* (2008), pp. 95–104
23. A.X. Liu, F. Chen, Privacy preserving collaborative enforcement of firewall policies in virtual private networks. IEEE Trans. Parallel Distrib. Syst. **22**(5), 887–895 (2011)
24. A.X. Liu, M.G. Gouda, Complete redundancy detection in firewalls, in *Proc. DBSec* (2005), pp. 196–209
25. A.X. Liu, M.G. Gouda, Diverse firewall design. IEEE Trans. Parallel Distrib. Syst. **19**(8), 1237–1251 (2008)
26. A.X. Liu, A.R. Khakpour, Quantifying and verifying reachability for access controlled networks. IEEE/ACM Trans. Netw. **21**, 551–565 (2013)
27. P. Matousek, J. Rab, O. Rysavy, M. Sveda, A formal model for network-wide security analysis, in *Proceedings of the IEEE International Conference and Workshop on the Engineering of Computer Based Systems* (2008)
28. D. Oppenheimer, A. Ganapathi, D.A. Patterson, Why do internet services fail, and what can be done about it? in *Proc. USENIX Symposium on Internet Technologies and Systems (USITS)* (2003)
29. S.C. Pohlig, M.E. Hellman, An improved algorithm for computing logarithms over GF(p) and its cryptographic significance. IEEE Trans. Inf. Theory **24**, 106–110 (1978)
30. D. Safford, D.L. Schales, D.K. Hess, Secure RPC authentication (SRA) for TELNET and FTP. Techical Report, 1993
31. Y. Sang, H. Shen, Efficient and secure protocols for privacy-preserving set operations. ACM Trans. Inf. Syst. Secur. **13**(1), 9:1–9:35 (2009)
32. S. Singh, F. Baboescu, G. Varghese, J. Wang, Packet classification using multidimensional cutting, in *Proc. SIGCOMM* (2003), pp. 213–224
33. Y.-W.E. Sung, C. Lund, M. Lyn, S. Rao, S. Sen, Modeling and understanding end-to-end class of service policies in operational networks, in *Proc. SIGCOMM* (2009), pp. 219–230
34. A. Wool, A quantitative study of firewall configuration errors. IEEE Comput. **37**(6), 62–67 (2004)
35. G.G. Xie, J. Khan, D.A. Maltz, H. Zhang, A. Greenberg, G. Hjálmtýsson, J. Rexford, On static reachability analysis of IP networks, in *Proc. INFOCOM* (2005), pp. 2170–2183
36. B. Zhang, T.S.E. Ng, G. Wang, Reachability monitoring and verification in enterprise networks, in *Proc. SIGCOMM (Poster)* (2008)

Chapter 8
Cross-Domain Privacy-Preserving Cooperative Firewall Optimization

8.1 Introduction

8.1.1 Background and Motivation

Firewalls are critical in securing private networks of businesses, institutions, and home networks. A firewall is often placed at the entrance between a private network and the external network so that it can check each incoming or outgoing packet and decide whether to accept or discard the packet based on its policy. A firewall policy is usually specified as a sequence of rules, called Access Control List (ACL), and each rule has a predicate over multiple packet header fields (i.e. source IP, destination IP, source port, destination port, and protocol type) and a decision (i.e. accept and discard) for the packets that match the predicate. The rules in a firewall policy typically follow the first-match semantics, where the decision for a packet is the decision of the first rule that the packet matches in the policy. Each physical interface of a router/firewall is configured with two ACLs: one for filtering outgoing packets and the other one for filtering incoming packets. In this chapter, we use *firewalls*, *firewall policies*, and *ACLs*, interchangeably.

The number of rules in a firewall significantly affects its throughput. Figure 8.1 shows the result of the performance test of iptables conducted by HiPAC [7]. It shows that increasing the number of rules in a firewall policy dramatically reduces the firewall throughput. Unfortunately, with the explosive growth of services deployed on the Internet, firewall policies are growing rapidly in size. Thus, optimizing firewall policies is crucial for improving network performance.

A. X. Liu, R. Li, *Algorithms for Data and Computation Privacy*, https://doi.org/10.1007/978-3-030-58896-0_8

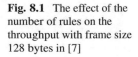

Fig. 8.1 The effect of the number of rules on the throughput with frame size 128 bytes in [7]

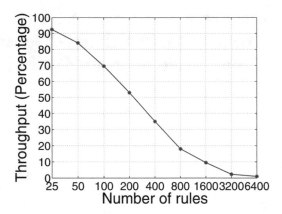

8.1.2   Limitation of Prior Work

Prior work on firewall optimization focuses on either intra-firewall optimization [6, 17–23] or inter-firewall optimization [2, 30] within one administrative domain where the privacy of firewall policies is not a concern. Intra-firewall optimization means optimizing a single firewall. It is achieved by either removing redundant rules [17, 18] or rewriting rules [6, 19–23]. Prior work on inter-firewall optimization requires two firewall policies without any privacy protection, and thus can only be used within one administrative domain. However, in reality, it is common that two firewalls belong to different administrative domains where firewall policies cannot be shared with each other. Keeping firewall policies confidential is important for two reasons. First, a firewall policy may have security holes that can be exploited by attackers. Quantitative studies have shown that most firewalls are misconfigured and have security holes [28]. Second, a firewall policy often contains private information, e.g., the IP addresses of servers, which can be used by attackers to launch more precise and targeted attacks.

8.1.3   Cross-Domain Inter-Firewall Optimization

To our best knowledge, no prior work focuses on cross-domain privacy-preserving inter-firewall optimization. This chapter represents the first step in exploring this unknown space. Specifically, we focus on removing inter-firewall policy redundancies in a privacy-preserving manner. Consider two adjacent firewalls 1 and 2 belonging to different administrative domains Net_1 and Net_2. Let FW_1 denote the policy on firewall 1's outgoing interface to firewall 2 and FW_2 denote the policy on firewall 2's incoming interface from firewall 1. For a rule r in FW_2, if all the packets that match r but do not match any rule above r in FW_2 are discarded by FW_1, rule r can be removed because such packets never come to FW_2. We call rule r an *inter-*

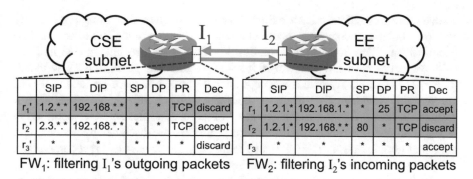

	SIP	DIP	SP	DP	PR	Dec
r_1'	1.2.*.*	192.168.*.*	*	*	TCP	discard
r_2'	2.3.*.*	192.168.*.*	*	*	TCP	accept
r_3'	*	*	*	*	*	discard

	SIP	DIP	SP	DP	PR	Dec
r_1	1.2.1.*	192.168.1.*	*	25	TCP	accept
r_2	1.2.1.*	192.168.*.*	80	*	TCP	discard
r_3	*	*	*	*	*	accept

FW$_1$: filtering I$_1$'s outgoing packets   FW$_2$: filtering I$_2$'s incoming packets

Fig. 8.2 Example inter-firewall redundant rules

firewall redundant rule with respect to FW_1. Note that FW_1 and FW_2 only filter the traffic from FW_1 to FW_2; the traffic from firewall 2's outgoing interface to firewall 1's incoming interface is guarded by other two separate policies. For simplicity, we assume that FW_1 and FW_2 have no intra-firewall redundancy as such redundancy can be removed using the proposed solutions [17, 18].

Figure 8.2 illustrates inter-firewall redundancy, where two adjacent routers belong to different administrative domains CSE and EE. The physical interfaces connecting two routers are denoted as I_1 and I_2, respectively. The rules of the two firewall policies FW_1 and FW_2, that are used to filter the traffic flowing from CSE to EE, are listed in two tables following the format used in Cisco Access Control Lists. Note that SIP, DIP, SP, DP, PR, and Dec denote source IP, destination IP, source port, destination port, protocol type, and decision, respectively. Clearly, all the packets that match r_1 and r_2 in FW_2 are discarded by r_1' in FW_1. Thus, r_1 and r_2 of FW_2 are inter-firewall redundant with respect to r_1' in FW_1.

8.1.4 Technical Challenges and Our Approach

The key challenge is to design a protocol that allows two adjacent firewalls to identify the inter-firewall redundancy with respect to each other without knowing the policy of the other firewall. While intra-firewall redundancy removal is complex [17, 18], inter-firewall redundancy removal with the privacy-preserving requirement is even harder. To determine whether a rule in FW_2 is inter-firewall redundant with respect to FW_1, Net_2 certainly needs some information about FW_1; yet, Net_2 cannot reveal FW_1 from such information.

A straightforward solution is to perform a privacy preserving comparison between two rules from two adjacent firewalls. Particularly, for each rule r in FW_2, this solution checks whether all possible packets that match rule r in FW_2 match a rule r' with the discard decision in FW_1. If rule r' exists, r is inter-firewall redundant with respect to r' in FW_1. However, because firewalls follow the first-match semantics and the rules in a firewall typically overlap, this solution is not only incorrect but also incomplete. Incorrect means that wrong redundant rules could be identified in FW_2. Suppose this solution identifies r as a redundant rule in FW_2 with respect to r'_2 in FW_1. However, if some packets that match rule r also match rule r'_1 (r'_1 is above r'_2) with the accept decision in FW_1, these packets will pass through FW_1 and then FW_2 needs to filter them with r. In this case, r is actually not redundant. Incomplete means that a portion of redundant rules could be identified in FW_2. If all possible packets that match rule r in FW_2 are discarded by not only one rule but multiple rules in FW_1, r is also redundant. However, the direct comparison solution cannot identify such redundancies.

Our basic idea is as follows. For each rule r in FW_2, we first compute a set of compact predicates representing the set of packets that match r but do not match the rules above r in FW_2. Then, for each predicate, we check whether all the packets that match the predicate are discarded by FW_1. If this condition holds for all the predicates computed from rule r, then rule r is redundant. To efficiently compute these predicates, we convert firewalls to firewall decision diagrams [18]. To allow the two firewalls to detect the redundant rules in FW_2 in a privacy-preserving manner, we develop a protocol so that two firewalls can detect such redundant rules without disclosing their policies to each other.

Our protocol applies to both stateful and stateless firewalls. The main difference between stateful and stateless firewalls is that stateful firewalls maintain a connection table. Upon receiving a packet, if it belongs to an established connection, it is automatically accepted without checking against the rules. Having the connection table or not does not affect our protocol.

8.1.5 Key Contributions

We make two key contributions. First, we propose a novel privacy-preserving protocol for detecting inter-firewall redundant rules in one firewall with respect to another firewall. This chapter represents the first effort along this unexplored direction. Second, we implemented our protocol and conducted extensive experiments on both real and synthetic firewall policies. The results on real firewall policies show that our protocol can remove as many as 49% of the rules in a firewall whereas the average is 19.4%. The communication cost is less than a few hundred KBs. Our protocol incurs no extra online packet processing overhead and the offline processing time is less than a few hundred seconds.

We organize the chapter as follows. We first review related work in Sect. 11.2. Then, we introduce our system model and threat model in Sect. 13.3. In Sect. 8.4, we present our privacy-preserving protocol for detecting inter-firewall redundant rules. In Sect. 8.5, we discuss remaining issues. In Sect. 8.6, we give security analysis results of our protocol. In Sect. 9.7, we present our experimental results. Finally, we conclude in Sect. 8.8.

8.2 Related Work

8.2.1 Firewall Redundancy Removal

Prior work on intra-firewall redundancy removal aims to detect redundant rules within a single firewall [12, 17, 18]. Gupta identified backward and forward redundant rules in a firewall [12]. Later, Liu et al. pointed out that the redundant rules identified by Gupta are incomplete, and proposed two methods for detecting all redundant rules [17, 18]. Prior work on inter-firewall redundancy removal requires the knowledge of two firewall policies and therefore is only applicable within one administrative domain [2, 30].

8.2.2 Collaborative Firewall Enforcement in VPN

Prior work on collaborative firewall enforcement in virtual private networks (VPNs) enforces firewall policies over encrypted VPN tunnels without leaking the privacy of the remote network's policy [5, 15]. The problems of collaborative firewall enforcement in VPNs and privacy-preserving inter-firewall optimization are fundamentally different. First, their purposes are different. The former focuses on enforcing a firewall policy over VPN tunnels in a privacy-preserving manner, whereas the latter focuses on removing inter-firewall redundant rules without disclosing their policies to each other. Second, their requirements are different. The former preserves the privacy of the remote network's policy, whereas the latter preserves the privacy of both policies.

8.3 System and Threat Models

8.3.1 System Model

A firewall FW is an ordered list of *rules*. Each *rule* has a *predicate* over d *fields* $F_1, \cdots, F_d$ and a *decision* for the packets that match the predicate. Firewalls usually check five fields: source IP, destination IP, source port, destination port, and protocol type. The length of these fields are 32, 32, 16, 16, and 8 bits, respectively. A *predicate* defines a set of packets over the d fields, and is specified as $F_1 \in T_1 \wedge \cdots \wedge F_d \in T_d$ where each T_i is a subset of F_i's domain $D(F_i)$. A packet over the d fields $F_1, \cdots, F_d$ is a d-tuple $(p_1, \cdots, p_d)$ where each p_i $(1 \leq i \leq d)$ is an element of $D(F_i)$. A packet $(p_1, \cdots, p_d)$ *matches* a rule $F_1 \in T_1 \wedge \cdots \wedge F_d \in T_d \rightarrow \langle decision \rangle$ if and only if the condition $p_1 \in T_1 \wedge \cdots \wedge p_d \in T_d$ holds. Typical firewall decisions include accept, discard, accept with logging, and discard with logging. Without loss of generality, we only consider accept and discard in this chapter. We call a rule with the accept decision an *accepting rule* and a rule with the discard decision a *discarding rule*. In a firewall policy, a packet may match multiple rules whose decisions are different. To resolve these conflicts, firewalls typically employ a first-match semantics where the decision for a packet p is the decision of the first rule that p matches. A *matching set* of r_i, $M(r_i)$, is the set of all possible packets that match the rule r_i [17]. A *resolving set* of r_i, $R(r_i)$, is the set of packets that match r_i but do not match any rule r_j above r_i ($j < i$), and $R(r_i)$ is equal to $M(r_i) - M(r_1) \cup \cdots \cup M(r_{i-1})$ [17].

Based on above concepts, we define inter-firewall redundant rules. Given two adjacent firewalls FW_1 and FW_2, where the traffic flow is from FW_1 to FW_2, a rule r in FW_2 is inter-firewall redundant with respect to FW_1 if and only if all the packets in r's resolving set are discarded by FW_1.

8.3.2   Threat Model

We adopt the semi-honest model in [9]. For two adjacent firewalls, we assume that they are semi-honest, i.e. each firewall follows our protocol correctly but each firewall may try to reveal the policy of the other firewall. The semi-honest model is realistic and well adopted [3, 29]. For example, this model is appropriate for large organizations that have many independent branches as well as for loosely connected alliances composed by multiple parties. While we are confident that all administrative domains follow mandate protocols, we may not guarantee that no corrupted employees are trying to reveal the private firewall policies of other parties. Also, it may be possible for one party to issue a sequence of inputs to try and reveal the other party's policy. For this attack to be successful, several assumptions have to be satisfied, one of them being that one firewall's policy remain constant. Another requirement is that, the number of times the protocol needs to be executed to reveal a significant amount of rules is computationally expensive.[1] Such malicious activity may be identified by the other party using anomaly detection approaches [13, 14, 25]. However, in our threat model, the inputs to the protocol are honest and crafting inputs to reveal the firewall policies is beyond our threat model. We leave investigation of privacy-preserving firewall optimization in the model with malicious participants to future work.

---

[1]It requires $\log w$ updates to reveal w-bit field. Given that rule has d-fields, the complexity is $d^{\log w}$ updates for a single rule whereby such high communication activity can be detected by anomaly detection approaches.

8.4 Privacy-Preserving Inter-Firewall Redundancy Removal

In this section, we present our privacy-preserving protocol for detecting inter-firewall redundant rules in FW_2 with respect to FW_1. To do this, we first converts each firewall to an equivalent sequence of non-overlapping rules. Because for any non-overlapping rule nr, the matching set of nr is equal to the resolving set of nr, i.e. $M(nr) = R(nr)$, we only need to compare non-overlapping rules generated from the two firewalls for detecting inter-firewall redundancy. Second, we divide this problem into two subproblems, *single-rule coverage redundancy detection* and *multi-rule coverage redundancy detection*, and then propose our privacy-preserving protocol for solving each subproblem. A rule nr is *covered* by one or multiple rules $nr'_{i_1} \cdots nr'_{i_k}$ ($k \geq 1$) if and only if $M(nr) \subseteq M(nr'_{i_1}) \cup \cdots \cup M(nr'_{i_k})$. The first subproblem checks whether a non-overlapping rule nr in FW_2 is covered by a non-overlapping discarding rule nr' in FW_1, i.e. $M(nr) \subseteq M(nr')$. The second subproblem checks whether a non-overlapping rule nr in FW_2 is covered by multiple non-overlapping discarding rules $nr'_{i_1} \cdots nr'_{i_k}$ ($k \geq 2$) in FW_1, i.e. $M(nr) \subseteq M(nr'_{i_1}) \cup \cdots \cup M(nr'_{i_k})$. Finally, after redundant non-overlapping rules generated from FW_2 are identified, we map them back to original rules in FW_2 and then identify the redundant ones.

The problem of checking whether $M(nr) \subseteq M(nr')$ boils down to the problem of checking whether one range $[a, b]$ in nr is contained by another range $[a', b']$ in nr', which further boils down to the problem of checking whether $a \subset [a', b']$ and $b \in [a', b']$. Thus, we first describe the privacy-preserving protocol for comparing a number and a range.

8.4.1 Privacy-Preserving Range Comparison

To check whether a number a from FW_2 is in a range $[a', b']$ from FW_1, we use a method similar to the prefix membership verification scheme in [15]. The basic idea is to convert the problem of checking whether $a \in [a', b']$ to the problem of checking whether two sets converted from a and $[a', b']$ have a common element. Our method consists of four steps:

1. *Prefix conversion.* It converts $[a', b']$ to a minimum number of prefixes, denoted as $\mathcal{T}([a', b'])$, whose union is $[a', b']$. For example, $\mathcal{T}([11, 15])=\{1011, 11**\}$.
2. *Prefix family construction.* It generates all the prefixes that contains a including a itself. This set of prefixes is called the prefix family of a, denoted as $\mathcal{F}(a)$. Let k be the bit length of a. The prefix family $\mathcal{F}(a)$ consists of $k + 1$ prefixes where the i-th prefix is obtained by replacing the last $i - 1$ bits of a by $*$. For example, as the binary representation of 12 is 1100, we have $\mathcal{F}(12)=\{1100, 110*, 11**, 1***, ****\}$. It is not difficult to prove that $a \in [a', b']$ if and only if $\mathcal{F}(a) \cap \mathcal{T}([a', b']) \neq \emptyset$.

3. *Prefix numericalization.* It converts the prefixes generated in the previous steps to concrete numbers such that we can encrypt them in the next step. We use the prefix numericalization scheme in [4]. Given a prefix $b_1 b_2 \cdots b_k * \cdots *$ of w bits, we first insert 1 after b_k. The bit 1 represents a separator between $b_1 b_2 \cdots b_k$ and $* \cdots *$. Then we replace every $*$ by 0. For example, 11** is converted to 11100. If the prefix does not contain *s, we place 1 at the end. For example, 1100 is converted to 11001.

4. *Comparison.* It checks whether $a \in [a', b']$ by checking whether $\mathcal{F}(a) \cap \mathcal{T}([a', b']) \neq \emptyset$, which boils down to checking whether two numbers are equal. We use commutative encryption to do this checking in a privacy-preserving manner. Given a number x and two encryption keys K_1 and K_2, a commutative encryption is a function that satisfies the property $((x)_{K_1})_{K_2} = ((x)_{K_2})_{K_1}$, i.e. encryption with key K_1 first and then K_2 is equivalent to encryption with key K_2 first and then K_1. Example commutative encryption algorithms are the Pohlig-Hellman Exponentiation Cipher [24] and Secure RPC Authentication (SRA) [26]. In our scheme, each domain chooses a private key. Let K_1, K_2 be the private keys chosen by Net_1 and Net_2, respectively. To check whether number v_1 from Net_1 is equal to number v_2 from Net_2 without disclosing the value of each number to the other party, Net_1 can first encrypt v_1 using key K_1 and sends $(x)_{K_1}$ to Net_2; similarly, Net_2 can first encrypt v_2 using key K_2 and sends $(x)_{K_2}$ to Net_1. Then, each party checks whether $v_1 = v_2$ by checking whether $((v_1)_{K_1})_{K_2} = ((v_2)_{K_2})_{K_1}$. Note that $((v_1)_{K_1})_{K_2} = ((v_2)_{K_2})_{K_1}$ if and only if $v_1 = v_2$. If $v_1 \neq v_2$, neither party can learn anything about the numbers being compared. Figure 8.3 illustrates the process of checking whether 12 from FW_2 is in the range [11, 15] from FW_1.

8.4.2 Processing Firewall FW_1

To detect the redundant rules in FW_2, Net_1 converts its firewall FW_1 to a set of non-overlapping rules. To preserve the privacy of FW_1, Net_1 first converts each range of a non-overlapping discarding rules from FW_1 to a set of prefixes. Second, Net_1

Fig. 8.3 Prefix membership verification

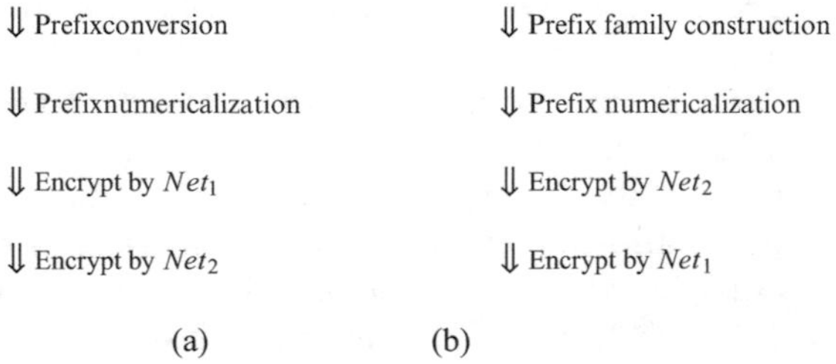

⇓ Prefixconversion   ⇓ Prefix family construction

⇓ Prefixnumericalization   ⇓ Prefix numericalization

⇓ Encrypt by Net_1 ⇓ Encrypt by Net_2

⇓ Encrypt by Net_2 ⇓ Encrypt by Net_1

(a)   (b)

and Net_2 encrypt these prefixes using commutative encryption. The conversion of FW_1 includes nine steps:

1. Net_1 first converts FW_1 to an equivalent firewall decision diagram (FDD) [10, 11]. An FDD for a firewall FW of a sequence of rules $\langle r_1, \cdots, r_n \rangle$ over fields $F_1, \cdots, F_d$ is an acyclic and directed graph that has five properties.

   (a) There is exactly one node that has no incoming edges. This node is called the *root*. The nodes that have no outgoing edge are called *terminal* nodes.
   (b) Each node v has a label, denoted $F(v)$. If v is a nonterminal node, then $F(v) \in \{F_1, \cdots, F_d\}$. If v is a terminal node, then $F(v)$ is a decision.
   (c) Each edge e, $u \to v$, is labeled with a non-empty set of integers, denoted $I(e)$, where $I(e)$ is a subset of the domain of u's label (i.e. $I(e) \subseteq D(F(u))$).
   (d) The set of all outgoing edges of a node v, denoted $E(v)$, satisfies two conditions: (a) *consistency*: $I(e) \cap I(e') = \emptyset$ for any two distinct edges e and e' in $E(v)$; (b) *completeness*: $\bigcup_{e \in E(v)} I(e) = D(F(v))$.
   (e) A directed path from the root to a terminal node is called a *decision path*. No two nodes on a decision path have the same label. Each path in the FDD corresponds to a non-overlapping rule. A *full-length ordered FDD* is an FDD where in each decision path all fields appear exactly once and in the same order. For ease of presentation, we use the term "FDD" to denote "full-length ordered FDD". An FDD construction algorithm, which converts a firewall policy to an equivalent FDD, is presented in [16]. Figure 8.4b shows the FDD constructed from Fig. 8.4a.

2. Net_1 reduces the FDD's size by merging isomorphic subgraphs. An FDD f is *reduced* if and only if it satisfies two conditions: (a) no two nodes in f are isomorphic; (b) no two nodes have more than one edge between them. Two nodes v and v' in an FDD are *isomorphic* if and only if v and v' satisfy one of the following two conditions: (a) both v and v' are terminal nodes with identical labels; (b) both v and v' are nonterminal nodes and there is a one-to-one correspondence between the outgoing edges of v and the outgoing edges of v' such that every two corresponding edges have identical labels and they both point to the same node. Figure 8.4c shows the FDD reduced from the FDD in Fig. 8.4b.

3. Net_1 extracts non-overlapping discarding rules. Net_1 does not extract non-overlapping accepting rules because the packets accepted by FW_1 are passed to FW_2. Note that a non-overlapping rule from FW_2 that is covered by these discarding rules from FW_1 is redundant. Figure 8.4d shows the discarding non-overlapping rules extracted from the reduced FDD in Fig. 8.4c.

4. Net_1 converts each range to a set of prefixes. Figure 8.4e shows the prefixes generated from Fig. 8.4d.

5. Net_1 unions all these prefix sets and then permutes the prefixes. Figure 8.4f shows the resulting prefix list. Note that the resulting list does not include duplicate prefixes. The benefits are twofold. In terms of efficiency, it avoids encrypting and sending duplicate prefixes for both parties, and hence, signifi-

Fig. 8.4 The conversion of FW_1

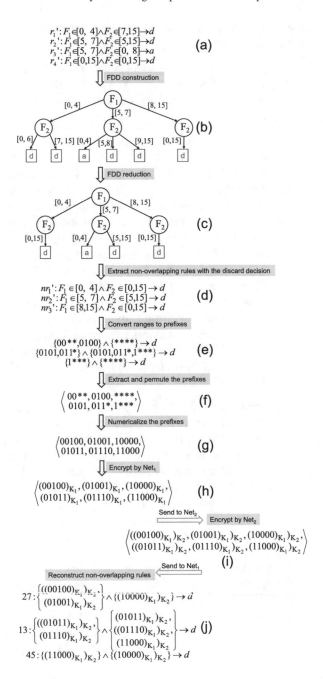

cantly reduces computation and communication costs. In terms of security, Net_2 cannot reconstruct the non-overlapping rules from FW_1, because Net_2 does not know which prefix belongs to which field of which rule. However, Net_1 knows such information and it can reconstruct these non-overlapping rules.

6. Net_1 numericalizes and encrypts each prefix using K_1, and then sends to Net_2. Figure 8.4g and h show the numericalized and encrypted prefixes, respectively.
7. Net_2 further encrypts these prefixes with K_2 and sends them back to Net_1 as shown in Fig. 8.4i.
8. Net_1 reconstructs its non-overlapping discarding rules from the double encrypted prefixes because Net_1 knows which prefix belongs to which field of which rule.
9. For each reconstructed non-overlapping rule, Net_1 assigns a distinct random index to it. These indices are used for Net_2 to identify the redundant non-overlapping rules from FW_2. For example, in Fig. 8.4j, Net_1 assigns its three rules with three random indices: 27, 13, and 45. The detailed discussion is in Sect. 8.4.4.

8.4.3   Processing Firewall FW_2

In order to compare two firewalls in a privacy-preserving manner, Net_2 and Net_1 convert firewall FW_2 to d sets of double encrypted numbers, where d is the number of fields. The conversion of FW_2 includes five steps:

1. Net_2 converts FW_2 to an equivalent all-match FDD. All-match FDDs differ from FDDs on terminal nodes. In an all-match FDD, each terminal node is labeled with a nonempty set of rule sequence numbers, whereas in an FDD each terminal node is labeled with a decision. For rule r_i ($1 \leq i \leq n$), we call i the *sequence number* of r_i. The set of rule sequence numbers labeled on a terminal node consists of the sequence numbers of all the rules that overlaps with the decision path ending with this terminal node. Given a decision path $\mathcal{P}$, $(v_1 e_1 \cdots v_d e_d v_{d+1})$, the matching set of $\mathcal{P}$ is defined as the set of all packets that satisfy $F(v_1) \in I(e_1) \wedge \cdots \wedge F(v_d) \in I(e_d)$. We use $M(\mathcal{P})$ to denote the matching set of $\mathcal{P}$. More formally, in an all-match FDD, for any decision path $\mathcal{P} : (v_1 e_1 \cdots v_d e_d v_{d+1})$, if $M(\mathcal{P}) \cap M(r_i) \neq \emptyset$, then $M(\mathcal{P}) \subseteq M(r_i)$ and $i \in F(v_{d+1})$. Figure 8.4b shows the all-match FDD generated from Fig. 8.4a. Considering the terminal node of the fourth path in Fig. 8.4b, its label {2, 4} means that $M(\mathcal{P}) \subseteq M(r_2)$, $M(\mathcal{P}) \subseteq M(r_4)$, $M(\mathcal{P}) \cap M(r_1) = \emptyset$, and $M(\mathcal{P}) \cap M(r_3) = \emptyset$. An all-match FDD not only represents a firewall in a non-overlapping fashion but also represents the overlapping relationship among rules. The reason of converting FW_2 to an all-match FDD is that later Net_2 needs the rule sequence numbers to identify inter-firewall redundant rules in FW_2.
2. Net_2 extracts all non-overlapping rules from the all-match FDD. Figure 8.5c shows the non-overlapping rules extracted from Fig. 8.5b. For each range $[a, b]$

Fig. 8.5 The conversion of FW_2

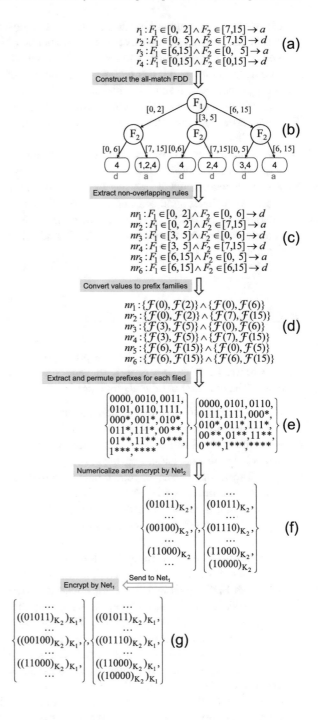

of a non-overlapping rule, Net_2 generates two prefix families $\mathcal{F}(a)$ and $\mathcal{F}(b)$. Figure 8.5d shows the result from Fig. 8.5c.

3. For every field F_k, Net_2 unions all prefix families of all the non-overlapping rules into one prefix set and permutes the prefixes. Considering the first field F_1 in Fig. 8.5d, Net_2 unions $\mathcal{F}(0)$, $\mathcal{F}(2)$, $\mathcal{F}(3)$, $\mathcal{F}(5)$, $\mathcal{F}(6)$ and $\mathcal{F}(15)$ to obtain the first prefix set in Fig. 8.5e. The benefits of this step are similar to those of Step (5) in FW_1's conversion. In terms of efficiency, it avoids encrypting and sending the duplicate prefixes for each field, and hence, significantly reduces the computation and communication costs. In terms of security, Net_1 cannot reconstruct the non-overlapping rules of FW_2, because Net_1 does not know which prefix belongs to which rule in FW_2. However, Net_2 knows such information, which will be used to identify redundant non-overlapping rules later. Note that, the ordering of the fields cannot be permuted because Net_1 needs to perform comparison of the prefixes with only those prefixes from the corresponding fields.

4. Net_2 numericalizes and encrypts the prefixes using its private K_2, and sends them to Net_1. Figure 8.5f shows the prefixes.

5. Net_1 further encrypts these prefixes using key K_1.

8.4.4   Single-Rule Coverage Redundancy Detection

After processing the two firewalls, Net_1 has a sequence of double encrypted non-overlapping rules obtained from FW_1 and d sets of double encrypted numbers obtained from FW_2. Let $(F_1 \in \mathcal{T}_1) \wedge \cdots \wedge (F_d \in \mathcal{T}_d) \rightarrow discard$ denote a double encrypted rule, where $\mathcal{T}_i$ is a set of double encrypted numbers. Let $\mathbb{T}_1, \cdots, \mathbb{T}_d$ denote the d sets of double encrypted numbers from FW_2. Figure 8.6a shows the double encrypted non-overlapping rules generated from Figs. 8.4 and 8.6b shows the double encrypted numbers generated from Fig. 8.5. For each field F_i ($1 \leq i \leq d$) and for each number a in $\mathbb{T}_i$, Net_1 checks whether there exists a double encrypted rule $(F_1 \in \mathcal{T}_1) \wedge \cdots \wedge (F_d \in \mathcal{T}_d) \rightarrow discard$ such that $a \in \mathcal{T}_i$. If rule r_i satisfies this condition, then Net_1 associates the rule index i with a. As there maybe multiple rules that satisfy this condition, eventually Net_1 associates a set of rule indices with a. If no rule satisfies this condition, Net_1 associates an empty set with a. Considering the number $((01011)_{K_2})_{K_1}$, only the rule with index 13 contains it because $((01011)_{K_2})_{K_1} = ((01011)_{K_1})_{K_2}$; thus, Net_1 associates $((01011)_{K_2})_{K_1}$ with $\{13\}$. Finally, Net_1 replaces each number in $\mathbb{T}_1, \cdots, \mathbb{T}_d$ with its corresponding set of rule indices, and sends them to Net_2.

Upon receiving the sets from Net_1, for each prefix family, Net_2 finds the index of the rule that overlaps with the prefix family. For a non-overlapping rule nr from FW_2, if all its prefix families overlap with the same discarding rule nr' from FW_1, nr is covered by nr' and hence, nr is redundant. For example, in Fig. 8.6d, nr_1 is redundant, because $\mathcal{F}(0)$, $\mathcal{F}(2)$, $\mathcal{F}(0)$ and $\mathcal{F}(6)$ overlap with rule 27 from FW_1. Similarly, nr_2 is redundant. Note that $\mathcal{F}(v) : j_1, \ldots, j_k$ denotes that $\mathcal{F}(v)$ overlaps with non-overlapping rules $j_1, \ldots, j_k$ from FW_1.

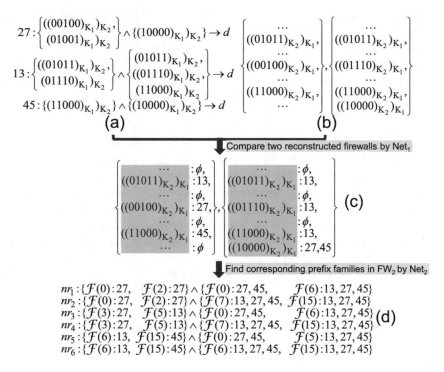

Fig. 8.6 Comparison of two firewalls

8.4.5 *Multi-Rule Coverage Redundancy Detection*

To detect multi-rule coverage redundancy, our basic idea is to combine all the non-overlapping discarding rules from FW_1 to a set of new rules so that for any arbitrary rule from FW_2, if it is covered by multiple non-overlapping discarding rules from FW_1, it is covered by a rule from these new rules. More formally, let $nr'_1, \cdots, nr'_l$ denote the non-overlapping discarding rules from FW_1 and $\{s'_1, \cdots, s'_g\}$ denote the set of new rules generated from $nr'_1, \cdots, nr'_l$. For any rule nr from FW_2, if a non-overlapping rule nr from FW_2 is multi-rule coverage redundant, i.e., $M(nr) \subseteq M(nr'_{i_1}) \cup \cdots \cup M(nr'_{i_k})$ where $nr'_{i_1} \cdots nr'_{i_k}$ ($k \geq 2$) from FW_1, there is a rule s'_j ($1 \leq j \leq g$) that covers nr, i.e., $M(nr) \subseteq M(s'_j)$. Thus, after Net_1 computes the set of new rules from FW_1, we reduce the problem of multi-rule coverage redundancy detection to single-rule coverage redundancy detection. Then, two parties Net_1 and Net_2 can cooperatively run our protocol proposed in this section to identify the non-overlapping single-rule and multi-rule coverage redundant rules from FW_2 at the same time. However, the key question is how to compute the set of new rules $s'_1, \cdots, s'_g$.

A straightforward method is to compute all possible rules that are covered by a single or multiple non-overlapping discarding rules among $nr'_1, \cdots, nr'_l$. All these rules form the set of new rules $s'_1, \cdots, s'_g$. However, this method incurs two major drawbacks. First, the time and space complexities of this method can be significant because the number of all these rules could be huge. Second, due to the huge number of these rules, the communication and computation costs increase significantly. The relationship between these costs and the number of rules is discussed in Sect. 8.6.2.

Our solution is to compute only the *largest* rules that are covered by a single or multiple non-overlapping discarding rules among $nr'_1, \cdots, nr'_l$. The term *largest* can be explained as follows. Without considering the decision, a firewall rule with d fields can be denoted as a hyperrectangle over a d-dimensional space. Then, l non-overlapping discarding rules $nr'_1, \cdots, nr'_l$ are l hyperrectangles over a d-dimensional space. The new rules $s'_1, \cdots, s'_g$ are also the hyperrectangles. The term *largest* means that if a hyperrectangle s^*_j contains the hyperrectangle s'_j but is larger than s'_j, s^*_j has some parts which are not covered by all the l hyperrectangles $nr'_1, \cdots, nr'_l$. For example, the non-overlapping discarding rules nr'_1, nr'_2, nr'_3 in Fig. 8.4d can be illustrated as three filled rectangles in Fig. 8.7. Figure 8.7 also shows three new rules s'_1, s'_2, s'_3 generated from nr'_1, nr'_2, nr'_3, where s'_1, s'_2, and s'_3 are illustrated as different dashed rectangles. Note that s'_1 is the same as nr'_1, and s'_3 is the same as nr'_3. Note that the values of two fields F_1 and F_2 are integers. Thus, we can combine three ranges [0, 4], [5, 7], [8, 15] to a range [0, 15] for the field F_1 of s'_2.

More formally, we can define a largest rule s'_j ($1 \leq j \leq g$) as follows.

1. $M(s'_j) \subseteq M(nr'_1) \cup \cdots \cup M(nr'_l)$.
2. For any rule s^*_j that $M(s^*_j) \supset M(s'_j)$,
   $M(s^*_j) \not\subseteq M(nr'_1) \cup \cdots \cup M(nr'_l)$.

Fig. 8.7 Three largest rules generated from Fig. 8.4d

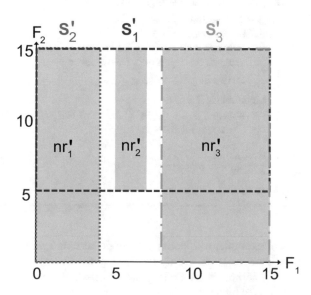

Given the set of all largest rules $s'_1, \cdots, s'_g$ generated from $nr'_1, \cdots, nr'_l$, for any rule nr, if nr is covered by one or multiple rules in $nr'_1, \cdots, nr'_l$, there exists a largest rule s'_j ($1 \leq j \leq g$) which covers nr. We have the following theorem.

Theorem 8.1 *Given the set of all largest rules $s'_1, \cdots, s'_g$ generated from $nr'_1, \cdots, nr'_l$, for any rule nr, if $M(nr) \subseteq M(nr'_1) \cup \cdots \cup M(nr'_l)$, there exists a largest rule s'_j ($1 \leq j \leq g$) which satisfies the condition $M(nr) \subseteq M(s'_j)$.*

Proof If nr is a largest rule, it is included in $s'_1, \cdots, s'_g$.

If nr is not a largest rule, we prove it by contradiction. If there exists no largest rule among $s'_1, \cdots, s'_g$ which covers nr, we can generate all possible rules which satisfy two conditions: (1) the matching set of each of these rules is the superset of $M(nr)$; (2) each of these rules is covered by $nr'_1, \cdots, nr'_l$. Among all these generated rules, there exists at least a largest rule otherwise the number of these rules is infinite. However, $M(nr'_1) \cup \cdots \cup M(nr'_l)$ is a finite domain.   □

Next, we discuss how to compute the set of all the largest rules $S = \{s'_1, \cdots, s'_g\}$ from the non-overlapping discarding rules $nr'_1, \cdots, nr'_l$. Our idea is to first compute the largest rules for every two rules among $nr'_1, \cdots, nr'_l$. Repeat computing the largest rules for every two rules in the previous step until the resulting rules do not change. Finally, the resulting rules is the set of all the largest rules $s'_1, \cdots, s'_g$. Note that it is trivial to compute the largest rules from two rules. This algorithm is shown in Algorithm 1.

Algorithm 1: Computation of the set of largest rules

Input: l non-overlapping rules $nr'_1, \cdots, nr'_l$.
Output: The set of all the largest rules S

1 Initialize S, $S := \{nr'_1, \cdots, nr'_l\}$;
2 **while** *S has been changed* **do**
3   **for** *every two rules s'_i, s'_j ($i \neq j$) in S* **do**
4   compute the largest rules from s'_i and s'_j;
5   add the largest rules to $\hat{S}$;
6   **for** *each rule $\hat{s}_i$ in $\hat{S}$* **do**
7   **if** *there is a rule $\hat{s}_j$ ($j \neq i$) in $\hat{S}$ such that $M(\hat{s}_j) \supset M(\hat{s}_i)$* **then**
8   remove $\hat{s}_i$ from $\hat{S}$;
9      $S := \hat{S}$;
10     $\hat{S} := \emptyset$;
11 **return** S;

For example, to identify the single-rule and multiple-rule coverage redundancy simultaneously, Net_1 only needs to perform one more step between Fig. 8.4d and e. Net_1 computes all the largest rules from the non-overlapping discarding rules in Fig. 8.4d, which are

$$s_1' : F_1 \in [0, 4] \wedge F_2 \in [0, 15] \to d$$
$$s_2' : F_1 \in [0, 15] \wedge F_2 \in [5, 15] \to d$$
$$s_3' : F_1 \in [8, 15] \wedge F_2 \in [0, 15] \to d$$

Finally, Net_2 can identify that $nr_4 : F_1 \in [3, 15] \wedge F_2 \in [7, 15] \to d$ is redundant because nr_4 is covered the by the rule s_2'.

8.4.6   Identification and Removal of Redundant Rules

After single-rule and multi-rule coverage redundancy detection, Net_2 identifies the redundant non-overlapping rules in FW_2. Next, Net_2 needs to identify which original rules are inter-firewall redundant. As each path in the all-match FDD of FW_2 corresponds to a non-overlapping rule, we call the paths that correspond to the redundant non-overlapping rules *redundant paths* and the remaining paths *effective paths*. For example, in Fig. 8.8, the dashed paths are the redundant paths that correspond to nr_1, nr_2 and nr_4 in Fig. 8.5c, respectively. Finally, Net_2 identifies redundant rules based on Theorem 8.2.

Theorem 8.2   *Given firewall $FW_2 : \langle r_1, \cdots, r_n \rangle$ with no intra-firewall redundancy and its all-match FDD, rule r_i is inter-firewall redundant with respect to FW_1 if and only if two conditions hold: (1) there is a redundant path whose terminal node contains sequence number i; (2) there is no effective path whose terminal node contains i as the smallest element.*

Proof   Let $\{\mathcal{P}_1, \cdots, \mathcal{P}_m\}$ denote all paths in FW_2's all-match FDD. According to the theorems in [17, 18], the resolving set of each rule r_i $(1 \le i \le n)$ in firewall FW_2 satisfies the condition $R(r_i) = \cup_{k=1}^{k=t} M(\mathcal{P}_{j_k})$ $(1 \le j_k \le m)$, where $\mathcal{P}_{j_1}, \cdots, \mathcal{P}_{j_t}$ are all the paths whose terminal nodes contain i as the smallest element. Based on the definition of inter-firewall redundant rules in Sect. 8.3.1, rule r_i is inter-firewall redundant if and only if all the packets in $\cup_{k=1}^{k=t} M(\mathcal{P}_{j_k})$ are discarded by FW_1. Thus, each path $\mathcal{P}_{j_k}$ $(1 \le k \le t)$ is a redundant path. In other words, all the paths $\mathcal{P}_{j_1}, \cdots, \mathcal{P}_{j_t}$ whose terminal nodes contain i as the smallest element are redundant paths. $\square$

Fig. 8.8 Identification of redundant rules in FW_2

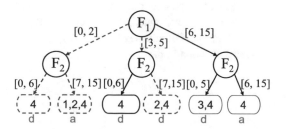

Considering redundant paths in Fig. 8.8, Net_2 identifies that r_1 and r_2 are inter-firewall redundant with respect to FW_1.

Theorem 8.3 *The privacy-preserving inter-firewall redundancy removal protocol is a* complete *inter-firewall redundancy removal scheme.*

Proof Suppose that our proposed protocol is not a complete scheme and hence it cannot detect all inter-firewall redundant rules in FW_2. Assume that rule r_i is inter-firewall redundant in FW_2 but it is not detected by our protocol. According to Theorem 8.2, $R(r_i) = \cup_{k=1}^{k=t} M(\mathcal{P}_{j_k})$ ($1 \leq j_k \leq m$) and $\mathcal{P}_{j_1}, \cdots, \mathcal{P}_{j_t}$ are redundant paths in FW_2's all-match FDD. Thus, some paths in $\{\mathcal{P}_{j_1}, \cdots, \mathcal{P}_{j_t}\}$ cannot be identified as redundant paths by our protocol. This conclusion violates the fact that our protocol can identify all the redundant paths in FW_2's all-match FDD.   □

8.5   Firewall Update After Optimization

If FW_1 or FW_2 changes after inter-firewall optimization, the inter-firewall redundant rules identified by the optimization may not be inter-firewall redundant anymore. In this section, we discuss our solution to address firewall update. There are five possible cases under this scenario.

1. Net_2 changes the decisions of some rules in FW_2. In this case, neither party needs to take actions because the inter-firewall redundancy detection does not consider the decisions of the rules in FW_2.
2. Net_1 changes the decisions of some rules from discard to accept in FW_1. In this case, Net_1 needs to notify Net_2 which non-overlapping rules (indices of these rules) from FW_1 are changed. Using this information, Net_2 checks if there were any rules in FW_2 that were removed due to these rules, and then adds the affected rules back into FW_2.
3. Net_1 changes the decisions of some rules from accept to discard in FW_1. In this case, Net_2 can run our cooperative optimization protocol again to possibly identify more inter-firewall redundant rules in FW_2.
4. Net_1 adds or removes some rules in FW_1. In this case, since the resolving sets of some rules in FW_1 may change, a rule in FW_2 that used to be inter-firewall redundant maybe not redundant anymore. It is important for Net_2 to run our optimization protocol again.
5. Net_2 adds or removes some rules in FW_2. Similar to the fourth case, since the resolving sets of some rules in FW_2 may change, it is important for Net_2 to run our protocol again.

8.6 Security and Complexity Analysis

8.6.1 Security Analysis

To analyze the security of our protocol, we first describe the commutative encryption and its properties. Let Key denote a set of private keys and Dom denote a finite domain. A commutative encryption f is a computable function $f:Key \times Dom \rightarrow Dom$ that satisfies the following four properties. (1) Secrecy: For any x and key K, given $(x)_K$, it is computationally infeasible to compute K. (2) Commutativity: For any x, K_1, and K_2, we have $((x)_{K_1})_{K_2} = ((x)_{K_2})_{K_1}$. (3) For any x, y, and K, if $x \neq y$, we have $(x)_K \neq (y)_K$. (4) The distribution of $(x)_K$ is indistinguishable from the distribution of x. Note that, for ease of presentation, in the rest of this section, any x, y, or z is an element of Dom, any K, K_1, or K_2 is an element of Key, and $(x)_K$ denotes $f(x, K)$.

In the conversion of FW_1, for each non-overlapping rule nr' from FW_1, let $V_{F_j}(nr')$ denote the prefix set for the field F_j, e.g., in Fig. 8.4e, $V_{F_1}(nr'_1)$ denotes $\{00**, 0100\}$. In the conversion of FW_2, let U_{F_j} denote the prefix set for the field F_j after removing duplicate prefixes, e.g., in Fig. 8.5e, U_{F_1} denotes the first prefix set. Our cooperative optimization protocol essentially compares $V_{F_j}(nr')$ and U_{F_j} in a privacy-preserving manner. We have the following theorem.

Theorem 8.4 *If both parties Net_1 and Net_2 are semi-honest, after comparing two sets $V_{F_j}(nr')$ and U_{F_j} using our protocol, Net_1 learns only the size $|U_{F_j}|$ and the intersection $V_{F_j}(nr') \cap U_{F_j}$, and Net_2 learns only the size $|V_{F_j}(nr')|$ and the intersection $V_{F_j}(nr') \cap U_{F_j}$.*

Proof According to the theorems in multi-party secure computation [1, 8], if we can prove that the distribution of the Net_1's view of our protocol cannot be distinguished from a simulation that uses only $V_{F_j}(nr')$, $V_{F_j}(nr') \cap U_{F_j}$, and $|U_{F_j}|$, then Net_1 cannot learn anything else except $V_{F_j}(nr') \cap U_{F_j}$ and $|U_{F_j}|$. Note that Net_1's view of our protocol is the information that Net_1 gains from FW_2.

Without loss of generality, we only prove that Net_1 learns only the size $|U_{F_j}|$ and the intersection $V_{F_j}(nr') \cap U_{F_j}$. The simulator for Net_1 uses key K_1 to create a set from $V_{F_j}(nr')$ and $V_{F_j}(nr') \cap U_{F_j}$ as follows

$$Y_S = \{\underbrace{(x_1)_{K_1}, \cdots, (x_m)_{K_1}}_{x_i \in V_{F_j}(nr') \cap U_{F_j}}, \underbrace{z_{m+1}, \cdots, z_n}_{n-m=|V_{F_j}(nr')-U_{F_j}|} \}$$

where $z_{m+1}, \cdots, z_n$ are random values generated by the simulator and they are uniformly distributed in the finite domain Dom. According to the theorems in [1], Net_1 cannot distinguish the distribution of Y_S's elements from that in

$$Y_R = \{\underbrace{(x_1)_{K_1}, \cdots, (x_m)_{K_1}}_{x_i \in V_{F_j}(nr') \cap U_{F_j}}, \underbrace{(x_{m+1})_{K_1}, \cdots, (x_n)_{K_1}}_{x_i \in V_{F_j}(nr')-U_{F_j}} \}$$

The Net_1's view of our protocol corresponds to Y_R. Therefore, the distribution of the Net_1's view of our protocol cannot be distinguished from this simulation.   □

Next, we analyze the information learned by Net_1 and Net_2. After implementing our protocol, Net_1 knows the converted firewalls of FW_1 and FW_2, e.g., Fig. 8.4j and Fig. 8.5g, and Net_2 knows the comparison result, e.g., Fig. 8.6d. On Net_1 side, for each field F_j ($1 \leq j \leq d$), it knows only $|U_{F_j}|$ and $V_{F_j}(nr') \cap U_{F_j}$, and it cannot reveal the rules of FW_2 for two reasons. First, in $V_{F_j}(nr') \cap U_{F_j}$, a numericalized prefix can be generated from many different numbers. For example, a prefix of IP addresses (32 bits) $b_1 b_2 \cdots b_k * \cdots *$ can be generated from 2^{32-k} different IP addresses. Second, even if Net_1 finds the number for a prefix in $V_{F_j}(nr') \cap U_{F_j}$, Net_1 doesn't know which rule in FW_2 contains that number. On Net_2 side, it only knows that the prefix x in $\mathcal{F}(x)$ belongs to which non-overlapping rules in FW_1. But such information is not enough to reveal the rules in FW_1.

8.6.2   Complexity Analysis

Let n_1 and n_2 be the number of rules in two adjacent firewalls FW_1 and FW_2, respectively, and d be the number of fields in both firewalls. For simplicity, we assume that the numbers in different fields have the same length, say w bits. We first analyze the computation, space, and communication costs for the conversion of FW_1. Based on the theorem in [16], the maximum number of non-overlapping rules generated from the FDD is $(2n_1 - 1)^d$. Each non-overlapping rule consists of d w-bit intervals and each interval can be converted to at most $2w - 2$ prefixes. Thus, the maximum number of prefixes generated from these non-overlapping rules is $d(2w - 2)(2n_1 - 1)^d$. Note that the total number of prefixes cannot exceed 2^{w+1} because Net_1 puts all prefixes into one set. Thus, the computation cost of encryption by Net_1 is $\min(d(2w - 2)(2n_1 - 1)^d, 2^{w+1})$. Therefore, for the conversion of FW_1, the computation cost of Net_1 is $\min(O(dwn_1^d), O(n_1^d + 2^w))$, the space cost of Net_1 is $O(dwn_1^d)$, the communication cost is $\min(O(dwn_1^d), O(2^w))$, and the computation cost of Net_2 is $\min(O(dwn_1^d), O(2^w))$. Similarly, for the conversion of FW_2, the computation cost of Net_2 is $\min(O(dwn_2^d), O(n_2^d + 2^w d))$, the space cost of Net_2 is $O(dwn_2^d)$, the communication cost is $\min(O(dwn_2^d), O(2^w d))$, and the computation cost of Net_1 is $\min(O(dwn_2^d), O(2^w d))$.

The computation and communication costs of firewall update depend on the different cases in Sect. 8.5. There is no cost for Case (1) in Sect. 8.5. Case (2) only incurs the computation and communication costs of firewall comparison. For Cases (3), (4), and (5), the computation and communication costs of firewall update are the overall costs of our protocol because we need to rerun our protocol for these three cases. Note that if a firewall is updated frequently, our protocol may not be applicable for this scenario due to significant computation and communication costs of running our protocol many times.

8.7 Experimental Results

We evaluate the effectiveness of our protocol on real firewalls and evaluate the efficiency of our protocol on both real and synthetic firewalls. We implemented our protocol using Java 1.6.0. Our experiments were carried out on a PC running Linux with 2 Intel Xeon cores and 16GB of memory.

8.7.1 Evaluation Setup

We conducted experiments over five groups of two real adjacent firewalls. Each firewall examines five fields, source IP, destination IP, source port, destination port, and protocol. The number of rules ranges from dozens to thousands. In implementing the commutative encryption, we used the Pohlig-Hellman algorithm [24] with a 1024-bit prime modulus and 160-bit encryption keys. To evaluate the effectiveness, we conducted our experiments over these five groups of adjacent firewalls. To evaluate the efficiency, for two firewalls in each group, we measured the processing time, the comparison time, and the communication cost of both parties.

Due to security concerns, it is difficult to obtain a large number of real adjacent firewalls. To further evaluate the efficiency, we generated a large number of synthetic firewalls based on Singh et al.'s method [27]. The synthetic firewalls also examine the same five fields as real firewalls. The number of rules in the synthetic firewalls ranges from 200 to 2000, and for each number, we generated 10 synthetic firewalls. To measure the efficiency, we first processed each synthetic firewall as FW_1 and then measured the processing time and communication cost of two parties. Second, we processed each synthetic firewall as FW_2 and measured the processing time and communication cost. Third, we measured the comparison time for every two synthetic firewalls. We did not evaluate the effectiveness of our protocol on synthetic firewalls because they are generated randomly and independently without considering whether two firewalls are adjacent or not.

8.7.2 Methodology

In this section, we define the metrics to measure the effectiveness of our protocol. Given our firewall optimization algorithm A, and two adjacent firewalls FW_1 and FW_2, we use $A(FW_1, FW_2)$ to denote a set of inter-firewall redundant rules in FW_2. Let $|FW|$ denote the number of rules in FW and $|A(FW_1, FW_2)|$ denote the number of inter-firewall redundant rules in FW_2. To evaluate the effectiveness, we define a *redundancy ratio* $\beta(A(FW_1, FW_2)) = \frac{|A(FW_1, FW_2)|}{|FW_2|}$. This ratio $\beta(A(FW_1, FW_2))$ measures what percentage of rules are inter-firewall redundant in FW_2.

8.7.3   Effectiveness and Efficiency on Real Policies

Table 8.1 shows the redundancy ratios for five real firewall groups. Column 1 shows the names of five real firewall groups. Columns 2 and 3 show the names of firewalls FW_1 and FW_2, respectively. Column 4 shows the number of rules in firewall FW_2. Figure 8.9 shows the processing time and communication cost of two parties Net_1 and Net_2 when processing FW_1; Fig. 8.10 shows the processing time and communication cost of the two parties when processing FW_2. Figure 8.11 shows the comparison time of each group. Figure 8.12 shows the overall processing time and communication cost of implementing our protocol on real firewalls. Note that the processing time in Fig. 8.12 does not include the communication time between two parties.

Our Protocol Achieves Significant Redundancy Ratio on Four Real Firewall Groups For five real firewall groups, our protocol achieves an average redundancy ratio of 19.4%. Particularly, for the firewall group Host, our protocol achieves 49.6% redundancy ratio, which implies that almost half of rules in Host2 are inter-firewall redundant rules. For firewall groups Econ, Ath, and Comp, our protocol achieves 14.4%–17.1% redundancy ratios, which implies that about 15% of rules in FW_2 are redundant in these three groups. Only for one firewall group Wan, our protocol achieves 1.0% redundancy ratio. From these results, we observed that most adjacent real firewalls, have many inter-firewall redundant rules. Thus, our protocol

Table 8.1 Redundancy ratios for five real firewall groups

Group	FW_1	FW_2	$|FW_2|$	Redundancy ratio
Econ	Econ1	Econ2	129	17.1%
Host	Host1	Host2	139	49.6%
Wan	Wan1	Wan2	511	1.0%
Ath	Ath1	Ath2	1308	14.4%
Comp	Comp1	Comp2	3928	14.7%

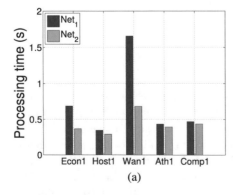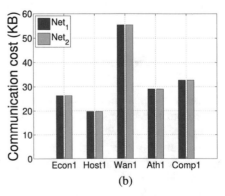

Fig. 8.9 Processing FW_1 on real firewalls. (**a**) Processing time. (**b**) Communication cost

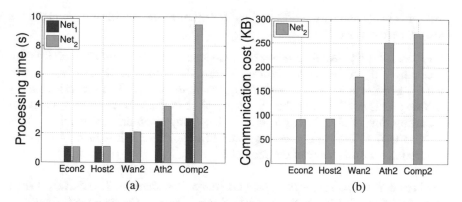

Fig. 8.10 Processing FW_2 on real firewalls. (**a**) Processing time. (**b**) Communication cost

Fig. 8.11 Comparing two real firewalls

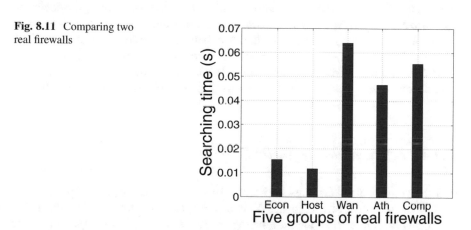

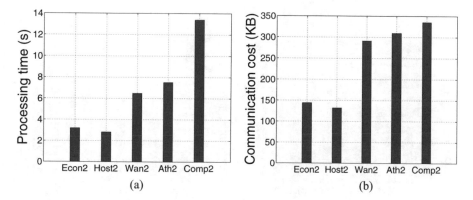

Fig. 8.12 Total processing time and communication cost on real firewalls. (**a**) Processing time. (**b**) Communication cost

could effectively remove inter-firewall redundant rules and significantly improve the network performance.

Our Protocol Is Efficient for Processing and Comparing Two Real Firewalls   When processing FW_1 in the five real firewall groups, the processing time of Net_1 is less than 2 s and the processing time of Net_2 is less than 1 s. When processing FW_2 in those real firewall groups, the processing time of Net_1 is less than 4 s and the processing time of Net_2 is less than 10 s. The comparison time of two firewalls is less than 0.07 s. The total processing time of two parties is less than 14 s, which demonstrates the efficiency of our protocol.

Our Protocol Is Efficient for the Communication Cost Between Two Parties   When processing firewall FW_1 in the five real firewall groups, the communication cost from Net_1 to Net_2 and that from Net_2 to Net_1 are less than 60 KB. Note that the communication cost from Net_1 to Net_2 and that from Net_2 to Net_1 are the same because Net_1 and Net_2 encrypt the same number of values and the encrypted values have the same length, i.e. 1024 bits in our experiments. When processing FW_2 in those real firewall groups, the communication cost from Net_2 to Net_1 is less than 300 KB. The total communication cost between two parties is less than 350 KB, which can be sent through the current network (e.g., DSL network) around 10 s.

8.7.4   Efficiency on Synthetic Policies

For the synthetic firewalls, Figs. 8.13 and 8.14 show the average processing time and communication cost of two parties Net_1 and Net_2 for processing FW_1 and FW_2, respectively. Figure 8.15 shows the average comparison time for every two synthetic firewalls. Figure 8.16 shows the overall processing time and communication cost of

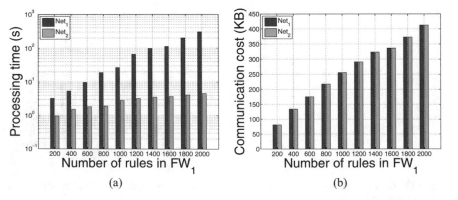

Fig. 8.13 Processing FW_1 on synthetic firewalls. (**a**) Ave. processing time. (**b**) Ave. communication cost

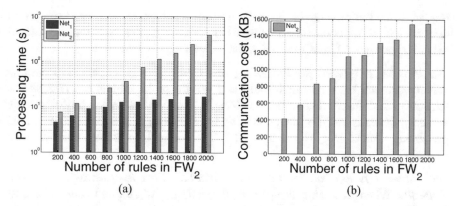

Fig. 8.14 Processing FW_2 on synthetic firewalls. (**a**) Ave. processing time. (**b**) Ave. communication cost

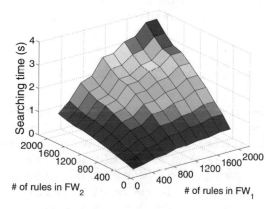

Fig. 8.15 Comparing two synthetic firewalls

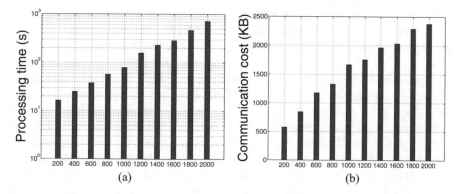

Fig. 8.16 Total processing time and communication cost on synthetic firewalls. (**a**) Processing time. (**b**) Communication cost

implementing our protocol on synthetic firewalls. The processing time in Fig. 8.16 does not include the communication time between two parties. Note that the vertical axis of three Figs. 8.13a, 8.14a, and 8.16a are in a logarithmic scale.

Our Protocol Is Efficient for Processing and Comparing Two Synthetic Firewalls When processing the synthetic firewalls as FW_1, the processing time of Net_1 is less than 300 s and the processing time of Net_2 is less than 5 s. When processing the synthetic firewalls as FW_2, the processing time of Net_1 is less than 400 s and the processing time of Net_2 is less than 20 s. The comparison time of two synthetic firewalls is less than 4 s.

Our Protocol Is Efficient for the Communication Cost Between Two Synthetic Firewalls When processing the synthetic firewalls as FW_1, the communication cost from Net_1 to Net_2 and that from Net_2 to Net_1 grow linearly with the number of rules in FW_1, and both costs are less than 420 KB. Similarly, when processing synthetic firewalls as FW_2, the communication cost from Net_2 to Net_1 grows linearly with the number of rules in FW_2, and the communication cost from Net_2 to Net_1 is less than 1600 KB.

8.8   Conclusions and Future Work

In this work, we identified an important problem, cross-domain privacy-preserving inter-firewall redundancy detection. We propose a novel privacy-preserving protocol for detecting such redundancy. We implemented our protocol in Java and conducted extensive evaluation. The results on real firewall policies show that our protocol can remove as many as 49% of the rules in a firewall whereas the average is 19.4%.

Our protocol is applicable for identifying the inter-firewall redundancy of firewalls with a few thousands of rules, e.g., 2000 rules. However, it is still expensive to compare two firewalls with many thousands of rules, e.g., 5000 rules. Reducing the complexity of our protocol needs to be further studied. In our work, we have demonstrated rule optimization, from FW_1 to FW_2, we note that, a similar rule optimization is possible in the opposite direction, i.e., FW_2 to FW_1. In the first scenario, FW_1 to FW_2, it is FW_1 that is improving the performance load of FW_2 and in return FW_2 is improving the performance of FW_1 in a vice-versa manner. All this is being achieved the without FW_1 or FW_2 revealing each other's policies thus allowing for a proper administrative separation. Our protocol is most beneficial if both parties are willing to benefit from it and can collaborate in a mutual manner. There are many special cases that could be explored based on our current protocol. For example, there may be hosts or Network Address Translation (NAT) devices between two adjacent firewalls. Our current protocol cannot be directly applied to such cases. Extending our protocol to these cases could be an interesting topic, and requires further investigation.

References

1. R. Agrawal, A. Evfimievski, R. Srikant, Information sharing across private databases, in *Proceedings of ACM SIGMOD* (2003), pp. 86–97
2. E. Al-Shaer, H. Hamed, Discovery of policy anomalies in distributed firewalls, in *Proceedings of IEEE INFOCOM* (2004), pp. 2605–2616
3. J. Brickell, V. Shmatikov, Privacy-preserving graph algorithms in the semi-honest model, in *Proceedings of ASIACRYPT* (2010), pp. 236–252
4. Y.-K. Chang, Fast binary and multiway prefix searches for packet forwarding. Comput. Netw. **51**(3), 588–605 (2007)
5. J. Cheng, H. Yang, S.H. Wong, S. Lu, Design and implementation of cross-domain cooperative firewall, in *Proceedings of IEEE ICNP* (2007)
6. Q. Dong, S. Banerjee, J. Wang, D. Agrawal, A. Shukla, Packet classifiers in ternary CAMs can be smaller, in *Proceedings of ACM SIGMETRICS* (2006), pp. 311–322
7. Firewall throughput test, http://www.hipac.org/performance_tests/results.html.
8. O. Goldreich, Secure multi-party computations. Working draft. Version 1.4 edition (2002)
9. O. Goldreich, *Foundations of Cryptography: Volume II (Basic Applications)* (Cambridge University Press, Cambridge, 2004)
10. M.G. Gouda, A.X. Liu, Firewall design: consistency, completeness and compactness, in *Proceedings of IEEE ICDCS* (2004), pp. 320–327
11. M.G. Gouda, A.X. Liu, Structured firewall design. Comput. Netw. J. **51**(4), 1106–1120 (2007)
12. P. Gupta, Algorithms for routing lookups and packet classification. PhD thesis, Stanford University, 2000
13. C. Kruegel, T. Toth, E. Kirda, Service specific anomaly detection for network intrusion detection, in *Proceedings of ACM SAC* (2002), pp. 201–208
14. W. Lee, D. Xiang, Information-theoretic measures for anomaly detection, in *Proceedings of IEEE S&P* (2001), pp. 130–143
15. A.X. Liu, F. Chen, Collaborative enforcement of firewall policies in virtual private networks, in *Proceedings of ACM PODC* (2008), 95–104
16. A.X. Liu, M.G. Gouda, Diverse firewall design. IEEE Trans. Parallel Distrib. Syst. **19**(8), 1237–1251 (2008)
17. A.X. Liu, M.G. Gouda, Complete redundancy removal for packet classifiers in TCAMs. IEEE Trans. Parallel Distrib. Syst. **21**(4), 424–437 (2010)
18. A.X. Liu, C.R. Meiners, Y. Zhou, All-match based complete redundancy removal for packet classifiers in TCAMs, in *Proceedings of IEEE INFOCOM* (2008), 574–582
19. A.X. Liu, E. Torng, C. Meiners, Firewall compressor: an algorithm for minimizing firewall policies, in *Proceedings of IEEE INFOCOM* (2008)
20. A.X. Liu, C.R. Meiners, E. Torng, TCAM razor: a systematic approach towards minimizing packet classifiers in TCAMs. IEEE/ACM Trans. Netw. **18**(2), 490–500 (2009)
21. C.R. Meiners, A.X. Liu, E. Torng, TCAM Razor: a systematic approach towards minimizing packet classifiers in TCAMs, in *Proceedings of IEEE ICNP* (2007), pp. 266–275
22. C.R. Meiners, A.X. Liu, E. Torng, Bit weaving: a non-prefix approach to compressing packet classifiers in TCAMs, in *Proceedings of IEEE ICNP* (2009), pp. 93–102
23. C.R. Meiners, A.X. Liu, E. Torng, Topological transformation approaches to optimizing TCAM-based packet processing systems, in *Proceedings of ACM SIGMETRICS* (2009), pp. 73–84
24. S.C. Pohlig, M.E. Hellman, An improved algorithm for computing logarithms over GF(p) and its cryptographic significance. IEEE Trans. Inf. Theory **24**, 106–110 (1978)
25. R. Sekar, A. Gupta, J. Frullo, T. Shanbhag, A. Tiwari, H. Yang, S. Zhou, Specification-based anomaly detection: a new approach for detecting network intrusions, in *Proceedings of ACM CCS* (2002), pp. 265–274
26. D. Safford, D.L. Schales, D.K. Hess, Secure RPC authentication (SRA) for TELNET and FTP. Techn. Rep., 1993

27. S. Singh, F. Baboescu, G. Varghese, J. Wang, Packet classification using multidimensional cutting, in *Proceedings of ACM SIGCOMM* (2003)
28. A. Wool, A quantitative study of firewall configuration errors. IEEE Comput. **37**(6), 62–67 (2004)
29. Z. Yang, S. Zhong, R.N. Wright, Privacy-preserving classification of customer data without loss of accuracy, in *Proceedings of SIAM* (2005)
30. L. Yuan, H. Chen, J. Mai, C.-N. Chuah, Z. Su, P. Mohapatra, Fireman: a toolkit for firewall modeling and analysis, in *Proceedings of IEEE S&P* (2006), pp. 199–213

Chapter 9
Privacy Preserving String Matching for Cloud Computing

9.1 Introduction

9.1.1 Motivation

Advances in cloud computing have redefined the landscape of modern information technology as seen by the popularity of cloud service providers such as Amazon, Microsoft Azure and Google App Engine. Data storage outsourcing is a prime application in cloud computing, which allows organizations to provide reliable data services to users without concerning with the data management overheads. But, there are several practical apprehensions regarding the privacy of the outsourced data and these concerns are a major hindrance towards the uninhibited adoption of cloud storage services. Generally, the cloud service provider does not attempt to violate data privacy, there are internal factors like malicious employees who will abuse the client data at the first available opportunity. Also, cloud computing servers are prone to serious external threats like malware and botnets, which may not be reported publicly.

In this chapter, we consider the popular cloud storage model, which is composed of three entities: the data owner, the cloud server and the authorized users. The data owner stores the data on the cloud server and authorizes the users to issue different queries on the outsourced data. To protect the data, the data owner encrypts the data prior to outsourcing and shares the decryption keys with the authorized users. However, the encryption is a major hindrance to perform regular data access operations, such as searching for documents containing specific keywords or patterns. For instance, the Google$^{(tm)}$ search engine supports rich functionality like, find documents containing, *"terms appearing in the text of the page"*, *"terms appearing anywhere in title of the page"* and so on. Therefore, there is a crucial need for techniques to support a rich set of querying functionality on the encrypted data without violating the privacy of the users.

A. X. Liu, R. Li, *Algorithms for Data and Computation Privacy*, https://doi.org/10.1007/978-3-030-58896-0_9

9.1.2   Problem Statement

Our work focuses on the problem of privacy preserving *string pattern* queries on keywords in outsourced documents or database records. A *string pattern* query is a sequence of characters. A keyword is said to *match* a string pattern query, if the query string is either identical to the keyword or is *contained* as a sub-string of the keyword. For example, given a string pattern query, "*late*" where the "*" denotes any other characters, a sample list of matching keywords are: *"ablate, contemplate, plates, elated"* and so on. In other words, it is necessary to examine every possible sub-string [1, 2] of the keyword as the query string can occur anywhere inside the keyword.

To describe the problem in the context of cloud computing, initially, the data owner has a set of documents, $\mathbf{D} = \{D_1, \cdots, D_n\}$ where each document contains a set of distinct keywords, $D_i(W) = \{w_1, \cdots, w_p\}$. Before outsourcing the data to the cloud, the data owner computes an index $\mathbf{I}$ on the documents' keywords, encrypts the documents and stores the encrypted documents, along with the index, on the cloud server. Now, to search for query string pattern in these encrypted documents, an authorized user computes an encrypted query or a *"trapdoor"*, using the string pattern query p, and submits it to the cloud server. The server processes the trapdoor on the index $\mathbf{I}$ and retrieves all documents, D_i such that, p matches at least one keyword $w \in D_i(W)$ for $1 \leq i \leq n$. There are two major challenges in this process: (a) the index $\mathbf{I}$ should not leak any information regarding the keywords (e.g., size and content) and (b) the string query processing technique should be efficient and scalable to large collections of keywords.

9.1.3   Adversary and Security Model

We adopt the semi-honest adversary model [3] for the cloud server and any passive adversaries. In this model, the cloud server *honestly* adheres to the communication protocols and the query processing algorithms, but is *curious* to learn additional information about the user by observing the data processed in the search protocol. Our goal is to construct a *secure index*, which is secure in the strong *semantic security against adaptive chosen keyword attack* (IND-CKA) security model described in [4]. We assume that the index and the trapdoor construction relies on symmetric key encryption algorithms, i.e., our solution is a symmetric searchable encryption (SSE) [5, 6] scheme. To prove security in IND-CKA model, an adversary is given two distinct document sets $\mathbf{D_0}$ and $\mathbf{D_1}$, containing nearly equal number of keywords and with some amount of overlap and *one* secure index $\mathbf{I_b}$ for $\mathbf{D_b}$ where $b = 0$ or $b = 1$. Finally, the adversary is challenged to output the correct value of b with non-negligible probability. An IND-CKA secure index does not necessarily hide the number of keywords in a document, the *search* patterns of the users, i.e., the history of the trapdoors used, and the *access* patterns, i.e., the documents retrieved due to the search queries.

9.1.4 Limitation of Prior Art

Prior secure string pattern matching schemes under the secure multi-party computation model have high communication and computational complexity (e.g., exponentiations and garbled circuit evaluations) [7–10].

Several symmetric key based searchable encryption techniques [4–6, 11–16] have focused on privacy preserving *exact* keyword matching in cloud computing. We note that, keyword matching problem is an instance of the string pattern matching problem where the pattern query is a *whole* keyword, i.e., the complete query must match a stored keyword. The work in [17] proposed a similarity based keyword matching solution, in which the cloud server retrieves keywords *similar* to a given query string by using a predefined hamming distance as the similarity measure. However, the similarity of string pattern query cannot be measured by hamming distance as a matching keyword can be of arbitrary length and we are only interested in the *exact* matching of a query sub-string within the keyword.

All the SSE solutions discussed above cannot address the privacy preserving string query pattern matching problem considered in our work. In this work, for the first time ever, we describe an efficient privacy preserving approach for executing string pattern queries over encrypted cloud data. Unless specified otherwise, we will use the term "string pattern" and "pattern", interchangeably in our work.

9.1.5 Proposed Approach

Our approach has two building blocks: a string pattern matching mechanism with strong privacy guarantees and an efficient index structure for fast processing of string pattern queries. First, our pattern matching approach is based on a simple intuition, i.e., if a pattern query matches a keyword then the pattern *must* be a sub-string of the keyword. Therefore, for each keyword in the document data set, we encrypt *every* possible sub-string of the keyword and store the encrypted sub-strings in the secure index. With this approach, we reduce the problem of pattern matching to that of comparing a query trapdoor with the encrypted sub-strings of the keyword. Second, to achieve fast searching, we arrange the encrypted sub-strings in a highly balanced binary tree structure, the *Pattern Aware Secure Search* tree (PASStree), in which each tree node corresponds to a Bloom filter encoding of a set of the encrypted sub-strings. The PASStree is built in a top-down manner. The root node of the PASStree stores all the encrypted sub-strings corresponding to all the keywords. Any two child nodes store an equal sized partition of the set of sub-strings stored in their parent node and each leaf node corresponds to the encrypted sub-strings of a distinct keyword. This ensures that the PASStree satisfies the index indistinguishability [4] property as the size of each Bloom filter depends only on the number of encrypted sub-strings stored and not on the content of the sub-strings.

9.1.6   Technical Challenges and Solutions

The first major challenge is, improving the efficiency of search on the PASStree by imposing some order on the encrypted sub-strings. Without any ordering, every pattern query can induce a worst case search complexity scenario over the PASStree causing a major performance bottleneck. To overcome this, we devise a novel similarity based clustering technique to cluster the keywords in the PASStree and narrow the search towards the matching keywords. The similarity between two keywords is calculated using multiple independent dimensions to prevent any leakage of content similarity due to the PASStree organization.

The second major challenge is, to retrieve the most relevant documents for a given pattern query, because a pattern query can match any sub-string at any location in a keyword and hence, it is essential to *rank* the matching keywords by relevance. Towards this, we leverage the structure of the PASStree in the following manner: for each regular Bloom filter in the PASStree, we associate an additional Bloom filter, called the *sub-string prefix* (SP) Bloom filter to determine the position of the query sub-string within a keyword. Based on the different SP Bloom filter matches, the matching keywords are relatively ordered without leaking any other additional information about the similarity of the keywords.

9.1.7   Key Contributions

Our key contributions are as follows. (a) We take the first step towards exploring the solution space for the problem of privacy preserving string pattern matching over encrypted data in the symmetric searchable encryption setting. (b) We describe PASStree, a secure searchable index structure, which processes a pattern query in logarithmic time complexity for each possible matching keyword. (c) We devise a relevance ranking algorithm by leveraging the structure of the PASStree to ensure that the most relevant documents of the pattern query are returned in that order. (d) We prove the security of our algorithm under the *semantic security against adaptive chosen keyword attack* IND-CKA. (e) We performed comprehensive experimentation on real-life data sets and show that we achieve 100% accuracy in retrieving all matching keywords with query processing time in the order of few milliseconds for an index over a keyword space of 100,000 keywords.

9.2 Related Work

Secure pattern matching has received much attention in the secure multi-party communication community and several interesting protocols [7–10] have been proposed with applications to secure DNA matching and discrete finite-automaton (DFA) evaluation. These solutions address different variations of pattern matching over encrypted data, such as exact pattern matching with index location reporting, wild-card matching, and non-binary hamming distance matching. Although these protocols have extensive pattern matching capabilities, they require expensive computations, such as exponentiations [7, 8, 10, 18], and large communication overhead [9], unsuitable for user oriented cloud computing.

Several symmetric key based efficient techniques [4–6, 11–14, 16] have been proposed for exact keyword search. However, adopting these solutions for string pattern matching will result in impractical index sizes. Even the recently proposed approach from [15], which is highly storage efficient, cannot solve the string pattern query problem considered in our work. We note that, our approach can be super-imposed over most of these schemes, since the leaf nodes of the PASStree correspond to keywords and therefore, it is possible to incorporate useful features such as dynamic updates[12] to the cloud data.

The work in [17] proposes a technique to search for keywords *similar* to the search keyword on the encrypted data The authors describe an error-correction technique to handle mistakes in user inputs such as typos or incorrect spellings, based on a predefined hamming distance metric. However, the index size stored in this approach grows polynomially with respect to the desired hamming distance. In [13], the authors use *cosine similarity* metric, which is based on the Term-Frequency Inverse-Document-Frequency (TF-IDF) ranking metric, to rank the search results when multiple keywords are searched. However, the focus of [13] is to return the best ranked documents for multiple keyword search and not on pattern matching. In summary, compared to the other symmetric key approaches, our PASStree maintains a smaller index and does not need to predefine the similarity metrics.

9.3 Pattern Aware Secure Search Tree

In this section, we formally describe the construction of PASStree, our index structure to support pattern queries. Our PASStree description begins with our string pattern matching approach, followed by the structural description of PASStree, the description of the privacy preserving measures for PASStree and finally, the query processing approach.

9.3.1 String Pattern Matching

For a given document D, a keyword $w \in D(W)$ is defined as a sequence of characters over a text alphabet $\sum$ and a string pattern $p \in \sum^l$ is defined as a string of l contiguous characters over the same alphabet. Any sub-string of w, denoted by w_{ab}, is a sequence of characters starting from position a and ending at position b, $\forall$ $1 \le a \le b \le |w|$. We denote $S(w) = \cup_{a,b=1}^{a,b=|w|}$, as the set of all sub-strings of the keyword w. We note that, a string pattern p *matches* the keyword w if and only if $p \in S(w)$, i.e., p is a sub-string of w. Next, we denote the set of all sub-strings of all keywords in the document set $\mathbf{D}$ as: $\mathbf{S} = \cup S(w_j)$ where $j = 1$ to $j = |D_i(W)|$ and $i = 1$ to $|\mathbf{D}|$. In our work, we assume that the cardinality of this set, $|\mathbf{S}| = N$, i.e., there are N distinct keywords across all the documents.

Using this formulation, the problem of string pattern matching is reduced to that of membership testing on a set of sub-strings. Thus, our string pattern matching approach is as follows: given a pattern p and document set $\mathbf{D}$, we explicitly generate and store $\mathbf{S}$. In the basic search process, we examine each sub-string in $\mathbf{S}$ and report the mth keyword w_m as a matching keyword, if p is identical to $w_m[a, b]$ where $1 \le a, b \le |w_m|$. However, as linear searching is expensive, we describe an efficient tree index structure, the PASStree, which stores the sub-strings of the keywords in a binary tree structure and performs the search in logarithmic complexity.

9.3.2 PASStree Structure

To reduce the overhead of matching the pattern query, p, with each keyword w_i, we organize $\mathbf{S}$ in a complete binary tree and narrow the search to only those keywords that possibly match the pattern. We describe PASStree—Pattern Aware Secure Search tree, a highly balanced binary tree, to store $S(w_1), \cdots, S(w_N)$, without revealing any content similarities of the keywords.

PASStree Construction For an input of N keywords, the PASStree consists of $2N$ distinctly labeled nodes arranged as follows: a root node, $N - 1$ intermediate nodes, and N leaf nodes Each tree node is associated with a unique Bloom filter [19], which is an efficient storage data structure used for performing set membership testing over large data sets. The Bloom filter is a bit-array of size M where all the bits are initially set to zero. Each Bloom filter is associated with set of q independent hash functions: $h_1, h_2, \cdots, h_q$, where each hash function hashes an input element into the range $[0, M - 1]$. Given a set A of elements, to store an element $a \in A$ in the Bloom filter, we hash a using each of the hash functions as follows: $h_1(a), h_2(a), \cdots, h_q(a)$ and set the respective Bloom filter array positions to 1. After storing all elements from A, to check if a query element b belongs to A, the query element is hashed using each of the q hash functions. After hashing, b is declared to belong to A, only if, all the Bloom filter bits in the hashed locations are equal to 1. Note that, this property of

Bloom filters is useful for the string pattern matching problem since we are checking if the query string pattern is a member of the set of all sub-strings of keywords in the document set. Now, we state two fundamental properties of a PASStree index structure. First, the Bloom filter associated with each leaf node stores the set of all sub-strings $S(w_i)$ of a unique keyword w_i. Second, at the intermediate tree nodes, the Bloom filters store the union of the elements stored in the respective Bloom filters of the child nodes. Typically, the size of a parent Bloom filter is approximately twice as big as any of its child Bloom filters.

The root node R stores the sub-strings of all the keywords, i.e., the root node stores S, where each sub-string is stored using the standard Bloom filter hashing approach [19]. Now, we create two child nodes for the root node and denote them by the binary tree terminology, as R_{left} and R_{right} child nodes. Next, the set S is partitioned into two mutually exclusive sub-sets, S_1 and S_2 where each sub-set is associated with one child node, i.e., S_1 is stored in R_{left} and S_2 is stored in R_{right}. The partitioning satisfies the following important conditions: $|R_{left}| = |R_{right}|$ if $|S|$ is even, and $||R_{left}| - |R_{right}|| = 1$ if $|S|$ is odd. The partitioning is repeated recursively until each leaf node is associated with a single set $S(w)$ of a distinct keyword w. Based on the balancing conditions, this partitioning approach ensures that the height of the PASStree is $\log N$.

Since the expected output of the pattern query is the set of documents containing the matching keywords, the PASStree incorporates an inverted table index, i.e., for each distinct keyword we maintain a list of document identifiers for documents containing the keyword. For a given keyword w, the document identifier list is denoted by $L(w) = \{D_a, D_b, \cdots, Dv\}$. Given a keyword w, we add a pointer from the corresponding leaf node in the PASStree to $L(w)$, and if any pattern matches this leaf node, the list of identifiers is included in the output.

PASStree Search To process a query over the PASStree, the approach is as follows. We denote the root of the PASStree by R and R_{left} and R_{right} to denote the logical left and right subtrees of R, respectively. The identifiers of R_{left} and R_{right} are chosen uniformly at random and stored along with the Bloom filter corresponding to R, i.e., as a tuple $\langle R, ID(R_{left}), ID(R_{right}) \rangle$ where $ID(X)$ is the identifier of X. For a given pattern query, we first check the R Bloom filter and if a match is found, we proceed further down the PASStree. If R_{left} or R_{right} report a match, the search continues further in that sub-tree and if no Bloom filter reports a match, meaning that no keyword contains this pattern, we stop exploring that sub-tree further. The output of the algorithm is the list of documents that are associated with the leaf nodes An illustrative PASStree is shown in Fig. 9.1.

Theorem 9.1 (Logarithmic Complexity) *For a given query string p, the PASStree search algorithm finds all matching leaf nodes in a complexity of $O(E \log N)$ where N is the total number of leaf nodes in the PASStree and E is the number of leaf nodes matching p.*

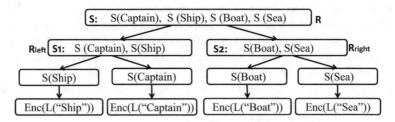

Fig. 9.1 PASStree example

Proof First, we show the search time complexity of a pattern p, which matches only one leaf node. At each level from the root node, the search algorithm checks the nodes R_{left} and R_{right}. Since the pattern query matches only one leaf node, the search algorithm proceeds along the sub-tree where the match is found and does not explore the other sub-tree. Therefore, the search algorithm performs at most two Bloom filter verifications at each level in the PASStree until the leaf node, which translates to at most $2 \log N$ complexity.

Next, we consider the case where the pattern p matches at most E leaf nodes. In the worst case scenario, the E leaf nodes will be found in E different sub-trees Given that the cost of verification along each independent sub-tree is $2 \log N$, the aggregated complexity of searching for pattern p is $2E \log N$. If E is of the order of N, say, $\frac{N}{c}$ for some c, the complexity of searching in PASStree is $O(N \log N)$. This result proves that the PASStree achieves polynomial time complexity in worst-case and achieves logarithmic complexity if a pattern matches only a small number of keywords.   □

9.3.3   Preserving Privacy of Bloom Filters

As the Bloom filter data is available on the cloud server, an adversary can make some inferences regarding the data directly or indirectly. For instance, the parameters of the Bloom filter, the hash functions and the bit-array size, need to made public since the cloud server needs to perform the set membership operation. The Bloom filter size M-bits depends on the number of distinct keywords denoted by $|D_i(W)|$ for a document D_i and the number of sub-strings in each keyword. Using this information, an adversary can perform brute force dictionary attacks and determine the content or the number of elements stored in the Bloom filter. Furthermore, the common bit positions between two different Bloom filters can be used to infer the common elements stored in two different Bloom filters. To address these concerns, we describe our privacy preserving approach to protect the content of the Bloom filters.

Secure Trapdoor Generation   We assume that the data owner and the authorized users share a t-bit common secret master key, $K \in \{0, 1\}^t$, and agree on a common secure one-way hash function $\mathcal{H}$, such as SHA-2. The data owner computes q secret keys as follows: $K_1 = K||1, K_2 = K||2, \cdots , K_q = K||q$. Now, for each unique sub-string $w_{ab} \in S(w)$ of a keyword $w \in D_i$, we compute q secure one-way hashes as follows: $\mathcal{H}(K_1, w_{ab}), \mathcal{H}(K_2, w_{ab}), \cdots , \mathcal{H}(K_q, w_{ab})$. This approach ensures the privacy of the sub-string w_{ab}, as it is easy to compute a one-way hash, given K and w_{ab}, but it is computationally infeasible to determine w_{ab}, given these one-way hashes.

Sub-string Randomization   Storing the one-way hashes of the sub-strings into various Bloom filters in the PASStree does not prevent passive inference, i.e., an adversary can examine the Bloom filters for common locations and determine the common elements directly. Therefore, we use the randomizing approach from [4] while storing an identical hash value in different Bloom filters. We note that, each PASStree tree node has a distinct label, $\mathcal{L}_z$. Using this label, we compute the q Bloom filter hashes as follows:$\mathcal{H}(\mathcal{L}_z, \mathcal{H}(K_1, w_{ab}))\%M$, $\mathcal{H}(\mathcal{L}_z, \mathcal{H}(K_2, w_{ab}))\%M, \cdots , \mathcal{H}(\mathcal{L}_z, \mathcal{H}(K_q, w_{ab}))\%M$. Since the PASStree node labels are chosen uniformly at random, the sub-string w_{ab}, will hash into different bit-positions across two Bloom filters of two different PASStree nodes, thereby, eliminating correlation based attacks.

Blinding the Bloom Filters   Finally, we blind each Bloom filter [4], at the same distance from the PASStree root, by inserting $(|W| - |T|) * V_r$ random 1s into the different Bloom locations. Here, $|T|$ is the number of distinct sub-strings in the Bloom filter, $|W|$ is the maximal number of sub-strings stored in a Bloom filter at the same level and V_r is a random integer constant. This ensures that all Bloom filters at the same distance from the PASStree root node contain the same number of 1s regardless of the number of sub-strings stored. This blinding is necessary to provide security against the passive inference of common elements across two Bloom filters.

9.3.4   Query Trapdoor Generation and Processing

The user specifies a string $p \in \sum$ as a pattern query and generates the trapdoor, T_p as follows: $\mathcal{H}(K_1, p), \mathcal{H}(K_2, p), \cdots , \mathcal{H}(K_q, p)$. The cloud server executes the search algorithm, as described in Sect. 9.3.2, starting from the root as follows: $\mathcal{H}(\mathcal{L}_R, \mathcal{H}(K_1, p))\%M, \mathcal{H}(\mathcal{L}_R, \mathcal{H}(K_2, p))\%M, \cdots , \mathcal{H}(\mathcal{L}_R, \mathcal{H}(K_q, p))\%M$ where $\mathcal{L}_R$ is the label of the root Bloom filter. If all the hashed locations are set to 1, the p is a sub-string of one or more keywords and the search proceeds along the children of the root node. Proceeding thus, the leaf nodes matching the trapdoor are declared to matching the query string pattern and the corresponding list of the documents are retrieved.

9.4   PASStree+

The PASStree construction does not take advantage of the similarity of different keywords and hence, might result in the worst case search behavior in many scenarios. In this section, we first describe the technical challenge involved in search optimization and present a novel heuristic algorithm towards this challenge.

9.4.1   Challenge in Search Optimization

During the PASStree search, if a pattern is found in both the sub-trees, T_{left} and T_{right}, the search algorithm proceeds along both the paths and results in maximum possible paths being explored along the length of the PASStree. This scenario arises due to the unstructured partitioning of the keyword set at a PASStree node, S_a into two keyword sets S_{aa} and S_{bb} in such a way that both the sets might end up sharing many common sub-strings. Hence, it is desirable to achieve PASStree node partitioning while minimizing $S_{aa} \cap S_{bb}$, i.e., the number of common sub-strings across two partitions should be minimal while satisfying the constraint: $||S_{aa}| - |S_{bb}|| \leq 1$. This problem is a variant of the well-known set partitioning problem and can be shown to be NP-hard in a straightforward manner and can be solved using a greedy heuristic. The key intuition to improving the search efficiency of the PASStree is to group keywords, matching similar query sting patterns, into common sub-tree locations.

9.4.2   Optimizing PASStree

To overcome the challenges in search optimization, we describe the construction of PASStree+, an enhanced version of PASStree, which uses a novel heuristic algorithm for the partitioning problem to optimize the search efficiency. First, our heuristic algorithm computes the similarity of the keyword pairs using a similarity metric that not only takes into account the pattern similarity of the keyword pairs, but also the distribution of the keyword pairs across the document set. Second, using the similarity coefficients as keyword weights, our algorithm uses a scalable clustering approach to partition the keyword set.

Keyword Pair Similarity Estimation We make an important observation that, if two keywords share many patterns then it would be desirable that these two keywords are placed in the same partition, because if the user searches for a pattern common to both the keywords, then the PASStree exploration will be focused only along this partition. Therefore, our approach to improving the search efficiency is to arrange two or more keywords in the same partition by measuring the number of sub-strings they have in common. For instance, given two keywords w_1 and w_2, where $S(w_1) \in$

$\mathbf{S_{aa}}$ and where $S(w_2) \in \mathbf{S_{bb}}$, we can re-arrange them into the same partition, $\mathbf{S_{aa}}$ or $\mathbf{S_{bb}}$, if they share many common sub-strings. We quantify this metric, using the Jaccard similarity coefficient technique [20], as follows:

$$SS_c = \frac{|S(w_1) \cap S(w_2)|}{|S(w_1) \cup S(w_2)|} \tag{9.1}$$

where SS_c stands for *sub-string similarity co-efficient*. Since this approach does not group the keywords based on a lexical ordering, it does not violate the privacy of the content in the generated PASStree.

But, using only this approach might create partitions purely on a syntactic basis and not on the semantic relation between the keywords. Therefore, it would be desirable to group together common patterns that occur within the same document, as it lead to more relevant documents with respect to the pattern query. For instance, if two keywords, "Shipper" and "Shipment", with common pattern "Ship", are in the same document, then this document is probably most relevant to this pattern. Based on this, we identify two additional metrics for grouping keywords: (a) PS_c *phrase similarity co-efficient*, which measures the fraction of documents in which the two keywords occur as a *phrase*, i.e., one after another, and (b) DS_c *document similarity co-efficient*, which measures the fraction of documents in which the two keywords occur within the same document, but not as a phrase. These two metrics are computed using Jaccard similarity technique as follows. The first metric PS_c is given by following equation: $PS_c = \frac{|L(w_1 \to w_2)| + |L(w_2 \to w_1)|}{|L(w_1 \cap \cancel{w}_2)| + |L(w_2 \cap \cancel{w}_1)| + |L(w_1 \cap w_2)|}$ where $L(w_1 \to w_2)$ indicates the list of documents in which w_1 and w_2 occur as a phrase; $|L(w_1 \cap \cancel{w}_2)|$ is the number of documents containing only w_1 but not w_2 and so on. The second metric DS_c is as follows: $DS_c = \frac{|L(w_1 \cap w_2)|}{|L(w_1 \cap \cancel{w}_2)| + |L(w_2 \cap \cancel{w}_1)| + |L(w_1 \cap w_2)|}$. Based on these metrics, we quantify the similarity coefficient $S_c(w_1, w_2)$ of a keyword pair, w_1 and w_2, as the sum of the individual Jaccard similarity coefficients: $S_c(w_1, w_2) = SS_c + PS_c + DS_c$

Partitioning Using Clustering We use CLARA [21], a well known clustering algorithm, to partition a keyword set based on the keyword pair similarity. CLARA clusters the keywords around a representative keyword, called a medoid, MED, such that all the keywords share a high S_c with the medoid of a cluster. The medoids are chosen from a sample space of randomly selected keywords from the complete keyword set. Through thorough experimental analysis, [21] suggests that 5 sample spaces of size $40 + 2k$ give satisfactory results, where k is the number of required clusters. In our partitioning problem, we need 2 clusters, thus $k = 2$ and the corresponding sample space is of size 44. Finally, as suggested by Kaufman and Rousseeuw [21], to get the best possible medoids, we perform 5 iterations and balance the clusters to contain equal number of items.

9.5   Ranking Search Results

As a query string pattern can match several keywords in the document set, it is necessary to determine the relative importance of a matching keyword to the query string. We define *ranking* as an ordering of the matching leaf nodes with respect to a query string This implies that for two different string patterns matching the same set of leaf nodes, the ranking of the leaf nodes will be likely to be distinct. Note that, our definition of *ranking* is different from the conventional ranking defined in works such as [13]. *Ranking Heuristic.* We use a simple metric to quantify the relevance of a keyword to a given pattern: the position of the first occurrence of the pattern in the keyword determines the *rank* of the keyword with respect to the pattern. We have adopted this strategy as it is used in popular search engines such as Google$^{(tm)}$ and there may be other suitable alternative strategies depending on the application domain. Formally, if the characters in a keyword w are numbered as $1, 2, \cdots, |w|$, and if a given query sub-string p begins at the jth position of w, then the rank of w is j with respect to p where a smaller j means a higher rank. For example, for a query string *Ship*, a set of matching keywords *Shipment*, *Shipper*, *Worship*, will be ranked 1, 1 and 2 respectively, based on the position of *Ship* in these keywords. Therefore, to return the most relevant documents to the user, the matching keywords, i.e., the leaf nodes of the PASStree are ranked high to low based on the ranks of the respective keywords for the pattern string query.

9.5.1   Recording Matching Positions

To determine the position of the matching string pattern in a keyword, we use a heuristic approach leveraging the structure of the PASStree and store additional information in the PASStree to record the matching positions. For each PASStree node, we store an auxiliary Bloom filter, called the *sub-string prefix* (SP) Bloom filter. For uniformity, we denote the regular Bloom filter as the R Bloom filter. For a PASStree node at a distance d from the leaf nodes, the corresponding SP Bloom filter stores *all* possible prefixes of the node's keywords for the sub-strings at the dth positions of the keywords. For instance, at a leaf node, the SP Bloom filter stores all the prefixes of the keyword, corresponding to sub-strings at 1st position, e.g., given keyword *"Ship"*, the SP Bloom filter stores, *"S, Sh, Shi, Ship"*. Next, the SP Bloom filter at the parent node of the leaf nodes stores all the prefixes corresponding to the sub-strings found at the 2nd position in the keywords and so on. At the child nodes of the PASStree root, the SP Bloom filter stores all the prefixes corresponding to any substrings still remaining. The storage technique is same as that described in Sect. 9.3, where each SP Bloom filter has a distinct identifier, and the same set of cryptographic keys are used as done within the regular Bloom filters of the PASStree nodes.

9.5.2 Ranking Algorithm

Our ranking approach assigns ranks in ascending order, i.e., 1 is highest and so on. The key intuition of the ranking algorithm is as follows: if a query string, say "p", matches an SP filter of a leaf node, then this leaf node receives the highest rank of 1. If an intermediate SP filter node matches the query string, then the ranking of the matching leaf nodes in this node's sub-tree is decided by the distance of the SP filter node from the leaf node, i.e., the farther the SP node, the lower its rank. The detailed approach is described as follows.

At each PASStree node, the search algorithm performs two checks: once in the regular Bloom filter and another in the SP Bloom filter. If there is a match in SP Bloom filter, then the height d_i of the matching PASStree node and the identifier BF_{id} of the PASStree node Bloom filter are recorded as: $M_i =< d_i, BF_{id} >$ are recorded in the set $R = R \cup M_i$ where R sorts the tuples in ascending order of the d_i values. When the search terminates, the ranking algorithm, chooses the first $M_i =< d_i, BF_{id} >$ from R, and assigns the highest rank to all the matching leaf nodes within the subtree of the PASStree node corresponding to BF_{id}, and moves to the next node in R. Proceeding in this manner, all the matching leaf nodes in the PASStree are arranged in the ranked order.

9.6 Security Analysis

9.6.1 Security Model

To achieve IND-CKA security, our PASStree structure uses *keyed* one-way hash functions as pseudo-random functions whose output cannot be distinguished from a truly random function with non-negligible probability [22]. We have used SHA − 2 for our scheme as the pseudo-random function $\mathcal{H}$ and AES as the encryption algorithm Enc for the documents. From [6, 22], in the simulation based security model, a searchable symmetric encryption (SSE) scheme is IND-CKA secure if any probabilistic polynomial-time adversary cannot distinguish between the trapdoors generated by a real index using pseudo-random functions and a simulated index using truly random functions, with non-negligible probability. The important part of our proof is the construction of a polynomial time simulator, which can simulate the PASStree and hence, show the IND-CKA security conclusively. A probabilistic polynomial-time adversary interacts with the simulator as well as the real index and is challenged to distinguish between the results of the two indexes with non-negligible probability. We consider a *non-adaptive adversary*, i.e., prior to the simulation game, the adversary is not allowed to see the history of any search results or the PASStree.

9.6.2   Security Proof

Without loss of generality, the PASStree can be viewed as a list of Bloom filters, where each Bloom filter stores the sub-strings corresponding to a distinct keyword and matches different string patterns. The leaf node points to a list of document identifiers containing the keyword and the list can be encrypted as well using well known techniques from [6] and [23]. Therefore, proving the PASStree IND-CKA secure is equivalent to proving that each Bloom filter is IND-CKA secure with the following properties: (a) the Bloom filter bits do not reveal the content of the stored strings and (b) any two Bloom filters storing the same number of strings, with possibly overlapping strings, are indistinguishable to any probabilistic polynomial-time adversary. Given that the Bloom filter identifiers are distinct and random, the same pattern is stored in different locations across different Bloom filters. We use the key length s as the security parameter in following discussion.

History H_q. Let $\mathbf{D} = \{D_1, D_2, \cdots, D_n\}$ denote the set of document identifiers where D_i denotes the ith document. The history H_q is defined as $H_q = \{\mathbf{D}, p_1, p_2, \cdots, p_q\}$, where the set $\mathbf{D}$ consists of document identifiers matching one or more query string patterns p_1 to p_q. An important requirement is that q must be polynomial in the security parameter s, the key size, in order for the adversary to be polynomially bounded.

Adversary View A_v. This is the view of the adversary of a history H_q. Each query pattern, p_i generates a pseudo-random trapdoor T_{p_i} using the secret key $K \in \{0, 1\}^s$. The adversary view is: the set of trapdoors corresponding to the query strings denoted by $\mathbf{T}$, the secure index $\mathcal{I}$ for $\mathbf{D}$ and the set of the encrypted documents, $Enc_K(D)=\{Enc_K(D_1), \cdots, Enc_K(D_n)\}$, corresponding to the returned document identifiers. Formally, $A_v(H_q) = \{\mathbf{T}; \mathcal{I}; Enc_K(D)\}$.

Result Trace This is defined as the *access* and *search* patterns observed by the adversary after $\mathbf{T}$ is processed on the encrypted index $\mathcal{I}$. The access pattern is the set of matching document identifiers, $M(T)=\{ m(T_{p_1}), \cdots, m(T_{p_q})\}$ where $m(T_{p_i})$ denotes the set of matching document identifiers for trapdoor T_{p_i}. The search pattern is a symmetric binary matrix Π_T defined over T, such that, $\Pi_T[p, q] = 1$ if $T_p = T_q$, for, $1 \leq p, q \leq \sigma^{|T_i|}$. We denote the matching result trace over H_q as: $M_{(H_q)} = \{M(T), \Pi_T[p, q]\}$.

Theorem 9.2 (IND-CKA Security Proof) *The PASStree scheme is IND-CKA secure under a pseudo-random function f and the symmetric encryption algorithm Enc.*

Proof We show that given a real matching result trace $M_{(H_q)}$, it is possible to construct a polynomial time simulator $S = \{S_0, S_q\}$ simulating an adversary's view with non-negligible probability. We denote the simulated index as $\mathcal{I}^*$, the simulated encrypted documents as, $Enc_K(D^*)$ and the trapdoors as $\mathbf{T}^*$. Recall that, each Bloom filter matches a distinct set of trapdoors, which are visible in the result trace of the query. Let ID_j denote the unique identifier of a Bloom filter. The expected result of the simulator is to output trapdoors based on the chosen query string history submitted by the adversary. The adversary should not be able distinguish between these trapdoors and the trapdoors generated by a real PASStree with non-negligible probability.

Step 1. Index Simulation To simulate the index I^*, we generate $2N$ random identifiers corresponding to the number of Bloom filters in the index and associate a *depth* label with each string to denote its distance from the root. We generate random strings $Enc_K(D^*)$, such that each simulated string has the same size as an original encrypted document in $Enc_K(D)$ and $|Enc_K(D^*)| = |Enc_K(D)|$.

Step 2. Simulator State S_0 For H_q, where $q = 0$, we denote the simulator state by S_0. We construct the adversary view as follows: $A_v^*(H_0) = \{Enc_K(D^*), I^*, T^*\}$, where T^* denotes the set of trapdoors. To generate T^*, each document identifier $Enc_K(D^*)$ corresponds to a set of matching trapdoors. The length of each trapdoor is given by a pseudo-random function and the maximum possible number of trapdoors matching an identifier is given by the average maximum number, denoted by δ, of sub-strings of a keyword. Therefore, we generate $(\delta + 1) * |Enc_K(D^*)|$ random trapdoors and uniformly associate at most $\delta + 1$ trapdoors for each data item in $Enc_K(D^*)$. Note that, some trapdoors might repeat, which is desirable as two documents might match the same trapdoor. This distribution is consistent with the trapdoor distribution in the original index I, i.e., this simulated index satisfies all the structural properties of a real PASStree index. Now, given that $SHA - 2$ is pseudo-random and the probability of trapdoor distribution is uniform, the index I^* is indistinguishable by any probabilistic polynomial time adversary.

Step 3. Simulator State S_q For H_q where $q \geq 1$, we denote the simulator state by S_q. The simulator constructs the adversary view as follows: $A_v^*(H_q) = \{Enc_K(D^*), I^*, T^*, T_q\}$ where T_q are trapdoors corresponding to the query trace. Let p be the number of document identifiers in the trace. To construct I^*, given M_{H_q}, we construct the set of matching document identifiers for each trapdoor. For each document identifier in the trace, $Enc_K(D_p)$, the simulator associates the corresponding real trapdoor from $M(T_i)$ and if more than one trapdoor matches the document identifier, then the simulator generates a union of the trapdoors. As $q < |\mathbf{D}|$, the simulator generates $1 \leq i \leq |\mathbf{D}| - q + 1$ random strings, $Enc_K^*(D_i)$ of size $|Enc_K(D)|$ each and associates up to $\delta + 1$ trapdoors uniformly, as done in Step 2, ensuring that these strings do not match any strings from $M(T_i)$.

However, this construction cannot handle the cases where an adversary generates sub-strings from a single keyword and submits them to the history. For instance, the trapdoors corresponding to $Stop, top, op$ and $flop$ will result a set of common document identifiers as some of these patterns will be found in the same documents. Therefore, in such cases, the adversary expects to see some of the document identifiers to repeat within the result trace and if this does not happen, the adversary will be able to distinguish between a real and simulated index. To address this scenario, we take the document identifiers from the real trace and for each of the random Bloom filter identifiers, we associate a unique sub-set of these identifiers. This ensures that given any q query trapdoors, the intersection of the document identifiers induced due to this q query history is non-empty and therefore, indistinguishable from a real index. The simulator maintains an auxiliary state $\mathcal{ST}_q$ to remember the association between the trapdoors and the matching document identifiers. The simulator outputs: $\{Enc_K(D^*), \mathcal{I}^*, T^*, T_q\}$. Since all the steps performed by the simulator are polynomial and hence, the simulator runs in polynomial time complexity.

Now, if a probabilistic polynomial time adversary issues a query string pattern over any document identifier matching the set M_{H_q} the simulator gives the correct trapdoors. For any other query string pattern, the trapdoors given by simulator are indistinguishable due to pseudo-random function. Finally, since each Bloom filter contains sufficient blinding, our scheme is proven secure under the IND-CKA model.

□

9.7   Performance Evaluation

9.7.1   Experimental Methodology

To evaluate the performance of our approach, we considered three key parameters to design the experimental configurations: the data size, the PASStree type, and the pattern query result size. Based on these parameters we have done a thorough experimental evaluation of the index size, index construction time, the query processing time and the ranking precision.

9.7.1.1   Data Sets

The number of keywords is the most important factor in the PASStree evaluation and we select document collections containing different sized keywords set. We chose two real-life data sets: the Wikipedia archival pages from year 2010 and the *Enron* email dataset, containing mails of Enron employees over a certain period. We denote the Wikipedia data set by $WIKI$ and the Enron data set by $ENRON$. The $WIKI$ data set consists of 10,000 documents, chosen out of a 10 million plus corpus, where each document contains an average of 100 distinct keywords, not counting the general stop-words such as, "a, an, the, there" and so on. We chose distinct collections of $WIKI$ documents containing, on an average, 1000, 5000, 25,000, 50,000 and 100,000 keywords, and averaged the results over 5 different collections for each keyword size configuration. For instance, to get one instance of 1000 keywords data set, we chose up to 100–150 distinct documents and similarly, for the other 4 instances of 1000 keywords data set, we chose four more distinct document collections. We ran the PASStree and PASStree+ algorithms on each of these five different 1000 keywords data sets and averaged the results. Similar experiments were repeated for the other keyword data set sizes as well.

The $ENRON$ email data set consisted of 10,000 documents, chosen out of 0.6 million corpus, where each document contained an average of 10 distinct keywords, besides the stop words. Each $ENRON$ document corresponds to an email between a *Sender* and a *Receiver* with the email header and content exchanged. For the $ENRON$ data set, we considered different document collections containing, 4000, 6000, 8000, 10,000 and 12,000, distinct keywords and averaged the results over 5 different collections for each configuration. The keyword data set configuration is similar to the $WIKI$ data set configuration.

9.7.1.2 Implementation Details

The PASStree was implemented in C++ and the experiments were conducted on desktop PC running Linux Ubuntu 12.10 with $4GB$ memory and *3.3GHz Intel(R) Core(TM) i3-2120k* processor. To encrypt the keywords we use the Advanced Encryption Standard (AES) algorithm with a 128-bit master key and $HMAC - SHA2$ as the secure hash function for the Bloom filter encoding. We set the Bloom filter parameter, $M/N = 10$, where M is the Bloom filter size and N is the number of elements and the number of Bloom filter hash functions: $q = 7$. We chose $t = 256$ as the bit-length for each of the K_i where $1 \leq i \leq q$ keys used to compute the trapdoor hashes over an encrypted pattern query.

9.7.1.3 Query Types

For the $WIKI$ data set, we considered string pattern queries where the user retrieves documents containing keywords that match a sub-string. We denote these queries as *sub-string* queries. For the $ENRON$ data set, we considered queries that wish to retrieve emails between a particular $SENDER$ to a particular receiver $RECEIVER$. Since our PASStree approach includes the co-occurrence of the two keywords as one of the similarity metrics, this experiment is useful to determine whether PASStree can achieve multi-keyword phrase search effectively. We denote these queries as $SENDER/RECEIVER$ queries. For $SENDER/RECEIVER$ queries in Enron data set, the individual keywords from sender and receiver are extracted. An example $SENDER/RECEIVER$ query is: *"From: Grant Colleean To: Market Status"*, which is converted to a set of 4 keywords query: *Grant, Colleean, Market* and *Status*. The query is performed on individual keywords and the results are accumulated.

Next, the query result size, i.e., number of matches for a query string, is an important factor affecting the performance of the PASStree and therefore, we chose the *sub-string* and $SENDER/RECEIVER$ queries, which have different query result sizes ranging from: $10, 20, \cdots, 100$. We averaged each of the experiments

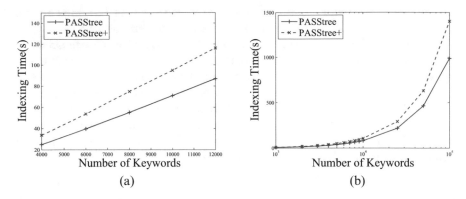

Fig. 9.2 Index construction time. (**a**) ENRON. (**b**) WIKI

over 10 different trials, e.g., choosing 10 distinct queries resulting in 10 different
matching leaf nodes and recording the average of the metrics involved.

9.7.2   PASStree Construction and Size

Our experimental evaluation shows that the PASStree construction time is small for
large data sets and the index size is either comparable or smaller to existing works.
Figures 9.2a and b show the construction time for PASStree and PASStree+ over
different sized keyword sets, and as expected, PASStree construction is faster. For
reasonably large sized sets of 1000 to 10,000 keywords, the construction time is
less than 100 s, and for very large keyword sizes, >10,000, the construction time is
between 100 to 1500 s.

To compare the size of PASStree PASStree+, we chose several existing privacy
preserving keyword search schemes. The scheme in [15] is denoted as *Blind Seer*
wherein this scheme uses a Bloom tree to index documents instead of keywords.
This scheme is highly space efficient but can only support keyword queries.
The scheme in [17] supports similarity based search using hamming distance as
similarity metric and we denote this scheme by *Fuzzy* $d = x$ where x is the chosen
hamming distance. The index sizes in this scheme are very high and cannot support
some queries like "*Immun*" to match keywords like "*Immunization*", because the
hamming distance is $d = 7$ and for this value of d the index size is prohibitive.
Finally, we compare with the scheme in [24] and denote it by *KRB Tree*, which
supports dynamic keyword search. Figure 9.3a and b, show that the PASStree size
is much smaller than the *Fuzzy* scheme and comparable to the other keyword only
search schemes. These results show that PASStree sizes are very reasonable even
for large keyword spaces and therefore, is suitable for practical deployment.

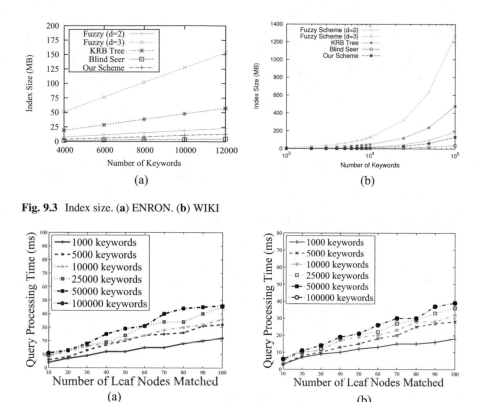

Fig. 9.3 Index size. (**a**) ENRON. (**b**) WIKI

Fig. 9.4 Query time for WIKI. (**a**) PASStree. (**b**) PASStree+

9.7.3 Query Processing Speed and Accuracy

Our experiments show that the pattern query matching achieves 100% *accuracy and the query processing time is very efficient over large data sets.* Figures 9.4 and 9.5 show the query processing times over PASStree and PASStree+ for different keyword sets for various query result sizes. While PASStree+ is faster than PASStree, as is expected, both the structures execute large queries within few 10s of milliseconds, which is very fast considering the data set sizes.

9.7.4 Ranking Precision

Our ranking approach is very effective in returning the most relevant matching documents. For the sake of experiments, we maintained a ranked list of documents at the leaf nodes and compared the relative ranking of the PASStree results with

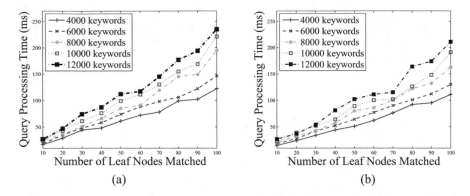

Fig. 9.5   Query time for ENRON. (**a**) PASStree. (**b**) PASStree+

this ranked list. We measured the *ranking precision* as L'/L where L' denotes the number of top-ranked documents returned in the PASStree results and L denotes the actual number of top-ranked documents. The experiments show that, for the $WIKI$ data, the ranking precision is between 90% to 100%, whereas, for the $ENRON$ data, the values are between 90% to 100% on an average, with an odd value falling to 70%.

9.8   Conclusion and Future Work

In this work, we presented the first approach towards privacy preserving string pattern matching in cloud computing. We described PASStree, a privacy preserving pattern matching index structure along with novel algorithms to solve the various challenges in this problem. Our PASStree structure can process pattern queries in a fast and efficient manner over several thousands of keywords. The results of our scheme demonstrate the need to further explore the rich problem space of privacy preserving pattern matching in cloud computing. We also demonstrated strong security guarantees, which shows that our approach can be deployed in practical systems. The future scope of this work lies in exploring more expressive pattern querying mechanisms for user friendly cloud computing data applications.

References

1. R. Grossi, J. Vitter, Compressed suffix arrays and suffix trees with applications to text indexing and string matching. SIAM J. Comput. **35**(2), 378–407 (2005)
2. P. Ferragina, G. Manzini, *Opportunistic Data Structures with Applications*. FOCS (IEEE Computer Society, Washington, 2000)

3. R. Canetti, U. Feige, O. Goldreich, M. Naor, Adaptively secure multi-party computation, in *STOC '96: Proceedings of the Twenty-Eighth Annual ACM Symposium on Theory of Computing* (1996), pp. 639–648
4. Eujin-Goh, Secure indexes (2004). Stanford University Technical Report
5. D. Song, D. Wagner, A. Perrig, Practical techniques for searches on encrypted data, in *IEEE S&P Symposium* (2000)
6. R. Curtmola, J. Garay, S. Kamara, R. Ostrovsky, Searchable symmetric encryption: improved definitions and efficient constructions. J. Comput. Sec. **19**, 895–934 (2011)
7. J.R. Troncoso-Pastoriza, S. Katzenbeisser, M. Celik, Privacy preserving error resilient DNA searching through oblivious automata, in *CCS '07: Proceedings of the 14th ACM Conference on Computer and Communications Security* (2007), pp. 519–528
8. J. Katz, L. Malka, Secure text processing with applications to private DNA matching, in *CCS '10: Proceedings of the 17th ACM Conference on Computer and Communications Security* (2010), pp. 485–492
9. P. Mohassel, S. Niksefat, S. Sadeghian, B. Sadeghiyan, An efficient protocol for oblivious DFA evaluation and applications, in *Cryptographers' Track at the RSA Conference* (2012), pp. 398–415
10. J. Baron, K. El Defrawy, K. Minkovich, R. Ostrovsky, E. Tressler, 5PM: secure pattern matching, in *International Conference on Security and Cryptography for Networks* (Springer, Berlin, 2012), pp. 222–240
11. Y.-C. Chang, M. Mitzenmacher, Privacy preserving keyword searches on remote encrypted data, in *Third International Conference on Applied Cryptography and Network Security* (2005)
12. S. Kamara, C. Papamanthou, T. Roeder, Dynamic searchable symmetric encryption, in *Computer and Communications Security* (2012)
13. W. Sun, B. Wang, N. Cao, M. Li, W. Lou, Y.T. Hou, H. Li, Privacy-preserving multi-keyword text search in the cloud supporting similarity-based ranking, in *ASIA CCS '13: Proceedings of the 8th ACM SIGSAC Symposium on Information, Computer and Communications Security* (2013), pp. 71–82
14. N. Cao, C. Wang, M. Li, K. Ren, W. Lou, Privacy-preserving multi-keyword ranked search over encrypted cloud data. IEEE Trans. Parallel Distrib. Syst. **25**(1), 222–233 (2014)
15. V. Pappas, F. Krell, B. Vo, V. Kolesnikov, T. Malkin, S. G. Choi, W. George, A. Keromytis, S. Bellovin, Blind seer: a scalable private DBMS, in *IEEE S&P Symposium* (2014)
16. D. Cash, J. Jaeger, S. Jarecki, C. Jutla, H. Krawczyk, M.-C. Rosu, M. Steiner, Dynamic searchable encryption in very-large databases: data structures and implementation, in *ISOC Network and Distributed System Security Symposium* (2014)
17. J. Li, Q. Wang, C. Wang, N. Cao, K. Ren, W. Lou, Fuzzy keyword search over encrypted data in cloud computing, in *2010 Proceedings IEEE INFOCOM* (2010), pp. 441–445
18. C. Hazay, T. Toft, Computationally secure pattern matching in the presence of malicious adversaries. J. Crypt. 358–395 (2014)
19. B. H. Bloom, Space time tradeoffs in in hash coding with allowable errors. Commun. ACM **13**, 422–426 (1970)
20. A.K. Jain, R.C. Dubes, *Algorithms for Clustering Data* (Prentice-Hall, Inc., Upper Saddle River, 1988)
21. L. Kaufman, P.J. Rousseeuw, *Finding Groups in Data: An Introduction to Cluster Analysis.* Wiley Series in Probability and Statistics (1990)
22. J. Katz, Y. Lindell, *Introduction to Modern Cryptography* (Chapman & Hall, London/CRC Press, Boca Raton, 2007)
23. X. Zou, Y.-S. Dai, E. Bertino, A practical and flexible key management mechanism for trusted collaborative computing, in *IEEE INFOCOM* (2008)
24. S. Kamara, C. Papamanthou, Parallel and dynamic searchable symmetric encryption, in *Financial Cryptography*. Lecture Notes in Computer Science, vol. 7859 (2013), pp. 258–274

Chapter 10
Privacy Preserving Information Hub Identification in Social Networks

10.1 Introduction

10.1.1 Background and Motivation

In a social network, a user that has a large number of interactions with other users is defined as an *information hub* (or simply a *hub*) [1]. An interaction refers to the transmission of information by one user to another user. For example, an interaction from user A to user B in online social networks may be the action when user A posts a message or comment on user B's profile. Hubs play important roles in the spread or subversion of propaganda, ideologies, or gossips in social networks. Taking the advertising industry as an example, instead of giving free product samples to random people, to improve the effectiveness of word of mouth advertising and increase recommendation based product adoption, they may want to give free samples to hubs only [2]. For example, CNN reported that Samsung used social networks information to target dissatisfied owners of Apple iPhone 4 in a recent advertisement campaign [3]. Samsung first monitored Twitter feeds to identify dissatisfied iPhone 4 owners who are the most active in terms of communicating with their friends (i.e. hubs) and are therefore most influential in spreading word of mouth recommendation, then offered free GalaxyS phones to some of them. Furthermore, observing adoption of products or trends at hubs helps to predict the eventual total sale of a product [2]. For instance, advertisers can observe the impact of distributing free samples to hubs to predict the future successfulness of a product. Due to limited advertisement budget (e.g., free product samples), advertisers want to identify the top-k nodes in a social network. Suri and Narahari [4] defined these as, "for any given positive integer k, the top-k nodes in a social network, based on a certain measure appropriate for the social network." In the context of this research, that measure is information. Therefore, identifying top-k information hubs in social networks is an important problem.

A. X. Liu, R. Li, *Algorithms for Data and Computation Privacy*, https://doi.org/10.1007/978-3-030-58896-0_10

10.1.2   Limitations of Prior Art

Prior methods for computing top-k information hubs (e.g., [5] and [6]), are mostly centralized assuming the availability of either interaction or friendship graphs. The interaction graph of a social network is a directed multigraph [7] whose nodes represent users and directed links represent the existence of a directed pairwise interaction. Each link is labeled with a time stamp that indicates when the interaction occurred. The friendship graph of a social network consists of nodes representing users and undirected links representing the friend relationship among users. Figure 10.1 shows the conceptual depiction of the friendship graph between users and the overlaid interaction graph. However, centralized computation of top-k information hubs is mostly unrealistic for parties such as advertisers because online social networking companies are reluctant to share their interaction or friendship graphs due to privacy concerns and regulations [8]. Furthermore, advertisers cannot even directly collect interaction or friendship information from social network sites by means such as crawling because for many online social networking companies such as Facebook [9], unauthorized data collection is a violation of their terms of service.

10.1.3   Proposed Solution

In this chapter, we propose a distributed and privacy preserving algorithm for computing top-k information hubs in social networks. Distributed algorithms for computing top-k information hubs have to be privacy preserving because users are typically hesitant to disclose explicit information about their friendship links or interaction information due to privacy concerns [10]. To preserve the privacy of user interactions, our algorithm is distributed and does not require the advertiser to know

Fig. 10.1 Conceptual depiction of the friendship graph between users and the overlaid interaction graph

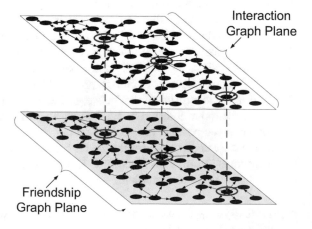

Interaction Graph Plane

Friendship Graph Plane

users' friendship associations or interactions. There are three technical challenges in designing such an algorithm. First, the problem of inferring a user's salience (whose ground truth resides in the interaction graph) from the corresponding friendship graph is inherently difficult because an interaction graph has more information than its corresponding friendship graph. Furthermore, a friendship graph is directed or undirected (and un-weighted), whereas the interaction graph is a directed multigraph. Second, the complete friendship graph itself may not be available to the parties interested in identifying hubs. Third, preserving users' privacy in this computation is difficult as any information exchange involved in this computation should not contain any personal information.

We now present an overview of our proposed solutions to the above-mentioned technical challenges. To address the first challenge, we apply principal component centrality (PCC), a new measure of centrality we introduced in [11], to the friendship graphs. The intuition behind PCC is that a user who is connected to well-connected users (even if the user himself is poorly connected) has a more central status. For example, a poorly connected person who has a direct connection with a well-connected representative in some population may be capable of propagating an opinion well by simply convincing the representative. Unlike other measures of user influence (e.g., eigenvector centrality [12, 13]), PCC takes into consideration the fact that social networks can be multi-polar consisting of multiple communities with few connections between them. However, since PCC applies to symmetric matrices, it does not apply to social graphs in which relationships are not bi-directional. We extend PCC's definition to the Generalized PCC which is applicable to non-symmetric matrices as well, i.e. it is applicable to social graphs in which relationships are directional.

To address the second challenge of friendship graph data availability, we distribute the computation of PCC among users and therefore do not require a central entity to access the friendship graph. Advertisers can utilize existing functionality in popular online social networks (such as *groups* and *pages* in Facebook [14]) to implement our proposed distributed method. Motivation for user participation in decentralized PCC computation may range from tangible incentives such as receiving free samples from advertisers (e.g., [3]), to intangible incentives such as bragging rights about one's popularity (e.g., [15]). We decentralize the PCC computation using the Kempe-McSherry (KM) algorithm [16]. These iterative algorithms compute eigenvalues and eigenvectors that are essential for computing nodes' PCCs. Our decentralized algorithm restricts the set of users that a particular user has to communicate with to its immediate friends. Furthermore, the memory requirement at each user of this algorithm grows only linearly with the number of friends. Hence, one of the contributions of this work is extending the original centralized PCC approach to a more practical distributed PCC form. This new distributed PCC form is an accurate and robust centrality measure that is capable of identifying all salient users in a social graph using a truly decentralized and scalable method. Finally only a numeric vector representing intermediate eigenvector entries are exchanged between users. It is impossible to reverse-engineer users' friendship associations from these intermediate scores.

10.1.4   Results and Findings

We evaluated the effectiveness of our proposed technique using three real-world data sets: The first two are Facebook data sets [17] containing about six million users and more than 40 million friendship links. In this data set relationships are reciprocated, i.e. links between users are undirected (if user A is friends with user B, that implies user B is also friends with user A). The third data set consists of a little over two million Twitter users and their activity. The Twitter data set differs from the Facebook data sets in that relationships between users are not necessarily reciprocated, i.e. links between users are directed (if user A follows user B, that does not imply that user B also follows user A). We have four major findings from our results. First, there is indeed close correlation between the PCC of nodes in the friendship graph and corresponding dynamic user interaction data. We envision that this correlation can be exploited for other purposes as well. Second, the computation of PCC can be effectively distributed across individual users in a social graph without compromising its accuracy. This eliminates the requirement of a central authority for identifying hubs. Third, the accuracy of PCC improves as we use more eigenvectors in its computation. Further, the appropriate number of eigenvectors required in the computation of PCC for real-world social networks is around 10-20. Fourth, the accuracy (in terms of number of correctly identified top-k users and their estimated rank) of PCC improves as the duration of interaction data used for comparison is increased from 1 month, to 6 month to more than a year. This essentially shows that PCC scores reflect the flow of information between users of a social network over long time periods.

10.1.5   Key Contributions

We make four key contributions in this chapter. First, we propose a novel method to infer information lying in the interaction graph (i.e. hub identification) from the friendship graph in social networks without using the interaction data. Earlier works are limited to solving this problem using complete interaction graph data. Second, our proposed method, first of its kind, allows third parties (other than social network owners) to solve this problem. We use a distributed method to overcome the requirement of a central authority. Third, our proposed method preserves the privacy of users, i.e., users do not release any personal information to other users. We achieve this objective by letting each user share only some real numbers that cannot be reverse-engineered. Finally, we evaluate the effectiveness of our proposed technique using real-world Facebook data sets that are publicly available. The results of our analysis show that the proposed approach improves the accuracy of finding the top-k user set by approximately 50% over existing measures. Furthermore, the proposed technique accurately estimates the rank of individual users.

The rest of the chapter proceeds as follows. In Sect. 10.2, we present an overview of related work. We provide the details of our proposed approach in Sect. 10.3. We also provide the analysis of the data set used for evaluating our proposed technique in Sect. 10.4.1. We then provide the detailed results of our evaluation in the rest of Sect. 10.4. Finally, we conclude the chapter in Sect. 10.5.

10.2   Related Work

Besides work on hub identification using user interaction data [5, 6] mentioned in Sect. 10.1, we provide an overview of other research on influence maximization, a different but related problem. Several algorithms have been proposed for identifying influential users in social networks [4, 18–22]. The objective function for this influence maximization problem is to maximize the number of users that are part of information flows initiated by the top-k influential users. In contrast, our method uses friendship graphs, is fully distributed, and is privacy-preserving, while such work uses user interaction data and is centralized and is not privacy-preserving.

Kempe et al. studied this influence maximization problem for the first time, proved it is NP-hard, and proposed a heuristics-based algorithm that achieves 63% of the optimal result in most cases and outperforms degree and distance centrality heuristics [19]. Suri and Narahari later proposed Shapley value based heuristic for solving this problem [4]. Zou et al. studied the same problem with an additional constraint of latency [22]. Estevez et al. proposed an algorithm called the Set Covering Greedy (SCG) algorithm, which takes into account the intuition that we should prefer to select nodes in different neighborhoods rather than selecting highly connected nodes lying in the same neighborhood [18]. Kimura et al. studied the influence maximization problem with respect to two widely-used fundamental stochastic information diffusion models in networks, and proposed a solution utilizing tools from bond percolation and graph theory [20, 21].

Algorithms that forgo using interaction data use structural information like the friendship graph. They are based on centrality measures computed from friendship graph topologies. Marsden [23] used degree, closeness, betweenness and eigenvector centrality measures. This is followed by Shi et al. in [24] who used the same centrality measures, i.e. degree, closeness, betweenness and pagerank [25–27] (which is just an iterative algorithm to compute eigenvector centrality). However, as Borgatti showed in [28], degree, closeness and betweenness centrality are inappropriate measures of centrality for influence processes. Degree centrality is a good measure of the rate of immediate rate of spread of influence from nodes in the short-term. Betweenness and closeness centrality are ill-suited for the problem at hand because the definitions underlying them assume that the flow on the network does not replicate and occurs only along shortest paths. Therefore, the performance of Marsden's use of eigenvector centrality and Shi's use of Pagerank form the baseline for comparison against our proposed algorithm. Canright, Engø-Monsen and Jelasity [29] described a distributed and privacy preserving algorithm for the computation of eigenvector centrality/PageRank.

10.3   Proposed Solution

This section presents our proposed technique for identifying information hubs in social networks. We model the information flow as an influence process. The underlying rationale for doing so is rooted in the assumption that in social networks people (nodes) with more friends (connections) send and receive more messages. Furthermore, people will receive more messages from friends that send/receive a lot of traffic than from those that send/receive fewer messages. This information flow can be modeled as an influence process. According to Borgatti's two dimensional taxonomy of node centrality measures in [28], the appropriate measure to quantify nodes' influence is eigenvector centrality (EVC) [12, 13].

10.3.1   Eigenvector Centrality

Let $\mathbf{A}$ denote the adjacency matrix of a graph $G(V, E)$ consisting of the set of nodes $V = \{v_1, v_2, v_3, \ldots, v_N\}$ of size N and set of undirected edges E. When a link is present between two nodes v_i and v_j, both $A_{i,j}$ and $A_{j,i}$ are set to 1 and set to 0 otherwise. Let $\Gamma(v_i)$ denote the neighborhood of v_i, the set of nodes v_i is connected to directly. EVC of a node is recursively defined as proportional to the number of its neighbors and their respective EVCs. Let $x(i)$ be the EVC score of a node v_i. Then,

$$x(i) = \frac{1}{\lambda_1} \sum_{v_j \in \Gamma(v_i)} x(j) = \frac{1}{\lambda_1} \sum_{j=1}^{N} A_{i,j} x(j) \tag{10.1}$$

Here λ_1 is a constant (later found to be the principal eigenvalue of $\mathbf{A}$). Equation (10.1) can be rewritten in vector form Eq. (10.2) where $\mathbf{x}_1 = [x(1), x(2), x(3), \ldots, x(N)]^T$ is the vector of EVC scores of all nodes.

$$\mathbf{x}_1 = \frac{1}{\lambda_1} \mathbf{A} \mathbf{x}_1 \quad \Longleftrightarrow \quad \lambda_1 \mathbf{x}_1 = \mathbf{A} \mathbf{x}_1 \tag{10.2}$$

Equation (10.2) is the well-known eigenvector equation where this centrality takes its name from. Obviously several eigenvalue/eigenvector pairs exist for an adjacency matrix $\mathbf{A}$. Here, λ_1 is the largest of all eigenvalues of $\mathbf{A}$ by magnitude. If λ_i is any other eigenvalue of $\mathbf{A}$ then $|\lambda_1| > |\lambda_i|$. The eigenvector $\mathbf{x}_1 = [x_1(1), x_1(2), \ldots, x_1(N)]^T$ corresponding to the principal eigenvalue is the principal eigenvector. Thus, the vector of node EVCs is equivalent to the principal eigenvector. The EVC of a node v_i is the corresponding element $\mathbf{x}_1(i)$ of the principal eigenvector $\mathbf{x}_1$.

10.3.2 Motivation for Principal Component Centrality

As we demonstrated in [11], in networks of multiple communities with sparse connectivity between communities, EVC assigns centrality scores to nodes according to their location with respect to the most dominant community. We also gave an elaborate example illustrating the relationship between successive eigenvectors and their interpretation in terms of the network topology of the graph adjacency matrix they are obtained from. When applied to large networks, EVC fails to assign significant scores to a large fraction of nodes. The principal eigenvector is "pulled" in the direction of the largest community. The motivation for using PCC as a measure of node influence may be understood by looking at EVC in the context of principal component analysis (PCA) [30]. In PCA, when feature vectors are extracted from an $N \times N$ covariance matrix of N random variables, the principal eigenvector is the most dominant feature vector, i.e. the direction in N-dimensional hyperspace along which the spread of data points is greatest. Similarly, the second eigenvector (corresponding to the second largest eigenvalue) is representative of the second most significant feature of the data set. The second eigenvector may also be thought of as the most significant feature after the data points are collapsed along the direction of the principal eigenvector. Eigendecomposition of a covariance matrix is the performed using the well-known PCA. PCA is used to compute the eigenvectors $\mathbf{x}_1, \mathbf{x}_2, \mathbf{x}_3, \ldots, \mathbf{x}_N$ and eigenvalues $\lambda_1, \lambda_2, \lambda_3, \ldots, \lambda_N$ of the graph G's adjacency matrix $\mathbf{A}$. Readers interested in a deeper coverage of the intuitive meaning of eigenvectors and eigenvalues of a graph adjacency matrix are referred to Ilyas and Radha [11].

10.3.3 Definition of PCC

While EVC assigns centrality to nodes according to their location with respect to the most dominant community in a graph G, PCC takes into consideration additional communities. We define the PCC of a node in a graph as its Euclidean distance/ℓ^2 norm from the origin in the P-dimensional eigenspace. The basis vectors of that eigenspace are the P most significant eigenvectors of the adjacency matrix A of the graph G under consideration. For a graph G, its N eigenvalues $|\lambda_1| \geq |\lambda_2| \geq \ldots \geq |\lambda_N|$ correspond to the normalized eigenvectors $\mathbf{x}_1, \mathbf{x}_2, \ldots, \mathbf{x}_N$, respectively. The eigenvector/eigenvalue pairs are indexed in descending order of magnitude of eigenvalues. When $P = 1$, PCC equals a scaled version of EVC. The parameter P in PCC can be used as a tuning parameter to adjust the number of eigenvectors included in PCC.

Let $\mathbf{X}$ denote the $N \times N$ matrix of concatenated eigenvectors $\mathbf{X} = [\mathbf{x}_1 \mathbf{x}_2 \ldots \mathbf{x}_N]$ and let $\Lambda = [\lambda_1 \lambda_2 \ldots \lambda_N]^T$ be the vector of eigenvalues. Furthermore, if $P < N$ (typically $P \ll N$) and if matrix $\mathbf{X}$ has dimensions $N \times N$, then $\mathbf{X}_{N \times P}$ will denote the submatrix of $\mathbf{X}$ consisting of the first N rows and first P columns. Then PCC can be expressed in matrix form as:

$$\mathbf{C}_P = \sqrt{((\mathbf{AX}_{N \times P}) \odot (\mathbf{AX}_{N \times P})) \, \mathbf{1}_{P \times 1}} \tag{10.3}$$

The '$\odot$' operator is the Hadamard (or entrywise product or Schur product) operator and $\mathbf{1}_{P \times 1}$ is a vector of 1s of length P. Equation (10.3) can also be expressed in terms of the eigenvalue and eigenvector matrices Λ and $\mathbf{X}$, of the adjacency matrix $\mathbf{A}$:

$$\mathbf{C}_P = \sqrt{(\mathbf{X}_{N \times P} \odot \mathbf{X}_{N \times P})(\Lambda_{P \times 1} \odot \Lambda_{P \times 1})}. \tag{10.4}$$

10.3.4   Generalized PCC

So far, we have assumed that the adjacency matrix of social networks is symmetric. This limits application of the PCC, as it has been defined in the preceding section, to undirected graphs. However, in several social network services, relationships between users is one-directional and not necessarily reciprocated. The adjacency matrix of such a network is non-symmetric, and with exception of the principal eigenvalue and eigenvector all subsequent eigenvalues and eigenvectors may be complex. To extend the possible use of PCC to social networks whose topology is best captured by directed graphs, we generalize the definition of PCC as follows.

$$\mathbf{C}_P = \sqrt{|(\mathbf{X}_{N \times P} \odot \mathbf{X}_{N \times P})| \, |(\Lambda_{P \times 1} \odot \Lambda_{P \times 1})|}. \tag{10.5}$$

Node PCCs as defined in Eqs. (10.3)–(10.5) are not normalized. To allow interpretation of centrality scores, Ruhnau advocated in [31] that they should be normalized by either the Euclidean norm (ℓ_2 norm) or the maximum norm (ℓ_∞ i.e. the maximum centrality score) of the centrality vector. For the remainder of this chapter the PCC vector will be normalized by the ℓ_∞ norm, thereby restricting all entries to the range [0, 1].

We demonstrate PCC on a small-scale example, a graph consisting of two Barabási-Albert graphs [32], one consisting of 100 nodes in one community that is sparsely connected with another Barabási-Albert graph of 50 nodes. Figure 10.2 demonstrates the effect of changing number of eigenvectors P for PCC $\mathbf{C}_P$ from 1 (Fig. 10.2a) for EVC to 5 (Fig. 10.2b), 10 (Fig. 10.2c) and 100 (Fig. 10.2d). As this example shows, EVC is only able to assign significant centrality to the most well connected node in the larger of the two subgraphs. As P is raised to 5 and 10,

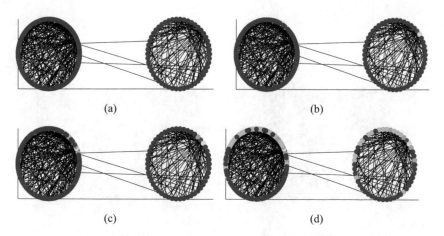

Fig. 10.2 PCC of nodes in a network consisting of two Barabási-Albert graphs of 100 and 50 nodes connected by a few links when computed using the most significant (a) $C_1(i)$, (b) $C_5(i)$, (c) $C_{10}(i)$, and (d) $C_{100}(i)$ eigenvectors. Warm node colors represent high PCC, cold node colors represent low PCC

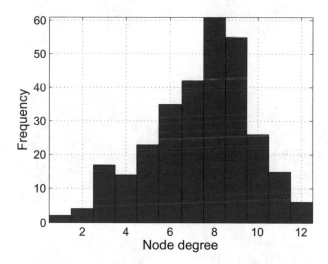

Fig. 10.3 Degree distribution of a geometric mesh graph of 300 nodes

gradually more nodes are assigned significant centrality scores, even some in the smaller subgraph of 50 nodes.

For an illustrated example of PCC applied to a graph whose hubs are less prominent, refer to the example of the geometric mesh graph with a non-scale free distribution in Fig. 10.4 and its graph's degree distribution in Fig. 10.3. A more detailed demonstration of PCC on a graph with a degree distribution not resembling a scale free distribution is available in [33].

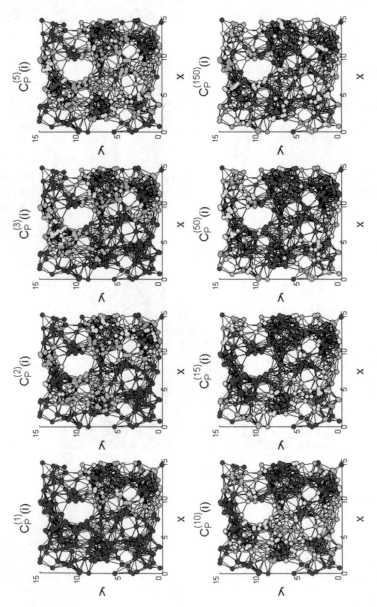

Fig. 10.4 PCC applied to a geometric mesh graph of 300 nodes. Warm node colors represent high PCC, cold node colors represent low PCC

10.3.5   Selection of Number of Eigenvectors

The cost of computing an eigenvector can be significant for large matrices, favoring the use of as few eigenvectors for PCC as are necessary. To determine appropriate number of eigenvectors (P_{app}), we consider the phase angle ϕ as a function of P. The phase angle $\phi(P)$ of a PCC vector $\mathbf{C}_P$ is defined as its angle with the EVC vector $\mathbf{C}_E$ and is defined mathematically in Eq. (10.6).

$$\phi(P) = \arccos\left(\frac{\mathbf{C}_P}{|\mathbf{C}_P|} \cdot \frac{\mathbf{C}_E}{|\mathbf{C}_E|}\right) \tag{10.6}$$

When the phase angle function is plotted for a range of P, the value of P at which ϕ begins approaching its final steady value is used for that particular graph (P_{app}) [11]. The selection of P_{app} can be made as,

$$P_{app} = min\{\phi(P+1) - \phi(P)\} \quad \in [-\epsilon, \epsilon], \forall [P, N], \tag{10.7}$$

where ϵ is a small real number. It is our observation that the value of P_{app} is close to the number of well-connected communities in a social graph.

10.3.6   Decentralized Eigendecomposition Algorithm

The massive sizes of social networks require a method whose space and time complexity scales well with the number of nodes and links between them. According to Eq. (10.3), for a node to compute its own PCC score it needs to know its corresponding entries in the first P eigenvectors $\mathbf{x}_1, \mathbf{x}_2 \ldots \mathbf{x}_P$ of the adjacency matrix $\mathbf{A}$, as well as who its neighbors are, i.e. the entries in its corresponding row of A. Although many decentralized algorithms for computing eigenvectors of a matrix exist, many of them are not designed to minimize the communication overhead between participating nodes. We discuss 2 well-known distributed algorithms in the following text.

In [16] Kempe and McSherry developed a decentralized algorithm for the computation of the first P most significant eigenvectors. Their approach differs from other algorithms in that each node is only required to communicate with neighbor nodes. This means that the computational complexity of the algorithm at every node, and the volume of messages exchanged by each node scales only linearly with the number of its neighbors and linearly with the number of eigenvectors that are computed. Furthermore, the time for the algorithm to converge is $O(\tau_{mix} \log N)$, where N is the total number of nodes in the graph and τ_{mix} is the mixing time of the Markov chain with a transition matrix that is the row-normalized version of $\mathbf{A}$. Although the Power method with deflation's [34, 35] overhead and convergence properties vary greatly from those of the KM algorithm, the iterative components of the KM algorithm are very similar to those of the power method when it is used in the computation of the principal eigenvector only. Both algorithms perform a deterministic simulation of a random walk. For detailed coverage of the KM algorithm we refer the reader to [16].

The principal advantage of the KM algorithm is its lower message exchange overhead. Given the degree of each node in a graph, the number of messages exchanged network-wide in each iteration of the KM algorithm is deterministic. In each iteration, every node sends a message to all nodes it is connected with. Therefore, the number of messages exchanged is twice the number of edges in the graph.

Kempe reported the error of the ℓ_2 norm of the space spanned by R_P, the projection of P most significant eigenvectors on $\mathbf{A}$, and $R_{P'}$, the projection of P most significant eigenvectors by KM-algorithm onto $\mathbf{A}$, with high probability as follows.

$$\|\mathbf{R}_P - \mathbf{R}_{P'}\|_2 \leq O\left(\left|\frac{\lambda_{P+1}}{\lambda_P}\right|^t \cdot N\right) + 3\epsilon^{4t} \tag{10.8}$$

Here, t denotes the number of iterations for which the KM algorithm executes. Clearly, since $\lambda_{P+1} < \lambda_P$, the fractional term will be decreasing with t at a geometric rate. Figure 10.5 shows a plot of average mean squared error (MSE) between the actual and estimated top-k eigenvectors (using the KM algorithm) for random graphs of 100 nodes. We report average MSE values for varying number of eigenvectors (k) and number of iterations (t). Each point in the plot is an average of 1000 independent runs and the confidence intervals are too small to be shown. As expected from Eq. (10.8), we observe that average MSE values sharply decrease approximately at a geometric rate for increasing number of iterations. Furthermore, for a given number of iterations, average MSE values increase for larger k values.

From the above discussions of the KM algorithm, we conclude the following:

- The KM algorithm never requires a node to communicate beyond its immediate neighbors. This implies that the communication overhead of the KM algorithm scales linearly with the number of computed eigenvectors.
- Kempe et al. reported near perfect convergence for their algorithm, which is also verified from our observations in Fig. 10.5.

For these reasons, we choose to use the KM algorithm for the distributed computation of eigenvectors for PCC.

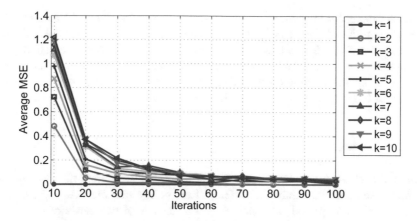

Fig. 10.5 Average mean squared error (MSE) for the KM algorithm reported for varying values of number of eigenvectors (k) and number of iterations (t)

10.4 Performance Evaluation

10.4.1 Data Sets

We now present details of the data sets used to evaluate the efficacy of our proposed technique.

10.4.1.1 Facebook A and Facebook B

In our study, we use two independently collected data sets from Facebook [17]. We use both data sets to demonstrate that our proposed solution is not biased in favor of any particular data set. The data sets are labeled data set A and data set B here-onwards. As Wilson et al. describe in [17], at the time of collection in April 2008 Facebook had 67 million subscribers of whom 44.3 million belonged to a regional network (regional networks were defined on the basis of geography and institutions). Each regional network forms a community of nodes that are strongly intra-connected but sparsely connected to other communities. Their crawler performed a breadth-first-search and collected data from the 22 largest regional networks. The crawler was initialized with 50 randomly seeded user profiles. Wilson et al. verified the completeness of their coverage of regional networks by performing 5 simultaneous crawls of the San Francisco regional network, each seeded by a different number of seed user IDs varying from 50 to 5000. The difference in the number of users discovered between crawls was a mere 0.1%. Therefore, we can conclude that the coverage of users in these data sets is fairly complete. The data contained in data set A and data set B is from different regions.

Each data set further consists of two types of graphs. First, we have an undirected friendship graph where the nodes represent users and links represent the friendship between two users. Second, we have a directed pair-wise user interaction graph where the nodes represent users and the directed links represent the interaction from one user to another. The interaction data spans a time duration of 1 year. Note that we use the interaction data only to evaluate the ground truth.

10.4.1.2 Twitter

The third data set comprises of the follower graph between more than two million Twitter users, and the number of different tweets they sent out over the course of the data collection period. This data set, too, consists of two types of data. First, we have an directed follower graph where the nodes represent users and each link represents subscription by a user to another user's Twitter feed. It is different from the two Facebook data sets A and B because the nature of relationships between Twitter users is fundamentally different. Twitter does not have a friendship graph like Facebook; Instead, it has a follower graph of directional, non-reciprocal relationships. Second, we have users' Twitter activity history. It includes all of the following:

- **Tweets—T:** The number of original tweets authored by a user during the data collection period.
- **Retweets—RT:** The number of retweets made by a user during the data collection period.
- **Retweeted—RTT:** The number of times other users retweeted a tweet sourced by the user under consideration.
- **Tweets+Retweets—TRT:** The number of tweets and retweets (T+RT) sent by a user during the data collection period.

The data collection period spans 1 week. Note that we use the activity history data only as the ground truth.

Table 10.1 provides the basic statistics of the friendship and follower graphs analyzed in this study. We note that the number of users in data set A are slightly more than those in data set B. We also note that the ratio of the number of friendship links to the number of users for data set A is $\sim$7.6, which is slightly more than $\sim$7.1 for data set B. The same ratio is an order of magnitude larger for the Twitter data set C. This difference in ratio is reflected in the values of average clustering coefficients of data sets A and B. Moreover, the number of cliques in the friendship graph of data set A is more than those in data set B. However, we observe that the transitivity value (defined as the fraction of possible triangles that are actually triangles) for data set A is less than the respective value of data set B.

Figures 10.6, 10.7 and 10.8 show the plots of degree distributions for graphs of all three data sets. In Figs. 10.6a, 10.7a and 10.8a we plot the histograms of one thousand bins in which we have grouped users. Although the distribution does not follow a power-law exactly, it fits it reasonably well as shown by straightness on

Table 10.1 Basic statistics of the friendship graphs analyzed in this study

Property	FB data set A	FB data set B	Twitter data set C
# Users	3,097,165	2,937,612	2,082,187
# Friendship links	23,667,394	20,959,854	102,143,769
Average clustering coefficient	0.0979	0.0901	–
# Cliques	28,889,110	27,593,398	–
Transitivity	0.0477	0.04832	–

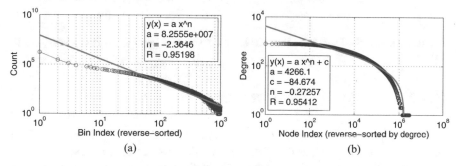

Fig. 10.6 Degree distribution of friendship graph for Facebook data set A. (**a**) Power law. (**b**) Zipf-like

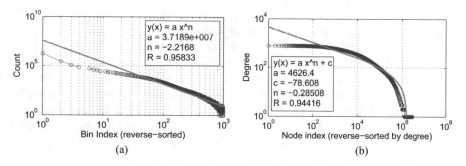

Fig. 10.7 Degree distribution of friendship graph for Facebook data set B. (**a**) Power law. (**b**) Zipf-like

log-log scale and verified by high goodness-of-fit (R^2) values for data set A and data set B. This observation is in accordance with the result of recent studies that have shown that the degree distribution of many online social networks is power-law [36]. An equivalent representation is shown in Figs. 10.6b, 10.7b and 10.8b where users are reverse-sorted by their degree. Note that the estimated values of model parameters are similar for data sets A and B.

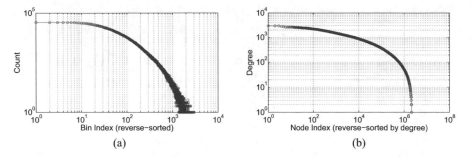

Fig. 10.8 Degree distribution of friendship graph for Twitter data set C. (**a**) Power law. (**b**) Zipf-like

10.4.2   Selection of PCC Parameter

We can compute the PCC vector $\mathbf{C}_P$ for a range of number of eigenvectors P. Note that at $P = 1$ the PCC $\mathbf{C}_1$ is the EVC $\mathbf{C}_E$, which serves as the measure of baseline comparison, as mentioned in [24] and [23]. Although we will be comparing PCC with EVC for a range of values of P in some of our subsequent analysis, we will try to determine the "appropriate" number of eigenvectors for PCC (denoted by P_{app}). We do this by means of plotting the phase angle function defined in Eq. (10.6). Figure 10.9a, b and c plot the phase angle functions of all three data sets A, B and C, respectively, for the range of $P = 1$ to 100. Incidentally, For data sets A, B and C, the phase angle function rises quickly initially until $P = 6$ and rises only very slowly thereafter. Using Eq. (10.7), the P_{app} values are 10, 20 and 26 for data sets A, B and C, respectively. The difference in P_{app} values for data sets A and B can be explained by differences in their network structures. In terms of PCC computation, this indicates that all nodes can be reached from a given node in lesser number of hops on average. In other words, fewer number of eigenvectors (denoted by P_{app}) are enough to approximate the steady-state PCC value.

10.4.3   Comparison with Ground Truth

Now that we have identified an appropriate number of eigenvectors for PCC for both data sets, we devote the remaining section to evaluating its accuracy by comparing the results to the ground truth, i.e. interaction data. For both data sets A and B, we have interaction graphs spanning 1 month, 6 months, and 1 year time periods. For the Twitter data set C, we have four different activity measurements, namely each user's tweets, retweets, the number of times he/she was retweeted, and the sum of the number of tweets and retweets.

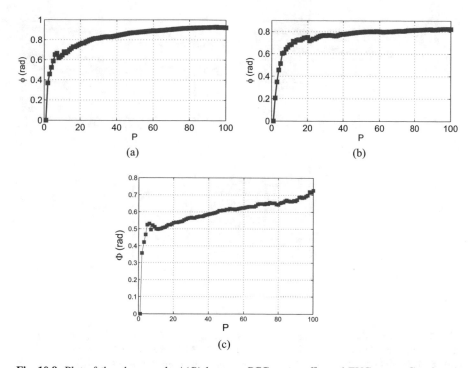

Fig. 10.9 Plot of the phase angle $\phi(P)$ between PCC vectors $\mathbf{C}_P$ and EVC vector $\mathbf{C}_E$ plotted against number of feature vectors P for (**a**) Facebook data set A, (**b**) Facebook data set B, (**c**) Twitter data set C

10.4.3.1   Verification of Optimal PCC Parameter

Recall that the PCC scores for individual users are calculated using only information from the friendship graph. We compare the PCC of nodes against their actual flows over various time periods to get a sense of the time period over which PCC best predicts the flow.

   We have used a symmetric measure called Pearson's product-moment coefficient to quantify the similarity between the output of PCC and the ground truth from interaction data. The Pearson's product-moment coefficient ρ is defined in Eq. (14.1). Here E is the expectation operator, σ refers to standard-deviation, and μ denotes mean value.

$$\rho(\mathbf{C}_P, \vartheta) = \frac{E[(\mathbf{C}_P - \mu_{\mathbf{C}_P})(\vartheta - \mu_\vartheta)]}{\sigma_{\mathbf{C}_P}\sigma_\vartheta} \tag{10.9}$$

Figure 10.10 shows the plots of correlation coefficients $\rho(\mathbf{C}_P, \vartheta)$ as a function of number of eigenvectors for the range $1 \leq P \leq 100$. Figure 10.10a plots $\rho(\mathbf{C}_P, \vartheta)$ for flows collected over 1 month, 6 months and the entire collection time period (labeled 'All') for data set A. Figure 10.10b does the same for data

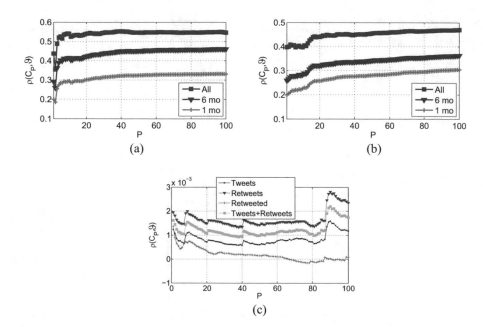

Fig. 10.10 Correlation coefficients ρ of PCC $\mathbf{C}_P$ and, (**a**) flow count of Facebook data set A $(\vartheta(A))$, (**b**) flow count of Facebook data set B $(\vartheta(B))$, (**c**) tweets/retweets/retweeted/tweet+retweet counts of Twitter data set C. The correlation coefficients are plotted as functions of the number of eigenvectors P and plotted separately for each interaction graph

set B. Figure 10.10c plots the Pearson's product-moment coefficient of various PCC vectors C_1 through C_{100} with T, RT, RTT and TRT.

For the Facebook data sets, we make two major observations from these plots. First, we note that the value of ρ generally increases with increasing number of eigenvectors P for computing PCC. It rises quickly to reach its steady-state value for both data sets. For Facebook data set A, ρ reaches close to its steady-state value at around 10 eigenvectors. Whereas, for Facebook data set B, ρ reaches close to its steady-state value at around 20 eigenvectors. Note that the steady-state values for ρ are reached at P_{app} values selected in the previous subsection. This observation verifies the merit of using phase angle for selection of appropriate value of P in PCC computation.

Second, we note that the correlation coefficients are higher for interaction data collected over longer periods of time. This observation follows our intuition that the trends in short-term interaction data can deviate from our expectations in steady-state friendship graph; However, the trends in long-term interaction data show greater similarity with the underlying friendship graph. This observation remains consistent across both Facebook data sets.

For the Twitter data set the values of ρ change much more erratically with P. More importantly though, we note that RT (the number of times a user retweets) is the user activity that is most correlated with his/her PCC score.

10.4.3.2 Accuracy of PCC in Predicting Top-2000 Users

To further evaluate the accuracy of PCC in finding information hubs, we analyze the overlap between the set of top-2000 users by PCC (denoted by $S_{2000}(\mathbf{C}_P)$) and the ground truth. Note that the choice of 2000 nodes in the following analysis is purely arbitrary. The results of our analysis for different set sizes are qualitatively similar. Let the cardinality of the intersection set of the first k nodes by PCC and the first k nodes by flow/activity ϑ be denoted by $I_k(\mathbf{C}_P, \vartheta)$ and defined in Eq. (10.10) below.

$$I_k(\mathbf{C}_P, \vartheta) = |S_k(\mathbf{C}_P) \cap S_k(\vartheta)| \qquad (10.10)$$

Figure 10.11a and b plot I_{2000} for data sets A and B, respectively. We evaluate separately for interaction data of different durations. As expected, the cardinality of the intersection set increases with the number of eigenvectors used in computation of PCC. In both figures, the data points at $P = 1$ represent the baseline for our comparison, i.e. EVC.

Figure 10.11c plots I_{2000} for data sets C. Clearly, the cardinality of the intersection sets is an order of magnitude lower than we observe for the Facebook data sets A and B.

For data set A, the cardinality of the intersection set of the top-2000 nodes by EVC and top-2000 nodes by flow ϑ, the cardinality of the intersection set

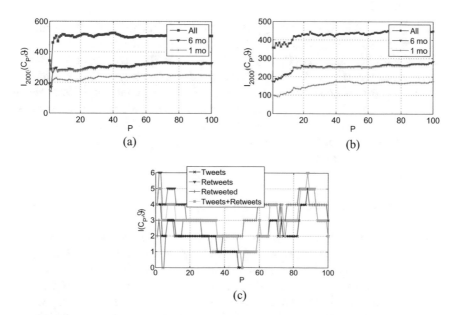

(a)

(b)

(c)

Fig. 10.11 Size of the intersection set in (**a**) Facebook data set A, (**b**) Facebook data set B, (**c**) Twitter data set C, for varying number of eigenvectors used in computation of PCC

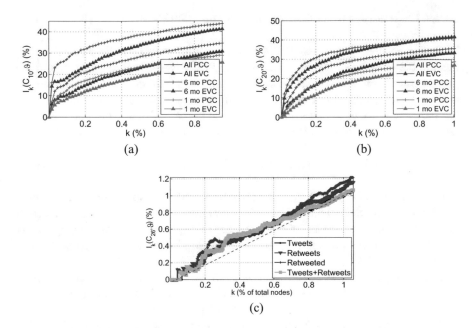

Fig. 10.12 Cardinality of the intersection set in (**a**) Facebook data set A, (**b**) Facebook data set B, (**c**) Twitter data set C, for varying fraction of nodes in graph

$I_{2000}(\mathbf{C}_E, \vartheta)$ is 342. At $P = 10$, $I_{2000}(\mathbf{C}_{10}, \vartheta) = 513$ for data set A. These numbers represent an increases of 50.0%. For Facebook data set B intersection cardinality of EVC set with flow are $I_{2000}(\mathbf{C}_E, \vartheta) = 358$. At $P = 20$, $I_{2000}(\mathbf{C}_{20}, \vartheta) = 426$ for data set A, an increase of 19.0%. For the remainder of this section, we fix the values of P at P_{app} for both data sets A and B. We see greater agreement between the list of nodes generated by PCC score with flow data collected over a longer durations.

For data set C, the cardinality of the intersection set of the top-2000 nodes by PCC and top-2000 nodes by user activity ϑ is denoted by $I_{2000}(\mathbf{C}_P, \vartheta)$. At $P = 26$, $I_{2000}(\mathbf{C}_{10}, \vartheta)$ for data set A.

10.4.3.3 Accuracy of PCC in Predicting Top-k Users

Figure 10.12a, b and c plot I_k set for top-k users for data sets A, B and C, respectively. We observe an increasing trend for I_k as we increase the bracket size of top-k users. We also note that the cardinality of the intersection set increases for increasing durations of interaction data. The overlap approaches 40% of k for top-1% users. Moreover, we observe that the results for Facebook data set A are slightly better than those of Facebook data set B. The same results for the Twitter data set C, however, are less positive.

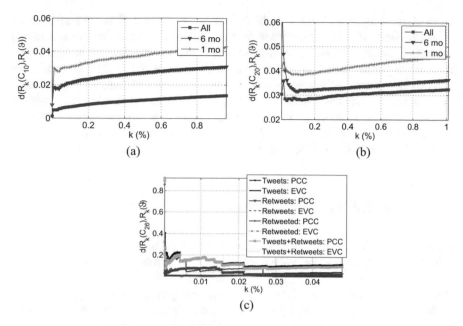

Fig. 10.13 Distance between ordered lists computed by PCC and interaction data using (**a**) Facebook data set A, (**b**) Facebook data set B, (**c**) Twitter data set C, for varying fraction of nodes in graph

10.4.3.4   Accuracy of PCC in Rank Prediction

The evaluation described till now focuses on the number of users that are common in top-k set assembled with respect to PCC scores and node degree in directed interaction graph. In a more fine-grained analysis, we are also interested in quantifying the accuracy of ranks assigned using PCC scores. Towards this end, we compute the difference between ranks assigned by PCC and those determined using data from interaction graph. Moreover, the significance of correct ranking of high-ranked users is more important than low-ranked users. To accomplish these objectives, we have devised a distance metric to compare the relevance of two ordered lists. We denote the list of nodes of length k in descending order of $\mathbf{C}_P$ by $\mathcal{R}_k(\mathbf{C}_P)$ and the list of nodes of length k in descending order of interaction graph degree by $\mathcal{R}_k(\vartheta)$. The distance is normalized in the range [0, 1], where 0 correspond to the perfect match between two given order lists, and vice-versa. We define the normalized distance $d \in [0, 1]$ between these two ordered lists as:

$$d\left(\mathcal{R}_k(\mathbf{C}_P), \mathcal{R}_k(\vartheta)\right) = \frac{\sum_{i \in \mathcal{R}_k(\vartheta)} \left[\frac{w_i |\mathcal{R}_k(\mathbf{C}_P(i)) - \mathcal{R}_k(\vartheta(i))|}{N - 2i + 1} \right]}{\sum_{i \in \mathcal{R}_k(\vartheta)} w_i} \tag{10.11}$$

Here w_i is the degree of user i in the interaction graph and N is the total number of users. Figure 10.13a, b and c show the variation in distance between two ordered lists as we increase its size k for data sets A, B and C, respectively. Similar to the intersection results for the Facebook data sets, we first note that the best results are achieved when comparison is done with interaction data of longer time duration. Second, we note that the results slightly degrade for increasing values of k. Third, it is evident that the results for Facebook data set A are better than those for Facebook data set B. For example, $d \approx 0.01$ at $k = 0.5\%$ of N for data set A, whereas $d \approx 0.03$ at $k = 0.5\%$ of N for data set B.

10.5   Conclusions

Information hubs in social networks play important roles in the speed and depth of information diffusion. Identifying hubs helps us to harness their power to pursue social good at local, national, and global levels. In this chapter, we propose the first friendship graph based, fully distributed, and privacy-preserving method for identifying hubs in online social networks. Unlike prior work, our method can be used to identify hubs by parties other than social network owners as we do not require any entity to access interaction or friendship graphs. We evaluated PCC and Generalized PCC using data collected from Facebook and Twitter. The Facebook data sets used in this study were collected over the period of more than a year and contain data from about six million users. The Twitter dataset was collected over a shorter period of time of only 1 week. The results of our analysis on the Facebook data sets showed that our proposed approach better (in terms of number of correctly identified top-k nodes and their estimated rank) identifies the top-k information hubs in a social network. For the Twitter dataset we used the generalized form of the PCC. The results on the Twitter dataset still demonstrate an improvement vs. random selection of top-k nodes as well as EVC, but only slightly. Based on the trend in the Facebook data set where results correlated better with user behavior over longer periods of time, we explain the difference in performance by the fact that that the Twitter data set was collected over a very short period of 1 week.

References

1. G. Caldarelli, *Scale-Free Networks* (Oxford University Press, Oxford, 2007)
2. J. Goldenberg, S. Han, D.R. Lehmann, J.W. Hong, The role of hubs in the adoption processes. J. Mark. Amer. Mark. Asso. **73**, 1–13 (2008)
3. D. Geere, Samsung offers free phones to frustrated iPhone users. CNN Tech (2010). http://www.cnn.com/2010/TECH/mobile/07/24/samsung.replacing.iphones/
4. N. Rama Suri, Y. Narahari, Determining the top-k nodes in social networks using the Shapley value, in *Proceedings of the 7th International Conference on Autonomous Agents and Multiagent Systems (AAMAS)* (2008)

5. J. Leskovec, A. Krause, C. Guestrin, C. Faloutsos, J. VanBriesen, N. Glance, Cost-effective outbreak detection in networks, in *Proceedings of the 13th ACM SIGKDD International Conference on Knowledge Discovery and Data mining (KDD)* (2007)

6. A. Goyal, F. Bonchi, L.V.S. Lakshmanan, Discovering leaders from community actions, in *Proceeding of the 17th ACM Conference on Information and Knowledge Management (CIKM)* (2008)

7. B. Bollobas, *Modern Graph Theory* (Springer, Berlin, 1998)

8. Facebook Advertising (2010). http://www.facebook.com/advertising/

9. Statement of Rights and Responsibilities (2010). http://www.facebook.com/terms.php

10. E. Zheleva, L. Getoor, To join or not to join: The illusion of privacy in social networks with mixed public and private user profiles, in *Proceedings of the 18th International World Wide Web conference (WWW)* (2009)

11. M.U. Ilyas. H. Radha, A KLT-inspired node centrality for identifying influential neighborhoods in graphs, in *Proceedings of the 44th Annual Conference on Information Sciences and Systems (CISS)* (2010)

12. P. Bonacich, Factoring and weighting approaches to status scores and clique identification. J. Math. Sociol. **2**(1), 113–120 (1972)

13. P. Bonacich, Technique for analyzing overlapping memberships. Sociol. Methodol. **4**, 176–185 (1972)

14. Facebook Pages (2010). http://www.facebook.com/advertising/

15. R. Shahbaz, how high is your popularity? (2010). 12120 monthly users. http://www.facebook.com/apps/application.php?id=174042725891

16. D. Kempe, F. McSherry, A decentralized algorithm for spectral analysis. J. Comp. Syst. Sci. **74**(1), 70–83 (2008)

17. C. Wilson, B. Boe, A. Sala, K.P.N. Puttaswamy, B.Y. Zhao, User interactions in social networks and their implications, in *Proceedings of the ACM European Conference on Computer Systems (EuroSys)* (2009)

18. P.A. Estevez, P. Vera, K. Saito, Selecting the most influential nodes in social networks, in *Proceedings of the International Joint Conference on Neural Networks (IJCNN)* (2007)

19. D. Kempe, J. Kleinberg, E. Tardos, Maximizing the spread of influence through a social network, in *Proceedings of the 9th ACM SIGKDD International Conference on Knowledge Discovery and Data mining (KDD)* (2003)

20. M. Kimura, K. Saito, R. Nakano, Extracting influential nodes for information diffusion on a social network, in *Proceedings of the 22nd National Conference on Artificial Intelligence (AAAI)* (2007)

21. M. Kimura, K. Saito, R. Nakano, H. Motoda, Finding influential nodes in a social network from information diffusion data, in *Springer Social Computing and Behavioral Modeling* (Springer, Boston, 2009)

22. F. Zou, Z. Zhang, W. Wu, Latency-bounded minimum influential node selection in social networks, in *Proceedings of the 4th International Conference on Wireless Algorithms, Systems, and Applications (WASA)* (2009)

23. P.V. Marsden, Egocentric and sociocentric measures of network centrality. Soc. Netw. **24**(4), 407–422 (2002)

24. X. Shi, M. Bonner, L.A. Adamic, A.C. Gilbert, The very small world of the well-connected, in *Proceedings of the 19th ACM Conference on Hypertext and Hypermedia (HT)* (2008)

25. K. Sankaralingam, S. Sethumadhavan, J.C. Browne, Distributed pagerank for p2p systems, in *Proceedings of the 12th IEEE International Symposium on High Performance Distributed Computing (HPDC)* (2003)

26. A.N. Langville, C.D. Meyer, P. FernÁndez, Googleís pagerank and beyond: the science of search engine rankings. Math. Intell. **30**(1), 68–69 (2008)

27. C. Kohlschütter, P. Chirita, W. Nejdl, Efficient parallel computation of pagerank, in *Proceedings of the 28th European Conference on IR Research (ECIR)* (2006), pp. 241–252

28. S.P. Borgatti, Centrality and network flow. Soc. Netw. **27**(1), 55–71 (2005)

29. G. Canright, K. Engø-Monsen, M. Jelasity, Efficient and robust fully distributed power method with an application to link analysis, in *Department of Computer Science, University of Bologna, Technical Report UBLCS-2005-17* (2005), pp. 2005–17
30. R.O. Duda, P.E. Hart, D.G. Stork, *Pattern Classification*, 2nd edn. (Wiley, New York, 2001)
31. B. Ruhnau, Eigenvector-centrality–a node-centrality? Soc. Netw. **22**(4), 357–365 (2000)
32. A.L. Barabási, R. Albert, Emergence of scaling in random networks. Science **286**(5439), 509 (1999)
33. M.U. Ilyas, H. Radha, A KLT-inspired node centrality for identifying influential neighborhoods in graphs, in *2010 44th Annual Conference on Information Sciences and Systems (CISS)* (IEEE, Piscataway, 2010), pp. 1–7
34. C. Lanczos, *An Iteration Method for the Solution of the Eigenvalue Problem of Linear Differential and Integral Operators* (Institute for Numerical Analysis, Los Angeles, 1949)
35. R.B. Lehoucq, D.C. Sorensen, Deflation techniques for an implicitly restarted arnoldi iteration. SIAM J. Matrix Analy. Appl. **17**, 789 (1996)
36. A. Mislove, M. Marcon, K.P. Gummadi, P. Druschel, B. Bhattacharjee, Measurement and analysis of online social networks, in *Proceedings of the 7th ACM SIGCOMM Conference on Internet Measurement (IMC)*, San Diego (2007)

Part III
Differential Privacy

Chapter 11
Publishing Social Network Data with Privacy Guarantees

11.1 Introduction

11.1.1 Background and Motivation

Online Social Networks (OSNs) have become an essential part of modern life. Billions of users connect and share information using OSNs such as Facebook and Twitter. Graphs obtained from these OSNs can provide useful insights on various fundamental societal phenomena such as epidemiology, information dissemination, marketing, and sentiment flow [1–5]. Various analysis methods [6–10] have been applied to OSNs by explicitly exploring its graph structure, such as clustering analysis for automatically identifying online communities and node influence analysis for recognizing the influential nodes in social networks. The basis of all these analysis is to represent a social network graph by an adjacency matrix and then represent individual nodes by vectors derived from the top eigenvectors of the adjacency matrix. Thus, all these analysis methods require real social network graphs.

Unfortunately, OSN companies often refuse to publish their social network graphs due to privacy concerns. Social network graphs contain sensitive information about individuals such as an user's topological characteristics in a graph (e.g., number of social ties, influence in a community, etc.). From the user perspective, the sensitive information revealed from a social network graph can be exploited in many ways such as fraud and spam [11]. From the OSN perspective, disclosing sensitive user information may put them in the risk of violating privacy laws. A natural way to bridge the gap is to anonymize original social network graphs (by means such as removing identifiers) and publish the anonymized ones. For example, Netflix published anonymized movie ratings of 500,000 subscribers and AOL published search queries of 658,000 users [12, 13]. However, such anonymization is vulnerable to privacy attacks where attackers can identify personal information by linking two or more separately innocuous databases [14, 15]. For example, recently, de-anonymization attacks were successful on Netflix and AOL datasets, which resulted in Netflix and AOL being sued [12, 13].

11.1.2 Problem Statement

In this chapter, we aim to develop a scheme for publishing eigen-vectors of social network graphs with differential privacy guarantees. Recently, differential privacy has become the widely accepted criteria for privacy preserving data publishing because it provides strongest privacy guarantees for publishing sensitive datasets [16–18]. The concept of differential privacy was proposed by Dwork in the context of statistical databases, where a trusted party holds a dataset D containing sensitive information (e.g., medical records) and wants to publish a dataset D' that provides the same global statistical information as D while preserving the private information of each individual user. Given a database D and its neighbor database D' differing from D in only one record, according to differential privacy, any information that can be learned from the database D can also be learned from D', irrespective of the presence or absence of a record.

Our targeted differential privacy preserving social graph publishing scheme should satisfy the following two requirements. First, the published dataset should maintain the utility of the original dataset. As many analysis of social networks are based on the top eigenvectors of the adjacency matrices derived from social networks, the utility of the published dataset will be measured by how well the top eigenvectors of the published data can be approximated to the eigenvectors of the original data. Second, the scheme should guarantee differential privacy, that is, an adversary should learn nothing more about any individual from the published data, regardless of the presence or absence of the record of any particular individual in the dataset. We emphasize that these two goals are often conflicting: to achieve differential privacy, sufficiently large amount of random noise has to be added to the published data, which could result in a large error in approximating the top eigenvectors of the original data. The goal of this chapter is to achieve a proper tradeoff between privacy and utility.

11.1.3 Limitations of Prior Art

Given an original $n \times n$ matrix, some schemes have been proposed to perturb this matrix by adding random noise and then publish the perturbed $n \times n$ matrix [19, 20]. The key limitation of such schemes is that they are computationally unpractical as they are not designed to handle large matrices such as the adjacency matrices of OSN graphs. The value of n, which is the number of users in an OSN, can be in the scale of millions or even billions. For example, as of September 2013, Facebook has over a billion monthly active users. Even when the input to such schemes are sparse matrices such as OSN adjacency matrices, the output of such schemes are dense matrices, which are difficult to store efficiently. A one billion times one billion dense matrix requires storage of about 800 petabytes. It is practically infeasible to apply any useful operation (such as computing eigenvectors) on such large matrices. Recently, Wang et al. proposed a scheme called LNPP, which perturbs the eigenvectors of the original matrices by adding random noise and then publishes the perturbed eigenvectors [21]. Although this reduces computation cost and storage space, it requires a large amount of random perturbation in order to preserve differential privacy, which leads to poor estimation of the top eigenvectors of large OSNs.

11.1.4 Proposed Approach

In this chapter, we propose a random matrix approach to address the above limitation by leveraging the theories of random matrix and differential privacy. Our key idea is to first project each row of an adjacency matrix into a low dimensional space using random projection, and then perturb the projected matrix with random noise, and finally publish the perturbed and projected matrix. Given an $n \times n$ adjacency matrix A of a social network graph, with m projections and k eigenvectors, we output an $n \times m$ ($0 < k \leq m \ll n$) randomly perturbed matrix $\widehat{A}$ where the top k eigenvectors of A are close to the k eigenvectors of $\widehat{A}$ (in terms of both vector directions and magnitude). The random projection is critical in our approach. First, it significantly reduces the size of the matrix to be published because $n \times m \ll n \times n$, addressing the limitations of prior art. Second, based on the theory of random matrix [22], we can preserve the top eigenvectors of the adjacency matrix using random projection. Third, the random projection step itself has the ability of achieving differential privacy, which makes it possible to ensure differential privacy in the second step by introducing a *small* random perturbation [23, 24].

11.1.5 Technical Challenges

There are three key technical challenges. The first challenge is to prove that random projection plus random perturbation preserve differential privacy. The second challenge is to prove that the random noise required to achieve differential privacy is small. We address these two challenges by leveraging the theory of random matrix and differential privacy. The third challenge is to validate the proposed approach and demonstrate the utility preservation of eigen-spectrum. We address this challenge by evaluating the utility of the published data for three different applications that require the spectral information of an OSN graph. We use publicly available datasets of Facebook, Live Journal and Pokec social networks [25, 26]. The first application is OSN node clustering, which has been widely used for OSN applications such as community detection [27, 28]. We focus on spectral clustering algorithms as they are based on the eigenvectors of adjacency matrices. The second application is OSN node ranking, which has been widely used for OSN applications such as influential node identification [29]. We focus on principal component centrality based algorithms as they are based on the eigenvectors of adjacency matrices. The third application is OSN node classification, which has been widely used for OSN applications such as spammer identification and sybil node detection [30]. We focus on linear classification algorithms as they use the eigenvectors of adjacency matrices as feature vectors. Note that our approach published the eigen-spectrum of the social network graph. Reconstructing the social network graph from the eigen spectrum is computationally expensive and in our evaluation we only evaluate preservation of the eigen spectrum of the graph.

11.1.6 Key Contributions

We make three key contributions in this chapter. First, we propose a random matrix approach to OSN data publishing, which achieves space efficiency by reducing the dimensions of adjacency matrices and achieves differential privacy by adding a small amount of noise. Second, we formally prove that our scheme achieves differential privacy and that the amount of added noise is small. We present theoretical error bounds for approximating top$-k$ eigenvectors. Third, we validate our random matrix approach on three different applications: node clustering, node ranking, and node classification, which require the spectral information of a graph. Our experimental results show that even for high values of noise variance $\sigma = 1$, our scheme preserves the utility of the dataset. For node clustering, our scheme achieves high clustering quality defined by normalized mutual information, which is more than 0.7. For node ranking, our scheme can correctly recover 80% of the most influential nodes. For node classification with 16 classes, our scheme obtains an accuracy of 70% with fivefold cross validation. We also compare our results with the LNPP scheme, which represents the state-of-the-art [21]. The LNPP scheme directly perturbs the eigenvector of the original data by a Laplacian noise; in contrast, we first use random projections to reduce the size of the adjacency matrix and then compute the eigenvectors. Our experimental results show that for high noise variance $\sigma = 1$, our approach achieves high clustering quality of 0.74, which is normalized mutual information; for LNPP, the same amount of noise completely destroys the clustering of nodes in the original dataset. For node ranking, our approach correctly identifies 80% of the most influential nodes, whereas LNPP correctly identifies less than 1% of the most influential nodes.

11.2   Related Work

11.2.1   Differential Privacy

An ideal privacy guarantee is defined by Dalenius in 1977, according to which an attacker having some background knowledge of the data should not be able to learn anything new about an individual regardless of its access to the database. However, such ideal guarantees are impossible to achieve. The seminal work of Dwork on differential privacy provides formal privacy guarantees that do not depend on an adversary's background knowledge.

The notion of differential privacy was developed through a series of research work presented in [31–33]. Popular differential private mechanisms that are used in publishing sensitive datasets include Laplace mechanism [31] and the Exponential mechanism [34], which add Laplace noise and exponential noise, respectively. A general overview of the research work on differential privacy is in [24, 35, 36].

11.2.2   Differential Privacy in Data Publishing

In recent years, works on privacy preserving graph data publishing have adopted two types of approaches. First is publishing entire graphs where the output graph is an anonymized version of the original graph. Second is publishing some intermediate and sanitized form of the original graph. To these ends, approaches aim to achieve edge privacy or node privacy. In this work, we propose a random matrix approach that preserves edge-privacy and publishes the eigen-spectrum of the input graph. TmF [37], EdgeFlip [38], and HRG-MCMC [39] are approaches that target edge privacy and publish entire graphs. For edge privacy, some schemes perturb an $n \times n$ matrix by adding random noise and then publish the perturbed $n \times n$ matrix [19, 20]. Given a large $n \times n$ matrix, no matter dense or spare, all these schemes outputs another large dense matrix of size $n \times n$. The key limitation of such schemes is that they are computationally unpractical as in large OSNs, n is in the scale of millions or even billions.

Most prior works target edge privacy and publish processed form of the original graphs which can be used to extract important statistics about the original graph [21, 32, 33, 40–45]. Chen et al. [40], propose a data-dependent solution by identifying and reconstructing the dense regions of a graph's adjacency matrix. Sala et al. presented a scheme to share meaningful graph datasets, based on the $dk - graph$ model, while preserving differential privacy [41]. Wang and Wu [42] use dK-series to summarize the graph into a distribution of degree correlations. In [32], Blum et al. propose to publish the covariance matrix of the original data contaminated by random noise. Hay et al. proposed a scheme to preserve the degree distribution of a social network graph [43]. Kenthapadi developed a differential private algorithm that preserves distance between any two samples in a given database [33]. Although these studies deal with differential private publication of social network data, none of them address the utility of preserving the eigenvectors of the graph, the central theme of this work.

Another category of related work is towards preserving the utility of eigen-spectrum of the input matrix. In [23, 24], the authors show that random projection by itself can preserve both the differential privacy and the eigen-spectrum of a given matrix provided appropriate modification is made to the original matrix. In [23], Proserpio et al. present a randomized response approach that achieves the preservation of differential privacy and top eigenvectors by inverting each feature attribute with a fixed probability. Hardt and Roth proposed an iterative algorithm to compute differential private eigenvectors [46]. This scheme generates large dense matrix of $n \times n$ at each iteration. Sampling approaches based on the exponential mechanism have been proposed for computing differential private singular vectors [19, 20]. Since these approaches require sampling very high dimensional vectors from a random distribution, they are computationally infeasible for large social networks. In [21], Wang et al. propose to publish eigenvectors perturbed by Laplacian random noise, which unfortunately requires a large amount of random perturbation for differential privacy preservation and consequentially leads to poor utility of data.

There are some efforts on preserving the node-privacy of social network data [47–50]. Node privacy is challenging to achieve due to high sensitivity of many graph queries. Insertion or deletion of a single node in the graph can cause large variations in the output of the graph queries [43, 51]. Chen et al. [47] compute Lipschitz extensions for subgraph counts and other relevant statistics. Raskhodnikova et al. [50] also compute Lipschitz extension and use the generalized exponential mechanism for achieve node privacy and publish degree distribution of the input graph. Blocki et al. [48] and Kasiviswanathan et al. [49] achieve node privacy on sparse graph by projecting input graphs to a set of graphs with a certain maximum degree.

11.3   Random Matrix Approach

In this section, we first present the proposed approach for differential private publication of eigen-vectors of social network graph based on random matrix theory. We then present its guarantee on differential privacy and the approximation of eigenvectors.

Let G be a binary graph representing the connectivity of a social network, and $A \in \{0, 1\}^{n \times n}$ be the adjacency matrix representing the graph, where $A_{i,j} = 1$ if there is an edge between nodes i and j, and $A_{i,j} = 0$, otherwise.[1] By assuming that the graph is undirected, A will be a symmetric matrix, i.e. $A_{i,j} = A_{j,i}$ for any $0 \leq i < n$ and $0 \leq j < n$. The first step of our approach is to generate two Gaussian random matrices $P \in \mathbb{R}^{n \times m}$ and $Q \in \mathbb{R}^{n \times m}$, where $m \ll n$ is the number of random projections. Here, each entry of P is sampled independently from a Gaussian distribution $\mathcal{N}(0, 1/m)$, and each entry of Q is sampled independently from another Gaussian distribution $\mathcal{N}(0, \sigma^2)$, where the value of σ will be discussed later. Using Gaussian random matrix P, we compute the projection matrix $A_p \in \mathbb{R}^{n \times m}$ by $A_p = A \times P$, which projects each row of A from a high dimensional space $\mathbb{R}^n$ to into a low dimensional space $\mathbb{R}^m$. We then perturb A_p with the Gaussian random matrix Q by $\widehat{A} = A_p + Q$, and publish $\widehat{A}$ to the external world. Algorithm 1 highlights the key steps of the proposed routine for publishing the social network graph.

Algorithm 1: $\widehat{A} = \texttt{Publish}(A, m, \sigma^2)$

Input: (1) symmetric adjacency matrix $A \in \mathbb{R}^{n \times n}$
       (2) the number of random projections $m < n$
       (3) variance for random noise σ^2
Output: $\widehat{A}$

1 Compute a random projection matrix P, with $P_{i,j} \sim \mathcal{N}(0, 1/m)$
2 Compute a random perturbation matrix Q, with $Q_{i,j} \sim \mathcal{N}(0, \sigma^2)$
3 Compute the projected matrix $A_p = AP$
4 Compute the randomly perturbed matrix $\widehat{A} = A_p + Q$

Compared to the existing approaches for differential private publication of social network graphs, the proposed algorithm is advantageous in three aspects:

- The proposed algorithm is computationally efficient as it does not require either storing or manipulating a *dense* matrix of $n \times n$.
- The random projection matrix P allows us to preserve the top eigenvectors of A due to the theory of random matrix.
- The joint effort of the random projection P and the random perturbation Q preserves differential privacy. This unique feature allows us to introduce a small amount of random perturbation for differential privacy preservation, thus improving the utility of data.

Next, we give a theoretical analysis of two main aspects of publishing differential private eigen-vectors of graphs of OSNs. First, we formally prove that our random matrix approach to publishing eigen-vectors of OSN graphs guarantees differential privacy. Second, we give theoretical error bounds for approximating top$-k$ eigen-vectors.

---

[1]Note that each row of an adjacency matrix represents an individual and the values in that row can be considered as attributes associated to that individual. In the case of graph's adjacency matrix, the attributes are binary that represent the edges corresponding to the individual in a graph.

11.3.1   Theoretical Guarantee on Differential Privacy

Basic Differential Privacy   According to differential privacy, an adversary (regardless of its background knowledge) can learn nothing more about an individual, regardless of whether the individual's record is present or absent in the data. For a dataset D, a standard mechanism to achieve differential privacy is to add random noise to the true output of a function $f(D)$. The sensitivity δf of this function is defined as the maximum change in the output when a single record is added or removed from the dataset. More formally, sensitivity is defined as:

$$\delta f = max_{D,D'}||f(D) - f(D')|| \tag{11.1}$$

If the sensitivity of the function is high, this means that a small change in D produces a large change in the output $||f(D) - f(D')||$, which reveals the presence or absence of a record in D. Therefore, for high sensitivity functions, a large amount of noise is required to minimize the effect in the output of $f(D)$. However, if the function has low sensitivity, differential privacy is achieved with smaller noise, which also maintains the utility of the output. Therefore, for a dataset D, the function should be designed such that its sensitivity is low and the output gives meaningful results. Depending on the sensitivity of the function or a set of functions, a privacy budget is assigned for a dataset. There are two main methodologies adopted when using the privacy budget: Interactive, Non-interactive. Interactive methods specify a privacy budget that the user can spend for querying the original database through a privacy preserving mechanism [52]. Such interactive approaches allow users to post multiple queries to the original dataset. Depending upon the sensitivity of the query the output of the query is perturbed i.e., for high sensitivity queries the perturbation introduced is large and the privacy budget used is also large. Non-Interactive methods utilize privacy-preserving data publishing which publish the output of a query function that consumes all the privacy budget. The original data is queried only once and the result is made available to the user [41].

Differential Privacy on Graphs   In case of social network graph datasets, a high sensitivity function is computing eigenvectors of a graph's adjacency matrix A. The sensitivity of the function can be calculated by analyzing the output eigenvectors when an edge is added or removed from the graph. Before we show the guarantee on differential privacy, we first introduce the definition of (ϵ, δ)-*Differential Privacy* in the context of Graph dataset [37]. Two graphs G1 = (V1, E1) and G2 = (V2, E2) are neighbors if $V1 = V2$, $E1 \subset E2$ and $|E2| = |E1| + 1$. A (randomized) algorithm $\mathcal{A}$ satisfies (ϵ, δ)-differential privacy, if for any two neighboring graphs G1 and G2 and for all sets of possible outputs $D \subseteq Range(\mathcal{A})$, we have

$$\Pr\left(\mathcal{A}(G1) \in D\right) \leq e^{\epsilon} \Pr\left(\mathcal{A}(G2) \in D\right) + \delta, \tag{11.2}$$

where the probability is computed over the random coin tosses of the algorithm.

The choice of node privacy as compared to edge privacy directly impacts the amount of noise that should be added to achieve strong differential privacy guarantees. A change in the presence or absence of a node directly affects multiple edges, which increases the sensitivity of the function and hence more noise is required to achieve privacy [53]. As a result the utility of the published graph is reduced. The tradeoff between utility and privacy has been previously tackled by designing a task specific differential private mechanism that maximizes utility. However, work by Wu et al. suggests that mechanisms can be designed to tune for high utility or high privacy [54]. They propose mechanisms that are privacy centric and use different parameters to tune for privacy. They also propose mechanisms that can be adapted for privacy centric or utility centric queries by tuning different parameters. We propose a utility centric mechanism and focus on edge privacy.

To understand the implication of (ϵ, δ)-differential privacy, consider the database $X \in \{0, 1\}^{n \times m}$ as a binary matrix. Let $p_{i,j} := \Pr(X_{i,j} = 1)$ represent the prior knowledge of an attacker about X, and let $p'_{i,j} = \Pr(X_{i,j} = 1 | \mathcal{A}(X))$ represent his knowledge about X after observing the output $\mathcal{A}(X)$ from algorithm $\mathcal{A}$. Then, if an algorithm $\mathcal{A}$ satisfies (ϵ, δ)-differential privacy, then with a probability $1 - \delta$, for any $i \in [n]$ and $j \in [m]$, the following condition holds:

$$\left| \ln p_{i,j} - \ln p'_{i,j} \right| \leq \epsilon$$

In other words, the additional information gained by observing $\mathcal{A}(X)$ is bounded by ϵ. Thus, parameter $\epsilon > 0$ determines the degree of differential privacy: the smaller the ϵ, the less the amount of information will be revealed. Parameter $\delta \in (0, 1)$ is introduced to account the rare events when the two probabilities $\Pr(\mathcal{A}(X) \in D)$ and $\Pr(\mathcal{A}(X_0) \in D)$ may differ significantly from each other.

Theorem 11.1 *Assuming $\delta < 1/2$, $n \geq 2$, and*

$$\sigma \geq \frac{1}{\epsilon} \sqrt{10 \left(\epsilon + \ln \frac{1}{2\delta} \right) \ln \frac{n}{\delta}}$$

Then, Algorithm 1 satisfies (ϵ, δ)-differential privacy w.r.t. a change in an individual person's attribute.

The key feature of Theorem 11.1 is that the variance for generating the random perturbation matrix Q is $O(\ln n)$, almost independent from the size of social network. As a result, we can ensure differential privacy for the published $\widehat{A}$ for a very large social network by only introducing a Gaussian noise with small variance, an important feature that allows us to simultaneously preserve both the utility and differential privacy. Our definition of differential privacy is a generalized version of ϵ-differential privacy which can be viewed as $(\epsilon, 0)$-differential privacy.

To prove that Algorithm 1 is differential private, we need the following Theorem from [33]

Lemma 11.1 (Theorem 1 [33]) *Define the ℓ_2-sensitivity of the projection matrix P as $w_2(P) = \max\limits_{1 \leq i \leq n} |P_{i,*}|_2$, where $P_{i,*}$ represents the ith row of matrix P. Assuming $\delta < 1/2$, and*

$$\sigma \geq \frac{w_2(P)}{\epsilon} \sqrt{2 \left(\epsilon + \ln \frac{1}{2\delta} \right)}$$

Then Algorithm 1 satisfies (ϵ, δ)-differential privacy w.r.t. a change in an individual person's attribute.

In order to bound $w_2(P)$, we rely on the following concentration for χ^2 distribution.

Lemma 11.2 (Tail Bounds for the χ^2 Distribution) *Let $X_1, \ldots, X_d$ be independent draws from $\mathcal{N}(0, 1)$. Therefore, for any $0 < \delta < 1$, we have, with a probability $1 - \delta$,*

$$\sum_{i=1}^{d} X_i^2 \leq d + 2\sqrt{d \ln \frac{1}{\delta}} + 2 \ln \frac{1}{\delta}$$

Define

$$z_i^2 = \sum_{j=1}^{m} P_{i,j}^2$$

Evidently, according to the definition of $w_2^2(P)$, we have

$$w_2^2(P) = \max_{1 \leq i \leq n} z_i^2$$

Since $P_{i,j} \sim \mathcal{N}(0, 1/m)$, we have mz_i^2 follow the χ^2 distribution of d freedom. Using Lemma 11.2, we have, with a probability $1 - \delta$,

$$z_i^2 \leq 1 + 2\sqrt{\frac{1}{m} \ln \frac{1}{\delta}} + \frac{2}{m} \ln \frac{1}{\delta} \tag{11.3}$$

By taking the union bound, we have, with a probability $1 - \delta$

$$w_2^2(P) = \max_{1 \leq i \leq m} z_i^2 \leq 1 + 2\sqrt{\frac{1}{m} \ln \frac{n}{\delta}} + \frac{2}{m} \ln \frac{n}{\delta} \leq 2 \tag{11.4}$$

where the last inequality follows from $m \geq 4 \ln(n/\delta)$. We complete the proof by combining the result from Lemma 11.1 and the inequality in (11.4). Inequality (11.4) comes from the inequality (11.3). According to inequality (11.3), each z_i

can fail inequality (11.3) with a probability at most δ. Then, for all z_i, to ensure that the chance for inequality (11.3) to fail with probability at most δ, we can simply replace δ in (11.3) with δ/n, which immediately leads to the inequality (11.4). Therefore, theorem 1 holds because of Lemma 11.1 and inequality (11.4).

11.3.2 Theoretical Guarantee on Eigenvector Approximation

Let $u_1, \ldots, u_n$ be the eigenvectors of the adjacency matrix A ranked in the descending order of eigenvalues $\lambda_1, \ldots, \lambda_n$. Let k be the number of top eigenvectors of interests. Let $\widetilde{\mathbf{u}}_1, \ldots, \widetilde{\mathbf{u}}_k$ be the first k eigenvectors of $\widehat{A}$. Define the approximation error for the first k eigenvectors as

$$\mathcal{E}^2 = \max_{1 \leq i \leq k} |\mathbf{u}_i - \widetilde{\mathbf{u}}_i|^2$$

Our goal is to show that the approximation error $\mathcal{E}^2$ will be small when the number of random projections m is sufficiently large.

Theorem 11.2 *Assume (i) $m \geq c(k + k \ln k)$, where c is an universal constant given in [55], (ii) $n \geq 4(m + 1) \ln(12m)$ and (iii) $\lambda_k - \lambda_{k+1} \geq 2\sigma\sqrt{2n}$. Then, with a probability at least $1/2$, we have*

$$\mathcal{E}^2 \leq \frac{16\sigma^2 n}{(\lambda_k - \lambda_{k+1})^2} + \frac{32}{\lambda_k^2} \sum_{i=k+1}^{n} \lambda_i^2$$

The corollary below simplifies the result in Theorem 11.2 by assuming that λ_k is significantly larger than the eigenvalues $\lambda_{k+1}, \ldots, \lambda_n$.

Corollary 11.1 *Assume (i) $\lambda_k = \Theta(n/k)$, and (ii) $\sum_{i=k+1}^{n} \lambda_i^2 = O(n)$. Under the same assumption for m and n as Theorem 11.2, we have, with a probability at least $1/2$,*

$$\mathcal{E} \leq O\left(k\left[\frac{\sigma}{\sqrt{n}} + \frac{1}{\sqrt{n}}\right]\right)$$

As indicated by Theorem 11.2 and Corollary 11.1, under the assumptions (1) λ_k is significantly larger than eigenvalues $\lambda_{k+1}, \ldots, \lambda_n$, (2) the number of random projections m is sufficiently larger than k, and (3) n is significantly larger than the number of random projections m, we will have the approximation error $\mathcal{E} \propto O(k/\sqrt{n})$ in recovering the eigenvectors of the adjacency matrix A. Prior work has shown that large social graphs have good expansion properties [56]. Graphs with good expansion have large spectral gaps i.e., λ_k is significantly larger than $\lambda_k + 1, \ldots, \lambda_n$. Therefore, for large online social networks we assume a large spectral gap. We also note that according to Corollary 11.1, the approximation error is proportional to σ, which measures the amount of random perturbation needed for differential privacy preservation. This is consistent with our intuition, i.e., the smaller the random perturbation, the more accurate the approximation of eigenvectors.

Next, we prove Theorem 11.2. Let $A \in \mathbb{R}^{n \times n}$ be the adjacency matrix, $A_p = AP$, and $\widehat{A} = A_p + Q$. Let $\widehat{\mathbf{u}}_1, \ldots, \widehat{\mathbf{u}}_k$ be the first k eigenvectors of matrix A_p. Define $U = (\mathbf{u}_1, \ldots, \mathbf{u}_k)$, $\widehat{U} = (\widehat{\mathbf{u}}_1, \ldots, \widehat{\mathbf{u}}_k)$, and $\widetilde{U} = (\widetilde{\mathbf{u}}_1, \ldots, \widetilde{\mathbf{u}}_k)$. For each of these matrices, we define a projection operator, denoted by P_k, $\widehat{P}_k$ and $\widetilde{P}_k$, as

$$P_k = \sum_{i=1}^{k} \mathbf{u}_i \mathbf{u}_i^\top = UU^\top$$

$$\widehat{P}_k = \sum_{i=1}^{k} \widehat{\mathbf{u}}_i \widehat{\mathbf{u}}_i^\top = \widehat{U}\widehat{U}^\top$$

$$\widetilde{P}_k = \sum_{i=1}^{k} \widetilde{\mathbf{u}}_i \widetilde{\mathbf{u}}_i^\top = \widetilde{U}\widetilde{U}^\top$$

We first bound the approximation error $\mathcal{E}^2$ by the difference between projection operators, i.e.,

$$\mathcal{E}^2 = \max_{1 \leq i \leq k} |\mathbf{u}_i - \widetilde{\mathbf{u}}_i|^2 \leq \|UU^\top - \widetilde{U}\widetilde{U}^\top\|_2 = \|P_k - \widetilde{P}_k\|_2$$

where $\| \cdot \|_2$ stands for the spectral norm of matrix. Using the fact that

$$\mathcal{E}^2 \leq \|P_k - \widetilde{P}_k\|_2^2 = \|P_k - \widehat{P}_k + \widehat{P}_k - \widetilde{P}_k\|_2^2$$

$$\leq 2\|P_k - \widehat{P}_k\|_2^2 + 2\|P_k - \widetilde{P}_k\|_2^2$$

$$\leq 2\|P_k - \widehat{P}_k\|_F^2 + 2\|P_k - \widetilde{P}_k\|_2^2 \tag{11.5}$$

where $\| \cdot \|_F$ stands for the Frobenius norm of matrix, below we will bound $\|P_k - \widehat{P}_k\|_F$ and $\|P_k - \widetilde{P}_k\|_F$, separately.

To bound $\|P_k - \widehat{P}_k\|_F$, we need the following theorem for random matrix.

Lemma 11.3 (Theorem 14 [55]) *Assume $0 < \epsilon \leq 1$ and $m \geq c(k/\epsilon + k \ln k)$, where c is some universal constant. Then, with a probability at least 2/3, we have*

$$\|A - \widehat{P}_k(A)\|_F \leq (1 + \epsilon)\|A - P_k(A)\|_F,$$

Since

$$\|A - \widehat{P}_k(A)\|_F \geq -\|A - P_k(A)\|_F + \|P_k(A) - \widehat{P}_k(A)\|_F$$

$$= -\|A - P_k(A)\|_F - \|P_k(A) + \widehat{P}_k P_k(A) + \widehat{P}_k P_k(A) - \widehat{P}_k(A)\|_F$$

$$\geq -\|A-P_k(A)\|_F+\|P_k(A)-\widehat{P}_kP_k(A)\|_F-|\widehat{P}_k(A-P_k(A))\|_F$$

$$\geq \|P_k(A)-\widehat{P}_kP_k(A)\|-2\|A-P_k(A)\|_F>,$$

combining with the result from Lemma 11.3, we have, with a probability at least $2/3$,

$$\|(P_k - \widehat{P}_kP_k)(A)\|_F \leq (3+\epsilon)|A - P_k(A)|_F \tag{11.6}$$

Since

$$\|(P_k - \widehat{P}_kP_k)(A)\|_F$$
$$= \|(P_kP_k - \widehat{P}_kP_k)(A)\|_F = \|(P_k - \widehat{P}_k)P_k(A)\|_F$$
$$\geq \|P_k - \widehat{P}_k\|_F\|P_k(A)\|_2 = \lambda_k\|P_k - \widehat{P}_k\|_F$$

combining with the inequality in (11.6), we have, with a probability at least $2/3$,

$$\|P_k - \widehat{P}_k\|_F \leq \frac{3+\epsilon}{\lambda_k}|A - P_k(A)|_F \tag{11.7}$$

In order to bound $\|\widehat{P}_k - \widetilde{P}_k\|_2$, we use the Davis-Kahan $\sin\Theta$ theorem given as below.

Lemma 11.4 *Let A and $\tilde{A}$ be two symmetric matrices. Let $\{\mathbf{u}_i\}_{i=1}^k$ and $\{\widetilde{\mathbf{u}}_i\}_{i=1}^k$ be the first k eigenvectors of A and $\tilde{A}$, respectively. Let $\lambda_k(A)$ denote the kth eigenvalue of A. Then, we have*

$$\|P_k - \widetilde{P}_k\|_2 \leq \frac{\|A - \tilde{A}\|_2}{\lambda_k(A) - \lambda_{k+1}(\tilde{A})}$$

if $\lambda_k(A) > \lambda_{k+1}(\tilde{A})$, where $P_k = \sum_{i=1}^k \mathbf{u}_k\mathbf{u}_k^\top$ and $\widetilde{P}_k = \sum_{i=1}^k \widetilde{\mathbf{u}}_i\widetilde{\mathbf{u}}_i^\top$.

Using Lemma 11.4 and the fact

$$\lambda_{k+1}(\widehat{A}) \leq \lambda_{k+1}(A_p) + \|A_p - \widehat{A}\|_2 = \lambda_k + \|Q\|_2$$

we have

$$\|\widehat{P}_k - \widetilde{P}_k\|_2 \leq \frac{\|A_p - \widehat{A}\|_2}{\lambda_k(A_p) - \lambda_{k+1}(\widehat{A})}$$

$$\leq \frac{\|Q\|_2}{\lambda_k - \lambda_{k+1} - \|Q\|_2}$$

Under the assumption that $\lambda_k - \lambda_{k+1} \geq 2\|Q\|_2$, we have

$$\|\widehat{P}_k - \widetilde{P}_k\|_2 \le \frac{2\|Q\|_2}{\lambda_k - \lambda_{k+1}}$$

In order to bound the spectral norm of Q, we need the following lemma from random matrix.

Lemma 11.5 *Let $A \in \mathbb{R}^{r \times m}$ be a standard Gaussian random matrix. For any $0 < \epsilon \le 1/2$, with a probability at least $1 - \delta$, we have*

$$\left\|\frac{1}{m} A A^\top - I\right\|_2 \le \epsilon$$

provided

$$m \ge \frac{4(r+1)}{\epsilon^2} \ln \frac{2r}{\delta}$$

Using Lemma 11.5 and the fact that $Q_{i,j} \sim \mathcal{N}(0, \sigma^2)$, we have, with a probability at least $5/6$

$$\|Q Q^\top\|_2 \le (1 + \eta)\sigma^2 n$$

where

$$n \ge \frac{4(m+1)}{\eta^2} \ln(12m)$$

As a result, we have, with a probability at least $5/6$,

$$\|Q\|_2 \le \sigma \sqrt{(1 + \eta)n}$$

and therefore

$$\|\widehat{P}_k - \widetilde{P}_k\|_2 \le \frac{2\sigma}{\lambda_k - \lambda_{k+1}} \sqrt{(1 + \eta)n} \tag{11.8}$$

We complete the proof by combining the bounds for $\|P_k - \widehat{P}_k\|_F$ and $\|\widehat{P}_k - \widetilde{P}_k\|_2$ in (11.7) and (11.8) and plugging them into the inequality in (11.5).

11.4   Experimental Results

To demonstrate the effectiveness of our differential private random matrix approach and to illustrate the utility preservation of eigen-spectrum, we perform experiments over graphs obtained from three different online social networks. We analyze the impact of perturbation by evaluating the utility of the published data for two different applications which require spectral information of a graph. First, we consider clustering of social networks, which has been widely used for community detection in social networks. We choose spectral clustering algorithm that depends on the eigenvectors of the adjacency matrix. Next, we examine the problem of identifying the ranks of influential nodes in a social network graph.

For the evaluation purposes, we obtain clusters and node ranks from the published graph data, and compare the results against those obtained from the original graph data. We give a brief description of the results obtained for each of the applications of graph spectra in the subsequent sections.

11.4.1 Dataset

In our evaluation we use three different social network graphs from Fcaebook, Live Journal and Pokec. We use the Facebook data set collected by Wilson et al. from Facebook [26]. The social graphs of Live Journal and Pokec were obtained from publicly available SNAP graph library [57, 58]. The choice of these social networks is based on two main requirements. First, the network should be large enough so that it is a true representation of real online social structure. A small network not only under-represents the social structure, but also produces biased results. Second, the number of edges in the network should be sufficiently large in order to reveal the interesting structure of the network. For all three benchmark datasets, the ratio of the number of edges to the number of nodes is between 7 and 20. Table 11.1 provides the basic statistics of the social network graphs.

Figure 11.1 shows degree distribution of three online social networks on log-log scale. We can see that the data follows a power law distribution which is a characteristic of social network degree distribution.

11.4.2 Node Clustering

Clustering is a widely used technique for identifying groups of similar instances in a data. Clustering has applications in community detection, targeted marketing, bioinformatics etc. Social networks posses large amount of information which can be utilized in extensive data mining applications. Large complex graphs can

Table 11.1 Dataset description

Network	Nodes	Edges
Facebook	3, 097, 165	23, 667, 394
Pokec	1, 632, 803	30, 622, 564
LiveJournal	3, 997, 962	34, 681, 189

Fig. 11.1 Degree distribution
of three datasets

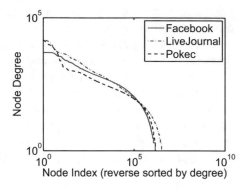

Algorithm 2: Spectral clustering

Input: (1) Adjacency Matrix $A \in \mathbb{R}^{n \times n}$
      (2) Number of clusters k
Output: Clusters $C_1, \ldots, C_k$

1 Compute first k eigenvectors $\mathbf{u}_1, .., \mathbf{u}_k$ of A
2 Get matrix $U \in \mathbb{R}^{n \times k}$ where ith column of U is $\mathbf{u}_i$
3 Obtain clusters by applying $k-$means clustering on matrix U

---

be obtained from social networks which represent relationships among individual users. One of the key research questions is the understanding of community structure present in large social network graphs. Social networking platforms possess strong community structure of users, which can be captured by clustering nodes of a social network graph. Detecting communities can help in identifying structural position of nodes in a community. Nodes with a central position in a community have influence in the community. Similarly, nodes lying at the intersection of two communities are important for maintaining links between communities. Disclosure of the identity of such nodes having important structural properties results in serious privacy issues. Therefore, in order to protect an individual's privacy it is crucial for data publishers to provide rigorous privacy guarantees for the data to be published.

In our experiments, we use spectral clustering for evaluating our privacy-preserving random matrix approach. Spectral clustering has many fundamental advantages over other clustering algorithms [59]. Unlike other clustering algorithms, spectral clustering is particularly suitable for social networks, since it requires an adjacency matrix as an input and not a feature representation of the data. For social network data graph G represented by the binary adjacency matrix A, spectral clustering techniques utilize the eigen-spectrum of A to perform clustering [59]. The basic idea is to view clustering as a graph partition problem, and divide the graph into several disjoint subgraphs by only removing the edges that connect nodes with small similarities. Algorithm 2 gives the standard clustering algorithm, and Algorithm 3 states the key steps of differential private spectral clustering algorithm. Algorithm 3 differs from Algorithm 2 in that it calls the publish routine in Algorithm 1 to obtain a differential private matrix which represents the structure of a social network.

Algorithm 3: Differential private spectral clustering

Input: (1) adjacency matrix $A \in \mathbb{R}^{n \times n}$
      (2) number of clusters k
      (3) the number of random projections $m < n$
      (4) variance for random noise σ^2
Output: Clusters $C_1, \ldots, C_k$

1 Compute a differential private matrix for social network A by $\widehat{A} = \text{Publish}(A, m, \sigma^2)$
2 Compute first k eigenvectors $\widetilde{u}_1, .., \widetilde{u}_k$ of $\widehat{A}$
3 Get matrix $U \in \mathbb{R}^{n \times k}$ where ith column of U is $\widetilde{u}_i$
4 Obtain clusters by applying $k-$means clustering on matrix U

To evaluate the utility of the published data for clustering, we utilize normalize mutual information (NMI) as a measure to evaluate the clustering quality [60]. Although *Purity* is a simpler evaluation measure, high purity is easy to achieve for large number of clusters and cannot be used to evaluate trade off between clustering quality and number of clusters. NMI allows us to evaluate this tradeoff by normalizing mutual information $I(\omega; C)$ as described in Eq. (11.9).

$$NMI = \frac{I(\omega; C)}{[H(\omega) + H(C)]/2},$$
(11.9)

where H is entropy which measures the uniformity of the distribution of nodes in a set of clusters, $\omega = w_1, \ldots, w_k$ is a set of clusters and $C = c_1, \ldots, c_k$ is a set of classes or ground truth. NMI is bounded between 0 and 1, and the larger the NMI, the better the clustering performance is.

We perform extensive experiments over the datasets to evaluate our approach. We now give a stepwise explanation of our evaluation protocol. Since we donot have ground truth about the communities in the datasets, we employ an exhaustive approach to evaluate clustering over the original data and generate the ground truth communities. First, for a given value of k we generate 5 different sets of clusters from Algorithm 2, represented as C_i for $i = 1, .., 5$. Since spectral clustering employs $k-$means, each set C_i can have different cluster distributions. Therefore, to evaluate the consistency in cluster distribution, NMI values are obtained for $\binom{5}{2}$ different pairs of sets represented as (C_i, C_j), where $i \neq j$ and average value is reported. Then, another 5 cluster sets are obtained through Algorithm 3, represented as ω_i for $i = 1, \ldots, 5$. Finally, to evaluate cluster sets ω_i, NMI values are obtained using C_i as the ground truth. In this case NMI values are obtained for each pair $(\omega_i, C_j) \forall i, j \in 1, \ldots, 5$ and average value is reported.

Since one of the advantages of the proposed approach is its low sensitivity towards noise, we evaluate the clustering results for three different values of σ, where $\sigma = 0.1, 0.5$ and 1. We note that these values of random noise were suggested in [20], based on which we build our theoretical foundation. For each σ, we evaluate clustering for two different number of random projections $m = 20, 200$.

Figures 11.2, 11.3 and 11.4 shows NMI values obtained for four different values of k, where symbol O represents the NMI values obtained by using the original data. It is not surprising to observe that the clustering quality deteriorates with increasing number of clusters. This is because the larger the number of clusters, the more the challenging the problem is. Overall, we observe that $m = 200$ yields significantly better clustering performance than $m = 20$. When the random perturbation is small (i.e. $\sigma = 0.1$), our approach with $m = 200$ random projections yields similar clustering performance as spectral clustering using the original data. This is consistent with our theoretical result given in Theorem 11.2, i.e. with sufficiently large number of random projections, the approximation error in recovering the eigenvectors of the original data can be as small as $O(1/\sqrt{n})$. Finally, we observe that the clustering performance declines with larger noise for random perturbation. However, even with random noise as large as $\sigma = 1$, the clustering performance using the differential private copy of the social network graph still yield descent performance with NMI ≥ 0.70. This is again consistent with our theoretical result: the approximation error of eigenvectors is $O(\sigma/\sqrt{n})$, and therefore will be small as long as σ is significantly smaller than $\sqrt{n}$. Finally, Table 11.2 shows the memory required for the published data matrix and the time required to compute the random projection query over the graph matrix. It is not surprising to see that both

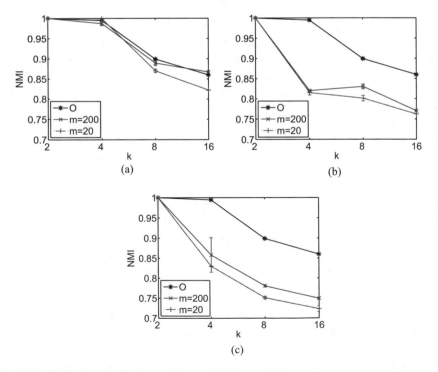

Fig. 11.2 NMI values for Facebook. (**a**) $\sigma = 0.1$. (**b**) $\sigma = 0.5$. (**c**) $\sigma = 1$

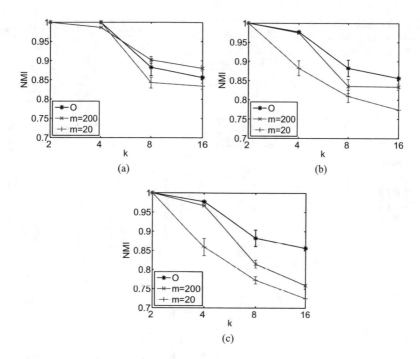

Fig. 11.3 NMI values for Live Journal. (**a**) $\sigma = 0.1$. (**b**) $\sigma = 0.5$. (**c**) $\sigma = 1$

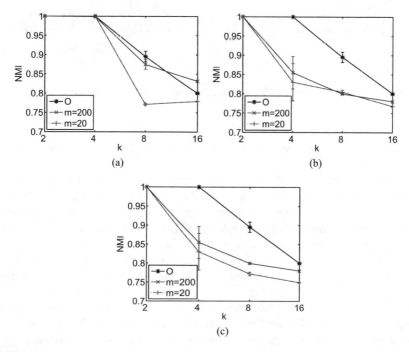

Fig. 11.4 NMI values for Pokec. (**a**) $\sigma = 0.1$. (**b**) $\sigma = 0.5$. (**c**) $\sigma = 1$

Table 11.2 Memory utilization and running time for the proposed algorithm

Dataset	Facebook	Pokec	LiveJournal
Memory (MB) $m = 200$	4955	2612	6396
Memory (MB) $m = 20$	495	261	639
Time (s) $m = 200$	150	97	211
Time (s) $m = 20$	6.15	4.60	8.15

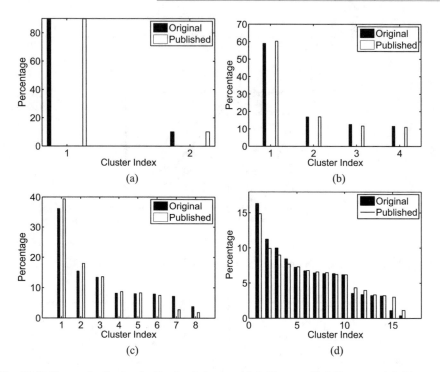

Fig. 11.5 Cluster distribution for Facebook dataset. (**a**) 2-Clusters. (**b**) 4-Clusters. (**c**) 8-Clusters. (**d**) 16-Clusters

the memory requirement and running time increases significantly with increasing number of random projections.

To show the variation in the cluster distribution, we select clusters obtained from Facebook data for $k = 200$ and $\sigma = 1$. Figures 11.5, 11.6 and 11.7 shows the percentage of nodes present in clusters obtained from the original and published data. Note that perturbation has little to no effect over small number of clusters as the distribution of nodes is identical.

We compare our results with an approach presented in [21], which directly perturbs the eigenvector of the original data by a Laplacian noise. We refer to this approach as (LNPP) for short. We note that we did not compare to the other approaches for differential private eigen decomposition because they are computationally infeasible for the large social networks studied in our experiments. We implement the LNPP mechanism and evaluate the clustering performance by

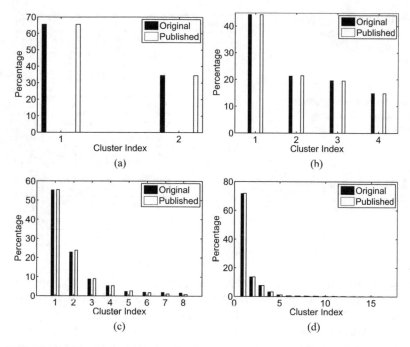

Fig. 11.6 Cluster Distribution for Live Journal Dataset. (**a**) 2-Clusters. (**b**) 4-Clusters. (**c**) 8-Clusters. (**d**) 16-Clusters

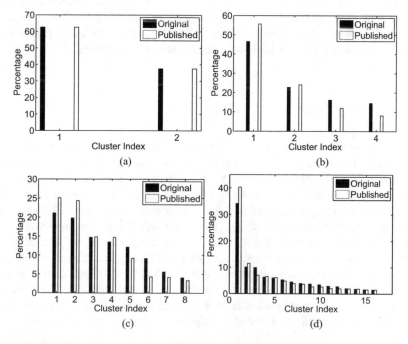

Fig. 11.7 Cluster Distribution for Pokec Dataset. (**a**) 2-Clusters. (**b**) 4-Clusters. (**c**) 8-Clusters. (**d**) 16-Clusters

Table 11.3 Clustering result (measured in NMI) using LNPP Approach [21] for $\sigma = 1$

Cluster	2	4	8	16
Facebook	$9.1E–8$	$8.8E–7$	$4.1E–6$	$1.3E–5$
LiveJournal	$9.7E–7$	$3.2E–6$	$3.6E–6$	$1.1E–5$
Pokec	$1.1E–7$	$3.5E–6$	$5.8E–6$	$2.6E–5$

Table 11.4 Clustering result (measured in NMI) using Pygmalion

Cluster	2	4	8	16
Facebook	0.98	0.97	0.94	0.91
LiveJournal	0.99	0.99	0.97	0.97
Pokec	0.98	0.88	0.87	0.81

Table 11.5 Clustering result (measured in NMI) using RW

Cluster	2	4	8	16
Facebook	0.70	0.76	0.75	0.70
LiveJournal	0.99	0.82	0.79	0.80
Pokec	0.97	0.89	0.85	0.85

comparing it to the clustering results generated by the original adjacency matrix. Table 11.3 gives NMI results using LNPP over different datasets for $\sigma = 1$. It is clear that LNPP performs significantly worse than the proposed algorithm in clustering. We also compare the clustering performance of *Pygmalion*, a differential privacy based algorithm proposed by Sala et al. in [41] and a random walk based algorithm (RW) presented in [61]. Tables 11.4 and 11.5 give the NMI results for these approaches. The results show that these approaches, in comparison to our random matrix approach provide high utility for the spectral clustering algorithm that use the eigen-spectrum of the social network graphs. Note that we did not include the clustering performance of LNPP in Figs. 11.2, 11.3 and 11.4 because of its poor performance that basically overlaps with the horizontal axis.

11.4.3   Node Ranking

Identifying information hubs in a social network is an important problem. An information hub refers to a node which occupies a central position in the community and has a large number of connections with other users. Such central nodes play an important role in information diffusion. Advertising agencies, can utilize information about top-t influential nodes for word-of-mouth advertisements [62]. Therefore, the preservation of privacy of such influential nodes is important.

Influential node analysis require information about the eigen-spectrum of the social network graph. Eigen-vector centrality (EVC) is a measure to quantify the influence of a node in a social network [63]. EVC is mathematically related to several other influence measures such as [64–66]. EVC requires the computation of eigen-vectors and assigns ranks to nodes according to their location in the most dominant community. EVC of an adjacency matrix is defined as its principle eigenvector. We employ principal component centrality (PCC) which is based on EVC measure to rank the nodes [67]. Let k denote the number of eigen vectors to be computed. Let U denote the $n \times k$ matrix whose ith column represents the ith eigenvector of an $n \times n$ adjacency matrix A. Then PCC can be expressed as:

$$C_k = \sqrt{(AU_{n \times k}) \bigodot (AU_{n \times k}) 1_{k \times 1}} \qquad (11.10)$$

Where C_k is an $n \times 1$ vector containing PCC score of each node. Nodes with highest PCC scores are considered the influential nodes. Similar to the clustering approach, Algorithm 4 gives the standard PCC algorithm, and Algorithm 5 states the key steps of differential private PCC algorithm.

Algorithm 4: Principal component centrality

Input: (1) Adjacency Matrix $A \subset \mathbb{R}^{n \times n}$
       (2) number of top eigenvectors k
Output: PCC score C_k

1   Compute first k eigenvectors $\mathbf{u}_1, .., \mathbf{u}_k$ of A
2   Get matrix $U \in \mathbb{R}^{n \times k}$ where ith column of U is $\mathbf{u}_i$
3   Obtain PCC scores C_k using Eq. (11.11)

Algorithm 5: Differential private principal component centrality

---

Input: (1) adjacency matrix $A \in \mathbb{R}^{n \times n}$
       (2) number of top eigenvectors k
       (3) the number of random projections $m < n$
       (4) variance for random noise σ^2
Output: PCC score $\hat{C}_k$

1   Compute a differential private matrix for social network A by $\widehat{A} = \texttt{Publish}(A, m, \sigma^2)$
2   Compute first k eigenvectors $\tilde{\mathbf{u}}_1, .., \tilde{\mathbf{u}}_k$ of $\widehat{A}$
3   Get matrix $U \in \mathbb{R}^{n \times k}$ where ith column of U is $\tilde{\mathbf{u}}_i$
4   Obtain PCC scores $\hat{C}_k$ using Eq. (11.11)

We evaluate the utility preservation of the published data by evaluating the accuracy with which influential nodes with high ranks are identified. First, for a given value of k, eigenvectors corresponding to the k largest eigenvalues are computed from the original adjacency matrix and used to obtain PCC scores of all the nodes in a graph using Algorithm 4 (denoted as C_k). Then, a second set of k eigenvectors is computed from the published data i.e., after applying matrix randomization using Algorithm 5. This second set is then used to obtain another vector containing PCC scores denoted as $\hat{C}_k$. The original scores C_k and the published scores $\hat{C}_k$ are then compared in two different ways. For all experiments, we compute PCC scores by varying the number of eigenvectors in the range $k = 2, 4, 8, 16$.

In the first evaluation, we use Mean Square Error (MSE) to compute the error between score values of C_k and $\hat{C}_k$. We report $n \times MSE$ in our study in order to

Table 11.6 $n \times$ MSE using the proposed approach

# of eigenvectors	2	4	8	16
Facebook	$2.6e^{-26}$	$2.9e^{-4}$	0.021	0.013
Live Journal	$4.0e^{-4}$	0.006	0.034	0.719
Pokec	$3.0e^{-4}$	0.005	0.009	0.019

Table 11.7 $n \times$ MSE using baseline LNPP

# of eigenvectors	2	4	8	16
Facebook	1.83	1.83	1.67	1.64
Live Journal	1.96	1.96	1.88	1.92
Pokec	1.79	1.63	1.62	1.55

Table 11.8 $n \times$ MSE using Pygmalion

# of eigenvectors	2	4	8	16
Facebook	0.04	0.06	0.09	0.12
Live Journal	0.22	0.31	0.37	0.56
Pokec	0.04	0.05	0.05	0.21

Table 11.9 $n \times$ MSE using RW

# of eigenvectors	2	4	8	16
Facebook	0.01	0.008	0.02	0.03
Live Journal	0.02	0.04	0.06	0.09
Pokec	0.03	0.04	0.04	0.05

alleviate the scaling factor induced by the size of social networks. In the second evaluation, we identify two sets of top t influential nodes based on the PCC scores computed from the original data as well as from the published data. We then evaluate the performance of our algorithm by measuring the percentage of overlapped nodes between these two sets. Table 11.6 gives the values of Mean Square Error (MSE) between PCC scores obtained from the original and published data. We also compare these results with the LNPP approach, Pygmalion proposed by Sala et al. , and random walk based approach by Mittal et al. . For comparison, we show in Tables 11.7, 11.8, and 11.9 the MSE results for the three approaches respectively. It is clear that the proposed algorithm yields significantly more accurate estimation of PCC scores than LNPP. In most cases, the proposed approach is 100 times more accurate than LNPP. MSE values for Pygmalion and RW show that these approaches perform significantly better than LNPP and outperform our random matrix approach when using 16 eigen-vectors for Live Journal social network. However the random matrix approach performs better for smaller number of eigen-vectors.

In the second evaluation, we measure the percentage of nodes correctly identified as the top$-t$ influential nodes. First, we obtain two sets T and $\hat{T}$ that contain the top$-t$ most influential nodes measured by the PCC scores given by C_k and $\hat{C}_k$. Then the percentage of nodes common to both T and $\hat{T}$ is computed. We consider top 10, 100, 1000 and 10,000 ranked nodes. Figure 11.8 shows the percentage of nodes correctly identified as the top$-t$ influential nodes for the three datasets. Figures 11.9, 11.10, and 11.11 show the results for LNPP, Pygmalion, and RW approaches. We can see that for all case, the proposed algorithm is able to recover at least 80% of

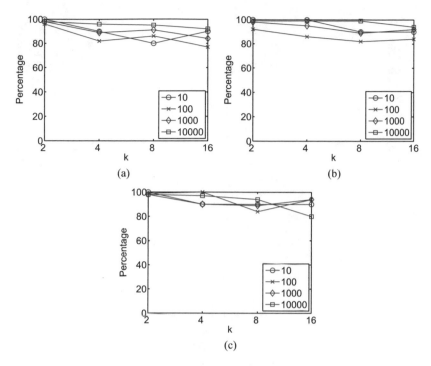

Fig. 11.8 Percentage of preserved ranks using random matrix approach. (**a**) Facebook. (**b**) LiveJournal. (**c**) Pokec

the most influential nodes. In contrast, LNPP fails to preserve the most influential nodes as the percentage of nodes correctly identified as the top$-t$ influential nodes is less than 1% for all cases. When looking at top-t influential nodes, Pygmalion and RW do not preserve the ranks. Pygmalion has better rank preservation of top nodes for Facebook and Pokec datasets.

11.5 Utility Comparison

In this section, we compare anonymization techniques by evaluating the utility of eigen vectors after anonymizing graph data. To perform a fair comparison, we integrate our approach with the state-of-the-art Secure Graph data publishing and sharing system (SecGraph) [68]. SecGraph provides implementations of 11 graph data anonymization schemes. The system also provides implementations of several graph utility metrics which can be used to test the utility preservation of an anonymization scheme. We implement and integrate our random matrix approach to SecGraph's anonymization module (AM). As our random matrix approach is focused on preserving the utility of eigen-vectors of a graph's adjacency matrix,

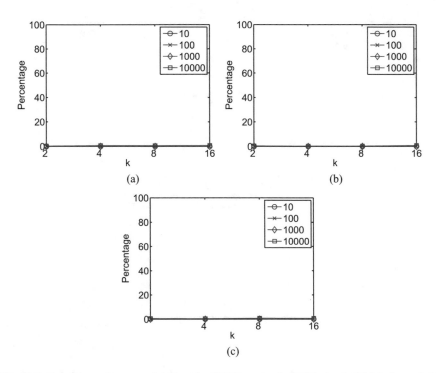

Fig. 11.9 Percentage of preserved ranks using LNPP approach. (**a**) Facebook. (**b**) LiveJournal. (**c**) Pokec

we use the implementation of Eigen-Vector (EV) similarity in the utility module of SecGraph.

In order to keep our evaluations consistent, we anonymize the Facebook, Live Journal, and Pokec graph datasets using three different schemes. In comparison to graph datasets used in [68], our datasets are many times larger and represent real online social networks which have several millions of nodes and edges. The anonymization of these large graphs present significant computational challenges and only some anonymization approaches output anonymized graphs in real time. Furthermore, to evaluate other utilities through SecGraph, we need to reconstruct the adjacency matrix $\hat{A}$. This is because other approaches implemented in SecGraph, require $\hat{A}$ as an input. The spectral decomposition of $\hat{A}$ can be defined in terms of the published eigen-spectrum of the input matrix A i.e., eigen-vectors $\widetilde{\mathbf{u}}_1, .., \widetilde{\mathbf{u}}_k$ and eigen-values $\widetilde{\lambda}_1, .., \widetilde{\lambda}_k$ as follows:

$$\hat{A} = \sum_{i}^{n} \widetilde{\lambda}_i \widetilde{\mathbf{u}}_\mathbf{i} \widetilde{\mathbf{u}}_\mathbf{i}^\mathbf{T} \qquad (11.11)$$

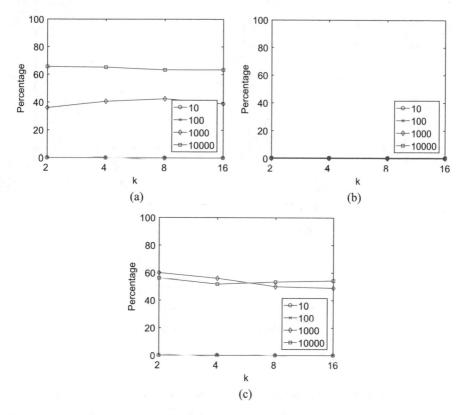

Fig. 11.10 Percentage of preserved ranks using Pygmalion. (**a**) Facebook. (**b**) LiveJournal. (**c**) Pokec

Rank-k approximation of $\hat{A}$ can be computed by using the published eigen-vectors and eigen-values [69]. The rank-k approximation is obtained as $\sum_i^k \tilde{\lambda}_i \tilde{\mathbf{u}}_i \tilde{\mathbf{u}}_i^T = \widetilde{\mathbf{U}}_{\mathbf{k}} \mathbf{D} \widetilde{\mathbf{U}}_{\mathbf{k}}^T$ The approximation of $\hat{A}$ is non-binary. A binary version can be obtained through rounding heuristics such as those used in [21]. Reconstruction of adjacency matrices of large graphs is computationally expensive. Therefore, we limit our comparisons to only graph's spectral properties. For comparison purposes, we use Pygmalion proposed by Sala et al. in [41], a random walk based algorithm (RW) by Mittal et al. [61], LNPP approach by Wang et al. [21], and our random matrix approach (RM). We chose these algorithms because of their realistic processing times. We ran these experiments on a dedicated machine with 2.5 Ghz 10-core Intel Xeon E5-2670v2 processor and 128 GB of RAM. Table 11.10 shows the time taken in seconds by each algorithm to anonymize the three graphs. From the table, we see that the random matrix approach outperforms other anonymization schemes in terms of processing time (Table 11.11).

Next we evaluate the utility preservation of the three anonymization schemes. First, we anonymize the original graph using an anonymization scheme. Second,

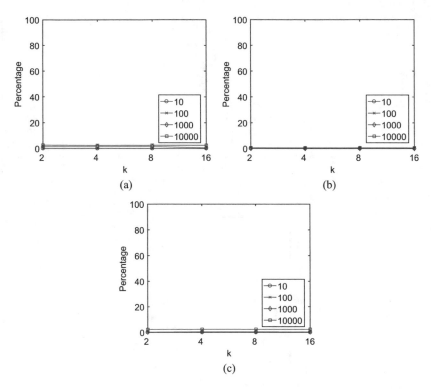

Fig. 11.11 Percentage of preserved ranks using RW. (**a**) Facebook. (**b**) LiveJournal. (**c**) Pokec

Table 11.10 Time taken in seconds to anonymize graph datasets

OSN	Pygmalion	RW	RP
Facebook	3078	479	78
Live Journal	1912	493	55
Pokec	4368	329	43

we compute first k eigen-vectors $\mathbf{u}_1, .., \mathbf{u}_k$ of the original graph and eigen-vectors $\widetilde{\mathbf{u}}_1, .., \widetilde{\mathbf{u}}_k$ of the anonymized graph. Note that for the random matrix approach, we skip the second step as it generates eigen-vectors $\widetilde{\mathbf{u}}_1, .., \widetilde{\mathbf{u}}_k$ in the anonymization step. Finally, we compute the ratios between pairs of eigen-vectors as calculated in [68]. For Pygmalion, we use the value of $\epsilon = 300$. For the random walk based scheme presented in [61], we use the value of random walk step $t = 2$. For the random matrix approach, we use number of random projections $m = 200$ and variance of random noise $\sigma^2 = 1$. For each pair of eigen-vectors $< \mathbf{u}_k, \widetilde{\mathbf{u}}_k >$, where $k \in 1, 2, \ldots, 16$, we report the ratios in Table 13.1. From this table we see that all approaches except LNPP yield high eigen-vector utility for the three graph datasets. RW approach performs poorly on Facebook dataset across majority of eigen-vectors. When looking at top 5 eigen-vectors, RW and Pygmalion performs poorly as compared to the random matrix approach (RM).

Table 11.11 Utility of eigen vectors after anonymization using SecGraph

OSN	Method	1	2	3	4	5	6	7	8	9	10	11	12	13	14	15	16
FB	Pyg.	1.09	0.76	0.92	0.96	1.01	1.00	0.99	0.96	0.96	0.81	1.00	0.99	0.87	1.00	0.95	0.99
FB	RW	0.13	0.49	1.55	0.21	0.34	0.54	0.68	1.01	0.98	0.60	1.33	0.47	0.63	0.15	0.55	0.99
FB	RM	0.95	1.07	0.99	1.14	1.08	1.23	1.08	0.91	1.03	0.71	0.92	0.88	0.67	1.13	1.08	0.59
FB	LNPP	0.002	0.001	0.002	0.008	0.001	0.00	0.004	0.00	0.004	0.001	0.003	0.002	0.005	0.002	0.001	0.006
LJ	Pyg.	0.73	0.48	0.51	0.98	1.08	1.05	0.99	1.01	1.07	0.94	0.94	0.99	1.00	1.00	0.90	1.00
LJ	RW	0.84	0.12	0.13	0.15	0.11	1.00	1.00	0.15	1.00	1.00	1.00	1.00	0.99	0.99	1.00	1.00
LJ	RM	0.94	1.10	0.91	0.93	1.02	0.89	0.92	1.00	0.85	0.46	0.86	0.93	0.84	1.07	1.11	1.04
LJ	LNPP	0.003	0.001	0.003	0.001	0.004	0.003	0.003	0.006	0.003	0.004	0.004	0.002	0.006	0.006	0.004	0.001
Pokec	Pyg.	0.98	0.87	1.00	1.00	0.65	0.89	1.00	1.03	0.99	0.91	0.97	0.90	0.72	1.10	1.04	0.99
Pokec	RW	1.02	1.09	1.00	1.06	1.01	0.78	0.96	0.94	1.00	0.96	0.94	0.98	0.99	0.55	1.09	1.05
Pokec	RM	0.99	0.64	1.10	1.01	0.97	1.07	1.20	1.02	1.03	0.66	0.51	0.90	1.08	1.05	1.04	1.08
Pokec	LNPP	0.008	0.004	0.007	0.003	0.00	0.010	0.001	0.006	0.008	0.002	0.006	0.005	0.007	0.002	0.001	0.007

SecGraph also provides a De-Anonymization module (DM) that consists of implementations of several structure based de-anonymization attacks (SDA). Since, the random matrix approach generates $\widetilde{\mathbf{u}}_1, .., \widetilde{\mathbf{u}}_k$ in the anonymization step, it does not publish an anonymized graph. Therefore, all SDA approaches implemented in SecGraph are not applicable to our random matrix approach and we limit our analysis to the utility module of the SecGraph system. Furthermore, an anonymized version of the input graph can be obtained by reconstructing the adjacency matrix $\hat{A}$. However, this approach is computationally prohibitively expensive for large adjacency matrices of real world social networks. Thus, we limit our experiments to the utility comparisons of eigen-spectrum only.

11.6 Conclusions

In this chapter, we propose a random matrix approach to publishing eigen-vectors of an OSN graph, which achieves space efficiency by reducing the dimensions of adjacency matrices and achieves differential privacy by adding a small amount of noise. The key advantage of our work over prior art is that our proposed random matrix approach achieves both space efficiency and utility preservation, whereas prior work either loses space efficiency (due to outputting large $n \times n$ matrices) or utility preservation (due to the addition of a large amount of noise). We formally prove that our scheme achieves differential privacy and that the amount of added noise is small. Furthermore, we validated our random matrix approach on three different applications: node clustering, node ranking, and node classification, which require the spectral information of a graph. Our experimental results show that even for high values of noise variance $\sigma = 1$, our scheme preserves the utility of the dataset. We also provide a utility comparison of our random matrix approach with two well know graph anonymization approaches. The results show that the random matrix approach is computationally cheap and preserves eigen vector utility more than other anonymization approaches.

References

1. Y.Y. Ahn, S. Han, H. Kwak, S. Moon, H. Jeong, Analysis of topological characteristics of huge online social networking services, in *Proceedings of the 16th International Conference on World Wide Web* (ACM, New York, 2007), pp. 835–844
2. E.M. Rogers, *Diffusion of Innovations* (Simon and Schuster, New York, 1995)
3. D. Gruhl, R. Guha, D. Liben-Nowell, A. Tomkins, Information diffusion through blogspace, in *Proceedings of the 13th International Conference on World Wide Web* (ACM, New York, 2004), pp. 491–501
4. P. Domingos. M. Richardson, Mining the network value of customers, in *Proceedings of the 7th ACM SIGKDD International Conference on Knowledge Discovery and Data Mining* (ACM, New York, 2001), pp. 57–66

5. M. Richardson, P. Domingos, Mining knowledge-sharing sites for viral marketing, in *Proceedings of the 8th ACM SIGKDD International Conference on Knowledge Discovery and Data Mining* (ACM, New York, 2002), pp. 61–70

6. M. Girvan. M.E.J. Newman, Community structure in social and biological networks. Proc. Nat. Acad. Sci. **99**(12), 7821–7826 (2002)

7. N. Du, B. Wu, X. Pei, B. Wang, L. Xu. Community detection in large-scale social networks, in *Proceedings of the 9th WebKDD and 1st SNA-KDD Workshop on Web Mining and Social Network Analysis* (ACM, New York, 2007), pp. 16–25

8. M. Cha, A. Mislove, K.P. Gummadi, A measurement-driven analysis of information propagation in the flickr social network, in *Proceedings of the 18th International Conference on World Wide Web* (ACM, New York, 2009), pp. 721–730

9. D. Kempe, J. Kleinberg, É. Tardos, Maximizing the spread of influence through a social network, in *Proceedings of the 9th ACM SIGKDD International Conference on Knowledge Discovery and Data Mining* (ACM, New York, 2003), pp. 137–146

10. H. Kwak, C. Lee, H. Park, S. Moon, What is twitter, a social network or a news media? in *Proceedings of the 19th International Conference on World Wide Web* (ACM, New York, 2010), pp. 591–600

11. K. Thomas, D.M. Nicol, The koobface botnet and the rise of social malware, in *Proceedings of 5th International Conference on Malicious and Unwanted Software* (IEEE, Piscataway, 2010), pp. 63–70

12. S. Hansell, AOL removes search data on vast group of web users. New York Times, 8 (2006)

13. A. Narayanan, V. Shmatikov, Robust de-anonymization of large sparse datasets, in *Proceedings of IEEE Symposium on Security and Privacy* (IEEE, Piscataway, 2008), pp. 111–125

14. L. Backstrom, C. Dwork, J. Kleinberg, Wherefore art thou r3579x?: Anonymized social networks, hidden patterns, and structural steganography, in *Proceedings of the 16th International Conference on World Wide Web* (ACM, New York, 2007), pp. 181–190

15. A. Narayanan, V. Shmatikov, De-anonymizing social networks, in *Proceedings of IEEE Symposium on Security and Privacy* (IEEE, Piscataway, 2009), pp. 173–187

16. C. Dwork, Differential privacy, in *Automata, Languages and Programming*. Lecture Notes in Computer Science, vol. 4052 (Springer, Berlin, 2006), pp. 1–12

17. C. Dwork, Differential privacy: A survey of results, in *Theory and Applications of Models of Computation* (Springer, Berlin, 2008), pp. 1–19

18. C. Dwork, The differential privacy frontier, in *Theory of Cryptography* (Springer, Berlin, 2009), pp. 496–502

19. K. Chaudhuri, A. Sarwate, K. Sinha, Near-optimal differentially private principal components, in *Advances in Neural Information Processing Systems*, vol. 25 (2012), pp. 998–1006

20. M. Kapralov, K. Talwar, M. Kapralov, K. Talwar, On differentially private low rank approximation, in *Proceedings of the 24rd Symposium on Discrete Algorithms (SODA)* (2012)

21. Y. Wang, X. Wu, L. Wu, Differential privacy preserving spectral graph analysis, in *Advances in Knowledge Discovery and Data Mining*, ed. by J. Pei, V.S. Tseng, L. Cao, H. Motoda, G. Xu. Lecture Notes in Computer Science, vol. 7819 (Springer, Berlin, 2013), pp. 329–340

22. N. Halko, P.G. Martinsson, J.A. Tropp, Finding structure with randomness: probabilistic algorithms for constructing approximate matrix decompositions. SIAM Rev. **53**(2), 217–288 (2011)

23. D. Proserpio, S. Goldberg, F. McSherry, A workflow for differentially-private graph synthesis, in *Proceedings of the ACM Workshop on Online Social Networks* (ACM, New York, 2012), pp. 13–18

24. J. Blocki, A. Blum, A. Datta, O. Sheffet, The Johnson-Lindenstrauss transform itself preserves differential privacy, in *Proceedings of the 53rd IEEE Annual Symposium on Foundations of Computer Science* (IEEE, Piscataway, 2012), pp. 410–419

25. Stanford large network dataset collection (2014). http://snap.stanford.edu/data/

26. C. Wilson, B. Boe, A. Sala, K.P.N. Puttaswamy, B.Y. Zhao, User interactions in social networks and their implications, in *Proceedings of the 4th ACM European Conference on Computer Systems* (ACM, New York, 2009), pp. 205–218

27. D. Verma, M. Meila, A comparison of spectral clustering algorithms. Technical Report (2003)
28. B. Luo, R.C. Wilson, E.R. Hancock, Spectral embedding of graphs. Pattern Recogn. **36**, 2213–2230 (2003)
29. M.U Ilyas, H. Radha, Identifying influential nodes in online social networks using principal component centrality, in *Proceedings of IEEE International Conference on Communications* (IEEE, Piscataway, 2011), pp. 1–5
30. S. Fortunato, Community detection in graphs. Phys. Rep. **486**, 75–174 (2010)
31. C. Dwork, F. McSherry, K. Nissim, A. Smith, Calibrating noise to sensitivity in private data analysis, in *Theory of Cryptography* (Springer, Berlin, 2006), pp. 265–284
32. A. Blum, C. Dwork, F. McSherry, K. Nissim, Practical privacy: The SuLQ framework. in *Proceedings of the Twenty-Fourth ACM SIGMOD-SIGACT-SIGART Symposium on Principles of Database Systems* (ACM, New York, 2005), pp. 128–138
33. K. Kenthapadi, A. Korolova, I. Mironov, N. Mishra, Privacy via the Johnson-Lindenstrauss transform (2012). Preprint arXiv:1204.2606
34. F. McSherry, K. Talwar, Mechanism design via differential privacy, in *48th Annual IEEE Symposium on Foundations of Computer Science, 2007. FOCS'07* (IEEE, Piscataway, 2007), pp. 94–103
35. C. Dwork, A firm foundation for private data analysis. Commun. ACM **54**(1), 86–95 (2011)
36. C. Dwork, A. Smith, Differential privacy for statistics: what we know and what we want to learn. J. Priv. Confid. **1**, 2010, pp. 135–154
37. H.H. Nguyen, A. Imine, M. Rusinowitch, Differentially private publication of social graphs at linear cost, in *Proceedings of the IEEE/ACM International Conference on Advances in Social Networks Analysis and Mining, ASONAM* (2015), pp. 596–599
38. Y. Mülle, C. Clifton, K. Böhm, Privacy-integrated graph clustering through differential privacy, in *EDBT/ICDT Workshops* (2015), pp. 247–254
39. Q. Xiao, R. Chen, K.-L. Tan, Differentially private network data release via structural inference, in *Proceedings of the 20th ACM SIGKDD International Conference on Knowledge Discovery and Data Mining, KDD* (2014), pp. 911–920
40. R. Chen, B.C. Fung, P.S. Yu, B.C. Desai, Correlated network data publication via differential privacy. The VLDB J. **23**(4), 653–676 (2014)
41. A. Sala, X. Zhao, C. Wilson, H. Zheng, B.Y. Zhao, Sharing graphs using differentially private graph models, in *Proceedings of the ACM SIGCOMM Internet Measurement Conference* (ACM, New York, 2011), pp. 81–98
42. Y. Wang, X. Wu, Preserving differential privacy in degree-correlation based graph generation. Trans. Data Privacy **6**(2), 127–145 (2013)
43. M. Hay, C. Li, G. Miklau, D. Jensen, Accurate estimation of the degree distribution of private networks, in *Proceedings of the 9th IEEE International Conference on Data Mining* (IEEE, Piscataway, 2009), pp. 169–178
44. D. Mir, R.N. Wright, A differentially private estimator for the stochastic kronecker graph model, in *Proceedings of the Joint EDBT/ICDT Workshops* (ACM, New Yrok, 2012), pp. 167–176
45. W. Lu, G. Miklau, Exponential random graph estimation under differential privacy, in *Proceedings of the 20th ACM SIGKDD International Conference on Knowledge Discovery and Data Mining, KDD* (2014), pp. 921–930
46. M. Hardt, A. Roth, Beyond worst-case analysis in private singular vector computation (2012). Preprint arXiv:1211.0975
47. S. Chen, S. Zhou, Recursive mechanism: Towards node differential privacy and unrestricted joins, in *Proceedings of the 2013 ACM SIGMOD International Conference on Management of Data, SIGMOD '13* (2013), pp. 653–664
48. J. Blocki, A. Blum, A. Datta, O. Sheffet, Differentially private data analysis of social networks via restricted sensitivity, in *Proceedings of the 4th Conference on Innovations in Theoretical Computer Science, ITCS '13* (2013), pp. 87–96
49. S.P. Kasiviswanathan, K. Nissim, S. Raskhodnikova, A. Smith, Analyzing graphs with node differential privacy, in *Proceedings of the 10th Theory of Cryptography Conference on Theory of Cryptography, TCC* (2013), pp. 457–476

50. S. Raskhodnikova, A. Smith, Lipschitz extensions for node-private graph statistics and the generalized exponential mechanism, in *IEEE 57th Annual Symposium on Foundations of Computer Science (FOCS)* (2016), pp. 495–504

51. V. Karwa, S. Raskhodnikova, A. Smith, G. Yaroslavtsev, Private analysis of graph structure. ACM Trans. Database Syst. **39**(3), 22:1–22:33 (2014)

52. A. Friedman, A. Schuster, Data mining with differential privacy, in *Proceedings of the 16th ACM SIGKDD International Conference on Knowledge Discovery and Data Mining, KDD '10* (2010), pp. 493–502

53. D. Kifer, A. Machanavajjhala, No free lunch in data privacy, in *Proceedings of ACM SIGMOD International Conference on Management of data* (2011)

54. G. Wu, X. Xia, Y. He, The policies of designing differentially private mechanisms: Utility first vs. privacy first (2017). Preprint arXiv:1702.02721

55. T. Sarlos, Improved approximation algorithms for large matrices via random projections, in *Proceedings of the 47th Annual IEEE Symposium on Foundations of Computer Science, FOCS '06* (2006), pp. 143–152

56. F.D. Malliaros, V. Megalooikonomou, Expansion properties of large social graphs, in *DASFAA Workshops* (Springer, Berlin, 2011), pp. 311–322

57. L. Takac, M. Zabovsky, Data analysis in public social networks, in *International Scientific Conference and International Workshop Present Day Trends of Innovations* (2012)

58. J. Yang, J. Leskovec, Defining and evaluating network communities based on ground-truth, in *Proceedings of the ACM SIGKDD Workshop on Mining Data Semantics* (ACM, New Yrok, 2012), p. 3

59. U. Von Luxburg, A tutorial on spectral clustering. Stat. Comput. **17**(4), 395–416 (2007)

60. S. Guiaşu, *Information Theory with Applications* (McGraw-Hill, New York, 1977)

61. P. Mittal, C. Papamanthou, D. Song, Preserving link privacy in social network based systems (2012). Preprint arXiv:1208.6189

62. H. Ma, H. Yang, M.R. Lyu, I. King, Mining social networks using heat diffusion processes for marketing candidates selection, in *Proceedings of the 17th ACM Conference on Information and Knowledge Management* (ACM, New York, 2008), pp. 233–242

63. P. Bonacich, Factoring and weighting approaches to status scores and clique identification. J. Math. Sociol. **2**(1), 113–120 (1972)

64. L. Katz, A new status index derived from sociometric analysis. Psychometrika **18**(1), 39–43 (1953)

65. M. Taylor, Influence structures. Sociometry **32**, 490–502 (1969)

66. C. Hoede, A new status score for actors in a social network, in *Twente University Department of Applied Mathematics (Memorandum no. 243)* (1978)

67. M.U. Ilyas, M.Z. Shafiq, A.X. Liu, H. Radha, A distributed and privacy preserving algorithm for identifying information hubs in social networks, in *2011 Proceedings IEEE INFOCOM* (IEEE, Piscataway, 2011), pp. 561–565

68. S. Ji, W. Li, P. Mittal, X. Hu, R. Beyah, Secgraph: A uniform and open-source evaluation system for graph data anonymization and de-anonymization, in *24th USENIX Security Symposium* (2015), pp. 303–318

69. I. Markovsky, *Low Rank Approximation: Algorithms, Implementation, Applications* (Springer, London, 2011)

Chapter 12
Predictable Privacy-Preserving Mobile Crowd Sensing

12.1 Introduction

In recent years, the proliferation of sensor-equipped smartphones, wearable devices, and implantable medical devices has enabled many novel applications to collect sensor data from the crowd through *mobile crowd sensing* (MCS) [1, 2], in which sensor data is contributed by the "grassroot" devices to complete sensing tasks collaboratively. In general, this new sensing paradigm has led to two types of applications: *community statistics analysis* and *collaborative learning*.

In community statistics analysis, the data collectors, or the application publishers are interested in deriving important statistics about certain groups of people or around certain physical areas. One important application is community health monitoring [3, 4], in which the health statistics of the community (e.g., average, distribution, etc.) needs to be monitored or derived. On the other hand, in collaborative learning, participating users contribute sensor data as training samples to build classifiers collaboratively. For example, users may contribute audio features to build classification models that recognize different environments that a user is in [5]. We envision that mobile crowd sensing continues to gain its popularity as the rise of wearable and edge computing, especially the big data analytics for healthcare [6].

In MCS, to aggregate data from participating users, a cloud server architecture is usually employed [5]. Since the local sensor data contains or can be used to derive users' private information, uploading the data to the cloud and enabling third parties to access the data inevitably exposes participants under the risk of privacy leakage [7]. To protect users' privacy, current mobile operating systems like Android and iOS require users to grant permissions to apps before they can access the sensor data. However, due to the lack of an efficient approach to analyze the privacy leakage of different applications, users are usually not fully aware of the underlying risks when they grant permissions to these apps. As a result, the privacy concerns inevitably hinder the participants from contributing data in the crowd sensing systems.

A. X. Liu, R. Li, *Algorithms for Data and Computation Privacy*,
https://doi.org/10.1007/978-3-030-58896-0_12

To address the privacy concerns, most existing work focuses on privacy issues of particular types of sensor data, such as location privacy when users need to grant the apps with the GPS permission [8]. To enable collaboration over privately collected user data, PoolView [9] provides a data perturbation based technique that hides user data while allowing applications to derive community statistics. Pickle [5] further proposes a regression based technique to learn classification models from crowdsourcing data while ensuring certain privacy protection. While the above work provides important insights that the privacy of MCS applications can be protected using different techniques, currently there are still several practical issues need to be addressed to achieve the *predictable privacy-preserving MCS*.

Typical MCS systems generally involve *two roles*, the application publisher, and the data-contributing users. To help users understand the privacy risks, the degree of private data leakage needs to be explicitly quantified. Furthermore, for different privacy settings, the application utility sacrifice also needs to be theoretically analyzed and accurately predicted, so that both data contributors and application users clearly understand their risks/utilities in MCS applications. Different types of sensor data (e.g., accelerometer, heart rate, GPS, etc.) and different data aggregators (e.g., average, histogram, classifier, etc.) are required in MCS applications. Therefore, it should be generally applied to different MCS applications regardless of the sensor types and data aggregators used.

In this chapter, *our focus therefore is on understanding the accurate privacy-accuracy trade-offs for different types of MCS applications, and designing generic application frameworks for predictable privacy-preserving MCS*. To achieve so, we first investigate the design principles of perturbation-based privacy protection algorithm and its performance against data reconstruction attacks. We then propose our *Salus*[1] algorithm, which preserves differential privacy and is resilient against data reconstruction attacks. Next, we analyze the efficiency of data protection using the Salus algorithm when different levels of privacy budgets are used. A theoretical lower bound on the reconstruction error is given against any reconstruction attacks. To understand the utility sacrifice under different privacy settings, we then derive *asymptotically tight error bounds* for three most widely used data aggregators required by the MCS applications: average (AVG), histogram (HIST), and classifier (CLS). This helps application publishers understand the additional errors introduced by different privacy settings set by users. Finally, with all these insights, we design and implement the P^3 framework for predictable privacy-preserving MCS.

12.2   Related Work

Mobile Privacy Protecting the privacy of mobile devices has received increasing attentions in the mobile computing community recently [10] due to the proliferation

---

[1] Salus was a Roman goddess of safety.

of mobile crowdsourcing in different applications [11, 12]. To prevent the sensitive data from data reconstruction attacks, PoolView [9] uses a synthesis user model to introduce correlation among noises. The research that is closest to ours is a group of work that perturbs sensor data or feature vectors before transmitting them to a cloud [9, 13]. However, although they provide important insights on different aspects of private data protections on mobile platforms, none of them provides quantified privacy risk and utility analysis. To account for the temporal correlations, [14] proposes a systematic solution to protect the location privacy based on the characteristics of the location data. This solution derives the lower bound of "δ-location set" based differential privacy, but is specially designed for location data and cannot be easily generalized to all sensor types in MCS applications. To protect the privacy in mobile crowd sensing, INCEPTION [15] further proposes a systematic solution for incentive management, data perturbation, and data aggregation in MCS applications.

Differential Privacy Differential privacy [16] is a popular quantification of privacy for data release in statistical database. Differential privacy has also been used to protect the location privacy in crowdsourcing [8, 17]. The authors in [18] apply differential privacy in the medical applications and analyze the risks of patients with different privacy budgets used.Hardt and Talwar [19] gives tight upper and lower bounds on the errors of differentially private mechanisms that answer linear queries. Our work differs from the above work in that, in addition to quantifying the privacy risks, we also explicitly analyze the data distortion of different privacy budgets and bridge it with the utilities of MCS applications.

Privacy-Utility Trade-Off A body of research work has been focusing on optimizing the privacy-utility trade-off in data mining [20–22]. Unlike the above existing work, P^3 focuses on the privacy-utility analysis on MCS applications, and it generalizes the privacy-utility quantification for different types of sensors and different data aggregators particularly required in MCS applications.

Cryptography The protection of privacy has received significant attention in the data mining community, where the private data is usually protected through the cryptography approach. The homomorphic encryption [23, 24] and secure multi-party computation [25] are usually adopted to derive community aggregations from private user input. However, under the model of collaborative mobile sensing, such schemes are vulnerable to collusion attacks.

12.3 Privacy of MCS

12.3.1 Threat Model

To enable predictable privacy-preserving MCS, we consider the typical mobile crowd sensing scenario which involves one central data aggregation cloud server and multiple data-contributing users. The cloud server collects data contributed by different users and aggregates the sensing data to support applications mainly in two categories: community statistics analysis and collaborative learning. In MCS, typically the cloud server is untrusted. We assume an *active (malicious) adversary* model, in which the adversary knows the exact privacy protection algorithm used, and can misbehave in any way, such as conducting data reconstruction attacks. In P^3, our objective is therefore to hide the sensitive private information while allowing the server to compute useful aggregation results required by different applications.

12.3.2   Data Reconstruction Attack

In data protection, data perturbation is a common practice that exploits random noise injection to achieve the *differential privacy* [26]. However, research has shown that the original data can be largely reconstructed from the noisy input [9]. This poses significant risks to the perturbation-based algorithms in MCS, in which the key concern of privacy protection is to avoid the original data being obtained by the adversary. In general, two categories of data reconstruction attacks exist in the literature: the *Principle Component Analysis (PCA) based attack* [25] and *Spectral Filtering (SF) based attack* [27]. The key ideas behind these attacks are to exploit the correlation that exists among the original data to filter out the injected random noises. In MCS, since each user is usually required to upload multiple samples, *temporal correlation* generally exists in the uploaded data. For example, in health monitoring applications, heart rate data needs to be continuously uploaded to the server. Since consecutive sensor values tend to stay similar, high temporal correlation exists among consecutive sensor values. This correlation may help the adversary to reverse-engineer the original data.

12.4   Differentially Private Mechanisms for Privacy-Preserving MCS

12.4.1   Models and Definitions

12.4.1.1   Overview of the System Model

We consider an MCS system that recruits n users, who are indexed by $i = 1, \ldots, n$. The system runs for T rounds. In each round $t \in \{1, \ldots, T\}$, each user i has some local sensor data $x_{i,t}$ to upload to a cloud server, and the server is to compute an aggregation function $g(X_t)$ over the collection $X_t = \{x_{1,t}, \ldots, x_{n,t}\}$ (e.g., average, maximum, histogram, etc.). Let $\mathcal{D}$ be the universe from which each data value $x_{i,t}$ is drawn from, then $X_t \in \mathcal{D}^n$ and we call the collection $X = \{X_1, \ldots, X_T\} = \{x_{i,t}\} \in \mathcal{D}^{n \times T}$ a *dataset*.

For a concrete example, consider a system that collects each user's height and then calculates the average height of all the users. In this case, $\mathcal{D} = [0, 3]$ (assuming that no one is higher than 3 meters), and $g(\cdot)$ is the average function. A more complex example is a medical research system. In this case, $\mathcal{D} = \mathbb{R}^k$ is the k-dimensional Euclidean space, where k is the dimension of the feature vector of users' health data, and $g(\cdot)$ computes some medical statistics of the users or learns classification models.

12.4.1.2 Differential Privacy

We adopt the standard differential privacy [26] as our formal definition of privacy. We first define the concept of *neighboring datasets*:

Definition 12.1 (Neighboring Datasets) Two datasets $X = \{x_{i,t}\} \in \mathcal{D}^{n \times T}$ and $X' = \{x'_{i,t}\} \in \mathcal{D}^{n \times T}$ are neighboring datasets (denoted by $X \sim X'$) iff $|\{(i, t)|x_{i,t} \neq x'_{i,t}\}| \leq 1$.

In other words, $X \sim X'$ iff the users' data is different for at most one user in at most one round. Note that here the neighboring is defined to be per-record instead of per-user. In the latter case the noise would be too large to be useful, while we will show in the later sections that following this definition we can still achieve practical privacy protection using our proposed algorithm. After we have defined neighboring datasets, we can then define differential privacy for an input perturbation scheme:

Definition 12.2 (ϵ-Differential Privacy) An input perturbation scheme $\mathcal{A}$ preserves ϵ-differential privacy iff

$$\Pr[\mathcal{A}(X) \in S] \leq e^{\epsilon} \Pr[\mathcal{A}(X') \in S]$$

for any datasets $X \sim X'$ and any subset $S \subseteq \text{Range}(\mathcal{A})$.

Definition 12.2 guarantees that any perturbation result occurs with similar probabilities for neighboring datasets. In other words, one user cannot have a significant impact on the output of $\mathcal{A}$, and in this sense the users' privacy is protected. The privacy parameter ϵ measures the maximum "privacy leakage," and usually it is called the *privacy budget*.

12.4.1.3 Sensitivity

The data sensitivity quantifies the maximum change of the data values.

Definition 12.3 (Sensitivity) The sensitivity σ is defined as

$$\sigma = \max_{X \sim X'} \|X - X'\|_1.$$

Recall that if $X \sim X'$, then there can be at most one user i^* and one round t^* such that $x_{i^*,t^*} \neq x'_{i^*,t^*}$, and $\|X - X'\|_1 = \|x_{i^*,t^*} - x'_{i^*,t^*}\|_1$. Therefore the sensitivity σ measures the maximum change of any user's data (in terms of ℓ^1 norm). Next, we will show that differential privacy can be achieved by adding random noise that is calibrated according to the sensitivity.

12.4.1.4   Laplacian Random Variables and Vectors

A random variable Y has Laplacian distribution with parameter b if its p.d.f. $f_Y(y) = \frac{1}{2b} \exp\left(-\frac{|y|}{b}\right)$. We call Y a Laplacian random variable, and we denote it by $Y \sim \text{Lap}(b)$. Given k i.i.d. random variables $Y_i \sim \text{Lap}(b)$, $i = 1, \ldots, k$, we call the vector $Y = (Y_1, \ldots, Y_k)$ a Laplacian random vector, and we denote it by $Y \sim \text{Lap}(b)^k$.

12.4.2   The Basic Laplacian Mechanism

One of the basic approaches to achieve differential privacy is via Laplacian mechanism [16]. The general Laplacian mechanism considers an arbitrary *query* q that maps an input X to an m-dimensional real vector. It defines the *sensitivity of the query* $\sigma_q = \max_{X \sim X'} \|q(X) - q(X')\|_1$, and it achieves ϵ-differential privacy by outputting $q(X) + \text{Lap}(\frac{\sigma_q}{\epsilon})^m$. Set q to be the identity function, we find that the input perturbation scheme depicted in Algorithm 1 preserves ϵ-differential privacy:[2]

Algorithm 1: The basic Laplacian mechanism for user i

Input: Privacy budget ϵ, Sensitivity σ, Data dimension k
1 **for** *round* $t = 1, \ldots, T$ **do**
2     $Y_{i,t} \leftarrow \text{Lap}(\frac{\sigma}{\epsilon})^k$;
3   Upload $x_{i,t} + Y_{i,t}$;

A drawback of Algorithm 1 is that it is vulnerable to *data reconstruction attack*. In Algorithm 1, the noises $Y_{i,t}$'s are i.i.d. and their distribution is publicly known. Meanwhile, in practice, a user's data in different rounds is usually correlated. These properties may be exploited by the adversary to remove the noise and recover the

---

[2]The notation $Y_{i,t} \leftarrow \text{Lap}(\frac{\sigma}{\epsilon})^k$ means independently drawing a random vector $Y_{i,t}$ according to $\text{Lap}(\frac{\sigma}{\epsilon})^k$ distribution.

original data. For example, in [25], the authors use principal component analysis (PCA) to reconstruct the original data. Since the original data is correlated, most of its principal components are negligible except for the first a few ones. The principle components of the i.i.d. noise, however, are roughly the same due to their independence. By keeping the first a few principal components and discarding the rest, the authors of [25] are able to remove most of the noise without hurting the original data too much. Another similar attack using spectral filtering (SF) is presented in [27], which also recovers the original data by exploiting the different patterns between a real-world data matrix and a random matrix.

Figure 12.1a demonstrates the risks of the basic Laplacian mechanisms (denoted as "Basic" in the figure) facing data reconstruction attacks. The heart rate sensor data is collected by one user and uploaded to the cloud server. The raw data is protected by the basic Laplacian mechanism. We can see that although the basic Laplacian scheme injects a significant amount of noises to the original data, the original data can be largely recovered from the noisy inputs using either PCA or SF based techniques. This makes it less adequate in protecting the sensor values collected by users in MCS. Moreover, it is still unknown how the accuracy of the final aggregation result $g(X_t)$ depends on the system parameters of the input perturbation scheme such as ϵ, σ, k, n.

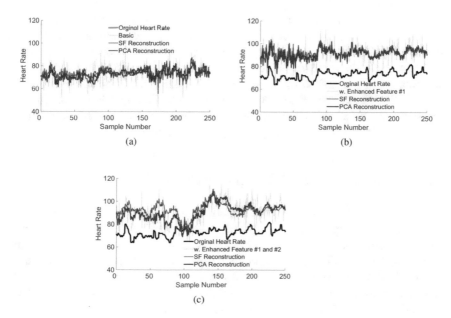

Fig. 12.1 The resilience of Salus against data reconstruction attacks. (**a**) The basic Laplacian mechanism is vunerable to data reconstruction attacks. (**b**) The permanent noise component introduces random shifts to the original data. (**c**) The Salus algorithm protects both the value and trend of the original data

12.4.3   The Salus Algorithm

To address the limitation, we propose Salus, an input perturbation algorithm that is light-weight, provides *strong resilience against data reconstruction attacks* and *predictable utilities*. Salus provides several enhanced features to the basic Laplacian mechanisms:

12.4.3.1   Enhanced Feature #1: Value Protection

We notice that the major threat of the data reconstruction comes from the i.i.d. property of the injected noises. To improve the resilience of input perturbation schemes against data reconstruction attacks, one potential countermeasure is to introduce correlations to the injected noises.

For example, in addition to $Y_{i,t}$, a user i could add one more noise component Ψ_i to its original data $x_{i,t}$ in each round t, where Ψ_i is a random vector drawn from $\text{Lap}(\frac{\sigma}{\epsilon})^k$ distribution as well. Notice that the noise Ψ_i does not change over time, and hence we call it the *permanent noise component*. By introducing the permanent noise Ψ_i, now the noise in round t_1 (which is $Y_{i,t_1} + \Psi_i$) is correlated with the noise in round t_2 (which is $Y_{i,t_2} + \Psi_i$).

The permanent noise component provides one important feature in privacy protection: value protection. Since Ψ_i is drawn at the beginning and is reused in all the following rounds, no known correlation-based data reconstruction attack is able to remove Ψ_i from the noisy input efficiently. As a result, the value of the raw data is always masked by Ψ_i and is protected. Figure 12.1b demonstrates the effect of Ψ_i. The quality of the data reconstructed by both techniques significantly degrades with Ψ_i added. The permanent noise component essentially introduces a random shift to the original data uploaded in each round.

12.4.3.2   Enhanced Feature #2: Trend Protection

However, Fig. 12.1b also reveals one important limitation with only enhanced Feature #1 added. In Fig. 12.1b, although the values of raw data are "hidden," another private information about the data, *the data evolution trend*, is still unprotected. Protecting data evolution trend is important especially in MCS applications because the trend of the sensing data is usually considered as sensitive. For example, in weight sensing applications, the user might want to hide the fact that he is gaining/losing weight during the data collection campaign.

To further protect the data's trend, we introduce the noise component $\Lambda_{i,t}$, which we call it the *dynamic noise component*. The $\Lambda_{i,t}$ in round t is generated as follows: with probability p (where p is a parameter), $\Lambda_{i,t} = \Lambda_{i,t-1}$; with the rest probability, $\Lambda_{i,t}$ is a new random vector that is independently drawn from $\text{Lap}(\frac{\sigma}{\epsilon})^k$ distribution. By generating the dynamic noise component in this way, it breaches the original data evolution trend. Notice that the dynamic noise $\Lambda_{i,t}$ in round t and the dynamic noise $\Lambda_{i,t+1}$ in round $t + 1$ are also correlated, therefore they cannot be easily removed by the data reconstruction processes. As shown in Fig. 12.1c, with the permanent and dynamic noise components, both the raw value and evolution trend of heart rate data are protected against data reconstruction attacks.

12.4.3.3   The Final Salus Algorithm

The following Algorithm 2 depicts the final Salus algorithm. For each user i, the original data is perturbed by all the noise components before uploading to the server to achieve different privacy protection features. The final perturbed data is then uploaded to the cloud server to support different MCS applications.

Here we want to point out that the noises $Y_{i,t}$ can be viewed as a special dynamic noise with $p = 0$, and the noise Ψ_i can be viewed as a special dynamic noise with $p = 1$. In other words, these three seemingly different types of noise components in Salus are in fact from the same family. This observation provides a more structural perspective to inspect our algorithm.

Algorithm 2: The Salus perturbation algorithm for user i

Input: Privacy budget ϵ, Sensitivity σ, Data dimension k, Probability parameter p

1   $\Psi_i \leftarrow \text{Lap}(\frac{\sigma}{\epsilon})^k$;

2   $\Lambda_{i,0} \leftarrow \text{Lap}(\frac{\sigma}{\epsilon})^k$;

3   **for** *round* $t = 1, \ldots, T$ **do**

4   $\quad$ $Y_{i,t} \leftarrow \text{Lap}(\frac{\sigma}{\epsilon})^k$;

5   $\quad$ Independently toss a biased coin which comes up HEADS with probability p;

6   $\quad$ $\Lambda_{i,t} \leftarrow \begin{cases} \Lambda_{i,t-1} & \text{if the coin comes up HEADS} \\ \text{Lap}(\frac{\sigma}{\epsilon})^k & \text{if the coin comes up TAILS} \end{cases}$;

7   $\quad$ Upload $x_{i,t} + Y_{i,t} + \Psi_i + \Lambda_{i,t}$;

12.4.3.4   Privacy Analysis of Salus Algorithm

Theorem 12.1 *The Salus input perturbation algorithm in Algorithm 2 preserves ϵ-differential privacy.*

Proof Consider an arbitrary pair of neighboring datasets $X = \{x_{i,t}\}$ and $X' = \{x'_{i,t}\}$, and fix the noises Ψ_i and $\Lambda_{i,t}$'s for now. Let $\hat{X} = \{x_{i,t} + \Psi_i + \Lambda_{i,t}\}$ and $\hat{X}' = \{x'_{i,t} + \Psi_i + \Lambda_{i,t}\}$ be the datasets that is obtained by adding $\Psi_i + \Lambda_{i,t}$ to each $x_{i,t}$ and $x'_{i,t}$, respectively. It then follows that $\hat{X} \sim \hat{X}'$, and $\|\hat{X} - \hat{X}'\|_1 = \|X - X'\|_1 \leq \sigma$.

For fixed Ψ_i and $\Lambda_{i,t}$'s, the execution of Algorithm 2 with X and X' is the same to an execution of Algorithm 1 with $\hat{X}$ and $\hat{X}'$ respectively. Let $\mathcal{A}_2$ denote the Salus input perturbation scheme in Algorithm 2. Since Algorithm 1 preserves ϵ-differential privacy, we have

$$\Pr[\mathcal{A}_2(X) \in S | \Psi_i, \Lambda_{i,1}, \ldots, \Lambda_{i,T}]$$

$$\leq e^\epsilon \Pr[\mathcal{A}_2(X') \in S | \Psi_i, \Lambda_{i,1}, \ldots, \Lambda_{i,T}] \qquad (12.1)$$

for any subset $S \subseteq \text{Range}(\mathcal{A}_2)$. Take expectation over both sides of (12.1), we then get

$$\Pr[\mathcal{A}_2(X) \in S] \leq e^\epsilon \Pr[\mathcal{A}_2(X') \in S]$$

for any subset $S \subseteq \text{Range}(\mathcal{A}_2)$.   □

By varying privacy budget ϵ in *Salus*, the degree of data protection and utility sacrifice can be explicit quantified, as we will show in Sects. 12.5 and 12.6.

12.5   Role User: The Privacy Quantification

12.5.1   Data Reconstruction Error: A Quantitative Analysis

In this section, we analyze Salus from the perspective of data-contributing users to study its privacy risks in different settings. Recall that Salus is parameterized by the privacy budget ϵ, and the amount of injected noise is proportional to $\frac{\sigma}{\epsilon}$. Since σ is fixed for a particular type of sensor data to be uploaded, ϵ controls the degree of data protection in the MCS applications. To aid users understand their privacy risks intuitively, it becomes crucial to understand *how different ϵ's correspond to different privacy risks.*

In P^3, the privacy risk is defined to be the degree of private data disclosure, that is, the degree of "difference" between the original sensor data and the data that can be reconstructed by the adversary. A smaller distance between the original data and the reconstructed data indicates that the adversary gets a more accurate estimation on the users' private data, and hence the users have higher privacy leakage. On the other hand, a larger such distance indicates that the original data is better hidden from the adversary, and as a result, lower privacy risks are posed to the users. To measure such distances, we define the average normalized data reconstruction errors (ANEs). For arbitrary user i, the ANE is defined as:

$$\text{ANE} = \frac{\sum_{t=1}^{T} \|x_{i,t} - r_{i,t}\|_1}{\sigma T},$$

where $x_{i,t}$ is the data vector uploaded by user i at round t, and $r_{i,t}$ is the reconstructed data for $x_{i,t}$ by the adversary. The ANE measures the normalized average error of the data reconstruction. For example, imagine that a user i uploads his/her heart rate data $x_{i,t} = 75$ to the cloud server at round t. The adversary obtains this value, performs data reconstruction attacks and obtains a reconstructed value $r_{i,t} = 50$. If the possible heart rate values range from 50 to 150, the data sensitivity $\sigma = 100$. In this example, the user only uploads data for one round, and we have ANE $= |50 - 75|/100 = 0.25$, indicating that the average error is $100 \times 0.25 = 25$. If the ANE is calculated over many rounds, it approaches to the expected reconstruction error per round by the law of large numbers. In this way, the ANE gives users intuitive risk assessments to their private data leakage in MCS applications.

We evaluate the impact of c on protecting different types of sensors on mobile devices. As shown in Table 12.1, we divide the sensors into three different categories based on their major applications: human quantification, environment monitoring, and miscellaneous sensors. To quantify human, accelerometers and gyroscopes are widely used to detect human activities. Heart rate, skin temperatures, and galvanic skin response (GSR) sensors provide human biometric measurements and can be used to support applications such as human emotion detection. The environment monitoring sensors include ambient temperature, humidity, light, pressure, and magnetic. The miscellaneous sensors include the widely used GPS sensor, and the MFCC features extracted from audio clips which are usually used for context recognition [5]. For GPS, we use the large-scale T-Drive dataset [28] with around 15 millions GPS records to analyze the ANEs under data reconstruction attacks. All these sensors are widely used in MCS applications. To study the impact of different ϵ used in Salus, we vary the ϵ from 1 to 30 for each sensor and obtain the ANEs to analyze the corresponding privacy risks. Figure 12.2 shows the change of ANEs by varying ϵ values for four types of sensors: accelerometer, heart rate, GPS and MFCC. Note that here we do not show the other sensors due to similar results. We can see that the ANEs of the raw Salus uploaded data (where ANEs are computed with no data reconstruction performed), the ANEs of PCA reconstruction, and the ANEs of SF based reconstruction decrease as ϵ increases for all different sensors, and the decreasing pattern is similar regardless of the sensor type. Also, the ANEs with data reconstruction is almost the same as the raw Salus uploaded data without any data reconstruction, which indicates that with Salus, the data reconstruction attacks do not give the adversary any privilege to estimate the private sensor data more accurately. Table 12.1 summarizes the smallest ANEs of all sensors using either PCA or SF under different ϵ, we can see that the ANEs of different sensors remains consistent under different ϵ values, regardless that their data dimensions and data sensitivities are different.

Implications of Privacy Analysis Results Two major insights can be gained from the results. (1) From the results shown in Table 12.1, the ANE which quantifies the reconstruction error is *sensor independent*, and this indicates that the results can be applied to arbitrary type of sensors in MCS applications. This is an important feature since it *generalizes* the privacy risk assessment to all MCS applications that require different sensors. Although similar numerical errors of different sensors will have different impact on different applications, ANEs capture the relative 'shift' of

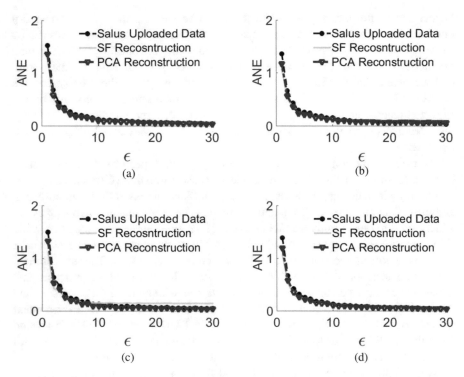

Fig. 12.2 The ANEs with different privacy budget ϵ set in Salus. (**a**) Accelerometer. (**b**) Heart rate sensor. (**c**) GPS. (**d**) MFCC (Audio)

Table 12.1 The ANE of different sensors using different privacy budgets ϵ in Salus

Privacy budget ϵ	1	2	3	4	5	6–15	16–30
Accelerometer	1.36	0.58	0.37	0.30	0.22	[0.07,0.17]	<0.07
Gyroscope	1.20	0.57	0.41	0.34	0.23	[0.07,0.18]	<0.07
Heart rate	1.25	0.57	0.37	0.24	0.21	[0.08,0.21]	<0.08
Skin temperature	1.28	0.58	0.36	0.30	0.22	[0.07,0.19]	<0.08
GSR	1.27	0.56	0.39	0.29	0.21	[0.08,0.20]	<0.08
Temperature	1.20	0.57	0.44	0.27	0.18	[0.07,0.14]	<0.07
Humidity	1.28	0.57	0.30	0.24	0.19	[0.07,0.18]	<0.07
Light	1.28	0.62	0.36	0.27	0.26	[0.08,0.18]	<0.08
Pressure	1.29	0.52	0.33	0.31	0.18	[0.06,0.14]	<0.06
Magnetic	1.22	0.61	0.38	0.25	0.24	[0.06,0.18]	<0.06
GPS	1.38	0.61	0.45	0.32	0.26	[0.09,0.21]	<0.09
MFCC (Audio)	1.20	0.58	0.36	0.27	0.22	[0.08,0.20]	<0.08

the data and directly quantify the private data leakage, which can be used for users to understand how accurately their private data can be recovered under the data reconstruction attacks using the current privacy budget. (2) The ANE deceases as the privacy budget ϵ increases. Use the same example of heart rate, when $\epsilon = 5$, the ANE is about 0.21, the average heart rate reconstruction error equals $100 \times 0.21 = 21$, which is sufficient to hide the heart rate values for most users. When ϵ grows to 10, the ANE is about 0.13, resulting in an average reconstruction error of 13, which still reasonably hides the real heart rate values. Even when ϵ increases to 15, most ANEs are still greater than 0.08, with the average reconstruction error of 8. When ϵ is greater than 16, the ANEs become smaller than 0.08 and it is less useful to protect the private heart rate value. This enables users participating in MCS applications to intuitively understand their private data leakage with different configuration of ϵ in Salus.

12.5.2   Data Reconstruction Error: A Lower Bound

In the previous subsection, we investigate the ANEs of some popular reconstruction algorithms by numerical studies. In this subsection, we show a lower bound on ANE of arbitrary data reconstruction algorithm, demonstrating that the privacy protection is universal.

We consider a particular user i throughout this subsection. To simplify notations, we will drop the i's in all the subscripts. Let X be user i's dataset, Salus's output $\tilde{X}$ can be written as $\tilde{X} = X + Z$, where Z is the introduced noise. Let $\mathcal{R}$ be any reconstruction algorithm, we will show that $\mathbb{E}\left[\|\mathcal{R}(\tilde{X}) - X\|_1\right] = \tilde{\Omega}(\frac{\sigma}{\epsilon \cdot T})$. Since ANE $= \frac{1}{\sigma T}\|\mathcal{R}(\tilde{X}) - X\|_1$, this implies that any reconstruction algorithm must suffer $\tilde{\Omega}(\frac{1}{\epsilon \cdot T^2})$ ANE on average.

Before we move on to the formal statement and proof of the lower bound, we note that *it is necessary to assume a distribution over the original dataset X*. To see why, let's imagine the case that $X = x_0$ with probability 1 for some x_0. In this extreme case, no matter what fancy manipulation we perform on X, the reconstruction algorithm can simply ignore its input and always outputs x_0, resulting a zero ANE. Technically, the distribution over X measures the reconstruction algorithm's prior knowledge over the dataset. Privacy protection is possible only when the prior knowledge is weak, that is, the distribution of X is sufficiently "noisy" or "flat".

In this chapter, we assume that there exists a constant $\gamma > 0$ such that $\frac{\Pr[X=x]}{\Pr[X=x']} \leq e^{\gamma\|x-x'\|_1}$ for any x and x'. Intuitively, this means the density of X changes smoothly in any neighborhood.[3]

Finally, for simplicity, we consider the case $k = 1$, i.e., the users' data is 1-dimensional in each round. This is sufficient for the purpose of showing a lower bound, and our approach can be easily generalized to cases where $k > 1$.

---

[3]This assumption is for the purpose of clearer presentation, and similar (but messier) lower bound can be shown with weaker assumptions.

Theorem 12.2 *The expected ANE of any reconstruction algorithm $\mathcal{R}$ is $\Omega(\frac{1}{\epsilon T^2} \cdot e^{-\frac{3\gamma\epsilon}{\sigma}})$.*

Proof Since ANE $= \frac{1}{\sigma T}\|\mathcal{R}(\tilde{X}) - X\|_1$, it suffices to show that $\mathbb{E}\left[\|\mathcal{R}(\tilde{X}) - X\|_1\right] = \Omega(\frac{\sigma}{\epsilon T} \cdot e^{-\frac{3\gamma\epsilon}{\sigma}})$.

W.l.o.g we can assume that $\mathcal{R}$ is deterministic, because for any randomized algorithm, we can first fix its coin flips, prove a lower bound and then take expectation over the coin flips.

Let $U = \|\mathcal{R}(\tilde{X}) - \tilde{X}\|_1$ and $V = \|X - \tilde{X}\|_1$, there are two cases:

Case 1. $\Pr\left[U < \frac{18T\sigma}{\epsilon}\right] \geq \frac{1}{2}$: In this case, there must exist an integer $\ell \in \{1, \cdots, 18T\}$ such that $\Pr\left[U \in \left[\frac{(\ell-1)\sigma}{\epsilon}, \frac{\ell\sigma}{\epsilon}\right)\right] \geq \frac{1}{36T}$.

Denote $I_0 = \left[\frac{(\ell-1)\sigma}{\epsilon}, \frac{\ell\sigma}{\epsilon}\right)$, $I_1 = \left[\frac{(\ell-2)\sigma}{\epsilon}, \frac{(\ell+1)\sigma}{\epsilon}\right)$. Since $\|\mathcal{R}(\tilde{X}) - X\|_1 = \|(\mathcal{R}(\tilde{X}) - \tilde{X}) - (X - \tilde{X})\|_1 \geq |U - V|$, and $|U - V| \geq \frac{\sigma}{\epsilon}$ when $U \in I_0$ and $V \notin I_1$, we have that

$$\mathbb{E}\left[\|\mathcal{R}(\tilde{X}) - X\|_1 \,\middle|\, U \in I_0, V \notin I_1\right] \geq \frac{\sigma}{\epsilon}.$$

In the rest of this proof, we will show that $\Pr[U \in I_0, V \notin I_1] = \Omega(\frac{1}{T} \cdot e^{-\frac{3\gamma\sigma}{\epsilon}})$. We then obtain the desired result because $\mathbb{E}\left[\|\mathcal{R}(\tilde{X}) - X\|_1\right] \geq \mathbb{E}\left[\|\mathcal{R}(\tilde{X}) - X\|_1 \,\middle|\, U \in I_0, V \notin I_1\right] \cdot \Pr[U \in I_0, V \notin I_1]$.

Recall that $\Pr\left[\tilde{X} = \tilde{x}|X = x\right] \geq e^{-\epsilon} \Pr\left[\tilde{X} = \tilde{x}|X = x'\right]$ for any x, x' with $\|x - x'\|_1 \leq \sigma$ and any $\tilde{x}$ (Theorem 12.1). An immediate corollary is that

$$\Pr\left[\tilde{X} = \tilde{x}|X = x\right] \geq e^{-\epsilon\|x-x'\|_1/\sigma} \Pr\left[\tilde{X} = \tilde{x}|X = x'\right]$$

for any x, x' and $\tilde{x}$.

Define interval $I_2 = \left[\frac{(\ell+1)\sigma}{\epsilon}, \frac{(\ell+4)\sigma}{\epsilon}\right)$. Fix $\tilde{x}$, let $S_0 = \{\tilde{x}|\|\mathcal{R}(\tilde{x}) - \tilde{x}\|_1 \in I_0\}$, $S_1(\tilde{x}) = \{x|\|x - \tilde{x}\|_1 \in I_1\}$, and $S_2(\tilde{x}) = \{x|\|x - \tilde{x}\|_1 \in I_2\}$. Then it is possible to construct a one-to-one mapping such that for each point $x \in S_1(\tilde{x})$, there is a corresponding point $x' \in S_2(\tilde{x})$ with $\|x' - x\|_1 \leq \frac{3\sigma}{\epsilon}$. We thus have

$$\Pr[U \in I_0, V \notin I_1] \geq \Pr[U \in I_0, V \in I_2]$$

$$= \int_{\tilde{x}\in S_0} \int_{x\in S_2(\tilde{x})} \Pr\left[\tilde{X} = \tilde{x}|X = x\right] \cdot \Pr[X = x]\, dx\, d\tilde{x}$$

$$\geq \int_{\tilde{x}\in S_0} \int_{x'\in S_1(\tilde{x})} e^{-\frac{\epsilon}{\sigma} \cdot \frac{3\sigma}{\epsilon}} \Pr\left[\tilde{X} = \tilde{x}|X = x'\right]$$

$$\cdot e^{-\gamma \cdot \frac{3\sigma}{\epsilon}} \Pr[X = x'] \, dx' \, d\tilde{x}$$

$$= e^{-(3 + \frac{3\gamma\sigma}{\epsilon})} \Pr[U \in I_0, V \in I_1]. \tag{12.2}$$

In the meanwhile,

$$\Pr[U \in I_0, V \notin I_1] + \Pr[U \in I_0, V \in I_1]$$

$$= \Pr[U \in I_0] \geq \frac{1}{36T}. \tag{12.3}$$

Combine (12.2) and (12.3), we solve that

$$\Pr[U \in I_0, V \notin I_1] \geq \frac{e^{-(3 + \frac{3\gamma\sigma}{\epsilon})}}{1 + e^{-(3 + \frac{3\gamma\sigma}{\epsilon})}} \cdot \frac{1}{36T} = \Omega\left(\frac{1}{T} \cdot e^{-\frac{3\gamma\sigma}{\epsilon}}\right).$$

Case 2. $\Pr\left[U < \frac{18T\sigma}{\epsilon}\right] < \frac{1}{2}$: First notice that $V = \|X - \tilde{X}\|_1 = \|Z\|_1$ is sum of $3T$ $\mathrm{Exp}(\frac{\epsilon}{\sigma})$ random variables, hence $\mathbb{E}[V] = \frac{3T\sigma}{\epsilon}$. By Markov's inequality, $\Pr[V > \frac{9T\sigma}{\epsilon}] \leq \frac{1}{3}$. Since $\Pr[AB] \geq 1 - \Pr[\bar{A}] - \Pr[\bar{B}]$ for any events A and B, it follows that

$$\Pr[U \geq 18T\sigma/\epsilon, V \leq 9T\sigma/\epsilon]$$

$$\geq 1 - \Pr[U < 18T\sigma/\epsilon] - \Pr[V > 9T\sigma/\epsilon] > \frac{1}{6}. \tag{12.4}$$

On the other hand, $\|\mathcal{R}(\tilde{X}) - X\|_1 = \|(\mathcal{R}(\tilde{X}) - \tilde{X}) - (X - \tilde{X})\|_1 \geq U - V$, by linearity of expectation, we get

$$\mathbb{E}\left[\|\mathcal{R}(\tilde{X}) - X\|_1 \big| U \geq 18T\sigma/\epsilon, V \leq 9T\sigma/\epsilon\right]$$

$$\geq \mathbb{E}\left[U - V \big| U \geq 18T\sigma/\epsilon, V \leq 9T\sigma/\epsilon\right]$$

$$\geq \frac{18T\sigma}{\epsilon} - \frac{9T\sigma}{\epsilon} = \frac{9T\sigma}{\epsilon}. \tag{12.5}$$

Combine (12.4) and (12.5), we finally get

$$\mathbb{E}\left[\|\mathcal{R}(\tilde{X}) - X\|_1\right]$$

$$\geq \mathbb{E}\left[\|\mathcal{R}(\tilde{X}) - X\|_1 \big| U \geq 18T\sigma/\epsilon, V \leq 9T\sigma/\epsilon\right]$$

$$\cdot \Pr[U \geq 18T\sigma/\epsilon, V \leq 9T\sigma/\epsilon]$$

$$> \frac{9T\sigma}{\epsilon} \cdot \frac{1}{6} = \Omega\left(\frac{T\sigma}{\epsilon}\right),$$

which is also $\Omega\left(\frac{\sigma}{\epsilon T} \cdot e^{-\frac{3\gamma\epsilon}{\sigma}}\right)$. □

From Theorem 12.2, we see that the reconstruction error of any algorithm is inherently lower bounded by the term $\frac{1}{\epsilon}$, which coincides with the hyperbolic curves shown in Fig. 12.2. We also notice that the error gets smaller as T increases. This is consistent to our intuitions, because more data (even if it is noisy) is always more helpful for denoising. The extreme case given earlier in this section corresponds to a $\gamma = \infty$, in which case our lower bound becomes trivial, and the attacker can indeed perfectly reconstruct the data. On the other hand, if $\gamma = O(\frac{\sigma}{\epsilon})$, then the term $e^{-\frac{3\gamma\epsilon}{\sigma}}$ is bounded by a constant and X's distribution no longer has significant impact on the asymptotic behavior of the lower bound.

12.6   Role Application Publisher: The Utility Prediction

From the application publishers' points of view, one of the key concerns is to understand the utility sacrifice due to the injected noises for privacy protection. In this section, we study the impact on the application utility under different privacy settings set by users, i.e., the privacy budget ϵ used in Salus.

In P^3, we consider two categories of mobile crowd sensing applications: community statistics analysis and collaborative learning. In the first category, we are interested in learning community characteristics, e.g., average. This type of applications are commonly seen in the collaborative sensing literature [27, 29]. The second category is collaborative learning where participants contribute training data to build classification models [30]. In this chapter, we discuss three important aggregators: average (AVG), histogram (HIST) and classifiers (CLS).

Next, we will derive asymptotic tight error bounds of these three aggregators with respect to ϵ.

12.6.1   Average (AVG)

The average aggregator over a dataset X_t is defined as:

$$\text{AVG}(X_t) = \frac{1}{n}\sum_{i=1}^{n} x_{i,t}. \tag{12.6}$$

In crowd sensing applications, understanding the average of certain sensing data in the community is important to support applications such as finding out the average temperature, activity level, heart rate, etc. We have the following theorem:

Theorem 12.3 *For any $X_t = \{x_{i,t}\} \in \mathcal{D}^n$, let $\tilde{X}_t = \{x_{i,t} + Y_{i,t} + \Psi_i + \Lambda_{i,t}\}$ be the perturbation results of the Salus algorithm, then*

$$\Pr\left[\left\|\mathrm{AVG}(\tilde{X}_t) - \mathrm{AVG}(X_t)\right\|_1 \leq \frac{2k\sigma}{\epsilon}\sqrt{\frac{6\ln(2k/\delta)}{n}}\right] \geq 1 - \delta$$

for any $\delta \in (0, 1)$ and $n \geq \frac{1}{3}\ln(2k/\delta)$.

That is, with probability $1 - \delta$, the average of the perturbed data is $O(n^{-\frac{1}{2}})$ away from the true average, hence we get better aggregation result as more users participate. Also note that the error is proportional to $\frac{1}{\epsilon}$ (fixing other parameters).

Before we give the formal proof to Theorem 12.3, we first introduce some useful technical lemmas. The following Lemma 12.1 upper-bounds the sum of n i.i.d. Laplacian random variables. It is a direct corollary of Corollary 2.9 in [31].

Lemma 12.1 *Suppose $Y_1, \ldots, Y_n \sim \mathrm{Lap}(b)$ are i.i.d. random variables. Let $Y = \sum_{i=1}^{n} Y_i$, then for any $\delta \in (0, 1)$ and any $n \geq \ln \frac{2}{\delta}$,*

$$\Pr\left[|Y| > b\sqrt{8n\ln(2/\delta)}\right] \leq \delta.$$

We can also generalize Lemma 12.1 to random vectors:

Lemma 12.2 *Suppose $Y_1, \ldots, Y_n \sim \mathrm{Lap}(b)^k$ are i.i.d. k-dimensional random vectors. Let $Y = \sum_{i=1}^{n} Y_i$, then for any $\delta \in (0, 1)$ and any $n \geq \ln \frac{2k}{\delta}$,*

$$\Pr\left[\|Y\|_1 > kb\sqrt{8n\ln(2k/\delta)}\right] \leq \delta.$$

Proof Let us denote $Y_i = (Y_i^{(1)}, \ldots, Y_i^{(k)})$, where $Y_i^{(j)} \sim \mathrm{Lap}(b)$ is the jth component in the vector Y_i. Then

$$\|Y\|_1 = \sum_{j=1}^{k}\left|\sum_{i=1}^{n} Y_i^{(j)}\right|,$$

and $\|Y\|_1 > kb\sqrt{8n\ln(2k/\delta)}$ implies that $\left|\sum_{i=1}^{n} Y_i^{(j)}\right| > b\sqrt{8n\ln(2k/\delta)}$ for some $j = 1, \ldots, k$. Therefore,

$$\Pr[\|Y\|_1 > kb\sqrt{8n\ln(2k/\delta)}]$$

$$\leq \Pr\left[\exists j : \left|\sum_{i=1}^{n} Y_i^{(j)}\right| > b\sqrt{8n \ln(2k/\delta)}\right]$$

$$\leq \sum_{j=1}^{k} \Pr\left[\left|\sum_{i=1}^{n} Y_i^{(j)}\right| > b\sqrt{8n \ln(2k/\delta)}\right] \&\& \qquad \text{(by union bound)}$$

$$\leq \sum_{j=1}^{k} (\delta/k)\&\& \qquad \qquad \text{(by Lemma 12.1)}$$

$$= \delta.$$

$\square$

We are now ready to prove Theorem 12.3:

Proof To show Theorem 12.3, it is equivalent to showing

$$\Pr\left[n\left\|\text{AVG}(\tilde{X}_t) - \text{AVG}(X_t)\right\|_1 > \frac{2k\sigma}{\epsilon}\sqrt{6n \ln(2k/\delta)}\right] \leq \delta$$

for any $\delta \in (0, 1)$ and $n \geq \frac{1}{3}\ln(2k/\delta)$.

By definition,

$$n\left\|\text{AVG}(\tilde{X}_t) - \text{AVG}(X_t)\right\|_1 = \left\|\sum_{i=1}^{n}(Y_{i,t} + \Psi_i + \Lambda_{i,t})\right\|_1,$$

which is the ℓ^1 norm of sum of $3n$ i.i.d. $\text{Lap}(\frac{\sigma}{\epsilon})^k$ random vectors, Theorem 12.3 is then proved by applying Lemma 12.2. $\square$

Figure 12.3 shows the error of the average aggregator over the heart rate data collected from 20 participants. As ϵ increases, the error decreases correspondingly. When ϵ is greater than 5, the error of the average aggregator becomes smaller than 3. For all ϵ, the derived error bound provides an asymptotic tight bound of the error, with a constant scaling factor.

Fig. 12.3 The AVG error and error bound with respect to different privacy budget ϵ

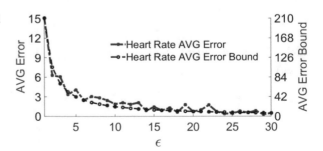

12.6.2 Histogram (HIST)

Histogram is an important tool that summarizes community statistics. For example, in collaborative mobile sensing applications we might be interested in asking questions such as "To be the top 10% in the community, how many steps I should walk each day?", or, "Is my heart rate too fast and falls into the top 5% of the community?", etc. Let $\mathcal{D}_1, \ldots, \mathcal{D}_m$ be a partition of $\mathcal{D}$ (recall that $\mathcal{D}$ is the universe from which the data $x_{i,t}$ is drawn), the histogram aggregator $\mathrm{HIST}(X_t)$ is a sequence of m reals $(h_1, \ldots, h_m)$, where

$$h_j = \frac{1}{n}|X_t \cap \mathcal{D}_j|. \tag{12.7}$$

We can imagine $\mathcal{D}_1, \ldots, \mathcal{D}_m$ as m buckets and h_j is the fraction of elements in X_t that fall in the jth bucket $\mathcal{D}_j$.

Before we analyze the "error" of HIST, we first need to define the distance between histograms. We adopt the standard statistical distance in this chapter:

Definition 12.4 (Statistical Distance) The statistical distance $d(\mathcal{H}, \mathcal{H}')$ between two histograms $\mathcal{H} = (h_1, \ldots, h_m)$ and $\mathcal{H}' = (h'_1, \ldots, h'_m)$ is defined to be

$$d(\mathcal{H}, \mathcal{H}') = \frac{1}{2}\sum_{i=1}^{m}|h_i - h'_i|. \tag{12.8}$$

$d(\mathrm{HIST}(\tilde{X}_t), \mathrm{HIST}(X_t)) \in [0, 1]$ quantifies the differences between the ground truth histogram and the aggregated histogram, and can be viewed as the error of the histogram aggregator. we now derive a bound for $d(\mathrm{HIST}(\tilde{X}_t), \mathrm{HIST}(X_t))$.

Let Q_i be the probability that $x_{i,t}$ and $x_{i,t} + Y_{i,t} + \Psi_i + \Lambda_{i,t}$ fall in different buckets. The value of Q_i depends on $x_{i,t}$'s position and $Y_{i,t} + \Psi_i + \Lambda_{i,t}$'s distribution. For example, if $x_{i,t}$ is near boundary of some bucket, then it is very likely that it goes to a different bucket after adding the perturbation $Y_{i,t} + \Psi_i + \Lambda_{i,t}$, in which case Q_i is large. Let $\bar{Q} = \frac{1}{n}\sum_{i=1}^{n} Q_i$ be the average probability that a data point in X_t falls into a different bucket after the perturbation, we have:

Theorem 12.4 *For any $X_t = \{x_{i,t}\} \in \mathcal{D}^n$, let $\tilde{X}_t = \{x_{i,t} + Y_{i,t} + \Psi_i + \Lambda_{i,t}\}$ be the perturbation results of the Salus algorithm, then*

$$\Pr\left[d(\mathrm{HIST}(\tilde{X}_t), \mathrm{HIST}(X_t)) \leq \bar{Q} + \sqrt{\frac{2\ln(1/\delta)}{n}}\right] \geq 1 - \delta$$

for any $\delta \in (0, 1)$.

There is no simple bound for $\bar{Q}$. In fact, $\bar{Q}$ can be very large if every $x_{i,t}$ is near the boundary of some bucket. However, in such a bad case, the data is so sensitive that $d(\mathrm{HIST}(\tilde{X}_t), \mathrm{HIST}(X_t))$ is inherently large for *any* input perturbation scheme.

In practice, we can estimate $\bar{Q}$ by assuming that all the data is near the "center" of each bucket. For example, if the data is 1-dimensional, and the bucket is equal-sized intervals, where each interval is of length L, then $\bar{Q}$ is approximately $e^{-\epsilon L/2\sigma}$. Following we give the formal proof to Theorem 12.4:

Proof To show Theorem 12.4, it is equivalent to showing

$$\Pr\left[d(\mathrm{HIST}(\tilde{X}_t), \mathrm{HIST}(X_t)) > \bar{Q} + \sqrt{\frac{2\ln(1/\delta)}{n}} \right] \le \delta$$

for any $\delta \in (0, 1)$.

We first need to introduce some notations. Let $Z_i = Y_{i,t} + \Psi_i + \Lambda_{i,t}$ be user i's noise. Recall that $X_t = \{x_{1,t}, \ldots, x_{n,t}\}$ is the n users' original data, we define $X^{(0)} = X_t$, and

$$X^{(i)} = \{x_{1,t} + Z_1, \ldots, x_{i,t} + Z_i, x_{i+1,t}, \ldots, x_{n,t}\}.$$

That is, $X^{(i)}$ is obtained from X_t by perturbing the first i elements of X_t. Obviously, $\tilde{X}_t = X^{(n)}$. For simplicity, let us write $\mathcal{H}_i = \mathrm{HIST}(X^{(i)})$. Our goal is to upper-bound $d(\mathcal{H}_n, \mathcal{H}_0)$.

Given $Z_1, \ldots, Z_{i-1}, \mathcal{H}_{i-1}$ is fixed. If $x_{i,t}$ and $x_{i,t} + Z_i$ fall in the same bucket (i.e., both $x_{i,t}$ and $x_{i,t} + Z_i$ are in the same $\mathcal{D}_j$), then $d(\mathcal{H}_i, \mathcal{H}_{i-1}) = 0$; otherwise, $d(\mathcal{H}_i, \mathcal{H}_{i-1}) = \frac{1}{n}$ (because moving one point from one bucket to another bucket can cause the distance changed by $\frac{1}{n}$). Recall that the probability for $x_{i,t}$ and $x_{i,t} + Z_i$ being in different buckets is Q_i, therefore:

$$\mathbb{E}\left[d(\mathcal{H}_i, \mathcal{H}_{i-1}) - \frac{1}{n}Q_i \,\Big|\, Z_1, \ldots, Z_{i-1} \right] = 0. \tag{12.9}$$

Let $D_i = \sum_{j=1}^{i}\left(d(\mathcal{H}_j, \mathcal{H}_{j-1}) - \frac{1}{n}Q_j \right)$. According to (12.9), the random variables $D_0 = 0, D_1, D_2, \ldots, D_n$ form a martingale. Since $d(\mathcal{H}_i, \mathcal{H}_{i-1}) \in [0, \frac{1}{n}]$, we have that $|D_i - D_{i-1}| = \left| d(\mathcal{H}_i, \mathcal{H}_{i-1}) - \frac{1}{n}Q_i \right| \le \frac{1}{n}$. Then, by Azuma-Hoeffding Inequality,

$$\Pr[D_n - D_0 \ge \lambda] \le e^{-\lambda^2 n/2}. \tag{12.10}$$

Notice that $D_n = \sum_{i=1}^{n} d(\mathcal{H}_i, \mathcal{H}_{i-1}) - \bar{Q}$ (where $\bar{Q} = \frac{1}{n}\sum_{i=1}^{n} Q_i$) and $D_0 = 0$, substitute this to (12.10), we get

$$\Pr\left[\sum_{i=1}^{n} d(\mathcal{H}_i, \mathcal{H}_{i-1}) \ge \bar{Q} + \lambda \right] \le e^{-\lambda^2 n/2}.$$

Fig. 12.4 The HIST error
and error bound with respect
to different ϵ using bucket
size 10

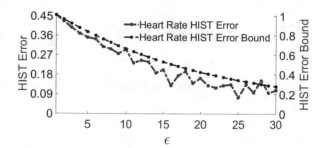

Since $d(\mathcal{H}_n, \mathcal{H}_0) \leq \sum_{i=1}^{n} d(\mathcal{H}_i, \mathcal{H}_{i-1})$, we finally get

$$\Pr\left[d(\mathcal{H}_n, \mathcal{H}_0) \geq \bar{Q} + \lambda\right] \leq e^{-\lambda^2 n/2},$$

or

$$\Pr\left[d(\mathcal{H}_n, \mathcal{H}_0) \geq \bar{Q} + \sqrt{\frac{2\ln(\delta^{-1})}{n}}\right] \leq \delta.$$

$\square$

Figure 12.4 shows the histogram error and the error bound as ϵ increases (fixing other parameters). We can see that the derived error bound provides a close estimation to the ground truth error by a constant scaling factor. This enables the applications to predict their performances when using different ϵ. In this example, when ϵ is greater than 20, the histogram error is less than 0.18, which indicates that a close estimation can be obtained to the ground truth histogram using the perturbed input data.

12.6.3   Classifiers (CLS)

Classifiers such as kNN and SVM are important tools in collaborative learning applications, and we would like to understand how our Salus perturbation algorithm affects the classification accuracy of the classifiers. However, since the classification algorithms are usually complex (some are even iterative), it will be very challenging to directly derive theoretical error bounds for different classification algorithms. Instead, in P^3 we take an indirect approach: in this section, we give a theoretical bound for the "random shift" of each data $x_{i,t}$; and we experimentally show how the classification accuracy changes depending on the "random shift."

Formally, we can view each $x_{i,t}$ as a point in k-dimensional Euclidean space, and adding noise to $x_{i,t}$ in Salus moves the point from its original position to a (random) new position as illustrated in Fig. 12.5. In this figure, two classes of accelerometer

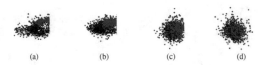

Fig. 12.5 Effect of the random shift caused by different privacy budget ϵ in Salus. (**a**) Original. (**b**) $\epsilon = 30$. (**c**) $\epsilon = 5$. (**d**) $\epsilon = 1$

Fig. 12.6 Classification accuracy changes with different Δd

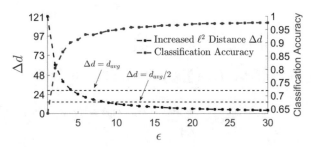

data that represent two different activities (using phone and brushing teeth) are visualized in the 3-dimensional space. As ϵ gets smaller, more noises are injected and the data points in the two classes shift randomly and merge together. Intuitively, the degree of random shift (the increased ℓ^2 distance of each data point) affects the final classification accuracy: larger random shift may imply higher accuracy lost in classification due to the fact that they are merged together and become hard to be classified.

To validate this intuition, we run different classification algorithms on datasets from UCI Repository of Machine Learning Databases: iris [32], skinseg [33], balance [34], and activity [35]. Let d_{avg} represent the average original ℓ^2 distance between the data points of two classes, and Δd represent the increased ℓ^2 distance of each data point after noise injection. Therefore $\Delta d = \|Y_{i,t} + \Psi_i + \Lambda_{i,t}\|_2$. Figure 12.6 shows the changes of kNN classification accuracy on the activity dataset using different privacy budget ϵ. Here we omit the results of SVM due to similar results. We can see that as ϵ increases, Δd decreases accordingly, indicating less random shifts with larger ϵ; the classification accuracy also increases accordingly. In this example when ϵ is greater than 6, Δd is less than $d_{\text{avg}}/2$, and the classification accuracy is almost not affected by the noise injection. This can be intuitively understood as follows: when ϵ is large, the injected noise is small, and the increased ℓ^2 distance of each class is less than half of the original ℓ^2 distance between the two classes, in which case the data points are unlikely to cross the separating hyper plane of the two classes, and hence this poses minimum impact on the classification accuracy. When ϵ decreases to 3, Δd approaches to d_{avg}, and the accuracy starts to drop fast. When ϵ is smaller than 3, Δd exceeds d_{avg}, and the classification accuracy drops dramatically and the classifier's utility is significantly degraded by noise injection. Figure 12.7 shows the classification accuracies with different increased ℓ^2 ratios, where the increased ℓ^2 ratio is defined to be $\Delta d/d_{\text{avg}}$. For all datasets, when the ratio is smaller than 0.5 (i.e., Δd is less than half of d_{avg}), the classification

Fig. 12.7 Impact of increased ℓ^2 ratio to classification accuracy

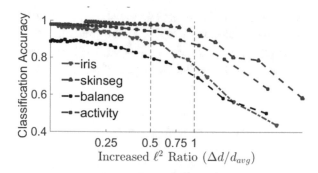

accuracy remains similar to the original accuracy when no noise is injected. When the ratio increases from 0.5 to 1, the accuracy degradation speeds up, and when the ratio grows larger than 1, the classification accuracy significantly degrades. These results imply that $\Delta d / d_{\text{avg}}$ plays an important role in estimating the impact of the privacy protection mechanisms on the classifiers' utility.

Since d_{avg} depends on the original data characteristics and is fixed for particular type of training data, Δd affected by the privacy budget ϵ uniquely determines the classifiers' final utilities. To quantify the impact of ϵ on the classification utility, we have the following theorem for Δd:

Theorem 12.5

$$\Pr\left[\Delta d \leq \frac{3\sigma\sqrt{k}}{\epsilon}\ln(3k/\delta)\right] \geq 1 - \delta$$

for any $\delta \in (0, 1)$.

Proof To show Theorem 12.5, it is equivalent to showing

$$\Pr\left[\left\|Y_{i,t} + \Psi_i + \Lambda_{i,t}\right\|_2 > \frac{3\sigma\sqrt{k}}{\epsilon}\ln(3k/\delta)\right] \leq \delta$$

for any $\delta \in (0, 1)$. Let $Y_{i,t}^{(j)}$, $\Psi_i^{(j)}$ and $\Lambda_{i,t}^{(j)}$ be the jth component of the random vector $Y_{i,t}$, Ψ_i and $\Lambda_{i,t}$, respectively. By the definition of ℓ^2 norm,

$$\left\|Y_{i,t} + \Psi_i + \Lambda_{i,t}\right\|_2 = \left(\sum_{j=1}^{k}\left(Y_{i,t}^{(j)} + \Psi_i^{(j)} + \Lambda_{i,t}^{(j)}\right)^2\right)^{1/2}$$

$$\leq \left(\sum_{j=1}^{k} 3\left(\left|Y_{i,t}^{(j)}\right|^2 + \left|\Psi_i^{(j)}\right|^2 + \left|\Lambda_{i,t}^{(j)}\right|^2\right)\right)^{1/2}$$

Notice that all these $3k$ random variables $Y_{i,t}^{(j)}$'s, $\Psi_i^{(j)}$'s and $\Lambda_{i,t}^{(j)}$'s are i.i.d. Lap$(\frac{\sigma}{\epsilon})$ random variables. For simplicity, let us rename them as $Z_1, \ldots, Z_{3k}$.

If $\|Y_{i,t} + \Psi_i + \Lambda_{i,t}\|_2 > \frac{3\sigma\sqrt{k}}{\epsilon}\ln(3k/\delta)$, then we must have $|Z_\ell| > \frac{\sigma}{\epsilon}\ln(3k/\delta)$ for some $\ell = 1, \ldots, 3k$. Otherwise, if $|Z_\ell| \leq \frac{\sigma}{\epsilon}\ln(3k/\delta)$ for all $\ell = 1, \ldots, 3k$, we will have

$$\|Y_{i,t} + \Psi_i + \Lambda_{i,t}\|_2 \leq \left(3\sum_{\ell=1}^{3k}|Z_\ell|^2\right)^{1/2} \leq \frac{3\sigma\sqrt{k}}{\epsilon}\ln(3k/\delta),$$

contradiction. It then follows that

$$\Pr\left[\|Y_{i,t} + \Psi_i + \Lambda_{i,t}\|_2 > \frac{3\sigma\sqrt{k}}{\epsilon}\ln(3k/\delta)\right]$$

$$\leq \Pr\left[\exists \ell : |Z_\ell| \leq \frac{\sigma}{\epsilon}\ln(3k/\delta)\right]$$

$$\leq \sum_{\ell=1}^{3k}\Pr\left[|Z_\ell| \leq \frac{\sigma}{\epsilon}\ln(3k/\delta)\right] \qquad \text{(by union bound)}$$

$$= \sum_{\ell=1}^{3k}(\delta/3k) \qquad \text{(since } |Z_\ell| \sim \text{Exp}(\frac{\sigma}{\epsilon}) \text{ is exponentially distributed)}$$

$$= \delta.$$

$\square$

As shown in Fig. 12.8, the derived Δd bound provides an asymptotic tight bound on the increased ℓ^2 distance with a constant scaling factor. As discussed above, once Δd is known, the classification accuracy degrading can be estimated by finding the ratio between Δd and d_{avg}. If the ratio is smaller than 0.5, then the classification accuracy is expected to remain similar to the case without perturbation.

Implications of Utility Analysis Results In this section, we study three aggregators, AVG, HIST, and CLS, which are essential in MCS applications. We show

Fig. 12.8 The Δd and Δd bound with respect to different privacy budget ϵ

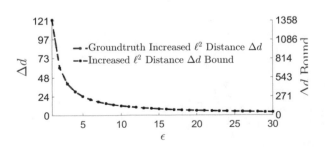

that asymptotic tight bounds can be derived for AVG, HIST, and Δd that indirectly reflects the utility of CLS. For all these derived bounds, constant scaling factors applied to scale the bound to the actual error. These constant factors are independent with the data, but only relate to different application settings, such as number of users n and the probability δ used. Once the application setting is fixed, such scaling factors can be easily determined by the cloud server using random training inputs for some ϵ. For example, by applying the Salus algorithm to the random input data and finding the scaling factor for $\epsilon = 1$, the scaling factor can be reused to estimate the error for arbitrary ϵ values using the derived bounds. This property enables application developers to understand the impact of different ϵ and specify their utility requirements in terms of ϵ.

12.7   The P^3 Framework for Predictable Privacy-Preserving MCS

In light of the above findings, we propose P^3 to support predictable privacy-preserving MCS applications. The P^3 architecture is shown in Fig. 12.9.

(1) *Utility Analyzer.* Before publishing data collection tasks, the application publishers first need to decide their data collection settings, including sensor type, number of users, aggregators, etc. After analyzing the utilities, the application publishers are allowed to specify their utility requirements in terms of the minimum acceptable privacy budget ϵ_a. Consider the heart rate example shown in Fig. 12.3. Suppose that an application publisher wants to find the average heart rate from 20 users. Suppose the maximum average error the application can tolerate is 3, the minimum acceptable privacy budget is determined to be 5, since ϵ smaller than 5 will result in larger average errors than 3 as shown in Fig. 12.3. Therefore, ϵ_a is set to be 5 in this data collection task. For CLS, to analyze the utility of different ϵ, the application publishers first need to

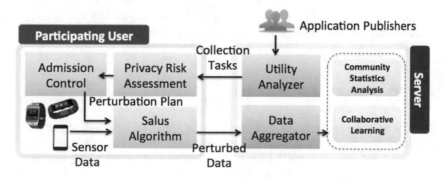

Fig. 12.9 P^3 architecture

gather d_{avg} from users. To collect this information, *metadata collection tasks* are first published. Users can submit the d_{avg} between different classes to help application publishers decide the ϵ_a used in CLS tasks.

After determining the ϵ_a, the application publisher then publishes *data collection tasks*. Each data collection task consists of five elements: *{aggregator; sensor type; number of users n; the minimum acceptable privacy budget ϵ_a; and Misc}*. Aggregators can be AVG, HIST, or CLS. Sensor type specifies what sensor data to collect, such as accelerometer, heart rate, GSR, etc. n specifies the total number users that need to be recruited, and ϵ_a indicates the utility requirement of the application. Finally, Misc part is optional and is used for task publishers to specify other misc information such as detailed task descriptions, incentives, or different training classes required by the CLS aggregator.

(2) *Privacy Risk Assessment.* The goal of privacy risk assessment is to provide users with intuitive understanding on their private date leakage before they participate in data collection tasks. Using the results shown in Table 12.1, the risk assessment provides the average reconstruction error estimation to the private data. For example, if $\epsilon_a = 5$ is specified by the data collection task, regardless of the sensor type, the corresponding ANE is about 0.21. And the users will be alerted that the average reconstruction error is 21 if the task collects heart rate data. This enables users to intuitively understand the level of private data leakage with ϵ_a and to decide whether to participate in the data collection.

(3) *Admission Control.* The admission control module enables general users to grant permissions to data collection tasks after the risk assessment. Users can specify their maximum privacy budget ϵ_u such that he/she will only join the data collection tasks when $\epsilon_u \geq \epsilon_a$.

(4) *Salus Perturbator.* After a user joins a data collection task, the Salus algorithm with the privacy budget set to ϵ_a is applied on the raw sensor data to protect the privacy before uploading them to the cloud server. The Salus perturbator ensures that the required application utility can be achieved with the ϵ_a. On the other hand, the user data will also be protected by ensuring that the degree of data leakage in terms of ANE will stick to the ϵ_a.

(5) *Data Aggregator.* The data aggregator takes the perturbed data from all participants and performs the aggregation operations such as AVG, HIST, or CLS. The final aggregated results are used to support different MCS applications for community statistic analysis or collaborative learning.

12.8   Performance Evaluation

In this section, we evaluate the performance of P^3 with system evaluations and two real-world case studies. The goals of evaluations are summarized as follows: (1) To analyze the privacy protection in terms of ANEs with different ϵ_u's determined by the data-contributing users; (2) To study the system overhead of P^3; (3) Through cases studies, to analyze the utility guarantee of P^3 with different ϵ_a set by application publishers in real MCS applications, and to demonstrate that P^3 can be used in practice to efficiently support real-world MCS applications, including community statistics analysis and collaborative learning.

12.8.1 Privacy Protection

In P^3, the Salus plays the key role in protecting data privacy of MCS applications, especially those with strong temporal correlations in data. To understand the effectiveness of Salus, we evaluate ANEs against data reconstruction attacks comparing with the state-of-the-art. INCEPTION [15] is an effective data privacy protection framework especially designed for MCS applications using data perturbation mechanisms. We evaluate the ANEs under both PCA and SF data reconstruction attacks. The integrated results are shown in Fig. 12.10. As the figure shows, Salus has larger ANEs over all the privacy budgets ϵ, reflecting that the reconstruction errors are always larger and the data is better protected comparing to INCEPTION. On average, the ANEs of Salus are 39.1% larger than that of INCEPTION, while using Salus also provides accurate utility predictions. These results show that Salus has high effectiveness against data reconstruction attacks given high temporal correlation in the MCS data.

12.8.2 System Overhead

In MCS applications, data is usually collected and contributed by resource-constrained devices, therefore understanding the system overhead is crucial for any privacy protection mechanism. To understand the computation and energy overhead,

Fig. 12.10 Privacy protection comparison between Salus and the state-of-the-art

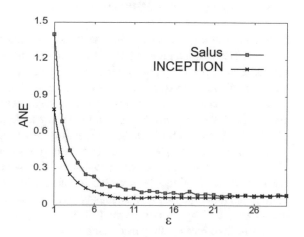

Table 12.2 System computation and energy overhead

Window size	Time (ms)	Power (mW)	Energy (mJ)
100	0.454	7.5	0.0034
200	0.869	7.5	0.0047
300	1.307	7.5	0.0098
400	1.673	7.5	0.0125
500	2.089	7.5	0.0157

Fig. 12.11 The maximum privacy budget ϵ_u specified by 20 participants in the admission control

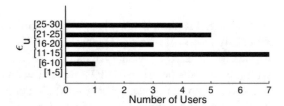

we evaluate the computation time and power consumption using a Lenovo K50-15 smartphone running Android 5.1 in an accelerometer-based activity learning system, which is a typical MCS application. We vary the window size from 100 to 500 samples to measure the computation time and power consumption. As shown in Table 12.2, we can see that the computation time of running Salus ranges from 0.454 to 2.089 ms, incurring only 0.0024–0.0157 mJ additional energy overhead. Since the perturbed data is of the same size as the original data, no additional transmission overhead is incurred. Since the computation overhead of Salus is insensitive to the sensor type, the measurement results illustrate that little system overhead is incurred using Salus for privacy protection in MCS applications.

12.8.3   Case Studies

12.8.3.1   Community Health Survey

In this case study, we survey the health conditions of a community of research students. We recruit a group of 20 participants from the community and collect their sensor data. In particular, we are interested in finding the heart rate average and the heart rate distribution (histogram) of this community.

To get an accurate estimation of the average heart rate, we set the maximum error to be 3, which gives the minimum privacy budget $\epsilon_a = 5$ using the analysis of Fig. 12.3. We then publish the data collection task {aggregator = AVG; sensor type = heart rate; $n = 20$; $\epsilon_a = 5$} to collect the data for computing community average.

To provide the risk assessment to users, the average heart rate reconstruction errors calculated using ANEs shown in Table 12.1 are shown to the users to help them understand the private data leakage with different ϵ. Figure 12.11 summarizes the ϵ_u specified by 20 participants in this study. All of the users select $\epsilon_u > 5$ and more than half of the participants select $\epsilon_u > 15$. Since the ϵ_a set in the data

Fig. 12.12 The AVG error
with ϵ_a set to 5 equals to 2.77
after data aggregation

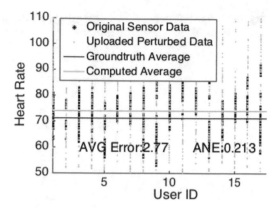

collection task is 5, all of the users participate in the data collection task. The Salus
algorithm is then used to perturb the private heart rate data in P^3 with $\epsilon_a = 5$ to
guarantee the privacy of users while ensuring the application's utility. To obtain the
ground truth, we also collect the raw sensor data in the case studies.

After collecting the perturbed data from users, the data is used as input to the data
aggregator to aggregate the community average. Figure 12.12 shows the uploaded
heart rate data by 20 participants, we can see that the computed average is 74.29, and
the ground truth average is 71.52, resulting an error of 2.77. The error satisfies the
utility requirement of the application publisher since the expected error is 3 using
$\epsilon_a = 5$. This shows that the selected $\epsilon_a = 5$ ensures that the AVG error is less
than 3. To analyze the private data leakage in this process, we calculate the ANE for
all users and the average ANE is 0.213, which is consistent with the results shown
in Table 12.1 with $\epsilon_u = 5$, indicating that the degree of private data leakage is
controlled at the level acceptable by all participating users.

To compute the distribution of heart rate in this community, the HIST aggregator
is used. Since the HIST error quantifies the difference between two normalized histograms, for this application a HIST error less than 0.2 (20% difference between two
histograms) provides a good estimation to the ground truth heart rate distribution.
Following the utility analysis shown in Fig. 12.4, we choose $\epsilon_a = 20$ to achieve
a small HIST error. The data collection task then becomes {aggregator = HIST;
sensor type = heart rate; $n = 20$; $\epsilon_a = 20$}. The privacy budgets ϵ_u set by the
users are the same as the previous task shown in Fig. 12.11. Therefore, 45% of the
users who set their privacy budget ϵ_u greater than 20 participate in this experiment.
Figure 12.13 shows the comparison between the ground truth histogram and the
aggregated histogram using the data perturbed by Salus algorithm with $\epsilon_a = 20$.
The HIST error between two histograms is 0.15, which is less than 0.2 required by
the application. We compute the ANE of all the uploaded data, the final average
ANE for all users is 0.075, which also achieves the required degree of protection for
$\epsilon_a = 20$.

Fig. 12.13 The HIST error
with ϵ_a set to 20

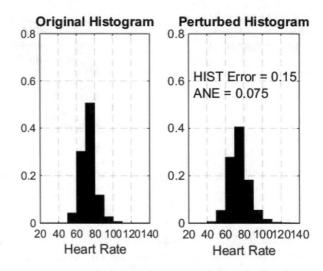

12.8.3.2   Collaborative Emotion Classification

Emotion classification plays an important role in elderly care. The authors in [36] demonstrates the feasibility to use heart rate, GSR, and skin temperatures sensor to classify users' emotion states. In this case study, we use Microsoft Band to collect the heart rate, GSR, and skin temperature from users to build classification models collaboratively. To demonstrate the effectiveness of P^3, we recruit the same 20 participants in this experiment. To induce stress safely into the participants, the Stroop Color-Word Interference Test [37] is conducted to collect the sensor data in stressful/non-stressful states.

Before publishing the data collection tasks, the utility analyzer first needs to collect the d_{avg} from all the users. In this study, the feature vectors contain three sensor readings: {heart rate, GSR, skin temperature}, and two classes are being classified: the non-stressful state and the stressful state. After collecting d_{avg}, the server computes the increased ℓ^2 ratio $\Delta d/d_{\text{avg}}$ with respect to ϵ as discussed in Sect. 12.6. Figure 12.14 shows the estimated ratio with different privacy budget ϵ_a. To ensure that the classification accuracy will not degrade significantly due to privacy protection, a ratio less than 0.5 is required as discussed previously. As shown in Fig. 12.14, when $\epsilon = 16$, $\Delta d/d_{\text{avg}}$ is about 0.25, and when $\epsilon = 8$, $\Delta d/d_{\text{avg}}$ increases to about 0.5. To demonstrate the classification utility changes, we publish two data collection tasks with $\epsilon_a = 16$ and $\epsilon_a = 8$ to measure the performance. In addition, we build two additional classifiers using the raw sensor data with no perturbation, and using $\epsilon_a = 1$ as comparisons.

The users are asked to specify their ϵ_u in the admission control module as their privacy requirements. Since heart rate is considered to be the most sensitive data among these three sensors, all of them adopt the same privacy setting shown in

Fig. 12.14 The predicted increased ℓ^2 ratio $\Delta d/d_{avg}$ with different ϵ

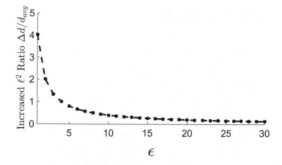

Fig. 12.15 The classification accuracy with different ϵ_a

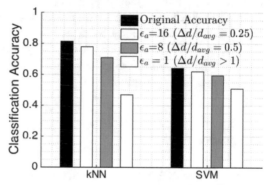

Fig. 12.11. Figure 12.15 shows the classification results for the collected data. We build two classifiers, kNN and SVM, using the uploaded data. The original emotion classification accuracy built with the unperturbed sensor data is 81.5% for kNN and 64.2% for SVM, respectively. From Fig. 12.15, we see that when ϵ is set to 8 (in which case $\Delta d/d_{avg} = 0.25$) or 16 (in which case $\Delta d/d_{avg} = 0.5$), the accuracy sacrifices are small and they remain similar to the original accuracy. This result indicates, as we estimated previously, that the classification accuracies are not substantially affected by the privacy protection when ϵ_a is greater than 8. On the other hand, when $\epsilon_a = 1$, $\Delta d/d_{avg}$ is greater than 1, and the accuracies of both classifiers quickly degrade. When $\epsilon_a = 8$, the final average ANE for all three sensors is 0.19, which is consistent with the results shown in Table 12.1. Since all participating users are required to have an ϵ_u greater than or equal to 8, this indicates that the users' data achieves their desired level of protection. Finally, it is worth noting that although there are only two classes here, it can be easily generalized to arbitrary number of classes by setting d_{avg} to be the average ℓ^2 distances between all different classes.

12.9   Conclusions

In this chapter, we study the privacy issues of mobile crowd sensing system. To support privacy-preserving MCS, we first propose the Salus algorithm, an ϵ-differentially private perturbation algorithm that is resilient against data reconstruction attacks and provides quantifiable utility. Next, to address the practical issues, we further quantify the privacy risks and the application utilities in terms of the privacy budget ϵ used in Salus. Measurement results and case studies show that for different types of sensors and different aggregators (AVG, HIST, CLS), the privacy risks can be explicitly quantified and the utility can be accurately estimated. In light of these benefits gained, we finally design and implement P^3, an application framework that successfully balances both the user and application requirements for practical privacy-preserving MCS. We believe that the tractability, generality, and the usability will make P^3 a promising framework to support future privacy-preserving MCS applications.

References

1. H. Ma, D. Zhao, P. Yuan, Opportunities in mobile crowd sensing. Commun. Mag. IEEE **52**, 29–35 (2014)
2. X. Hao, L. Xu, N.D. Lane, X. Liu, T. Moscibroda, Density-aware compressive crowdsensing, in *2017 16th ACM/IEEE International Conference on Information Processing in Sensor Networks (IPSN)*(ACM/IEEE, New York/Piscataway, 2017), pp. 29–39
3. A. ResearchKit. https://www.apple.com/researchkit/
4. S. Li, C. Xu, J. Wang, Y. Zhang, R.E. Howard, P. Zhang, Z. Jia, A. Bonde, Monitoring a person's heart rate and respiratory rate on a shared bed using geophones, in *Proceedings of the 15th ACM Conference on Embedded Network Sensor Systems SenSys* (ACM, New York, 2017)
5. B. Liu, Y. Jiang, F. Sha, R. Govindan, Cloud-enabled privacy-preserving collaborative learning for mobile sensing, in *Proceedings of the 10th ACM Conference on Embedded Network Sensor Systems SenSys* (ACM, New York, 2012)
6. J. Sun, C.K. Reddy, Big data analytics for healthcare, in *Special Interest Group on Knowledge Discovery and Data Mining* (ACM, New York, 2013)
7. S. Eberz, A. Patané, N. Paoletti, M. Kwiatkowska, M. Roeschlin, I. Martinovic, Broken hearted: How to attack ECG biometrics, in *NDSS Symposium* (2017)
8. N.E. Bordenabe, K. Chatzikokolakis, C. Palamidessi, Optimal Geo-indistinguishable mechanisms for location privacy. In *Proceedings of the 2014 ACM SIGSAC Conference on Computer and Communications Security* (ACM, New York, 2014)
9. R.K. Ganti, N. Pham, Y.-E. Tsai, T.F. Abdelzaher, PoolView: Stream privacy for grassroots participatory sensing. In *Proceedings of the 6th ACM Conference on Embedded Network Sensor Systems* (ACM, New York, 2008)
10. Y. Shen, H. Wen, C. Luo, W. Xu, T. Zhang, W. Hu, D. Rus, GaitLock: Protect virtual and augmented reality headsets using gait. IEEE Trans. Dependable Secure Comput. **6**, 484–497 (2018)
11. C. Luo, H. Hong, M.C. Chan, J. Li, X. Zhang, Z. Ming, Mpiloc: self-calibrating multi-floor indoor localization exploiting participatory sensing. IEEE Trans. Mobile Comput. **17**(1), 141–154 (2018)

12. C. Luo, L. Cheng, M.C. Chan, Y. Gu, J. Li, Z. Ming, Pallas: self-bootstrapping fine-grained passive indoor localization using WiFi monitors. IEEE Trans. Mobile Comput. **16**(2), 466–481 (2017)
13. K.-P. Lin, M.-S. Chen, On the design and analysis of the privacy-preserving SVM classifier. IEEE Trans. Knowl. Data Eng. **23**, 1704–1717 (2011)
14. Y. Xiao, L. Xiong, Protecting locations with differential privacy under temporal correlations, in *Proceedings of the 22nd ACM SIGSAC Conference on Computer and Communications Security* (ACM, New York, 2015)
15. H. Jin, L. Su, H. Xiao, K. Nahrstedt, Inception: Incentivizing privacy-preserving data aggregation for mobile crowd sensing systems. In *Proceedings of the 17th ACM International Symposium on Mobile Ad Hoc Networking and Computing* (ACM, New York, 2016)
16. C. Dwork, A. Roth, The algorithmic foundations of differential privacy. Theor. Comput. Sci. **9**, 211–407 (2013)
17. H. To, G. Ghinita, C. Shahabi, A framework for protecting worker location privacy in spatial crowdsourcing. Proc. VLDB Endow. **7**, 919–930 (2014)
18. M. Fredrikson, E. Lantz, S. Jha, S. Lin, D. Page, T. Ristenpart, Privacy in pharmacogenetics: An end-to-end case study of personalized warfarin dosing, in *Proceedings of USENIX Security* (2014)
19. M. Hardt, K. Talwar, On the geometry of differential privacy, in *Proceedings of the Forty-Second ACM Symposium on Theory of Computing* (ACM, New York, 2010)
20. V. Rastogi, D. Suciu, S. Hong, The boundary between privacy and utility in data publishing, in *Proceedings of the 33rd International Conference on Very Large Data Bases VLDB Endowment* (2007)
21. T. Li, N. Li, On the tradeoff between privacy and utility in data publishing, in *Proceedings of the 15th ACM SIGKDD International Conference on Knowledge Discovery and Data Mining* (ACM, New York, 2009)
22. A. Ghosh, T. Roughgarden, M. Sundararajan, Universally utility-maximizing privacy mechanisms. SIAM J. Comput. **41**, 1673–1693 (2012)
23. R.A. Popa, C. Redfield, N. Zeldovich, H. Balakrishnan, CryptDB: Protecting confidentiality with encrypted query processing, in *Proceedings of the Twenty-Third ACM Symposium on Operating Systems Principles* (ACM, New York, 2011)
24. H. Shafagh, A. Hithnawi, A. Dröscher, S. Duquennoy, W. Hu, Talos: Encrypted query processing for the internet of things, in *Proceedings of the 13th ACM Conference on Embedded Networked Sensor Systems* (ACM, New York, 2015)
25. Z. Huang, W. Du, B. Chen, Deriving private information from randomized data, in *Proceedings of the 2005 ACM SIGMOD International Conference on Management of Data* (ACM, New York, 2005)
26. C. Dwork, Differential privacy, in *Encyclopedia of Cryptography and Security* (Springer, Berlin, 2011)
27. H. Kargupta, S. Datta, Q. Wang, K. Sivakumar, On the privacy preserving properties of random data perturbation techniques, in *Third IEEE International Conference on Data Mining* (IEEE, Piscataway, 2003)
28. J. Yuan, Y. Zheng, X. Xie, G. Sun, Driving with knowledge from the physical world, in *Proceedings of the 17th ACM SIGKDD International Conference on Knowledge Discovery and Data Mining* (ACM, New York, 2011)
29. R.K. Rana, C.T. Chou, S.S. Kanhere, N. Bulusu, W. Hu, Ear-phone: An end-to-end participatory urban noise mapping system. In *Proceedings of the 9th ACM/IEEE International Conference on Information Processing in Sensor Networks* (IEEE/ACM, Piscataway/New York, 2010)
30. C. Luo, M.C. Chan, Socialweaver: Collaborative inference of human conversation networks using smartphones, in *Proceedings of the 11th ACM Conference on Embedded Networked Sensor Systems* (ACM, New York, 2013)
31. T.-H. Hubert Chan, E. Shi, D. Song, Private and continual release of statistics. ACM Trans. Inf. Syst. Security **14**, 1–24 (2011)

32. M. Marshall, Iris data set, in *UCI Machine Learning Repository* (1988)
33. A. Dhall, R. Bhatt, Skin segmentation dataset, in *UCI Machine Learning Repository* (2012)
34. T. Hume, Balance scale data set, in *UCI Machine Learning Repository* (1994)
35. A. Sgorbissa, B. Bruno, F. Mastrogiovanni, Adl recognition data set, in *UCI Machine Learning Repository* (2014)
36. G.E. Sakr, I.H. Elhajj, H.A.-S. Huijer, Support vector machines to define and detect agitation transition. IEEE Trans. Affect. Comput. **1**, 98–108 (2010)
37. J.R. Stroop, Studies of interference in serial verbal reactions. J. Exp. Psychol. **18**, 643–662 (1935)

Chapter 13
Differentially Private and Budget Limited Bandit Learning over Matroids

13.1 Introduction

The Multi-Armed Bandit (MAB) problem is a classical problem in machine learning, and can be applied to many networking problems such as adaptive routing, jamming defence and quality control in crowdsourcing [1, 2]. In the basic model of MAB, there are a set of k slot machines (or called "arms") and a gambler (or called "player"). Whenever an arm is pulled, it provides a random reward sampled from an unknown distribution specific to that arm. The problem of the player is to select exactly one arm to pull at each time step, such that the expected sum of rewards that they receive for a given time period is maximized. The performance of the player is usually measured by the "regret", i.e., the expected difference of the total reward gained by the player and the reward gained by an omniscient genie. To achieve a low regret, the key challenge faced by the player is to balance the tradeoff between "exploration" and "exploitation" at each time step, where exploration refers to pulling less-known arms to obtain more statistics about them, and exploitation means pulling the most rewarding arm according to the current empirical knowledge about all arms. Indeed, this problem is encountered in many real applications. For example, in an adaptive routing scenario [3], a router is faced with a set of routing paths with unknown delays, and has to handle the exploration vs. exploitation tradeoff to select the routing path with the minimum delay for the routing requests arriving online.

In this chapter, we consider a new MAB model that extends the basic model of MAB on several important aspects. The first extension is that we introduce a union of matroid constraints into arm-pulling, instead of forbidding the player to pull exactly one arm at each time step. Roughly speaking, a pair (E, M) is called a matroid if and only if: (1) E is a finite set (called the ground set), (2) M is a collection of subsets of E (called the independent sets), and (3) M satisfies

A. X. Liu, R. Li, *Algorithms for Data and Computation Privacy*, https://doi.org/10.1007/978-3-030-58896-0_13

some pre-defined axioms.[1] Indeed, the concept of matroid plays a fundamental role in combinatorics. It can be used as the "meta structure" to model numerous optimization problems in various areas such as network theory, geometry, topology, and coding theory [4–8], as the feasible solutions of many optimization problems (e.g., the minimum spanning tree problem) are essentially the independent sets of a single matroid, which is a special case of a union of matroid constraints as studied in this chapter. Hence, the algorithms designed for a union of matroids can be directly applied to numerous applications. In our problem, we model the set of all arms as the ground set E, and we allow the player to pull the arms in an independent set of any matroid defined on the ground set E at each step. By this extension, we are able to handle more complex problems appeared in many applications such as online advertising, online recommendation, wireless routing, and dynamic channel allocation, where the action unit taken at each time is a combinatorial object.

The second extension is that, in our model pulling an arm incurs a cost, and the player has a limited budget for pulling arms. More specifically, we assume that pulling any arm incurs a random cost which is sampled from an unknown distribution specific to that arm, and the pulling continues until the given budget B is used up. This extension is based on the observation that the player usually has to consume substantial resources for pulling the arms in many applications. Under this consideration, our problem turns into a Budgeted MAB (BMAB) problem [9–12].

The third extension is that we require the arm-pulling policy to achieve ϵ-differential privacy. In practice, the arms' costs and rewards can be important private information whose leakage causes undesirable losses. In this work, we address this problem based on the concept of Differential Privacy (DP) [13]. Roughly speaking, DP ensures that any change of a single input entity does not make "significant" changes on the output, hence the individual entity's privacy is protected. In our model, this implies that any single change on the rewards/costs of an arm pulled in the history should not result in a significant change on the arm-selection at next time.

In summary, our problem is to design an MAB algorithm that is differentially private, budget limited, and the arms pulled at each time step satisfy a union of matroid constraints. The goal is to minimize the regret. To the best of our knowledge, this problem has never been studied.

Due to the wide applications of matroids, our problem has many potential applications. For example, in a network backbone construction problem [7], an Internet Service Provider (ISP) may need to learn minimum spanning trees for constructing a network backbone under a stochastic environment, where the total construction cost is constrained by the ISP's budget. It turns out that this problem can be formulated as a graphic matroid bandit with budget constraint. Another application example is the online pricing problem for crowdsourcing, where the posted prices for multiple tasks should be selected for each crowdsourcing worker

---

[1] We will clarify these axioms in Sect. 13.3.1.

to incentivize their participation, and the total reward/payment should not exceed a predefined budget. Moreover, the workers may require to protect the privacy of their private costs for participation. This problem can be formulated as a partition matroid bandit with budget constraint. We will explain this example in more details in Sect. 13.3.3.

13.1.1 Limitations of Prior Art

Most previous work on MAB has assumed that pulling the arms incurs no costs, hence the player can pull the arms as many times as they wish (e.g., [14]). Recently, some studies consider the BMAB model, but most of them have forced the player to obey the rule of $A_t \in S_1$ [9, 10, 12, 15–18], and only one proposal [11] has relaxed this rule to $A_t \in S_L (L \geq 1)$, where A_t denotes the set of arms pulled at any time step t, S_i denotes the set $\{S | S \subseteq E \wedge |S| = i\}$ for any $1 \leq i \leq |E|$, and E denotes the set of all arms. Indeed, these arm-pulling constraints are just special cases of our matroid constraints, as we will show in Sect. 13.3.1. However, a lot of practical problems cannot be modeled by restricting $A_t \in S_L$, such as the advertising application described above. Moreover, even under the simplest setting of $A_t \in S_1$, existing BMAB studies only achieve asymptotic regret bounds under the case of stochastic arm-pulling costs with unknown expectations [10–12], i.e., their regret bounds are logarithmic to the budget B only when B is sufficiently large. It is difficult to adapt existing BMAB algorithms to handle matroid constraints as the regret bounds of existing BMAB algorithms designed for $A_t \in S_1$ are all linear with respect to k, which is the number of arms. If we use these algorithms to solve our problem in a brute-force manner, i.e., regarding each independent set in the matroid as a "super arm", we will get an exponential searching space for finding the optimal super arm, hence both of the time complexity and the regret bound will be exponential with respect to k. The only BMAB study [11] that considers multiple pulls (they allow $A_t \in S_L$) has used a time-consuming LP-solving technique specifically designed for their problem. Their approach did not exploit any properties of matroids, hence cannot be adapted to the case of general matroid constraints on arm-pulling.

None of existing BMAB algorithms has taken the privacy issue into account. Clearly, introducing DP into BMAB would inevitably make the problem harder, as the extra noises (or randomness) introduced to guarantee DP makes it harder to identify the optimal arms that should be selected by an omniscient genie.

13.1.2 Proposed Approach

In this work, we first leverage the martingale theory to study the Bayesian setting where the cost/reward distributions of all arms are known in advance, which reveals that an arm-pulling policy leading to low regret is always pulling the "optimal super arm" in the matroid which has the maximal ratio of the total expected reward with respect to the total expected cost. Based on this observation, we try to identify the optimal super arm at each time step using the empirical knowledge learned about the arms, but this leads to a complex non-linear 0–1 optimization problem with an exponential number of feasible solutions. To address this challenge, we propose a divide-and-conquer approach to reduce the searching complexity. More specifically, we first divide the searching space into k subspaces, where the ith subspace consists of a group of super arms containing arm i. Indeed, each arm i serves as a "sentinel arm" of the ith subspace, and we use the empirical knowledge on the sentinel arm i as the "sketched" knowledge on the other arms lies in the ith subspace. With this method, we further propose a parametric searching process to find the best super arm in each subspace, and the parametric searching process achieves polynomial time complexity by exploiting the special properties of the matroids. Finally, we select the best one among the best super arms found in all sub-spaces, hence we get the optimal super arm in polynomial time complexity.

To handle the privacy issue, we use a hybrid mechanism [19] to generate noisy means of the pulled arms, then design a specific additive "exploration factor" to rectify the deviation caused by the Laplace noises brought by the hybrid mechanism. The noisy means of the arms together with the exploration factors are used as the empirical knowledge about the arms, which is further used to search the optimal super arm by the processes described above. By the exploration factors and the optimality of our searching process, we prove that the super arm selected at each time step gradually converges to the real optimal one (in a probabilistic sense), hence get a uniform logarithmic regret bound. Finally, as the hybrid mechanism achieves differential privacy and DP is immune to post-processing [13], we prove that our algorithm also achieves differential privacy.

13.1.3   Advantages over Prior Art

Our approach advances the state of the art in four key aspects.

First, we adopt a more general BMAB model than that in prior studies, as we consider both general matroid constraints and differential privacy in arm-pulling. Our model subsumes the arm-pulling models of $A_t \in \mathcal{S}_L$ in previous studies [9–12, 17, 18] as our special cases, hence it has broader applications.

Second, our algorithm achieves a uniform $O(\log(\frac{B}{\epsilon} \log \frac{B}{\epsilon}))$ regret bound and ϵ-differential privacy simultaneously, and achieves a uniform $O(\log B)$ regret bound (for any $B > 0$) when the privacy concern is absent. This implies that we improve the theoretical bounds of prior BMAB algorithms under the case of random arm-pulling costs with unknown expectations, as prior studies only propose asymptotic logarithmic regret bounds with respect to B (e.g., [10–12]).

Third, experimental results show that our algorithm has significantly better regret performance compared with the best prior algorithms [11, 20] under their settings of $A_t \in S_L$.

Fourth, the processing speed of our algorithm is more than 20 times faster than the closest BMAB algorithm [11] in performance evaluation, as [11] use a time-consuming LP-solving approach while our algorithm is purely combinatorial. Therefore, our algorithm scales better to the case of large number of arms.

The rest of our chapter proceeds as follows. We review the related work in Sect. 13.2 and clarify our problem statement in Sect. 13.3. We provide some bounds on the optimal solution, which are used in our algorithm design and regret analysis in Sects. 13.5 and 13.6. The experimental results are shown in Sect. 13.7 before we conclude this chapter in Sect. 13.8.

13.2   Related Work

We review several lines of related work in the following:

13.2.1   MAB Algorithms Without Budgets

Traditional MAB algorithms only work under the Single-Pull (SP) setting of $A_t \in S_1$. When Multiple-Pulls (MP) is allowed (i.e., more than one arm can be pulled at each time step), [21] have considered the case that exactly L out of k arms can be pulled at each time (i.e., $A_t \in S_L$), and [1, 22–27] have considered the more general combinatorial bandit problem. More specifically, [1] have proposed an algorithm with the regret bound of $O\left(\frac{m^3 k \Xi_{max}}{\Xi_{min}^2} \log(T)\right)$, where $m \leq k$ is the maximum number of arms contained in a "super arm" and Ξ_{min} is the difference between the expected reward of the best super arm and that of the second-best super arm. Chen et al. [23] have provided an improved regret bound of $O\left(\frac{m^2 k}{\Xi_{min}} \log(T)\right)$, while [24] and [27] have further improved Chen et al.'s regret bound to $O\left(\frac{mk}{\Xi_{min}} \log(T)\right)$ and $O\left(\frac{\sqrt{mk}}{\Xi_{min}} \log(T)\right)$, respectively. Wang and Chen [25] and Chen et al. [26] have extended the combinatorial bandit model to include more general reward functions and probabilistically triggered arms. Wen et al. [28], Talebi et al. [29], and Vaswani et al. [30] have designed combinatorial bandit algorithms for the shortest-path routing and influence maximization problems.

Very recently, the pioneer work in [6, 7] and [8] has considered a single matroid basis constraint in MAB algorithm design, and proposed some nice regret bounds. More specifically, [7] have provided a matroid bandit algorithm with the regret bound of $O(\frac{k-m}{\Xi_{min}} \log T)$. Talebi and Proutiere [6] have also achieved the

$O(\frac{k-m}{\Xi_{\min}} \log T)$ regret bound, but with a strictly smaller constant in $O(\cdot)$. Chen et al. [8] aim to identify a best matroid basis using as few samples as possible, which is a totally different goal from regret minimization. However, all these studies have not considered the arm-pulling costs and the budget constraint, and the arms selected in each round under their model must be a matroid basis. Moreover, their model does not consider random stopping times. A close look reveals that the regret analysis in [7] and [6] is based on a simple arm-selection policy, i.e., greedily selecting the arms according to the non-increasing order of the (estimated) expected rewards of each arm. Unfortunately, such a simple arm-pulling policy (and the corresponding regret analysis) cannot be applied to our problem, as we need to select the arms by holistically considering multiple aspects including the random rewards, random costs and the budget constraint. In summary, the methods proposed in [7, 8] and [6] are not suitable for BMAB.

13.2.2   MAB Algorithms with Budgets

Existing BMAB algorithms have adopted different assumptions on the arm-pulling costs, which can be classified as follows: (1) Static Costs (SC) vs. Random Costs (RC): The SC model denotes the case that the arm-pulling costs are static and known, while RC denotes the setting of random arm-pulling costs. (2) Partial Knowledge (PK) vs. No Knowledge (NK): In the PK setting, there is a known positive lower bound on the expectations of the arm-pulling costs, while there is no such knowledge under the NK setting.

Tran-Thanh et al. [9, 17] have investigated the SP+SC setting and presented a uniform regret bound of $O(\log B)$. Ding et al. [18] have studied the RC+SP case both under NK and PK. However, [12] prove that the algorithms proposed in [18] have linear regrets of $O(B)$, and they propose a uniform regret bound of $O(\log B)$ for RC+PK and an asymptotic regret bound of $O(\log^{1+\varepsilon} B)$ for RC+NK where $\varepsilon > 0$. Nevertheless, [12] have left it as an open problem deriving a uniform logarithmic regret bound under the RC+NK setting. Xia et al. [10] have applied Thompson sampling to BMAB under the SP+RC+NK setting and claimed a regret bound of $O(\log B)$ for $B \in \mathbb{N}$, but it is not clear if this bound holds for a general budget. Very recently, [11] have considered the case of MP+RC+NK and proposed a regret bound of $O(\log B + (B/\mu_{min}^c) \exp\{-\mu_{min}^c B/2\})$ (μ_{min}^c denotes the minimum expected cost of all arms), which asymptotically approaches $O(\log B)$. For clarity, we summarize the regret bounds of these related work in Table 13.1.

All of the BMAB studies listed above have assumed that the stopping time of the arm-pulling is fully controlled by a unique budget B, which is also adopted in this chapter. Besides, there exist some other studies which use different assumptions [15, 16, 31, 32]. More specifically, [15] and [16] assume a known stopping time T and propose distribution-free regret bounds of $\tilde{O}(\sqrt{T})$ (hiding multiplicative logarithmic terms) for their model. Combes et al. [31] have considered arm-pulling costs and

Table 13.1 The results of some BMAB algorithms. A_t denotes the set of arms pulled at any time t. The asymptotic and uniform regret bounds are denoted by O and $\mathcal{O}$, respectively. More specifically, $O(\log B)$ represents a regret bound which is logarithmic to any $B > 0$; $\mathcal{O}(\log B)$ represents a regret bound which is logarithmic to B only when B is sufficiently large. The abbreviations "SC", "RC", "PK" and "NK" denote "static costs", "random costs", "partial knowledge" and "no knowledge", respectively.

| | | RC | | | |
	SC	PK	NK	Pulls	DP
Tran-Thanh et al. [9]	$O(\log B)$	–	–	$A_t \in S_1$	–
Flajolet and Jaillet [12]	–	$O(\log B)$	$O(\log^{1+\varepsilon} B)$	$A_t \in S_1$	–
Xia et al. [10]	–	–	$O(\log B)$	$A_t \in S_1$	–
Xia et al. [11]	–	–	$O(\log B)$	$A_t \in S_L$	–
This work	–	–	$O(\log B)$	$A_t \in \mathcal{I}$	$O\left(\frac{\log B}{\epsilon} \log\left(\frac{\log B}{\epsilon}\right)\right)$

adapted the KL-UCB algorithm [33] to their problem, but they assume that there is an independent budget constraint on each arm, instead of a holistic budget limit. Wu et al. [32] have considered a contextual bandit problem with budget and time constraints, where the player can observe some context information before playing arms. Due to the discrepancies on the problem models, it would be hard to adapt these work and their regret bounds to our case.

In summary, it can be seen that almost all of the above studies related to BMAB have only considered the single-pull setting [9, 10, 12, 15–18, 32], and none of them has studied the privacy issue.

13.2.3 Privacy-Aware Online Learning

Compared with the BMAB studies, the proposals on privacy-preserving online learning are relatively few. Jain et al. [34] have considered the differentially private online learning problem in the full information setting. Thakurta and Smith [35] have studied the differentially private adversarial bandit problem. Very recently, [36] have presented a private MAB algorithm under the stochastic bandit setting with a regret bound of $O(\frac{\log^2 T}{\epsilon^2})$, and [20] have improved this bound to $O(\log T + \epsilon^{-1})$. However, it is noted that none of these work has considered multiple-pulls or the budget constraint on arm-pulling.

13.3 Problem Statement

In this section, we first introduce the concepts on matroids, then propose the formal definition on our problem. We also give an application example of our problem.

13.3.1 Matroids

A matroid is a structure that abstracts and generalizes the notion of linear independence in vector spaces. The formal definition of matroid is given in Definition 13.1:

Definition 13.1 (Matroid [4, 37]) Let E be a finite set (called the ground set) and $\mathcal{M}$ be a family of subsets of E (called the independent sets). The pair $(E, \mathcal{M})$ is called a matroid if $\emptyset \in \mathcal{M}$ and the following two axioms are satisfied:

1. $\forall G \in \mathcal{M}; H \subseteq G \Rightarrow H \in \mathcal{M}$ (called the hereditary property).
2. $\forall H, G \in \mathcal{M}; |H| < |G| \Rightarrow \exists x \in G \backslash H; H \cup \{x\} \in \mathcal{M}$ (called the exchange property).

Besides, any $G \in \mathcal{M}$ is called a basis of the matroid $(E, \mathcal{M})$ iff $\{J | G \subset J \wedge J \in \mathcal{M}\} = \emptyset$. The set of all bases of $(E, \mathcal{M})$ is denoted by $\mathcal{B}(\mathcal{M})$. Note that all bases have the same cardinality. The cardinality of any basis is called the rank of the matroid $(E, \mathcal{M})$.

There are numerous special matroid structures that satisfy Definition 13.1, such as uniform matroid, partition matroid, graphic matroid and transversal matroid [4]. Please refer to the online supplement for the definitions of these matroid structures.

The concept of Matroid is fundamental in combinatorial optimization, as it has many important applications [4]. For example, in a graphic matroid built upon a connected undirected graph G, the set of all bases is exactly the set of all spanning trees in G.

Recall that the previous BMAB studies have only considered the case of $A_t \in \mathcal{S}_L(L \geq 1)$. Using Definition 13.3, we can verify that $\mathcal{S}_L$ is exactly the set of all bases in a uniform matroid. However, previous BMAB studies lack generality as they cannot handle any other matroid constraints.

13.3.2 DP-Aware BMAB Over Matroids

We assume that there are a budget B and a set of k arms. Any arm $i \in [k] \triangleq \{1, \cdots, k\}$ is associated with a random reward $\hat{v}_{i,t}$ and a random cost $\hat{c}_{i,t}$ for any time step (or called "round") $t \in \mathbb{N}$. We assume that $\hat{c}_{i,1}, \hat{c}_{i,2}, \cdots$ (or $\hat{v}_{i,1}, \hat{v}_{i,2}, \cdots$) are independent and identically distributed according to some unknown distribution with the support $[0, 1]$. We use c_i and v_i to denote $\mathbb{E}\{\hat{c}_{i,t}\}$ and $\mathbb{E}\{\hat{v}_{i,t}\}$, respectively, where $v_i, c_i > 0$. When a set of arms $A_t \subseteq [k]$ is pulled at time t, the player observes the values in $\{\hat{v}_{i,t}, \hat{c}_{i,t} | i \in A_t\}$, receives a reward $\hat{V}(A_t) = \sum_{i \in A_t} r_i \hat{v}_{i,t}$ and pays a cost $\hat{C}(A_t) = \sum_{i \in A_t} s_i \hat{c}_{i,t}$, where $r_i, s_i > 0$ are predefined coefficients for any arm $i \in [k]$. Without loss of generality, we assume $c_1 \leq c_2 \cdots \leq c_k$ and we denote $\min_{i \in [k]} s_i c_i$ by μ.

We generalize the models in previous BMAB studies by considering a union of matroid constraints (or matroid basis constraints) for arm-pulling. More specifically, we assume that there are $\hbar$ matroids defined on the set of arms, which are denoted by $([k], \mathcal{I}_1), ([k], \mathcal{I}_2), \cdots, ([k], \mathcal{I}_\hbar)$. Let $\mathcal{I} = \bigcup_{j \in [\hbar]} \bar{\mathcal{I}}_j \backslash \{\emptyset\}$ where $\bar{\mathcal{I}}_j$ either equals $\mathcal{I}_j$ or equals $\mathcal{B}(\mathcal{I}_j)$. The player is allowed to select a set of arms $A_t \in \mathcal{I}$ to pull at each round t under the budget B.

At each round t, an *arm-pulling policy* $\mathcal{P}$ selects $A_t^{\mathcal{P}} \in \mathcal{I}$ to pull depending on the arms pulled in all previous rounds and their observed costs and rewards. Let $N^{\mathcal{P}} = \min\{t | \sum_{j=1}^{t} \hat{C}(A_j^{\mathcal{P}}) > B\}$. The total expected reward of policy $\mathcal{P}$ is defined as $TR(\mathcal{P}) = \mathbb{E}\left\{\sum_{t=1}^{N^{\mathcal{P}}-1} \hat{V}(A_t^{\mathcal{P}})\right\}$, where the expectation is taken with respect to the random generation of the arms' costs/rewards and the internal randomization of $\mathcal{P}$. Let $\mathcal{P}^*$ be an arm-pulling policy such that $TR(\mathcal{P}^*)$ is maximized. The regret of any arm-pulling policy $\mathcal{P}$ is defined as $\text{Reg}(\mathcal{P}) = TR(\mathcal{P}^*) - TR(\mathcal{P})$.

The concept of DP was first proposed in [13]. Intuitively, any algorithm satisfies DP if its output is not affected "too much" (in distribution) when there is only one single perturbation in its input data. In our problem, the input data for any arm-pulling policy $\mathcal{P}$ is the arms' rewards and costs in all time slots, which can be denoted by an infinite multiset $\mathcal{D} = \{\hat{v}_{i,t}, \hat{c}_{i,t} | i \in [k] \wedge t \in \mathbb{Z}^+\}$; and the output is the set $\mathcal{A}^{\mathcal{P}}$ of actions taken by $\mathcal{P}$, i.e., $\mathcal{A}^{\mathcal{P}} = \{A_1^{\mathcal{P}}, A_2^{\mathcal{P}}, \cdots, A_{N^{\mathcal{P}}}^{\mathcal{P}}\}$. Let $\Sigma_{\mathcal{P}}$ denote the set of all possible outputs of $\mathcal{P}$ (i.e., the range of $\mathcal{P}$). We call $(\mathcal{D}, \mathcal{D}')$ a neighboring pair if $\mathcal{D}'$ is a multiset that differs from $\mathcal{D}$ only in one data element (e.g., $\mathcal{D}$ and $\mathcal{D}'$ only differ in the value of $\hat{v}_{3,5}$). An ϵ-differentially private arm-pulling policy can be defined as follows:

Definition 13.2 (ϵ-Differentially Private Arm-Pulling Policy) Given $\epsilon \in [0, 1]$, an arm-pulling policy $\mathcal{P}$ satisfies ϵ-differential privacy if $\mathbb{P}\{\mathcal{A}^{\mathcal{P}} \in \Sigma' | \mathcal{D}\} \leq \exp(\epsilon)\mathbb{P}\{\mathcal{A}^{\mathcal{P}} \in \Sigma' | \mathcal{D}'\}$ holds for any neighboring pair $(\mathcal{D}, \mathcal{D}')$ and any $\Sigma' \subseteq \Sigma_{\mathcal{P}}$.

Based on the above definitions, our goal is to seek an ϵ-differentially private arm-pulling policy $\mathcal{P}$ such that $\text{Reg}(\mathcal{P})$ is minimized.

For convenience, we define $C(S) = \sum_{i \in S} s_i c_i$ and $V(S) = \sum_{i \in S} r_i v_i$ ($\forall S \subseteq [k]$). Throughout the chapter, we use bold letters to denote vectors. For example, the symbol $\hat{\mathbf{c}}_t$ denotes the vector $\langle \hat{c}_{1,t} \cdots \hat{c}_{k,t} \rangle$. When the arm-pulling policy $\mathcal{P}$ is clear from context, we will use A_t and N to denote $A_t^{\mathcal{P}}$ and $N^{\mathcal{P}}$, respectively.

13.3.3 An Example in Crowdsourcing

To help the readers understand our problem formulation, we describe an application of our model in this section, which is about a dynamic pricing problem in crowdsourcing.

Suppose that a crowdsourcing task owner has b kinds of tasks $\mathcal{T} = \{\mathcal{T}_1, \mathcal{T}_2, \cdots, \mathcal{T}_b\}$ to be crowdsourced, and there is a group of crowdsourcing workers $U_1, U_2, \cdots, U_m$ who arrive sequentially in an arbitrary order.[2] We assume that completing each task in $\mathcal{T}_i (\forall i \in [b])$ brings the task owner a revenue of e_i, and each user $U_n (n \in [m])$ holds a random private cost $o_{i,n}$ for performing a task in any $\mathcal{T}_i \in \mathcal{T}$, which is drawn independently from an unknown distribution characterized by the c.d.f. F_i. To incentivize the users' participation, the task owner needs to select a set $G_n \subseteq E = [b] \times \mathcal{L}$ of take-it-or-leave-it prices and post them to any user U_n, where $\mathcal{L} = \{\ell_1, \cdots, \ell_q\}$ is a candidate set of prices for paying the users. More specifically, any element $(i, \ell_j) \in G_n$ indicates that user U_n would get a payment ℓ_j if she/he performs a task in $\mathcal{T}_i$. To avoid ambiguous pricing, G_n should satisfy $G_n \in \mathcal{B}(\mathcal{M}) = \{S | (S \subseteq E) \wedge (\forall i \in [b] : |S \cap E_i| = 1)\}$, where $\forall i \in [b] : E_i = \{(i, \ell_j) | \ell_j \in \mathcal{L}\}$. Note that this is exactly a matroid basis constraint, i.e., G_n must be a basis of the partition matroid $(E, \mathcal{M})$ where $\mathcal{M} = \{S | (S \subseteq E) \wedge (\forall i \in [b] : |S \cap E_i| \leq 1)\}$.

If the user U_n accepts any price $(i, \ell_j) \in G_n$ (i.e., $o_{i,n} \leq \ell_j$), she/he will perform a task in $\mathcal{T}_i$ assigned by the task owner, and the task owner would get a revenue of e_i under a cost/payment of ℓ_j. Note that the cost and revenue of the task owner are both random as $o_{i,n}$ is random. Suppose that the task owner wants to maximize her/his revenue under a budget B for the total payment. This is exactly a BMAB problem under a matroid basis constraint, where each posted price $(i, \ell_j) \in E$ can be considered as an arm in BMAB. Finally, as the workers may care about the privacy on their costs of performing tasks [39], the prices selected for U_n (i.e., G_n) should not leak the information about the costs of the users $U_1, \cdots, U_{n-1}$ under differential privacy. It can be seen that this problem is an instance of the DP-aware BMAB problem formulated in Sect. 13.3.2.

13.4   Bounding the Optimal Policy

In this section, we will give an upper bound on $TR(\mathcal{P}^*)$, under the assumption that the distributions of the arms' rewards/costs are known in advance. As a byproduct, we will also give an upper bound on the $N^{\mathcal{P}}$ of any given arm-pulling policy $\mathcal{P}$, which will be used in the regret analysis of our algorithm.

To get these bounds, we construct a martingale for any arm-pulling policy $\mathcal{P}$ as follows. Let $(\mathcal{F}_t)_{t \in \mathbb{N}}$ be the natural filtration generated by the revealed rewards and costs of the arms pulled by $\mathcal{P}$. So $N^{\mathcal{P}}$ is a stopping time with respect to $(\mathcal{F}_t)_{t \in \mathbb{N}}$. Actually, we can bound the expectation of $N^{\mathcal{P}}$ by using the Hoeffding's inequality (Lemma 13.12), which is shown in Lemma 13.1:

Lemma 13.1 *Let* $\gamma = \sum_{i \in [k]} s_i$. *For any arm-pulling policy* $\mathcal{P}$, *we have* $\mathbb{E}\{N^{\mathcal{P}}\} \leq$
$2 + \frac{\sqrt{2}B}{(\sqrt{2}-1)\mu} + \left(1 + \frac{\gamma^2}{\mu^2}\right) \exp\left\{-\frac{\mu^2}{\gamma^2}\right\}.$

---

[2]This crowdsourcing model follows the paradigm of some popular commercial crowdsourcing platforms, such as Amazon's Mechanical Turk [38].

Define $X_t = \hat{C}(A_t^{\mathcal{P}})$ for any $t \in [N^{\mathcal{P}}]$ and $X_t = 0$ for any $t \notin [N^{\mathcal{P}}]$. Define $Y_t = \sum_{j=1}^{t}(X_j - \mathbb{E}\{X_j\})$. Using Lemma 13.1 and the definition of martingales [40], we can get:

Lemma 13.2 *The random process* $Y_1, Y_2, \cdots$ *is a martingale with respect to the filtration* $(\mathcal{F}_t)_{t \in \mathbb{N}}$.

Proof of Lemma 13.2: Clearly, Y_t is $\mathcal{F}_t$-measurable for any t. Note that $\mathbb{E}\{Y_{t+1}| \mathcal{F}_t\} = Y_t + \mathbb{E}\{X_{t+1} - \mathbb{E}\{X_{t+1}\}\} = Y_t$. Besides, we have $\mathbb{E}\{|Y_t|\} \leq 2\gamma \mathbb{E}\{N^{\mathcal{P}}\} < \infty$ according to Lemma 13.1. So $Y_1, Y_2, \cdots$ is a martingale with respect to $(\mathcal{F}_t)_{t \in \mathbb{N}}$.

□

With Lemmas 13.1 and 13.2, we can use the optional stopping theorem (Lemma 13.13) to prove:

$$B + \gamma \geq \mathbb{E}\left\{\sum_{j=1}^{N^{\mathcal{P}}} X_j\right\} = \mathbb{E}\left\{\sum_{j=1}^{N^{\mathcal{P}}} \mathbb{E}\{X_j\}\right\} \geq \mu \mathbb{E}\{N^{\mathcal{P}}\} \qquad (13.1)$$

which immediately gives us a tighter bound on $\mathbb{E}\{N^{\mathcal{P}}\}$ shown in Lemma 13.3.

Lemma 13.3 $\mathbb{E}\{N^{\mathcal{P}}\} \leq (B + \gamma)/\mu$.

More importantly, Eq. (13.1) can be used to prove the following theorem:

Theorem 13.1 *Let* $\rho(S) = V(S)/C(S)$ *for any* $S \subseteq [k]$. *Let* $S^* = \arg\max_{S \in I} \rho(S)$. *We have* $TR(\mathcal{P}^*) \leq (B + \gamma)\rho^*$ *where* $\rho^* \triangleq \rho(S^*)$. *Moreover, the policy of always pulling* S^* *has an expected total reward of at least* $B\rho^* - V(S^*)$.

It can be seen that Theorem 13.1 actually suggests a greedy strategy to solve our problem, i.e., we can achieve a low regret by selecting a subset of arms in $[k]$ at each time which has the maximum ratio of total expected reward vs. total expected cost. In the sequel, we will apply this idea to our algorithms design.

13.5 Algorithm Design

In this section, we introduce an algorithm called OPBM to address our problem. OPBM follows the greedy strategy suggested by Theorem 13.1, i.e., it tries to pull S^* based on the empirical means of the played arms. However, the design of OPBM is non-trivial due to the following reasons. Firstly, we need to find a mechanism to guarantee the differential privacy in OPBM. Secondly, we need to find an efficient way to implement OPBM, as a naive enumeration approach for finding S^* leads to prohibitive time complexity. In the sequel, we will explain in detail how we overcome these hurdles in OPBM.

13.5.1 Ensuring Differential Privacy

Traditional MAB algorithms directly use the empirical means of the rewards/costs of the arms played in the history as the empirical knowledge about them, based on which the arms played in the next round are selected. However, this method compromises differential privacy. Therefore, we introduce the hybrid mechanism proposed in [19] to get "noisy" empirical means of the arms for our algorithm design. In the sequel, we briefly explain the hybrid mechanism.

The input of the hybrid mechanism is any data stream $\dashv_1, \dashv_2, \cdots$. The hybrid mechanism generates random numbers drawn from Laplace distributions (i.e., Laplace noises) and adds these Laplace noises into $Q(n) = \sum_{j=1}^{n} \dashv_j$ for any n, then publishes the result $\widetilde{Q}(n)$. It is proved that $\widetilde{Q}(n)$ guarantees ϵ-differential privacy. To optimize the utility of $\widetilde{Q}(n)$ (i.e., reduce the error of $\widetilde{Q}(n)$), the hybrid mechanism tries to reduce the number of Laplace noises added in $\widetilde{Q}(n)$ based on a binary tree, so $\widetilde{Q}(n)$ only contains a logarithmic number of Laplace noises with respect to n. Due to this reason, it has been shown that the hybrid mechanism has the following nice property:

Lemma 13.4 ([19, 20]) *For any $h \leq n^{-a}$ where $a > 0$, the total error of the hybrid mechanism for summing any n numbers $\dashv_1, \cdots, \dashv_n$ is bounded by $\frac{\sqrt{8}}{\epsilon} \ln \left(\frac{4}{h} \right) \ln n + \frac{\sqrt{8}}{\epsilon} \ln \left(\frac{4}{h} \right)$ with probability of at least $1 - h$.*

In OPBM, we use the observed rewards of any arm i as the input to the hybrid mechanism, hence get the noisy empirical mean of arm i's reward at any time step t (denoted by $\widetilde{v}_{i,t}$). Similarly, we also get the noisy empirical mean of arm i's cost at any time t (denoted by $\widetilde{c}_{i,t}$). That is, we will run two hybrid mechanisms for each arm to achieve differential privacy. We set $\widetilde{v}_{i,0} = \widetilde{c}_{i,0} = 0$, and set $\widetilde{v}_{i,t} = \widetilde{v}_{i,t-1}$, $\widetilde{c}_{i,t} = \widetilde{c}_{i,t-1}$ if arm i is not pulled at time t. As the hybrid mechanism achieves differential privacy by adding Laplace noises that could be negative, $\widetilde{v}_{i,t}$ and $\widetilde{c}_{i,t}$ also could take negative values, which impedes us from deriving an elegant regret bound of our algorithm. To address this problem, we define $\widetilde{v}'_{i,t} = \widetilde{v}_{i,t}$ when $\widetilde{v}_{i,t} \geq 0$, and define $\widetilde{v}'_{i,t} = 0$ otherwise. Similarly, we define $\widetilde{c}'_{i,t} = \widetilde{c}_{i,t}$ when $\widetilde{c}_{i,t} \geq 0$, and define $\widetilde{c}'_{i,t} = 0$ otherwise. Note that such a mapping does not affect the ϵ-differential privacy achieved by the hybrid mechanism, as differential privacy is immune to post-processing [13].

13.5.2 The OPBM Algorithm

Based on the hybrid mechanism, we propose the OPBM algorithm, as shown in Algorithm 3. The OPBM algorithm iterates until the leftover budget $B_t \triangleq B - \sum_{j=1}^{t} \hat{C}(A_j)$ is negative. At each time t, it first gets the noisy means through the hybrid mechanism, then tries to select $A_t = \arg \max_{S \in \mathcal{I}} \Upsilon(S, \widetilde{\mathbf{v}}'_{t-1}, \widetilde{\mathbf{c}}'_{t-1}, \boldsymbol{\theta}_{t-1})$,

$$\Upsilon(A_t, \widetilde{\mathbf{v}}'_{t-1}, \widetilde{\mathbf{c}}'_{t-1}, \boldsymbol{\theta}_{t-1}) = \frac{\sum_{i \in A_t} r_i \widetilde{v}'_{i,t-1}}{\sum_{i \in A_t} s_i \widetilde{c}'_{i,t-1}} + \frac{\left(\sum_{i \in A_t} r_i \theta_{i,t-1} + \frac{\varsigma \sum_{i \in A_t} s_i \theta_{i,t-1}}{\min_{i \in A_t} \max\{\widetilde{c}'_{i,t-1} - \theta_{i,t-1}, 0\}} \right)}{\sum_{i \in A_t} s_i \widetilde{c}'_{i,t-1}} \quad (13.2)$$

Fig. 13.1 The function for selecting A_t

Algorithm 3: The OPBM algorithm

Input: $B, k, \mathcal{I}, \mathbf{r}, \mathbf{s}, \epsilon \in [0, 1]$.
Output: The arms pulled at each time t, the stopping time N
1 Play each arm once and update the parameters; ;
2 **while** $B_{t-1} \geq 0$ **do**
3   Get the noisy means $\widetilde{\mathbf{v}}_{t-1}$ and $\widetilde{\mathbf{c}}_{t-1}$ from the hybrid mechanisms with ϵ differential privacy;
4      $A_t \leftarrow$ **Select**$(\widetilde{\mathbf{v}}'_{t-1}, \widetilde{\mathbf{c}}'_{t-1}, \boldsymbol{\theta}_{t-1}, \mathbf{r}, \mathbf{s}, \mathcal{I})$;
5   Play the arms in A_t and update the parameters in $\{n_{i,t} | i \in [k]\}$, where $n_{i,t}$ is the number of times that arm i has been played from time 1 to time t;
6      $B_t \leftarrow B_{t-1} - \hat{C}(A_t); t \leftarrow t + 1$
7 $N \leftarrow \min\{t | \sum_{j=1}^{t} \hat{C}(A_j) > B\}$;
8 **return** $(\langle A_1, \cdots, A_N \rangle, N)$

---

where the function Υ is clarified in Eq. (13.2) (Fig. 13.1). The parameter ς appeared in Eq. (13.2) is defined as a constant, i.e., $\varsigma \triangleq \frac{\max_{i \in [k]} r_i}{\min_{i \in [k]} s_i}$; and the parameter $\theta_{i,t-1}$ appeared in Eq. (13.2) is defined as follows:

$$\forall i, t : \theta_{i,t} \triangleq \lambda_{i,t} + \xi_{i,t}; \lambda_{i,t} \triangleq \sqrt{3 \ln t / (2 n_{i,t})}; \xi_{i,t} \triangleq \frac{\sqrt{8}}{n_{i,t} \epsilon} \ln \left(4 t^3 \right) (1 + \ln n_{i,t}).$$

The parameters $\theta_{i,t}, \xi_{i,t}$ and $\lambda_{i,t}$ listed above are designed based on the confidence bounds of the costs/rewards of the arms. Intuitively, the first additive factor in Eq. (13.2) (i.e., $\frac{\sum_{i \in A_t} r_i \widetilde{v}'_{i,t-1}}{\sum_{i \in A_t} s_i \widetilde{c}'_{i,t-1}}$) can be understood as an "exploitation factor", which implies that the current empirical knowledge of arms (i.e., $\widetilde{\mathbf{v}}_{t-1}, \widetilde{\mathbf{c}}_{t-1}$) is used to find S^*; and the second additive factor in Eq. (13.2) can be understood as an "exploration factor", which is designed to compensate for the estimation error introduced by using the noisy empirical means of the arms.

It can be seen that selecting A_t based on Eq. (13.2) involves solving a non-linear optimization problem under matroid constraints, which is not a standard fractional optimization problem considered by traditional optimization approaches [11, 41, 42]. Therefore, we design a novel algorithm (Algorithm 4) that can solve it optimally. Algorithm 4 is a purely combinatorial algorithm, hence it is more efficient than LP-based algorithms, as we will show in the performance evaluation section.

In Algorithm 4, we adopt a divide-and-conquer approach to find an element in any $\bar{\mathcal{I}}_w$ which maximizes the function Υ. More specifically, we first assign each arm i a pseudo index $f(i) \triangleq \max\{\widetilde{c}'_{i,t-1} - \theta_{i,t-1}, 0\}$ and sort all arms into $\{u_1, \cdots, u_k\}$

Algorithm 4: Select($\widetilde{\mathbf{v}}'_{t-1}, \widetilde{\mathbf{c}}'_{t-1}, \boldsymbol{\theta}_{t-1}, \mathbf{r}, \mathbf{s}, \mathcal{I}$)

---

1   $\mathcal{X} \leftarrow \emptyset$; Sort $[k]$ into $\{u_1, \cdots, u_k\}$ such that $\forall i \in [k-1] : f(u_i) \leq f(u_{i+1})$;

2   **for** $w = 1$ **to** $\hbar$ **do**

3   **for** $i = 1$ **to** k **do**

4   **if** $\{u_i\} \notin \mathcal{I}_w$ **then continue if** $f(u_i) = 0$ **then**

5           $\lfloor$ **return** *any basis in* $\mathcal{I}_w$ *that contains* u_i

6         $\iota_i \leftarrow \frac{\varsigma}{f(u_i)}$; $x_i \leftarrow 0$; $y_i \leftarrow \infty$;

7   **for** $l = 1$ **to** $k - i$ **do**

8           $\lfloor$ $p[l] = u_{i+l}$

9   **for** $l = k - i$ **to** 2 **do**

10   **for** $q = 1$ **to** $l - 1$ **do**

11             $e \leftarrow p[q]$; $h \leftarrow p[q+1]$;

12   **if** $\beta(e) = \beta(h)$ **then**

13               $\lfloor$ $g \leftarrow \arg\max_{j \in \{e,h\}} \varphi(j, \iota_i)$; ;

14   **else**

15               $\delta_i \leftarrow \frac{\varphi(e, \iota_i) - \varphi(h, \iota_i)}{\beta(e) - \beta(h)}$;

16   **if** $\delta_i \in (x_i, y_i)$ **then**

17                 $\langle D_i, z \rangle \leftarrow$ **Search**$(i, \iota_i, \delta_i, w, \mathbf{u})$;

18   **if** $D_i = \emptyset$ **then goto** line 3 **if** $z = 0$ **then**

19                   $\mathcal{X} \leftarrow \mathcal{X} \cup \{D_i\}$;;

20   **goto** line 3

21   **if** $z > 0$ **then** $x_i \leftarrow \delta_i$ **if** $z < 0$ **then** $y_i \leftarrow \delta_i$

22   **if** $\delta_i \geq y_i$ **then**

23                 $\lfloor$ $g \leftarrow \mathbf{1}\{\beta(e) > \beta(h)\} \cdot e + \mathbf{1}\{\beta(e) < \beta(h)\} \cdot h$

24   **if** $\delta_i \leq x_i$ **then**

25                 $\lfloor$ $g \leftarrow \mathbf{1}\{\beta(e) > \beta(h)\} \cdot h + \mathbf{1}\{\beta(e) < \beta(h)\} \cdot e$;

26   **if** $g \neq e$ **then** $p[q] \leftrightarrow p[q+1]$

27         $\mathcal{X} \leftarrow$ **PostSearch**$(i, \iota_i, w, x_i, y_i, u_i, \mathcal{X}, p[1 \ldots k-i])$

28 **return** $A_t \leftarrow \arg\max_{S \in \mathcal{X}} \Upsilon(S, \widetilde{v}'_{t-1}, \widetilde{c}'_{t-1}, \boldsymbol{\theta}_{t-1})$;

---

according to the non-decreasing order of their pseudo indexes (line 1), then partition the searching space $\bar{\mathcal{I}}_w (\forall i)$ into k subsets $K_{1,w}, \cdots, K_{k,w}$, where $K_{i,w} = \{S | (S \in \bar{\mathcal{I}}_w) \wedge (S \cap \{u_1, \cdots, u_i\} = \{u_i\})\}$. Based on this partition, we try to identify $D_i^* \in K_{i,w} (\forall i)$ such that $\delta_i^* \triangleq \sum_{j \in D_i^*} \varphi(j, \iota_i) / \sum_{j \in D_i^*} \beta(j)$ is maximized, where

$$\varphi(i, \iota_i) \triangleq r_i \widetilde{v}'_{i,t-1} + r_i \theta_{i,t-1} + \iota_i s_i \theta_{i,t-1}; \quad \iota_i \triangleq \varsigma / f(u_i); \quad \beta(i) \triangleq s_i \widetilde{c}'_{i,t-1}.$$

From Eq. (13.2), it would not be hard to see that $D_i^* = \arg\max_{S \in K_{i,w}} \Upsilon(S, \widetilde{v}'_{t-1}, \widetilde{c}'_{t-1}, \boldsymbol{\theta}_{t-1})$. Indeed, with this divide-and-conquer method, we can use the value of $f(u_i)$ as the "sketched" knowledge of the values in $\{f(u_j) | i \leq j \leq k\}$, and hence bypass the difficulty introduced by the "min max" denominator appeared in Eq. (13.2). Note that we also handle the special case of $f(u_i) = 0$ by pulling a matroid basis containing u_i (line 5), which implies that Algorithm 3 correctly finds A_t when the min max denominator appeared in Eq. (13.2) is 0.

Next, we explain how Algorithm 4 can find D_i^* optimally. Algorithm 4 maintains two variables x_i, y_i as the guesses of the lower and upper bounds of δ_i^*, respectively, and also maintains a variable δ_i as the guess of δ_i^*. Let $M(a) \triangleq \max\{\sum_{j \in S} \tau(a, j) | S \in K_{i,w}\}$ where $\tau(a, j) \triangleq \varphi(j, \iota_i) - a\beta(j) (\forall a \in \mathbb{R}, \forall j \in [k])$. It is not hard to see: $M(\delta_i) \geq 0 \Rightarrow \delta_i \leq \delta_i^*$, $M(\delta_i) \leq 0 \Rightarrow \delta_i \geq \delta_i^*$ and $M(\delta_i) = 0 \Leftrightarrow \delta_i = \delta_i^*$ as $M(\delta_i^*) = 0$. Based on this observation, Algorithm 4 tries to make the guesses (i.e., x_i, y_i and δ_i) more accurate by a parametric sorting process (lines 6–26). In the parametric sorting process, Algorithm 4 calls Algorithm 5 (line 17) to decide how to adjust the values of x_i, y_i, and Algorithm 5 actually tries to calculate $M(\delta_i)$ using a greedy searching process over $\bar{I}_w$. Once Algorithm 5 outputs $D_i = \arg\max_{S \in K_{i,w}} \sum_{j \in S} \tau(\delta_i, j)$ satisfying $\sum_{j \in D_i} \tau(\delta_i, j) = 0$, it implies $D_i = D_i^*$ due to the reason that $M(\delta_i) = 0 \Leftrightarrow \delta_i = \delta_i^*$. If this never happens in the parametric sorting process (i.e., D_i^* remains unfound), Algorithm 4 can still iteratively adjust the values of x_i, y_i, δ_i according to the outputs of Algorithm 5, and finally gets a refined $[x_i, y_i]$ satisfying $\delta_i^* \in [x_i, y_i]$ and a permutation $p[1], \cdots, p[k-i]$ of $u_{i+1}, \cdots, u_k$ satisfying $\forall a \in [x_i, y_i] : \tau(a, p[1]) \geq \cdots \geq \tau(a, p[k-i])$ when the parametric sorting process terminates. In that case, Algorithm 4 calls Algorithm 6 (line 27) to employ a second round greedy searching process similar to that in Algorithm 5 to identify D_i^* based on the rule of $M(\delta_i) = 0 \Leftrightarrow \delta_i = \delta_i^*$. Finally, after the D_i^*'s are found for each $u_i \in [k]$ (if it exists), we choose the one that maximizes the function Υ shown in Eq. (13.2) (line 28). More detailed explanations on Algorithm 4 can be found in the proofs of Lemma 13.5 and Theorem 13.2.

Algorithm 5: Search($i, \iota_i, \delta_i, w, \mathbf{u}$)

---

1 for $j = 1$ **to** k **do**
2 $\tau(\delta_i, j) = \varphi(j, \iota_i) - \delta_i \beta(j); \tau'(\delta_i, j) = \tau(\delta_i, j)$;
3   **if** $\bar{I}_w = \mathcal{B}(I_w)$ **then**
4 $\tau'(\delta_i, j) = \tau(\delta_i, j) + \sum_{l=1}^{k} |\tau(\delta_i, l)| + 1$;

5 Sort $[k] \backslash \{u_1, \cdots, u_i\}$ into $\{m_1, \cdots, m_{k-i}\}$ such that $\forall j \in [k-i-1]$: $\tau'(\delta_i, m_j) \geq \tau'(\delta_i, m_{j+1})$;
6 $D_i \leftarrow \{u_i\}$;
7 for $j = 1$ **to** $k - i$ **do**
8   **if** $D_i \cup \{m_j\} \in I_w \wedge \tau'(\delta_i, m_j) > 0$ **then**
9 $D_i \leftarrow D_i \cup \{m_j\}$

10 if $\bar{I}_w = \mathcal{B}(I_w) \wedge D_i \notin \mathcal{B}(I_w)$ **then** $D_i \leftarrow \emptyset$ **return** $\langle D_i, \sum_{j \in D_i} \tau(\delta_i, j) \rangle$

Lemma 13.5 *Let* $K_{i,w} = \{S | S \cap \{u_1, \cdots, u_i\} = \{u_i\} \wedge S \in \bar{I}_w\}$. *If* $K_{i,w} = \emptyset$, *then Algorithm 5 outputs* $D_i = \emptyset$. *Otherwise, Algorithm 5 outputs* $D_i = \arg\max_{S \in K_{i,w}} \sum_{j \in S} \tau(\delta_i, j)$.

Algorithm 6: PostSearch($i, \iota_i, w, x_i, y_i, u_i, \mathcal{X}, p[1 \ldots k - i]$)

---

1 $S_{-1} \leftarrow \emptyset; p[0] \leftarrow u_i$;

2   **for** $l = 0$ **to** $k - i$ **do**

3 $S_l \leftarrow S_{l-1} \cup \{p[l]\}$;

4   **if** $S_l \notin \mathcal{I}_w$ **then** $S_l \leftarrow S_{l-1}$ **else**

5 $\delta_i^l \leftarrow (\sum_{j \in S_l} \varphi(j, \iota_i))/(\sum_{j \in S_l} \beta(j))$;

6   **if** $\delta_i^l \in [x_i, y_i]$ **then** $\mathcal{X} \leftarrow \mathcal{X} \cup \{S_l\}$ **if** $\bar{\mathcal{I}}_w = \mathcal{B}(\mathcal{I}_w) \wedge S_l \notin \mathcal{B}(\mathcal{I}_w)$ **then** $\mathcal{X} \leftarrow \mathcal{X} \backslash \{S_l\}$

7   **return** $\mathcal{X}$

Proof If $K_{i,w} \neq \emptyset$, then there must exist D_i' which satisfies $D_i' \in \bar{\mathcal{I}}_w$ and $D_i' \cap \{u_1, \cdots, u_i\} = \{u_i\}$ and $\sum_{j \in D_i'} \tau'(\delta_i, j)$ is maximized. We assume $\forall j \in D_i' \backslash \{u_i\} : \tau'(\delta_i, j) > 0$ (because otherwise we can remove any $j \in D_i' \backslash \{u_i\}$ satisfying $\tau'(\delta_i, j) \leq 0$). In such a case, we can prove:

(i) $|D_i'| = |D_i|$:

     Clearly, D_i' can be written as $\{u_i, m_{a_1}, m_{a_2}, \cdots, m_{a_q}\}$ such that $\tau'(\delta_i, m_{a_1}) \geq \tau'(\delta_i, m_{a_2}) \geq \cdots \geq \tau'(\delta_i, m_{a_q}) > 0$ where $q = |D_i'| - 1$. According to Algorithm 5, D_i can also be written as $\{u_i, m_{b_1}, m_{b_2}, \cdots, m_{b_o}\}$ such that $\tau'(\delta_i, m_{b_1}) \geq \tau'(\delta_i, m_{b_2}) \geq \cdots \geq \tau'(\delta_i, m_{b_o}) > 0$ where $o = |D_i| - 1$. According to the exchange property of any matroid, we know that $|D_i'| \geq |D_i|$. If $|D_i'| > |D_i|$, then there must exist $m' \in D_i' \backslash D_i$ such that $D_i \cup \{m'\} \in \mathcal{I}$, which contradicts with the greedy strategy of Algorithm 5 (i.e., the for loop in lines 6–8), as m' should be in D_i. Therefore, we have $|D_i'| = |D_i|$.

(ii) $\sum_{j \in D_i'} \tau'(\delta_i, j) = \sum_{j \in D_i} \tau'(\delta_i, j)$:

     If $\sum_{j \in D_i'} \tau'(\delta_i, j) > \sum_{j \in D_i} \tau'(\delta_i, j)$, there must exist $l = \min\{j | j \in [q] \wedge \tau'(\delta_i, m_{a_j}) > \tau'(\delta_i, m_{b_j})\}$. Let $\bar{D}_i = \{u_i, m_{b_1}, m_{b_2}, \cdots, m_{b_{l-1}}\}$ and $\bar{D}_i' = \{u_i, m_{a_1}, m_{a_2}, \cdots, m_{a_l}\}$. Using the exchange property of any matroid, we know that there must exist $m_{a_p} \in \bar{D}_i' \backslash \bar{D}_i$ such that $\bar{D}_i \cup \{m_{a_p}\} \in \mathcal{I}$ and $\tau'(\delta_i, m_{a_p}) > \tau'(\delta_i, m_{b_l})$. Therefore, m_{a_p} should have been selected before m_{b_l} in the loop of lines 6–8 of Algorithm 5. This contradicts with the greedy strategy of Algorithm 5 again.

The above reasoning has proved (i) and (ii). In the case of $\bar{\mathcal{I}}_w = \mathcal{I}_w$, we have $\forall j \in [k] : \tau(\delta_i, j) = \tau'(\delta_i, j)$. Moreover, D_i' must exist, as $\{u_i\} \in \mathcal{I}_w$ (see line 4 of Algorithm 4). So Algorithm 5 returns the correct D_i.

In the case of $\bar{\mathcal{I}}_w = \mathcal{B}(\mathcal{I}_w)$, if $K_{i,w} \neq \emptyset$, then D_i' must exist and D_i' must be a basis (because $\forall j \in [k] : \tau'(\delta_i, j) > 0$). According to (i) which is proved above, if D_i is not a basis, we must know $Q = \emptyset$, so it is correct for us to return $D_i = \emptyset$. When D_i is a basis, suppose that there exists another basis D_i'' such that $\sum_{j \in D_i''} \tau(\delta_i, j) > \sum_{j \in D_i} \tau(\delta_i, j)$, we must have $\sum_{j \in D_i''} \tau'(\delta_i, j) > \sum_{j \in D_i} \tau'(\delta_i, j)$ as $|D_i''| = |D_i|$

and $\tau'(\delta_i, j) - \tau(\delta_i, j)$ is just a common constant (see line 4 of Algorithm 5); this contradicts with (ii). So it is correct to return D_i. □

Theorem 13.2 *Suppose that there is an independence oracle for the matroids considered by our algorithm. Algorithm 4 can correctly find an A_t that maximizes the function Υ shown in Eq. (13.2), and has the time complexity of $O(k^4)$.*

Proof To show the correctness of Algorithm 4, it is sufficient to prove that the algorithm can correctly find D_i^* (if it exists) for any given $u_i, \bar{\mathcal{I}}_w$, such that $D_i^* \cap \{u_1, \cdots, u_i\} = \{u_i\}$, $D_i^* \in \bar{\mathcal{I}}_w$ and $\delta_i^* = \sum_{j \in D_i^*} \varphi(j, \iota_i)/\sum_{j \in D_i^*} \beta(j)$ is maximized. To see this, we first prove that we always have $\delta_i^* \in [x_i, y_i]$ when Algorithm 4 executes. Note that this is true when line 6 is executed. After that, $[x_i, y_i]$ only changes when line 21 or 21 is executed.

Note that $z = \sum_{j \in D_i} \tau(\delta_i, j)$. If $z > 0$ in line 21, then we have $\sum_{j \in D_i} \tau(\delta_i^*, j) \leq 0 < z = \sum_{j \in D_i} \tau(\delta_i, j)$, so we know that $\delta_i^* > \delta_i$ and setting x_i to δ_i in line 21 still ensures $\delta_i^* \in [x_i, y_i]$. If $z < 0$, we have $\sum_{j \in D_i^*} \tau(\delta_i, j) \leq \sum_{j \in D_i} \tau(\delta_i, j) = z < 0 = \sum_{j \in D_i^*} \tau(\delta_i^*, j)$, so we know that $\delta_i > \delta_i^*$ and setting y_i to δ_i in line 21 still ensures $\delta_i^* \in [x_i, y_i]$. Note that the above reasoning also implies $\delta_i^* = \delta_i$ when $z = 0$. In this case, we have already found $D_i^* = D_i$, so we put D_i into the bag X and check u_{i+1} (line 19).

Next, we prove that, when lines 13, 23 or 25 is executed, we always have $\forall a \in [x_i, y_i] : g = \arg\max_{j \in \{e, h\}} \tau(a, j)$. Clearly this holds for line 13. When line 23 or line 25 is executed, we must have $\delta_i \geq y_i \geq a$ or $\delta_i \leq x_i \leq a$, respectively; hence $g = \arg\max_{j \in \{e, h\}} \tau(a, j)$ can also be easily proved by the instructions in lines 23 and 25, where $\mathbf{1}(\cdot)$ is the indicator function.

According to the above reasoning, we have $\delta_i^* \in [x_i, y_i]$ and $\forall a \in [x_i, y_i] : \tau(a, p[1]) \geq \cdots \geq \tau(a, p[k - i])$ when Algorithm 6 is called. Therefore, we create a set of new guesses $S_0, \cdots, S_{k-i}$ on D_i^* in Algorithm 6. As Algorithm 6 employs a similar greedy search process with that in Algorithm 5, we can prove that $D_i^* \in \{S_0, \cdots, S_{k-i}\}$ by very similar reasoning with that in Lemma 13.5. After $\{S_0, \cdots, S_{k-i}\}$ is obtained, Algorithm 6 checks each S_j and put it into X if S_j does not conflict with the fact of $\delta_i^* \in [x_i, y_i]$ and satisfies the required matroid constraints (lines 5–6 of Algorithm 6).

Finally, after all the D_i^*'s have been collected into the set X, we return the one with the maximum value on function Υ (line 28 of Algorithm 4), which guarantees that an optimal solution is found.

It can be seen that any of the for-loops in lines 3, 9 or 10 of Algorithm 4 costs $O(k)$ time in the worst case, while Algorithm 5 (or Algorithm 6) also costs $O(k)$ time. Therefore, the total time complexity of **Algorithm** 4 is $O(k^4)$. □

As the selection of A_t is a mapping from the noisy means of the arms to $\mathcal{I}$, we can also prove:

Theorem 13.3 *OPBM achieves ϵ-differential privacy.*

Proof We use the notations introduced in Definition 13.2 to prove the theorem. Let $\mathcal{P}$ denote the arm-selection policy of OPBM. Let $\mathcal{H} = \{S_1, S_2, \cdots\} \in \Sigma_{\mathcal{P}}$ be any possible output of OPBM, where S_t denotes the set of arms selected at time slot t. Let $\tilde{\mathbf{v}}_{(i)} = \{\tilde{v}'_{i,t} | t \geq 1 \wedge i \in S_t\}$ denote the sequence of noisy means of arm i's rewards when arm i is selected in $\mathcal{H}$. Similarly, let $\tilde{\mathbf{c}}_{(i)} = \{\tilde{c}'_{i,t} | t \geq 1 \wedge i \in S_t\}$ denote the sequence of noisy means of arm i's costs. Let $\tilde{\mathbf{vc}} = \{\tilde{\mathbf{v}}_{(1)}, \tilde{\mathbf{c}}_{(1)}, \cdots, \tilde{\mathbf{v}}_{(k)}, \tilde{\mathbf{c}}_{(k)}\}$ denote the collection of the $2k$ sequences of noisy means of all arms. Let $\mathcal{H}_{vc}$ denote the set of all possible values of $\tilde{\mathbf{vc}}$ that makes OPBM output $\mathcal{H}$. We can prove

$$\mathbb{P}\{\tilde{\mathbf{vc}} \in \mathcal{H}_{vc}|\mathcal{D}\} \leq \exp(\epsilon) \cdot \mathbb{P}\{\tilde{\mathbf{vc}} \in \mathcal{H}_{vc}|\mathcal{D}'\} \tag{13.3}$$

Equation (13.3) can be explained as follows. Each element in $\tilde{\mathbf{vc}}$ is a sequence generated by using a hybrid mechanism (and some post-processing), as described in Sect. 13.5.1. Therefore, each sequence in $\tilde{\mathbf{vc}}$ achieves ϵ-differential privacy. Besides, a single perturbation on $\mathcal{D}$ affects at most one of the $2k$ hybrid mechanisms according to Definition 13.2. Moreover, the input data to the $2k$ hybrid mechanisms are $2k$ mutually disjoint subsets of the input data $\mathcal{D}$. Therefore, according to the parallel composition theorem of differential privacy [43], $\tilde{\mathbf{vc}}$ achieves ϵ-differential privacy, which proves (13.3).

With Eq. (13.3), the theorem can be easily proved by the fact that differential privacy is immune to post-processing [13]. More specifically, we have

$$\mathbb{P}\{\mathcal{A}^P = \mathcal{H}|\mathcal{D}\} = \mathbb{P}\{\tilde{\mathbf{vc}} \in \mathcal{H}_{vc}|\mathcal{D}\} \leq \exp(\epsilon) \cdot \mathbb{P}\{\tilde{\mathbf{vc}} \in \mathcal{H}_{vc}|\mathcal{D}'\}$$
$$= \exp(\epsilon) \cdot \mathbb{P}\{\mathcal{A}^P = \mathcal{H}|\mathcal{D}'\} \tag{13.4}$$

Hence, the theorem follows. $\square$

13.6 Regret Analysis

In this section, we give the regret analysis of the OPBM algorithm. We first introduce several important events as follows:

$$\mathcal{E}_{1,t} = \{\forall i \in [k] : |\bar{v}_{i,t} - v_i| \leq \lambda_{i,t}\}; \mathcal{E}_{2,t} = \{\forall i \in [k] : |\bar{c}_{i,t} - c_i| \leq \lambda_{i,t}\}; \tag{13.5}$$

$$\mathcal{E}_{3,t} = \{\forall i \in [k] : |\tilde{v}_{i,t} - \bar{v}_{i,t}| \leq \xi_{i,t}\}; \mathcal{E}_{4,t} = \{\forall i \in [k] : |\tilde{c}_{i,t} - \bar{c}_{i,t}| \leq \xi_{i,t}\}; \tag{13.6}$$

$$\mathcal{E}_{5,t} = \mathcal{E}_{1,t} \wedge \mathcal{E}_{2,t} \wedge \mathcal{E}_{3,t} \wedge \mathcal{E}_{4,t} \tag{13.7}$$

where $\bar{v}_{i,t}$ and $\bar{c}_{i,t}$ are the empirical means of arm i's reward and cost at time t (without noise). Using the Hoeffding's inequality and the properties of hybrid mechanism, we know that these events must happen with high probability, as is proved by the following lemma:

Lemma 13.6 $\mathbb{E}\left\{\sum_{t=k+1}^{N} \mathbf{1}\{\bigcup_{j=1}^{4} \neg\mathcal{E}_{j,t-1}\}\right\} \leq \frac{4k\pi^2}{3}$.

Intuitively, if the knowledge learned about the reward and cost of each single arm is accurate enough, then the value of $\Upsilon(A_t, \tilde{\mathbf{v}}_{t-1}, \tilde{\mathbf{c}}_{t-1}, \boldsymbol{\theta}_{t-1})$ should also be close to $\rho(A_t)$. Indeed, we need the knowledge on the arms to be accurate enough such that the elements in $\tilde{I}$ can be differentiated from the elements in I^*, where $\tilde{I} \triangleq \{S|S \in I \wedge \rho(S) < \rho(S^*)\}$ and $I^* \triangleq I\backslash\tilde{I}$. When event $\mathcal{E}_{5,t-1}$ happens, quantifying such an accuracy level boils down to quantifying the number of arm-pulling times; as the more times the arms are pulled for, the smaller the "error bound" $\theta_{i,t}$ should be; hence the second additive factor in the function Υ should also be small. We clarify these ideas by Lemmas 13.7, 13.8, 13.9, and 13.10. More specifically, Lemma 13.10 reveals that any $S \in \tilde{I}$ cannot be selected by OPBM when the arms in S have been played for a sufficient number of times quantified by a function $\tilde{\Phi}$, and Lemmas 13.7, 13.8, and 13.9 define the function $\tilde{\Phi}$ and show some useful properties of $\tilde{\Phi}$.

Lemma 13.7 ([44, 45]) *Let W be the Lambert function which satisfies $\forall x \in \mathbb{R} : x = W(x \exp(x))$. The equation $e^{-a_1 x} = a_0 (x - a_2)$ has the solution* $x = \frac{1}{a_1} W \left(\frac{a_1 \exp(-a_1 a_2)}{a_0} \right) + a_2$.

Lemma 13.8 *For any $S \in \tilde{I}$, let $\Delta_S = \rho(S^*) - \rho(S)$. Let $h(y) = \frac{\varsigma y}{(c_1-y)} \left(1 + \frac{1}{(c_1-2y)} \right)$. Let $d_0(\Delta_S)$ be the smaller root of the quadratic equation $2h(y) = \Delta_S$ (shown in Fig. 13.2). Define $d_1(\Delta_S) = \min\{\frac{c_1}{2}, d_0(\Delta_S), v_{min}\}$ where $v_{min} = \min_{i \in [k]} v_i$. Define*

$$\tilde{\Phi}(\Delta_S, t) = \frac{(8\sqrt{2}d_1(\Delta_S) + 1)\ln(4t^3)}{2\epsilon d_1^2(\Delta_S)} \left(\ln \left(\frac{(8\sqrt{2}d_1(\Delta_S) + 1)\ln(4t^3)}{2\epsilon d_1^2(\Delta_S)} \right) + 7 \right)$$

$$(13.8)$$

For any $i \in [k]$, if $n_{i,t} > \tilde{\Phi}(\Delta_S, t)$, then we have $\theta_{i,t} < d_1(\Delta_S)$.

Lemma 13.9 *For any $S, S' \in \tilde{I}$ satisfying $\Delta_S \geq \Delta_{S'}$, we have $d_1(\Delta_S) \geq d_1(\Delta_{S'})$ and $\tilde{\Phi}(\Delta_S, t) \leq \tilde{\Phi}(\Delta_{S'}, t)$.*

Lemma 13.10 *For any $S \in \tilde{I}$ and any $t \in [N - 1]$, if the events $\mathcal{E}_{5,t}$ and $\{\forall i \in S : n_{i,t} > \tilde{\Phi}(\Delta_S, t)\}$ both hold, then we must have $A_{t+1} \neq S$.*

With Lemma 13.10, we further provide Lemma 13.11 to analyze the total loss of OPBM caused by selecting the suboptimal arms in $\tilde{I}$, under the condition that $\mathcal{E}_{5,t-1}$ holds for all $t \geq k + 1$.

Lemma 13.11 *Define $\tilde{I}_i = \{S|i \in S \wedge S \in \tilde{I}\}$ for any $i \in [k]$. Suppose that $\tilde{I}_i = \{S_{i,1}, S_{i,2}, \cdots, S_{i,l_i}\}$ and $\Delta_{S_{i,1}} \geq \Delta_{S_{i,2}} \geq \cdots \geq \Delta_{S_{i,l_i}}$. Then we have:*

$$d_0(\Delta_S) = \frac{3\Delta_S c_1 + 2\varsigma + 2\varsigma c_1 - \sqrt{\Delta_S^2 c_1^2 + 4\varsigma^2 + 4\varsigma c_1^2(\varsigma - \Delta_S) + 12\varsigma c_1 \Delta_S + 8\varsigma^2 c_1}}{4\Delta_S + 8\varsigma} \tag{13.10}$$

Fig. 13.2 The closed-form expression of $d_0(\Delta_S)$

$$\sum_{t=k+1}^{N} \mathbf{1}\{A_t \in \widetilde{\mathcal{I}} \wedge \mathcal{E}_{5,t-1}\} \Delta_{A_t}$$

$$\leq \sum_{i=1}^{k} \widetilde{\Phi}(\Delta_{S_{i,l_i}}, N) \Delta_{S_{i,l_i}} + \sum_{i=1}^{k} \sum_{j=1}^{l_i - 1} \widetilde{\Phi}(\Delta_{S_{i,j}}, N)(\Delta_{S_{i,j}} - \Delta_{S_{i,j+1}})$$

Now we propose the regret bound of OPBM, as shown by Theorem 13.4. The proof of Theorem 13.4 uses Theorem 13.1 to get an upper bound of the expected reward of an optimal policy, and it derives the regret bound by leveraging the results of Lemma 13.11 and Jensen's inequality.

Theorem 13.4 *The regret of OPBM is upper bounded by* $O(\frac{km}{\epsilon\Delta_{\min}}(\ln B)\ln(\frac{\ln B}{\epsilon\Delta_{\min}}))$, *where* $\Delta_{\min} = \min_{S \in \widetilde{\mathcal{I}}} \Delta_S$ *is the minimum gap between* S^* *and any* $S \in \widetilde{\mathcal{I}}$, *and* $m = \max\{|S||S \in \widetilde{\mathcal{I}}\}$ *is the maximum number of arms pulled in each round. More specifically, the regret bound can be written as:*

$$\sum_{i=1}^{k} \varrho \widetilde{\Phi}\left(\Delta_{S_{i,l_i}}, b\right) \Delta_{S_{i,l_i}} + \sum_{i=1}^{k} \varrho \int_{\Delta_{S_{i,l_i}}}^{\Delta_{S_{i,1}}} \widetilde{\Phi}(x, b)\, dx + (\frac{4\pi^2}{3} + 1)k\varrho\Delta_{max} + \gamma\rho^* + \omega$$

$$\tag{13.9}$$

where $\varrho = \max\{C(S)|S \in \widetilde{\mathcal{I}}\}$, $\Delta_{max} = \max_{S \in \widetilde{\mathcal{I}}} \Delta_S$, $\omega = \sum_{j \in [k]} r_j$ *and* $b = \frac{B+\gamma}{\mu}$.

It is noted that the regret analysis for OPBM can be smoothly adapted to the case where DP is not requested. In that case, we can revise OPBM by replacing the input of Algorithm 4 by the un-noisy means of the arms' rewards and costs, and $\xi_{i,t}$ will be set to 0. With the similar analysis, we get the following bound:

Theorem 13.5 *For any* $S \in \widetilde{\mathcal{I}}$, *define* $\Phi(\Delta_S, t) = \max\{\frac{6}{c_1^2}, \frac{3}{2d_0^2(\Delta_S)}\}\ln t$. *The regret of the non-private OPBM algorithm is upper-bounded by*

$$\sum_{i=1}^{k} \varrho\Phi\left(\Delta_{S_{i,l_i}}, b\right) \Delta_{S_{i,l_i}} + \sum_{i=1}^{k} \varrho \int_{\Delta_{S_{i,l_i}}}^{\Delta_{S_{i,1}}} \Phi(x, b)\, dx$$

$$+(\frac{4\pi^2}{3} + 1)k\varrho\Delta_{max} + \gamma\rho^* + \omega = O(\frac{km \ln B}{\Delta_{\min}})$$

Although [6, 7] have proposed tighter regret bounds for the matroid bandit problem without a budget constraint, their regret analysis heavily relies on the nice properties of their simplified problem model. More specifically, they have assumed that arm-pulling incurs no costs, and any policy must pull k arms in each round. Using these nice properties, they have designed a simple greedy algorithm that selects k arms in each round based on the non-increasing order of the arms' estimated rewards, and they have got a small regret bound by constructing a bijective mapping from any sub-optimal solution to an optimal matroid basis, as well as by decomposing the total regret into k parts corresponding to k single optimal arms. Unfortunately, their regret analysis method cannot be applied to our problem, as the arm-pulling policies considered in our problem could have heterogeneous stopping time and select different number of arms due to the arm-pulling costs, and applying their greedy searching process could result in selecting arms with very high costs. Perhaps it is possible to improve our regret bound by designing a regret-decomposition method similar to that proposed in [6, 7], but this is highly non-trivial due to the correlation of the arm-pulling rewards and costs, and we plan to study it in our future work.

13.7 Performance Evaluation

In this section, we conduct numerical experiments to evaluate the performance of our algorithm and compare it to state-of-the-art MAB algorithms.

13.7.1 Experimental Setup

As none of the previous BMAB studies can handle general matroid constraints, we can only compare our algorithms with the existing algorithms under their settings of $A_t \in S_L (L \geq 1)$. Therefore, we implemented two representative MAB algorithms including MRCB [11] and DP-UCB-INT [20] for comparison purposes. MRCB is the only BMAB algorithm that allows multiple-pulls (they allow $A_t \in S_L$ and $L > 1$), and it is shown in [11] that MRCB outperforms other BMAB algorithms such as KUBE [9] and BTS [10]. We adapted MRCB to achieve DP by feeding it with the data output by the hybrid mechanism, as we did in OPBM. The DP-UCB-INT algorithm is the best-known differentially private bandit algorithm under the single-pull setting (i.e., $A_t \in S_1$) without a budget limit, and we adapted it to the budgeted case by selecting an arm with the maximum ratio of reward to cost in each round, where both of the reward and cost are estimated by the DP-aware method (with low data noise) proposed in [20]. We also used the best parameter settings reported in [11] and [20], e.g., setting $\kappa = 2^{-4}$ in MRCB to get its best performance.

To validate our algorithms under general matroid constraints, we also generate several matroid instances including a partition matroid $([k], M_p)$, a transversal matroid ($[k]$, $\mathcal{M}_t$) and a graphic matroid ($[k]$, $\mathcal{M}_g$), where k is set to 50. These matroids are all randomly generated and each of them has the rank of 20.

In our experiments, the arms' rewards and costs follow a mixture of heterogeneous distributions including Gaussian, beta, and exponential distributions, and all these distributions are truncated to have the support $[0, 1]$. In each run of the simulations, the expectations/variances of the Gaussian/exponential distributions and the shape parameters of the beta distributions are all uniformly sampled from $(0, 1)$. The reported data in each of our figures are the average of 100 simulation runs. All experiments were conducted on a PC equipped with Intel(R) Pentium(R) Processor G3250 3.20GHz CPU and 16GB memory. As MRCB is LP-based, we used IBM ILOG CPLEX as the LP solver [46].

13.7.2 Metrics

We use two metrics including regret and running time to evaluate the performance of our implemented algorithms. The regret performance is crucial for MAB algorithms, and we use $B\rho^*$ to approximate $TR(\mathcal{P}^*)$ in the evaluation (see Theorem 13.1). The time efficiency is important for any MAB algorithm considering multiple-pulls, as the arm-selection is much more complex than that in the single-pull case, so the scalability issue cannot be neglected.

13.7.3 Regret Performance

In Fig. 13.3, we compare OPBM and MRCB under the case of $A_t \in \mathcal{S}_L$ where $L > 1$. It can be seen that the regret of both OPBM and MRCB increases when the number of k increases, as more arms can make it harder to identify the optimal solution. However, OPBM greatly outperforms MRCB no matter how the values of k and L change, and varying the privacy level ϵ also does not reverse the OPBM's superiority.

In Fig. 13.4, we compare OPBM with DP-UCB-INT under the case of single-pull. As expected, the results show that the regret of OPBM outperforms DP-UCB-INT under different settings of k and ϵ. We also notice that the regrets of all algorithms increase when ϵ decreases, which can be explained by the fact that more noises have to be added for a smaller ϵ, so it would be more difficult to gain accurate knowledge about the arms.

In Fig. 13.5, we evaluate the performance of OPBM on several matroid constraints that cannot be handled by prior BMAB algorithms. More specifically, we require that $A_t \in \mathcal{B}(\mathcal{M}_p)$, $A_t \in \mathcal{B}(\mathcal{M}_g)$ and $A_t \in \mathcal{B}(\mathcal{M}_t)$ in Fig. 13.5a–c, respectively, where $\mathcal{M}_p$, $\mathcal{M}_t$ and $\mathcal{M}_g$ are explained in Sect. 13.7.1. It can be seen that the growth speed of OPBM's regret slows down under different settings of ϵ

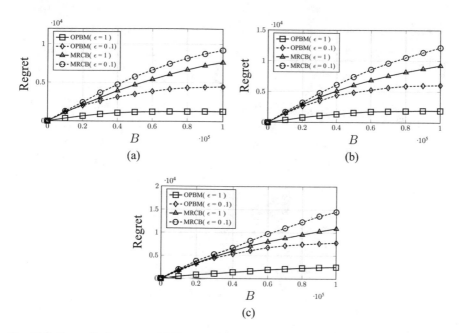

Fig. 13.3 Regret Performance of OPBM and MRCB. (**a**) $k = 10$, $L = 5$. (**b**) $k = 20$, $L = 10$. (**c**) $k = 50$, $L = 20$

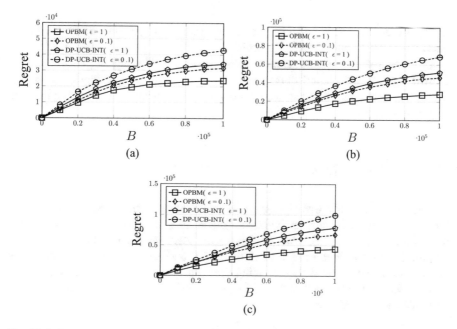

Fig. 13.4 Regret performance of OPBM and DP-UCB-INT. (**a**) $k = 10$, $L = 1$. (**b**) $k = 20$, $L = 1$. (**c**) $k = 50$, $L = 1$

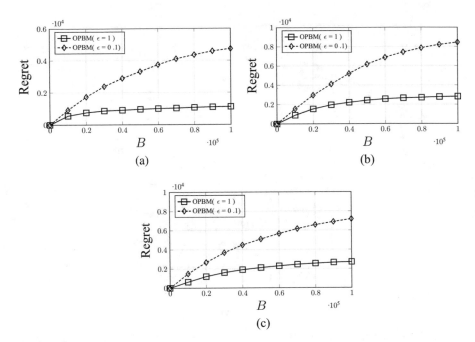

Fig. 13.5 Regret performance of OPBM under general matroid constraints. (**a**) Partition matroid. (**b**) Graphic matroid. (**c**) Transversal matroid

when B increases. This corroborates the logarithmic regret bounds that we have proved for OPBM under general matroid constraints.

In summary, our experimental results show: (1) The regret performance of OPBM significantly outperforms previous studies under their settings of $A_t \in \mathcal{S}_L$. (2) OPBM performs well under general matroid constraints that cannot be handled by previous work.

13.7.4 Time Efficiency

As MRCB is the only BMAB algorithm that allows multiple-pulls, we compare OPBM and MRCB's running time under the setting of $A_t \in \mathcal{S}_L(L > 1)$, and the results are shown in Table 13.2. In Table 13.2, each integer pair listed in the first and the fourth rows denotes the value of (k, L), and each number appeared in the other rows indicates the average running time per round. It can be seen that MRCB is more than 20 times slower than OPBM. Therefore, OPBM scales better to the case of large number of arms.

Table 13.2 Running time of OPBM and MRCB (ms/round)

	(100, 30)	(200, 100)	(300, 150)	(500, 200)	(800, 300)	(1000, 400)
OPBM	0.11	0.31	0.48	0.85	1.14	1.96
MRCB	2.85	7.23	11.77	23.73	34.42	82.74

13.8 Conclusion

In this study, we have made the first step towards designing differentially private BMAB algorithms under general matroid constraints for arm-pulling. More specifically, our model allows that the arms selected at each round satisfy a union of multiple matroid (or matroid basis) constraints, and the total rewards or costs incurred at each round are linear combinations of the rewards or costs of pulling individual arms. Moreover, we have adopted a general RC+NK model for arm-pulling costs, which means that the arms' costs are random with unknown expectations. We have proposed a novel algorithm called OPBM for our problem, and the nice features of OPBM include: (1) OPBM is the first algorithm that is capable of handling general matroid constraints in BMAB, and the arm-pulling models in previous studies can be considered as the special cases of ours. (2) OPBM achieves a uniform $O\left(\frac{\ln B}{\epsilon} \ln\left(\frac{\ln B}{\epsilon}\right)\right)$ regret bound and ϵ-differential privacy. (3) When DP is not required, OPBM achieves a uniform regret bound of $O(\ln B)$, which improves the asymptotic regret bound proposed in prior BMAB studies under the RC+NK setting. (4) Compared with some LP-based solutions in prior studies, OPBM is a purely combinatorial algorithm with lower time complexity, hence it scales better to the case of large number of arms. (5) Performance evaluation show that the regret performance of OPBM significantly outperforms the related studies under their settings, with a more than 20 times faster processing speed.

Although we are the first to provide a budget-constrained matroid bandit algorithm, our algorithm still has some limitations. In the future work, we will consider more kinds of constraints (e.g., the matroid-intersection constraint) in our problem model. Moreover, as discussed in Sect. 13.6, we also plan to investigate some regret decomposition methods similar to that in [6, 7] to provide a tighter regret bound for our problem.

Appendix: Missing Definitions, Lemmas and Proofs

Definition 13.3 (Uniform Matroid [4]) The pair $(E, \mathcal{M})$ is called a uniform matroid if $\mathcal{M} = \{S | S \subseteq E \wedge |S| \leq L\}$, where L is a non-negative integer.

Definition 13.4 (Partition Matroid [4]) Suppose that $E_1, E_2, \cdots, E_\ell$ is a partition of the ground set E and $z_1, \cdots, z_\ell$ are predefined integers. The pair $(E, \mathcal{M})$ is called a partition matroid if $\mathcal{M} = \{S | (S \subseteq E) \wedge (\forall i \in [\ell] : |S \cap E_i| \leq z_i)\}$.

Definition 13.5 (Graphic Matroid [4]) Let $G = (V, E)$ denote an undirected graph whose node set is V and edge set is E. The pair (E, M) is called a graphic matroid if M is the set of all the forests in G.

Definition 13.6 (Transversal Matroid [4]) Let $G = (E, V, J)$ denote a bipartite graph whose node partition has the parts E and V, with J denoting the set of edges. For any matching K in G, let $K(E)$ denote the endpoints of K in E. The pair (E, M) is called a transversal matroid if $M = \{K(E) | K \text{ is a matching in } G\} \cup \{\emptyset\}$.

Lemma 13.12 ([47]) *Let $Z_1, Z_2, \cdots, Z_n$ be a sequence of random variables with common support $[0,1]$. If $\mathbb{E}\{Z_i | Z_1, Z_2, \cdots, Z_{i-1}\} \leq \psi$ for any $i \leq n$, then we have $\mathbf{Pr}\{\sum_{i=1}^{n} Z_i \geq n\psi + \ell\} \leq e^{-2\ell^2/n}$ for any $\ell > 0$. If $\mathbb{E}\{Z_i | Z_1, Z_2, \cdots, Z_{i-1}\} \geq \psi$ for any $i \leq n$, then we have $\mathbf{Pr}\{\sum_{i=1}^{n} Z_i \leq n\psi - \ell\} \leq e^{-2\ell^2/n}$ for any $\ell > 0$.*

Lemma 13.13 ([40]) *Let $(Y_t)_{t\in\mathbb{N}}$ be a martingale and τ a stopping time, both with respect to the filtration $(\mathcal{F}_t)_{t\in\mathbb{N}}$. Then we have $\mathbb{E}\{Y_\tau\} = \mathbb{E}\{Y_1\}$ provided that the following conditions hold:*

1. $\mathbb{E}\{\tau\} < \infty$;
2. $\mathbb{E}\{|Y_{t+1} - Y_t| | \mathcal{F}_t\} < a$ holds for all t and some constant a.

Proof of Lemma 13.1

Proof When $t \geq \frac{\sqrt{2}B}{(\sqrt{2}-1)\mu}$, using Lemma 13.12 we can get

$$\mathbb{P}\{N^{\mathcal{P}} \geq t+1\} \leq \mathbb{P}\left\{\sum_{j=1}^{t} \hat{C}(A_j^{\mathcal{P}}) \leq B\right\}$$

$$\leq \mathbb{P}\left\{\sum_{j=1}^{t} \frac{\hat{C}(A_j^{\mathcal{P}})}{\gamma} \leq \frac{t\mu}{\gamma} - \frac{t\mu}{\sqrt{2}\gamma}\right\} \leq \exp\left\{-\mu^2 t/\gamma^2\right\},$$

which can be used to prove

$$\mathbb{E}\{N^{\mathcal{P}}\} = \sum_{t=0}^{\infty} \mathbb{P}\{N^{\mathcal{P}} \geq t+1\}$$

$$\leq 2 + \frac{\sqrt{2}B}{(\sqrt{2}-1)\mu} + \sum_{t=1}^{\infty} \exp\left\{-\frac{\mu^2}{\gamma^2} t\right\}$$

$$\leq 2 + \frac{\sqrt{2}B}{(\sqrt{2}-1)\mu} + \left(1 + \frac{\gamma^2}{\mu^2}\right) \exp\left\{-\frac{\mu^2}{\gamma^2}\right\}$$

Hence the lemma follows.   □

Proof of Theorem 13.1

Proof Let $A_t^{\mathcal{P}^*}$ denote the set of arms pulled by $\mathcal{P}^*$ at round t and $N^{\mathcal{P}^*} = \min\{t| \sum_{j=1}^{t} \hat{C}(A_j^{\mathcal{P}}) > B\}$. Let $(\mathcal{F}_t)_{t\geq 0}$ denote the natural filtration [48] generated by the observations on the arms pulled by the policy $\mathcal{P}^*$. So $N^{\mathcal{P}^*}$ is a stopping time with respect to $(\mathcal{F}_t)_{t\geq 0}$ and we have

$$TR(\mathcal{P}^*) \leq \mathbb{E}\left\{\sum_{t=1}^{N^{\mathcal{P}^*}} \hat{V}(A_t^{\mathcal{P}^*})\right\} = \mathbb{E}\left\{\sum_{t=1}^{\infty} \hat{V}(A_t^{\mathcal{P}^*}) \cdot \mathbf{1}\{N^{\mathcal{P}^*} \geq t\}\right\} \qquad (13.10)$$

$$= \mathbb{E}\left\{\sum_{t=1}^{\infty} \sum_{S\in I} \hat{V}(S) \cdot \mathbf{1}\{A_t^{\mathcal{P}^*} = S; N^{\mathcal{P}^*} \geq t\}\right\} \qquad (13.11)$$

$$= \sum_{t=1}^{\infty} \sum_{S\in I} \mathbb{E}\left\{\hat{V}(S) \cdot \mathbf{1}\{A_t^{\mathcal{P}^*} = S; N^{\mathcal{P}^*} \geq t\}\right\} \qquad (13.12)$$

$$= \sum_{t=1}^{\infty} \sum_{S\in I} \mathbb{E}\left\{\mathbb{E}\left\{\hat{V}(S) \cdot \mathbf{1}\{A_t^{\mathcal{P}^*} = S; N^{\mathcal{P}^*} \geq t\} \mid \mathcal{F}_{t-1}\right\}\right\} \qquad (13.13)$$

$$= \sum_{t=1}^{\infty} \sum_{S\in I} \mathbb{E}\left\{\mathbb{E}\left\{\hat{V}(S) \mid \mathcal{F}_{t-1}\right\} \cdot \mathbf{1}\{A_t^{\mathcal{P}^*} = S; N^{\mathcal{P}^*} \geq t\}\right\} \qquad (13.14)$$

$$= \sum_{t=1}^{\infty} \sum_{S\in I} V(S) \cdot \mathbb{P}\{A_t^{\mathcal{P}^*} = S; N^{\mathcal{P}^*} \geq t\} \qquad (13.15)$$

where (13.12) is due to the linearity of expectation and the fact that $M \triangleq \sum_{t=1}^{\infty} \mathbb{E}\left\{|\sum_{S\in I} \hat{V}(S) \cdot \mathbf{1}\{A_t^{\mathcal{P}^*} = S; N^{\mathcal{P}^*} \geq t\}|\right\}$ converges (this can be seen from the fact that $M = \sum_{t=1}^{\infty} \sum_{S\in I} V(S) \cdot \mathbb{P}\{A_t^{\mathcal{P}} = S; N^{\mathcal{P}^*} \geq t\} \leq \mathbb{E}\{N^{\mathcal{P}^*}\} \cdot \sum_{i\in[k]} r_i$ according to (13.15), so M is bounded above due to Lemma 13.1 and hence it converges), and (13.14) is due to the fact that $\mathbf{1}\{A_t^{\mathcal{P}^*} = S; N^{\mathcal{P}^*} \geq t\}$ is $\mathcal{F}_{t-1}$-measurable (note that $N^{\mathcal{P}^*}$ is a stopping time and $A_t^{\mathcal{P}^*}$ is determined based on the observations from round 1 to round $t - 1$).

Using similar reasoning with (13.10)–(13.15), we also have

$$\mathbb{E}\left\{\sum_{t=1}^{N^{\mathcal{P}^*}} \hat{C}(A_t^{\mathcal{P}^*})\right\} = \sum_{t=1}^{\infty} \sum_{S\in I} C(S) \cdot \mathbb{P}\{A_t^{\mathcal{P}^*} = S; N^{\mathcal{P}^*} \geq t\} \qquad (13.16)$$

As $\sum_{t=1}^{N^{\mathcal{P}^*}-1} \hat{C}(A_t^{\mathcal{P}^*}) \leq B$, we have $\mathbb{E}\left\{\sum_{t=1}^{N^{\mathcal{P}^*}} \hat{C}(A_t^{\mathcal{P}^*})\right\} \leq B + \gamma$. Besides, we have $\forall S \in I : V(S) \leq \rho^* C(S)$. Combining these results with (13.15)–(13.16) gives us

$$TR(\mathcal{P}^*) \leq \sum_{t=1}^{\infty} \sum_{S\in I} \rho^* C(S) \cdot \mathbb{P}\{A_t^{\mathcal{P}^*} = S; N^{\mathcal{P}^*} \geq t\}$$

$$= \rho^* \mathbb{E}\left\{\sum_{t=1}^{N^{\mathcal{P}^*}} \hat{C}(A_t^{\mathcal{P}^*})\right\} \leq \rho^*(B + \gamma) \qquad (13.17)$$

Next, we prove $TR(\mathcal{P}') \geq B\rho^* - V(S^*)$, where $\mathcal{P}'$ denotes the policy that always plays S^*. Note that

$$TR(\mathcal{P}') = \mathbb{E}\left\{\sum_{t=1}^{N^{\mathcal{P}'}-1} \hat{V}(S^*)\right\} = \mathbb{E}\left\{\sum_{t=1}^{N^{\mathcal{P}'}} \hat{V}(S^*)\right\} - V(S^*) \quad (13.18)$$

Besides, using similar reasoning with (13.10)–(13.16), we have

$$\mathbb{E}\left\{\sum_{t=1}^{N^{\mathcal{P}'}} \hat{V}(S^*)\right\} = \sum_{t=1}^{\infty} V(S^*) \cdot \mathbb{P}\{N^{\mathcal{P}'} \geq t\} = \rho^* \sum_{t=1}^{\infty} C(S^*) \cdot \mathbb{P}\{N^{\mathcal{P}'} \geq t\}$$

$$= \rho^* \mathbb{E}\left\{\sum_{t=1}^{N^{\mathcal{P}'}} \hat{C}(S^*)\right\} \geq B\rho^* \quad (13.19)$$

Combining (13.18)–(13.19), we get $TR(\mathcal{P}') \geq B\rho^* - V(S^*)$.   □

Proof of Lemma 13.6

Proof Using Lemma 13.4, we have

$$\mathbb{E}\{\sum_{t=k+1}^{N} \mathbf{1}\{\neg\mathcal{E}_{3,t-1}\}\} \leq \sum_{t=k+1}^{\infty} \mathbb{P}\{\neg\mathcal{E}_{3,t-1}\}$$

$$\leq \sum_{i\in[k]} \sum_{t=k}^{\infty} \sum_{j=1}^{t} \mathbb{P}\left\{|\tilde{v}_{i,t} - \bar{v}_{i,t}| > \xi_{i,t}; n_{i,t} = j\right\}$$

$$\leq \sum_{i\in[k]} \sum_{t=1}^{\infty} \sum_{j=1}^{t} 2t^{-3} \leq k\pi^2/3 \quad (13.20)$$

Similarly, we can get $\sum_{t=k+1}^{\infty} \mathbb{P}\{\neg\mathcal{E}_{4,t-1}\} \leq \frac{k\pi^2}{3}$.

By using Lemma 13.12, we can also get $\sum_{t=k+1}^{\infty} \mathbb{P}\{\neg\mathcal{E}_{j,t-1}\} \leq \frac{k\pi^2}{3}$ for $j = 1, 2$. The lemma then follows by using the union bound.   □

Proof of Lemma 13.8

Proof By using Lemma 13.7 and the approximation of the Lambert function [20, 44], we know that

$$\forall n \in \mathbb{N}, z > 0 : n \geq z(\ln z + 7) \Rightarrow n \geq z \ln n + z \quad (13.21)$$

To satisfy $\theta_{i,t} < d_1(\Delta_S)$, it is sufficient to find $\alpha \in (0, 1)$ such that $(1-\alpha)d_1(\Delta_S) > \lambda_{i,t}$ and $\alpha d_1(\Delta_S) > \xi_{i,t}$. For $(1 - \alpha)d_1(\Delta_S) > \lambda_{i,t}$, we need $n_{i,t} > \frac{3\ln t}{2(1-\alpha)^2 d_1^2(\Delta_S)}$. For $\alpha d_1(\Delta_S) > \xi_{i,t}$, it is sufficient to have $n_{i,t} > \Gamma(\Delta_S, t)$ (due to Eq. (13.21)) where

$$\Gamma(\Delta_S, t) \triangleq \frac{\sqrt{8}\ln(4t^3)}{\epsilon\alpha d_1(\Delta_S)}\left(\ln\left(\frac{\sqrt{8}\ln(4t^3)}{\epsilon\alpha d_1(\Delta_S)}\right) + 7\right)$$

Let $\alpha = \frac{1}{2}\left(2 + \beta - \sqrt{\beta^2 + 4\beta}\right)$ where $\beta = 1/(4\sqrt{2}d_1(\Delta_S))$. As such, we have $\alpha \in (0, 1)$ and

$$\frac{\sqrt{8}}{\alpha d_1(\Delta_S)} = \frac{1}{2(1-\alpha)^2 d_1^2(\Delta_S)}, \tag{13.22}$$

which implies $\Gamma(\Delta_S, t) > \frac{3\ln t}{2(1-\alpha)^2 d_1^2(\Delta_S)}$. So we only need to ensure $n_{i,t} > \Gamma(\Delta_S, t)$ according to the above reasoning. Note that

$$\frac{\sqrt{8}}{\alpha d_1(\Delta_S)} = \frac{\sqrt{8}}{2d_1(\Delta_S)}\left(2 + \beta + \sqrt{\beta^2 + 4\beta}\right) < \sqrt{8}\frac{\beta + 2}{d_1(\Delta_S)} = \frac{(8\sqrt{2}d_1(\Delta_S) + 1)}{2d_1^2(\Delta_S)} \tag{13.23}$$

Therefore, we have $\widetilde{\Phi}(\Delta_S, t) \geq \Gamma(\Delta_S, t)$, hence the lemma follows. $\square$

Proof of Lemma 13.9

Proof According to Eq. (13.10), we have

$$d_0(\Delta_S) = \frac{2\Delta_S c_1^2}{3\Delta_S c_1 + 2\varsigma + 2\varsigma c_1 + \sqrt{\Delta_S^2 c_1^2 + 4\varsigma^2 + 4\varsigma^2 c_1^2 + (12\varsigma c_1 - 4\varsigma c_1^2)\Delta_S + 8\varsigma^2 c_1}} \tag{13.24}$$

So $d_0(\Delta_S)$ increases when Δ_S increases. Hence we have $d_0(\Delta_S) \geq d_0(\Delta_{S'})$, which implies $d_1(\Delta_S) \geq d_1(\Delta_{S'})$ and $\widetilde{\Phi}(\Delta_S, t) \leq \widetilde{\Phi}(\Delta_{S'}, t)$ according to the definitions of $d_1(\Delta_S)$ and $\widetilde{\Phi}(\Delta_S, t)$. $\square$

Proof of Lemma 13.10

Proof For convenience, we define $\sigma(S', \widetilde{\mathbf{v}}_t', \widetilde{\mathbf{c}}_t') = \sum_{i \in S'} r_i \widetilde{v}_{i,t}' / \sum_{i \in S'} s_i \widetilde{c}_{i,t}'$ and $\eta(S', \widetilde{\mathbf{c}}_t', \boldsymbol{\theta}_t) = \Upsilon(S', \widetilde{\mathbf{v}}_t', \widetilde{\mathbf{c}}_t', \boldsymbol{\theta}_t) - \sigma(S', \widetilde{\mathbf{v}}_t', \widetilde{\mathbf{c}}_t')$ for any $S' \in \mathcal{I}$. So we have $\sigma(S', \mathbf{v}, \mathbf{c}) = \rho(S')$ for any $S' \in \mathcal{I}$.

Let $x = \max_{i \in S} \theta_{i,t}$. According to Lemma 13.8, we have $x < \min\{\frac{c_1}{2}, d_0(\Delta_S), v_{min}\}$ when $n_{i,t} > \widetilde{\Phi}(\Delta_S, t)$ holds for all $\forall i \in S$. When $\mathcal{E}_{2,t}$ and $\mathcal{E}_{4,t}$ happen, we have $\forall i \in S : \widetilde{c}_{i,t} \geq \bar{c}_{i,t} - \xi_{i,t} \geq c_i - \theta_{i,t} \geq c_1 - x > 0$ and $\forall i \in S : c_i \geq \bar{c}_{i,t} - \lambda_{i,t} \geq \widetilde{c}_{i,t} - \theta_{i,t} \geq c_1 - 2x > 0$. When $\mathcal{E}_{1,t}$ and $\mathcal{E}_{3,t}$ happen, we have $\forall i \in S : \widetilde{v}_{i,t} \geq \bar{v}_{i,t} - \xi_{i,t} \geq v_i - \theta_{i,t} \geq v_{min} - \theta_{i,t} > 0$. Using these inequalities, we get

$$= \left| \frac{\sum_{i \in S} r_i \left(\widetilde{v}'_{i,t} - v_i\right) \sum_{i \in S} s_i c_i}{\sum_{i \in S} s_i \widetilde{c}'_{i,t} \sum_{i \in S} s_i c_i} + \frac{\sum_{i \in S} s_i \left(c_i - \widetilde{c}'_{i,t}\right) \sum_{i \in S} r_i v_i}{\sum_{i \in S} s_i \widetilde{c}'_{i,t} \sum_{i \in S} s_i c_i} \right|$$

$$\leq \frac{\sum_{i \in S} r_i |\widetilde{v}_{i,t} - v_i|}{\sum_{i \in S} s_i \widetilde{c}'_{i,t}} + \frac{\sum_{i \in S} s_i |c_i - \widetilde{c}_{i,t}| \sum_{i \in S} r_i v_i}{\sum_{i \in S} s_i \widetilde{c}'_{i,t} \sum_{i \in S} s_i c_i}$$

$$\leq \frac{\sum_{i \in S} r_i \theta_{i,t}}{\sum_{i \in S} s_i \widetilde{c}'_{i,t}} + \frac{\sum_{i \in S} r_i \sum_{i \in S} s_i \theta_{i,t}}{\sum_{i \in S} s_i \widetilde{c}'_{i,t} \sum_{i \in S} s_i c_i}$$

$$\leq \frac{1}{\sum_{i \in S} s_i \widetilde{c}'_{i,t}} \left(\sum_{i \in S} r_i \theta_{i,t} + \frac{\varsigma \sum_{i \in S} s_i \theta_{i,t}}{\min_{i \in S} \max\{\widetilde{c}_{i,t} - \theta_{i,t}, 0\}} \right)$$

$$= \eta(S, \widetilde{\mathbf{c}}'_t, \boldsymbol{\theta}_t)$$

$$\leq \frac{1}{\sum_{i \in S} s_i (c_1 - x)} \left(\sum_{i \in S} r_i x + \frac{\varsigma \sum_{i \in S} s_i x}{c_1 - 2x} \right)$$

$$\leq \frac{\varsigma x}{(c_1 - x)} + \frac{\varsigma x}{(c_1 - 2x)(c_1 - x)} = h(x) < \frac{\Delta_S}{2},$$

where the last inequality is due to $x < d_0(\Delta_S)$. This implies

$$\sigma(S, \widetilde{\mathbf{v}}'_t, \widetilde{\mathbf{c}}'_t) - \sigma(S, \mathbf{v}, \mathbf{c}) \leq \eta(S, \widetilde{\mathbf{c}}'_t, \boldsymbol{\theta}_t) < \frac{\Delta_S}{2} \qquad (13.25)$$

By similar reasoning, when $\mathcal{E}_{5,t}$ happens, we can get

$$\sigma(S^*, \mathbf{v}, \mathbf{c}) - \sigma(S^*, \widetilde{\mathbf{v}}'_t, \widetilde{\mathbf{c}}'_t) \leq \eta(S^*, \widetilde{\mathbf{c}}'_t, \boldsymbol{\theta}_t) \qquad (13.26)$$

Suppose by contradiction that $A_{t+1} = S$. Then, according to the selection rule in Algorithm 3, we can get

$$\sigma(S^*, \widetilde{\mathbf{v}}'_t, \widetilde{\mathbf{c}}'_t) + \eta(S^*, \widetilde{\mathbf{c}}'_t, \boldsymbol{\theta}_t) \leq \sigma(S, \widetilde{\mathbf{v}}'_t, \widetilde{\mathbf{c}}'_t) + \eta(S, \widetilde{\mathbf{c}}'_t, \boldsymbol{\theta}_t); \qquad (13.27)$$

Summing all these equations gives us

$$\sigma(S^*, \mathbf{v}, \mathbf{c}) - \sigma(S, \mathbf{v}, \mathbf{c}) \leq 2\eta(S, \widetilde{\mathbf{c}}'_t, \boldsymbol{\theta}_t) < \Delta_S,$$

which is a contradiction. Hence the lemma follows. □

Proof of Lemma 13.11

Proof The proof borrows some ideas from [23]. We first introduce a variable $\phi_{i,t}$. We set $\phi_{i,k} = 1$ for all $i \in [k]$. Given the values of $\phi_{i,t-1} : i \in [k]$, the values of $\phi_{i,t} : i \in [k]$ are set as follows. Let $j = \arg\min_{i \in A_t} \phi_{i,t-1}$ (ties broken arbitrarily). If $i = j$ and $A_t \in \widetilde{I}$ both hold, then we set $\phi_{i,t} = \phi_{i,t-1} + 1$, otherwise we set $\phi_{i,t} = \phi_{i,t-1}$. It can be seen that $n_{i,t} \geq \phi_{i,t}$ for any $i \in [k]$ and any $t \geq k$.

With the above definition on $\phi_{i,t}$, we can prove that

$$A_t \in \widetilde{I} \wedge \phi_{i,t} > \phi_{i,t-1} \wedge \phi_{i,t-1} > \widetilde{\Phi}(S_{i,j}, N) \wedge \mathcal{E}_{5,t-1}$$
$$\Rightarrow A_t \in \{S_{i,j+1}, S_{i,j+2}, \cdots, S_{i,l_i}\} \tag{13.28}$$

This can be explained as follows. if $\phi_{i,t} > \phi_{i,t-1}, \phi_{i,t-1} > \widetilde{\Phi}(S_{i,j}, N)$ and $\mathcal{E}_{5,t-1}$ all hold, then we must have $\forall i \in A_t : n_{i,t-1} > \widetilde{\Phi}(S_{i,j}, t-1)$ and hence $A_t \in \widetilde{I}_i \backslash \{S_{i,j}\}$ according to Lemma 13.11. Note that we also have $\widetilde{\Phi}(\Delta_{S_{i,1}}, N) \leq \widetilde{\Phi}(\Delta_{S_{i,2}}, N) \leq \cdots \leq \widetilde{\Phi}(\Delta_{S_{i,l_i}}, N)$ due to $\Delta_{S_{i,1}} \geq \Delta_{S_{i,2}} \geq \cdots \geq \Delta_{S_{i,l_i}}$ and Lemma 13.9. So we can use similar reasoning to get $A_t \in \widetilde{I}_i \backslash \{S_{i,1}, \cdots, S_{i,j-1}\}$, which proves (13.28). Based on (13.28), we can get:

$$\sum_{t=k+1}^{N} \mathbf{1}\{A_t \in \widetilde{I} \wedge \mathcal{E}_{5,t-1}\} \Delta_{A_t}$$

$$\leq \sum_{t=k+1}^{N} \sum_{i=1}^{k} \mathbf{1}\{A_t \in \widetilde{I} \wedge \phi_{i,t} > \phi_{i,t-1} \wedge \mathcal{E}_{5,t-1}\} \Delta_{A_t}$$

$$\leq \sum_{t=k+1}^{N} \sum_{i=1}^{k} \sum_{j=1}^{l_i} \mathbf{1}\{A_t \in \widetilde{I} \wedge \phi_{i,t} > \phi_{i,t-1} \wedge \mathcal{E}_{5,t-1} \wedge \phi_{i,t-1} \in (\widetilde{\Phi}(\Delta_{S_{i,j-1}}, N), \widetilde{\Phi}(\Delta_{S_{i,j}}, N)]\} \Delta_{A_t}$$

$$\leq \sum_{i=1}^{k} \sum_{j=1}^{l_i} \left(\widetilde{\Phi}(\Delta_{S_{i,j}}, N) - \widetilde{\Phi}(\Delta_{S_{i,j-1}}, N) \right) \Delta_{S_{i,j}}$$

$$= \sum_{i=1}^{k} \widetilde{\Phi}(\Delta_{S_{i,l_i}}, N) \Delta_{S_{i,l_i}} + \sum_{i=1}^{k} \sum_{j=1}^{l_i-1} \widetilde{\Phi}(\Delta_{S_{i,j}}, N)(\Delta_{S_{i,j}} - \Delta_{S_{i,j+1}}),$$

where $\widetilde{\Phi}(\Delta_{S_{i,0}}, N) \triangleq 0$. Hence the lemma follows. □

Proof of Theorem 13.4

Proof Using Theorem 13.1, the regret of OPBM is upper bounded by

$$\mathbb{E}\left\{(B+\gamma)\rho^* - \sum_{t=1}^{N-1}\hat{V}(A_t)\right\}$$

$$\leq \mathbb{E}\left\{\sum_{t=1}^{N}\left(\hat{C}(A_t)\rho^* - \hat{V}(A_t)\right)\right\} + \rho^*\mathbb{E}\left\{B - \sum_{t=1}^{N}\hat{C}(A_t)\right\} + \gamma\rho^* + \omega$$

$$\leq \mathbb{E}\left\{\sum_{t=1}^{N}\left(\hat{C}(A_t)\rho^* - \hat{V}(A_t)\right)\right\} + \gamma\rho^* + \omega \qquad (13.29)$$

Moreover, we have

$$\mathbb{E}\left\{\sum_{t=1}^{N}\left(\hat{C}(A_t)\rho^* - \hat{V}(A_t)\right)\right\}$$

$$\leq \sum_{t=1}^{\infty}\left(\mathbb{E}\left\{[\hat{C}(A_t)\rho^* - \hat{V}(A_t)]\cdot\mathbf{1}\{A_t \in \widetilde{I}; N \geq t\}\right\}\right.$$

$$\left. + \mathbb{E}\left\{[\hat{C}(A_t)\rho^* - \hat{V}(A_t)]\cdot\mathbf{1}\{A_t \in I^*; N \geq t\}\right\}\right)$$

$$\leq \varrho\sum_{t=1}^{\infty}\sum_{S\in\widetilde{I}}\Delta_S\mathbb{P}\{A_t = S; N \geq t\} = \varrho\mathbb{E}\left\{\sum_{t=1}^{N}\mathbf{1}\{A_t \in \widetilde{I}\}\Delta_{A_t}\right\} \qquad (13.30)$$

and

$$\mathbb{E}\left\{\sum_{t=1}^{N}\mathbf{1}\{A_t \in \widetilde{I}\}\Delta_{A_t}\right\} - k\Delta_{max}$$

$$\leq \mathbb{E}\left\{\sum_{t=k+1}^{N}\mathbf{1}\{A_t \in \widetilde{I} \wedge \mathcal{E}_{5,t-1}\}\Delta_{A_t}\right\} + \mathbb{E}\left\{\sum_{t=k+1}^{N}\mathbf{1}\{\neg\mathcal{E}_{5,t-1}\}\Delta_{A_t}\right\}$$

$$\leq \mathbb{E}\left\{\sum_{t=k+1}^{N}\mathbf{1}\{A_t \in \widetilde{I} \wedge \mathcal{E}_{5,t-1}\}\Delta_{A_t}\right\} + \frac{4k\pi^2}{3}\Delta_{max}$$

$$\leq \sum_{i=1}^{k}\mathbb{E}\{\widetilde{\Phi}(\Delta_{S_{i,l_i}}, N)\}\Delta_{S_{i,l_i}} + \sum_{i=1}^{k}\sum_{j=1}^{l_i-1}\mathbb{E}\{\widetilde{\Phi}(\Delta_{S_{i,j}}, N)\}(\Delta_{S_{i,j}} - \Delta_{S_{i,j+1}}) + \frac{4k\pi^2}{3}\Delta_{max}$$

$$\qquad (13.31)$$

where the second inequality is due to Lemma 13.6, and the last inequality is due to Lemma 13.11.

For any $S \in \widetilde{\mathcal{I}}$, let $d_S = \frac{8\sqrt{2}d_1(\Delta_S)+1}{2\epsilon d_1^2(\Delta_S)}$. Then we have $\widetilde{\Phi}(\Delta_S, t) = d_S \ln(4t^3)(\ln(d_S \ln(4t^3)) + 7)$. Let $g_S(x) = \widetilde{\Phi}(\Delta_S, x)$. We have

$$g_S''(x) = \frac{3d_S}{x^2 \ln(4x^3)}[3 - \ln(4x^3)(\ln(d_S \ln(4x^3)) + 8)]$$

Hence $g_S''(x) < 0$ when $x \geq 0.9$. As $N \geq 1$, we can get the following equation by using the Jensen's inequality and Lemma 13.3:

$$\forall S \in \widetilde{\mathcal{I}} : \mathbb{E}\{\widetilde{\Phi}(\Delta_S, N)\} = \mathbb{E}\{g_S(N)\} \leq g_S(\mathbb{E}\{N\})$$
$$= \widetilde{\Phi}(\Delta_S, \mathbb{E}(N)) \leq \widetilde{\Phi}\left(\Delta_S, \frac{B+\gamma}{\mu}\right)$$

Using this, we have

$$\sum_{i=1}^{k} \mathbb{E}\{\widetilde{\Phi}(\Delta_{S_{i,l_i}}, N)\}\Delta_{S_{i,l_i}} + \sum_{i=1}^{k}\sum_{j=1}^{l_i-1} \mathbb{E}\{\widetilde{\Phi}(\Delta_{S_{i,j}}, N)\}(\Delta_{S_{i,j}} - \Delta_{S_{i,j+1}})$$

$$\leq \sum_{i=1}^{k} \widetilde{\Phi}\left(\Delta_{S_{i,l_i}}, \frac{B+\gamma}{\mu}\right)\Delta_{S_{i,l_i}} + \sum_{i=1}^{k}\int_{\Delta_{S_{i,l_i}}}^{\Delta_{S_{i,1}}} \widetilde{\Phi}\left(x, \frac{B+\gamma}{\mu}\right)dx \quad (13.32)$$

Combining (13.29)–(13.32), we can get (13.9). Note that $\varrho = O(m)$, $\frac{1}{d_0(\Delta_{S_{i,l_i}})} = O(\frac{1}{\Delta_{S_{i,l_i}}})$ and $\Delta_{\min} = \min_{i \in [k]} \Delta_{S_{i,l_i}} = \min_{S \in \widetilde{\mathcal{I}}} \Delta_S$. So we have $\widetilde{\Phi}\left(\Delta_{S_{i,l_i}}, b\right) = O(\frac{1}{\epsilon \Delta_{\min}^2}(\ln B) \ln(\frac{\ln B}{\epsilon \Delta_{\min}}))$ and hence the regret bound is $O(\frac{km}{\epsilon \Delta_{\min}}(\ln B) \ln(\frac{\ln B}{\epsilon \Delta_{\min}}))$. $\qquad \square$

Proof of Theorem 13.5

Proof In the case that DP is neglected, we can set $\xi_{i,t} = 0$, hence $\theta_{i,t} = \lambda_{i,t}$. Then we can prove: $n_{i,t} > \Phi(\Delta_S, t) \Rightarrow \lambda_{i,t} < \min\{\frac{c_1}{2}, d_0(\Delta_S)\}$. The proof is similar to that of Lemma 13.8. With this, we can further prove: for any $S \in \widetilde{\mathcal{I}}$ and any $t \in [N-1]$, if the events $\mathcal{E}_{5,t}$ and $\{\forall i \in S : n_{i,t} > \Phi(\Delta_S, t)\}$ both hold, then we must have $A_{t+1} \neq S$. The proof is similar to that of Lemma 13.10. Then we can replace $\widetilde{\Phi}$ by Φ and get similar results with those of Lemma 13.11 and Theorem 13.4. So the claimed regret bound can be derived. $\qquad \square$

Table 13.3 Frequently used notation

Notation	Description
$\hat{v}_{i,t}, \hat{c}_{i,t}$	The random reward and cost of pulling arm i at time slot t, respectively
v_i, c_i	The expectation of $\hat{v}_{i,t}$ and $\hat{c}_{i,t}$, respectively
$\bar{v}_{i,t}, \bar{c}_{i,t}$	The empirical means of the reward and cost of arm i at time slot t, respectively
$\widetilde{v}_{i,t}, \widetilde{c}_{i,t}$	The noisy means of the reward and cost of arm i at time slot t, respectively
$\widetilde{v}'_{i,t}, \widetilde{c}'_{i,t}$	$\widetilde{v}'_{i,t} = \widetilde{v}_{i,t}$ if $\widetilde{v}_{i,t} > 0$, otherwise $\widetilde{v}'_{i,t} = 0$. $\widetilde{c}'_{i,t}$ is defined similarly
r_i, s_i	The predefined coefficients associated with arm i
k, B	k is the number of arms, and B is the budget
γ, μ	$\gamma = \sum_{i \in [k]} s_i$ and $\mu = \min_{i \in [k]} s_i c_i$
A_t	The set of arms pulled at time slot t
$\mathcal{I}$	All subsets of $[k]$ subject to a union of matroid constraints
$N^{\mathcal{P}}$	The stopping time of the budget-constrained arm-pulling policy $\mathcal{P}$
$n_{i,t}$	The number of times that arm i has been played from time slot 1 to time slot t
$C(S), V(S), \rho(S)$	$C(S) = \sum_{i \in S} s_i c_i$, $V(S) = \sum_{i \in S} r_i v_i$, $\rho(S) = V(S)/C(S)$
S^*, ρ^*	$S^* = \arg\max_{S \in \mathcal{I}} \rho(S), \rho^* = \rho(S^*)$
$\theta_{i,t}, \lambda_{i,t}, \xi_{i,t}$	$\theta_{i,t} = \lambda_{i,t} + \xi_{i,t}, \lambda_{i,t} = \sqrt{3 \ln t/(2n_{i,t})}$, $\xi_{i,t} = \frac{\sqrt{8}}{n_{i,t}\epsilon} \ln\left(4t^3\right)(1 + \ln n_{i,t})$
c_1, v_{min}, ς	$c_1 = \min_{i \in [k]} c_i, v_{min} = \min_{i \in [k]} v_i, \varsigma \triangleq \frac{\max_{i \in [k]} r_i}{\min_{i \in [k]} s_i}$
$\varphi(i, \iota_i), \iota_i, \beta(i)$	$\varphi(i, \iota_i) = r_i \widetilde{v}'_{i,t-1} + r_i \theta_{i,t-1} + \iota_i s_i \theta_{i,t-1}, \iota_i = \varsigma/f(u_i)$, $\beta(i) = s_i \widetilde{c}'_{i,t-1}$
$\tau(a, j), M(a)$	$\tau(a, j) = \varphi(j, \iota_i) - a\beta(j), M(a) = \max\{\sum_{j \in S} \tau(a, j)\|S \in K_{i,w}\}$
$\mathcal{I}^*, \widetilde{\mathcal{I}}, \widetilde{\mathcal{I}}_i$	$\widetilde{\mathcal{I}} = \{S \in \mathcal{I}\|\rho(S) < \rho(S^*)\}, \mathcal{I}^* = \mathcal{I} \backslash \widetilde{\mathcal{I}}, \widetilde{\mathcal{I}}_i = \{S\|i \in S \wedge S \in \widetilde{\mathcal{I}}\}$
$\Delta_S, \Delta_{\min}, \Delta_{\max}$	$\Delta_S = \rho(S^*) - \rho(S), \Delta_{\min} = \min_{S \in \widetilde{\mathcal{I}}} \Delta_S, \Delta_{\max} = \max_{S \in \widetilde{\mathcal{I}}} \Delta_S$
$S_{i,1}, S_{i,2}, \cdots, S_{i,l_i}$	All the sets in $\widetilde{\mathcal{I}}_i$ such that $\Delta_{S_{i,1}} \geq \Delta_{S_{i,2}} \geq \cdots \geq \Delta_{S_{i,l_i}}$
$d_0(\Delta_S)$	The value of $\frac{3\Delta_S c_1 + 2\varsigma + 2\varsigma c_1 - \sqrt{\Delta_S^2 c_1^2 + 4\varsigma^2 + 4\varsigma c_1^2(\varsigma - \Delta_S) + 12\varsigma c_1 \Delta_S + 8\varsigma^2 c_1}}{4\Delta_S + 8\varsigma} = O(\frac{1}{\Delta_S})$
$d_1(\Delta_S)$	The value of $\min\{c_1/2, d_0(\Delta_S), v_{min}\}$
$\widetilde{\Phi}(\Delta_S, t)$	The value of $\frac{(8\sqrt{2}d_1(\Delta_S)+1)\ln(4t^3)}{2\epsilon d_1^2(\Delta_S)}\left(\ln\left(\frac{(8\sqrt{2}d_1(\Delta_S)+1)\ln(4t^3)}{2\epsilon d_1^2(\Delta_S)}\right) + 7\right)$
$\Phi(\Delta_S, t)$	The value of $\max\{\frac{6}{c_1^2}, \frac{3}{2d_0^2(\Delta_S)}\} \ln t$
ϱ, m	$m = \max\{|S|\|S \in \mathcal{I}\}, \varrho = \max\{C(S)\|S \in \widetilde{\mathcal{I}}\} = O(m)$
ω, b	$\omega = \sum_{j \in [k]} r_j, b = (B + \gamma)/\mu$

References

1. Y. Gai, B. Krishnamachari, R. Jain, Combinatorial network optimization with unknown variables: multi-armed bandits with linear rewards and individual observations. IEEE/ACM Trans. Netw., **20**(5), 1466–1478 (2012)
2. C. Tekin, M. Liu, Online learning methods for networking. Found. Trends Netw. **8**(4), 281–409 (2015)
3. S. Bubeck, N. Cesa-Bianchi, Regret analysis of stochastic and nonstochastic multi-armed bandit problems. Found. Trends Mach. Learn. **5**(1), 1–122 (2012)
4. J. Oxley, *Matroid Theory* (Oxford University Press, Oxford, 2011)
5. T.H. Cormen, C.E. Leiserson, R.L. Rivest, C. Stein, *Introduction to Algorithms* (The MIT Press, Cambridge, 2009)
6. M.S. Talebi, A. Proutiere, An optimal algorithm for stochastic matroid bandit optimization, in *Proceedings of AAMAS* (2016), pp. 548–556
7. B. Kveton, Z. Wen, A. Ashkan, H. Eydgahi, B. Eriksson, Matroid bandits: Fast combinatorial optimization with learning, in *Proceedings of UAI* (2014), pp. 420–429
8. L. Chen, A. Gupta, J. Li, Pure exploration of multi-armed bandit under matroid constraints, in *Proceedings of COLT* (2016), pp. 647–669
9. L. Tran-Thanh, A. Chapman, A. Rogers, N.R Jennings, Knapsack based optimal policies for budget-limited multi-armed bandits, in *Proceedings of AAAI* (2012), pp. 1134–1140
10. Y. Xia, H. Li, T. Qin, N. Yu, T.-Y. Liu, Thompson sampling for budgeted multi-armed bandits, in *Proceedings of IJCAI* (2015), pp. 3960–3966
11. Y. Xia, T. Qin, W. Ma, N. Yu, T.-Y. Liu, Budgeted multi-armed bandits with multiple plays, in *Proceedings of IJCAI* (2016), pp. 2210–2216
12. A. Flajolet, P. Jaillet, Low regret bounds for bandits with knapsacks (2015). Preprint. arXiv:1510.01800
13. C. Dwork, A. Roth et al., The algorithmic foundations of differential privacy. Found. Trends Theor. Comput. Sci. **9**(3–4), 211–407 (2014)
14. P. Auer, N. Cesa-Bianchi, P. Fischer, Finite-time analysis of the multiarmed bandit problem. Mach. Learn. **47**(2–3), 235–256 (2002)
15. A. Badanidiyuru, R. Kleinberg, A. Slivkins, Bandits with knapsacks, in *Proceedings of FOCS* (2013), pp. 207–216
16. S. Agrawal, N.R. Devanur, Bandits with concave rewards and convex knapsacks, in *Proceedings of EC* (2014), pp. 989–1006
17. L. Tran-Thanh, A. Chapman, E.M. de Cote, A. Rogers, N.R. Jennings, Epsilon-first policies for budget-limited multi-armed bandits, in *Proceedings of AAAI* (2010), pp. 1211–1216
18. W. Ding, T. Qin, X.-D. Zhang, T.-Y. Liu, Multi-armed bandit with budget constraint and variable costs, in *Proceedings of AAAI* (2013), pp. 232–238
19. T.-H.H. Chan, E. Shi, D. Song, Private and continual release of statistics. ACM Trans. Inf. Syst. Secur. **14**(3), 26 (2011)
20. A.C.Y. Tossou, C. Dimitrakakis, Algorithms for differentially private multi-armed bandits, in *Proceedings of AAAI* (2016), pp. 2087–2093
21. J. Komiyama, J. Honda, H. Nakagawa, Optimal regret analysis of Thompson sampling in stochastic multi-armed bandit problem with multiple plays, in *Proceedings of ICML* (2015), pp. 1152–1161
22. S. Buccapatnam, A. Eryilmaz, N.B. Shroff, Stochastic bandits with side observations on networks, in *Proceedings of SIGMETRICS* (2014), pp. 289–300
23. W. Chen, Y. Wang, Y. Yuan, Combinatorial multi-armed bandit: general framework and applications, in *Proceedings of ICML* (2013), pp. 151–159
24. B. Kveton, Z. Wen, A. Ashkan, C. Szepesvari, Tight regret bounds for stochastic combinatorial semi-bandits, in *Proceedings of AISTATS* (2015), pp. 535–543
25. Q. Wang, W. Chen, Improving regret bounds for combinatorial semi-bandits with probabilistically triggered arms and its applications, in *Proceedings of NIPS* (2017), pp. 1161–1171

26. W. Chen, W. Hu, F. Li, J. Li, Y. Liu, P. Lu, Combinatorial multi-armed bandit with general reward functions, in *Proceedings of NIPS* (2016), pp. 1659–1667
27. R. Combes, M.S.T.M. Shahi, A. Proutiere et al., Combinatorial bandits revisited, in *Proceedings of NIPS* (2015), pp. 2116–2124
28. Z. Wen, B. Kveton, M. Valko, S. Vaswani, Online influence maximization under independent cascade model with semi-bandit feedback, in *Proceedings of NIPS* (2017), pp. 3026–3036
29. M.S. Talebi, Z. Zou, R. Combes, A. Proutière, M. Johansson, Stochastic online shortest path routing: The value of feedback. IEEE Trans. Autom. Control **63**(4), 915–930 (2018)
30. S. Vaswani, B. Kveton, Z. Wen, M. Ghavamzadeh, L.V.S. Lakshmanan, M. Schmidt, Model-independent online learning for influence maximization, in *Proceedings of ICML* (2017), pp. 3530–3539
31. R. Combes, C. Jiang, R. Srikant, Bandits with budgets: Regret lower bounds and optimal algorithms. ACM SIGMETRICS Perform. Eval. Rev. **43**(1), 245–257 (2015)
32. H. Wu, R. Srikant, X. Liu, C. Jiang, Algorithms with logarithmic or sublinear regret for constrained contextual bandits, in *Proceedings of NIPS* (2015), pp. 433–441
33. A. Garivier, O. Cappé, The KL-UCB algorithm for bounded stochastic bandits and beyond, in *Proceedings of COLT* (2011), pp. 359–376
34. P. Jain, P. Kothari, A. Thakurta, Differentially private online learning, in *Proceedings of COLT* (2012), pp. 24.1–24.34
35. A.G. Thakurta, A. Smith, (nearly) optimal algorithms for private online learning in full-information and bandit settings, in *Proceedings of NIPS* (2013), pp. 2733–2741
36. N. Mishra, A. Thakurta, (nearly) Optimal differentially private stochastic multi-arm bandits, in *Proceedings of UAI* (2015), pp. 592–601
37. G. Calinescu, C. Chekuri, M. Pál, J. Vondrák, Maximizing a monotone submodular function subject to a matroid constraint. SIAM J. Comput. **40**(6), 1740–1766 (2011)
38. Amazon mechanical turk (2005). https://www.mturk.com/mturk/welcome
39. H. Jin, L. Su, B. Ding, K. Nahrstedt, N. Borisov, Enabling privacy-preserving incentives for mobile crowd sensing systems, in *Proceedings of ICDCS* (2016), pp. 344–353
40. G. Grimmett, D. Stirzaker, *Probability and Random Processes* (Oxford University Press, Oxford, 2001)
41. C.A. Floudas, P.M. Pardalos, *Encyclopedia of Optimization* (Springer, New York, 2009)
42. N. Megiddo, Combinatorial optimization with rational objective functions. Math. Oper. Res. **4**(4), 414–424 (1979)
43. F.D. McSherry, Privacy integrated queries: an extensible platform for privacy-preserving data analysis, in *Proceedings of SIGMOD* (2009), pp. 19–30
44. D.A. Barry, J.-Y. Parlange, L. Li, H. Prommer, C.J. Cunningham, F. Stagnitti, Analytical approximations for real values of the lambert w-function. Math. Comput. Simul. **53**(1), 95–103 (2000)
45. S. Yi, P.W. Nelson, A.G. Ulsoy, *Time-delay Systems: Analysis and Control Using the Lambert W Function* (World Scientific, Singapore, 2010)
46. Ibm ilog cplex optimization studio (2009). https://www.ibm.com/developerworks/downloads/ws/ilogcplex/
47. W. Hoeffding, Probability inequalities for sums of bounded random variables. J. Am. Stat. Assoc. **58**(301), 13–30 (1963)
48. G. Gan, C. Ma, H. Xie, *Measure, Probability, and Mathematical Finance: A Problem-oriented Approach* (Wiley, Hoboken, 2014)

Part IV
Breaking Privacy

Chapter 14
Breaching Privacy in Encrypted Instant Messaging Networks

14.1 Introduction

The proliferation of online social networks has attracted the interest of computer scientists to mine the available social network data for developing behavior profiles of people. These profiles are often used for targeted marketing [1–3], web personalization [4], and even price discrimination on e-commerce portals [5, 6]. Recently, there has been increased interest in more fine-grained profiling by leveraging information about people's friendship networks. It has been shown that information from people's friendship networks can be used to infer their preferences and religious beliefs, and political affiliations [7–10].

There has been a lot of research on de-anonymizing people's friendship networks in online social networks such as Facebook, MySpace, Twitter [11, 12]. Surprisingly, little prior work has focused on de-anonymizing people's friendship link in instant messaging (IM) networks. IM services—such as Yahoo! Messenger, Skype, IRC, and ICQ—are popular tools to privately communicate with friends and family over the Internet. IM networks are different than other online social networks in various respects. For example, in contrast to online social networks, communication among users in IM networks is synchronous in nature and messages between two communicating users are routed through relay servers of the IM service provider.

The goal of this chapter is to identify the set of most likely IM users that a given user is communicating with during a fixed time period. Note that packet payloads in IM traffic are encrypted; therefore, payload information cannot be used for the identification. Therefore, to infer who a user is talking to, we will rely only on the information in packet header traces. Packet header traces contain information such as timestamp, source IP address, destination IP address, source port, destination port, and protocol type, and payload size of each packet. It is noteworthy that each packet in the IM traffic has as its source and destination IP addresses of a user computer and an IM relay server (or vice versa). At no point do two users

A. X. Liu, R. Li, *Algorithms for Data and Computation Privacy*,
https://doi.org/10.1007/978-3-030-58896-0_14

exchange packets directly with each other, i.e., there are no packets in which the two communicating users' IP addresses appear in the same packet. For this attack, we assume that IM service acts neutral, i.e., it neither facilitates the attacker nor actively participates in providing anonymity to the users using non-standard functionality. Our specific goal is to accurately identify a candidate set of top-k users with whom a given user possibly talked to using only the information available in packet header traces.

A natural approach to tackle this problem would be to match header information of packets entering and leaving IM relay servers. However, simply matching header information of packets entering and leaving IM servers is not feasible due the following reasons. First, a user may be talking to multiple users simultaneously. Second, IM relay servers typically serve thousands of users at a time. Third, the handling of duplicate packets that are the result of packet losses followed by re-transmissions. Forth, the handling of out-of-order packets. Finally, the handling of variable transmission delays, which are introduced by the IM relay servers.

In this chapter, we propose a wavelet-based scheme, called COmmunication Link De-anonymization (COLD), to accurately infer who's talking to whom using only the information available in packet header traces. Wavelet transform is a standard method for simultaneous time-frequency analysis and helps to correlate the temporal information in one-way (i.e. user-to-server or server-to-user) traffic logs across multiple time scales [13]. Wavelet analysis allows decomposition of traffic time series between a user and an IM relay server into several levels. All levels are associated with a coefficient value and contain different levels of frequency information starting from low to high. The original traffic time series can be reconstructed by combining all levels after weighing them with their respective coefficients. COLD leverages the multi-scale examination of traffic time series provided by wavelet analysis to overcome the aforementioned technical challenges. Given two candidate time series between an IM relay server and two users, COLD computes correlation between the vectors of wavelet coefficients for both time series to determine whether these users talked to each other.

We evaluate the effectiveness of COLD on a Yahoo! Messenger data set comprising of traffic collected over 10, 20, 30, 40, 50 and 60 min periods. We also compare COLD's performance to a baseline time series correlation (TSC) scheme, which represents the state of the art. The effectiveness is quantified in terms of hit rate for a fix-sized candidate set. The results of our experiments show that COLD achieves a hit rate of more than 90% for a candidate set size of 10. For slightly larger candidate set size of 20, COLD achieves almost 100% hit rate. In contrast, a baseline method using time series correlation could only achieve less than 5% hit rate for similar candidate set sizes.

We summarize the major contributions of this chapter as follows.

1. We define an attack for breaching communication privacy in encrypted IM networks using only the information available in packet header traces.
2. We propose COLD to infer who's talking to whom using wavelet based multi-scale analysis.

3. We conducted experiments using a real-world Yahoo! Messenger data set to evaluate the effectiveness of our proposed approach.

14.1.1   Chapter Organization

The rest of this chapter is organized as follows. Section 14.2 summarizes the related work. A detailed description of attack scenarios is provided in Sect. 14.3. Section 14.4 provides details of the proposed attack. In Sect. 14.5, we present the evaluation results on a real-world Yahoo! Messenger data set. Possible evasion techniques and their countermeasures are discussed in Sect. 14.6. Finally, Sect. 14.7 concludes the chapter.

14.2   Related Work

In this section, we provide details of the research work related to our study. To the best of our knowledge, no prior work has reported a successful attack to breach users' communication privacy in encrypted IM networks using only the information available in packet header traces. However, there is some relevant work in the area of mix network de-anonymization. We discuss it and other related studies below.

14.2.1   Mix Network De-anonymization

In the area of mix network, several studies have used correlation techniques for de-anonymization. However, most of these studies are limited to computing temporal correlation between traffic of two user-network links to find user-user links. Furthermore, de-anonymization of mix networks is fundamentally different from our problem in the following two aspects. First, mix network de-anonymization techniques require traffic logs from multiple points inside a mix network. In contrast, this study treats IM relay servers as a black box. Second, the size of user populations in mix network de-anonymization studies is only of the order of tens or hundreds. However, in real-life IM networks, thousands of users can simultaneously communicate with other users; therefore, presenting a more challenging problem. In [14], Troncoso and Danezis build a Markov Chain Monte Carlo inference engine to calculate probabilities of who is talking to whom in a mix network using network traces. However, they log network traces from multiple points in a mix network and the maximum network size studied in their chapter is limited to 10. In [15], Zhu et al. compute mutual information between aggregate inflow and outflow traffic statistics to decide if two users are talking to each other in a mix network. Similar to this study, they also log traffic from the edges of a mix network. However, their proposed approach requires traffic logs for longer time durations. In this chapter, we compare the results of COLD and the method proposed by Zhu et al. [15].

14.2.2 Social Network De-anonymization

There is also some related work in the field of social network de-anonymization. Narayanan and Shamitkov developed an algorithm to utilize sparsity in high-dimensional data sets for de-anonymization [16]. Later they developed a user re-identification algorithm that operated on anonymized social network data sets [17]. Other related studies use group membership information to identify users in a social network [7, 18]. IM networks also fall under the broader category of online social networks; however, our problem and the nature of the data available to us is different from those tackled in the aforementioned chapters. These studies focus on user identification using mainly topological information; whereas, we focus on link identification using dynamic user communication traffic.

14.3   Problem Description and Attack Scenarios

In this section, we first provide a summary of architectural details of IM services. We then provide the details of information available from traffic traces logged near IM relay servers. Finally, we describe two scenarios in which traffic can be logged for link de-anonymization.

14.3.1 IM Service Architecture

We first describe the architecture of a typical IM service. Consider the scenario depicted in Fig. 14.1 where two users v_1 and v_2 are communicating with each other via an IM service. When v_1 sends a message to v_2, the source IP address in packets containing this message correspond to v_1 and the destination IP address correspond to the IM relay server. These packets are received by the IM relay server after a random delay. After receiving a packet from v_1, the IM server first looks up the IP address of v_2. It then creates new packets with its IP address as source and IP address of v_2 as destination. These packets containing message from v_1 are then relayed by the IM relay server to v_2 and have the same contents. This process incurs an additional delay after which the new packet reaches v_2.

The network traffic logged near the IM relay server only contains header information because the packet payload contents are not useful due to encryption. The statistics recorded by the well-known traffic logging tools like Cisco's NetFlow include IP addresses, port numbers, protocol, packet size, and timestamp information [19]. As mentioned before, IP addresses are used to identify individual users of the IM service. IM traffic is filtered from rest of the traffic using a combination of protocol and port number information. We are left with only aggregated packet sizes and timestamp information for each flow. A logged entry for a flow is an aggregation of packets which may be sent to or received from the IM server. Due to aggregation, information about the direction of flow is lost for individual packets. Therefore, we make a realistic assumption that the direction information is not available in the logged traffic. An example of a similar publicly available data set is the Yahoo! Network Flows Data [20].

Referring to Fig. 14.1, each flow in the data set comprises of information about incoming and outgoing packets between an IM relay server and a user. Furthermore, individual users can be distinguished based on IP addresses in the IM traffic. In Fig. 14.1, traffic exchanged between v_1 and the IM relay server is represented by blue arrows and traffic exchanged between v_2 and the IM relay server is represented by red arrows. The timestamps and packet sizes are both discrete and in units of milliseconds. The packet sizes are typically recorded in bytes. The resulting signal for each flow is discrete in both time and amplitude as shown in Fig. 14.1. These sparse time domain traces of network traffic are referred to as *traffic signals* from now-onwards. It is interesting to simultaneously analyze traffic signals for both users v_1 and v_2. Note that every entry in v_1's traffic signal has a time-shifted (time delayed or advanced) matching entry of equal magnitude in v_2's traffic signal. These matches between each pair of entries are marked by broken lines joining traffic signals in Fig. 14.1. Matching entries across both traffic signals may not have the same order due to random end-to-end delays. For example, third message flow entry in v_2's trace appears as fourth entry in v_1's trace in Fig. 14.1.

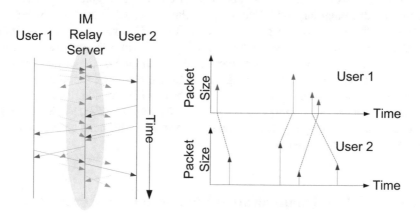

Fig. 14.1 Transforming logged traffic traces to user traffic signals

14.3.2   Attack Scenarios

We now consider two different scenarios in which traffic information necessary for the proposed attack can be obtained.

14.3.2.1   Scenario #1: Near IM Relay Servers

The first scenario assumes the capability to monitor incoming and outgoing traffic of an IM relay server or server farm. Figure 14.2a shows four users v_1, v_2, v_3 and v_4 connected to an IM relay server. The shaded circular region around the IM relay server marks the boundary across which network traffic is logged. For the scenario depicted in Fig. 14.2a, v_1 is communicating with v_2 and v_3 is communicating with v_4. Traffic signals for all users that are obtained after pre-processing their traffic flow logs. For each flow represented in a user's traffic signal, a corresponding flow entry can be observed in the traffic flow log. The IM relay servers also introduces a random delay between the time a message arrives at the IM relay server and the time it is relayed to the other user. Therefore, there will be a mismatch in the timestamps of the occurrences of a message in communicating users' traffic signals.

14.3.2.2   Scenario #2: Border Gateway

The second scenario assumes that all IM users communicating with each other are located in the same network. Many organizations, such as universities, connect to external networks and the Internet through one or more gateway routers. The incoming and outgoing traffic has to pass through a small number of gateway routers. In this scenario, it is possible to collect flow logs near the gateway routers of an organizational network. Figure 14.2b depicts the above-mentioned scenario. Here, v_1 and v_2 are in the same network and are communicating with each other via an IM relay server. All incoming and outgoing traffic of the network passes through the border gateway router near which it can be logged. The region near border gateway router is represented by the shaded region in Fig. 14.2b. The traffic signals obtained from pre-processing the flow logs have the same characteristics as described for the first scenario.

14.4   COLD: COmmunication Link De-anonymization

In this section, we present the details of our proposed method (COLD) to detect communication links between users in IM networks. We first introduce the overall architecture of COLD. We then provide details of each of its modules. Finally, we provide an easy-to-follow toy example of COLD on a small set of three IM users.

Fig. 14.2 Two attack
scenarios. (**a**) Collecting all
incoming and outgoing traffic
from IM relay server. (**b**)
Collecting all incoming and
outgoing traffic near border
gateway routers of an
organizational network

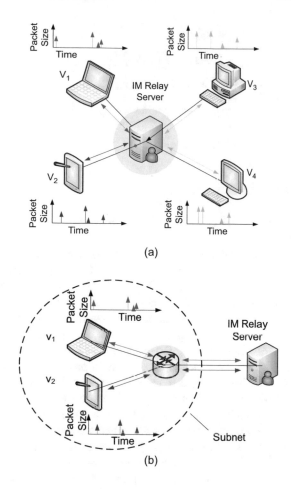

(a)

(b)

14.4.1   Architecture

Figure 14.3 shows the overall architecture of COLD. As mentioned in Sect. 14.3,
the logged traffic traces are separated for all users based on IP address information.
These user-wise separated traffic traces are further pre-processed and converted
to traffic signals. The traffic signals for all users are stored in a database. Note
that traffic signals of users may span different time durations. To overcome this
problem, we use zero-padding so that the lengths of traffic signals are consistent for
all users. After this pre-processing, wavelet transform is separately applied to all
users' traffic signals [13]. We then construct feature vectors for all users using the
computed wavelet coefficients. Now, to compare two given users, we compute the
correlation coefficient between their constructed feature vectors. Finally, the values
of the correlation coefficient are sorted to generate the candidate set. The details of
all modules of COLD are separately discussed in Fig. 14.3.

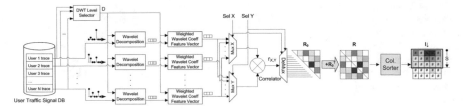

Fig. 14.3 COLD architecture

14.4.2   Details

14.4.2.1   Discrete Wavelet Transform

After pre-processing the traffic traces, we compute the discrete wavelet transform (DWT) of each user's traffic signal. This step is performed in the wavelet decomposition module shown in Fig. 14.3. The wavelet transform enables us to conduct a simultaneous time-frequency analysis. A traffic signal is decomposed into multiple time series, each containing information at different scales that range from coarse to fine. A time series at a coarse scale represents the low frequency or low pass information regarding the original time series. Likewise, a time series at a fine scale represents the high frequency or high pass information regarding the original time series. This allows us to compare traffic patterns of users at multiple time scales.

We have to select an appropriate wavelet function for our given problem. Since we are processing traffic signals of a large number of users, we want to select an efficient wavelet type. For our study, we have chosen the Haar wavelet function for wavelet decomposition [21]. We have chosen the Haar wavelet function because it is simple and is computationally and memory-wise efficient. Furthermore, the wavelet transform can be applied for varying decomposition levels to capture varying levels of detail. Choosing the optimal number of decomposition levels is important because this may lead to suppressing relevant and critical information that might be contained in one or more levels of the wavelet decomposition. Below, we discuss the method to select the optimal number of decomposition levels.

14.4.2.2   Choosing the Optimal Number of Decomposition Levels

Let $D \in \mathbb{Z}^+$ denote the optimal number of decomposition levels. Different methods have been proposed in the literature to select the optimal number of decomposition levels. In this chapter, we have used Coifman and Wickerhauser's well-known Shannon entropy-based method to select the optimal number of decomposition levels [22]. We applied this method to traffic signals of all users and then selected the optimal decomposition level at the 95th percentile. Now that we have selected the optimal number of decomposition levels, we can apply the wavelet transform on user traffic signals.

14.4.2.3   Coefficient Feature Vector

Once we have obtained the wavelet coefficients after applying the wavelet transform to a user's traffic signal, we need to convert them to a standard feature vector so that we can compare users' signals. Let $\mathcal{F}_X$ denote the feature vector of a user X. The coefficients that contain high frequency information are more numerous and such coefficients are assigned lower weights. Similarly, the coefficients that contain low frequency information are fewer and are assigned higher weights. The time signal corresponding to level 1 of the wavelet decomposition represents the coarsest features containing low frequency information, and level D refers to the highest level describing the most detailed features containing high frequency information. The level D feature coefficients are assigned weight 1, the level $D - 1$ coefficients are assigned weight 2, etc., and the level 1 coefficients are assigned weight 2^{D-1}. In general, the level d features are assigned a weight of 2^{D-d-1}. To produce the standard feature vector in which each coefficient is given the appropriate weight, we replace each coefficient by a vector of its copies of length equal to its weight, i.e. a wavelet coefficient of decomposition level d is replaced by a vector containing 2^{D-d-1} copies. This is equivalent to using the undecimated wavelet transform of users' traffic signals. By following this procedure, the total length of the feature vectors of all traffic signals becomes consistent.

14.4.2.4   Correlation

After applying the wavelet transform and post-processing coefficients to a user X's traffic signal, we obtain a feature vector denoted $\mathcal{F}_X$. To compare the feature vectors $\mathcal{F}_X$ and $\mathcal{F}_Y$ for two users X and Y, we have to compute their correlation. The sample correlation coefficient $r_{X,Y}$ of two discrete signals $\mathcal{F}_X$ and $\mathcal{F}_Y$, both of length L, is defined as,

$$r_{X,Y} = \frac{\sum_{i=1}^{L}(\mathcal{F}_X(i) - \overline{\mathcal{F}_X})(\mathcal{F}_Y(i) - \overline{\mathcal{F}_Y})}{(L-1)s_X s_Y}. \tag{14.1}$$

Here, $\mathcal{F}_X(i)$ is the ith element of the feature vector $\mathcal{F}_X$, $\overline{\mathcal{F}_X}$ is the sample mean of its elements, and s_X is the sample standard deviation of its elements. The values of the correlation coefficient lie in the closed interval $[-1, 1]$. The correlation coefficient values close to zero indicate no correlation; whereas, the values close to 1 and -1 respectively highlight strong correlation and anti-correlation. For this study, we only consider the magnitude of the correlation coefficient and discard its sign. After computing the correlation coefficient for all pairs of users, we get the upper triangular correlation matrix $\mathbf{R}_0$. $r_{i,j}$ is written into the ith row and the jth column of the correlation matrix $\mathbf{R}_0$. Conceptually, this correlation matrix is similar to the adjacency matrix of a weighted graph. We add to $\mathbf{R}_0$ its transpose to obtain $\mathbf{R}$.

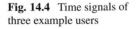

Fig. 14.4 Time signals of three example users

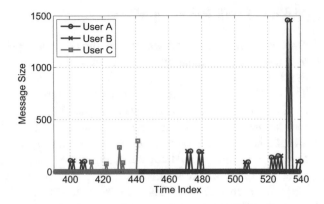

14.4.2.5   Candidate Set Generation

After obtaining the correlation matrix **R** whose elements are in the range of [0, 1] we need to generate, for each node, a sorted list of nodes in decreasing order of probability of communicating. This is done by sorting the node indices in descending order of correlation coefficients in every column of **R**. The resulting matrix will have the same size as **R** and is labeled **I** ↓. Suppose that the S most likely users that are communicating with user i is required. Then the user IDs contained in the top S rows of the i-th column of **I** ↓ is the sorted list of users i is most likely communicating with.

14.4.3   Example

We now provide a easy-to-follow toy example of COLD on three users (A, B, and C) in an IM network. Users A and B are communicating with each other while user C is not communicating with either user A or user B. Figure 14.4 shows the traffic signals for all three users. The traffic signals of users A and B are visibly similar to each other and significantly different from the traffic signal of user C. However, if we directly compute the correlation coefficients of users' time signals we get $r_{A,B} = -0.0046$, $r_{B,C} = -0.0053$, and $r_{A,C} = -0.0053$. Equivalently, the correlation matrix is:

$$\mathbf{R} = \begin{pmatrix} 1 & 0.0046 & 0.0053 \\ 0.0046 & 1 & 0.0053 \\ 0.0053 & 0.0053 & 1 \end{pmatrix}$$

This indicates that directly correlating users' traffic signal time series is not accurate.

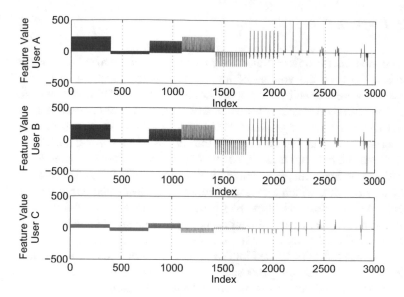

Fig. 14.5 Wavelet feature vectors of three example users

Let us now obtain the feature vectors for all users using the wavelet transform. Figure 14.5 shows the coefficient feature vectors for users A, B, and C. Note that the feature vectors at lower indices contain coarse grain or low frequency information. We observe significant similarity between the lower indices of the feature vectors of users A and B. Now when we compute the correlation coefficients of users' feature vectors we get $r_{A,B} = 0.7042$, $r_{B,C} = 0.0743$, and $r_{A,C} = 0.0742$. Equivalently, the correlation matrix is:

$$\mathbf{R} = \begin{pmatrix} 1 & 0.7042 & 0.0742 \\ 0.7042 & 1 & 0.0743 \\ 0.0742 & 0.0743 & 1 \end{pmatrix}$$

This clearly indicates the superiority of COLD (with the wavelet-based feature vectors) attack method compared to the direct correlation of users' traffic signals.

14.5   Experimental Results

In this section, we first describe the data set used for evaluating COLD, then define evaluation metrics, and finally present evaluation results.

14.5.1 Data Set

We collected a data set from Yahoo! Messenger IM network to validate our proposed approach. To keep the volume of logged data manageable, the users of Yahoo! Messenger were filtered by geographic location and restricted to the New York City area. This data set consists of traffic logs of Yahoo! Messenger user activity over a period of 60 min from the greater New York area, between 8 a.m. to 9 a.m. Using this data set, we create six data sets that are the subsets of the entire data. These consist of data over the only the first 10, 20, 30, 40, 50 and 60 min, i.e. from 8–8:10 a.m., 8–8:20 a.m., 8–8:30 a.m., 8–8:40 a.m., 8–8:50 a.m. and 8–9 a.m. To gauge the effect of the duration over which a data set is collected we evaluated our proposed COLD scheme on all six data sets. Table 14.1 lists, along with the time of day and duration, the number of logged users, number of messages exchanged between them, and the number of instant messaging sessions included in each data set.

The collected data is divided into two parts: input data and ground truth data, to systematically evaluate our proposed approach. Both data sets were collected with the assistance of Yahoo! and are described in the following text.

14.5.1.1 Input Data

The input data consists of *user-to-server* traffic traces that were collected similar to the scenario described in Fig. 14.2a. Figure 14.6 plots the volume of traffic logged in these traffic traces. The figure on top plots number of bytes per second against time. Similarly, the plot in the bottom figure plots the traffic volume in packets per second for the same period of time.

14.5.1.2 Ground Truth Data

The verification data contains a record of the actual *user-to-user* connections resulting from conversations between users. Therefore, the verification data contains the ground truth for given problem. Our proposed COLD scheme attempts to recreate the link structures between users contained in the verification data by only using information in the input data. Figure 14.7 is a plot of the degree distribution

Table 14.1 Data set statistics

Time	Duration	Users	Messages	Sessions
8–8:10a	10 min	3420	15,370	1968
8–8:20a	20 min	5405	33,192	3265
8–8:30a	30 min	7438	53,649	4661
8–8:40a	40 min	9513	75,810	6179
8–8:50a	50 min	11,684	99,721	7669
8–9a	60 min	13,953	126,694	9264

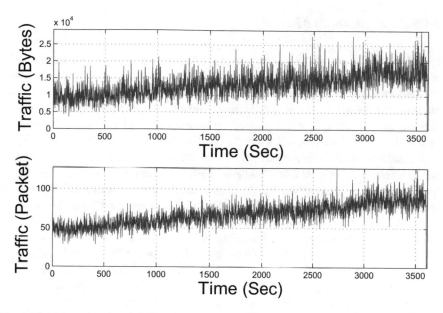

Fig. 14.6 Time series plot of traffic volume, in bytes and number of packets, over the entire 60 min time period from 8 to 9 a.m.

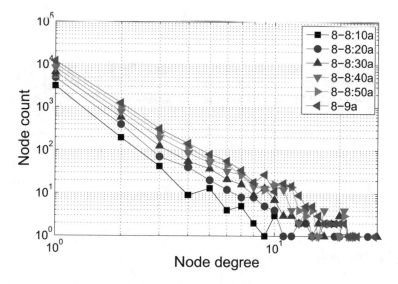

Fig. 14.7 Node degree distribution in our Yahoo! Messenger data set

of users observed in the verification data collected over 10 and 60 min time periods. The distribution is approximately linear on log-log scale over the range of degrees from 1 to 9 for the 10 min data, and from 1 to 11 for the 60 min data.

14.5.2   Evaluation Metrics

Let V denote the set of Yahoo! Messenger users $v_1, v_2, \ldots, v_N$. Furthermore, let E denote the set of actual communication links $u_1, u_2, \ldots, u_M$ of size M between N users captured in the verification data. Then $G(V, E)$ is the graph of users (or vertices) connected by the communication links (or edges) between them. Recall that the goal of the attack is to detect communication links $\widehat{U}$ that estimates the actual set of communication links in the verification data U. The graph $\widehat{G}(V, \widehat{U})$ is the outcome of the scheme that constitutes the attack. In the rest of this section, we compare our proposed COLD scheme with the baseline time series correlation (denoted by TSC here onwards). A graph that is obtained using COLD will be denoted by $\widehat{G}_C(V, \widehat{U}_C)$. A graph obtained using TSC is denoted by $\widehat{G}_T(V, \widehat{U}_T)$.

Consider the subset of vertices with degree δ in a graph $\widehat{G}(V, \widehat{U})$ obtained using either schemes. Now consider a candidate set C_i of size $S \geq \delta$ for every vertex v_i of degree δ. The candidate set C_i of a vertex v_i contains S vertices most likely to be v_i's neighbors, as determined by the COLD or TSC. We also define a neighborhood function denoted by $\Gamma_G()$. $\Gamma_G(v_i)$ returns the set of vertices in the graph G that are connected to vertex v_i. Furthermore, we define the node hit rate of a vertex v_i as the fraction of vertices in $\Gamma_G(v_i)$ that are also elements of candidate set C_i of size S. The node hit rate of vertex v_i is denoted $h_i(S)$ an is defined formally as follows.

$$h_i(S) = \frac{|\Gamma_G(v_i) \cap C_i(S)|}{|\Gamma_G(v_i)|} \tag{14.2}$$

The node hit rate can take values in the range of the closed interval $[0, 1]$. We also define the hit rate $H_{\widehat{G}}(S, \delta)$ for degree δ vertices of a graph $\widehat{G}(V, \widehat{U})$ as the average of their node hit rates $h_i(S)$ when candidate set sizes are S.

$$H_{\widehat{G}}(S, \delta) = \frac{\sum_{i=1, \delta_i = \delta}^{N} h_i(S)}{n_d} \tag{14.3}$$

Here n_d is the number of vertices in $\widehat{G}$ of degree δ. Just like the node hit rate, the hit rate can take values in the range of the closed interval $[0, 1]$.

14.5.3   Results

We compute the hit rates achieved using COLD on the 10, 20, 30, 40, 50 and 60 min data sets and compare them with the hit rates achieved by TSC. We further separate vertices by the number of packets they exchange over the duration of the data set, i.e. hit rates are computed separately for vertices exchanging 1–60, 61–70, 71–80, 81–90, 91–100, 101–110, and 111–120 packets. As we observed in the degree distributions of nodes in Fig. 14.7, data sets for all six durations are dominated by

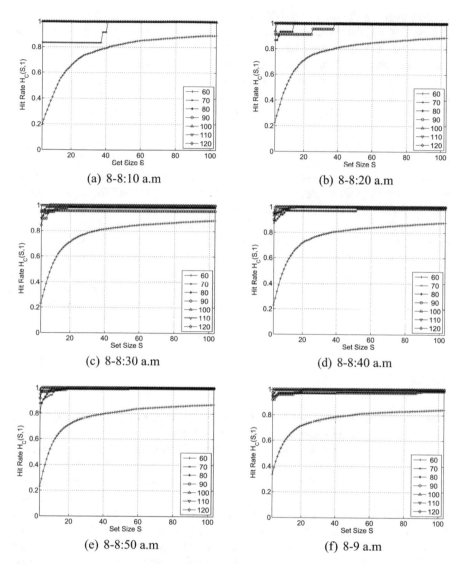

Fig. 14.8 Hit rates of COLD for vertices of degree 1 in the (**a**) 10 min data set, (**b**) 20 min data set, (**c**) 30 min data set, (**d**) 40 min data set, (**e**) 50 min data set, and (**f**) 60 min data set

nodes of degree 1. Therefore, in our evaluation we focus primarily on degree 1 vertices. Figure 14.8a–f plots the hit rates of degree 1 vertices as a function of set size S for COLD on 10, 20, 30, 40, 50, and 60 min data sets, respectively. Within each figure, hit rates are segregated according to the number of packets users send and receive over the duration the data was collected. As these six figures consistently show, the hit rate reaches between 0.9 and 1.0 for users exchanging 71 or more packets over the duration of the data sets. In case of the 20, 30, 40, 50, and 60 min data sets in Fig. 14.8b–f, this set of users is further extended to those exchanging 61 or more packets. In the 10 min data set in Fig. 14.8a users with 61–70 packets in their trace have a high hit rate of more than 0.80. However, the candidate set size S has to be increased all the way to 40 for the hit rate to reach close to 1.0. For users exchanging between 1–60 packets the hit rate starts out between 0.20 and 0.40. As the candidate set size is increased from 1 upward, the hit rate rises at a very similar rate in all six data sets.

We compare the accuracy of our proposed approach to that of the time series correlation (TSC) method. Similarly, Fig. 14.9a–f plots the hit rates of degree 1 vertices as a function of set size S for TSC on 10, 20, 30, 40, 50 and 60 min data sets, respectively. The baseline TSC method, which represents the state of the art, fails to deliver sufficient performance to be useful for any conceivable application, across all six data sets. With one slight exception, TSC fails to achieve a hit rate of even 0.20 even for candidate set size of as large as 100. The only exception is the group of users exchanging between 71–80 packets in the 10 min data set. However, even for this subset of users, TSC provides a hit rate of less than 0.30 at a set size greater than 70, i.e. at best, for users messaging with only one other person, in a set of 70 candidates TSC will include the actual instant messaging partner with a probability of only 0.30.

14.5.4   Discussions

These results provide us with several insights into the working of COLD. We separately discuss these insights in the following text.

First, there appears to be a very clear threshold value for the number of recorded packets beyond which the de-anonymization attack using COLD yields high hit rates. From the plots in Fig. 14.8 we observe that the hit rate for users containing more than 60 packets in their traffic traces is significantly higher, above 90%, even at very small candidate set sizes. On the other hand, the hit rate of users containing 60 packets or less in their traffic trace is significantly lower. This threshold value holds across all six data sets of different durations. More packet entries in traffic traces provide more points to match two communicating users' traces with each other. The greater number of data points also reduces the probability of a false match. Therefore, it is easier to identify communicating users that message each other more frequently.

Second, the hit rate of users, classified by the traffic they generate, is largely independent of the time duration over which the traces were collected. Rather, it is the actual number of message packets exchanged during that period that determines the hit rate. Hit rates for users exchanging the same number of packets over different periods of time are very similar. Therefore, we can state that we can identify two communicating users using COLD with great certainty as soon as they exchange more than 60 message packets.

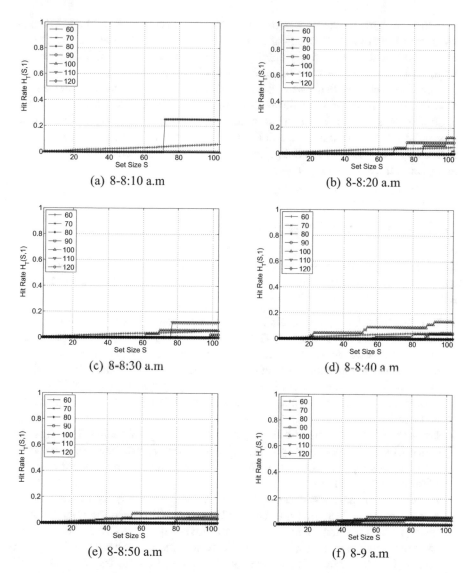

Fig. 14.9 Hit rates of TSC for vertices of degree 1 in the (**a**) 10 min data set, (**b**) 20 min data set, (**c**) 30 min data set, (**d**) 40 min data set, (**e**) 50 min data set, and (**f**) 60 min data set

Third, while we have already stated that the time period over which traffic traces are collected have only a weak effect on the hit rate. However, looking at the hit rate functions of users with 61–70, 71–80 and 81–90 packets in their traffic trace across different data sets, we observe that the hit rate function rises close to 1.0 at a faster rate in data sets collected over longer durations.

Fourth, judging by the time durations of the data sets (between 10 and 60 min), we conclude that the amount of data necessary to achieve a high hit rate by COLD can be collected in a relatively short period of time. Therefore, COLD does not require an extensive data collection effort to achieve high accuracy.

Finally, we observe that when TSC is applied to all data sets, the hit rate remains almost 0 for vertices of all traffic levels. This leads us to the conclusion that TSC is effectively unable to detect any communication links among users. We attribute this failure to the random phase delay of packet entries in traffic traces of two communicating users. These delays are a result of the bidirectional flow of traffic and jitter in the end-to-end delay.

14.6   Evasion and Countermeasures

This section presents some possible techniques that an adversary may utilize to evade the de-anonymization attack by COLD. We also discuss countermeasures to such evasion techniques below.

1. **Evasion by using proxy or NAT.** An adversary may access instant messaging network behind a proxy or a NAT to bypass the detection by the COLD attack algorithm. However, in this scenario, COLD will still detect the external IP address, which appears in the traffic traces collected outside the proxy or NAT. Once the external IP address is detected, our proposed approach will require additional traces collected inside the proxy or NAT to specifically pin-point the end-host.
2. **Evasion by IP spoofing.** An adversary may try to spoof source IP address to evade COLD. However, IP spoofing will not be successful because every end-user has to setup a connection with the IM relay server, which is not possible with spoofed IP address.
3. **Evasion by fragmentation/aggregation.** An adversary may try to break-down a large message into multiple smaller messages. However, fragmentation at the end-host into smaller packets will not adversely affect COLD because our approach relies on correlating the traffic traces that are collected entering and leaving the IM service. The smaller packets created due to fragmentation will appear the same in both sets of traffic traces. In fact, the increased number of packets would improve COLD's accuracy. On the other hand, an adversary may try to aggregate as many messages as possible into a single message to minimize the data available. However, the maximum packet size is limited by the IM service provider and maximum transmission unit (MTU) of the network.
4. **Evasion by changing packet sizes.** If an adversary tries to deliberately change packet sizes, e.g., by inserting garbage, they will appear the same in the two sets of traffic traces correlated by COLD. Therefore, changing packets sizes will not affect COLD.

5. **Evasion by random delays.** Adversaries may also add random small or long delays between their communications. The time delays introduced by end-host will not affect COLD because these delays appear the same in the two sets of traffic traces. In another scenario, random delays may be introduced by the IM network due to network congestion or other processing delays. These delays will affect COLD because they will be different across the two correlated traffic traces. However, COLD is robust to such delays as well because it utilizes binning techniques, which reduces their effect.
6. **Evasion by injecting noise packets.** Injecting random noise packets is unlikely to affect the accuracy of COLD as long as the noise packets follow the protocol utilized by the IM network. Packets that do not follow the protocol utilized by the IM network will be discarded by the IM network after sanity checks and will not appear in the second traffic trace collecting traffic exiting the IM network. To mitigate the effect of such noise packets, similar sanity checks can be deployed to check if the logged packets follow the protocol utilized by the IM network under study.
7. **Evasion by encryption.** Encryption is only applicable to the packet payloads and packet headers remain unaffected. The use of encryption cannot evade COLD because our proposed approach only utilizes fields in the packet header.

14.7 Conclusions

In this chapter, we present a novel attack to breach the privacy of IM communication services that allows an attacker to infer who's talking to whom with high accuracy. We proposed a wavelet-based scheme, called COLD, that allows us to examine and compare the time series of one-way (user-server) traffic logs at multiple scales. We evaluated the COLD attack algorithm using a real-world Yahoo! Messenger data set, which was specifically collected for this study. Our experimental results showed that COLD clearly outperforms the baseline time series correlation scheme.

Our proposed approach can also be applied to the related problems such as mix network de-anonymization. In the mix network de-anonymization problem, a set of mix servers can be treated as the black box and the traffic logs at the edges of the mix network can be correlated using COLD to detect communication links among end-users [23, 24].

References

1. X. Li, Informational cascades in IT adoption. Commun. ACM **47**(4), 93 (2004)
2. W.-S. Yang, J.-B. Dia, H.-C. Cheng, H.-T. Lin, Mining social networks for targeted advertising, in *39th Annual Hawaii International Conference on System Sciences (HICSS)* (2006)

3. Y. Zhang, Z. Wang, C. Xia, Identifying key users for targeted marketing by mining online social network, in *Advanced Information Networking and Applications Workshops (WAINA)* (2010)
4. E. Pariser, *The Filter Bubble: How the New Personalized Web is Changing What We Read and How We Think [chapterback]* (Penguin Books, New York, 2012)
5. A.M. Odlyzko, Privacy, economics, and price discrimination on the internet, in *Fifth International Conference on Electronic Commerce (ICEC)* (2003)
6. J. Mikians, L. Gyarmati, V. Erramilli, N. Laoutaris, Detecting price and search discrimination on the internet, in *HotNets* (2012)
7. E. Zheleva, L. Getoor, To join or not to join: The illusion of privacy in social networks with mixed public and private user profiles, in *World Wide Web (WWW) Conference* (2009)
8. A. Mislove, B. Viswanath, K.P. Gummadi, P. Druschel, You are who you know: inferring user profiles in online social networks, in *ACM International Conference on Web Search and Data Mining (WSDM)* (2010)
9. M. Balduzzi, C. Platzer, T. Holz, E. Kirda, D. Balzarotti, C. Kruegel, Abusing social networks for automated user profiling, in *Recent Advances in Intrusion Detection* (2010)
10. R. Heatherly, M. Kantarcioglu, B.M. Thuraisingham, Preventing private information inference attacks on social networks. IEEE Trans. Knowl. Data Eng. **25**(8), 1849 (2012)
11. D. Liben-Nowell, J. Kleinberg, The link prediction problem for social networks, in *CIKM '03: Proceedings of the 12th International Conference on Information and Knowledge Management, New York, NY* (ACM, New York, 2003), pp. 556–559
12. A. Clauset, C. Moore, M.E.J. Newman, Hierarchical structure and the prediction of missing links in networks. *Nature* **453**, 98–101 (2008)
13. S. Mallat, *A Wavelet Tour of Signal Processing* (Academic Press, New York, 1999)
14. C. Troncoso, G. Danezis, The Bayesian traffic analysis of mix networks, in *ACM Conference on Computer and Communications Security (CCS)* (2009)
15. Y. Zhu, X. Fu, R. Bettati, W. Zhao, Anonymity analysis of mix networks against flow-correlation attacks, in *IEEE Global Communications Conference (GLOBECOM)* (2005)
16. A. Narayanan, V. Shmatikov, Robust de-anonymization of large sparse datasets, in *IEEE Symposium on Security and Privacy* (2008)
17. A. Narayanan, V. Shmatikov, De-anonymizing social networks, in *IEEE Symposium on Security and Privacy* (2009)
18. G. Wondracek, T. Holz, E. Kirda, C. Kruegel, A practical attack to de-anonymize social network users, in *IEEE Symposium on Security and Privacy* (2010)
19. B. Claise, Cisco systems NetFlow services export version 9. Wikipedia, the free encyclopedia, October 2004
20. Yahoo! network flows data, version 1.0. Yahoo! Research Webscope Data Sets
21. W. Lu, A.A. Ghorbani, Network anomaly detection based on wavelet analysis. EURASIP J. Adv. Signal Process. (2009), 837601 (2008). https://doi.org/10.1155/2009/837601
22. R.R. Coifman, M.V. Wickerhauser, Entropy-based algorithms for best basis selection. IEEE Trans. Inf. Theory **38**(2 Part 2), 713–718 (1992)
23. M.-H. Wang, V. Shmatikov, Timing analysis in low-latency mix networks: attacks and defenses, in *European Symposium on Research in Computer Security (ESORICS)* (2006)
24. Y. Zhu, X. Fu, B. Gramham, R. Bettati, W. Zhao, Correlation-based traffic analysis attacks on anonymity networks. IEEE Trans. Parallel Distrib. Syst. (2009)

Printed in the United States
by Baker & Taylor Publisher Services